GEORGE
WASHINGTON

Also by Willard Sterne Randall

THOMAS JEFFERSON:
A Life

BENEDICT ARNOLD:
Patriot and Traitor

A LITTLE REVENGE:
Benjamin Franklin and His Son

BUILDING SIX (with Stephen D. Solomon)

JOURNALIST

THE PROPRIETARY HOUSE AT AMBOY

AMERICAN LIVES (with Nancy Nahra)

FOUNDING CITY (with David R. Boldt)

GEORGE WASHINGTON

· A LIFE ·

Willard Sterne Randall

A JOHN MACRAE / OWL BOOK

HENRY HOLT AND COMPANY · NEW YORK

Henry Holt and Company, LLC
Publishers since 1866
115 West 18th Street
New York, New York 10011

Henry Holt® is a registered trademark
of Henry Holt and Company, LLC.

Published in Canada by Fitzhenry & Whiteside Ltd.,
195 Allstate Parkway, Markham, Ontario L3R 4T8.

Library of Congress Cataloging-in-Publication Data
Randall, Willard Sterne.
George Washington: a life / Willard Randall.
p.   cm.
Includes bibliographical references and index.
"A John Macrae book."
ISBN 0-8050-5992-X
1. Washington, George, 1732–1799.   2. Presidents—United
States—Biography.   3. Generals—United States—Biography.
4. United States—Continental Army—Biography.   I. Title.
E312.R196   1997   97-19125
973.4'1'092—dc21   CIP
[B]

Henry Holt books are available for special promotions and
premiums. For details contact: Director, Special Markets.

First published in hardcover in 1997 by
Henry Holt and Company

First Owl Books Edition 1998

A John Macrae/Owl Book

Designed by Victoria Hartman

Printed in the United States of America

5 7 9 10 8 6 4

To my father,

Leslie Fairbanks Randall, Jr.

CONTENTS

MAPS

ACKNOWLEDGMENTS

This book began on cold winter mornings in 1969, very early mornings. I was the young special enterprise reporter for the *Philadelphia Evening & Sunday Bulletin*. My boss, features editor B. Dale Davis, asked me to talk to a collector of antique letters, Sol Feinstone, who was lending his vast collection of early American autographs to the American Philosophical Society. Davis said they included many letters by George and Martha Washington, among others. I had written what were called in the newsroom "history pieces" from time to time. Davis warned me that Feinstone was a bit of a "character," who had established strict conditions for a story, and he gave me the customary week to turn in a Sunday feature timed for Washington's birthday (when it still was celebrated separately).

A drive to Bucks County revealed just how much of a character Mr. Feinstone was. At the kitchen table overlooking the spot where he insisted Washington "really" crossed the Delaware (there's a state park called Washington's Crossing a mile farther south), we pored over one letter after another signed by Founding Fathers. Feinstone, who had made a fortune building and renting housing to the U.S. government in World War I, had bought an eighteenth-century farmhouse and crammed it with rare books and letters. I was allowed to look at any of them if I arrived at dawn and finished by noon and gave him a ride into center-city Philadelphia: he did not own a car. With the indulgence of my editor, I stretched that assignment for six weeks. I got up in the dark and drove for an hour and read hundreds of letters and at night raced through Douglas Southall Freeman's six-volume *George Washington* and every other biography of the founding father I could find. The result was "George Washington's Love Letters," my first effort at biography—and the vow that someday I would go back and write a full biography of the great warrior-president.

Over the years, as I have worked on biographies of others of the Revolutionary generation, I have continued to bootleg Washington research. The list of all the people who have helped me over those twenty-eight years is too long to set forth here, but they will see I have finally finished it with their help. A number of editors encouraged me over those years. Hiram Hayden and Harry Sions did not think I was crazy to turn from a journalism career to the writing of historical biography and did not roll their eyes when I talked of one day tackling Washington. Most especially biographer Catharine Drinker Bowen encouraged me. And it was Alan T. Williams who first urged me to write about Washington in a single volume.

In the course of the research I have traveled to the Henry E. Huntington Library in San Marino, California, where I began the research while working on my Jefferson biography and gained access to the records of Washington's financial dealings. At the William L. Clements Library of the University of Michigan, I studied both ends of Benedict Arnold's treason, the Arnold-Clinton-André correspondence and Washington's lightning reaction—and that of his dispirited troops. To Galen R. Wilson, then curator, I owe deep thanks. While researching the life of William Franklin and studying the Loyalists, I squirreled away much material on Washington, especially at the Library of the American Philosophical Society, where Director Whitfield J. Bell was the first of many staff to help me over the years.

On the trail of Arnold I was also on the lookout for Washington material: my thanks to Nicholas Westbrook of Fort Ticonderoga Museum and to Ann Van Arsdale of the Princeton University library with its treasures in the André De Coppet Collection. At the New York Historical Society, then-director James E. Mooney was as ever knowledgeable and gracious. At the J. Pierpont Morgan Library, despite renovations that made conditions all but impossible for the staff, Robert Parks arranged for me to study the Henry Knox Papers; I was ably assisted by Sylvie Merian, Inge Dupont, and Vanessa Pintado. As usual, I am in debt to the staff of the Historical Society of Pennsylvania and the New York Public Library. At Mount Vernon, Librarian Barbara McMillan not only showed me Washington's business records but helped me with my research into the history of the plantation, of slavery, and of Washington's family. Dennis Pogue, director of restoration at Mount Vernon, helped with his writings and his tours of basement, grounds, and farm.

Without fine libraries and free access to them such books would be impossible. Near my home in Vermont are the excellent collections of the Bailey/Howe Library at the University of Vermont, where Patricia Mardeusz and Jake Barickman were as usual helpful, and the much smaller but user-friendly library of St. Michael's College, where emeritus professor Vincent Narramore arranged privileges and where Director Pat Suozzi, General Services Librarian Mark McAteer, Reference Librarians Michelle McCaffrey and Steve Burks, and Interlibrary Loan Librarian

Kristin Hindes made hours of database and computer searches bearable. They brought me books from all over North America and then let me take out far more of them and keep them longer than I had any right to expect.

I owe special thanks to many people. Douglas Denby, president of John Cabot University in Rome, was wonderfully gracious and supportive as I worked on Washington between lectures on "American Lives" while I was Visiting Professor of History. Carole Ludwig and Daniel Fior-rentino of the staff of the United States embassy in Rome helpfully arranged a lecture tour where I tried out my Washington presidential material on audiences at John Cabot University and at the Centro Studii Americani in Rome and in Naples. There, Consul General Clark Ellis was most gracious in helping arrange for me to talk to students from the University of Naples and to the English-speaking community. Closer to home, Lincoln Brownell, ever alert, spotted a Washington letter on a bank wall that I would have missed; J. Robert Maguire provided valuable insights. Ray Lincoln, agent and friend, listened, read, thought, and advised as generously as ever.

I would like to thank my editor, Jack Macrae at Henry Holt, for his many innocent-sounding questions and for his careful, subtle editing. My thanks also to his assistant, Rachel Klauber-Speiden, and to copy editor Erin Clermont. Once again, Diann Varricchione gave up evenings and weekends to prepare the numerous drafts of the manuscript. And, most of all, I want to thank my wife, Nancy Nahra, for listening, for reading, for arguing, and for never giving up.

GEORGE
WASHINGTON

INTRODUCTION

*A*t *noon on* November 25, 1783, a day of bright skies and a chilling northwest wind, General George Washington's honor guard of a thousand handpicked officers and men gathered at Day's Tavern in Harlem. Shivering in worn navy blue jackets shabby from years of hard use, they waited for Washington's command to march south into Manhattan. Astride a magnificent gray horse, Washington was ready, at last, to take back New York City, the most important British post in America. The peace treaty ending the Revolutionary War and affirming American independence had been signed in Paris more than a year ago but Sir Guy Carleton, the British commander, would not leave until he had written orders from London. Washington, for his part, would not disband his army so long as a redcoat remained who could rekindle the fighting.

No one could have been more eager for peace than Washington. At fifty-one, he had spent the last eight and a half years in uniform. In those years he had been home to Mount Vernon for only three days; since the Continental Congress had given him command of a rustic rabble in 1775, he had lived in 280 borrowed houses. His once-auburn hair had gone gray; pale and haggard, his cougarlike head was wrinkled from a decade of worry, struggle, and sadness.

Yet there was something calm in his visage, and he was still imposing in the saddle. A giant for his time, a full head taller than most men, Washington's 209 pounds were spread over a taut six-foot-four-and-a-half-inch frame. Wherever he went, crowds gathered to see the ramrod-straight man on the tall warhorse. In the tedious months since Congress had signed the peace treaty, Washington had been plagued by mutinies over back pay. He narrowly averted a military coup earlier that year when an inept Congress could not pay his officers. As long as he kept his army in the field, he was considered the real leader of the new American republic and a potential rival to Congress. Whether he would retire or become a military dictator had aroused speculation all over Europe. In farewell orders to his troop commanders on November 2, he had announced his intention to retire from the service, but the public did not know it.

Washington's growing impatience was made worse by his own deteriorating financial condition. After ten years of revolution and civil warfare, George Washington was as broke as most Americans. People who owed him money had paid him off during the war with nearly worthless depreciated paper currency. Tenants on his 23,000 acres of western lands paid no rents year after year. His farms in Virginia had suffered from years of neglect. Washington had as much reason to rejoice as anyone in America when an express rider pelted down the Boston Post Road with word that, after all the years of hardship and bloodletting, the British were finally departing. Their massive defensive works, which entirely encircled Manhattan Island, were deserted. Washington swung into action. He had a careful plan: he would ride at the side of New York Governor George Clinton, who was to enter the town first, as a signal that Washington was turning over his power to a civil government. Next in the line of march was the honor guard commanded by his corpulent chief of artillery, Henry Knox, the only officer who had remained by his side since the opening days of the Revolution. So many others had betrayed or deserted him, but big Henry, bulking fully 280 pounds, was with him to the last. He would take over Fort George from the British garrison, raise the American flag, and fire the first salute to the astonishing American victory.

Promptly at noon, Knox and eight hundred of the best Continentals stepped off briskly, their shouldered muskets gleaming in the cold light. Mounted light infantry from West Point nudged their horses to a walk. Behind a detachment of field artillery towing three-pounders came a battalion of lean, hard Massachusetts men. As Washington rode down the narrow Post Road, reminders of the long and bitter war bombarded him. All of Manhattan Island had been turned into a fortified camp. Earthwork stockades, gun emplacements, and breastworks everywhere jutted skyward. No one spoke as they passed the ruins of Fort Washington, betrayed in the earliest days of fighting while Washington watched helplessly through a telescope from the New Jersey shore. Nearly three thousand men had been taken prisoner that day. Most of them had died of hunger, cold, disease, and brutal British treatment. Now, Washington's triumph tromped through a Harlem stripped of orchards and fences to provide firewood during seven years of enemy occupation. Washington could remember his first successful stand against British professionals: on Harlem Heights he'd had a single heartening moment in that disastrous summer of 1776. He rode past Kip's Bay (at present-day 30th Street), where, more typically, he had sworn and slashed with his saber at his terrified troops as they fled under fire from British men-of-war escorting redcoats ashore. He had spent so many of those early days on the run, the British taunting him with foxhunting calls hooting from their cornets.

At Bull's Head Tavern in the Bowery, Washington's parade ran headlong into a crowd on horseback. Refugees with sprigs of laurel stuck in their hats, representing victory, were returning from years of exile in the countryside. They mingled with retired officers who wore the black-and-white cockade of Franco-American union on their chests. How many of these men had quit Washington's army as the war had dragged on! Now they pressed in on him, to shake his hand. A cheering crowd filled Broadway. Washington found his new role of national hero uncomfortable.

Everywhere he went that last year of war, Washington saw signs he was emerging as the Revolution's hero. His birthday had been celebrated as a national holiday. In Bordentown, New Jersey, citizens celebrated news that the peace treaty had been signed by mounting his portrait in windows "encompassed with thirteen stars." The people of Upper Marlboro, Massachusetts, likened Washington to "an auspicious planet" with "his thirteen satellites." At St. Tammany's Day celebrations in Philadelphia, the band played "Great Washington." A college in Maryland was renamed after Washington, and an innkeeper in New Haven replaced the new moon on his sign with "the sign of Washington." Congress voted to erect an equestrian statue to him as soon as it built a permanent capital. There had been only one equestrian statue in America before this time, of King George III, torn down in New York City in 1776. As Washington led his troops into New York City, the Marine Anti-Britannic Society of Charleston, South Carolina, toasted him: "To the unexampled citizen and hero of the New World," while the more laconic *New Hampshire Gazette* reported:

> He comes! 'Tis mighty Washington!
> Words fail to tell all he has done![1]

But Washington had had enough of war, uniforms, flattery, and doggerel. The adulation of strangers vexed him. Too many of his best friends had died before this day. He only wanted to go home.

As he smilingly led his troops down Broadway, amid the cheering some in the crowd wept. One woman wrote:

> We had been accustomed for a long time to military display in all the finish and finery of [British] garrison life. The troops just leaving us were as if equipped for a show and with their scarlet uniforms and burnished arms made a brilliant display. The troops that marched in, on the contrary, were ill-clad and weather-beaten and made a forlorn appearance. But then, they were *our* troops and as I looked at them and thought upon all they had done and suffered for us, my heart and my eyes were full.[2]

Her eyes brimmed when Washington, easily recognizable as he raised his gold-trimmed hat in salute, passed by. He was smiling now. He had reason to be proud of these rail-thin men in faded uniforms as they marched along. He could remember the day when he had seen a barefoot soldier, naked underneath his filthy blanket, running from one log hut to another through the deep snow at Valley Forge. Today's threadbare victors reminded him of his long struggle to wring from the reluctant Congress enough money to feed and clothe his men. In the distance now, punctuating the cheers, Washington could hear the pounding tattoo of a thirteen-gun salute. Knox had taken over Fort George. The last redcoat had clambered into a waiting barge. The United States was free at last.

One

"A PROMPT AND

LITERAL OBEDIENCE"

In the normal course of events, George Washington would have become an Oxford don and followed the profession of his English father. As it turned out, he never went to college. He received the least formal schooling of any of the Founding Fathers and remained self-conscious about this lack all his life. What robbed Washington of a university education but spared him the impecunious existence of an Oxford don was a revolution in England in the mid-seventeenth century. Had not the English civil wars of the 1640s intervened, the Washingtons probably would never have left England. George Washington probably would have studied and taught at Oxford until, as a middle-aged bachelor, he gave up the austere existence of the scholar to become an obscure country parson, sitting below the salt at the table of the local lord of the manor.

George Washington was the first of his old English family to oppose a king. All of his English and American ancestors including his mother were staunch royalists. Several Washingtons were courtiers knighted by James I. William Washington married Anne Villiers, half-sister of the first Duke of Buckingham, the corrupt court favorite of King James. His younger brother, Thomas, was a page to Prince Charles I. Henry Washington was a celebrated colonel in Charles I's royalist army. Henry's sister married royalist Colonel William Legge. Their son was created the first Earl of Dartmouth; the second earl was British secretary of state at the outbreak of the American Revolution. Indeed, the first Washington to settle in America had to leave England because his family would *not* rebel against their king.

There is an enduring myth that Washington's family "was gentle but undistinguished," that "usually the Washingtons married their social betters," that George Washington "did not know his forebears and cared less," but recent research shows that Washington himself contributed to his own log-cabin image. As president, Washington responded to a request for information on his family origins from Sir Isaac Heard, Garter King of Arms in London, averring that he had "no document" to shed light on his English origins. All he would admit was that two brothers, John and Lawrence Washington, had "emigrated from the north of England" but "from whom they descended" he had no written record. But why would he feel the need to produce written records for the royal genealogists at Windsor Castle? He rejected a peerage during the Revolution and a monarch's crown during the constitutional crisis of 1787–1789. To the English, who must have known of his roots and certainly should have known better after a bitter civil war than to ask about them, he gave a short, cold answer. They were "of no moment," he said.[1]

He provided more details in written memoranda to Colonel David Humphreys, his plump, supercilious former aide who started to write Washington's first biography. He required Humphreys to show him a draft of the biography and then "consign them [the original notes] to the flames." He corrected Humphreys on important particulars, but only those he considered noteworthy. Humphreys wrote that Washington came from an "opulent" family in England and that "his ancestors, who transferred a considerable inheritance from their native to their adoptive country, had been in the New World from the year 1657" when two brothers "came to America over the Atlantic from Cumberland in England." If Washington knew more, he refused to cooperate.[2]

Just as he showed his detestation for the trappings of English nobility by refusing to wear a wig during the Constitutional Convention of 1787, Washington opposed the acceptance of any title or honors from any foreign government. His objection became part of the Constitution. But he was also a master diplomat. Many American revolutionaries traced their descent from English Puritans, the persecutors of his family. By the time of his presidency Washington could afford to downplay the importance of his ancestry, but as a young orphan in the deferential status-conscious royalist society of Virginia his ease of access to colonial drawing rooms and his ability to win rapid advancement in the military and in government, coupled with his success at courting a wealthy and socially prominent woman, all depended at least in part on the fact that both sides of his family came from impeccable English stock who were already part of the Virginia ruling class. Several had served in Virginia's House of Burgesses. Many were militia officers. Almost all held rank and status in the country gentry as county court justices and Church of England vestrymen.

The Washingtons today would be called a "county family" in England. Through his paternal grandmother, George Washington was descended from King Edward III and was related to the Churchills. Washington's paternal ancestors came from Sulgrave Manor, a Northamptonshire estate about seventy-five miles northwest of London. The size of the Washington family was its curse. Too often the land was divided and its money parceled out among heirs. George Washington's last English forebear, Lawrence, was fifteen when Sulgrave Manor was sold off in 1616. He had to leave the land and find some other respectable livelihood—the clergy or the military—or, all else failing, become a lawyer or merchant. But most of these required a university education. His great-uncle and uncle had gone to Oxford, where, at seventeen, Lawrence enrolled in Brasenose College.

He arrived at Oxford's high-water mark of enrollment. An unprecedented proportion of young Englishmen, many with little or no money, were matriculating during Oxford's brief democratization. In a boom unsurpassed until the nineteenth century, more Oxonians graduated to Parliament between 1620 and 1660 than at any time before the mid-twentieth century. Lawrence Washington proceeded to the bachelor of arts degree and was elected a Fellow on condition that he could not have an income of more than a few pounds sterling a year. Wealth was considered grounds for disqualification. If he married, he would have to leave. For six years, Washington shared bachelor digs at Brasenose. He bought out the furnishings of his predecessor, and added, for his own sleeping room, a four-poster bed and a large number of leather-bound books. In the basement, he kept hogsheads of beer; in the yard heifers, cows, and a hog for bacon. Students assembling in his chambers around a large table sat on leather chairs or cushions while Washington read and lectured on philosophy and interrogated them.

Lawrence Washington turned out to be a fine young bureaucrat before there was the word for one who climbs relentlessly up through an organization. At twenty-four he was appointed Lector of Brasenose, at twenty-nine the college's disciplinarian, one of two university proctors. He held sway over everyone in town and in gowns in Oxford. He patrolled the streets at night to enforce the curfews, pursuing malefactors into their houses and hauling back young lords from brothels and taverns. He ordered women found in college rooms to be flogged. From his rare perch of clerical and civil power, Washington fell into an intense internal struggle that destroyed him.

The English revolution, so much the precursor of the American Revolution, began in the English universities. Eager college students lined up to read from Bibles chained to churches so they wouldn't be stolen. The universities were thronged with poor students whose scant £10 tuition was paid by merchants who were secret Puritans. Lawrence Washington was appointed university proctor by Archbishop of Canterbury William Laud, the king's point man for the suppression of Puritanism, who was also chancellor of Oxford. On August 22, 1631, with King Charles I personally presiding, Laud denounced the principal officers of Oxford as heretics. Lawrence Washington's roommate and closest friend was fired. Four days later, Reverend Lawrence Washington, who was more acceptable to Laud, was appointed to replace his roommate. As Laud's willing agent on the Brasenose faculty, Reverend Washington carried out a thorough purge of Oxford's Puritan clergy.

Father Washington also caught the eye of a wealthy and unusually literate young widow, Amphilis Twigden of Great Tring Manor in Hertfordshire. When nine out of ten women in East Anglia couldn't sign their names, Amphilis wrote long, charming letters. Reverend Washington soon decided that Amphilis was better and more profitable company than Laud's plotting clerics. He risked his position by courting her. In search of a higher-salaried job, he outfitted himself expensively, strapped on a dress sword, and went off to London. He drew on connections at Charles I's court to collect his political debt. Archbishop Laud appointed him rector of the rich parish of Purleigh in Essex. He married Amphilis, and in 1633 she gave birth to their first son, John, the great-grandfather of George Washington and the first American Washington.

John Washington was expected to emulate his father and become an Oxford don. According to custom, Reverend Washington secured the king's recommendation for a "schollers' place" [sic] for eight-year-old John at Charterhouse School in London where he was to prepare for Oxford. But the Puritan backlash during the English civil wars brought a sudden end to Reverend Washington's cozy existence and dashed his son's academic prospects. The Puritans took a dim view of the jovial, amiable cleric who liked to have a pot of ale at one of Purleigh's pubs. The Puritans stripped some 2,800 Church of England curates of their benefices. Lawrence Washington was Puritan Enemy Number Nine on the list of "scandalous, malignant priests." Parliamentary inquisitors in Essex described him as "a common frequenter of ale-houses, not only himself sitting daily tippling there but also encouraging others in that beastly vice. [He] hath often been drunk."[3]

Out of work with six children, the Washingtons were spared from starvation only by their royalist relatives. Lawrence's aunt Margaret was married to Sir Edwin Sandys (connecting the Washingtons with the Churchills). Sandys was treasurer of the Virginia Company and an early investor in the transatlantic tobacco trade. He sheltered Washington's wife and children. Reverend Washington went off alone to Little Brasted in Essex, "a poor and miserable [parish] whose pulpit was only filled with difficulty," and lived in poverty and increasing tipsiness.[4]

Any chance Reverend Washington's sons had for a university education had been dashed. If his father had not been purged John probably would have gone to Oxford where, each year, an increasing proportion of freshmen had been following their fathers into the church. The year John was to matriculate, all known royalists were expelled. Instead, John Washington used his Sandys connections and a small inheritance to become the first Washington to go to sea and seek his fortune as a merchant adventurer. As the Puritan Commonwealth continued to make life precarious for young royalists, John Washington sailed to America, where the colony of Virginia had declared itself a royalist sanctuary.

*T*he father's catastrophe proved good fortune for the son. John Washington became apprenticed to a merchant. He learned to keep accounts in a counting house along the London waterfront where cargoes came from all over England's booming maritime empire. There were wonderful opportunities to make money as the English competed for trade routes with the Dutch, French, and Spanish. John Washington decided to get into the tobacco re-export business: more than 40 percent of all tobacco imported from the English colonies Virginia and Maryland was reshipped to European markets. By 1656, twenty-four-year-old John Washington knew the tobacco trade and navigation well enough to invest his inheritance in the cargo of the *Sea Horse,* a merchant ketch whose owner signed him on as first mate and junior partner. Young Washington could expect a handsome profit. At each port, he went ashore to trade tobacco. In Denmark, the *Sea Horse* docked at Copenhagen and Washington traveled alone to the royal city of Elsinore.

As part of his contract, young Washington agreed to cross the Atlantic Ocean to procure a new cargo of tobacco in Virginia. The ship anchored in the Potomac River in February 1657. While John was ashore, the *Sea Horse* blew aground during a storm and began to sink. Washington managed to repair and refloat the ship, but most of the tobacco was waterlogged and had to be jettisoned. His inheritance lost, John Washington decided then and there not to return to England. While ashore, he had met an elderly planter-exporter named Nathaniel Pope who latched on to the young Englishman as just the right bridegroom for his daughter. Here was the son of an Oxford don who knew the European tobacco markets! For father and prospective son-in-law, it was love at first sight. Pope, a rich tobacco planter and member of the Maryland Assembly with extensive landholdings, was the ideal model for a young merchant mariner on the make.

It is hard to tell whether Washington fell in love with Anne Pope or his prospects as heir-apparent, but he suddenly broke his contract with Captain Prescott, who refused to pay him and sailed away. Pope advanced Washington a hefty £80 in gold and dangled the bequest of 700 acres of riverfront land. Shortly afterward, John married Anne. Nathaniel Pope appointed Washington to administer his family's lands. In only a few years, John Washington assumed the same second-tier social status in Virginia that his family had long enjoyed in England, even if to settle in Virginia in the 1650s was like deciding today to emigrate to the Brazilian rain forest. After the manor houses of England, the Virginia Tidewater plantation houses were rude shacks in a wilderness.

John Washington's migration added two new elements to the Washington family character. From that time on, they relentlessly pursued money and land. By the age of thirty, John Washington succeeded as a merchant-planter. At a time when frontier land was still cheap and tobacco fetched a high price in England, George Washington's great-grandfather accumulated five thousand acres in ten years. He also received paid emoluments from the royal governor as county coroner, trustee of estates, guardian of children, justice of the county court, and most notably, lieutenant colonel in the Virginia militia, initiating another Washington family tradition.

In September 1659, John and Anne Washington's first son was born at about the same time he began to import indentured servants from England. He received "head rights" of fifty acres for each servant. He put the servants to work for five to seven years clearing, cultivating, and defending his land. In all, he "brought over" sixty-three white servants. His neighbors elected him to the Virginia House of Burgesses for the Northern Neck.

As his wealth increased, so did his family. Anne Pope Washington gave birth to five children in nine years and died. Washington remarried quickly, choosing Anne Gerrard, a woman already twice widowed. The second Mrs. Washington was a shrewd businesswoman who imported servants, something few women did. His second marriage brought Washington a mill and a tavern plus a courthouse and a jail, which he leased to the colonial government. He combined a sharp eye for real estate and a knack for inside trading. When speculators along the Potomac failed to perfect their titles to grants of royal lands by settling them fast enough, the lands reverted to the colony's government. Colonel Washington made a secret pact with the secretary of the colony. They had the land surveyed just before its original grant expired and then quickly patented it for themselves. By this inside trading, the tract where Little Hunting Creek emptied into the Potomac became the future site of Mount Vernon. Colonel Washington's half-share of this 5,000-acre boondoggle placed him squarely among the leading families of the Potomac region.

The first Colonel Washington's militia appointment helped touch off Bacon's Rebellion in September 1675, and cast a shadow over the Washington family name. When Indians raided Virginia from Maryland, Virginia's royal governor, William Berkeley, ordered Washington to call out the militia. The governor of Maryland gave Virginia permission to pursue the natives. Washington crossed the Potomac and learned that Indians had taken refuge in a makeshift fort.

Whether the Indians came out to parley or, seeing that the fort was about to fall, came out to surrender is unclear. According to testimony before an investigating committee of the Virginia House of Burgesses, Washington suggested marching the prisoners to the farm where the fighting had taken place to compare the markings of the Indians killed there with his live prisoners. The Marylanders later contended that Washington grew impatient with Indian denials and ordered his men to club the Indians to death. The surviving Indians gave him the nickname

Burner of Towns. The name became hereditary and was later applied to George Washington. Governor Berkeley gave John Washington only a stern reprimand. Undeterred, Washington continued to support the royalists during Bacon's Rebellion and made money by smuggling supplies to the Maryland shore even after Bacon's rebels seized his farms. Once again a Washington had upheld the king's side in an armed rebellion.

Colonel Washington died at forty-four. His estate was divided equally among his wife and three children, two sons and a daughter. The Washingtons traditionally took a dim view of the standard practice of primogeniture. His oldest son, Lawrence, George Washington's grandfather, received most of the land and a share in Washington's mill. Living the life of a young country gentleman, Lawrence made enough money from a string of public offices to support himself. He was elected a member of the House of Burgesses and sheriff of Westmoreland County. He was an aberration among Washingtons; he cared little for land speculation. Social status meant more to him. He married Mildred Warner, daughter of the late Speaker of the House of Burgesses and a member of the governor's council. George Washington's grandparents led a life of ease. They made a long wedding trip to England and had three children. Like his father, Lawrence died young. He was thirty-seven.

Their second son, Augustine, was only three when his father died. Gus, as everyone called him, grew into an amiable blond giant. He very nearly spent his life in England, where his mother and her new husband took him. When Mildred died, her husband plunked Gus into Appleby School in Westmoreland, England. The boy spent nearly four happy years in the English boarding school while his Virginia relatives went to court to break Mildred's will. They succeeded. Brought back to Virginia, Gus was raised by an uncle, John Washington, the sheriff of Stafford County. George Washington's father grew to over six feet tall and became known for his great strength and kindness. Not long after Gus's twenty-first birthday, he married Jane Butler, daughter of a lawyer and planter. Their marriage united 1,740 prime acres, a powerful attraction to Gus, who inherited the Washington acquisitiveness for land. A year after their marriage the young couple bought a fine piece of ground on a neck of land on the south bank of the Potomac. They built a modest one-and-a-half-story house named Wakefield. In this frontier farmhouse, George Washington was born.

Exactly where George Washington was born was for a long time a subject of intense scholarly controversy. Washington's well-meaning adopted grandson, George Washington Parke Custis, evidently erred when he marked the spot in 1815 with a small monument. The federal government bought twenty-one acres around the site in 1882 and erected a 51-foot shaft of granite near where the house had stood before it was destroyed by fire. As the bicentennial of Washington's birth approached, the Wakefield National Memorial Association erected a supposed replica of the house. Memorial House, built on the foundations of a 38- by 14-foot eighteenth-century-style building, became a national park. But further research revealed a much larger U-shaped foundation almost sixty feet long, centrally located on the plantation. For years, the civic group that had built the replica in the wrong place resisted the findings of archaeologists, refusing to tear down the reproduction and build a more authentic structure. Instead, they devoted their efforts to filling the ersatz house with period furniture. Only one small tilt-top table could be obtained that, according to tradition, came from the original house.[5]

What may be an exact replica of Washington's birthplace was built in 1825 several hundred miles to the south in Florence, Alabama, while Washington's heirs still inhabited Mount Vernon. It is a handsomely trimmed, one-and-a-half-story, three-bedroom brick house. Its most striking features are crow-step gables rising on both sides and two full Doric columns and two half-columns in front, making a relatively small house appear gracious and inviting. Like many houses of the era, it has a center hall flanked by living room and dining room. The high-ceilinged master bedroom is off the dining room. Upstairs, there are two more bedrooms under the eaves, separated by a sitting room. The largest room in the house is the kitchen, which is connected to the dining room by a generous pantry.

The original Wakefield was modest by Virginia Tidewater standards because Gus Washington used his money wisely to develop iron-ore mining and build furnaces on his lands. When England went to war with Sweden, English iron imports disappeared. An iron rush ensued in Virginia, and Gus Washington was the first out of the gate. In 1724, Washington discovered rich iron ore deposits about eight miles northeast of Fredericksburg. For half a dozen years, small amounts of iron ore had been mined in the Northern Neck and shipped to England. Through a Virginia partner, London investors offered Gus Washington a one-sixth interest in a new iron-mining and manufacturing works, the Principio Company, in exchange for the rights to his iron ore deposits. Washington went to London to negotiate for himself. He took along his two sons, Lawrence and Augustine, Jr., and enrolled them in his alma mater, Appleby. He returned to Virginia with a generous contract only to discover when he arrived home that his wife, who had stayed behind with their four-year-old daughter, was dead.

*F*ew mothers of American presidents have been praised or vilified more than Mary Ball Washington, the first president's tall, athletic, jut-jawed mother. In the early nineteenth century, early Washington biographer and Methodist clergyman Mason Weems invented the story that young Washington could not tell a lie after he cut down a cherry tree. The Reverend Jared Sparks, president of Harvard College and biographer of the Founding Fathers, sanitized Washington by bowdlerizing his letters (those that he didn't give away to autograph collectors). Both men busily grafted and pruned facts to form a Washington myth. Parson Weems and Jared Sparks deified Mary Ball Washington, or at least made her the mother of a god. As with so much else, the historians of the twentieth century have been busy not only chopping down George Washington but knocking his mother off her pedestal. On the occasion of Washington's bicentennial in 1932 one proclaimed that Mary Ball was "grasping, querulous and vulgar":

> She was a selfish and exacting mother whom most of her children avoided as soon and as early as they could, to whom they did their duty but rendered little love. It was this sainted mother of Washington who opposed almost everything that he did for the public good, who wished his sense of duty to end with his duty to her.[6]

Nineteenth-century mythmakers put Washington's mother in the log cabin with her godlike son. Twentieth-century chroniclers diminish her as a crude frontier type. But Washington's legend has become so powerful that another president, Harry S. Truman, wrote glowingly of George Washington as one of his favorite chief executives but put his mother down as "a strange woman" and a "miser" who "although she was really quite rich complained all her life that she was destitute."[7]

According to family records exhumed by Mary Ball Washington's brother, Joseph, Jr., a London barrister of Lincoln's Inn and a court official who left Virginia to live and practice law in England, the first Ball family came to America in 1657, the same year John Washington emigrated. The Balls, also royalists, sailed into exile with their entire household, family and servants. Settling in Lancaster County, William Ball established himself as a major planter and trader. After only two years in the colony he became a justice of the county court. He helped Governor Berkeley put down Bacon's Rebellion. He was rewarded by promotion to lieutenant colonel of county militia and served as a fellow officer of Lieutenant Colonel John Washington. When Colonel Ball died in 1680, he left his wife, Hannah, nine slaves as part of a sizable estate. His son, William II, George Washington's maternal grandfather, assumed his mantle in county politics and served in the House of Burgesses. He had six children. Widowed at fifty-eight, he married again, to a woman who could not write, a condition not uncommon among Virginia frontier women.

The first of William and Mary Ball's children was George Washington's mother, Mary Ball. During his sojourn in England, Gus Washington met Mary Ball, who was visiting relatives in London. At twenty-two she was already considered virtually a spinster—girls in Virginia usually married by eighteen. Mary Ball had gone to London to be introduced into English society. On her illiterate mother's side she was a Montague, a member of a famous landed family. George Washington's mother, Mary Ball, was only three years old when her father died. She was taken to her step-father's farm at Yeocomico, Virginia. Her mother married again, a fourth time; she died at thirty-five. Her chief gifts to her daughter were a devout Anglicanism and a love of horses.

Each time a parent or stepparent died, Mary Ball received a legacy in land, livestock, furniture, slaves, cash, and, usually, a good horse. When her mother died, she was sent to live with a half-sister. She learned what was expected of a Virginia gentlewoman: sewing, dancing, embroidery, the Anglican catechism (she had already learned to read and write), paint-ing, horseback riding, how to treat her slaves. She also became acquisitive and attached to all her possessions, especially her horses. By the time Mary was eighteen she had enough land and personal property to have been pursued by the usual coterie of Tidewater swains. But if she was, she may not have found anyone she would accept. Could it have been that there was something so strong and independent about her that every suitor seemed to back away?

For one thing, Mary Ball had developed a lifelong disregard for the opinions of others, especially about fashion. She far preferred the com-pany of horses to that of other people. She seemed to be happiest when she was eighteen and a brother-in-law bequeathed her a young dappled gray horse. Throwing a silk plush saddle over its back, she charged over fields and fences and through woods. She remained unconcerned that she was considered "a young woman of a mind that never was orderly." She had thick dark eyebrows, a strong-set jaw, and a high, intelligent-looking forehead. She remained single until Gus Washington's bereavement. The fact that the tall, gray-eyed, fair-haired widower Washington already had three children did not deter Mary Ball. They married in the spring of 1731. Eleven months later, on February 11, 1732, under the existing En-glish calendar (eleven days were later added to catch up with the rest of the world), their first son, George, was born. Into Wakefield, the Washing-ton's modest brick house on Pope's Creek, Mary crowded all the furni-ture she had inherited, jammed alongside the Washington family's accumulation.[8] When she was pregnant with George Washington, she ex-perienced a shock that may have shaped her relationship with the large child taking shape in her womb. One summer Sunday afternoon, while the family was having dinner with guests from church, a thunderstorm rolled in. A bolt of lightning struck the house and traveled down the chimney and hit a young girl who was visiting the Washingtons for Sun-day dinner. The electric current was so strong it fused the knife and fork she was using to cut her meat. She died instantly. The lightning hit with such force that it severely jolted the pregnant Mary Washington, who was sitting only a few feet away. From that time on, Mary Ball Washington cringed and tried to hide whenever lightning passed overhead, burying her face in her hands. For the moment, she recovered, but she became increasingly fearful over the years. She was so happy a few months later when a strong, sound baby was born that she traveled around the Tidewater showing off George Washington to all his cousins for an entire month, before she even had him baptized.

Mary Ball Washington never recovered fully from the shock she had seen and felt. She rarely traveled any farther than church on Sunday and her timorousness touched off a number of clashes with her family, especially her sons, whom she discouraged from taking any risks. In his choice of a military career, George Washington faced a long struggle against a mother who kept him from going to sea as a boy and embarrassed him in front of senior British officers when he was a young aide-de-camp. Even when he became a hero in the American Revolution, she could not understand; in fact she resented his desire to stray from her side and leave the safety of the farm to go off to war. She never understood her own role in shaping his need to act with courage in a very public way. Her step-granddaughter (the wife of Robert E. Lee) passed down the family tradition that Mary Ball Washington "required from those about her a prompt and literal obedience somewhat resembling that demanded by proper military subordination." She had no doubt of her own "mental power that enabled her rightly to judge and wisely to direct." From his boyhood, George Washington knew what an order sounded like—and the pain of disobeying one.[9]

George Washington did not sit down and write of his childhood, as Thomas Jefferson and Benjamin Franklin did. Nor, as Jefferson did, did he ever reminisce in old age for his granddaughter, leaving charming anecdotes to act as homilies for his grandchildren. He seems to have been ashamed of his impoverished childhood and his poor education and his fear of his mother. As soon as he could, he ran away from his boyhood world and fled into the woods, where he remade himself into a brave and tight-lipped young warrior. What little can be deduced about his childhood has to be gleaned from scant evidence. George Washington made himself as elusive as the white-tailed deer that abounded in the forests that he came to love, and he left few footprints in his writings.

What is indisputable is that George Washington grew up on a farm. His childhood world was filled with children, chickens, dogs, pigs, calves, horses, and as many as fifty slaves. From ten thousand woodland acres, most of it uncleared, his father, tall, affable, sandy-haired Gus Washington, harvested a modest living. He reinvested much of the produce of his and his slaves' labor in better land for his tobacco crops and iron-mining venture. By the time little George turned three and could walk unsupervised around the place, the U-shaped brick house on a knoll near present-day Oak Grove in Westmoreland County was becoming seriously overcrowded. The house was fairly spacious for the region, but as more children came and Gus's business and politics brought more guests and Mary crowded in more furniture, it was obvious that the house was inadequate.

To move to a better piece of land closer to his business interests, Gus Washington decided they should rent out the Pope's Creek farm and move forty miles upriver to a 2,500-acre farm he had assembled where Little Hunting Creek emptied into the Potomac. It was called Epsewasson; it would be years before anyone called it Mount Vernon. There were still no roads wider than a horse. For weeks, Gus Washington directed the slaves as they built large rafts, and he told them what furniture and farm implements went into which barrels for the long voyage upriver. On the appointed day, little George watched as the entire farm livestock and barrels went aboard the rafts. The slaves followed Gus's lead as they pushed with long poles out into the river, careful to stay in the shallows as close to the riverbank as they could and still avoid fallen trees.

George was used to playing with children from neighboring farms. At Epsewasson, more isolated than Wakefield, there were no neighborhood boys to play with. His companions were slave children. Most of the excitement at first swirled around the construction of a new house on the high bluff overlooking the Potomac. Gus Washington had designed a large, steeply sloped roof for the one-and-a-half-story brick farmhouse and a wide front porch and center hall to funnel breezes wafting up from the Potomac. Solid and unpretentious like the Washingtons, the house sat screened from the river by tall trees. At the water's edge Gus built a dock where his slaves rolled the thousand-pound hogsheads of tobacco to merchant ships that sailed downriver into the Chesapeake and on into the Atlantic toward London. Here a boy watched all the waterfront activity, daydreamed of ships, and learned to dangle a fishing line. In the distance, through his father's telescope, he could plainly make out an Indian village a mile across the river on the Maryland shore.

At Epsewasson he also began to learn about life and death. When he was scarcely three, his ten-year-old half-sister, Jane, so close to him for his first conscious years, died of one of the fevers that plagued the steaming, mosquito-infested Tidewater in summer. George began to equate the hot season with death and frequent funerals. Soon there was another baby in the house. By the time George was six, along came Betty and Samuel. George's mother always seemed to be bulging with pregnancy or holding a baby at her breast.

When George was five, he met his half-brothers Lawrence and Austin for the first time. Since their mother had died, they had lived in England. At Appleby School they had learned the classics. George was especially fond of Lawrence, who was sensitive, intelligent, and had elegant manners and speech littered with literary allusions. Lawrence had decided it was time to come home to Virginia. A new war for empire, this one called King George's War, loomed between England and France and their allies. Gus Washington turned over to Lawrence the house and farm at Epsewasson. As the firstborn son it would be his one day, anyway.

The boy George was busy learning how to help his mother and how to sit on a horse. At first, his father held him up in front and steadied him with a brawny arm when he needed it. George started out a lifetime on horseback clinging to fistful of the animal's mane. Soon he could take the reins himself, timorously at first, and ride a horse taller than he was. Even when his father was away he practiced, under the expert eye of his mother. From his father and his brother he learned how to fish and hunt, skills absolutely indispensable to life on the frontier. There was plenty to learn on the new farm, and at day's end when the blistering sun subsided, he could make magic visits down to the river. He imbibed the leisurely excitement of fishing patiently and quietly in the hot sun, learning a life-long hobby. At night, when the tide came in and there were crabs in the river, he watched how the grown-ups used lanterns to lure the shiny blue crustaceans to the surface and snare them with their nets.

When George was seven years old, the *Virginia Gazette* for January 11, 1740, carried a story that Admiral Edward Vernon was leading a British fleet to attack Cartagena, a heavily fortified Spanish fortress on the Darien Peninsula seacoast of Colombia. England was determined to break Spanish domination of the Caribbean. A war fever raged. Three weeks later the *Gazette* reported that Admiral Vernon was sailing with seven men-of-war to attack the Spanish fleet at Porto Bello. Actually the battle had already taken place—Vernon had captured the Spanish port in a bold surprise attack. He would have been content to seize the base at Porto Bello and from there control the Caribbean sea lanes, enjoying the proceeds of the phenomenal loot and prize money paid at auction for ships he had captured, but the British ministry in London wanted to oust the Spanish from Cartagena. It had been captured and ransomed in every British war with Spain since Sir Francis Drake had first sacked it in the 1580s, and after each war the Spanish had strengthened their fortifications until Cartagena became the strongest citadel in New Spain. The British government ordered Admiral Vernon to follow up his easy victory at Porto Bello with a land-and-sea attack on the Spanish settlements in Colombia.

For the first time English settlers in America were ordered to raise troops to serve in a British overseas expedition. Red-coated recruiting officers with drummers and flags marched from town to town. The martial stirrings quickly reached the Washington household. Between them, Virginia and Maryland were to raise a battalion of troops, one-fourth of the 3,000-man American regiment. Lawrence Washington immediately applied for a captaincy. As a third-generation Virginian with two high-ranking militia officers in his family and strong recommendations from members of the royal governor's executive council, Lawrence won the coveted commission. In a matter of weeks, Captain Washington raised his own company of one hundred green-uniformed Virginia troops. Lawrence was resplendent in his new scarlet breeches and navy blue jacket and gold-laced hat. A shiny brass officer's gorget hung from his neck; a crimson sash draped across his shoulder held his silver short-sword. Captain Washington soon led his contingent aboard a British troop transport and sailed south into what one British military historian has called "a howling fiasco" that "accomplished nothing but the strewing of the Spanish Main with English corpses."[10]

The expedition dragged on into the yellow fever season. Most of the Americans who did not die in the assault succumbed to the fetid troop ships. The Americans, blamed by the British for the expedition's failure, were assigned the deadly task of carrying the scaling ladders for the more experienced British storming parties. Captain Washington's company took part in silencing a battery at Cartagena. The bombastic Admiral Vernon praised him in his official report for his bravery, but a place at the officers' mess table aboard his flagship did little to compensate for 90 percent American casualties. These were mostly caused by an array of diseases—scurvy, dysentery, yellow fever, malaria—and beatings and starvation at the hands of British officers, who then pressed-ganged any Americans who had survived the land assault into service on Royal Navy ships to replace dead English sailors. By late October 1742, after an absence of two terrible tense years of waiting, Lawrence Washington returned to Virginia, but he never fully recovered his health.

*G*eorge Washington clung to scant memories of his father. Gus Washington's days at home at Ferry Farm became rarer as George's boyhood raced on. Far more frequently, George spent his days with his mother. Life in the Washington household revolved around the crowded kitchen and dining room, where an amazing array of meats were served after being roasted in the large fireplace. During Washington's boyhood, the nearby forests were still full of game. In 1739, when George was seven, a botanist visiting the Virginia frontier reported to a friend in England of finding

> deer in great plenty, bears, buffaloes, wolves, foxes, panthers, wild cats, elks, hares, squirrels (three or four sorts), raccoons, opossums, beavers, otters, muskrats, polecats, minks . . . porcupines, but they are very scarce. . . . Then, for fowls, wild turkeys very numerous, partridges, wild geese, swans, brants, cormorants, teal duck and mallard, black ducks and another sort we call summer ducks, plover two or three sorts, soris (a delicious eating bird in shape and [in] way of living like your water rails), heath fowls (called here improperly pheasants), wild pigeons in prodigious great flocks, fieldhares, woodcocks, snipes, herons, bitterns, eagles, larks as big as quails.[11]

This abundance not only encouraged George to eat but to learn to hunt—his father taught him to covet the white-tailed deer. As a young boy he practiced the arts of stealth and surprise in the woods and the quick accurate marksmanship that brought back game for the family even if it led to the overeating of meat. Few Virginians ate enough fruits and vegetables. It was game and corn, cornbread and game. Many Virginians ate meat as often as five times a day.

At home, where George's mother spent virtually all her time, the Washingtons enjoyed exceptional comforts for the time and place, especially considering that they lived a day's ride from the edge of the white man's civilization. There were probably framed English prints on the walls. Neighbors had displays of Roman ruins in gilded frames and Hogarth's rollicking prints and flowers. Mary's brother was a connoisseur of fine prints and delighted in sending from London the latest prints from the shops on the Strand. It is inconceivable, given his closeness with his sister, that he left her drawing room and dining room walls barer than those of her socially competitive neighbors.

Yet Gus and Mary Washington were not extravagant. They did not fall into the trap that left so many Virginians in permanent debt to their English factors. There was silver on the table, but it was mostly spoons. When Lawrence came home from England, he brought George's younger sister Betty a gift from Uncle Joseph. This high-water mark of luxury in the household was long remembered: six silver spoons, a chest of tea, a silver strainer and tongs, and a box full of sugar cubes "ready broke." Now the Washingtons could serve tea in the latest English fashion. An inventory of King George County taken in the early 1740s shows how typical the Washington household was among the second rank of Virginia plantations. The walls were painted and a mirror hung in the entry hallway. There were two tables for meals and eleven leather-bottomed chairs arranged around them. There was plenty of china on the tables, but it was not fine. Few glasses had survived Atlantic crossings. Sometimes there was linen on the table, but it was coarse.

What visitors from England noticed more was the sheer quantity of food, all of it homegrown or hunted nearby. Bread and meat were abundant, their consumption ample. An average family and its servants consumed fifty pounds of flour a day as they eagerly cut down forests to make way for wheat fields. The Washingtons had their own mill. They charged one-twelfth of the grain they ground for their hungry neighbors. The slaves were fed cornmeal and pork, receiving fixed rations each year at hog-killing time. In addition to pork, hominy grits, and cornbread, the master's family ate large quantities of game and beef, which cost a penny a pound in 1740. After a prayer of thanks to God, young George could launch into white or corn bread and either hot or (if there were no green vegetables to boil) cold meat, chicken, fish, and oysters. For Sunday dinner, served at noon and often shared with guests invited after the morning Anglican service, there could be greens, fish, roast pig, cheese, puddings—with plenty of liquor (preferably rum or brandy) for the parents. No wonder George grew so tall.

George's father was often away on his restless quest for more land and more ore, and when he was home he pursued more income from his lengthening string of county and colony offices. With the new town of Fredericksburg burgeoning just across the narrow Rappahannock, however, other people were now demanding his son's attention. Seven was the traditional age for a boy in Virginia to begin schooling. There are no records, but he apparently began to learn to read, write, and keep sums from a tutor, a convict indentured servant Gus bought to teach his children. George began to copy out lessons in a beautiful round scroll. By the time his brother Lawrence returned in his red-and-blue uniform, George was already crossing the river each morning to the log schoolhouse in Fredericksburg. There he was preparing for the day when, like his father and stepbrothers, he would cross the Atlantic to Appleby School, to be educated formally as an English gentleman. In all, George Washington received between seven and eight years of schooling. For nearly four years, he took the ferry each morning to Fredericksburg.

When he was not bending over his quill pen and inkstand, George Washington was practicing to become a superb rider and wrestler. He was generally healthy, although the unbalanced diet of the Tidewater, combined with his mother's slavish adherence to the application of herbs, may have given George a case of rickets, a disease associated with malnutrition, which left him with a thin, caved-in chest. His mother became increasingly parsimonious over the years, and even if there were a good doctor around she did not like to pay one. He later resented and rejected his mother's stinginess, and as an adult would rely heavily on doctors while rejecting herbal nostrums.

Whenever his father was home between trips to England and to the western Virginia frontier, George followed him around in the way young boys do. Boys were considered the charges of their fathers and girls were trained by their mothers. He accompanied his father on daily rounds of inspecting the slaves at their labors. He learned the techniques of giving orders and of gaining obedience from men. Little black boys he had once played with now had to carry out his every wish. On special occasions he rode with his father over to the iron furnace to watch the blast. What a thrill for a young boy! Or he would go along to watch the slaves work his father's new grist mill on Does Creek. He learned that free white men as well as slaves and bondservants had to work hard and get dirty if they wanted to prosper. He watched his father load the wagons at the furnace, hauling twice as much as any man who worked for him. He also watched when his father came home after a trip to the west, unstrapped his surveying tools, and locked them safely in a shed. These, his father told him, were the keys George would need to claim the lands to the west that everyone, including his father and all his friends, seemed always to be talking about.

George had just turned eleven on Easter in 1743 and was visiting his

Washington cousins at Chotank when a message arrived from his mother to hurry home. His father had been away for months on one of his periodic voyages to England and had returned home seriously ill. Whatever communicable disease had stricken him, the local verdict was "gout of the stomach." Modern medical experts deny there is any such disease, but whatever it was killed Gus Washington. His father's death before the age of fifty and his grandfather's at thirty-seven gave Washington the lasting impression that the Washingtons were not long-lived. Partly because of unhealthy conditions in the Tidewater, where undrained swamps produced malaria and where medicine was exceedingly primitive, few people reached old age. Roughly half the immigrants from England died within the first five years. His grandfather's death at thirty-seven was about average. But his obsession with the ages of dead antecedents gave George a gloomy, diffident manner. Of his eight siblings, two died in infancy and six between the ages of thirteen and sixty-four. George outlasted them all, not succumbing until he hastened his own death at sixty-seven. A robust constitution, inherited as much from his mother as his father, may account for the fact that George Washington outlived all of his male line, but his overriding impression was that he could not expect many years.

Yet Washington's intimations of his own mortality were certainly not a sign of hypochondria. He had the strength to survive, in addition to mumps, a severe case of smallpox, four encounters with malaria, which afflicted him from age sixteen to his dying day, as well as serious and protracted bouts of dysentery. He endured smallpox and malaria simultaneously. He had a brush with tuberculosis, suffered from typhoid fever, twice suffered near-fatal bouts of influenza, and, as president, was crippled for months by a staphylococcus infection of the hip and a serious attack of pneumonia. He was dosed with quinine so much for recurring malaria that he suffered marked hearing loss and was nearly deaf by the time he left the presidency. Only his mother lived to an age today considered old. Unimpressed that her son was by that time the first president of the United States, she died at eighty-two. But all the illness, death, and dying seemed to have some good side effects on Washington. From his boyhood he grew in patience, self-control, courage, and determination. War seemed to come as a relief for him. His adrenaline pumping, he was never healthier than when under the crushing responsibilities of command during the Revolutionary War. Here, at least, he could see his enemies.

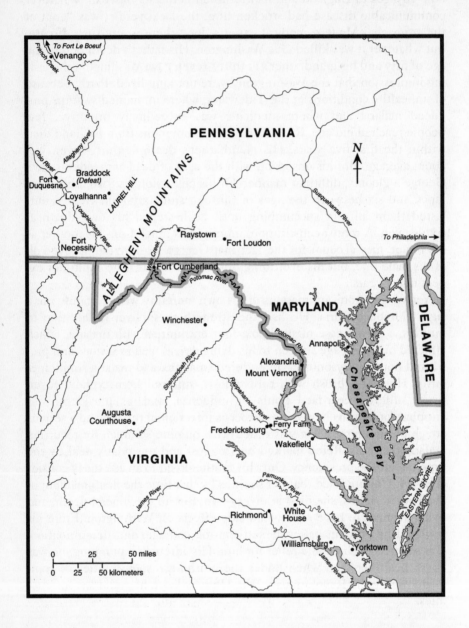

The region of George Washington's activities between 1732 and 1759, when he resigned his Virginia commission.

Two

"TAKE ALL ADMONITIONS THANKFULLY"

Barely eleven when his father died, George Washington's first duty as a young man was to read the prayers of the dead at his father's funeral in the family plot at Ferry Farm. Gus was buried, as he had wished, along Bridges Creek beside his grandfather and his father. There, surrounded by four generations of dead Washingtons, young George read the all-too-familiar Anglican words in his high-pitched boy's voice: "Man that is born of woman has a short time to live, and is full of misery." Three weeks later, on May 6, 1743, when Gus Washington's will was filed for probate at the county courthouse, the Washingtons learned how democratically Augustine Washington had divided his estate. He died owning more than 10,000 acres of Virginia in seven tracts as well as forty-nine slaves, about one in three able to work. He also left a one-sixth share in the Principio Iron Works and a small herd of cattle. In the spirit but not the letter of the law of primogeniture, he left Epsewasson and the larger share of his property to his firstborn son, Lawrence, who had been living there since returning from the Cartagena expedition. He had just planted his first crop and had renamed the plantation Mount Vernon in honor of his former commanding officer. Gus also left Lawrence his iron mining interests. To his second son, Augustine, Jr., whom everyone called Austin, he left the original Washington farm on Pope's Creek, which George would later pronounce the best part of his father's lands.

To George, his father left the largest share allotted to any of his five children by his second marriage. When he turned twenty-one, George was to receive the 260-acre Ferry Farm as well as some potentially valuable land along Aquia Creek: three town lots across the river in Fredericksburg; one-fifth of his father's personal property; some 2,100 acres of undeveloped land in the Deep Run tract; and ten slaves. By an elaborate legal arrangement, Gus Washington also planned for his family's more distant future: if one heir died, his land would go to another. Thus, if Lawrence died without an heir, the Mount Vernon farm would go to George unless Austin wanted to exchange it for yet another tract; if Lawrence married, then died, his widow and any heirs would inherit, but if they all died, Mount Vernon would revert to the next Washington bloodline. At eleven, George Washington became a slaveholder, even if his mother had the use of the slaves and their children until he turned twenty-one. Mary Ball Washington, wealthy enough to mark her as a target for imperious suitors, received one-fifth of her husband's personal property, the crops growing on three plantations, and five harvests on the Bridges Creek lands. She could establish her own plantation on Gus's Deep Run tract beside George's lands, where she was expected to move when she turned over Ferry Farm to her eldest son.

With his father away so frequently, George was accustomed to his mother's dominion, but now it was a ten-year sentence without possibility of appeal. In a way, he had always enjoyed more stature as the oldest of five children, but the single greatest shift at his father's death was in his prospects. He had always been led to expect to go to school in England once he had been prepared sufficiently by local tutors. Now on his horizon was Fredericksburg, no farther than across the river, unless he somehow managed to escape. It was at this point that George Washington learned what became one of his principal characteristics: he learned to be elusive, like an Indian. He made frequent small escapes whenever he could, fleeing his mother's demanding regime whenever possible to go visit his Chotank cousins or, best of all, Lawrence, who now carefully tucked George under his wing—careful not to rouse his stepmother, who considered the boy not only her firstborn, but *hers*.

Life at Ferry Farm became progressively more austere, the treatment of children and slaves stricter. Mary Washington insisted on discipline, on adherence to routines. She was especially strict about who could ride her horses. No one could ride her prize bay mare, inherited from her stepbrother. When young George ignored this rule and leaped on the horse one day, the horse reared and fell and tore a blood vessel in its neck and died. Mary Ball Washington may have never forgiven him: the seeds of a lifelong enmity had been planted by his strong-headed act. The only law at Ferry Farm was hers. Obsessed with a thousand trifles, she neglected larger interests. She did little to carry out her husband's wish that she prepare a new plantation for herself at Deep Run and move before George's twenty-first birthday. Instead, she concentrated on keeping the slaves at Ferry Farm tied down serving her whims. She was acquisitive without being a good investor or manager and allowed Ferry Farm to run down. Before long, young George could see that she was not conserving his estate or making any plans to leave it for a new farm of her own. In fact, it would take George not ten years but twenty-nine to dislodge his mother. More and more, Mary Ball Washington became convinced that her family owed her more than she had been left, that she should not have to provide for herself. She was determined to prepare George to take care of her. At first, that required getting him a practical schooling that would enable him to help out with the farm accounts.

*L*ater in his life, George Washington would almost never discuss his education. When David Humphreys submitted the first draft of his proposed biography of then-President Washington, he wrote at length on the subject. He noted that Washington's "father and oldest brothers had received their education in England" where "he would have been sent" if Washington's father hadn't died. "This was the common mode of disposing of the children of opulent families," Humphreys wrote. Apparently paraphrasing the notes Washington had given him, Humphreys added, "for such as were brought up at home were in danger of becoming indolent and helpless from the usual indulgence." He included "giving a horse and a servant to attend them as soon as they could ride" in this category of vice. Other damages he listed included becoming

> imperious and dissipated from the habit of commanding slaves and living in a measure without control. Those Virginians, educated in a domestic manner, who had fortitude enough to resist the temptations to which they were exposed in their youth, have commonly been distinguished by success in their various professions.

Washington left unchanged Humphreys's narrative of his early schooling. Young Washington, he wrote, was taught

> by a domestic tutor, which was then generally . . . the mode of education practiced in that part of the Continent. . . . He was betimes instructed in the principles of grammar, the theory of reasoning, on speaking, [in] the science of numbers, the elements of geography and the highest branches of mathematics [including] the art of [surveying and] composing together with the rudiments of geography [and] history and the studies which are not improperly termed "the humanities."[1]

Fortunately, the earliest surviving papers among the 20,000 documents George Washington did not destroy are his boyhood schoolwork. In three notebooks, there are 218 pages of his longhand exercises, mostly his practice exercises in mathematics and surveying. Much of what he read, studied, and copied to learn manners and mores can be found in these notebooks. When he was between ten and thirteen, a succession of tutors, as was customary at the time, put him to work copying out a variety of the legal instruments and forms he would need to manage a plantation.

Fully twenty pages of Washington's earliest notebook in the Library of Congress, entitled "1st Vol. Miscellaneous," were devoted to 110 rules for good behavior, the complete text of a sixteenth-century training manual prepared by French Jesuits for young noblemen. Proof that he was too young and naive to discard the rules that were totally inappropriate for a Virginia gentleman is that he copied all of them in a firm, flowing hand—as well as how to comport himself, he was learning handwriting. The Jesuit rules were to become a catechism to Washington, not only a code of conduct that he followed more faithfully than religious doctrine, but his own self-teaching school for manners. In the absence of a father, Lawrence was taking a growing interest in George's formation, and it is likely that the polished young captain lent him the book containing the kernel of a gentleman's code of chivalry that Lawrence himself had studied at the same age. The printer may well have been Benjamin Franklin, who ran off an edition of *Civilities Rules* in October 1730 and regularly distributed it to the bookstore of the *Virginia Gazette* in Williamsburg.

There were limits to what George could learn by observation and he already was developing a fondness for rules and order. His father had been away most of the time; his mother placed little value on order. How else was he to learn except by the book? Some were merely rules of etiquette; others reinforced the patriarchal system of deference in English society. Here is a sampler of some of Washington's favorite *Rules of Civility and Decent Behavior*, which he studied and then followed—and one day insisted others follow—the rest of his life:

Rule 1: Every action done in company ought to be with some sign of respect to those that are present.

Rule 4: In the presence of others, sing not to yourself with a humming noise nor drum with your fingers or feet.

Rule 5: If you cough, sneeze, sigh or yawn, do it not loud but privately. . . . Speak not in your yawning but put your handkerchief or hand before your face and turn aside.

Rule 6: Sleep not when others speak. Sit not when others stand. Speak not when you should hold your peace.

Rule 9: Spit not in the fire. . . . Neither put your hands into the flames to warm them nor set your feet upon the fire, especially if there be meat before it.

Rule 11: Shift not yourself in the sight of others nor gnaw your nails.

Rule 13: Kill no vermin [such] as fleas, lice, ticks, etc., in the sight of others. If you see filth or thick spittle, put your foot dexterously upon it. If it be upon the clothes of your companion, put it off privately. . . .

Rule 14: Turn not your back to others, especially in speaking. . . .

Rule 15: Keep your nails clean and short, also your hands and teeth clean yet without showing any great concern for them.

Nearly one-fifth of the rules governed good table manners. With a mother not known for putting out linen and china and dictating in small ways as well as large, George must have paid special attention. He internalized an attitude about food as well as a manual of arms for attacking it. He never took "great delight" in his victuals; he certainly didn't eat "with greediness."

How genteel this young Virginia gentleman must have looked when he ventured west toward the frontier with its rough-cut mountainmen: "Put not your meat to your mouth with your knife. . . . Neither spit forth the stones of any fruit pie upon a dish nor cast anything under the table. . . . [Don't] stoop much to [your] meat. . . . Keep your fingers clean and, when foul, wipe them on a corner of your table napkin. . . . Drink not nor talk with your mouth full. . . . Cleanse not your teeth with the table cloth, napkin, fork or knife. . . . Talk not with meat in your mouth."

Beyond good manners, Washington imbibed a moral code that became his civil religion and his guide in grooming himself into a gentleman and man of honor:

Rule 17: Be no flatterer.

Rule 19: Let your countenance be pleasant but, in serious matters, somewhat grave.

Rule 22: Show not yourself glad at the misfortune of another, though he were your enemy.

Rule 35: Let your discourse with men of business be short and comprehensive.

Rule 40: Strive not with your superiors in argument, but always submit your judgment to others with modesty.

Rule 49: Use no reproachful language against anyone; neither curse nor revile.

Rule 56: Associate yourself with men of good quality if you esteem your own reputation, for 'tis better to be alone than in bad company.

Rule 73: Think before you speak. Pronounce not imperfectly nor bring out your words too hastily but orderly and distinctly.

The last three rules that Washington copied into his notebook soared above the day-to-day details of the rest: Rule 108, "Honor and obey your natural parents although they be poor," and Rule 109, "Let your recreations be manful, not sinful," covered much of the curriculum desired for him by his mother and brother. Beyond all the others, the final rule, Rule 110, enjoined young Washington to "labor to keep alive in your breast that little spark of celestial fire called conscience."

Washington practiced these rules more closely than the precepts of any religion. In the absence of a father and in contention with his mother, he espoused them as dogma, and his personal code of conduct closely paralleled them. "Youth, in Washington's time, took precepts more seriously than now," observed Washington scholar John C. Fitzpatrick. "There was a decided strain of romance in the makeup of George Washington," added Fitzpatrick, "and it was precisely to this romantic strain that these rules strongly appealed."[2]

Just how seriously Washington insisted on these rules underscores their impact on him. Most obviously, Washington believed in Rule 17, "Be no flatterer." His need as a young man to toady to Lord Fairfax and then to British officers filled him with revulsion. When he became the first president and could set the tone for this office by deciding on how the president would be addressed and introduced at his weekly audiences, he insisted on being called nothing more flowery than "Mister President." He severely reprimanded an aide who announced him with a long string of pompous adjectives. He believed in the importance of appropriate behavior: no one ever accused him of being silly or playing the fool. He seems to have taken his cue from Rule 19: "Let your countenance be pleasant but in serious matters somewhat grave." His closest friend, George Mercer, wrote of him, when he was still a young man, "In conversation he looks you full in the face, is deliberate, deferential and engaging."

His frank, compassionate manner carried some of the spirit of Rule 22: "Show not yourself glad at the misfortune of another though he were your enemy." At the capture of the Hessian colonel Johann Rall, at Trenton, the man who had decimated his troops only weeks earlier, and after the surrender of Burgoyne and Cornwallis, he was generous and unfailingly considerate. He had no patience for arrogance or insubordination, as in the case of his dismissed second-in-command, Major General Charles Lee, but he was truly compassionate in the face of honest failure. "When a man does all he can," stated Rule 44, "though it succeed not well, blame not him that did it." No matter how exalted he became, honoring others by addressing them meticulously, according to their proper rank and station—Rule 39—was a lifelong rule he followed almost slavishly in his thousands of letters. His rage was to become legendary, even though there are few provable examples of it—the refusal of Lee to attack at Monmouth, the cowardice of Connecticut militia at Kip's Bay, the blundering of St. Clair at Ticonderoga and again in battle against the Indians—yet he seems to have labored mightily all his life to follow Rule 58: "In all causes of passion admit reason to govern." His idealistic impulses yielded to pragmatism. Even though, for much of his life, he was the embodiment of the restless, yearning, striving, revolutionary, the Age of Reason with all its rules of order made him feel more at home.

George Washington's schoolboy notebook contained not only a formula "to keep ink from freezing or molding," which he copied almost verbatim from the 1727 edition of George Fisher's *The Instructor: or, Young Man's Best Companion,* but two poems. One of them was "True Happiness." At the age of twelve he copied out lines whose selection hint how much he already yearned for the quiet home life that so long eluded him, that came to mean more to him, he often said, than fame:

> These are the things which, once possessed,
> Will make a life that's truly blessed:
> A good estate on healthy soil
> Not got by vice, nor yet by toil:
> Round a warm fire, a pleasant joke,
> With chimney ever free from smoke:
> A strength entire, a sparkling bowl,
> A quiet wife, a quiet soul,
> A mind as well as body whole:
> Prudent simplicity, constant friends,
> A diet which no art commends:
> A merry night without much drinking,
> A happy thought without much thinking:
> Each night by quiet sleep made short,
> A will to be but what thou art:
> Possessed of these, all else defy,
> And neither wish nor fear to die.[3]

Mount Vernon was becoming his ideal world, the "good estate on healthy soil," even if it was not always perfect. It was often smoke-filled in the days before the Franklin fireback was introduced, and for many years it was unfinished when he was away engaging in war and politics. He liked nothing better than sitting "round a warm fire" with a draft from the "sparkling bowl." One of the many dentists who made him artificial teeth reasoned that only by drinking a substantial quantity of port each day could he turn the dentures so dark so fast. At Mount Vernon he would one day be delighted to consume and share the cases of fine French wine his friend Thomas Jefferson sent him from France. After several failed courtships and his troublesome relations with his mother, he was completely content to settle down there with "a quiet wife, a quiet soul." He survived many serious illnesses that would have killed weaker men, not even counting all the lead fired at him, and came to value "a strength entire" that repeatedly awed weaker men around him.

Only political dealings with Congress ever seriously threatened his mental health. Most of all, "True Happiness" to him meant what the poem said it should: "Prudent simplicity, constant friends" and "A will to be what thou art" in the company of "constant friends." Nothing unsettled him more than betrayal. If he had trusted friends and an occasional "happy thought without much thinking," he had no "wish nor fear to die."

As if to juxtapose the means to this material Eden of a young English-American and an end, the same notebook contains twenty-eight legal forms that the young boy had to copy out, including standard deeds, wills, indentures, notes promissory, and bills of exchange designed specifically for Virginia. He rendered the sample accounts in tobacco; he used the names of all the Virginia counties, dating each exercise. By the age of nine, and from time to time over the next four years, a succession of tutors put George Washington to work learning the proper forms he would need to settle the property rights and disputes of a country squire. It is reasonably safe to speculate that he preserved the notebook more for its legal forms than for its poetry.

*G*eorge Washington could have settled for the safe, pleasant life of the middle-rung Virginia farmer. His inheritance guaranteed that someday he would own Ferry Farm and enough slaves to begin to work it. Each good crop he produced would buy him a few more slaves, a few more luxury goods ordered from the London merchant who sold his crop. In time, he might add to his land. Tall and handsome, he would no doubt attract the daughter of a landed planter. There was no reason for him to do more than read, write, keep accounts, ride his horse, play cards, go to parties as he grew older—and wait. He was certainly under no pressure from his mother to go away to college at William and Mary. He had wanted to go to England to school or to Williamsburg. It was out of the question. No one ever got a shilling out of the hand of Mary Ball Washington. When he finally summoned the courage to ask for music lessons, something a boy of his social standing had a right to expect, she would only agree to lend him the money. But did he know not to ask much of his mother? A comment years later, by a cousin who frequently visited Ferry Farm, suggests that George Washington grew up afraid of his mother. The cousin said that he himself was "ten times" more afraid of Mary Ball Washington than of his own mother.[4]

That George was receiving unsolicited tutoring on how to prepare for a future beyond Ferry Farm was carefully hidden from Washington's mother until he was fourteen. As each year passed, it became clear to all around her that she had no intention of vacating Ferry Farm when George turned twenty-one. Secretly, tactfully, Lawrence had begun to coach George, to prepare him for a military career, including arranging fencing lessons from a Dutch tutor in Fredericksburg. As one of the heroes of the Cartagena expedition, and as a young man with private English schooling, Lawrence had been welcomed at Admiral Vernon's table. He regaled George with stories of the refined company and exciting life of a British navy officer. When biographer Humphreys wrote that it was "the design of his father that he should be bred for an officer in the British navy," Washington disagreed.[5]

To carry out their plot, Lawrence Washington arranged for George to spend more and more time at Mount Vernon. He further arranged to have George tutored by the neighborhood Anglican priest. His education now was obviously aimed at preparing him for the exciting life of a mariner. He was put in a school where the teacher thought little of his earlier tutoring: the new teacher made him repeat much of what he had already studied, as is evidenced by the repetition in his second notebook. Just what the schoolmaster was called is one of the enduring little mysteries of American history, but that it was indeed a school is indicated in a 1756 letter from his friend George Mason, who writes Washington and mentions "my neighbor and your old schoolfellow," now Sergeant Piper.[6]

What George Washington learned under Captain Washington's watchful eye is easier to decipher. In his new notebook, he began to master geometry lessons, which he dated and signed on August 13, 1745, when he was thirteen. He became an enthusiastic and excellent mathematics student. According to a modern mathematician, he learned as much as a student today who takes all the courses required for a liberal arts graduate. In his notebooks were fifty pages of exercises that encapsulated the mathematical training needed by any planter, merchant, or merchant mariner of the time, giving young Washington a thorough grounding in currency and credit and Virginia rates of exchange. His second notebook contains nineteen pages of geometric theorems, definitions, and twenty-nine problems. It also contains the first evidence that he had found his father's surveying tools locked away in an outbuilding. George did eight pages of exercises in how to survey woodlands. Fifteen pages show he also carried out physics experiments, learning how to measure liquids and solids in a variety of containers and figuring the weight and measurements of planks. In 1746, as he turned fourteen, he pondered how to calculate "the ecclesiastical and civil calendar" (five pages); the "mensuration of plain superficies" (four pages); geographical definitions and problems (six pages). His early lessons in geometry included drills in the principles of geometry, which applied the elementary rules of surveying. His calendar drills were sophisticated. Among the section titles were "a description of the leap year, Dominical letter, golden number, cycle of the sun."[7]

By age fifteen George was ready to advance to dizzying heights for a young Virginia farm boy. His third notebook included decimals, simple interest, money conversion, geometry problems, rules and problems of the square root, plane trigonometry, and surveying. Surveying accounted for 39 of the 120 pages in this ultimate notebook. One-third of Washington's final notebook was devoted to the "Art of Surveying and Measuring of Land." In its pages, Washington proved that he was properly trained for a career as a "woodland" surveyor, mute evidence that the secret plan to make him a Royal Navy officer had, in that last year of study, fizzled.

*B*y age fourteen, George Washington had grown up right past other boys his age on his way to a towering height. At the time of his death his personal secretary measured him at six feet three and a half inches. A modern medical historian says this means he was at least one inch taller in his earlier years. As a teenage boy in the 1740s, he was a head taller than most boys his age. Were it not for his physical prowess in sports, one way boys settle such differences, his height could have marked him as somewhat of a freak. George Washington was always proud of his strength and endurance. He was to become, according to Thomas Jefferson (who traveled all over Europe, as well as most of America east of the Mississippi, and was an expert breeder of thoroughbred horses), "the greatest horseman of his age." He was an uncommonly good wrestler and rail-splitter, activities which, like riding, required great strength, control, and endurance. He was especially proud of his throwing arm. Mythmaking biographer Weems coined the legend of his pitching a silver dollar across the Potomac after sales of his life of Washington started to flag. Washington was always proud that he could throw a stone farther than anyone he knew—all the way over the Natural Bridge in Virginia. "I have several times heard him say," related his amanuensis Humphreys, that "he never met any man who could throw to so great a distance as himself and that, when standing in the valley beneath the Natural Bridge in Virginia, he has thrown one up to that stupendous arch."[8] Probably because he was so graceful on a horse, he learned easily to become a good dancer: French officers during the Revolution attested to his great ability in the minuet, marveling that any American could have learned its graceful intricacies so well.

Until George was thirteen, he lived with his mother during the school year. But in summers and on holidays, he broke free and visited his cousins, most of whom placed a higher value on social niceties than Mary Ball Washington did, and his brother Lawrence at Mount Vernon. In the portrait of Lawrence at Mount Vernon there is a kindly man with a high forehead and a sensitive mouth; in biographer Douglas Southall Freeman's memorable description, the person to whom, in a crowd, a stranger would go to make an inquiry. Courteous, deferential to the rich and powerful he came to know, he was politically savvy, serious about his Anglican religion, and an excellent marksman and horseman. Yet he was no Squire Western: he was cultivated, well-read, an easy, witty conversationalist. He dazzled young, tongue-tied George Washington.

Lawrence had torn down the simple farmhouse where George had spent three dimly remembered childhood years, planted crops, and built a more gracious house. It was a typical Tidewater redbrick manor house, two symmetrical stories with high-pitched eaves bookended by tall brick chimneys. A rectangle cut by a hallway, it featured a "hall room" upstairs above the entry foyer. Slightly extending the walls of the original house, Lawrence furnished it elegantly. Shortly after his father died, Lawrence had married the girl next door, Anne Fairfax, daughter of the wealthy scion of an English land baron whose house was visible two miles away. It was a fortuitous marriage for the Washington clan. One of the wealthiest and most powerful families in Virginia, the Fairfaxes assured Lawrence's place in the front rank of socially conscious Virginia society. During the English civil wars, the Fairfax family had remained loyal, like the Washingtons, to the Stuart kings. As a result, Charles II, from exile in France, conferred an enormous grant of land, 5.2 million acres of the northern part of Virginia and of West Virginia, on the Fairfaxes. It was not until the 1740s, however, that the English government that had displaced the Stuarts confirmed the ninety-year-old grant, making it possible for settlers to buy land and obtain clear title to it. When George Washington was thirteen, the constant dinner-table gossip about western land speculation reached the level of a fever. Word reached Belvoir, the home of George's new sister-in-law, that Lord Fairfax had won his long-standing lawsuit against Virginia. While George may not have been able to comprehend all that this meant, he began to listen carefully to talk of the Fairfaxes sending out an expedition to map the boundary line between their lands and the colony of Virginia and then to survey these new wilderness lands for new towns and settlements.

By this time, the serious youth was becoming a fixture at Belvoir, where Lawrence and his Nancy spent so much time. Lawrence Washington was a personable ally for the Fairfaxes, who had only recently taken up residence on their Virginia lands. Not only had Lawrence received control of a 4,000-acre dowry when he married Nancy, but he had been elected to the House of Burgesses. He also kept his post as adjutant general of the Virginia militia. Amid this atmosphere of power, elegance, and wealth, George Washington began to look beyond the backwater world of Ferry Farm. It was Lawrence's idea, one that evolved from his own glorious brush with shipboard life aboard Admiral Vernon's flagship, that the route to distinction for his own protégé was through a career in the Royal Navy. The plot he concocted with the aid of the Fairfaxes and their friends was to spirit George away from his domineering mother and onto a man-of-war where he would begin his illustrious career as a midshipman. If only they could have managed to outmaneuver Mary Ball Washington, George Washington might have spent his life in the British navy and very possibly might have fought on the other side in the American Revolution.

According to Washington's recollection nearly half a century later when he was president, his bags were already packed. "He was entered as a midshipman," wrote Humphreys, "and his baggage prepared for embarkation" when his mother stopped his seagoing career. She was determined to keep her firstborn son close to dry land and her house. Lawrence could give all the advice he liked and use all his connections and influence to help George, but not without her consent. Knowing this, Captain Washington had proceeded with all the secrecy and caution of a surprise attack. He lined up allies, ensured safe channels of communication. He obviously felt that George had a good enough education in manners, mathematics, and celestial navigation to take advantage of his own connections, including Admiral Vernon and Lord Fairfax, and rise in rank in the patronage-controlled Royal Navy. His closest friend and neighbor, Colonel William Fairfax, obviously agreed with him and was willing not only to lend his influence but to participate actively in the siege of Mary Ball Washington.

Just what exactly George's wishes were in the matter must be guessed. Later on, to biographer Humphreys, he would write only to correct Humphreys's assertion that George's father had wanted him to join the navy. "It was the design of his father that he should be bred for an officer in the British navy," Humphreys wrote. "His mental acquisitions and exterior accomplishments were calculated to give him distinction in that profession." No, not entirely true, noted President Washington. "It was rather the wish of my eldest brother (on whom the several concerns of the family had devolved), that this should take place and the mother was consulted by him."[9]

On September 8, 1746, the fourteen-year-old George took the ferry as usual across the Rappahannock to Fredericksburg, where he met Colonel Fairfax, who had ridden the twenty-five miles from Belvoir on his way to map the Fairfax-Virginia line. After preliminary news from Nancy Fairfax and Mount Vernon, Colonel Fairfax gave George two letters from Lawrence, one addressed to George and the other to his mother. The colonel explained that George was to read the letter from Lawrence to him but not to mention it to his mother. Lawrence evidently laid out his reasons for urging the boy to take this sudden opportunity to join the Royal Navy. George was to use his judgment to decide when to give the second letter to his mother. The first letter contained the arguments in favor of a life at sea. Not that the possibility was so alien that it needed much of a brief—the first Washington who had come to America had been a merchant mariner, and every generation since on both his mother and father's sides had sailed back and forth to England. Lawrence also urged his younger brother to hold firm in the face of his mother's objections and to keep Lawrence's name out of it. Lawrence obviously thought that if his stepmother suspected his manipulation, the plot would fail. Promising to protect Lawrence's (and Colonel Fairfax's) behind-the-scenes maneuvering, young George set out on his first military campaign.

Fairfax wrote back to Lawrence, "George has been with us and says he will be steady and thankfully follow your advice as his best friend."[10]

Part of the reason for the cloak-and-dagger meeting was that Colonel Fairfax and Captain Washington knew that Mary Ball Washington was not alone over at Ferry Farm. Dr. Archibald Spencer had arrived in Virginia shortly after Gus Washington's death in search of money and, undoubtedly, a wealthy widow. He had come from England to Boston, where he supported himself for a while by giving public demonstrations of his electrical apparatus. On a visit to his family in Boston, Philadelphia printer Benjamin Franklin saw one of the amateur electrician's shows and became entranced. Returning to Philadelphia, he invited Dr. Spencer to come to the Quaker town to give public lectures and demonstrations. When Dr. Spencer arrived, Franklin studied his experiments, bought his apparatus, and set off on five years of experiments that were to immortalize him. With fresh cash in his pockets, Dr. Spencer headed south to Williamsburg where he advertised in the *Virginia Gazette* that he would offer Virginians a "course of experimental philosophy." He became a frequent caller at Ferry Farm and undoubtedly a suitor of Mary Ball Washington.[11]

Exactly when young George Washington summoned up the courage to present his proposal for a seagoing career to his mother is uncertain, but the ship with its billet for a midshipman would not wait for long. Just which side Dr. Spencer took in the siege is also unclear: did he connive with the captain and the colonel or bolster the good widow's defenses? He probably connived. One account holds that "the Doctor was urged to use his influence to persuade the widow to look more favorably on the plan for George to go to sea." But Mary Ball Washington dug in her heels. Wrote a family friend a week later to Lawrence, waiting anxiously back at Mount Vernon: "She offers several trifling objections such as fond and unthinking mothers naturally suggest." He added she was increasingly reluctant to let George do it. "I find that one word against his going has more weight than ten for it."[12]

By now, the ship was sailing away and the besieged mother was successfully wielding her ultimate weapon: delay. She insisted on writing to her older brother in England. This appeal to the family lawyer and, in Mary Washington's eyes, paterfamilias of the family must have infuriated George. It may have been the end of Dr. Spencer's marital aspirations as well. Soon afterward, he disappeared from the scene, abandoning his pursuit of the land-rich, thirty-seven-year-old mistress of Ferry Farm. He left; George had to stay. The answer from England, as everyone anticipated, took six months and was a foregone conclusion. The irascible barrister Joseph Ball wrote his sister:

> I understand you are advised and have some thought of sending
> your son George to sea. I think he had better be put apprentice

to a tinker, for a common sailor before the mast has by no means the common liberty of the subject. For they will [impress] him from a ship where he has 50 shillings a month and make him take three and twenty, and [whip] him and staple him and use him like a Negro, or, rather, like a dog. And as for any considerable preferment in the Navy, it is not to be expected. There are always too many grasping for it here who have interest, and he has none.

And if he should get to be master of a Virginia ship (which will be very difficult to do) a planter that has three or four hundred acres of land and three or four slaves, if he be industrious, may live more comfortably, and leave his family in better bread then such a master of a ship can. . . . He must not be hasty to be rich but must go on gently and with patience as things will naturally go. This method, without aiming to be a fine gentleman before his time, will carry a man more comfortably and surely through the world than going to sea. . . .[13]

The long-awaited letter ended any brief hope young Washington may have had of a naval career. It also made it plain that Mary Ball Washington would not be vacating Ferry Farm in a hurry. The acquisitive widow had asked permission to fell trees and take other building materials from Joseph Ball's portion of a tract they shared to build herself a new house. It was her only attempt to carry out her late husband's wishes and leave Ferry Farm in time for George to take up his rightful inheritance, and she may have deliberately asked what she knew her brother would refuse. She didn't move and she never remarried. As the farm began to look more and more run-down, she settled into a long life of widowhood. It would be another quarter-century before she moved off the farm and into a house George built for her across the river in Fredericksburg. With no real inheritance to look forward to, without permission to pursue a military career, fourteen-year-old George Washington had only meager prospects.

The efforts of George's brother and sister-in-law and her family, neighbors, and old family friends had only alienated Mary Washington from her family. George would never again be close to his mother and he would ignore his uncle from that time forward. Probably out of a sense of obligation after the failed plot to liberate George, his brother Lawrence invited him to come to live with him at Mount Vernon, where he would personally take charge of his schooling. Leaving home (he never returned except for visits), George eagerly left behind the domination of his mother and stepped into an exciting new world of possibilities. As his writings in his notebooks show, George's anger and his disappointment would be slow to dissipate, but he would soon be caught up in adventures that left his mother and Ferry Farm very far behind.

Three

"WE WENT THROUGH

MOST BEAUTIFUL GROVES"

Since his father's death, Lawrence Washington had been busily transforming Mount Vernon into an English-style country manor. When Lawrence married Nancy Fairfax, she furnished Mount Vernon in the latest Georgian elegance. Nothing at Ferry Farm had prepared George for a house where everyone wore shoes and where there were separate parlors so that one group could dance or play music while another played whist and loo. But the scene at his neighbors', the Fairfaxes, was even more sophisticated. Thomas Fairfax, Oxford-educated sixth Baron Fairfax of Cameron, was the first English nobleman George Washington ever saw and was, indeed, the first ever to come to live in America. His arrival in 1747 at Belvoir, the plantation adjoining Lawrence Washington's Mount Vernon, came at a time when young George was already learning the rituals of behaving in Tidewater society. George could be forgiven at first for appearing a tongue-tied young bumpkin when he rode over to Belvoir and first saw its ensemble of drawing rooms, music room, dining room, and grand library filled with guests in the latest London fashions. Here, between rounds of cards, conversations by the fire, and riding to hounds, George Washington learned the rituals of deference, of "attendance and dependence" as he later scornfully put it, that he was one day to overthrow.[1]

Put to his studies in a small Anglican school in the neighborhood, George continued to master mathematics. Independently, he pursued his surveying studies, practicing on his brother's fields, filling his notebooks with calculations. At fifteen he plotted his brother's turnip field, his first professional undertaking. He began to read more, drawing on the library at Belvoir for volumes of history and plays. He read the first 143 numbers of Joseph Addison and Richard Steele's *Spectator*. According to local legend, Lord Fairfax had once been a drinking buddy of Addison in London. The dinner table and drawing room repartee was sprinkled with references to the *Spectator*. While he never attended college and had scant formal literary education, Washington devoured the *Spectator*, exposing himself to the wit and politics of England. In their stylish bantering his brother and his in-laws amplified these readings.

Addison and Steele's works were replete with heroes and antiheroes that influenced the tall, grave young Virginian. There was the old-fashioned, somewhat rustic Sir Roger de Coverly—how like Lord Fairfax he must have seemed to young Washington. Steele could have been describing either de Coverly or Fairfax in *Spectator* No. 2 as someone with "good sense," including "contradictions to the manners of the world." In his rumpled old clothes, Lord Fairfax gave no hint that he had enormous wealth. He was sure, like Sir Roger, that whenever there was a question whether he was right or everyone else was, "the world is in the wrong." Lord Fairfax, like de Coverly, was not fond of women and saw no reason to dress up for a society that revolved around them. Steele could have been describing Lord Fairfax when he wrote,

> It is said he keeps himself a bachelor by reason he was crossed
> in love. . . . He grew careless of himself and never dressed after-
> wards. He continues to wear a coat and doublet of the same cut
> that were in fashion at the time of his repulse.[2]

Choosing between the slovenly Lord Fairfax and the fashionable younger Fairfaxes, Washington emulated the younger set at Belvoir. He was especially drawn to George William Fairfax, Nancy Washington's brother. Seven years older, he was sufficiently immature to be the right companion for the precocious George Washington. Colonel William Fairfax, master of Belvoir, was more impressed with young George than with his own son. He encouraged their friendship by frequently inviting young Washington to ride, hunt, and make himself at home at Belvoir. Colonel Fairfax was the first Englishman to take a liking to this tall, intent young man and had a strong influence on him. The younger son of the fourth Lord Fairfax, he would not inherit much in England, yet he was barred by tradition from working for a living. He had taken the path of currying "interest," joining the Royal Navy at an early age. He had seconded Lawrence's recommendation that young George go to sea. Colonel Fairfax's own experience with the patronage system had been less successful than he advertised. His own patron had left the ship for another command and Fairfax had been left high and dry. His influential relatives had rescued him and bought him a commission in the army and then helped him find a political appointment as chief justice of the Bahamas. When he married a Bahamian-English colonist of less than noble family, rumors circulated in London that he had married a black woman. Plucked back to England, he was packed off to a customs office in Massachusetts. Finally, his cousin, Lord Fairfax, had appointed him his agent for land sales in Virginia.

It was Colonel Fairfax as much as Lawrence who introduced George to the world of Roman history and literature and to English aristocratic manners. George Washington later wrote that of all the Fairfaxes he was most indebted to the colonel. Fairfax also introduced him to his son, who had been sent "home" to England from the Bahamas at age six with a note to his relatives to grant "indulgences to a poor West India boy." After fifteen years of learning the classics and good manners, especially how to dress, George William was shipped off to rejoin his father, now in Virginia. At Belvoir, he translated English aristocracy for his young, more vigorous neighbor. What George learned of lasting interest from young Fairfax was how to dress in the latest fashion. Surrounded suddenly by all this sophistication, George had fresh reasons to consult his handwritten *Rules of Civility* and to pore over Addison and Steele's *Spectator*. If he did not yet have the confidence to attempt to join the banter around him, he would learn the vocabulary. What better example than Sir Andrew Freeport, "a person of indefatigable industry, strong reason and great experience"? Could young Washington see how Steele mocked this man of trade, a despicable word to the English ruling class? Or did he take Sir Andrew's pronouncements literally:

> It is a stupid and barbarous way to extend dominion by arms, for true power is to be got by arts and industry. . . . Diligence makes more lasting acquisitions than valor. . . . Sloth has ruined more nations than the sword. . . . A penny saved is a penny got.[3]

Fascinated by the endless talk at Belvoir of tobacco, trade, and land, and impressed by the military prestige of his scarlet-uniformed brother, young Washington could also identify with Addison and Steele's Captain Sentry, "a gentleman of great courage, good understanding but invincible modesty." How close to the bone did some of the *Spectator*'s words cut the gangling youth:

> He is one of those that deserve very well but are very awkward at putting their talents within the observation of such as should take notice of them. He was some years a captain and behaved himself with great gallantry in several engagements and at several sieges, but having a small estate of his own and being next heir to Sir Roger, he has quitted a way of life in which no man can rise suitably to his merit who is not something of a courtier as well as a soldier.[4]

From studying the pages of Addison and Steele, by watching Lawrence's deft maneuvering for favors and preferment, young Washington was finding the *Spectator* more a primer than a satirical tabloid:

> The man who would make a figure, especially in a military way, must get over all false modesty. . . . It is a civil cowardice to be backward in asserting what you ought to expect as it is a military fear to be slow in attacking when it is your duty. He is never overbearing though accustomed to command men in the utmost degree below him nor ever too obsequious from a habit of obeying men highly above him.[5]

In the pages of the *Spectator,* Washington may have first been exposed to a smattering of Greek and Latin. He memorized the expressions he read and heard around him over the years until, like any gentleman of the time, he could sprinkle his pages of correspondence and military orders with apt classical references. Addison and Steele were fond of using classical quotations to set up their themes. In the numbers of the *Spectator* Washington read, there were quotations from Horace, Lucretius, Juvenal, Ovid, Virgil, Persius, Martial, Homer, Tully. Horace admonished him: "Nothing can be pleasant without love and mirth: then live in love and mirth." Publius Syrus told him: "A pleasant companion in a journey is as good as a coach." Modern historians have been swayed too much by John Adams's partisan slurs on Washington's education (made when the unpopular Adams was jealous of Washington's popularity). They have contended that Washington had no classical training. But, according to the 1756 letter from his friend George Mason, when Washington went to school near Mount Vernon his teacher was a classically trained Anglican clergyman. Adams discounted Washington's self-education and his great ability to absorb knowledge from his erudite brother and friends. When official biographer David Humphreys wrote his account of Washington's early years, he noted that Washington learned the "rudiments" of "the humanities." Washington let these words stand.[6]

Washington also read every word he could find about the London theater, probably in *Gentleman's Magazine*. He attended amateur plays in Williamsburg and, later, on trips to Annapolis with Lawrence. Yet there is every indication from his later readings that he early acquired the lifelong habit of reading things practical. He delved enthusiastically into *A Panegyric to the Memory of Frederick, Late Duke of Schomberg* (not to be confused with Frederick the Great). He continued to attend the theater wherever he went, in war and peacetime. His choice of plays leaned heavily toward drama that taught moral lessons and contained a strong political message. He may have seen Shakespeare's *Richard III* when it was first performed in Williamsburg in 1757, but the first play he read was *Cato: A Tragedy*. He read it as early as 1745 when he was thirteen (probably an edition printed by Benjamin Franklin). It was his all-time favorite, a tale of an uncompromising, incorruptible general who defied tyranny and yet could be compassionate to those loyal to him. At the nadir of the American Revolution, in the misery of winter at Valley Forge, Washington had his officers perform Robert L'Estrange's 1732 version of *Cato* to improve the morale of his troops. The impressionable young Washington was inspired by Cato's stirring rhetoric. He would reread the work often and see the play several times when it became a favorite of early protestors against British imperial "slavery." From Joseph Addison's prologue to the 1713 edition, he read words whose meaning kept changing for him:

> Life in bondage is a worthless thing
> The inborn greatness of your soul we view
> You tread the paths frequented by the few.[7]

As he learned to defer to his lordly neighbor, Lord Fairfax, the passages he read had ironic resonances, espousing rebelliousness:

> Gods! Where's the worth that sets this people up
> Above your own, Numidia's tawny sons!
> Do they with tougher sinews bend the bow?
> Or flies the javelin swifter to its mark
> Launched from the vigor of a Roman arm?[8]

Forced to keep his objections to his mother's iron-handed domination to himself, he could find strength in the words of Cato:

> 'Tis not my talent to conceal my thoughts
> Or carry smiles or sunshine in my face.
> When discontent sits heavy at my heart . . . [9]

But the words that echoed down the years from the elegant library at Belvoir to the huts and frozen hillsides of Valley Forge were Cato's warning speech, written long ago at another time of plots and coups:

> Perfidious men! And will you thus dishonor
> Your past exploits, and sully all your wars?
> Do you confess 'twas not a zeal for Rome
> Nor love of liberty, nor thirst of honor
> Drew you thus far, but hopes to share the spoil
> Of conquered towns and plundered provinces?[10]

Young George Washington had lost his father, but he had gained a new world of companionship among elegant men and women. He was becoming respected not only for his personal grace but for his superb horsemanship. He had to learn to let Lord Fairfax reach the fox first. Yet there were times, whenever he had to go home to visit his mother at Ferry Farm to get permission to accept his many opportunities, when he was filled with frustration and rage. To conquer his anger he turned to the works of Lucius Annaeus Seneca. Most certainly, he read *Seneca's Morals by Way of Abstracts* in its 1719 London edition. Seneca was "the sharpest of all the stoics," wrote Lactantius, "the most lively describer of public vices and manners." From Seneca, young Washington drew advice on how to overcome his anger. "Anger is against nature," he read. "The subduing of the monster will do a great deal toward the establishment of human peace." He read of Caesar Augustus and of Philip of Macedon as they struggled to develop "wonderful patience."[11]

From Seneca as much as any source, he learned to loathe disputation: "A huge deal of time is spent in cavilling about words and captions, disputations that work us up to an edge and then nothing comes of it."[12] From words, he learned to prefer actions. "Virtue," he read, "is divided into two parts, contemplation and action. One part of virtue consists in discipline, the other in exercise, for we must first learn, then practice."[13] Seneca, a Spanish colonist writing under Roman rule, an outsider like Washington in English colonial society, taught him a code of ethics. He read of the prudence of a general who, even after he lost a battle, believed he had not needlessly lost the lives of his men. He studied Seneca's lessons in dignity and courage:

> He is the brave man whose splendor and authority is the least part of his greatness, that can look death in the face without trouble or surprise; who, if his body were to be broken upon the wheel or melted lead poured down his throat, would be less concerned for the pain itself than for the dignity of bearing it.[14]

Surrounded by smoother, richer, better-spoken and educated people, George Washington learned during that first year at Mount Vernon the badinage his brother and the Fairfaxes exchanged, but most of all from his studies of Seneca and quiet observations he developed the patience and the stoicism that were to become his hallmarks:

> May not an honest man then be allowed to be angry at the murder of his father or the ravishing of his sister or his daughter before his face? No, not at all.[15]

He also studied how to behave around women, something that was not covered in any of the *Rules of Civility*. From his mother, he had inherited a fierce desire for independence. From his sister-in-law Nancy he learned to relax in witty and charming company while he played cards with her, beat her at loo and whist, and then kept careful track of his winnings. A little gambling alleviated the humiliation of borrowing the money from his mother for his dancing and fencing lessons and the fancy clothes he needed at Belvoir.

*F*rom the somewhat effeminate courtliness of Lawrence Washington and his talkative, card-playing wife to the erudite decadence of Colonel Fairfax and his fastidious son, George Washington's new world acquired an oddly rustic gloss in the summer of 1747 with the arrival of Lord Fairfax himself, the fountainhead from which all this frontier opulence flowed. What interested Lord Fairfax were two things: selling land and pursuing foxes. Just before he arrived, a ship from England delivered at Belvoir's dock three English foxhounds, which Lord Fairfax had ordered sent out ahead of him to Virginia to improve the local breed.

The conviviality of Belvoir received a check with Lord Fairfax's arrival. Now, there were afternoons of attending on him, of listening to him rant about women, of streaking off with him on horseback after the fox. Lord Fairfax, impressed with young Washington's horsemanship, gave him pointers in the breeding of English and American horses that triggered George's passion for horse-raising and racing.

It was also brought to His Lordship's attention that George had another useful skill: by the age of sixteen, he had become thoroughly grounded in surveying. All he lacked was field experience beyond the simple running of lines at Ferry Farm and Mount Vernon, which he had practiced for two years. In autumn 1746, when Colonel Fairfax stopped off in Fredericksburg to deliver Lawrence's letters urging George to go to sea, he had been on his way west to join a party of surveyors and mapmakers locating the boundary line between Virginia and the Fairfax proprietorship. The expedition to map the Fairfax line took five months and was led by Peter Jefferson, father of Thomas Jefferson, and Joshua Fry, the royal surveyor and professor of mathematics at William and Mary College. The surveyors dragged chains and sighted along a seventy-six-mile line from the headspring of the Rappahannock across rugged mountains and through primeval forests to the source of the Potomac. Thomas Lewis, one of the surveying team, recorded that, to someone like George Washington from the flat Tidewater estuary, the Blue Ridge Mountains they had to climb on foot seemed "exceedingly high and very rocky," the ridges and ravines "prodigiously full of fallen timber." The horses that bore men and supplies starved or fell down precipices: many of the men dropped out. The rest came back filled with stories of adventure and of a vast unsettled territory.

The immense tract was still unsettled by whites, not only because Lord Fairfax had been contesting its ownership for decades in the courts but because the mountains and valleys were still the hunting grounds of the Indians, who considered it theirs. This second barrier had fallen in the summer of 1748 when colonial officials from Virginia, Maryland, and

Pennsylvania negotiated the Treaty of Lancaster. At the end of King George's War (1739–1748), Indian affairs in the forests from Williamsburg to Detroit had been left in turmoil. Territories conquered by the colonial rivals had been restored: the vast Ohio watershed had been left a no-white-man's land. The withdrawal of the French to Canada left the natives west of the Appalachians without ammunition or gunsmiths to repair the weapons they needed to hunt for food and clothing. In July 1748, fifty-five Indian chiefs and their families and retainers walked some five hundred miles to Lancaster, Pennsylvania, to seek new trading partners among the merchants and officials of the English middle colonies. In exchange for furs, Quaker merchants sold the Indians English iron kettles and woolen blankets at far lower prices than the French had charged them. They also sold them English-made hatchets, knives, and guns. Philadelphia merchants won an exclusive franchise on fur trading: a thousand miles of forests were opened up to the English colonists. Virginians won the agreement of the natives to allow them to hunt and trap and map the lands unmolested. It was now safe for Lord Fairfax to send an expedition into his five million acres, a wilderness empire he intended to map, plot, sell, and lease.

In the two years following the first mapping expedition, a fever of excitement had raged in the Virginia Tidewater as a new speculative land rush loomed. For years, the Northern Neck and the Shenandoah had been off-limits to settlers. With a cloud of dispute over the land titles, no one dared settle there. Now, in the drawing rooms at Mount Vernon and Belvoir, rich, fertile, vacant land only a few days' ride to the west dominated the conversation. Lord Fairfax and his cousin, Colonel Fairfax, laid plans for opening up the vast new Virginia frontier.

Lord Fairfax, too, had grown fond of the tall, elegantly mannered George Washington and was inclined to do the lad a favor. His best surveyor, James Genn, a member of the 1746 mapping team and a prominent surveyor of Prince William County, needed a strong young assistant to manhandle the supplies, care for the horses, clear the underbrush, haul the chains, carry the theodolite, and hold steady the rod for his sightings.

Young Washington's studies of surveying had progressed steadily, evolving alongside his mastery of trigonometry, exhibited by his third and final "miscellaneous" notebook. His struggles with the highest level of mathematics available in Virginia in 1747 show not only a tenacity that would serve him well in working out problems far from books and libraries, but a basic understanding of principles that would make him a master of selecting land for cultivation and, later, for fortifications and battlefields. His close reasoning, patience, and sharp eye for detail equipped him well. The surveying problems he puzzled over match exactly several that appeared in William Leybourn's *Compleat Surveyor*, the second edition, printed in London in 1657, at the time John Washington first sailed for Virginia. (George was probably using his grandfather's book and tools.) Leybourn's was probably the most practical and influential field guide to surveying. Its plain style was ideal for a bright young boy essentially teaching himself to survey. Washington struggled with the problem of "how to take an inaccessible distance at two stations," basic for figuring out not only wooded terrain in the Shenandoah but for artillery fire. He puzzled over "how to measure a field in which bog or marsh interferes with chaining," important in mapping and plotting much of the swampy Virginia wilderness Washington was to survey. It was quite a feat for a fifteen-year-old boy to learn "to measure" any piece of ground, be it ever so irregular, and to "cast up the content thereof in acres, rods and perches and likewise to examine ye truth of ye survey." Now the abstract exercises were to become concrete.[16]

As a young man George Washington often helped fence the fields he surveyed and by age sixteen he had developed powerful arms and tough hands. He also possessed what mattered most on a frontier expedition: endurance. A day's ride west of Mount Vernon and the Tidewater estuaries, the land of the backcountry began to rise. Two days out came the foothills of the Blue Ridge Mountains, the limit of white settlement. Forest clearings came farther apart; the houses were smaller. Few settlers had ventured into the Shenandoah Valley. No white man lived legally beyond the valley's western wall, the solid barrier of the Allegheny Mountains. Virginia claimed this land "from sea to sea" under its seventeenth-century charter, but, in fact, Indian hunting parties had kept the forests primeval.

On March 11, 1748, only a few weeks past his sixteenth birthday, George Washington set out on horseback from Belvoir with his twenty-three-year-old friend George William Fairfax. An embarrassed George had to stop to get his mother's reluctant permission to make the western trip. After George pointed out he would be paid as one of James Genn's chainmen, she gave her approval. That first day out, the Dumfries Road was hardpacked after the cold winter. It was necessary to complete the mission before spring: the theodolite could not be sighted through foliage. The two riders were exuberant. They rode forty miles, not stopping until they reached George Neville's plantation, which doubled as an unlicensed tavern for travelers. The next morning, surveyor Genn and his team of chainmen and hunters joined them and "we travelled over the Blue Ridge to Captain Ashby's on the Shenandoah River. . . . Nothing remarkable happened,"[17] Washington recorded in his first diary, his earliest surviving document.

Nothing remarkable happened! At sixteen, free from parental and patriarchal control and riding into the unspoiled Shenandoah, George Washington was metamorphosing from naive boy to typical eighteenth-century gentleman: unromantic, unimpressed by nature. That would come later, officially too late for him, in the Romantic Age, when people flocked to cities and began to romanticize life in the countryside and the forest. For now, George was caught up in being part of an adult mission to perform a highly technical and practical task in a wild place. Crossing through Ashby's Gap, by the third day out the surveying party reached Lord Fairfax's "quarter," his unsurveyed lands four miles farther north on the Shenandoah near Howell's Point. There, young Washington waxed as rhapsodic as he ever got in this primitive paradise: "We went through most beautiful groves of sugar trees and spent the best part of the day in admiring the trees and richness of the land."

George Washington was already knowledgeable about land, timber, terrain, crop yields, all part of the well-trained eighteenth-century surveyor's kitbag. He was able to cast a discerning eye on the commercial possibilities of the wilderness:

> *Monday 14th. We sent our baggage to Capt. Hites (near Frederick Town) went ourselves down the river about 16 miles to Capt. Isaac Pennington's (the land exceeding rich & fertile all the way produces abundance of grain, hemp, tobacco, etc.) in order to lay off some lands.*[18]

The scale of expectations in the west must have dazed the young man. At Frederick Town, now Winchester, at the head of the Shenandoah Valley, Washington encountered prosperous German settler Jost Hite, born in Strasbourg, Alsace, and arriving in America thirty years earlier. Settling first on the Hudson and then in Pennsylvania and finally, in 1731, purchasing 40,000 acres in Frederick County, Virginia, this successful land speculator eventually settled families on 94,000 acres he owned. The young surveyor's luck changed the fifth day out. It rained hard and harder.

> *We set out early with intent to run [lines] round the said land but being taken in a rain and it increasing very fast obliged us to return. It clearing about one o'clock & our time being too precious to lose, we a second time ventured out and worked hard till night and then returned to Pennington's.*[19]

Dragging heavy 33-foot wrought-iron chains with eight-inch links or shouldering the tripod and the circumferentor, which measured off the land, hacking brush and trees to make a clear path for the sightlines, and blazing marks on trees with an axe, young Washington was wet and cold and tired in a way he never experienced before. He had penetrated the wilderness to a point his *Rules of Civility* could not encompass.

> *We got our suppers & was lighted into a room & I not being so good a woodsman as the rest of the company stripped myself very orderly & went into the bed, as they called it, when to my surprise I found it to be*

nothing but a little straw matted together without sheets or anything else but only one threadbare blanket with double its weight of vermin, such as lice, fleas, etc. I was glad to get up (as soon as the light was carried from us) & put on my clothes and lay as my companions. Had we not been very tired, I am sure we should not have slept much that night. I made a promise not to sleep so, from that time forward choosing rather to sleep in open air before a fire.[20]

Arriving the next day at Winchester, the young gentleman-surveyor was delighted to wash—and made a note of it: "We cleaned ourselves to get rid of the game we had catched the night before." That night was more "agreeable" to George's taste. After a stroll around town, "we had a good dinner prepared for us [with] wine & rum punch in plenty and a good feather bed with clean sheets." From then on, where and how George Washington slept became noteworthy.

Blocked by flooding of the Potomac, which had been caused by the sudden runoff of snowmelt high in the Appalachians, Washington made the first of many visits to Warm Springs (now Bath, West Virginia). "We this day called to see the famed Warm Springs. We camped out in the field this night." After a three-day delay, the surveying party couldn't wait any longer for the floodwaters to recede. "We in the evening swam our horses over" to the Maryland shore. It was a dangerous passage in the fast-moving current and only a superb horseman would have stated its achievement so matter-of-factly. After leaving the horses in a pasture, they canoed "up the Maryland side all day in a continued rain." At the mouth of the South Branch of the Potomac, they followed "the worst road that ever was trod by man or beast." The rain continued, as did the flooding, and the road kept washing out. On March 23, on their eleventh day out, the rain stopped in midafternoon and the surveying party stumbled upon a group of thirty Indians, the first Washington had ever seen close up. They were "coming from war with only one scalp." Washington wrote that "we had some liquor with us of which we gave them part, it elevating their spirits, put them in the humor of dancing." Washington was fascinated and amused by the Indians more than fearful:

We had a war dance. Their manner of dancing is as follows: They clear a large circle and make a great fire in the middle, then seat themselves around it. The speaker makes a grand speech, telling them in what manner they are to dance. After he has finished, the best dancer jumps up as one awaked out of a sleep & runs & jumps about the ring in a most comical manner. He is followed by the rest. Then begins their musicians to play the music. [There] is a pot half [full] of water with a deerskin stretched over it as tight as it can & a gourd with some shot in it to rattle & a piece of an horse's tail tied to it to make it look fine. The

one keeps rattling and the other drumming, all the while the others
[are] dancing.[21]

So unimpressed was Washington at "being with the Indians all day"
the next day that he wrote "nothing remarkable was happening so shall
skip it."

More interesting to him was crossing the rain-swollen river in a canoe
while they "swum our horses over." As they canoed and camped ever
deeper into the wilderness, Washington was scandalized to see how raw
the way of life was becoming. They dined at the home of Squire Solomon
Hedges, a Quaker and justice of the peace for Frederick County. "When
we came to supper there was neither a cloth upon the table nor a knife to
eat with but, as good luck would have it, we had knives of [our] own."
Each day, they rode along the South Branch and surveyed riverfront
tracts. On a typical day, Washington recorded on March 29, 1748, they
"surveyed five hundred acres of land" for James Rutledge, who was buying it from Lord Fairfax, then rode to their next campsite at a place called
Stumps and "on our way shot two wild turkeys."[22]

They were already short of food, having outridden their supply line.
The next day, they laid out lots for four other settlers. Hunting fresh
game and working hard all day, young Washington became inured to the
hard outdoor life. He commented only when the weather turned foul:
"Last night was a blowing and rainy night." It must have been a miserable night, but he did not complain. He only reported that "our straw
catched a fire that we were laying upon & [we were] luckily preserved by
one of our men's awaking." Apparently, embers from the all-night camp-
fire inside their tent had blown into the straw in the high winds. The next
night, "a much more blustering night," they tried to sleep in their tents,
but "we had our tent carried quite off with the wind and [were] obliged
to lie the latter part of the night without covering."[23]

The stormy, cold, miserable conditions proved too much for the lordly
young George Fairfax, who left the party and turned back at this point.
After three weeks of roughing it, he headed for the comforts of the nearest inn. The remaining surveyors, old Genn and young George, struggled
on, accompanied now by large numbers of German settlers "that attended us through the woods as we went, showing their antic tricks. I really think they seem to be as ignorant a set of people as the Indians. They
would never speak English but, when spoken to, they speak all Dutch."[24]
Here, faced by a menacing, resentful crowd of squatters, was a young
provincial Englishman buttressed by his boyish intolerance.

Their tents blowing down every night or so smoky from drenched firewood that they had to leave them, they were dogged all day, day after
day, by crowds of taunting Germans. It did not dawn on the young surveyor's assistant that they were hated for coming into these woods and

making surveys for a new master who was disputing their right to remain on the land.

As they left this "company" behind, they traveled downriver, only to be caught in another ferocious rainstorm. "We got under a straw [thatch-roofed] house until the worst of it was over."[25] Thursday, April 7, was no better: "Rained successively all last night." But the hungry, bedraggled pair did feast on "a wild turkey that weighed 20 pounds" before they went out and surveyed 1,500 acres of land by one o'clock in the afternoon. Washington was happy to learn that his friend George Fairfax was at a farm nearby. "I then took my horse and went up to see him." They ate dinner together and, leading their horses, walked the two miles to the tavern where Genn was staying and back again "and slept in [Peter] Casey's house, which was the first night I had slept in a house since I came to the [South] Branch [of the Potomac]."[26] Those had been eighteen of the worst nights of his young life, but this was as close as the young stoic came to complaining. The amenities were not to last. By the next night, after laying off lots and riding around eight miles of impassable West Virginia ledge,

> we camped this night in the woods near a wild meadow where was a very large stack of hay. After we had pitched our tent & made a very large fire, we pulled out our knapsack in order to [refresh] ourselves. Everyone was his own cook. Our spits were forked sticks, our plate was a large chip. As for dishes, we had none.[27]

By now, after a full month in the wilderness, Washington was ready when George Fairfax proposed that they leave Genn and head home. Their mission was finished and George had his first pay in his pocket. "We took our farewell." They traveled over forty miles on horseback "over hills and mountains reaching Winchester, Virginia, at noon the next day." Washington's terse journal entry bespoke volumes of contentment at returning to civilization: "We dined in town and then went to Captain Hite's and lodged." Sure they would be home in a few days, they set off the next morning, intending to ride due east twenty miles through Williams Gap in the Shenandoahs, but the young surveyor got lost. Exhausted, they had to ride another twenty miles before they found the gap late that night. They rode on until they reached Bull Run in Fairfax County, in all covering fifty miles on horseback in a single day. On April 13, 1748, young Washington made his final notation: "Mister Fairfax got safe home and I myself safe to my brother's."[28]

George Washington's first journey to the west was one of the pivotal events of his life. It marked his virtual independence from his mother—once he had cash in his pocket from surveying, there were fewer occasions when he had to go to her and ask. He did not learn to save money, though. After he spent his earnings, a few months later, he had to borrow three shillings ninepence from her for dancing lessons. But now he usually had cash. He began to keep his own ledger book, even tallying his winnings and less frequent losses from whist and loo with his brother and sister-in-law. He kept track of every farthing he lent to friends and relatives. Whenever he was paid for surveying jobs, he bought fashionable clothes. He purchased a sword and took fencing lessons. He also was gaining a new kind of stature. Men who ventured out onto the frontier and returned safely earned respect they could receive no other way. Their retellings of their adventures made them the centerpiece of fireside society. George had left a boy; he returned a young man respected by other men. He had heard their talk, about hunting, about women, and he had worked hard beside them. Most of all the riches of the forested riverbanks and valleys dazzled him and he could foresee his own way to inestimable wealth and influence far beyond anything little Ferry Farm could offer him. With his skill as an experienced surveyor trained by the best man of his craft, George Washington at age sixteen was ready to begin to seek that fortune.

There were to be a few momentary distractions. In the spring of 1748, shortly after George returned from West Virginia with George William Fairfax, his friend went with his brother Lawrence to the colonial capital at Williamsburg for the April session of the House of Burgesses. Lawrence did not last long at the all-day legislative sessions and the late-night round of parties, balls, and drinking bouts in the taverns. He returned to Mount Vernon with a racking cough. But young Fairfax lingered at the dances in Williamsburg and when he returned it was with the announcement that he was engaged to marry a young woman he had met just before the surveying expedition. As the son of the president of Virginia's executive council, upper house of the colony's legislature, young Fairfax was a most eligible bachelor. His betrothal to Sarah Cary, daughter of a member of the House of Burgesses, linked two of Virginia's most powerful families.

For nearly a century, the Carys had been leaders in the Tidewater aristocracy. Sarah's grandfather had been rector of William and Mary College, where her father had studied before going on to Trinity College at Cambridge University in England. Both sides of her family were rich and cultivated. In the library at Ceelip, the Cary mansion on the James River, Sally, as she was called, had received a superior education for a young girl of her time, learning French and reading English literature. She was a slender eighteen when Fairfax brought her to rural Belvoir. Her only known portrait shows a playful, bright-eyed woman with a long neck, a high forehead, and long black hair. Used to the more rustic, horsey women of the Northern Neck, George Washington had never seen anyone so elegant and alluring. Beneath strong, dark eyebrows like his mother's were large, steady, wide-open eyes that gazed out frankly, and a mouth that was a cupid's bow. George Washington could not escape having her on his mind (never mind that she was marrying his best friend and closest neighbor), in or away from her company, for a good long time to come. She was, he would write on the eve of his own marriage fully ten years later, an "amiable beauty" so notable for her "mirth, good humor, ease of mind,"[29] a coquette who excited and baffled the solemn young Washington. Nearly forty years later, when a civil war and the Atlantic Ocean had forever separated them, he still looked back on those thrilling days at Belvoir when she was a playful eighteen-year-old bride still competing with all the other girls for attention and he a sixteen-year-old whose love could never be requited. Nothing had ever "been able to eradicate from my mind," he wrote her after the Revolution, "those happy moments, the happiest of my life, which I have enjoyed in your company."[30]

There is evidence that Sally Fairfax felt somewhat less smitten but nonetheless drawn to the tall, athletic young man who could ride a horse and dance the intricacies of the minuet in a way she had not seen surpassed in all the elegant balls and assembly rooms of the Tidewater. French officers would later attest that they had never seen anyone at Versailles who danced better than George Washington. Sally saw George's graceful talents developing early and may have responded to his pull over other men, struck by his physical presence, his rare inborn dignity, his flawless courtesy. Sally's fussy, aristocratic bridegroom was one of the first men who, despite his superior English education and his wealth, followed Washington's lead in matters small and large, and Sally Fairfax certainly noticed this.

There is no evidence of anything more than yearning between the young Washington and his friend's two years' older—and many years more mature—wife. Washington was capable of being a great romantic. This was only the first instance of his admiring a woman one-sidedly. For the time being, he danced with Sally, played cards with her, listened to her speak French. He relished occasions for the enchanting flirtation with a young Virginia belle. But that was all he could do. He was still a very young man with little money who sometimes couldn't even afford to buy enough corn to feed his horse to make the journey from Ferry Farm to the spring dances in Williamsburg. Instead, he consoled himself with fencing lessons in Fredericksburg and became an excellent swordsman.

*I*n the year after his first contact with the frontier, young Washington, mature in matters of business, frequently visited Ferry Farm to manage affairs neglected by his mother, who was letting the place run into the ground. With his newly honed surveying skills, he measured off and made extensive drawings of the place. He drew up his first deed with accompanying survey of a portion of the farm that was soon to be his, sell-ing it back to one of the estate's trustees, who had sold it to George's fa-ther. The transaction had been allowed under his father's will and probably provided cash for keeping up the farm. The sale lessened the value of George's inheritance still further. George went on busily perfect-ing his surveying skills and used some of the money from surveying jobs to pay the fees to obtain a surveyor's license in July 1749, less than six months after he turned seventeen.

Only two days after becoming licensed, he accepted his first full-fledged professional surveying commission. He measured off a tract of four hundred acres in the Shenandoah Valley being sold by Lord Fairfax. Doubtless through the influence of Colonel Fairfax, at the same time George also received appointment as county surveyor of Culpeper County at an annual £15 salary plus all the fees he could charge. The salary was small, but it sealed his escape from Ferry Farm. For the next several weeks he led his own surveying team to the frontier. Colonel Fairfax gave him plenty of work and paid him more than the going rate. If this was not proof of the young man's expertise, Washington routinely charged and was paid about £1 per thousand acres above the official rate decreed by the colonial government. Before he was eighteen, he was earning £125 a year from surveying, more cash than most Virginia planters saw in a year and as much as any skilled artisan in Williamsburg.

*I*n chilly November mountain weather in 1749, on a break from frontier surveying for Lord Fairfax, after receiving a letter from his "wor-thy friend" Richard (whose last name is a mystery), George Washington wrote a letter that described his new way of life:

You gave me the more pleasure as I received it amongst a parcel of barbarians and an uncouth set of people. . . . Since you re-ceived my letter on October last I have not sleeped above three nights or four in a bed but, after walking a good deal all the day, lay down before the fire upon a little hay, straw, fodder or bear-skin, whichever is to be had, with man, wife and children like a parcel of dogs or cats & happy is he that gets the berth nearest the fire. There's nothing would make it pass tolerably but a good reward. A doubloon is my constant gain every day that the weather will permit my going out, and sometimes six pistoles. The coldness of the weather will not allow my making a long stay, as the lodging is rather too cold for the time of year. I have never had my clothes off but lay and sleep in them like a Negro except the few nights I have lain in [a tavern in Winchester].[31]

On trips "home" to Belvoir, "my place of residence at present," George spent some of his earnings on the latest fashions. He carried a fine watch and, for one visit to Belvoir, he packed nine shirts, six linen waistcoats, a cloth waistcoat, six bands of linen to hold up his neckcloths (he took along four of them), and seven caps. He also wrote down "razor" at the top of the list of other things to take along: he had begun to shave.

As he neared eighteen and became aware of girls, the prose of his letters was as purple as his face must have been in their presence. To another Tidewater friend he wrote:

> There's a very agreeable young lady lives in the same house [Sally Fairfax's younger sister] but as that's only adding fuel to fire, it makes me the more uneasy, for by often and unavoidably being in company with her revives my former passion for her lowland beauty whereas, was I to live more retired from young women, I might in some measure alleviate my sorrows by burying that chaste and troublesome passion in the grave of oblivion or eternal forgetfulness.... Was I ever to attempt anything, I should only get a denial which would only be adding grief to uneasiness.[32]

As he earned higher fees from surveying, he consoled himself by beginning to set aside enough silver to acquire land. Taking land sometimes in lieu of cash for his work, he paid hard money for his first parcel, some 450 acres, at a place called Dutch George's in the Shenandoah Valley. Then he purchased one thousand rich acres along Bullskin Creek, a tributary of the Shenandoah River on the Virginia–West Virginia line, later that same year. He was eagerly plunging into western speculative fever at a time when his brother and all his Belvoir friends were making grandiose plans to carve up the vast western lands recently opened up by the Lancaster negotiations with the Indians.

In 1748, Lawrence and Austin Washington, Governor Robert Dinwiddie, and several other Virginia planters, many of them veterans of King George's War, formed the Ohio River Company and petitioned the crown in London for a grant to 200,000 acres in the Ohio Valley. Their grandiose plans provided a welcome distraction from George's attempts at polite chatter. George Washington at eighteen had a much better idea what to do in a forest than in a drawing room. His infatuations came and went with the social seasons at Belvoir. One of them, Frances Alexander, inspired him to write in his notebook this moonstruck and unfinished attempt at a sonnet:

> From your bright sparkling eyes, I was undone;
> Rays, you have more transparent than the sun,
> Amidst its glory in the rising day,
> None can you equal in your bright array;
> Constant in your calm and unspotted mind;

Equal to all, but will to none prove kind,
So knowing, seldom one so young, you'll find.
Ah! woe's me, that I should love and conceal
Long have I wished but never dare reveal
Even though severely love's pain I feel;
Xerxes that great, was not free from Cupid's dart,
And all the greatest heroes felt the smart.[33]

Before he could find the last lines to finish expressing his undying love
for Frances, he gave up and panted off after someone else. George
recorded lovesickness in solemn jottings in his journal. What young lady
could have kept a straight face as a six-foot-four suntanned giant in London finery recited these lines of yearning iambic pentameter:

Oh, ye gods, why should my poor restless heart
Stand to oppose thy might and power
At last to surrender to Cupid's feathered dart
And now lays bleeding every hour
For her that's pitiless of my grief and woes
And will not on me pity take.
I'll sleep among my most inveterate foes
And with gladness [wish] to wake.
In deluding sleepings let my eyelids close
That in an enraptured dream I may
In a soft lulling sleep and gentle repose
Possess those joys denied by day.[34]

George Washington was jolted out of his protracted adolescence
when Lawrence's intermittent bouts of coughing deepened into full-
blown tuberculosis, the dreaded killer of the eighteenth century.
Lawrence, the strongest influence on George, had been in poor health for
nearly a decade, ever since he had returned from the suicidal Cartagena
campaign. His chronic lung ailments had been only worsened by bouts of
depression that accompanied the births and deaths of three infants in the
past five years. It briefly seemed that his luck was improving in 1751
when his wife, Nancy, gave birth to a daughter, Sarah. The baby survived, but Lawrence gave himself little chance to get to know her. A
member of the House of Burgesses since 1744, he had obtained a leave
from his office after herbal treatments prescribed by Williamsburg doctors proved useless. He left his family behind and sailed to London to
seek the best medical care of the age, but nothing helped and he returned exhausted by the rough sea voyage to Virginia. Persuading George
to accompany him to the warm springs at Bath, West Virginia, already famous for their supposed curative powers, they reached the Alleghenies
during the cold, damp winter of 1750. Again, the trip only aggravated his

condition. Returning to Mount Vernon when his daughter was born, he tried the mountain spa again with George at his side. Nothing seemed to help.

Convinced that another winter in Virginia would kill him, Lawrence, his cough now persistent, decided his only hope was to seek a warmer climate in the winter of 1751. A merchant friend of Lord Fairfax recommended Barbados and gave Lawrence the name of a physician famed for curing tuberculosis. Recipient of so much generosity and kindness from his half-brother, George, now nineteen, with trepidation boarded ship for the first time for the voyage to Bridgetown in September 1751. It was to be George Washington's only ocean voyage. He was never eager for another.

*T*he voyage from the mouth of the Potomac to Barbados in the Leeward Islands was a surprise for the nineteen-year-old Washington, who had once thought that he might spend his life at sea. To be seasick on his first ocean voyage was to be expected, but nothing prepared him for the kind of violent tossing about he received in the small, 40-ton merchant ship *Success*, which took more than thirty-seven days during hurricane season to make the journey. With a crew of eight men and a cargo of lumber, barrel staves, corn, and herring, the *Success* sailed south along the North Carolina coast until it reached the latitude of Bermuda, then sailed due east. Miserably uncomfortable in their bunks until they overcame their seasickness, Lawrence and George were able to go out on deck by the tenth day. George kept a journal from the start, but only fragments of it survive. In the mid-nineteenth century, Harvard president and would-be biographer Jared Sparks took to giving away samples of Washington's handwriting as souvenirs for admirers and the early pages are lost. Washington scholars have reconstructed the chronology of his first and only lengthy sea journey and they speculate that the two brothers sailed on September 28, 1751.

Fashioning his own amateur ship's log, George divided a homemade hand-sewn notebook into neat columns and each day recorded their progress. He was obviously learning the ship's routines and the language of mariners. His entry for October 7, 1751, shows that, as their supply of fresh food became exhausted, he and his brother were able to cast hand fishing lines from the ship. After recording "but little wind at 5 Wt. & So (south southwest) with calm smooth sea and fair weather," he noted seeing "many fish swimming about us of which a dolphin we catched at noon, but [we] could not entice with a baited hook two barracudas which played under our stern for some hours. . . . The dolphin being small, we had it dressed for supper."

The day's catch provided welcome relief from the weevil- and maggot-ridden ship's biscuits that made up the bulk of their normal fare as they sailed into the tropics. Their luck did not hold the next day when "a large dolphin" swam around the ship and "would not be ensnared by any bait we could lay." Although they were hungry, the Washington brothers were basking in the "fine clear weather with moderate gales of wind and smooth sea." The chill dampness of the Tidewater winter seemed far away.[35]

The surveyor in Washington made him a compulsive note-taker. The swearing of the sailors around him added as many words to his vocabulary as the jargon of knots and sails he was memorizing. In his log, he began to mimic in cryptical form the words the sailors used as they responded to wind and storm. "RM: FS and DRFS" (reefed mainsail, foresail and double-reefed foresail) became his code for the sail plan set in response to the sudden strong storm that swept down on them after three weeks at sea. Washington recorded the scene in wonderfully clear, strong prose:

> *19 October 1751. Hard squalls of wind and rain with a fomented sea jostling in heaps occasioned by the wavering wind which, in 24 hours, veered the compass, not remaining two hours in any point. The seamen seemed disheartened, confessing they had never seen such weather before. It was universally surmised there had been a violent hurricane not far distant. A prodigy in the west appeared towards the sun's setting about 6 P.M., remarkable for its extraordinary redness.*

Actually, the sailors' speculations were understated. The day before Washington posted this entry in his journal, there had been a strong earthquake near Santo Domingo, which sent tidal waves of turbulence toward the little ship.[36]

The last two weeks of the storm-tossed five-week ocean voyage were enough to unnerve any landlubber, but Washington absorbed himself in his record-keeping, observing each day's point of departure, difference of latitude, latitude, meridian distance, difference of longitude, and longitude. Had he brought along his surveyor's sextant or did he spend all day at the helmsman's elbow? He would always keep track of his journeys, as if he were plotting his own course in the future, then comment on the obstacles he overcame. It was an unusual diary, in which he never recorded his emotions. The wild seas did not seem to dissuade him from staying above decks. Whether his ailing brother stayed in his bunk in the tiny cabin is another matter. Day after day, George noted the passing of other ships and the force of the storms in a diary that gives a rare glimpse of sea travel in the eighteenth century:

> *Saturday, 19th. Hard squalls of wind and rain . . .*
> *Sunday, 20th. A constant succession of hard winds, squalls of rain . . .*
> *Wednesday, 23rd. Calm . . . the wind freshened up at last . . . our bread is almost eaten up by weevils and maggots.*

Friday, 25th. At 9 P.M. struck two dolphins, one of which [we] lost. . . .
Dolphin dressed for dinner.[37]

Washington's prose was becoming more romantic as he mastered the colorful formulations of the mariner. There were "wavering but pleasant gales" one day, "buffeting and being tossed by a fickle and merciless ocean" the next. It was almost as if he were disappointed the morning of November 2, when he and his brother were jolted awake at first light:

> *We were greatly alarmed with the cry of "land" at 4 A.M. We quitted our beds with surprise and found the land plainly appearing at about 3 leagues [9 miles] distance when, by our reckonings, we should have been near 150 leagues to the windward. . . . Had we been three or four leagues more, we should have been out of sight of the island . . . probably not have discovered the error in time to have gained land for three or four weeks more.*[38]

Badly off course, nearly out of food and drinking water, the *Success* had nearly overshot its landfall, but at last, after thirty-seven days at sea, the ship tacked into Bridgetown harbor and dropped anchor. Young Washington stepped ashore into what he considered a tropical island paradise. In the library at Belvoir, he had prepared himself for the flora and fauna of the island by studying a handsome new book on Barbados, the Reverend Griffith Hughes's *Natural History of Barbados*, a folio volume issued in ten parts in London the year before. Both Lord Fairfax and Colonel William Fairfax, who had been an official on the island for many years, had been subscribers to the publishing project. When they landed, the Washington brothers were greeted by another subscriber, James Carter, chief justice of Barbados, who drove the Virginians to his home. George had another chance to peruse the botany book there. The next day, they were on their way to the home of Boston-born Major Gedney Clarke, a merchant and slave trader who was a close friend of Lord Fairfax and who owned some 3,000 acres of land in northern Virginia. Clarke's sister, Deborah, was Colonel Fairfax's wife. This close connection was to prove both blessing and curse to young Washington.

*T*he day after they landed, the Washingtons visited Dr. William Hilary, a specialist in lung disorders, who examined Lawrence and gave him a dose of fresh hope. His opinion was that Lawrence's disease was not so deeply seated that it could not be cured. The brothers set off at once to find suitable seaside lodgings outside Bridgetown, as the doctor recommended. While they combed the coastline for rental properties, George, accustomed to the more muted palette of Virginia, was struck by the lush tropical landscape. He made notes on the "avagado pear" and the "Pine Apple," which became two of his favorite foods. They eventually found a pricey apartment in the home of the commander of Fort James, which guarded the approaches to Bridgetown's teeming harbor. Their bachelor digs only a mile from town delighted George, who kept track of the comings and goings of the ships in the harbor.

The attitudes of the two brothers had never been more strikingly different. George wrote exuberantly to his mentor, Colonel Fairfax, that "the prospect is extensive by land and pleasant by sea, as we command the prospect of Carlisle Bay and all the shipping in such manner that none can go in or out without being open to our view." George loved to ride out and explore the tropical vegetation by day, then avail himself of Bridgetown's diversions. The Clarkes gave him a ticket to see his first professional London stage play, *George Barnwell, a Tragedy*, which was also a hit on Drury Lane that season. One of England's longest-running and most popular works, the romantic tearjerker about a debauched apprentice had been running for twenty years in London after high praise by critic Alexander Pope. Washington's lifelong love of the theater grew out of this first sight of a top-notch stage production. In contrast, the fragile and melancholy Lawrence Washington gave Barbados little chance. He missed his wife and year-old baby; he was homesick for Mount Vernon. He wrote home that he was already weary of all the dignitaries who insisted on entertaining them. He complained especially about the heat. He had to go indoors, which meant staying in his rented rooms, "by the first dawn of the day, for by the time the sun is half an hour high, it is as hot as any time of the day."39

For two weeks George, on the other hand, soaked up the sun, the sights, the social invitations. He shopped for presents for family and friends. He bought a barrel of limes for his future brother-in-law, Fielding Lewis. He toured his first fort and took detailed notes in his diary. "It's pretty strongly fortified and mounts 36 guns within the fortifications." He added, with some astonishment, that it also was ringed by outerworks bristling with immense cannon that fired 51-pound shot.

On the morning of November 17, 1751, George woke up feeling stiff and hot. His days of enchantment with Barbados were over. He had worried aloud to Lawrence after the initial visit to the Clarkes that there had been a case of smallpox in their house. Now, George's fever soared. His head ached terribly. Pain wracked his back and limbs. The next day, he was no better, and on the third day, the appearance of red spots on his forehead that quickly turned to papules left no doubt. One Washington was dying of tuberculosis. The other, nineteen-year-old George, had the other dread disease of the eighteenth century, smallpox. On the sixth day, when the papules turned into vesicles, George's temperature dropped temporarily and his pain abated, but the fever came back strongly the next day and the vesicles turned into pustules. Not until the twelfth day did George's pain lessen and the pustules dry up, leaving the young man itching all over. When the scabs finally fell off, he was left with "pits," the sign of survival and lifelong immunity. Historians have argued over the severity of his case. Some suggest he must have been inoculated in Virginia at an early age or he would have died in Barbados, but there is no evidence of this and, indeed, few doctors in Virginia braved public superstition against inoculation. As late as 1769, there were riots when inoculations were attempted in the Tidewater. George's own terse thirty-one-word diary entry on a disease that had such a profound effect on his fortunes years later leaves little doubt: "was strongly attacked with the smallpox." The simple truth is that someone lacking Washington's great strength probably would have died.[40]

One day after he was discharged as healed by his physician, George went to dinner at the home of the Clarkes, who, perhaps as much out of guilt as loyalty, had visited him frequently during his illness. After a week of these daily visits, George and Lawrence had the talk that had only been postponed by George's illness. Lawrence was discouraged and terribly homesick. He did not think he was getting any better. He was tired of the endless dinners and afraid to go driving, Barbados's principal diversion, because he thought it caused yellow fever. He was convinced the heat was bad for him. He also thought that the languid relaxation of the tropics was bad for him: "Our bodies are too much relaxed and require a winter to brace them up." He wanted to return to Virginia but he was afraid to go home in the wintertime. He asked George to sail at once for Virginia. He wasn't needed to nurse him. He was to bring news of his condition to his wife. If his health didn't improve shortly, tell her he would try a visit to Bermuda and, that failing, return to Virginia and again try the baths and the mountain air of Berkeley Springs. At a loss what to do or say, George, who was already anxious about missing the spring surveying season, agreed to sail at once.[41]

As he waved good-bye to his brother and sailed toward home aboard the *Industry,* George was almost immediately overcome by seasickness. The voyage back was as difficult and stormy as the voyage out. No wonder he put off another ocean crossing for the rest of his life. Tired of play-acting the mariner, he dropped most of the nautical verbiage from his journal and instead composed a 750-word essay on his observations of life in Barbados. He wrote down his earliest observations on social structure and economics, recording his earliest known thoughts on inequality. What struck him hardest about the Barbadians was the fact that, despite slave labor and astronomical profits from sugar cane and rum, many island planters were deeply in debt and were paying 8 percent interest—nearly triple the usury rate—to keep afloat their lives of luxury. He considered such debt a "cancer." How people with four hundred acres of sugar cane could be in debt "is most wonderful to me." Washington was also disturbed to find no "middling sort."[42] Barbadians were "either very rich or very poor." What he admired most was the constant state of military preparedness of the islanders, every man ready to be at his post in less than two hours and the island "one entire fortification." But it was at a great social cost. Planters were allowed by law to hire substitutes to serve in their place in the militia. Paid only £10 a year (about $1,000 today), these men and their families lived in poverty in hovels, their condition little better than the slaves. This law guaranteed that there would only be rich and poor.

Between bouts of being "very sick" from the heaving homebound ship, George Washington spent his nineteenth Christmas at sea—eating an Irish goose and assorted meats and drinking his share of rum toasts at the captain's table. The only other excitement came when he was robbed of £10 of hard-earned money he had locked away in his sea chest—two-thirds of his year's salary as Culpeper County surveyor. Thirty-eight days out of Bridgetown, he stepped ashore in Virginia and hired a horse to ride to Williamsburg to deliver a pouch of letters to the royal governor. The meeting between the royal governor, Robert Dinwiddie, and the serious young Virginian was to eventually reshape George Washington's life, but for the moment it merely meant an invitation to stay for dinner in the re-splendent governor's palace and a chat about Barbados and mutual friends there. Then Washington rode off, stopping only long enough to take in a cockfight with a few of his friends and relatives before going on to Mount Vernon to bring the bad news to Nancy Fairfax Washington.

George Washington did not record in his diary—which he kept except for the Revolutionary War years—many of the most important events in his life, including the death of his brother and closest friend, Lawrence. George and Lawrence had been together almost constantly for nearly a year by the time George sailed home to Virginia. He spent long hours visiting Lawrence's wife. He told her of Lawrence's condition and how much Lawrence wanted her to join him in Barbados, but everyone knew how hard the voyage would have been on an infant, and the wives of colonists were almost never asked to endure sea voyages. They de-cided to follow Lawrence's wishes and to wait, however anxiously, for him to come home. George did not linger at Mount Vernon. He paid his respects to the Fairfaxes at Belvoir and to his mother at Ferry Farm and did what he always did when he was dispirited. He rode off to the west, taking on a string of surveying jobs in winter in the mountains. He stayed in the Shenandoah fully two frigid months this time. He cleared £115 profit and added 552 acres to his Bullskin Creek tract in Frederick County.

The freezing months in the winter woods exacted their price. Wash-ington had scarcely returned to Ferry Farm before he collapsed with pleurisy. His health, he wrote, was "very low" and he was weak for weeks. His ennui had a second cause that may have accounted for his alacrity at heading west. He was in love. That spring, he had been en-chanted by sixteen-year-old Betty Fauntleroy, daughter of a Richmond County delegate to the House of Burgesses. George knew how to talk to her father as he did with other men; Fauntleroy was interested in ships and trade. But George grew mute around young women, and because he was so shy and so much taller than most women he might have been regarded as a bit frightening. Betty evinced no further interest after their first meeting and apparently made it pretty plain.

In May 1752, as soon as he recovered from the bout with pleurisy, twenty-year-old George dashed off a more serious plea, as was customary, for the help of Betty's father in his suit:

> *Sir:*
>
> I should have been down long before this, but my business in Frederick detained me somewhat longer than I expected and immediately on my return from thence I was taken with a violent pleurisy which has reduced me very low; but propose, as soon as I recover my strength, to wait on Miss Betty, in hopes of a revocation of the former cruel sentence, and see if I can meet with any alteration in my favor. I have enclosed a letter to her which should be much obliged to you for the delivery of it. I have nothing to add but my best respects to your good lady and family.[43]

Betty's reply, if there ever was one, has been lost, but she could have no idea that the grave young giant pursuing her would turn out to be the famous George Washington. Her rebuff was so emphatic that George suddenly lost interest in her. Years later, he would see her frequently when her second husband, Thomas Adams, a close friend of Thomas Jefferson, was a Virginia delegate to the Continental Congress.

George had no time to dwell on his rejection. After three more months in Barbados, the restless Lawrence Washington had sailed to Bermuda, where he arrived in chilly weather. His health worsened. To a friend, he wrote he felt "like a criminal condemned." Put on a grueling regimen by a Bermuda physician, he was taken off all meat and liquor, given a milk diet, and told to ride each day as long as he could. Reluctant to lose such a good patient, the physician told Lawrence that winter in Virginia "will most certainly destroy me." Lawrence had the Washington habit of deferring to medical authority but not George Washington's rugged constitution. He talked of staying on in Bermuda for a year, but he was indecisive. George decided he must go on with his work. He made a round of visits to relatives with his younger brother, Samuel. Then, on June 16, 1752, Lawrence came home, obviously dying. He wrote his will, dividing his property. He left George his share in his father's Fredericksburg town lots. Then, on July 26, his ordeal ended. George arrived at Mount Vernon in time for his beloved brother's death. It was left to him to arrange his funeral and to bury him.[44]

The will was to prove troublesome for years. Lawrence left his wife a life interest in Mount Vernon and half of the slaves. Their daughter was to inherit the bulk of his estate. Then, if Sarah died without issue, Mount Vernon was to go to George along with all his other Fairfax County lands. George was to administer the will at first and then act as bookkeeper and co-executor with his half-brother, Austin, Colonel Fairfax, George Fairfax, and two other close friends. It soon became obvious that Lawrence had left a mess, or in George's polite words, "utmost confusion." His years of peripatetic convalescence coupled with four years' neglect of his farms, heavy investment in the Ohio Company and the imminent failure of the Principio Iron Works, three lawsuits, and a host of small bills left no choice but an auction to satisfy creditors. George was in the crowd as Lawrence's personal effects were sold. He bought several cattle for £33. The tangled affair dragged on for three years. Lawrence's widow, Nancy, left with a toddler and little income, remarried within six months, not unusual at the time. She became the wife of George Lee, uncle of Lighthorse Harry Lee, who was to become George Washington's close friend and the father of Robert E. Lee. Nancy and Sarah abandoned Mount Vernon and moved to Lee's Westmoreland County plantation. George was forced to move back to Ferry Farm and his mother, but not for long. Before he turned twenty-one, using his new friendship with Governor Dinwiddie, George turned his back on his sorrows and became Virginia's youngest adjutant, launching his military career.[45]

Four

"I PUT MYSELF INTO INDIAN DRESS"

In the summer of 1752, in the weeks while Lawrence lay dying at Mount Vernon, twenty-year-old George Washington had to face the fact that, beyond his surveying work and the modest investments in land it afforded him, he had little potential to earn enough money to live in the style to which he had become accustomed. As co-executor of his brother's estate, he knew not to expect much. Ferry Farm, while it would be legally his when he turned twenty-one in a matter of months, was a small, hardscrabble operation with poor soil. Worse, his mother was showing no sign of moving out. She had written to England to ask her brother for advice on George's youthful seafaring plans. After her brother refused to allow her to clear timber and gather stone for building materials from his land, she procrastinated further when she learned that a neighbor was to operate a ferry. Its landing, she said, would diminish the value of her land. Employing one excuse or another not to build a new house on the land her husband had left her, she must have known that her dutiful son George would not evict her. She would in fact tarry another twenty years before he finally built her a house on one of his town lots across the river in Fredericksburg.

With his brother's house no longer available to him, George moved back to Ferry Farm and took over its active management, its crops and accounts. It does not seem to have been a question whether George could stay on at Mount Vernon as a caretaker or manager in the house that had been his home for so many years. The house was boarded up; the slaves divided up and taken away in wagons. For George, it was one more sudden shock, one more rejection.

But the years in the forests, at sea, and in the company of wealthy and powerful men had transformed him. He had grown restless, ambitious. He knew he would have to do something bold to catapult himself into the position in society to which he was entitled by heritage if not birth as a third son. Long ago he had aimed his sights at a military life. Blocked from a naval career, he had the constant example of Lawrence's scarlet uniform and how far it had taken him in the ranks of Virginia's elite. For four generations, Washingtons had distinguished themselves in the Virginia militia, Lawrence rising to its highest permanent (and salaried) post as adjutant general. George was presentable and an experienced frontiersman, but he had no military experience. He had to rely only on family connections, the patronage of the powerful Fairfaxes—and sheer nerve. Tired of holding the reins for his Belvoir neighbors and understudying Lawrence, he did not wait for his brother to die to apply for his adjutant general's post. Soliciting the patronage of family and friends (most important, Lord Fairfax) for the prestigious £100-a-year post, he left his dying brother's bedside long enough to dash to Williamsburg to ask an audience with Governor Dinwiddie.

George Washington knew he had made a strong impression on Dinwiddie. The new royal governor was a keen land speculator who had just arrived in Virginia with a mercantile fortune and he was a stockholder in the Ohio Company cofounded by Lawrence Washington. The governor was aware of young Washington's backing by the Fairfaxes. George William Fairfax was now a member of the governor's executive council. Dinwiddie probably had already signed patents for young Washington's own western land purchases. But none of this was quite enough to explain the effect that the twenty-year-old Washington had on him. He decided to throw some of his support behind him, but the post was not completely in his gift. A few months later, the governor and his executive council slugged out in private a decision to divide Lawrence's former post of honor into four districts. The council had initially intended only three. Washington, proud that he was receiving his first military distinction before he was twenty, was appointed with the rank of major to oversee militia training in the southernmost (and least important) district, between the James River and the North Carolina border. He was to receive a £100-a-year salary, roughly doubling his cash income. The job carried more prestige than threat of future military action. Any contact with external enemies would probably come from the northwest, closer to Indian country, not the swamps of the southeast.

He had not received his far-more-prestigious home district of northern Virginia, so Washington did not rush off to visit the southern district for a year and a half. For several months in 1753, he stayed home at Ferry Farm, borrowing all the military books he could. He studied how to train the captains of the companies in his assigned district and how they, in turn, were to muster, organize, and drill their own companies of militia. In September, according to Governor Dinwiddie's decree, the first colony-wide musters were to take place. Meanwhile, Major Washington continued to lobby the governor and his own patrons to help him win over the northern district adjutancy, which, since his brother had been the colony's sole adjutant general, he considered rightfully his.

It may have been at least in part to further this military ambition that, on September 1, 1752, he applied to join a new Masonic lodge being organized in Fredericksburg. George Washington was one of the first five initiates on November 4, paying an initiation fee of £2, 3 shillings to become registered as an Entered Apprentice. But Washington was not just forming a self-interested connection with the Masons. He would take his Mason's apron and trowel seriously. Eventually he became the highest-ranking Mason in the United States and brought to the order a durable political prestige. While he dutifully attended the church services of the established Church of England, he was bored with its priestcraft and from that time forward rarely was seen going to Anglican communion. He put his own interpretation on Civility Rule No. 108: "When you speak of God or his attributes let it be seriously and with reverence." He began in his letters to use the word *God* very seldom, substituting Masonic formulae: the Almighty, the Ruler of the Universe, Providence, the Supreme Being. He used these forms not only in private correspondence but, as commander in chief during the Revolution, in his General Orders.

As he came of age, Major Washington was usually busy making money at a time of life when many of the William and Mary–educated sons of Tidewater planters were carousing, courting, and getting married as they came into and began to race through their inheritances. Between 1749 when he was seventeen and 1753 when he finally won his quest to become adjutant general of northern Virginia, he plunged twice each year, spring and fall, into the wilderness with his surveying team of an assistant, two chainmen, and a hunter or two. He carried out nearly two hundred surveys. Like his great-grandfather and each generation of Washingtons over the past century, by hard work and frugality he was beginning to amass a sizable estate. When he came of age at twenty-one, he owned ten inherited slaves, the 224-acre Ferry Farm, three Fredericksburg town lots, and half (2,291 acres) of the Deep Run tract, all inherited from his father. In addition, he had bought some 2,000 acres of fertile Shenandoah Valley riverfront land—in all, he owned over 5,000 acres of unencumbered land, making him a noticeable landowner. He could look forward to income from an estate that could be expected to appreciate in value as more settlers poured over the mountains. He had also confirmed his inherited place in the class of landed Virginia proprietors. His growing wealth and influence may explain why he was, with no military experience, able to shoulder his way to the head of the line for colonial military preferment. A major at twenty, he held the most prestigious peacetime military post in the colony at age twenty-one. He was clearly emerging as one of Virginia's up-and-coming young leaders. It should have come as no surprise when he approached Governor Dinwiddie again in 1753, offering his services for the most important and dangerous mission that the governor had to assign—to go as the governor's deputy and official diplomatic envoy five hundred miles into the wilderness and tell the French to get out of English-claimed territory south of the Great Lakes or face military consequence.

*F*or more than seventy years, the English and the French had contested their claims to the vast trans-Appalachian region from the Great Lakes south to the Ohio River and west to the Mississippi. The French considered the Ohio Valley a necessary strategic corridor linking their militarily feeble southern trading bases at New Orleans and St. Louis with their Canadian strongholds. They feared that rapidly swelling English immigration would send a tidal wave of settlers over the mountains and into the fertile interior valleys. The English colonists had used three intercolonial wars—King William's War (1689–1697), Queen Anne's War (1702–1713), and King George's War (1739–1748)—as opportunities to drive back the French and wrest from them the lucrative fur trade with the Indians. But European diplomacy had neutralized each effort. In 1748, the end of the latest war provided what was no more than a breather to allow each side to rearm and make new alliances with the natives before resuming the struggle for dominion over the forests.

The power vacuum left in 1748 after the Treaty of Lancaster allowed Pennsylvania, Maryland, and Virginia traders to rush into the Ohio Valley region, thoroughly alarming the French. From the east, Quaker merchants set up trading posts and sent armed traders to what is now western Pennsylvania, Ohio, and Kentucky. From the south, the Ohio Company, headed by Virginia's Royal Governor Dinwiddie, began to build a highway into the Ohio Valley to link Virginia with the interior and to bring in settlers to buy its 200,000 acres and take out furs and farm produce. The Ohio Company, founded by Lawrence Washington and his friends in 1748, had successfully appealed to the British authorities in London to offer ship's passage to indentured servants who would work to clear and improve roads and farmsteads and build company trading posts for seven years, in return for the right to remain on the lands as leaseholders afterward. It was a great feudal leap backward in English America—except for the owners of the land, who could look forward to raising the rents and, each year, charging higher base rents to new leaseholders. George Washington eagerly joined the scheme at the moment when it was becoming bogged down in English politics. The Ohio Company had competition. Rival companies included the Greenbriar Company, the Loyal Land Company of Virginia, formed by Thomas Jefferson's father and his friends, and the Vandalia Company of Philadelphia, organized by Benjamin Franklin and his son William. The Ohio Company had promised to settle one hundred families in the Ohio Valley around a fort that they would build at stockholders' expense. They had to move quickly or lose the grant and all they had invested.

The French were moving just as quickly to scuttle the Virginians' plans. The intercolonial wars between England and France had, until the 1750s, kept the English colonists pinned to the east side of the Appalachians, affording the French a virtual monopoly on trade with native trappers west of the mountains. There were few English settlements more than one hundred miles from the Atlantic Ocean. The French enjoyed several advantages. From their administrative and military capital inside the walled city of Quebec (the largest city in either English or French America) they wielded centralized control over all French settlers and Indians on lands they claimed, with bureaucrats and garrisons in forts as far away as New Orleans kept in constant communication by a fast-moving fleet of couriers in canoes and, in winter, on snowshoes. One of their principal fears was that English expansion would sever these links. For years, the French had been building forts around the Great Lakes and along the principal rivers of the interior, where they not only kept soldiers and colonial administrators but carried out their lucrative trade with the natives.

While the French were well organized, they worried about the sheer numbers of the English settlers. In 1688, there had been more than eight times as many English in New England alone (100,000) as there were *habitants* in all of New France (12,000). To offset English numerical superiority, the French imported soldiers from their army, the best in Europe, offered them land and built them houses around their forts when they retired, and even supplied them with oxen, tools, and seeds. But far more of the French came not to settle in the severe northern climate but to get rich quick enough in the fur trade to go back to France and live in civilization with money in their pockets. Englishmen came to stay, to settle, to buy land they could never buy in England, to hunt and to fish, which they also could never do back home, and to put down roots. They could live in America far better than they could in England. The English colonies also attracted settlers from twenty other nations. The English, in addition to numbers, had other advantages, which in the long term were decisive. They controlled the Atlantic Ocean with the Royal Navy, which protected their supply lines in war and their colonial markets in peacetime. They also had more capital on their side as Englishmen reinvested the huge profits of trade with the colonies in America. Both rivals relied on alliances with natives who were longtime enemies, the French with the Algonquins and the English with the Iroquois, although these confederacies were fluid and had learned to play off the Europeans against one another to gain more weapons and supplies.

The resulting stalemate was about to burst like a beaver dam in a spring freshet, sweeping away the French. By 1750, eighty thousand French *habitants* were outnumbered by more than one million Englishmen pent up east of the Appalachians. But the French certainly had not conceded this in 1753 when George Washington volunteered to carry an ultimatum to them. Even if they were endowed with the prescience to foresee the eventual failure of New France, few Frenchmen could see that its demise would come in only a few years. Probably the clearest warning to the French court at Versailles—one that helped stiffen French resolve to resist English expansion in North America—came from a naval officer who accidentally governed New France from 1747 to 1749. Marquis Roland-Michel Barrin de la Galissonière was pressed into service as deputy governor when the newly appointed governor was captured by the British navy en route to his new post. Galissonière, an outsider who was not afflicted with the usual optimistic myopia of the French foreign service, came to the conclusion in two years in Canada that the British were actively planning to drive the French out of North America and that steps must be taken quickly to stop them. He believed that the only way to offset the English advantage in population and to prevent French expulsion was to build a line of well-garrisoned fortresses between Canada and the French colony of Louisiana, a permanent barrier to confine the British settlers east of the Appalachians and prevent them from outflanking the French colonies. He advocated a chain of military posts that housed trading stations to assure French ties with the natives in the Ohio and Illinois country, still a no-white-man's-land between Canada and Louisiana when the Ohio Company began its push into the region in 1749.

Galissonière realized that France's claim to the Ohio region was shaky. It depended on undocumented discoveries by LaSalle in 1679, supposedly the first white man to lay eyes on the region. But Englishmen had also paddled through the region earlier in the 1670s. Neither nation had left lasting proof of the validity of its claims. The English had improved their claim in 1715 when the French signed the Treaty of Utrecht, which confirmed that the Iroquois, masters of the region, were henceforth full British subjects. That claim was further enhanced by the Treaty of Lancaster of 1748 when the Iroquois sold hunting rights to the Ohio Valley to the Pennsylvanians. Alarmed by this treaty, Galissonière dispatched a French expedition in 1749 to travel along the Ohio River, make treaties with the Indians, and plant iron plates in the ground at the junction of every river and creek to claim the river's waters and adjoining lands for France.

Relieved of his duties in September 1749, just as the Ohio Company began erecting its first fort at Cumberland Gap in present-day western Maryland, Galissonière hurried back to France and published his *Memoire sur les colonies de la France dans l'Amérique septentrionale*. This remarkable document was influential in forming French opinion on the eve of another war for empire. While admitting that Canada was still weak, poor, sparsely populated, and an expensive drain on the French treasury, it

> is of the greatest importance and absolutely necessary not to neglect any means or spare any expense to assure the preserva-

tion of Canada, since it is only in this way that we can succeed in saving America from the ambitions of the British. . . . The progress of their empire in this part of the world is what is most capable of giving them superiority in Europe.[1]

Galissonière was not a flattering courtier but a clear-headed military man who was probably the first to make in print a linkage between French security in Canada and French security in Europe. French settlements in the American wilderness could prevent the English from deriving great benefit from their colonies. The French, with a better army, had a military advantage that could offset the numerical odds against them. They had better alliances with more Indian warriors and could organize, supply, and successfully lead them in warfare because the French colonists were more willing to live like Indians. Since the French were no match for the British navy on the Atlantic, they must take the initiative on the North American mainland and attack first.

Galissonière publicly warned the French to prepare for preemptive war against British expansionism. His comments came at exactly the moment the Ohio Company of Virginia began to carry out a new covert British strategy of expansion into the disputed Ohio country.

*E*ach bloody frontier war in the American forests had proven inconclusive, with European diplomats consistently treating their mainland American colonies as bargaining chips less valuable to them than the sugar-rich islands in the Caribbean or bases around the Mediterranean and Indian Oceans. By the mid-eighteenth century, the struggle for trade advantage had shifted to North America as American furs became all the rage of French courtiers at Versailles and their fashionable imitators outside France. The failure of European diplomats to define the boundaries between French and English settlements had led to King George's War, which started when George Washington was seven and continued until he was sixteen. During Washington's youth, the French continued to build forts along the Illinois and Missouri Rivers and began relocating settlers from Canada. The Treaty of Aix-la-Chapelle of 1748 ended King George's War but once again, to the disgust of Americans—the first time this name was being used—returned captured territories and fortresses.

The European treaty was almost immediately contradicted by the Treaty of Lancaster, Pennsylvania, which gave Anglo-American traders the right to barter with the natives in the forests of the Ohio River watershed. Benjamin Franklin was the official printer of Indian treaties. After attending the conference, he wrote, "If these Indians and their allies prove faithful to the English, there will be nothing to interrupt an intercourse between this province and that great river (the Ohio)."[2]

Pennsylvania officials followed up on the Lancaster Treaty by sending an expedition into the Ohio Valley in late summer 1748, conferring again with Indian leaders at Logstown, the Delaware Indian capital eighteen miles north of present-day Pittsburgh. A new rivalry, between Virginia and Pennsylvania, had begun. While the Pennsylvanians were riding and rowing to reach their new Indian customers, the Ohio Company of Virginia was taking a more methodical approach. The company was officially headed by the royal governor Thomas Lee, but Lawrence Washington was its prime mover. He had won the support of Tidewater planters for a plan to build a highway over the mountains from Blue Ridge to the Ohio Valley to link a series of fortified trading posts. The Ohio Company was thinking on a grand scale. When its charter was blocked by a majority in the governor's council who had friends in rival speculative ventures, the company applied directly to London for an official grant of 200,000 acres along the Ohio River. In exchange, they promised to settle one hundred inhabitants quickly to garrison a fort they would build. If they met this goal, they would receive a 300,000-acre bonus.

The Board of Trade in London acted with surprising alacrity, in March 1749 ordering the royal governor to grant the land. The Ohio Company immediately hired a noted professional explorer and Indian trader, Christopher Gist, to search for an appropriate site to build a combined company trading post and fort. Gist was given stock in the company and was instructed to placate any reluctant natives objecting to this latest English encroachment by insisting that private citizens, not the English government, were behind it.

In less than three years of receiving the go-ahead from the British government, the Ohio Company had blazed a highway some eighty miles through Virginia backcountry through Cumberland Gap and built a fort at Will's Creek. It was beginning to survey and sell land to settlers. The value of the Ohio Company's stock had climbed when Robert Dinwiddie, already an Ohio Company investor before his arrival, was appointed to the highest Virginia office and arrived from Scotland with fresh capital.

While Lawrence Washington was ailing in Barbados, the new royal governor met George Washington for the first time. Just before Lawrence's death, George went a second time to Williamsburg to meet Dinwiddie and to seek his nomination to the adjutancy. The third time they met, George came away with the best adjutant's district: Dinwiddie appointed him adjutant for the Northern Neck, his home district. The bluff, puffy-faced Glasgow merchant was learning a grudging respect for the opportunistic young Washington. By the time they met again, Dinwiddie knew that, as co-executor of Lawrence Washington's estate, George Washington was deeply involved in the affairs of the Ohio Company, and was now linked by business ties with the cream of Tidewater aristocrats, including Fairfaxes, Lees, Carters, Harrisons, and Masons. Sixty-year-old Dinwiddie was impressed with the persistence of this frontier-toughened yet elegant young man. Childless, he could see something of himself in the youthful Major Washington. Dinwiddie had served as inspector general of British Customs for all southern ports before his appointment as royal governor of Virginia; he brought a fortune and a personal financial stake in Virginia's land venture into territory now actively contested by the French. But at a time when there was no such thing as the modern notion of conflict of interest, other Ohio Company stockholders, in addition to the royal governor of Virginia, included the governors of Maryland and North Carolina and twenty members of the Virginia House of Burgesses, nine members of the Virginia governor's executive council, four politically potent London merchants, and a duke. Not only were George Washington's new colleagues among the richest Virginians, they were among the most powerful men in British America. No wonder the French considered the activities and interests of the Ohio Company only a subterfuge for an extension of British foreign policy.

To emphasize that it had not lost interest in the Ohio Valley, early in 1753 the French government at Versailles decided to reinforce its garrisons in Canada, sending, among other deployments, some 1,500 troops, a large force for the times, to Fort Le Boeuf on the southeast shore of Lake Erie in present-day Erie County, Pennsylvania. Their orders were to remove, by intimidation or by force, all English traders from the region between the Appalachians and the Ohio River, an area already swarming with merchants, traders, and trappers sent out by Philadelphia companies. At once, French troops began to arrest the English traders, sending them first to a jail in Quebec and then by ship to France. News of the harsh new French policy sent Virginia governor Dinwiddie running for his quill pen. His personal fortune as well as English prestige were at stake. In June 1753, he wrote to London to report the new hard-line French behavior and to seek instructions. Four months later, in nearly record turnaround time, he had his answer. He was to send an emissary to the French commander at Fort Le Boeuf, warning him that the region was British territory and that if he did not withdraw his troops and stop arresting Englishmen immediately, Virginia would "drive them off by force of arms."[3]

*S*ince his father's death, George Washington had been blessed with a series of fatherly benefactors. He found another substitute father in Governor Dinwiddie, who gradually made Washington his protégé between 1752, when George's brother died, and 1754, when Dinwiddie entrusted an untried twenty-two-year-old with command of a little army that may have fired the first shots of the Seven Years' War (called the French and Indian War only in America). Dinwiddie not only allowed Washington to rise rapidly in military rank and honor, but he seems to have taught him by his example a combination of self-assured, stubborn patriotism and self-interest. In correspondence in the critical years leading up to the frontier war with the French that was to launch George Washington's military career, Dinwiddie referred interchangeably to his wielding of the power of the British king, the colony of Virginia, and the Ohio Company, of which he became the dominant member. His mingling of roles had the blessing of the British government.

After three-quarters of a century of stripping troublesome proprietary groups of their colonial charters and replacing them with royal colonial governments, the British Board of Trade suddenly seemed to be reversing itself. Most Virginians had been shocked when the King's Privy Council had deeded the 5.2 million acres of Northern Neck to the Fairfax family, making it a virtually feudal principality within Virginia. The British government's decision to grant half a million acres of the Ohio Valley to the Ohio Company represented the privatization of British foreign policy. Whatever on-the-scene actions seemed necessary to the stockholders of the Ohio Company in Virginia became British policy. The third surprise came when new Royal Governor Dinwiddie arrived in 1751 on a ship loaded with cannon and supplies for the Ohio Company's fort and goods to trade with the Indians. The Crown had appointed Dinwiddie as governor not only knowing he was a major stockholder but probably because he was.

*I*n February 1753, the same week George Washington, just turned twenty-one, was sworn in as district adjutant general for northern Virginia, the French launched their campaign to fortify the Ohio Country. First they built a fortress at Presque Isle on a peninsula protruding into Lake Erie. By the spring of 1754, they had smoothed a fifteen-mile portage south to French Creek, a tributary of the Allegheny River, where they constructed Fort Le Boeuf (Fort Buffalo). By June 1754, the news that a force of eight hundred French was moving south to the forks of the Ohio, the Allegheny, and the Monongahela reached Governor Dinwiddie, who sent off dispatch riders to the governors of the other English colonies. Only Dinwiddie, who knew that the Ohio Company of Virginia had already begun building its second fort two miles south of the forks of the Ohio, seemed exercised by the French advance. The governors of New York and New England saw little cause for concern: their boundaries were already established. Maryland could not expand farther westward, and Pennsylvania, its western border limited to three hundred miles from the Delaware, was ruled by Quakers unwilling to provoke an armed conflict. Virginia would have to act alone.

Dinwiddie knew that authorities in London would share his alarm. "I hope you will think it necessary to prevent the French taking possession of the lands on the Ohio," he wrote to the Board of Trade. His answer came in slightly more than four months. A sloop-of-war brought explicit instructions signed by King George II himself. Word spread quickly that Virginia was to counter the French threat. As a preliminary step, Dinwiddie was to send a warning to the French to get out of Ohio Country. Dinwiddie summoned his executive council for an emergency meeting on October 27 to consider the king's instructions:

> If you shall find any number of persons, whether Indians or Europeans, shall presume to erect any fort or forts within the limits of our province of Virginia, you are to require them peaceably to depart, and not to persist in such unlawful proceedings. And if, not withstanding your admonitions, they do still endeavor to carry on any such unlawful and unjustifiable designs, we do hereby strictly charge and command you to drive them off with force of arms.[4]

The night before the council was to meet, Major Washington rode into Williamsburg. Washington had learned from Councillor Fairfax that an emissary would be chosen. An adjutant general, already an administrative deputy of the governor, would be suitable. Washington, youngest of the three adjutants and the most vigorous, was the most experienced frontiersman and was ready and eager to go.

But he was not the obvious choice to Dinwiddie or the council. Captain William Trent, a fur trader and interpreter who had already carried out an exploratory mission for the Ohio Company into the Ohio Country, had represented Virginia at a Logstown parley with the Iroquois in 1752 and had been well known in Indian country for many years. It was Trent who had brought word of the French advance to Dinwiddie. But Governor Dinwiddie mistrusted him and was reluctant to make him aware of all his dealings, even if he was already the company's man in charge of building its new fort on the Allegheny. Dinwiddie decided that Trent ought to rush completion of the fort. But could he find someone else to risk the journey deep into Indian country as winter approached?

On the night before the council meeting, Washington rode to the governor's palace in Williamsburg and made his case in private to Dinwiddie. He knew how important the mission would be. Dinwiddie, through Washington, would be interposing the English flag (even if it flew over a private fort) between Virginia and New France. Whoever carried this ultimatum would represent not only Virginia but England. It was a rare opportunity for honor for such a young man who was no more than a peacetime militia officer. But what Dinwiddie saw was enough to convince him. Not only was Washington eager to prove his loyalty to his king, but here was a frontier-toughened, physically powerful young man who had, by his surveying expeditions, already proven he had the strength and endurance to carry off a thousand-mile round trip in the wilderness. There was nothing soft about this young man. There was something avid, determined. His steady gray-eyed gaze and quiet, well-mannered demeanor were enough to hold the respect of subordinates or of officers of equal rank. If Washington had any drawback, it was that he could speak neither French nor Indian languages. But this was only a minor objection, and Washington quickly pointed out that he could take along an interpreter. His former fencing teacher, Jacob Van Braam of Fredericksburg, once a lieutenant in the Dutch army, also taught French.

When Washington left the governor's palace on October 26, 1754, he had won the governor's appointment as Virginia's emissary to the French. The next day, when the executive council met, "The Governor acquainted the Board that George Washington Esqr., Adjutant General for the Northern District, had offered himself to go properly commissioned to the commander of the French forces, to learn by what authority he presumes to make encroachments on His Majesty's lands in the Ohio." The council promptly accepted Major Washington's offer and issued the necessary commission. He would go as the governor's deputy to carry a letter drafted by a council committee to the French commander. The committee also drew up instructions to Washington to be signed by the governor. Washington was to present the letter and wait no longer than one week for an answer. Using his keen surveyor's eye for detail, he was to observe as closely as possible the extent of French military preparations, including troop strengths, dispositions, and armaments. He was to be half diplomat, half intelligence officer.[5]

Four days later, a buckskin-clad Washington was on his way. Stopping off at Ferry Farm to explain his mission to his nervous and disapproving mother, Washington cut short the visit, crossed over to Fredericksburg and hired Van Braam as his interpreter, then hurried northwest eighty miles along the Ohio Company's new road. At Wills Creek near Cumberland Gap, he retained German-born trader Christopher Gist as his guide, as well as two hunters and two fur traders. After only an overnight stop, the seven-man delegation set off north by northwest on November 15.

It took eight miserable days of slogging through heavy snows and rain across Laurel Mountain to reach the forks of the Ohio at present-day Pittsburgh. Major Washington paused for two days to inspect the Ohio Company site for a fort—and saw at once it was in the wrong place. He began to write a report for the company, explaining why the fort should be located at the confluence of the three rivers, not two miles downstream where Trent had situated it. As he waited for one of his hunters to arrive with a canoe to paddle him across the rain-swollen river, he visited the Forks and made a long note in his journal to impress on the council why the Virginia fort must be built at the Forks:

> *I spent some time in viewing the rivers and the land in the fork, which I think extremely well-situated for a fort, as it has the absolute command of both rivers. The land at the point is 20 or 25 feet above the common*

*surface of the water, and a considerable bottom of flat, well-timbered
land all around it, very convenient for building.*

Washington the surveyor was beginning to metamorphose into the
military engineer with shrewd eye and judgment for siting a fort, building
it, defending it. He chose well, correctly seeing the rivers, "each a quarter
of a mile or more across," as natural defenses, one "very rapid, swift-
running water," the other "deep and still." Recrossing the Allegheny that
night, Washington visited the Ohio Company's fort site the next day. It
was "greatly inferior," he recorded, standing on a gradual hillside that
would be easy to assault and expensive to fortify. An enemy could raise
artillery batteries from a short distance "without being exposed to a
single shot from the fort."

As freezing rain continued to pelt them, the party hiked through bare
woods for two more days over Indian trails to the Youghiogheny, then on
to its confluence with the Monongahela; a few miles more and they
forded the Allegheny. They trudged a dozen miles the last day. At sunset
on November 23, 1753, two weeks after leaving Fredericksburg, they saw
and smelled the welcome smoke of Logstown. They spent five days
there while Half King, sachem of the Shawnees and Shingas, chief of the
Delawares, recruited guides. Resting and talking with the revered old
chief, Washington learned to listen and reply to an Indian speech. He revealed little about the importance of his mission, only that he must deliver a letter to the French commander. But he could not fool the old
man, who told Washington that his tribesmen had already threatened to
drive out the French, only to be ridiculed by the French commander.

Setting out for the French headquarters at Fort Le Boeuf as soon as
four guides—Half King, Jeskakake, White Thunder, and Hunter—were
ready, Washington and his eleven-man party arrived at Venango on December 4. For the first time, Washington saw a fleur-de-lis flying over
American soil. "We found the French colors hoisted at a house they drove
Mr. John Frazer, an English subject, from." Frazer was one of the Pennsylvania traders the French had taken prisoner to Canada. Washington
delivered his missive to the commandant, Captain Phillippe Thomas de
Joncaire, sieur de Chabert: "He invited me to sup with them and treated
me with the greatest complaisance. The wine, as they dosed themselves
pretty plentifully with it, soon banished the restraint which at first appeared in their conversation and gave license to their tongues." Washington was learning one of the secrets of successful diplomacy—to drink less
than an adversary.

*They told me it was their absolute design to take possession of the Ohio,
and by G— they would do it, for though they were sensible that the English could raise two men for their one, yet they knew their [the English*

colonies] motions were too slow & dilatory to prevent any undertakings of theirs.[6]

The detailed intelligence Washington gathered from the three French officers and recorded was dead accurate, despite his lack of knowledge of any of the languages being spoken around him. During three days of cold, torrential rains, the talks over meals and endless rounds of drinks went on. His journal shows that, by the time he left Venango, he had an accurate picture not only of French intentions but of their timetable and the location and size of their fortifications, supplies, and garrisons.

On December 7, 1753, with four French soldiers added to its numbers, Washington's party rode northward for four days of what the young major described as "excessive rains, snows and bad traveling through many mires and swamps." English traders had been rounded up and herded off to Canadian jails along this route. Washington had reason to know fear for the first time. But he seems to have been absorbed in appraising the real estate around him: "We passed over much good land since we left Venango and through several extensive and very rich meadows, one of which was near four miles in length and considerably wide." On December 11, the bedraggled band of fifteen approached the palisades of Presque Isle on the Lake Erie shore. To his face, the French officer in charge greeted Major Washington cordially. Behind his back, the French professionals mocked him as "the buckskin general." It was several hours before the commandant of Fort Le Boeuf arrived. Washington had changed into his red adjutant-general's uniform by the time he was ushered by the second officer into the presence of Louis Le Gardeur de St. Pierre de Repentigny, an old, one-eyed veteran who, to Washington, had "much the air of a soldier." Washington presented Repentigny with the letter from Virginia's government: "I acquainted him with my business and offered my commission and letter." Repentigny had, in this superpower race, arrived on the frontier from Montreal only seven days before Washington. He took Washington's papers and adjourned "into a private apartment for the Captain to translate." After a while, Washington and his translator were invited in to peruse the translation, "which I did."[7]

On December 13, the French officers held a council of war. While they were distracted, Washington was busy. The French meeting "gave me an opportunity of taking the dimensions of the fort and making what observations I could," Washington wrote blandly in his diary. Later, he drew a detailed plan of the fort and submitted it to Governor Dinwiddie. He noted dimensions, surrounding waters, construction: "The bastions are made of piles drove into the ground and, about twelve feet above, sharp at top with portholes cut for cannon and small arms to fire through." Washington was getting a lesson in fort building while the French debated. He compiled a brilliant picture of a French frontier fort and its armaments gleaned during his brazen tour of the fortress:

There are eight 6 lb. pieces mounted, two in each bastion & one of 4 lb. before the gate. In the bastions are a guard house, chapel, doctor's lodgings and the commander's private store, round which is laid platforms for the cannon and men to stand on. There is several barracks without the fort for the soldiers' dwelling, covered some with bark, and some with boards & made chiefly of logs; there is also several other houses such as stables, smith's chaps, etc., all of which I have laid down exactly as they stand. . . . I could get no certain account of the number of men here [he estimated there were 100 plus their officers]. . . . I also gave orders to the people that were with me to take an exact account of the canoes [to be used] to convey their forces down in the Spring . . . and [was] told 50 of birch bark & 170 of pine besides many others that were blocked out.

Dinwiddie sent Washington's report along with his expert drawings and map of the Ohio Country to London to the Board of Trade, where it had a strong impact on British officials pondering the French buildup. The report, rushed into print at Williamsburg, was widely discussed in Virginia, making Washington's exploits a sensation.

On December 14, Washington noted, "the snow increased very fast." He had delivered Virginia's ultimatum to the French; now he had to worry about getting back. The horses, Washington noted, "daily got weaker." He sent them off unloaded to Venango with one of his guards. Washington made up his mind he could make better time by canoe.

Two clocks were ticking now. He had to beat the severe northern winter and he had to carry a detailed warning to Williamsburg to allow time to outfit a force and return to the Ohio Valley early the next spring before the French resumed their advance into the Ohio Valley. Washington had already discovered "many plots" by the French to woo the Indians to their side, including preventing the Indians from returning to Logstown with him. While the French commandant was stalling answering Virginia's ultimatum, he actively plied the Indians with promises of food and supplies. There had been a drought that summer; the natives' crops had failed, and they were hungry as they faced winter. The English and their Iroquois allies were far away. What could they do to help the Indians now? The French were near and ready to help.

The French design, according to Washington, was to enlist the natives to hunt down "all our straggling traders." When Washington demanded what gave Repentigny authority to seize Englishmen, "he told me the country belonged to them, that no Englishman had a right to trade upon their waters and that it had orders to make every person prisoner that attempted it." Indians led by French officers, Washington had learned, had not only taken English prisoners to Canada but had taken eight scalps. When Washington brought up the names of specific missing traders,

Repentigny suddenly presented him with an answer to the Virginia ultimatum. He would not withdraw his troops. Nothing the French were
doing "can be construed as an act of hostility or as contrary to the treaties
between the two Crowns." In his written reply of December 15, 1754, to
Governor Dinwiddie, Repentigny pointed out he had "receive[d] Mr.
Washington with the distinction" deserved by "his own great merit."[8]

As the French continued to delay the Indian leader's departure, Washington lost patience and left by canoe, taking only Gist and two Indians
to guide them. They paddled sixteen miles the first day. One of the Indian guides slipped away at the next Indian camp. Washington left the
other and hurried on with Gist in a single canoe. By December 21, their
fourth day on the river, they ran into hard-packed ice, "so hard," wrote
Gist, "we could not break our way through." They had to drag their
loaded canoe to open water, then repeatedly get out and wade in the
frigid water. As it became shallower, the loaded canoe jammed in the
rocks, "the water freezing to our clothes." The French overtook them,
but then their canoes overturned, "the brandy and wine floating in the
creek." After a weeklong ordeal on the river, Washington and Gist
reached Venango, the rest of their party, and their horses.[9]

When the Seneca chief Half King obfuscated about going on, Washington, sure the packhorses would not survive the journey, traded them
for Indian packs, "putting myself into Indian walking dress." Leaving
Van Braam and the rest of the party behind, Washington was

> determined to prosecute my journey the nearest way through the woods
> on foot [actually on showshoes]. I took my necessary papers, pulled off
> my clothes, tied myself up in a match coat and, with my pack at my
> back, with my papers and provisions in it and a gun, set out with Mr.
> Gist fitted in the same manner.

They only made it one day before they were attacked by "a party of
French Indians which had laid in wait for us." One fired from only fifteen
yards away "at Mr. Gist or me" but "fortunately missed." Before the Indian could reload, Washington seized him and took him away at gunpoint
as a hostage, not releasing him until late that night. Washington and Gist
trudged on all night "without making any stop." Outdistancing their pur-
suers, they went on all the next day, too, "traveling until it was quite
dark." They had hoped to find the Allegheny frozen over. Instead they
faced fast-moving chunks of ice.

"There was no way for us to get over," Washington later wrote, "but
upon a raft, which we set about [making] with but one poor hatchet and
got finished just after sunsetting, after a whole day's work. We got it
launched and [climbed] on board of it and set off, but before we got half
over, we were jammed in the ice. We expected every moment our raft
would sink and we perish." When Washington tried to stop the raft with

his setting pole until floating ice passed them, "it jerked me into ten feet of water." Washington saved himself "by catching hold of one of the raft logs." But they could not push the raft to either shore. They decided to leave the raft and swim to a small island. "The cold was so extreme severe that Mr. Gist got all his fingers and some of his toes froze." Washington did not comment on his own near drowning and frozen state. They slept in frozen clothes on the island and made it on foot across the ice to Venango the next day.

By the first day of 1755, Major Washington had bought a horse and saddle for each of them and set off south along the Monongahela. On the sixth day they passed an Ohio Company convoy with seventeen loaded packhorses on its way north to build the company's fort. The next day, they reached the company base at Cumberland Gap, "after as fatiguing a journey as it is possible to conceive." Stopping at Belvoir only long enough for a night's rest, Washington rode into Williamsburg on January 16, arriving at the governor's palace after a seventy-nine-day mission. In all, he had traveled over one thousand miles on horseback, in a canoe, and on snowshoes in terrible winter weather. He didn't complain, only noting in his journal that "from the first day of December till the 15th (of January) there was but one day [when it didn't] rain or snow incessantly." Preparing the journal for the governor, he concluded by writing, "I hope it will be sufficient to satisfy your honor with my proceedings."[10]

Five

"I HEARD BULLETS WHISTLE"

After a one-day stopover at Belvoir to recount his frontier adventures to the Fairfaxes, Major Washington dashed off to Williamsburg. During Washington's perilous errand into the wilderness, Governor Dinwiddie had found it impossible to squeeze a penny from the Assembly to defend the colony and its frontier land interests. Many burgesses and several members of his executive council belonged to the Ohio Company; even more belonged to rival land companies. They believed the governor was using scare tactics to raise taxes to further the schemes of his own company. Dinwiddie saw Washington's breathless report as just the impetus he needed. He ordered him to write up his notes at once and bring them to the governor's palace the next morning so he could lay them before his council.

Staying up through the night, Washington turned his sketchy diary entries into a compelling 7,000-word report calculated to leave indisputable the clear and present danger the French and their Indian allies posed to Virginia. He made explicit the firm refusal of the French commander to abandon his posts in the face of the English ultimatum. He removed any doubt of French intentions—or of his own bravery. He colored the truth only once when he said that the Indian who had fired at Gist could have been aiming at him "but fortunately missed." The ambush was not the most riveting part—the murder and scalping of seven Virginians by Indians loyal to the French ended Washington's dramatic rendering with a courtier's flourish. He hoped the governor would be "satisfied with my conduct." That had been his "aim" in undertaking the mission "and my chief study through the prosecution of it."[1]

Beating his deadline, Washington was surprised when his report divided official Williamsburg. The governor's friends praised his courage. His enemies whispered that the governor and his young courier, also an

Ohio Company stockholder, were conniving to use public funds for their own profit. Washington's report nonetheless created a sensation. Dinwiddie presented it that afternoon to the emergency session of his council and then rushed it off to the colony's official printer. He did not wait for the House of Burgesses to reconvene in the spring. Within the month, Washington's report was read throughout Virginia, reprinted in newspapers in other colonies, and, within weeks, in at least two newspapers in London.

Washington's report brought results. He had warned the governor of his fear that the French planned to build a new fort at Logstown on the Allegheny River in the spring unless Virginia built a fort at the Forks of the Ohio first. He proposed a fort where the three rivers converged (the site of present-day Golden Triangle Park in Pittsburgh). Governor Dinwiddie wrung funds from the Assembly to dispatch workers to build a fort just where Washington had recommended. They also authorized the governor to call up two hundred militia to protect it, as Washington advised. Washington, as adjutant of the Northern Neck, was ordered to raise half the troops. Another four hundred would join him as soon as the burgesses reconvened. Meanwhile, Dinwiddie was to call on the royal governors of other colonies and "friendly Indians" to send assistance. He promoted Washington to lieutenant colonel of a newly formed Virginia Regiment. Only five days after his return from Pennsylvania, Colonel Washington, not quite twenty-two years old, left Williamsburg to take up his first combat command. His life as an amateur soldier was over.

A large part of war is the waiting, as Washington soon learned. Traveling to the jumping-off place at Alexandria, it must have occurred to him that nobody knew how long it would take to raise troops and drill them, much less to march them over the mountains to the Monongahela, or how many wagons or horses it would take to transport their supplies— or even how to get the horses and wagons. Virginia had no trained officers, no experienced recruiters, no troops, no wagon train, no artillery, and few weapons. Just how fast he could begin the march depended, first, on raising men quickly. That responsibility rested with the county lieutenants, Lord Fairfax for the Northern Neck and James Patton in Augusta, an enormous frontier county that stretched from the Blue Ridge to the Mississippi. It should have been easy to raise two hundred men in such a vast area, but, Washington soon found, it was not. Arriving in Frederick, Maryland, to begin drilling Lord Fairfax's recruits, he found them nonexistent. His Lordship didn't even have a roll of men liable for military duty: in three weeks he had not recruited one man. And, despite recent Indian raids in Augusta County, that county likewise produced no volunteers. After losing an entire month, by February 11, a disenchanted Washington rode back to Williamsburg in time to report in person to the governor for the emergency meeting of the House of Burgesses.

As Washington waited and Dinwiddie fumed, the General Assembly convened on February 14. The governor delivered a passionate version of Washington's report. He warned that 1,500 French professional soldiers and their Indian allies were preparing to mount a spring offensive and would "build many more fortresses" in the Ohio Country. The governor appended Washington's journal and Captain Joncaire's reply to his own message and demanded a sizable appropriation. In committee, some burgesses, far from swayed, labeled Washington's journal, he later reported, "a fiction and a scheme to promote the interest of a private company." But at the session's end, the majority of the entire House of Burgesses honored Washington by voting him £50 to "testify approbation of his proceedings on his journey to the Ohio." It was George Washington's baptism of fire in dealing with a legislature and he long remembered it. After a hot debate, the burgesses then voted £10,000 for defense with the proviso that fourteen burgesses form a committee to account for the money. To Dinwiddie, this constituted a new and alarming infringement of the Crown's prerogatives. The burgesses had insisted on looking over the governor's shoulder and they had done it "very much in a republican way of thinking," complained the royal governor to London.[2]

Cash in hand, Dinwiddie set out to form a new Virginia Regiment and to hire six companies of fifty men each. In addition to per diem pay of fifteen pounds of tobacco, he added the incentive of a share in a 200,000-acre land grant on the Ohio River to be apportioned to veterans of the fort-building expedition according to rank. The governor also asserted his power to appoint all officers, including the commander. This last provision deeply interested young Washington. Two facts raised his hopes. Official recognition by the burgesses combined with Dinwiddie's insistence on keeping him on a militia captain's active-duty pay since his return from the Ohio made him believe he was at least a strong candidate for another promotion. He decided to tackle the governor head-on and ask for appointment as second in command of the new regiment. He knew he lacked the experience to be named overall commander. Quietly lining up support on the executive council, Washington approached Dinwiddie to inquire how much the second in command would be paid. He expressed his horror at the answer: fifteen shillings a day, the same as enlisted men, but with all supplies provided. While he quietly protested that this was far too low, he not so quietly set out to find a sponsor for his application. To Richard Corbin on the governor's council, he wrote to ask to be "thought worthy of the post of lieutenant colonel." Wisely setting out to prove his worthiness, Washington went to work recruiting. At Winchester, he rounded up twenty-five "slack, idle fellows" with no shoes and little clothing who wanted cash advances against their pay. Washington had to tell them he had no money and no clothing to give them. "They are perpetually teasing me," Washington wrote to Governor Dinwiddie, "but I am not able to advance the money, provided there was no risk in it, which there certainly is, and too great for me to run, though it would be nothing to the country."[3]

The governor was finding that it was not easy to commission a competent commanding officer for his new regiment. With no battle-seasoned officers to draw on, Dinwiddie finally settled on Joshua Fry, a tired old former professor of mathematics at the College of William and Mary, to be colonel of the regiment and lead the western expedition. Six years earlier, Fry, an able cartographer, had teamed up with Peter Jefferson to map the boundary between the Fairfax lands and Virginia. A respected frontiersman, Fry was good at dealing with subordinates. He had served as county lieutenant of Albemarle County for many years and was skilled at negotiating with the Indians. Washington had every reason to be pleased to be named his second in command with the rank of lieutenant colonel. Governor Dinwiddie conferred the appointments with praise—"the best we have"—but it was very faint praise: "but not so well acquainted with the arts of war as I could wish. . . . I hope for the protection of heaven."[4]

On March 20, the newly minted Colonel Washington responded frankly that he was seeking "honor" among Virginians, yet he was vexed that he was only to be paid 12 shillings, 6 pence a day, 20 percent less than the paltry sum the governor had mentioned earlier (some 15 pounds a month less). And his provisions were to be the same as any private soldier. Taken together, his compensation was far less than what a British officer of equal rank would receive, he pointed out. Rather than admit that he was offended or that his pride was hurt, he announced, in a visit to Colonel Fairfax, that he considered this a case of discrimination against colonial officers in general. He told Fairfax he was going to decline the commission. Fairfax, after trying to persuade the hotheaded younger man to retain his commission, promised to speak with the governor. If Washington would go ahead with his recruiting efforts, he promised to argue Washington's case for higher pay for all the Virginia officers. Agreeing to postpone his resignation, Washington turned his attention to Dinwiddie's instructions: he was to "march what soldiers you have immediately to the Ohio and escort some wagons with the necessary provisions." Colonel Fry would catch up later.[5]

Washington's first great opportunity had come. Barely twenty-two, he had been trusted with the vanguard of troops to be gathered from all over colonial America to defend not only Virginia's but Great Britain's interests against French expansion into the heartland of North America. He had in hand orders to act on the defensive,

> but in case any attempts are made to obstruct the works or interrupt our settlements by any persons whatsoever you are to restrain all such offenders and in case of resistance to make prisoners of or kill and destroy them.[6]

Second in command of the only English military force active in North America in the spring of 1754, George Washington found himself in an exposed and dangerous post with absolutely no military experience. In fact if not in name, he was in command of an important mission. His commanding officer, Colonel Fry, had been in the militia but had never been in combat. He was too old, fat, and slow to embrace danger for the first time. Governor Dinwiddie, learning from an Ohio Company trader that hundreds of French troops were canoeing down the Ohio, instructed Washington not to wait for Fry or for the troops promised by other colonies. He was to leave with all the men he could raise at once, race the French to the Forks of the Ohio, and build a substantial fort before they could.

After a month of frustrating paper shuffling at expedition headquarters in Alexandria, Washington was eager to move out, if only with 134 poorly trained, ill-equipped troops. He did not know that Dinwiddie had already made a serious blunder. In his haste, Dinwiddie bypassed the royal governor of South Carolina and appealed directly to the Catawba and Cherokee Indians to send him one thousand warriors. While his success depended on the aid of Indian auxiliaries, young Washington was not to wait for them. The governors of the other colonies touching on the Ohio Country, Pennsylvania and Maryland, had also promised aid, but their assemblies had not yet approved aid. That spring, cooperation in intercolonial defense was becoming an important issue as representatives of nine colonies met at Albany and adopted Benjamin Franklin's plan for a defensive union. The delegates to the convention ultimately voted unanimously for Franklin's plan but, back home, not one legislature was to adopt it.

As Colonel Washington tried to raise an army within Virginia, he was handicapped by a Virginia law that barred him from recruiting into his new regiment members of existing militia units, which were better armed and trained. The existing militia, as such, could not be used in the Ohio Valley because the question of whether the Forks lay within Virginia's borders remained unresolved. Militia could only be called up within Virginia for Virginia's defense. Reliable volunteers also were proving hard to find. It was illegal to recruit slaves or indentured servants, and many of the available men were English convicts transported to the colonies as an alternative to imprisonment. Washington was finding equally frustrating the task of commandeering horses and wagons to transport supplies for his incipient expedition, even though, under the feudal arrangements of Lord Fairfax's land sales in the Northern Neck, all settlers were required to volunteer for military service and provide whatever Washington requisitioned.

Washington was getting his first painful lesson in logistics. He made himself grossly unpopular in frontier clearings as he tried to talk farmers out of their horses and wagons, able to offer only promissory notes from the provincial government. One result was that the animals farmers would sell him were old and tired, the few wagons the horses would have to pull equally dilapidated. It took his first little wagon train eight days to reach Winchester, normally only two days' ride. A little good news awaited Washington at the frontier town of Winchester, a rude collection of sixty log buildings at the northern end of the Shenandoah Valley, at the western edge of settlement. He was welcomed by Captain Adam Stephen and a company of recruits. A thirty-year-old Scot educated as a physician in Edinburgh, Stephen had served aboard a Royal Navy hospital ship before coming to Virginia and was practicing medicine in Frederick, Maryland. He came highly recommended by Colonel William Fairfax. He came even more highly regarded by himself—he vastly overstated his experience in combat.

Supplies slowly trickled into Winchester. Another week vanished before, on April 16, Colonel Washington, a tall, earnest young commander in a blue-and-buff Virginia uniform, mounted his horse and led his roughshod little force of a dozen wagons and carts toward Wills Creek, 110 miles to the northwest. The horses wheezed under the weight of food, rum, tools, lead, and gunpowder as the wagons bumped over the rutted road. By the time Washington left Winchester, he received the grim news that the Virginia Company's half-finished stockade near the Forks of the Ohio had already fallen to the French.

*G*overnor Dinwiddie had sent Captain William Trent, a seasoned trader for the Virginia Company, ahead of Washington to the Forks of the Ohio with some forty Virginia Company woodsmen. On his own initiative, Trent had left his brother-in-law, Ensign Edward Ward, in command of the unfinished company fort. On April 13, Ward learned from his Indian scouts that a large French force was floating down the Ohio. He sent word to Trent to hurry back, then rode ten miles to try to persuade veteran trader John Frazer and his assistants at Venango to hurry south to reinforce the post. Frazer refused. Ward hurried back to the Forks to take command and try to finish its defenses. On April 17, the French commander, Captain Claude-Pierre Pecaudy de Contrecoeur, marched with some one thousand men up to the half-finished fort and demanded that Ward surrender. Without firing a shot, the Virginians withdrew. The French burned the Virginia outpost, then marched north to the Forks of the Ohio where Washington had argued that Virginia should build its fort. There the French began to build the far larger Fort Duquesne. With no loss of life, France had won a great strategic victory, taking control of the upper Ohio Valley and seriously challenging British claims to the interior of North America for the first time.

*Q*uickly learning from Indian runners that Contrecoeur was building a great new fortress, Colonel Washington kept his men moving northward as fast as frequent breakdowns of his supply wagons allowed. On April 22, Washington learned from Ensign Ward, who had made the trek from the surrendered company fort, the details of the rout near the Forks. The interview only fortified Washington's belief that he must play a key role in the west, that the Ohio Valley, with all its rich fur trade and millions of acres of fertile land, would be lost to the French forever unless he himself, at this moment, could dislodge them. He also was afraid that the English would lose their Indian allies in the Ohio region unless he made a show of force that could support them and keep their loyalty. The Delawares and Shawnees in their villages along the Ohio were, he knew, dependents of the Iroquois and, as such, English subjects. They were also shrewd and eager to keep their ties with the English, who gave them better barter rates for their furs than the French. But there were limits to their loyalty. They must now either throw their lot in with their new French neighbors or risk being killed by Canadian Indians fighting as auxiliaries to the French. There was another possibility, Washington knew. The Indians could, as they had before, simply leave the troubled region and head farther west, away from the white men. Ensign Ward brought Washington an important message from Half King, who had helped Washington on his winter mission. The Shawnee leader had sent appeals to the British governors of Virginia and Pennsylvania for help: "If you do not come to our aid soon, it is all over for us, and I think that we shall never be able to meet together again."[7]

With no time to consult Governor Dinwiddie and no sign of Colonel Fry, Washington believed that he must change the entire plan of the expedition or make a hasty and dangerous retreat, which, additionally, would end his brief military career in disgrace. Despite the fact that the French were now in actual possession of the Forks of the Ohio, Washington was able to persuade his officers that to retreat would only confirm French possession of the vast over-the-mountain region, not just the Ohio Valley but the western slope of the Allegheny Mountains. Only determined action, he argued, would reassure the natives. While a more experienced officer might have been more prudent and counseled the need to await reinforcements, Washington persuaded his officers that they must advance to the junction of Red Stone Creek and the Monongahela, some thirty-seven miles south of the Forks, where another Virginia Company outpost had already been staked out, and there wait either for Colonel Fry to bring up reinforcements or for more positive orders from Governor Dinwiddie. In this, his first council of war, Washington convinced his company commanders, all older and some more experienced than he was, to take a large risk by holding out against the French until reinforcements arrived.

He somehow had persuaded his men that their first and most essential task was also possible—to clear a wide enough roadway from Wills Creek at Cumberland Gap across sixty miles of mountain ridges through primeval forests to the mouth of Redstone Creek, a road that would be wide and smooth enough for heavy wagons and artillery. He actually believed he could do this with only a few score men and hand tools. He did not even have oxen to drag away felled trees. He had found a narrow trail, little more than a deer trail, which Virginia Company scouts had widened several years ago into a horse path at most four feet wide, and he blithely ordered it widened into a road fit for an army and its artillery. In the steamy early summer heat of a dense forest, tortured by the black flies of May, his 159 raw troops began the brutal hard work of felling thick trees, stripping off branches, hacking away the underbrush, and grubbing out rocks and tree stumps and filling in holes for the would-be wagon road. As they made the road a day at a time, they had to use it, hauling their provisions and munitions over it. Incredibly, they managed to cut a passable road for forty miles over several Appalachian ridges. On May 24, they crossed the longest and the steepest, Laurel Hill, and gazed down at a lush glen where two streams crisscrossed, known as Great Meadows. Here, in a natural bowl surrounded by dark forested hills, Washington decided to pitch his camp and ordered his men to make themselves huts. At last they could rest while the horses grazed and switched away the flies. In less than a month, George Washington and his three companies of 159 frontiersmen had cut the first road across the Allegheny Mountains into the Ohio Valley.

Washington felt, as he described it in a letter to Governor Horatio Sharpe of Maryland, a "glowing zeal" to take on the French. Probably because of his military inexperience, he was unwilling to retreat. Asking Maryland for reinforcements, he explained that the Indians needed his help and he must respond to their loyalty. He felt it was his duty to push on as far as he could so that, when reinforcements came, his force would be as far advanced toward the enemy as possible. He had no question, it seems, that he could retake the Forks of the Ohio with a few hundred unseasoned soldiers. The fact that a much superior force of veteran French troops was entrenched in a strong position did not faze him. His orders were to drive the French away. He would do just that.[8]

Besides burning zeal, one of the few things Washington really had going for him was his knowledge of the terrain. He had passed this way with his trained surveyor's eye twice before. He reasoned that the Redstone Creek site was the best jumping-off place from which to send artillery upriver to attack the French. At Redstone Creek, there were already warehouses for his supplies that could be adapted into a fort of sorts. He wrote to Dinwiddie to hurry along construction and shipments of boats to make an attack on the French by water and also to send along the Indians from the Carolinas. He apparently forgot—or decided to ignore—that Colonel Fry back in Winchester was in command. Washington went over his commanding officer's head by writing directly for aid from the governors of Virginia, Maryland, and Pennsylvania.

Washington dispatched Ensign Ward with an Indian escort to take his report directly to Governor Dinwiddie in Williamsburg. He had persuaded several young Indians to escort Ward on the long trek; he sent another back to Half King with this speech:

> This young man will inform you where he found a small part of our army, making towards you, clearing the roads for a great number of our warriors who are ready to follow us with our great guns, our ammunition and provisions.[9]

In the woods where he had spent so much of the past half-dozen years, George Washington was at home. He had learned to run a bluff in negotiating with the Indians, yet he was totally naive about colonial politics. He was wildly optimistic about his chances of significant reinforcement reaching him before the inevitable attack by the vastly superior French force nearby. Still, he seems to have expected Half King and his warriors to be first to come to his defense, in normal times a logical expectation of Indians who were legally British subjects. During five days of sending off messages and messengers, Washington, faced with danger, remained exuberant. For the first time, passion and emotion crept into his writing. He wrote to Governor Sharpe that his "interesting cause should rouse from the lethargy we have fallen into the heroic spirit of every free-born Englishman." He urged Marylanders to remember "the rights and privileges of our King" and rescue the Ohio Country "from the invasions of a usurping enemy." He preached patriotic defense of "our Majesty's property, his dignity and land."[10]

His youthful idealism began to crack around the edges when the forty woodsmen who had surrendered under Ensign Ward drifted into Washington's camp and refused to do any work unless they were paid two shillings a day, three times the eight pence daily Dinwiddie had authorized. Washington rightly feared this would demoralize his men. Captain Trent's woodsmen refused to follow Washington's orders when he tried to keep them away from his own men. Finally, they just drifted off. Work on the new road to Redstone Creek went ahead slowly. By May 1, Washington was ready to send ahead his artillery swivel guns, just arrived from Alexandria. Some days, Washington's column, hampered by heavy rains, advanced only two miles, the packhorses sinking into the muck or balking at the swollen streams. Several times the men had to stop and spend whole days building bridges.

The presence of such a large, growing, and noisy force of axemen, carpenters, and yelling wagoneers was sure to attract attention. On May 9, Washington learned from an Indian trader that he had seen a patrol of 5 Frenchmen reconnoitering his advance from a settlement only five miles away. Washington's trader friend Christopher Gist also brought word that Half King was marching to Washington's aid with 50 Shawnee warriors. Excited, Washington dispatched Captain Stephen with 25 men to meet him. While Stephen marched off, Washington pushed ahead with work on the road. He received encouragement almost daily from messengers. One brought word that Colonel Fry had finally arrived in Winchester with 100 men and was on his way. North Carolina was sending 350 men; Maryland 200; Quaker Pennsylvania, no men but £10,000. This last news promised to silence the grumbling of Washington's officers and men, already discontented that their pay was so much lower than that of British troops. From as far away as Boston, Governor Shirley wrote to promise that he would march north at the head of 600 troops to attack the French in Quebec and thus draw off some of the French pressure on Ohio Country. Washington reasoned that when all these troops went into action he would have a force evenly matched with the French. On May 17, Ensign Ward returned with more promises from Williamsburg. South Carolina's Independent Company of 100 red-coated regulars had reached Virginia and was quick-marching on its way. Two more companies from New York were expected in ten days.

If Washington for even a moment doubted whether he should confront the French, Governor Dinwiddie assured him in a letter that the officers who had already abandoned the Forks to the French were going to be court-martialed. Another disquieting note in Dinwiddie's dispatch was that the House of Burgesses had decided to limit officers' pay and meal allowances to the same rate as enlisted men, despite the fact that the officers of the Independent Companies on their way to assist them would be receiving much higher pay. Washington shrugged it off. This lack of support by the House of Burgesses with its implications for overall support of the expedition should have set off an alarm in him about his chances to receive other promised aid. Little food and only a small percentage of the troops promised had reached him.

But the men were not so willing to overlook that they had not been paid and would eventually be paid poorly. All the hard work and worry about the nearby French enemy now stopped as the officers under Washington staged something like a mutiny over pay. With Captain Robert Stobo acting as their chairman, a committee of officers drew up a petition to the legislature protesting their pay rates. Unless they were paid more, they threatened, they would resign en masse. Their work stoppage made the petition clearly insubordinate. Stobo brought it to Washington, who said that, while he had agreed all along that their pay was discriminatory, as the commanding officer he could not sign it, but would forward it to Governor Dinwiddie. Secretly, he accompanied the petition with a shrewd self-serving letter of his own, agreeing in principle with his subordinates but carefully distancing himself from their petition:

> Giving up my commission is quite contrary to my intentions. Nay, I ask it as a greater favor than any amongst the many I have received from your Honor to confirm it to me. But let me serve

voluntarily: then, I will, with the greatest pleasure in life, devote my services to the expedition without any other reward than the satisfaction of serving my country.

The letter, his first of many offers to serve without pay, also for the first time revealed a vein of rebellion beneath his obsequious surface:

I would rather prefer the great toil of a day-laborer and dig for a maintenance, provided I were reduced to the necessity, than serve upon such ignoble terms. For I really do not see why the lives of his Majesty's subjects in Virginia should be in less value than of those in other parts of his American dominions, especially when it is well-known that we must undergo double their hardships.

Washington said he was determined not to go against his own men and accept a lower pay rate than other American officers.[11]

Sending off the protest to Williamsburg, Washington set out with a lieutenant, three soldiers, and an Indian guide in a canoe on a risky reconnaisance of the French positions. They paddled ten miles closer to the French before the Indian guide balked. Washington bribed the guide to go on by offering him his ruffled shirt and a gaudy matchcoat. Camping overnight, they paddled the next day until they came to the first of a series of waterfalls that dropped forty feet in two miles. Any hope of a waterborne assault on the French fort evaporated and they turned back. Discouraged at the accumulation of barriers to his expedition, Washington returned to Redstone Creek. He arrived in time to receive a warning from Half King's Shawnee scouts that the French were probing in strength close to his camp. Washington at first discounted it but decided to send out his own scouts, who found nothing.

Two days later, on May 24, 1754, his companion from the Fort Le Boeuf expedition, Christopher Gist, rode into the Great Meadows camp to report that the day before, a sizable French detachment had shown up at his farm, twelve miles to the north. Gist had followed their tracks to within five miles of Washington's camp. A few hours later, another messenger from Half King pelted into camp with word that the Shawnees had discovered the thirty-five French bivouacked nearby and could lead the Virginians to them. Washington snapped into action.

The fact that France and England were at peace did not seem to dissuade Washington, his officers, or his men. Their orders, authorized by the King's Privy Council and transmitted by Governor Dinwiddie, were to "drive the French from the Ohio," although Dinwiddie later insisted he had ordered Washington to act on the defensive. The absence of an official declaration of war did not seem to prevent an armed clash between the imperial rivals. Washington himself had warned the French to leave and with Dinwiddie's ultimatum had implied the consequences. Washington wanted to fight. He wanted to attack the French before they could attack him. There was no reason, other than prudence, to await reinforcements. The only real question was whether Half King and his Shawnees would fight. Washington assured Half King by messenger that massive reinforcements were on the way. As far as he knew, this was the truth: Dinwiddie had assured him help was coming. Whether or not Half King was responding truthfully, he answered by courier that he hated the French, that they had murdered and then boiled and eaten his father; of course he would fight at the side of the English.

On May 27, Washington gave orders to gather the wagons and munitions and build a defensive stockade in Great Meadows in case the French attacked in his absence. Then, at ten that night, Washington set out with six Shawnees and forty Virginians, half the men in his command. All night, they clambered single file through the forest, "having marched in small path and heavy rain and a night as dark as it is possible to conceive," he reported to the governor. "We were frequently tumbling over one another and often so lost that 15 or 20 minutes' search would not find the path again." He lost track of seven men along the way. At sunrise on May 28, they met Half King, who had only managed to persuade five of his warriors, not fifty, to join him. Washington concealed his disappointment and did not hesitate: would Half King send out scouts to find the French? He and his men then waited quietly. He instructed them that there was to be no talking and no pipe-smoking. They hid along one side of the forest path as Washington tensely waited, crouching, on the other side.

It was only minutes before the Indian scouts returned. They had found the French, about forty of them, encamped only half a mile away. They were sleeping in makeshift huts, all unsuspecting "in a very obscure place surrounded by rocks." The French party, commanded by young Ensign Joseph Coulon de Villiers, Sieur de Jumonville, had been sent out from the Forks' new French bastion, Fort Duquesne, with orders to warn the Virginians to leave French territory. According to their written orders, they were also to scout the Virginians' position and strength. While Jumonville's orders were little different from Washington's of six months earlier, he and his men were armed and came as a military force. They were concealing their movements. Both sides, French and English, were maneuvering for advantage on disputed territory still being negotiated in Paris by an international commission. Neither side belonged there. Both sides understood that their presence and actions almost inevitably would lead to armed conflict. An English fort, although unfinished, had been seized by a French military force. Washington, a British subject, albeit a colonial, had orders to oust the French.[12]

Characteristically, that British subject decided to strike first. Dividing his thirty-three soldiers and a handful of Half King's warriors into three squads, Washington led the column that would attack from the right. The scouts said that the French were camped in a depression in front of a high rock barrier. Washington would come up on the exposed right side; Adam Stephen and his squad would attack from the left. The Indians were to work around to the French rear to block their escape. Creeping within a hundred yards of the French camp, Washington studied the position through his telescope. Were his men ready? Seconds passed before the answer came back: ready. Leaping up, Washington bawled the order to attack. He took the French entirely by surprise. "They said they called to us not to fire," Washington wrote Dinwiddie, "but I know that to be false for I was the first man that approached them and the first whom they saw." The French "immediately ran to their arms and fired briskly till they were defeated." As the French scrambled for their weapons and tried to find cover, the Virginians fired a volley. Washington and his men concealed themselves among the rocks and kept up a withering fire for fully fifteen minutes. Frenchmen who tried to flee ran into the arms of waiting Indians. When the French surrendered and the firing stopped, ten French soldiers lay dead or wounded, including Jumonville. The French commander had attempted to escape only to be tomahawked. The Indians rushed in and brained and scalped the dead and the wounded. By the time Washington could stop their grisly ritual, ten bloody corpses lay scattered among rocks and trees. Washington decided to leave them there unburied as a warning to the French. Only one French-man escaped. He carried the alarming news back to Fort Duquesne.[13]

To his brother Jack, Washington wrote, "I fortunately escaped without a wound, though the right wing where I stood was exposed to and re-ceived all the enemy's fire and was the part where the man [a Virginian] was killed and the rest [two others] wounded." Washington remained vague in his reports and letters about exactly who had killed Jumonville. Under duress, he would later admit in writing that he was responsible for the Frenchman's death. At the time, on the day of the clash, to his diary he confided, "We killed Mr. de Jumonville; the commander of that party, as also nine others. . . . The Indians scalped the dead." Whether he had actually fired a fatal shot or given the order that directed the fifteen-minute fusillade, Washington had his first taste of combat, of killing men, of exulting over his own prowess in battle. He was elated, but in fact Washington had single-handedly touched off the forest war that soon led to the worldwide Seven Years' War. He ordered the twenty French pris-oners marched off toward the Great Meadows. Along with his report he sent Jumonville's scalp to the governor and his council and told him that Half King was sending the other scalps "to all the nations of Indians in union with them."[14]

In his euphoria, did Washington consider how exposed he and his men were? They were fifty miles from one thousand professional French sol-diers and fifty miles from their own exposed base. There were probably other large French patrols in the area. Marching his men back to the

Great Meadows, Washington sent off his twenty prisoners under guard to Winchester with a request for reinforcements and his advice that the prisoners be treated as spies. The French survivors claimed they had been on a diplomatic mission to warn off Washington. "I fancy they will have the assurance of asking the privileges due to an embassy when in strict justice they ought to be hanged for spies of the worst sort." In his official report, Washington told the Assembly that he had not fired at first, that he had ordered his men to fire only after the French went for their muskets and dived for cover on seeing the Virginians rush toward them. But Washington was stunned when his French prisoners insisted they were on a diplomatic mission. Before sending Dinwiddie a report of his actions, he poured out his thoughts in his diary as he always did when he was troubled or wanted to work out a problem on paper before composing an official version. What he confided to his diary was slightly different from his official report:

> *We formed ourselves for an engagement, marching one after the other in the Indian manner. We were advanced pretty near to them, as we thought, when they discovered us, whereupon I ordered my company to fire. Mine was supported by [Captain] Waggoner and my company and his received the whole fire of the French during the greatest part of the action which only lasted a quarter hour before the enemy was routed. We killed Mr. de Jumonville, the Commander. The Indians scalped the dead. I marched on with the prisoners.* They informed me that they had been sent with a summons to order me to depart *[Washington's emphasis]. A plausible pretense to discover our camp and to obtain the knowledge of our forces and our situation!*[15]

But Washington obviously was worried by the French claim to diplomatic immunity from attack. "It was so clear that they were come to reconnoiter. Instead of coming as an ambassador, publicly, in an open manner, they came secretly and sought after the most hidden retreats, more like deserters than ambassadors." The French version, carried by the only French soldier who escaped and then embroidered by the French commandant, Contrecoeur, was that Jumonville's party was under a flag of truce and that Jumonville was actually reading the French governor's diplomatic dispatch aloud to the English when the Virginians gunned them down. This version quickly found its way to France, where it was reported to the English ambassador during peace talks.[16]

There is reason to question whether Washington understood completely, at first, the consequences of his bold attack. Had he been more restrained, he could have at least postponed an armed conflict briefly, at least long enough to receive reinforcements—in which case the French and English would be evenly matched—or to receive orders to withdraw to undisputed Virginia soil, where Virginia militia could be pressed into service if other provinces broke their promises of armed assistance. If Washington had chosen to treat Jumonville as a diplomat rather than an enemy, the uneasy truce between England and France probably would not have lasted much longer. English colonists hailed the news of Washington's attack on Jumonville as a heroic blow against French depredations in Ohio Country. Washington became a hero to British-Americans who considered the lands west of the Allegheny Mountains theirs for the taking. Once he had led Virginia's little army into the wilderness, the proud, ambitious young Washington certainly would not have followed Jumonville's order to leave. Contrecoeur at Fort Duquesne would have been forced to carry out his orders to drive out the English or risk his own ouster by the reinforced Virginians.

In any event, Washington's attack and the killing of a French nobleman along with a third of his men gave the French commander all the justification he needed to do whatever he wanted. While Washington sent off his prisoners and waited for reinforcements, Contrecoeur prepared a major attack, should Washington be imprudent enough to remain within striking distance. When the French commander learned that Washington was staying in the rickety stockade in the Great Meadows, he launched a retaliatory counterattack led by Louis Coulon de Villiers, older brother of the slain Jumonville. While French soldiers primed their weapons and climbed into the war canoes of their Ottawa allies, Washington, back at Great Meadows, wrote an exuberant letter to Jack, adding as a postscript, "I heard the bullets whistle, and believe me there is something charming in the sound."[17]

When the jubilation of his first victory subsided a bit, Washington had to face the reality of his action and its probable consequences. He was completely exposed nearly fifty miles west of the Cumberland Gap, deep in Indian country. He must either risk a counterattack by a much larger force or wipe out the honor he had just won by retreating, probably losing most of his equipment and certainly some of his men to Indians outflanking him. He could not expect the French to remain passive after he had initiated hostilities with them. With one thousand French soldiers only a few days' march away and hundreds more within easy reach of his position, Washington could only hope that a large number of his own reinforcements arrived quickly in the glen he was now belatedly fortifying.

As he awaited help, he sent men into the forests to cut down, strip, and drag out oak logs nine or ten feet long. He put other men to work in the angle formed by the two streams he had chosen to defend. He laid out the fort himself, plotting the works after taking careful measurements with his theodolite. According to his plan, his men dug a circular trench two feet deep and fifty-three feet in diameter. They split the logs in half and then dropped them on end into the trench, interspersing thinner logs between them to fill in any gaps. Washington supervised as his men hoisted the logs and packed the dirt around their bases to form a crude circular palisade, at its highest point only eight feet above the ground. Then he indicated where a door was to be cut, gun ports cut out. Inside the palisades, in the center, he ordered them to build a log shelter for gunpowder, food, and other supplies. The problem with all of this was that the little fort was in a swampy hollow formed by hillsides that were covered with trees within easy musket range.

All Washington could do now was to push his men as hard as he could to prepare for the expected retaliation. Ten days after the skirmish with Jumonville's patrol, a courier brought word to Washington that Colonel Fry had died when he fell from a horse. Governor Dinwiddie had promoted Washington to full colonel and given him responsibility for the Virginia Regiment. At twenty-two, Washington was now the highest-ranking field officer in Virginia. All five Virginia companies had by now reached him at the Great Meadows fort. A reinforcement of 181 Virginians under the new lieutenant colonel, George Muse, arrived on June 9. One of the three companies was led by Captain Robert Stobo, a former Glasgow merchant who had arrived weeks earlier with ten servants he had press-ganged into military service and his own covered wagon, its cargo including about 125 gallons of wine and a butt of fine Madeira. In Captain Andrew Lewis and Lieutenant George Mercer, the other new company commanders, Washington found two new friends who were inexperienced officers but versatile and courageous men. Few of the new recruits had ever fired a gun. They brought along nine swivel guns for the fort, all the artillery available.

A few days later, the South Carolina Independent Company of one hundred redcoats driving a herd of sixty cattle arrived, commanded by British army captain James Mackay. By mid-June, three hundred more colonial troops arrived. Captain Mackay was a feisty Scot with a regular army commission who refused to take orders from Washington or any other colonial officer. He ordered his company to set up its own camp with its own passwords and countersigns, and he refused to allow his men to perform any labor, including construction on the fort or road building, unless they were paid extra. Added to the humiliation of a captain, a lower grade officer, refusing to follow his orders, Colonel Washington had no money to pay anyone and had to watch helplessly as his own men did all the hard work while the regulars lazed in their camp. Morale became a serious problem. Washington's officers were disgruntled at the disparity in their pay; his enlisted men were fuming at the laziness of the redcoats.

After the redcoats had been with his Virginians less than twenty-four hours, Washington decided that if he could not order Mackay to march off, he would remove himself and his men from the possibility of additional friction by resuming his road-building march to Redstone Creek. When Mackay refused to accept the daily passwords from a colonial officer, Washington added a postscript to his long report to Dinwiddie with an angry outburst: if he could not give the garrison's parole and countersign to the regulars, "then who is to give it? Am *I* to issue these orders to a Company? Or is an independent captain to prescribe rules to the Virginia Regiment? This is the question. But its absurdity is obvious! Two commanders are so incompatible that we cannot be as useful to one another, or the public, as we ought."[18]

Whether Washington chose this moment to share with any of his officers an abusive letter he received from Dinwiddie is unclear, but at this moment the governor wrote to upbraid Washington for his handling of the officers' pay crisis. No one else, except perhaps his mother, ever excoriated George Washington as often or as severely. He chided him for complaining and for passing along his subordinates' protest: "The hardships complained of are such as usually attend on a military life, and are considered by soldiers rather as opportunities of glory than objects of discouragement." Wounded by Dinwiddie's scolding at this his hour of triumph, Washington nonetheless followed Colonel Fairfax's advice to be careful not to lose Dinwiddie's patronage over the pay issue. Washington wrote back to the governor that his complaints over pay and morale were serious, not frivolous: "I am much concerned that your Honor should seem to charge me with ingratitude. I retain a true sense of your kindness and want nothing but opportunity to give testimony to my willingness to oblige."[19]

Then, as if to prove himself more than a mere courtier, Washington decided to march his men across Chestnut Ridge the twelve miles to Christopher Gist's plantation for a conference with Shawnee and Delaware Indian leaders and British colonial officials assembling there. He left Captain Mackay's Independent Company to hold the fort at Great Meadows. Packing up horses, wagons, and the heavy swivel guns, he had his men march smartly out of the fort. After a two-day slog, he found that several prominent traders had gathered with the Indians at Gist's trading post (near present-day Mount Braddock, Pennsylvania) to discuss their reactions to the new and powerful French presence. Washington had heard at Great Meadows that once-loyal Delawares and Shawnees were now defecting to the French, despite the fact that they were tributaries to the Iroquois Confederacy, who were British subjects and unquestionably loyal. In the three-day conference at Gist's, Delaware and Shawnee leaders professed continued loyalty, but after they saw how weak was Washington's force and how low his supplies, their speeches became laced with evasions and sarcastic remarks. They had seen how numerous and well-provisioned the French were. It was obvious to them which side would win. Washington, despite the able assistance of Half King, failed to move them with his main speech. "We have engaged in this war in order to assist and protect you," he told the

sachems with an earnest face. Privately, Washington had come to the conclusion that he could never rely on the Indians, "those treacherous dev-
ils," as he called them.[20]

One week later, as his weary men worked on the road near Gist's,
Washington received more bad news. An Indian chief he had met at
Logstown the past winter and still trusted said he had visited the new
French fort and reported that reinforcements had arrived from Canada
and that now there were 1,600 French troops at the fort. Shortly, some
900 of them, along with 400 or 500 Indians, would attack Washington's
force and drive it from Ohio Country. For weeks, Washington had been
indecisive, at first choosing Redstone, then Great Meadows as his base
fort. Now he shifted his plan again and decided to make a stand at Gist's
trading post, an odd place to defend because it could so easily be bypassed. He pulled back his patrols and road-building crews and sent an
urgent request to Captain Mackay to join him. Obliging a fellow officer in
distress, Mackay marched his 100 redcoats all night, arriving on June 29.
By now, Washington was worried. As the men frantically built what they
were calling a "hog pen fort" out of Gist's thin fence rails, Half King and
his dozen remaining Indians grumbled that there were more provisions
and a stronger fort at Great Meadows. In a council of war, Washington listened as his officers pointed out that the French could easily overwhelm
the divided forces and attack the Virginia backcountry. Washington
agreed to fall back on the fortified base camp at Great Meadows and
build it up while they awaited reinforcements.

At this point it is highly likely that Washington was willing to withdraw
his force all the way back to Wills Creek at Cumberland Gap, temporarily
leaving the Ohio Valley. If only he could be sure his tiny army could survive the fifty-mile march over terrible roads, and that they had enough
food and ammunition to fight off the French and their swarming Indian
confederates, who would undoubtedly attack him in the open. But any
hope of a timely retreat dissipated as his wagons broke down and his
horses stumbled toward Great Meadows under their loads. Mackay's regulars refused to help carry the nine heavy swivel guns and the ammunition. Washington's burdened and exhausted men, subsisting only on corn
and uncured beef from cattle killed along the road, needed three days to
stagger back to Great Meadows. By the time the hungry soldiers reached
their base camp, the combined tally of Virginia and Carolina troops fit for
duty was down to 284. More than a hundred were too sick from dysentery
and exhaustion to fight or do hard labor. To go another forty or fifty miles
with a well-armed and rested French army closing in on them was unthinkable. Colonel Washington realized he would have to make his stand
in the hollow of Great Meadows. He now fatalistically named the place
"Fort Necessity."

Washington had seen only a few forts, and he had no real idea how to design one. He had wasted more than a month building a road instead of a substantial fort on high, defensible ground. But he was not alone in the blame for throwing together a patchwork of defenses in a swamp. None of the other newly minted officers were military engineers. Starting with a small central stockade, which he made far too small, Washington had his men cut down oak trees of ten-inch diameter, split them in half, and carry them to the site. Each ten-foot length of green wood weighed about 250 pounds. His tired, hungry men had to go farther and farther into the woods to find the right trees of uniform diameter to make the logs fit together. Without oxen, they then had to lug the logs on their shoulders up to a mile in the fierce summer heat. They dropped them into the round trench, flat side outward with their bark still in place. To fill any chinks, they trimmed smaller trees, lashing the crosspieces with thongs they cut out of rawhide. The crude fence protruded only eight feet above ground. With hatchets, the sweating work crews pierced gun slits for their muskets and gun ports for the swivel guns. Working outward, Washington designed parallel trenches four feet wide at the top and about two feet at the bottom. This part of the task went quickly; the men dug down easily in the soft earth, making trenches two feet deep for the men to stand in when they fired at the enemy. The men piled the dirt in front of them to make shoulder-high breastworks. In all, they entrenched about a quarter-acre of ground on the three sides of the round stockade, leaving the creek side open. At the center of the fort, Washington laid out a log storehouse fourteen feet square and ordered a makeshift roof of hides tied over it. Here he placed gunpowder, flour, and rum.

By nightfall on July 2, the defensive works finished, Washington ordered a nighttime reconnaissance of the French advance. As his officers called the roll, he discovered that all the Indians, including Half King, his warriors, their squaws, and children, had vanished. Angry and humiliated, Washington realized that the natives had stayed just long enough to feed themselves on his meager supplies and then leave with a complete description of his new defensive works and the exact state of his provisions. In fact, the Indians had fallen victim to rumors from other Indians that a huge French force was bearing down on this pitiful Virginia outpost and that they had better flee rather than be slaughtered. In their eyes, such a desertion was only sensible. But Washington's faith in Indians was forever shaken. Sending out his own scouts, soldiers who knew nothing about tracking men, Washington only further weakened his defenses.

At dawn on July 3, 1754, a shot rang out. A shout followed. A man fell, wounded. Washington yelled to his men to take their positions. His second in command, Lieutenant Colonel Muse, and Captain Mackay ordered their men into the trenches of the works outside the fort. Stobo, now a major, lighted the matches for his swivel guns atop the parapets. It had rained all day the day before. The trenches were already half-filled with water as the men jumped into them. They wrapped garments around their gunstocks, trying to protect their priming powder as they peered anxiously toward the trees on the slopes surrounding them. The rain was beginning to fill up the bowl where Washington had built his fort. The shot was a false alarm. The men picked up their shovels and kept digging.

At about 11 A.M., one of the sentries sighted the French marching out of the trees on high ground to the west and fired at them. Washington ordered his men to form up and march *outside* the earthworks. But the French stayed in the woods and fired a volley from concealment, filed off "to another point of woods" and fired again. They refused to fight in the open. Washington had hoped to draw the French down from the tree line and close enough for his marksmen on the parapets to gun them down. One Virginia officer believed Washington was trying to seize part of the wooded heights but was driven back. When the French opened fire, at six hundred yards, they were too far off. Refusing Washington's gambit, they ran to within sixty yards of the breastworks. Dropping to the ground, they began to fire with murderous accuracy. Washington's men fell back first to the inner trenches. The Indians charged, but a volley from the trenches and blasts from two swivel guns drove them back, leaving many dead and wounded. Then, as the French firing intensified, Lieutenant Colonel Muse ordered his Virginians to retreat from the outerworks inside the stockade. That left the Independent Company exposed and forced it, too, to withdraw to the fort. Washington was furious. This was not in his plan. He had not given any order to retreat. Now the enemy could press even closer, and fire on the fort from its own outer trenches.[21]

Firing mostly from the high ground, concealed behind trees within musket range, the French poured a steady fusillade on the men cringing for cover inside the crowded, low stockade. Between six and eight o'clock that evening, according to the French commander, the firing from the fort became "even brisker." Washington had ordered the palisades around the swivel guns torn down to allow a wider field of fire. But then, the rain fell even heavier, "the most tremendous rain that could be conceived," Washington later wrote. His situation was hopeless. The French, sheltered by the dense cover of the trees, had picked off all the horses, cattle, even the dogs, which could have fed the British garrison. Escape was impossible. Lead balls had chewed up the stockade's uprights, showering the defenders with splinters. "They, then, from every little rising, tree, stump, stone and bush, kept up a constant, galling fire upon us." Years later, Washington told an aide how "dismal" he found the Indian war cries. In the crossfire from three sides, men were killed or wounded whenever they dared to raise their heads to fire at the French hidden in the trees. As the rains continued, cartridge boxes became soaked, muskets misfired. The rain even seeped into the driest spot in the supply building, finding its way into cracks in the barrels and ruining most of the gunpowder.[22]

By eight in the evening, few shots came from the little fort. One-third of its defenders—128 of his 293 men—had been killed or wounded; one-half of the remainder were too ill to fight. Washington's own manservant and his horses had been killed. With no dry gunpowder, only a few bayonets were left to stave off the inevitable French charge. To make matters worse, as if to prepare themselves for the impending arrival of Indian scalping parties, many of the able-bodied had broken into the supply building and imbibed generous quantities of rum.

Washington, racing around the fort from one calamity to another, could not know that the French were also running low on ammunition and that their commander was worried about losing control of the natives. Just at twilight, just past eight, after nine hours of firing, Washington heard a call from the French: *"Voulez-vous parler?"* When one of his two interpreters told him what the summons meant, he refused. The French only wanted to get inside the fort to see its layout, to spy out how to make a fresh assault. Several minutes passed. Again, a call in French. Would an officer who could speak French receive an offer? Washington alone could not make this decision, but the facts were clear. A third of his men were dead or dying. All his gunpowder was wet. Only two bags of flour and a little bacon, not even enough food for a few days, remained. There were no draught animals to aid their escape. He had finally faced the bitter fact that no reinforcements were coming. Without any Indians to help him, his men faced the full wrath of vengeful French and eager natives if his fort were overrun. Disheartened, Washington decided that his only recourse was to send two French-speaking officers, William La Péyronie and Jacob Van Braam, under a flag of truce to the French lines.

They came back quickly. The French commander Villiers declared that his orders were not to start a war but only to expel the English from French territory. Villiers had much on which to congratulate himself and orders not to turn the eviction of Washington's little force into another general war with the English. He had avenged his younger brother's death. With only five hundred French-Canadian militia and only a handful of regulars, he had skillfully used rumors passed by Indians to convince Washington that, in the forests around him, were more than a thousand professional French soldiers and hundreds of bloodthirsty Indians, when in fact, the French and English had been nearly evenly matched. If the English left the fort and returned to Virginia, they would not be prisoners of war. Péyronie, an intelligent, well-educated Frenchman, had begun the talks but, critically wounded, either during the parley or just afterward, collapsed soon after his return. Washington considered the French offer too vague. He sent back Van Braam, his trusted former fencing master and the interpreter on his winter mission to

Fort Le Boeuf. He had no idea how limited Van Braam's ability to translate French into English was.

This time the French commander offered Washington written articles of capitulation. He read them aloud to Van Braam so there would be no question what the blurred, water-blotched handwriting said. The preamble stated that the French intended "only to avenge" the death of Jumonville. Van Braam could not translate the next word. In the guttering candlelight of Washington's makeshift command post, it looked as if it were *l'assailir*. Witnesses later had trouble remembering whether Van Braam translated it as "death" or "loss" or "killing." What the French later contended they had written had only one possible meaning: assassination. If Washington signed his name to such an admission, he was taking full responsibility, on behalf of Virginia and the English, for the murder of a French diplomat. Washington later said that what came next was what made him willing to sign: *un de nos officiers*. That was easy, "one of our officers."

What concerned Washington more at the moment was that, after guaranteeing the Virginians' safe passage, the French wanted to "reserve" to themselves all his artillery "and munitions of war." This meant that Washington and his men would have to leave behind their guns and gunpowder and walk fifty miles through forests swarming with hostile Indians whom Villiers could only promise to restrain. Overall, the surrender terms seemed honorable to Washington. He balked only at this one, which he considered an invitation to mass murder. Again, he refused to sign. The French commander ended the impasse with a single stroke of his pen through the offending words. He had achieved enough. Washington's surrender was equivalent to a treaty recognizing French claims to Ohio Country. The French were now in sole possession of the western slopes of the Alleghenies and all of the tributaries of the Ohio River, consolidating their total control of the interior of North America. And, under his parole, his word of honor, Washington and his regiment could not set foot west of the mountains for at least a year.[23]

Once Washington selected two officers to leave as hostages for the twenty-two prisoners he had sent to Virginia, he was free to march out with his men. It was midnight, July 3, a date Washington always remembered with sadness. As he signed his name the rain stopped. The only sounds while Coulon de Villiers scrawled his signature were the moaning of the wounded and the rhythmic clang and thud of picks and shovels as both sides buried their dead.

When news of the debacle reached Governor Dinwiddie, at first he denied its importance. He went on firing off orders that made it clear he expected Washington to regroup, gather reinforcements, counterattack. Reaching Wills Creek, Washington was trying to keep a few hundred men together to defend the strategic Cumberland Gap. If the

French took it, the interior of Virginia would lie exposed and defenseless. A few days after his 165 remaining soldiers staggered into Wills Creek, as one later recalled,

> Sixteen men went in a body to Colonel Washington telling him that, as they came to settle the lands, which now they had no more thoughts of doing, they were determined to return home. Colonel Washington endeavored to persuade them to stay, promising to procure them some gratuity from the government of Virginia for all their trouble and losses. But he could not prevail with them . . . they went off in a body.[24]

Not only were the men bitter about losing the land they had been promised, but they were, Washington reported, in terrible shape. Despite French assurances, the Indians had looted the baggage of Washington and his men as they marched out of Fort Necessity. Even Washington's theodolite was missing. The men had barely made it the seventy miles back to the Cumberland Gap. "The chief part are almost naked and scarcely a man has either shoes, stockings or hat." Washington added bitterly that the local merchants would not give his men credit to buy clothes. "There is not a man that has a blanket to secure him from cold or wet."[25]

Dinwiddie continued to pressure Washington to fight on—which Washington considered sheer madness. His little army was melting away. "The soldiers are deserting constantly," he wrote Dinwiddie on August 20. Washington turned from persuasion to coercion. He arrested twenty-five men when they tried to march off. To his friend and mentor Colonel William Fairfax, Washington wrote secretly and sarcastically of the governor's latest chimerical scheme to evict the French. Another campaign at this time was "morally impossible." Dinwiddie wanted him to raid deep into Indian country and burn the corn crop feeding the French at Fort Duquesne. "I am a little surprised when it is known we must pass the French fort and the Ohio to go to Logstown. How this can be done with inferior numbers, under the disadvantages we labor, I see not." Then, in a scathing critique, Washington shredded Dinwiddie's plan. Soon after this, Dinwiddie stripped George Washington of his command. Yet, when Dinwiddie promoted a new colonel over him, Washington was carefully subordinate. He wrote that he would march where he was ordered "if no more than ten men follows me which I believe will be the full amount."[26]

Dinwiddie's downgrading of Washington could not have come at a worse time. Washington had become a hero along the American frontier since the fatal clash with Jumonville. He had clung to this newfound fame despite the loss of Fort Necessity and a third of his men at Great Meadows. His name was being mentioned in governors' reports to the king and printed in the London newspapers for the first time. As a war fever gripped England, young Washington became the symbol of English resistance to French imperial expansion in the New World. Even though he had to walk all the way back to the Cumberland Gap with his portmanteau strapped to his saddlehorse, George Washington emerged from the Ohio Valley the young man of the hour in English America. His journals and letters were reprinted in newspapers throughout the colonies.

A few men, important public figures, including Sir William Johnson of New York, England's expert in dealing with the Indians, remained unimpressed. "I wish Washington had acted with the prudence and circumspection requisite in an officer of rank. I can't help saying he was very wrong in many respects and I doubt not his being too ambitious of acquiring all the honor, or as much as he could, before the rest joined him." Johnson also faulted Washington for listening to reports given him by would-be deserters from the French, especially the Mingo Indians at the conference at Gist's plantation. This "did not show him at all the soldier." Rumors had been "the rock on which they split," according to Johnson's analysis. "He should rather have avoided an engagement until all our troops were assembled." Washington would have been even more dismayed if he had heard the criticism of Half King, who told the Pennsylvania agent for Indian affairs, Conrad Weiser, that Washington would not take the advice of Indians and commanded them as if they were his slaves. He blamed Washington for building "that little thing upon the meadow" and for thinking "the French would come up to him in open field." Moreover, he said Washington had been indecisive and had lost a full month before beginning to build a fort. Half King believed that if Washington had known how to build a proper fort, he could have beaten the French.[27]

It would be several years before Washington learned how he was being mocked by the victorious French commander at Fort Necessity. Villiers's comments in his memoirs eventually appeared in print in Paris. Translated into English during the Seven Years' War, they were excerpted in London newspapers and then reprinted in Philadelphia in 1757. The Frenchman's words stung Washington:

> We made the English consent to sign that they had assassinated my brother in his camp. We had hostages for the security of the French who were in their power. We made them abandon the King's country. We obliged them to leave their cannon, nine pieces. We destroyed their horses and cattle and made them sign that the favors granted were evidence that we wanted to use them as friends.[28]

The official English verdict, if possible, was even more devastating. In the confused evacuation of Fort Necessity, Washington had lost his diary. It fell into the hands of Villiers, who read it and passed it along to

Contrecoeur at Fort Duquesne, who forwarded it to Governor General Duquesne in Quebec. Eventually, it found its way back to the French archives in Quebec. A contemporary copy was discovered recently in the Contrecoeur papers at Laval University. Duquesne's letter of transmittal back to Contrecoeur on September 8, 1754, called Washington "the most impertinent of all men." Duquesne added that Washington "has wit only in the degree that he is cunning with credulous savages. For the rest, he lies very much to justify the assassination of Sieur de Jumonville, which has turned on him, and which he had the stupidity to confess in his capitulation!" Duquesne went on to call Washington a "blunderer": "There is nothing more unworthy and lower, and even blacker, than the sentiments and the way of thinking of this Washington. It would have been a pleasure to read his outrageous journal under his very nose."[29]

Governor Dinwiddie considered Washington's mission a fiasco. As a result of his defeat, the French were able to destroy not only Fort Necessity but also Redstone Fort and Gist's trading post, obliterating virtually every trace of the expensive five-year-long Virginia Company investment in the Ohio Valley. Dinwiddie's get-richer-quick scheme was over. Using his official government position to exact retribution for his personal losses, he punished Washington by announcing still another reshuffling of the Virginia militia. There would be only companies with captains. From colonel and then lieutenant colonel of an independent regiment, Washington would have to revert to the rank of militia captain, an obvious demotion that would be taken publicly as a mark of his disgrace. Or he could resign his commission.

Privately, Washington was grateful that he and so many of his men had escaped alive. Twenty years later, as he led the fight for American independence from arbitrary British rule, he still marked the third of July as a pivotal anniversary in his life. "I did not let the 3rd pass without a grateful remembrance of the escape we had," he wrote to Adam Stephen, his subordinate at Fort Necessity, from his Revolutionary War headquarters in New York City in July 1776. Publicly, however, Washington bitterly resented the denunciations of Governor Dinwiddie and other British officials. For his part, Dinwiddie wrote to a merchant friend in England that Virginians were lucky that Washington's defeat had not been worse. The French could have marched unopposed across the colony to the sea "without the least danger." The governor quite publicly pointed to an early warning he had sent to Washington on June first before the battle not "to make any hazardous attempts against a too-numerous enemy" and again, on June 27: "I wish you had suspended your going to Red Stone [sic] Creek till you were joined by the other forces." Dinwiddie blamed Washington's defeat on his failure to heed the governor's advice. He made a case that Washington was reckless and insubordinate. Later, he even claimed that he had ordered Washington not to attack the French until "the whole forces were joined in a body." Dinwiddie lashed out not only at Washington but at the governors of Maryland, New York, and North Carolina, who had pledged timely reinforcements. New York sent them so late that they did not reach Winchester until the week *after* the surrender—and then with no weapons.[30]

The New Yorkers were marching into Winchester as Washington received orders from the governor on July 11 to ride to Williamsburg and report in person. Washington stopped long enough at Fredericksburg to reassure his mother that he was safe, then rode on. He already knew that she had not spent the entire time he was away worrying about him. A friend, Speaker of the House of Burgesses John Robinson, wrote him that he saw Mrs. Washington frequently and had recently danced with her.

In the capital, Washington found himself and his expedition the talk of everyone. To his utter amazement, he had become famous. Even his signing of an admission that he had "assassinated" Jumonville was being transformed into a denunciation of the Dutch translator, Van Braam. If there was more than one scapegoat, the other was Lieutenant Colonel Muse, who had ignored Washington's order to stay with his men in the trenches to keep the French out of musket range of the stockade. Muse admitted his cowardice but charged there were others "as bad as he." Everyone was relieved when Muse resigned. Some of the blame was being apportioned to the Indians, some to Pennsylvania traders who had promised to supply flour to the men when they did not have any, but, in all the finger pointing, no blame attached to Washington. Two days after he arrived in Williamsburg, the *Virginia Gazette* cleared its editorial throat and delivered its verdict on his expedition:

> Thus have a few brave men been exposed to be butchered by the negligence of those who, in obedience to their Sovereign's command, ought to have been with them many months before. Had the companies from New York been as expeditious as Captain Mackay's from South Carolina, our camp would have been secure from the insults of the French.

Many Virginians, lionizing their own soldiers, eagerly blamed New York for the disaster. Yet a few, like Landon Carter, Tidewater magnate and member of the governor's executive council, called Washington's surrender "the most disgraceful capitulation that ever was made."[31]

Washington's own words reverberated as far as London. A line in a letter to his brother Jack, "I have heard the bullets whistle and there is something charming in the sound," wound up being quoted in a *Gentleman's Magazine* article on the Jumonville affair. King George II, reading it, turned to a courtier and commented: "He would not say so if he had been used to hear many." But the verdict came from Governor Dinwiddie, who abolished Washington's colonelcy. He appealed to London to send him a professional army, to be paid by colonial taxpayers, to counterattack the

French. He was supported not only by his superiors in England but by other colonial officials, who were unwilling to risk any longer a rich forest empire to the hands of amateurs. New York superintendent of Indian affairs William Johnson wrote gloomily, "I can foresee the ruin of this country very shortly without the immediate interposition of his Majesty and Parliament. Nothing else will save us."[32]

When Washington learned that his colonelcy had been eliminated, first he became disconsolate, then bitter. He did not even dignify Dinwiddie's offer of a new captain's commission. While he admitted that "my inclinations are strongly bent to arms," he vowed to give up his military aspirations and turn to a planter's life. Suddenly, his brother's estate at Mount Vernon had become available to him. He decided to turn his back on a military career. Just after Christmas in 1754, he rented the property and his sister-in-law's eighteen slaves. In only one year, he had become Virginia's youngest captain, then colonel, a hero, a loser in his first pitched battle—and a civilian again. He arrived at Mount Vernon sick at heart, ill in health, and broke. Only the letters of his former comrades cheered him. From Williamsburg, Captain La Péyronie, recovering from his wound, wrote Washington, "Thank God, I meet always with a good wish for you from every mouth."

Six

"TO OBEY THE CALL OF HONOR"

*E**ver since he was a boy*, George Washington had been able to find peace at Mount Vernon at times of misery. His earliest memories were of the farm, once called Epsewasson, where his father had brought the family on a barge to live in a new, lowbrowed farmhouse that looked out over a high bluff to the Potomac. They had moved when he was six to remote Ferry Farm, where, when he was scarcely eleven, he had seen his father die. His half-brother Lawrence, who had transformed Epsewasson into a handsome two-story manor house and renamed it Mount Vernon, brought George back to live there amid a cheerful, lively, sophisticated circle of friends. When Lawrence was dying of tuberculosis, George had hurried back from Barbados to Mount Vernon to comfort Lawrence's young wife, Nancy. He found not only the tears of a young wife but the infant prattle of Lawrence's little daughter, Sarah. Awkward, lonely George Washington learned the distraction from care that came with dandling a little child upon his knee.

But Mount Vernon was able to repel as well as attract him. The death of Lawrence Washington was a deep wound that George stanched by escaping into the woods. Lawrence's widow shut down Mount Vernon and moved away when she remarried. Under the terms of Lawrence's will, the place went to his widow in lifetime trust and then to their daughter at her majority unless the child died, breaking the bloodline of inheritance; in that case, when the widow died, George would inherit it. This unhappy eventuality had always seemed remote and unthinkable, but the child, Sarah Washington, had died, and Lawrence's widow wanted nothing more to do with Mount Vernon. She and her new husband, Colonel George Lee, agreed to lease all of the estate—2,298 acres, a grist mill, the manor house, outbuilding, and eighteen resident slaves—to George, who would inherit it anyway. Consoling himself after his frustrating year as a soldier,

Washington decided he would become a planter. While a contractor and the servants refurbished Mount Vernon, George lived and worked in borrowed quarters at nearby Belvoir proffered by his mentor, Colonel Fairfax.

George Washington was just beginning to absorb the effects of a year of great change. He had emerged from complete obscurity as a district adjutant, nothing more in peacetime than a muster-master of once-a-week local militia drills, to become field commander of Virginia's first permanent military force. He was the man on horseback defending the colony against the French. In the popular perception, he symbolized Virginia's honor: he was a young hero. *Honor* was a word terribly important in Tidewater drawing-room society at the time. Yet, to Washington at least, his status after a year of dizzying changes had never felt more ambiguous. He was not even sure he was still a colonel. At a time when honor, a remnant from a chivalric past of knights, lords, and places at court, still had a meaning close to the modern word *reputation,* young Washington was depending on the public's estimation of his honor to advance his military career. He was an eighteenth-century knight-errant. Because he had been born without a great feudal patrimony, he needed money. One route was to win appointment to a high public office, something usually reserved for the kin of English nobles. The other path to wealth was to win land bounties for his public services. To achieve this, he must hold on to his colonelcy in the face of Governor Dinwiddie's vindictive refusal to second the Assembly's acknowledgment of his public-spirited suffering on the frontier.

On November 15, 1754, a letter arrived for him at Fairfax's Belvoir land office that Washington hoped would finally enable him to put an end to the embarrassing tiff with Governor Dinwiddie. It had taken eleven days for the letter from Governor Horatio Sharpe of Maryland to travel from Annapolis, a distance of little more than one hundred miles. Sharpe had just been designated by the British government as commander-in-chief of militia in the southern colonies. Dinwiddie and his council had asked Sharpe to intervene in the smoldering dispute over pay and rank that had put Washington and his fellow officers at loggerheads with Virginia's governor. Sharpe wanted to keep Washington out on the frontier at the head of his experienced troops, but he was growing impatient with all the controversy. Sharpe basically took the side of a fellow royal governor. He offered Washington one last chance to resolve the dispute.

A more youthful Washington barely a year earlier had bowed and scraped and wangled his way to an appointment as courier to the French, but now he was no longer willing to play the humble sycophant. He was boiling over with a sense of injustice at Dinwiddie's arbitrary and capricious changes in the colony's military policies. And he was outraged at the English militia system, which allowed any arrogant, doddering, low-ranking, half-pay British army pensioner who could find his way to Virginia to outrank him and give orders to him, the commander of the colony's own forces. In the months since his regiment's rout at Fort Necessity, Washington had become disillusioned with the royal governor, the man who so recently had embodied for him decisive and farseeing action. He had come to believe Dinwiddie an unscrupulous fool. He was appalled when Dinwiddie, unable to grasp the thoroughness of Washington's defeat at Fort Necessity, prodded him for six weeks to counterattack with one hundred exhausted, barefoot, hungry, disorganized soldiers. He was bitter when Dinwiddie promoted an old compatriot from Scotland, erstwhile North Carolina militia colonel George Innes, over Washington's head to replace Joshua Fry. It further angered Washington when Dinwiddie kept on appointing officers willy-nilly without consulting him or discussing their qualifications with him. He probably had learned from Colonel Fairfax that Dinwiddie had written to England for a pad of blank officers' commissions he could fill out as he wanted. Any of the royal appointments, even to a captaincy, would outrank Washington or any other American provincial officer.

Washington could no longer sit by respectfully when the royal governor commissioned a deputy adjutant for Washington's home district, the Northern Neck. Worse, the deputy's commission entitled him to put in a bill for £65, two-thirds of Washington's meager £100 salary, for any duties the deputy performed while Washington was on active duty on the frontier. This appointment undermined Washington's financial security, something he could ill afford to tolerate. He felt he was doing enough for his country already. He had put aside his thriving surveying business, and while he was away at the front he was unable to clear his land or plant crops. Dinwiddie's thoughtlessness about Washington's adjutancy moved the young officer to ignore Colonel Fairfax's advice about tiptoeing around the irascible governor.

More than a few pounds sterling were at stake in Washington's growing dissatisfaction with the royal governor's arbitrary treatment of him. Washington considered Dinwiddie mean-spirited when he wrote that the deaths and desertions of Washington's men would effect "great savings" in the colony's military budget. And he thought the governor, while technically on firm legal ground, had acted immorally when he dishonored the terms of Washington's surrender at Fort Necessity. Dinwiddie insisted that Washington had no authority to promise to exchange prisoners he had taken in the clash with Jumonville: as they were no longer in his hands, he should not have promised to exchange them for officers he had to give up as hostages to the French. Washington objected, too, to the new conscription law, proposed by the governor and passed by the Assembly, which drafted only vagrants between the ages of twenty-one and fifty for a year's military service. Too many of Washington's unruly recruits already fitted this category.

Washington galloped off to Williamsburg to protest the deputy's appointment. He was going to point out that deputies usually received less than half this amount, but when he dismounted at the governor's palace, he was informed by a servant that the governor was too busy to see him. In fact, Dinwiddie was closeted with the governors of Maryland and North Carolina over the worsening frontier crisis.[1]

Washington was left with a door closing in his face to ponder his only alternative, Governor Sharpe's letter, and Sharpe was not asking his opinions. All he wanted to know was whether Washington would reconsider his resignation. Governor Sharpe had assured him that under the new scheme of command Dinwiddie's crony, Colonel Innes, would not give Washington orders but would only be the post commander at Fort Cumberland. Washington would also be spared the embarrassment of taking orders from officers who had been his subordinates when he had fought earlier on the frontier. Sharpe enclosed a letter to Dinwiddie that gave written assurance of his promises. Washington was to forward it to the Virginia governor. If he accepted Sharpe's offer, Washington would "hold" his "post." But his post in what? Dinwiddie was already disbanding the Virginia Regiment into several independent companies with only captains in charge and was offering Washington a captaincy in only one of them. Did Sharpe mean something else, some other assignment after his regiment was disbanded? And would he still be a colonel? It was all too vague and irregular. Washington could not possibly accept Sharpe's offer. No, he would not accept an empty rank; he would not accept a demotion in his real rank. But it was obvious that Governor Sharpe really had done all he could: he could not give Washington a colonel's commission. Only Virginia's governor could do that. Yet Sharpe also had no authority to insist on Washington's demotion. As politely as possible, twenty-two-year-old George Washington, wearing the Virginia colonel's uniform he was entitled to wear, bent over his borrowed desk at Belvoir and answered the governor of Maryland:

> You make mention in your letter of my continuing in the service and retaining my colonel's commission. This idea has filled me with surprise for if you think me capable of holding a commission that has neither rank nor emolument annexed to it, you must entertain a very contemptible opinion of my weakness and believe me more empty than the commission itself. I shall have the consolation of knowing that I have opened the way when the smallness of our numbers exposed us to attacks of a superior enemy, that I have hitherto stood the heat and brunt of the day and escaped untouched in time of extreme danger and that I have the thanks of my country for the services I have rendered it.

But he could not compromise where his sense of honor was concerned. He would not tolerate public humiliation by the royal governor of Virginia. He assured Colonel William Fitzhugh, second in command to

Governor Sharpe, "of my reluctance to quit the service," but he had "to obey the call of honor and the advice of my friends." He decided to decline Sharpe's offer. "My inclinations are strongly bent to arms," he wrote, but he could not give in to Dinwiddie. In November 1754, George Washington resigned as colonel of the Virginia Regiment.[2]

*O*ne month later, on December 17, 1754, before a large gathering of family and friends, George Washington signed a lease for Mount Vernon and its eighteen slaves. He agreed to pay 15,000 pounds of tobacco every Christmas Day. He managed to rent the estate for a little more than double his net pay as district adjutant. Whatever he grew on the place after he paid taxes and cared for the slaves would be pure profit. Depressed after his resignation, weakened by another bout of dysentery and a relapse of the malaria he had contracted in Bermuda, he nevertheless now immersed himself in his plans for major repairs to the manor house he so loved. He dug out surveys he had made as a boy. He was still too weak to travel over the Christmas holidays, but his friends at Belvoir, now his constant companions, buoyed him up. He consoled himself and recuperated during weeks of leisurely card-playing and gossiping with the Fairfaxes.

He was especially fond of George Fairfax's effervescent young wife. Sally Fairfax was two years older than Washington, a difference that mattered less now to the young officer who had come back so self-assured after his year on the frontier. When George Fairfax had married eighteen-year-old Sally six years earlier, George Washington had been a tongue-tied and blushing sixteen-year-old. During the intervening years, he had made desultory attempts at courting a handful of young women, all of whom were uninterested in him. After returning from the frontier, Washington showed no particular attraction to any one woman. He went to his share of Williamsburg parties and there were the inevitable church socials and the house parties of neighbors, but, more and more, he preferred the lively social world of Belvoir and, more and more that winter, he spent afternoons and evenings in the company of his friend's witty, wide-eyed, teasing wife. If ever either one skirted near an illicit sexual liaison, there is no proof of it, but George Washington could not stand to be very far, very long, from Sally. And because he was more than satisfied with her playful company, with just the sight and sound of her elegant beauty, because he could dance with her and play endless rounds of whist and billiards and enjoy her banter, he made no attempt to seek a wife, a natural expectation for someone of his age, rank, and wealth. He just liked to be around Sally Fairfax. If there was anything more to it than that, he did not yet realize it.

*D*uring the night of February 19–20, 1755, the flagship of a Royal Navy squadron, *Centurion*, and two other men-of-war, *Syren* and *Norwich*, dropped anchor off Norfolk, Virginia. On board *Centurion* was

Major General Edward Braddock, a stocky, blunt forty-five-year veteran of the regular army, a military oddity who, despite decades in the Coldstream Guards, had rarely been in combat. Braddock had been dispatched from Ireland with two regiments of redcoats, the 44th and the 48th Regiments of Foot, and a train of artillery with orders to lead a major offensive to drive the French from the Ohio Valley. Washington's defeat at Fort Necessity and the subsequent flight of English frontier families and fur traders from the west slope of the Appalachian Mountains had finally convinced the divided British ministry in London that the French were making a serious attempt to dominate North America. Some British leaders believed that neither the French nor the British wanted to resume all-out war and that they therefore should risk pushing the French back to the territories they had controlled at the end of King George's War in 1748.

When the English government learned from Dinwiddie that the French had built Fort Duquesne at the head of the Ohio River, British officials converged hastily at Whitehall for an emergency meeting of the King's Privy Councillors to decide their response. They found they were crucially divided. King George II declared his "utter aversion" to sending British troops to North America to fight the French. England and France were still at peace, still negotiating the final details of the treaty ending the last war. He did not want to endanger that peace. But the Earl of Halifax, president of the Board of Trade and Plantations and technically the man in charge of colonial policy, insisted on joint Anglo-American seizure of Fort Niagara, on the Niagara River between Lake Erie and Lake Ontario, as well as an attack on Fort Saint Frédéric, at Crown Point at the southern end of Lake Champlain. He argued that attacks on these two major French bases would force the French to withdraw to Canada and would, moreover, be far easier than a long and difficult expedition over the Allegheny Mountains against Fort Duquesne. But Prince William Augustus, the Duke of Cumberland, the bellicose son of the king and head of the British army, was an inveterate enemy of the French. He was widely known as "the Butcher of Culloden" for his brutal repression of the French-supported Scottish Rising of 1745 that had ended with the bloody Battle of Culloden in the Scottish Highlands. It was Cumberland who insisted on confronting the French in the Ohio Valley by sending a British expeditionary force against Fort Duquesne, and it was Cumberland who won out. He chose Major General Braddock, a veteran officer of the Coldstream Guards, and he selected two regiments of redcoats disgraced during the 1745 Scottish revolt. In the American wilderness they would have a chance to redeem themselves. Parliament voted £50,000 as an initial appropriation but virtually gave Braddock carte blanche. Braddock's expedition was supposed to intimidate the French into abandoning all the forts they had built in the past few years on Lake Erie and in the Ohio Valley. He was to raise two additional regiments made up of colonial troops, and he was to strike fast before the French could further consolidate their position.

George Washington, no longer involved in Williamsburg politics, knew little of the Braddock expedition until he read about it in the *Virginia Gazette*. While his friends, especially Colonel Fairfax, kept him up to date on Virginia politics, he had been showing little interest. He heard in December that Governor Sharpe had ridden to Will's Creek in western Maryland and found that everything Washington had said about conditions there was true. The troops were in miserable shape; the post, renamed Fort Cumberland, was indefensible. Sharpe had sent a contingent of Maryland troops to reinforce its Virginia garrison. By February, word arrived in Virginia from London that Sharpe along with Dinwiddie's new Virginia companies were to be replaced by 1,500 British army regulars to fight in the over-the-mountains wilderness. Braddock's orders were to march through northern Virginia and cross the Alleghenies, destroy Fort Duquesne, and then lead his army northward to assist two new American regiments, led by Governor William Shirley of New York and Sir William Pepperell of Massachusetts, in clearing out the French from their forts at Niagara and on Lake Champlain. At the same time, other English and colonial forces were to evict the French from three forts in Nova Scotia. All of this presupposed there would be little French objection to the British ministry's chastisement.

The expedition carried with it several innate handicaps. The British ministry evidently included no one who had ever seen the distances and obstacles involved. The natural jumping-off place for Braddock would have been Philadelphia, not Alexandria, Virginia. A more direct route to the Forks of the Ohio ran due west through Pennsylvania. The soldiers assigned to Braddock were mostly cast-offs of other British regiments, men with little discipline and less combat experience. They were to be augmented by seven hundred Americans. The British inspector general, Sir John St. Clair, called them "a very indifferent lot." And the French, who had been negotiating peace with the British all winter, knew all about the British plans and were able to rush well-trained reinforcements from France to their garrisons in French Canada. In Virginia, as soon as he learned of the British strategy, Governor Dinwiddie designated Fort Cumberland, still the Virginia Company's property, as the advance base for Braddock's expedition. Any improvements made to the post would enhance the value of the company's properties whether or not Wills Creek was a suitable jumping-off point. The delighted governor began to issue contracts to cronies to build up a mountain of supplies for the British expedition.

As news leaked out of the fresh British offensive, Washington became increasingly interested in offering his services to Braddock, even if, by volunteering to join a British march over the Alleghenies, he was violating his parole—his written word of honor signed at Fort Necessity—that he would not set foot on French-claimed land for one year. He refused to seek one of the new captain's commissions from Dinwiddie. He learned that Braddock had brought with him three young aides who would serve as members of his official "family." One was the son of the governor of Massachusetts, another the kinsman of the governor of Pennsylvania. They were doing exactly what Washington wanted to do, closely studying the "military arts" from a master of military procedure. Could not a Virginian expect a similar billet among Braddock's aides since the campaign was to be launched from Virginia and supported by Virginians? To be a volunteer would obviate all the touchy problems of rank and commission. But could he afford to forgo an officer's pay?

In another insulting about-face at the same time, Dinwiddie had coldly put Washington off when he requested his year's back pay. The expenses for leasing and making major repairs to Mount Vernon were already stretching his savings and he hesitated to borrow against his future crops. His mother showed no sign of vacating Ferry Farm or providing any income from it. Washington had left his ten inherited slaves with her to avoid another run-in over money. He needed an income from his lands; he had planned to work not only Mount Vernon but also his burgeoning Bullskin Creek plantation near Frederick, Maryland, and he would have to hire a manager for both properties if he volunteered as an aide.

But if he ever considered making peace with Dinwiddie and accepting a new paid post, he banished any thought of it when he read the first order posted by Braddock on his arrival in Virginia. As Washington had feared, an edict from the government in England declared that all royal commissions would "take rank before all troops which may serve by commission from any of the governors." To accept a position that would make him subservient to every British officer, he wrote, was "too degrading." His only hope of service now was to subsidize his own expenses and serve as a volunteer. More than anything else, George Washington wanted to be a British army officer. He saw a natural opportunity to win a commission by distinguishing himself while serving as Braddock's aide.[3]

Washington decided that he would first subtly campaign to win appointment as an aide-de-camp. When Braddock arrived at Alexandria, Lord Fairfax and his friends hosted a round of lavish entertainments for the general and his officers. It was a simple matter for the Fairfaxes to invite Washington and arrange his introduction. There, amid the feasting, Washington spent a giddy evening surrounded by elegant British officers and the elite of Virginia society, including Sally Fairfax and her circle of beautiful young women friends, all of them competing for Braddock's attention. As the next stage of his siege, Washington sent Braddock a sugary letter of welcome that listed his own past services. He wanted to be sure Braddock was aware not only of his existence but of his eagerness to serve. In the patronage system of the times, Washington's blatant quest for a new sponsor was normal and expected, especially since he had lost Dinwiddie's favor.

On March 14, 1755, a red-coated courier delivered to Washington at Mount Vernon a letter from Braddock's headquarters. Robert Orme, Braddock's chief of staff, had written:

> *Sir:*
> The General having been informed that you expressed some desire to make the campaign but have declined it upon the disagreeableness that you thought might arise from the regulation of command has ordered me to acquaint you that he will be very glad of your company in his family by which all inconveniences of that kind will be obviated. I shall think myself very happy to form an acquaintance with a person so universally esteemed.[4]

Washington immediately and honestly answered Braddock's aide. He wanted nothing more than to attach himself to this veteran Coldstream Guard. He bluntly told Braddock his motive: "I wish for nothing more earnestly than to attain a small degree of knowledge in the military art." But Washington had a problem—money—and could not explain his money constraints clearly to this English gentleman. His answer must have surprised these English aristocrats, so indiscreet was it:

> The inconveniences that must necessarily arise, as some proceedings in a late space (I mean before the General's arrival) had, in some measure, abated the edge of my intentions and determined me to lead a life of greater inactivity and into which I was just entering at no small expense, the business whereof must greatly suffer in my absence.[5]

Hemming and hawing, Washington could not bring himself to say that he could not afford to accept the general's invitation. But Braddock graciously overlooked Washington's gaffe. A few weeks later, when Washington presented himself to Braddock at his Alexandria headquarters, he obtained permission to delay joining the expedition until he hired a farm manager and planted his tobacco crop. He wrote Major Orme that "these things, sir, will not I hope be thought unreasonable when it's considered how unprepared I am at present to quit a family and estate scarcely settled and in the utmost confusion." Braddock, who must have been somewhat bemused, sent back permission for Washington to come and go from his official family "whenever you find it necessary."[6]

Washington's latest enlistment did not get off to a propitious start. He was not prepared for the surprise visit his mother paid him at Mount

Vernon the day before he was to leave for camp. She traveled there with his brother Jack, who had agreed to manage George's farms. Washington was trying to wind up last-minute business and pack to overtake Braddock when she arrived. This rare sortie away from Ferry Farm was the first time she had seen Mount Vernon since George was three years old and it was a small farmhouse. Lawrence had never invited her. Now, not waiting for an invitation from George, she came to plead with her son not to resume his military career. George found a moment to slip away from her and dash off a message to Major Orme at Braddock's headquarters:

> The arrival of a good deal of company (among whom is my mother, alarmed with the report of my attending your fortunes), prevents me the pleasure of waiting upon you today as intended; therefore, I beg you'll be kind enough to make my compliments and excuse to the General.[7]

That she should choose this moment to meddle in his affairs and delay his departure—he was now twenty-three and a public figure successful in his own right—perturbed Washington. But it did not change his mind. The next day, April 23, with Jack at his side, he said good-bye to her and rode away.

*G*eorge Washington saw his first British army late in March 1755. He had never seen anything like it and he loved the spectacle. Sixteen British troop transports disgorged boatload after boatload of red-coated regulars at the dock of the new town of Alexandria. They were the first British regulars ever to land on Virginia soil and they were probably not at all what a young British-American colonel had imagined. The soldiers were, according to British inspector general Sir John St. Clair, "the sweepings of Chelsea," many of them given the choice of enlisting or going to prison. Many others were rejects from other British regiments who had been dumped on the 44th and 48th Regiments of Foot, which, under other officers, had disgraced themselves by running away under fire from the young pretender, Prince Charles, at the Battle of Preston Pans. But compared to the shambling, poorly clad country bumpkins Washington was used to leading, one thousand British regulars in red coats and buff breeches trimmed with brightly burnished brass marching down Alexandria's only street behind forty pounding drums, three dozen shrill fifes, and fluttering flags with the rose-and-thistle-wreathed Roman numerals of the 44th and 48th Regiments of Foot were a stirring sight. The soldiers were in remarkably good physical shape after being cooped up for two months on shipboard during a winter Atlantic crossing, but they were in a foul mood because they considered themselves deported from English soil and dumped in the wilds of America as something of a punishment. To improve their morale, shortly after he landed Braddock had given each man a twenty-shilling bonus. The men promptly bought up all the peach brandy in town and went on a one-week bender, ignoring the risks of punishment. But their commander had also given a hint of what they could expect when he decreed, as soon as they landed, that deserters, even temporary ones, would be hanged and lesser offenders punished commensurately. Up to five hundred lashes would be meted out for a variety of lesser offenses.

Just as Braddock knew how to run a tight camp, he knew how to organize an expedition, especially the paperwork. Sixty years old, the son of a major in the Coldstream Guards, he had built a reputation for training men, no matter how refractory they seemed, even if he had only taken slight part in a few minor battles. Tall, broad-shouldered, paunchy, he could, when the mood moved him, tell military stories for hours to the delight of younger officers in his suite, which he called, as was the custom of the time, his "family." He could also be brutally undiplomatic and his officers had to study how to anticipate his outbursts and then try to stay beyond his reach.

After three weeks of negotiations with Braddock's chief of staff, George Washington joined Braddock's staff as an unpaid aide-de-camp and was brevetted as a regular army captain. He often had the general all to himself. According to Washington's own account, the two men, the tall, serious, young Virginian, already a seasoned courtier, and the barrel-chested, blowsy old braggadocio general, hit it off. One soldier recognized the makings of another good one. It would be many years before a more mature Washington put into writing his views on the red-faced general who, in the next few months, became so much his father figure. Braddock's

> good and bad qualities were intimately blended. He was brave
> even to a fault and in regular service would have done honor to
> his profession. His attachments were strong and having no dis-
> guise about him, both [these qualities] appeared in full force.
> He was generous and disinterested but plain and blunt in his
> manner even to rudeness.[8]

On Braddock's arrival in Alexandria, he had moved into merchant John Carlyle's fine new brick Georgian mansion along the river, at Fairfax and Cameron Streets. His entourage included a secretary, three aides, a dozen servants, and a thirty-man guard detail. Carlyle, appointed by Dinwiddie as commissary of Virginia, was married to Sally Fairfax's sister, and the couple frequently entertained Washington. During Braddock's stay in Alexandria, Carlyle had to pass an ensign and the guards to get in and out of his own house, which he had taken two years to build meticulously. As Braddock spent fully two months planning his first step and holding conferences with royal governors and Indian emissaries, Carlyle learned to despise the plodding commander and the officers around him, who "professed" to be afraid of "nothing but that the French and Indians would not give them a meeting and try their courage." Carlyle was especially irked that Braddock and his staff ignored the advice of Americans about what they could expect once they crossed the mountains. "We knew the numbers, etc., of the French," he wrote to his brother in Scotland. He "endeavored to set them right but to no purpose":

> They despised us and [the French] and by some means or another came in so prejudiced against us and our country [Virginia] that they used us like an enemy's country and took everything they wanted and paid nothing or very little for it, and when complaints were made to the commanding officers, they cursed the country and [its] inhabitants, calling us the spawn of convicts, the sweepings of the jails, etc., which made their company very disagreeable. The general and his aides-de-camp, secretary and servants lodged with me. He took everything he wanted, abused my house and furniture and made me little or no satisfaction.[9]

If Washington had the same view of Braddock, he chose to overlook many of his shortcomings. He took the time to observe Braddock's organizational skills. He learned that Braddock did not trust provincial troops to fight under their own officers. Virginians were being recruited directly into regular army units. He also saw Braddock form a low opinion of colonial officials as the general presided over the largest intercolonial conference ever held in America. His meetings with representatives of Pennsylvania, New York, Maryland, Virginia, and North and South Carolina revealed that they expected the British government to pick up the entire tab for the expedition to oust the French and make the west safe for English settlers. The British had only agreed to send Braddock after Governor Dinwiddie had promised that the colonies would assess special taxes and pool their funds to share the costs of Braddock's expedition. Now he was being told that the colonial legislatures would never consent to cooperate in a common fund. But after his many run-ins with the devious Dinwiddie, this only made Washington more sympathetic to Braddock. He did not shy away from the dyspeptic Braddock, even when the general raged. He attached himself even more closely to Braddock than he had to Lord Fairfax, or to Dinwiddie. Braddock openly rewarded him with his patronage. By granting him the temporary rank of regular army captain he allowed him to issue commissions to his own ensigns to fill slots in the two new American regiments he was creating. Thus, Washington was able to begin to build his own loyal following.

Immersing himself in the details of army life, Washington studied firsthand how to be a general. Each day, he borrowed the orders of the day and copied them into his journal, learning to emulate their forms and their language. He also made friends with Braddock's aides and officers. He especially liked the garrulous Horatio Gates of New York, the illegitimate son of the majordomo of the Duke of Leeds. Washington also was friendly with the much older Lieutenant Colonel Thomas Gage and got to know the slovenly, dog-loving Charles Lee. Gage graciously shared his portable library of military manuals and pamphlets with the young Virginian, who had seen only a handful of books on war before. Most of the British officers cheerfully answered Washington's endless questions. He also found time to enjoy the camaraderie of veterans from the Fort Necessity campaign. For the first time in years, Washington seemed completely content.

After nine days on the road, on May 1, 1755, Washington arrived in Frederick, Maryland, and joined Braddock's army, the largest ever assembled by the English in North America, as it uncoiled west along both banks of the Potomac over bad roads toward Fort Cumberland. He was never able to leave behind his money troubles. He had set out with four horses, light baggage, a single pair of boots, and little cash. Horses were hard to find within reach of Braddock's army, and Washington's were not the best. Blacksmiths to keep them shod had all been gobbled up by the British army. One of Washington's horses died on the way to the Shenandoah; the other three came up lame from being ridden on rough roads without shoes. Even after he borrowed Sally Fairfax's saddle horse, it took Washington five days to make a two-day ride. When he did get to Winchester, it took him another four days to find a horse of his own, and then only after he dashed off an urgent plea for a £50 loan from Lord Fairfax, who was vacationing nearby at present-day Greenbriar.

When Washington finally overtook Braddock, he found the general embroiled in controversy over his attempts to find the 2,500 horses and 200 wagons to haul supplies, food, munitions, and personal baggage the 110 miles from Fort Cumberland to the Ohio River. Governor Sharpe of Maryland had promised there would be enough wagons, horses, and cattle waiting at Wills Creek when the footsore army stumbled into the Virginia Company's fort there. There were none. For several days, Braddock seriously considered calling off the expedition.

Only a clever ruse by Benjamin Franklin, chairman of the defense committee of the Quaker-dominated Pennsylvania Assembly, finally produced the horses and Conestoga wagons that got the army rolling again. Franklin had attended the governor's conference in Alexandria and noticed that Sir John Sinclair, the British quartermaster general in charge of rounding up transportation and supplies, wore a Hussar-like caped jacket over one shoulder as he rode from farm to farm in Virginia and Maryland, trying to bully farmers into selling or renting him their steeds. Even the inducement of fifteen shillings a day for a four-horse team and wagon—as much as a skilled artisan made in one week—was not enough. Franklin told Braddock that, in Pennsylvania, every farmer had his own covered wagon and team. With Braddock's blessing, Franklin went back to Philadelphia to his printing press and printed up a notice that warned the German farmers, many of whom had seen such capes all too frequently during wars in Europe before they emigrated to America, that "Sir John St. Clair, the Hussar" was coming "with a body of soldiers" to seize their wagons and burn their farms unless they cooperated. Soon enough, some 150 Conestoga wagons, their teams, and drivers were hurrying southwest toward Braddock's army. Franklin also hired 1,500 packhorses and received the only written praise any colonist ever received from Braddock. But Braddock would not listen even to Franklin about the common sense of attacking Indians with a four- or five-hundred-mule cavalcade of wagons that could be "cut like a thread into several pieces." In his autobiography he recorded Braddock's dismissive reaction: "These savages may indeed be a formidable enemy to your raw American militia, but upon the King's regulars it is impossible they should make any impression."[10]

In his privileged new position in British councils of war, George Washington promptly made what was probably his first suggestion to Braddock and his staff. He knew from recent experience how hard it was to find reliable wagons. He also knew how poor the roads were to the northwest. He urged Braddock to think about employing pack trains of horses instead of the slow, heavy Conestogas that required building a wide, graded roadway. Horses would be more suitable for narrow trails through the wilderness. But Braddock was addicted to moving vast quantities of artillery equipment and ammunition by wagon train, even if it meant laboriously building roads ahead of him. He thanked Washington but ignored his advice.

While they waited for transport, Washington had time for letters. He wrote to Jack that there was "no probability of marching the army from Wills Creek till the latter end of this month (May) or the first of next, so that you may imagine time will hang heavy upon my hands." He wrote his mother a brief letter. He addressed her coolly and formally as "Honoured Madame." Using almost the same words he had written to Jack, he added, "I am very happy in the General's family and I am treated with a complaisant freedom which is quite agreeable so that I have no occasion to doubt the satisfaction I proposed in making this campaign." He concluded just as stiffly as he had begun: "As we have met with nothing worth relating, I shall only beg my love to my brothers and sisters and compliments to friends. I am, Honoured Madam, your most dutiful and obedient son." But not "affectionate."[11]

One week later, May 10, a brief twelve-word order appeared in Braddock's headquarters orderly book: "Mr. Washington is appointed aide-decamp to His Excellency General Braddock." George Washington had found his vocation and he was terribly proud of it. But this time he did not write to his mother or even to Sally. He contented himself with messages he sent through Jack at Mount Vernon. He knew Jack would tell everyone else and hand his letters around:

> The General has appointed me one of his aides-de-camps, in which character I shall serve this campaign agreeably enough as I am thereby freed from all commands but his and give orders to all which must be implicitly obeyed. I have now a good opportunity and shall not neglect it of forming an acquaintance which may be serviceable hereafter if I can find it worthwhile pushing my fortune in the military way.

He exaggerated his authority to give orders. He could only transmit Braddock's orders to British and American officers. What was true was that Washington was on the staff of the highest-ranking British officer in North America.[12]

He heard only once more from his mother during the 1755 campaign. He was at Fort Cumberland just before the gaudy red-clad army trudged through the narrow gap in the Allegheny range into daytime-dark forests. A letter arrived from Ferry Farm, delivered by one of his mother's friends. She demanded that he find her a "Dutch man," an indentured servant to help her on the farm. And would he also send her some butter? But no fresh beef, vegetables, or butter had reached the army for weeks since it marched out of Alexandria. Braddock's officers had cow's milk, biscuits, and cheese provided by Benjamin Franklin, but the common soldiers were already becoming sick from subsisting on Royal Navy rations of salt beef. In the heat, dust, and noise of an army camp, how could Washington help smiling? Patiently as he could, he wrote her again. It was not "in my power" to "supply you with a Dutch man." He was deep in the Appalachian wilderness with only fond memories of such a luxury as butter. "We are quite out of that part of the country where either are to be had. There are few or no inhabitants where we now lie encamped and butter cannot be had here to supply the wants of the camp." He knew that she was going, whether he invited her or not, to Mount Vernon while he was away. In any case, he now invited her. "I hope you will spend the chief part of your time at Mount Vernon, as you say, where I am certain everything will be ordered as much for your satisfaction as possible in the situation we are in."[13]

With few military duties in the month of enforced idleness before the army moved westward, Washington had time to think about home, especially about Sally Fairfax. His first day away from Belvoir, loneliness and homesickness had overtaken him and he began to write to her. No letters came from home, not a word from Sally. After that first letter to her, when no reply came, he wrote to Jack and to Sally's sister. He tried to get them to persuade her to write to him. But if Washington was too smitten with a married woman to avoid involving her in a correspondence that was considered out of bounds, Sally was not willing to jeopardize his position let alone hers by responding. She did not answer any of the three letters he wrote her over the next six weeks' time. When Sally's sister-in-law learned that Washington was persisting, she wrote to him and told him to stop troubling Sally and wait until he came home to find some "unknown she (who) may recompense you for all the trials past."[14]

But it was difficult to talk Washington out of an idea once it took shape in his head. He had become obsessed with Sally's friendship and may not have thought there was any danger in it. When he rode to Williamsburg in an attempt to collect £50 he thought the colony owed him for possessions he had lost at Fort Necessity, he stopped off at Belvoir to see Sally. This time, it was Sally who, ever so gently, rebuked him. He must not write her any more letters. Yet even her pleading was not enough. From Bullskin on his ride back to Braddock's army, he wrote to her again on April 30:

> *Dear Madam,*
> In order to engage your correspondence I think it expedient just to deserve it, which I shall endeavor to do by embracing the earliest and every opportunity of writing to you. It will be needless to expatiate on the pleasures that communication of this kind will afford me. It shall suffice to say a correspondence with my friends is the greatest satisfaction I expect to enjoy in the course of this campaign and that none of my friends are able to convey more real delight than you can to whom I stand indebted for so many obligations.

She did not answer him. Washington did not seem to understand that, as a married woman, moreover a woman married to his closest friend and neighbor, Sally was less free than he was. That, or his reasoning, did not enter into it. He was in love and desperate to hear from her.[15]

Two weeks passed. When no letter came from Sally, he enclosed a letter to her with a letter to Jack. As a cover he asked Jack to find him another pair of boots. "Wearing boots is quite the mode and mine are in a declining state. I must beg the favor of you to procure me a pair that is good and neat." He suggested that he send his boots and any letters to him through Sally Fairfax's brother-in-law, John Carlyle, who had frequent communication with the army. Washington was inexperienced in resorting to ruses and back channels. The rest of the letter was filled with news that Jack already knew. No doubt Washington was writing it to be repeated to Sally. The letter he enclosed to her was probably his first attempt at an epistolary flirtation:

Dear Madam,

I have, at last, with great pains and difficulty discovered the reason why Mrs. [Letitia Lee] Wardrop is a greater favorite with General Braddock than Mrs. Fairfax and met with more respect at the late review in Alexandria.

The cause I shall communicate after rallying you for neglecting the means that introduced her to his favor which, to say truth, was in part a present of delicious cake and potted woodcocks that wrought such wonders upon the heart of the General as well as upon those of the gentlemen [of Braddock's suite] that they became instant admirers not only of the charms but of the politeness of this fair lady. I hope you will favor me with your correspondence since you see my willing desire to deserve the honor.[16]

Washington did not have time to send the letter to Jack to forward to Sally. The very next day Braddock sent him on a mission that took him—and the letter—to Belvoir where he could present it in person to Sally. Braddock ordered him to ride to Williamsburg to fetch £4,000 in cash to pay the troops. Washington stopped off at Belvoir to see Sally, whose husband was away in Williamsburg at an emergency session of the legislature. In his official memorandum of the mission, Washington wrote that "I was detained a day in getting horses." In truth, he left Belvoir for the capital riding Sally's personal saddle horse. There was no time to stop again as he raced back toward the front. He arrived in Winchester in a foul mood on May 28; he described the town as "this vile hole." He had requested a cavalry escort as he carried the money the last dangerous leg of the 300-mile trip, but no one awaited him and he had little luck raising a militia troop. "You may, with almost equal success, attempt to raise the dead to life again," he wrote to his brother, "as the force of this county."[17]

When still no letter came from Sally three weeks later, Washington, now at Fort Cumberland, resorted to a stratagem. He wrote her a letter that he sent not to Belvoir where her husband would see it, but under cover of a letter to her sister, Sarah Fairfax Carlyle, which he enclosed with a letter he had no particular reason to write to her husband. A letter to John Carlyle, the purchasing agent for supplies for Braddock, was routine for someone on Braddock's staff. He inquired "after your health," gave Carlyle the latest news from camp (but none he probably didn't already know), and added, as if an afterthought, "The enclosed is to my good friend Mrs. Carlyle, who I hope will not suffer our former correspondence to drop." He didn't mention to Carlyle that his wife had directed Washington to stop writing to her married sister. The letter to her contained little but the same news he had just written to her husband, little except these words, which may explain the elaborate flanking maneuver: "I have no higher expectation in view than an intimate correspondence with my friends. I hope in that I shall not be disappointed, especially by you and Mrs. Fairfax." To Sally, he enclosed this note:

When I had the happiness to see you last, you expressed an inclination to be informed of my safe arrival in camp with the charge that was entrusted to my care but at the same time desired it might be communicated in a letter to somebody of your acquaintance. This I took as a gentle rebuke and polite manner of forbidding my corresponding with you. [I] conceive this opinion is not idly founded when I reflect that I have hitherto found it impractical to engage one moment of your attention. If I am right in this, I hope you will excuse the present presumption and lay the imputation to [elation] at my successful arrival. If, on the contrary, these are fearful apprehensions only, how easy it is to remove my suspicions, enliven my spirits and make me happier than the day is long by honoring me with a correspondence which you did once partly promise to do.[18]

And then there was no more time for letters.

Seven

"I HAD FOUR BULLETS
THROUGH MY COAT"

Finally everything was ready. From Fort Cumberland, turned overnight from a small stockaded Virginia Company trading post into a jerry-built fortress, Braddock sent off his troops, two regiments of redcoats from Ireland plus independent companies of regulars from New York and the Carolinas, along with twelve companies of Virginia militia—in all 2,100 fighting men. The 150-mile route through northern Virginia had crossed over into Maryland, then snaked back into Virginia and over into Maryland again to Fort Cumberland. The crude road, sometimes only twelve feet wide and a quagmire after the spring rains, was clogged with men, horse-drawn wagons, and herds of cattle. In the daytime, the soldiers baked as they labored in heavy woolen uniforms. At night, they shivered. Some nights it snowed. Braddock's quartermaster general, Sir John St. Clair, had trained many of the colonial volunteers as "pioneers," workmen with axes and shovels who chopped down the trees blazed by British engineers who were laying the road and then hurriedly filled and leveled it ahead of the backed-up stop-and-start column of redcoats.

Logistical considerations often had to give way to politics. In observing Braddock closely for three months, Washington was able to make a case study of all the failures and frustrations the British experienced in trying to deal smoothly with their colonies even during an emergency. He watched as Braddock butted his head against the two chronic American problems, lack of cooperation among the colonies and erratic relations with the Indians. Washington learned that Dinwiddie had complicated both by refusing to work through other colonial governors in his dealing with the Indians. As the result of his chintzy offers of customary gifts to the Cherokees and the Catawbas and his refusal to respect the normal diplomatic channels, virtually none of the expected thousand southern Indians had shown up. The northern tribes, since the fiasco at Fort

Necessity more than ever convinced that the French would win in a wilderness war, were staying safely neutral in their longhouses. What few Indians appeared left after a series of run-ins with Braddock. Shingas brought in a delegation of Delawares, Shawnees, and Mingoes. Braddock insulted them by declaring that "no savage should inherit the land" the British army liberated from the French. They immediately went over to the French. One chief's son was mistaken for an enemy Indian and shot dead. Another fifty Mingo warriors arrived from Pennsylvania. When the Indians insisted their wives be allowed to join them, Braddock refused, then relented. After several wild nights involving rum, soldiers, and Indian women, Braddock ordered all Indian women out of his camp—and the Indian men followed them. Only eight native guides remained. Their leader, Scaroyady, later called Braddock "a bad man" who "looked upon us as dogs and would never hear anything that was said to him."[1]

To replace the Indians and to screen his advance, Braddock organized twelve Virginia companies of light infantry. Washington became their self-appointed spokesman and advocate. Weeks of Braddock's time went into intercolonial diplomacy as he tried unsuccessfully to get the governors to make their legislatures honor Dinwiddie's pledge of a joint war chest. All the planning, arguing, and mobilizing slowed down the expedition and added a great deal of noise that completely destroyed any element of a surprise attack. Taking seriously the elaborate English show of force, the French rushed three thousand professional soldiers across the Atlantic to Canada, breaking with tradition by employing regulars instead of relying on *habitants* impressed into the Canadian militia. For the first time, two European armies of professional soldiers faced each other in North America, girding to vie for its control.

At a cabinet meeting in London on April 10, 1755, even as Braddock bickered with colonial officials in Virginia, the British ministry, under heavy pressure from the Duke of Cumberland and taking note of the French reinforcements, broke off negotiations with the French. The cabinet ordered a Royal Navy squadron to intercept "any French ships of war or ships having troops or warlike stores on board." Thirteen men-of-war sailed on April 27, 1755. It was tantamount to a declaration of war made without the knowledge or consent of Parliament or any of the American colonies. The British ministry was almost unanimous in its belief that a show of force would make the French abandon their new line of forts. When the British navy intercepted two troop-laden French men-of-war on June 8, while Braddock's army was lumbering west toward the Ohio, France recalled its ambassador from London. The Seven Years' War was the climactic struggle for control of half of North America and trade routes and colonies around the world. It formally began one year after Washington opened fire on Jumonville's drowsy soldiers.

All through the month of June 1755, Braddock's spit-and-polish parade ground army retraced the route so familiar to Washington through the oak forests until it squeezed through the Cumberland Gap and emerged on the rockier, thinly covered western slope of the Alleghenies. The long red line sometimes advanced only half a mile a day. Yet Washington could not make Braddock, as he wrote John Carlyle, "see the absurdity of the route." Braddock saw his road as a "tremendous building opportunity of transporting the heavy artillery over the mountains, which I believe will compose the greatest difficulty in the campaign." Artillery had never been brought to bear in the American interior and Braddock believed it would be decisive, especially against the Indians, who had never faced its fire. Riding in Braddock's suite all day except when he carried orders to unit commanders, Washington gave the general advice whenever he was asked for it. In his one year as a militia officer, Washington had formed a low opinion of American militia. He called them "a parcel of banditti" at this time. He was now thoroughly enamored of the British military system. He undoubtedly approved of British use of colonials to do all the menial work just so long as they were well paid. The British paid in gold and they paid bonuses for extra duty. Every soldier was beautifully dressed, equipped, and armed. The British had allowed double the usual number of washerwomen, some sixty of them, to accompany the troops from Ireland. The brutal hard work of building a road and moving an army was meted out to teamsters hired on the frontier and to "pioneer" labor brigades, which cut down trees marked with an axe by royal engineers and then cleared brush, built bridges, and pried up or blasted out boulders to widen and lengthen the Virginia Company's road through Great Meadows and north over Chestnut Ridge to Christopher Gist's trading post. Washington did not record his emotions as he rode past the burned remains of Fort Necessity almost a year to the day after his humiliation there.[2]

At the end of each day of frustrating delays, there were assemblies of the army to witness the reading of the rolls and the punishment of recalcitrant English and American soldiers. One young Virginia frontiersman, an eighteen-year-old teamster named Daniel Morgan, was flogged at one of these assemblies for allegedly striking a British sergeant. For the rest of his life, Morgan was easily persuaded to allow any doubter to pull up his shirt and touch and count what he said were five hundred and one scars from a British lash. At the somber evening gatherings along Braddock's line of march, Washington was learning the routines and apportionment of brutal army discipline.

It was also the Americans who more often than not were assigned to shield the regulars from ambushes by pro-French Indians on their flanks and rear. As the army inched forward with far too few of its own Indian allies to protect it, the French-led Shawnees slipped around and behind it, picking off up to a dozen redcoats in a day, burning half a dozen farms near Fort Cumberland, killing and scalping settlers. Still, Braddock kept his force intact and moving. Stopping to camp for the night often as early as three in the afternoon, the army made biscuits and broiled freshly slaughtered beef over smoky greenwood fires. The tower of smoke was visible for miles. Washington was relieved by the chance to climb down from the jarring all-day ride. Like so many others, he was suffering from what British doctors recorded as "the bloody flux," dysentery. Around the smoldering campfires, into the eerie nights, soldiers newly arrived from Ireland and England listened to frontiersmen's stories of Indian scalpings and torture and the feasting of wolves on human carcasses. Nervous sentries, choking back their fear, called out paroles and countersigns in the pitch-black forest beyond the campfires' glow.

As supplies and transport lagged far behind his expectations, Braddock's mood did not improve. He categorically berated all things American. Washington found himself in the role of defender of his fellow colonists. When beef ordered from a Maryland contractor showed up rotten, Braddock had him arrested. Washington was growing weary of Braddock's anti-American tirades. He wrote to his neighbor, William Fairfax:

> The general, by frequent breaches of contracts, has lost all degree of patience and for want of that consideration and moderation which should be used by a man of sense upon these occasions, will, I fear, represent us [at] home in a light we little deserve. Instead of blaming the individuals as he ought, he charges all his disappointments to a public supineness and looks upon the country, I believe, as void of both honor and honesty. We have frequent disputes on this head which are maintained with warmth on both sides, especially on his. [He] is incapable of giving up any point he asserts, let it be ever so incompatible with reason.[3]

In what may have been his first sustained political arguments, Washington upheld American honor against an onslaught by a raging British general who did not possess his humility or self-restraint. At times, it was a good thing he had the freedom of the unpaid volunteer. In their weeks together as they headed west, real affection developed between Braddock and his young aide. For his part, Braddock sometimes bore Washington's youthful nerve with good-natured patience. At Fort Cumberland, after he watched redcoats drill all day and fire in platoon formation, Washington, his thumbs thrust in his vest pockets, lectured Braddock that these European tactics would not repel an Indian attack in the forest. Braddock, turning to his other officers, chuckled gruffly and said, "What think you of this from a beardless boy?" Washington failed to realize that Braddock, informed that he would face French professionals, felt compelled to teach European tactics.[4]

Braddock's slow march averaged only two miles a day. Old, tired horses hauling 1,300-pound cannon and tons of ammunition and supplies dragged along behind hundreds of axemen swinging away in the sweltering heat. The red-faced Braddock had every reason for annoyance. At this rate, it would be late autumn before he reached the French fortress. His supplies would be too low to make it through a northern winter. Worse, his plodding progress was giving the French ample time to bring reinforcements from Canada. He began calling his advisers in one at a time to his command tent and asking them for suggestions how to speed things up. Colonel Washington was one of the first he summoned. For weeks, Washington later said, he had been urging Braddock and his senior officers to modify the march, especially since they lacked a strong contingent of Indians to scour the woods around them for the enemy. He wrote years later that the British, "instead of pushing on with vigor, without regarding a little rough road," were "halting to level every mole hill and to erect bridges over every brook." Washington

> used every proper occasion till [I] was taken sick to impress the General and the principal officers around him with the necessity of opposing the nature of [our] defense to the mode of attack which, more than probably, [we] would experience from the Canadian French and their Indians.[5]

To Colonel Fairfax at Belvoir he wrote to brood that nine hundred French regulars were coming "to reinforce the French on the Ohio: we shall have more to do than go up the hills to come down again." But this young volunteer who had lost his only battle had made little or no impression on professional officers who had complete faith in British discipline and experience under fire. When Braddock summoned him, this time in private, he had an answer ready. Obviously, he had prepared himself for just such an occasion. Washington was, Braddock knew, the only British officer who knew the terrain. This time, Braddock listened closely. Washington gave drastic advice. Divide the army. Split it in two. Send a fast-moving, handpicked force of the best troops with some artillery ahead to attack Fort Duquesne as fast as possible. Allow the baggage and the other slower troops to come along behind, building the supply road as fast as they could. Later, Braddock called in his senior officers and asked them what they thought of dividing his command and accelerating his attack. He did not attribute the idea to Washington. A majority of British officers, including Lieutenant Colonel Gage, his senior regimental commander, agreed.[6]

In a council of war at Fort Cumberland, Braddock ordered Gage to select 1,300 of the best men, including the 44th Regiment and four companies of Virginia light infantry, and take along no more than thirty wagons and some light artillery to form an advance force. Braddock would come behind him with his headquarters unit and about 350 redcoats. The 200-odd sick and most of the wagons and pioneers were to be sent back to the rear guard, made up of the 48th Regiment under Colonel Thomas

Dunbar. The advance force would march between the enemy and the wagon train to protect it. Washington was proud that Braddock adopted his plan. He heard that General St. Clair and the regimental commanders supported it, but he was careful not to take any credit for it at the time. He let all of Braddock's subordinates believe it was the general's idea and not his young uncommissioned provincial aide's. Later, he wrote a memorandum recording it as his idea, dated it, and sent it under seal to his family.

By this time, Washington was becoming seriously ill. Dysentery was rampant in the camp. Seventy serious cases had been caused by the rotten beef and rancid bacon provided by contractors. He was running a high fever and suffering from a severe headache. Depleted, after days of it, no doubt dehydrated and suffering from a touch of sunstroke as well, he kept up with Braddock for five more days. By June 23, however, he was delirious and too weak to sit on his horse. He had to ride in a supply wagon, in agony from the cramps and the jouncing over the raw dirt road. "My illness was too violent to suffer me to ride," he remembered thirty years later:

> I was indebted to a covered wagon for some part of my transportation, but even in this I could not continue, for the jostling was so great. I was left upon the road with a guard and necessaries to await the arrival of Colonel Dunbar's detachment, which was two days' march behind, the General giving me his word and honor that I should be brought up before he reached the French fort.[7]

Alarmed over his aide's condition, Braddock finally ordered Washington to the rear, worried that he would die if he continued on the march. Braddock gave specific orders that Washington was to be given some of his precious Doctor James's Powders, a compound of phosphate of lime and oxide of antimony that Washington called "the most excellent medicine in the world, for it gave me immediate ease." As Braddock's army left the supply base at Squaw Creek behind, Washington lay seriously ill in a makeshift field hospital awaiting the arrival of Dunbar's rear guard. He was treated for a week by Braddock's body servant, Thomas Bishop, until he, too, was stricken. Then Washington hired a nurse for eight days who put him on a milk diet. Slowly, Washington recovered, or at least stopped getting worse.[8]

By late June, Washington could not stand to convalesce any longer. He hitched a ride in a supply wagon. Braddock had reached the Youghiogheny River, twenty-five miles from the French fort. Washington was about to cross the river when an army doctor stopped him, checked him over, and refused to let him pass. Washington was, as he wrote Orme, still "excessively weak" and had a fever. For five more anxious days, Washington waited, sipping milk and worrying that he wouldn't be allowed to rejoin

Braddock in time for the attack. By his best estimate, Braddock would reach Fort Duquesne on July 10, maybe even a day earlier. To Captain Orme, with Braddock on the march, Washington wrote to plead for a countermand to the doctor's order and a ride to the front. "My fevers are very moderate and I hope are near a crisis." But it was raining hard and the road was too mired for a wagon to haul him. Washington brooded about "the difficulty in getting to you." He would, he said, "gladly give £500" rather than miss being in on the kill at Fort Duquesne. Braddock wouldn't attack without him, would he? "The General has given me his word and honor in the most solemn manner." Washington had grown terribly lonely, too. He wrote to Jack, that, except for letters from him and an overseer at Mount Vernon, he had received no mail from his family or friends. "You may thank my friends for the letters I have received," he wrote sarcastically, "which has not been one from any mortal since I left Fairfax."[9]

On July 8, Washington was finally strong enough to persuade a doctor to issue a pass that enabled him, although still feeling "very weak and low," to climb into a Conestoga wagon that overtook the general ten miles east of Fort Duquesne as he was preparing his orders for the elaborate assault the next morning. Washington arrived just in time to join the crowd of officers in Braddock's tent for the final council of war. The advance guard of 1,300 chosen men were to secure a ford of the Youghiogheny, cross it, and march two miles through the Narrows, a pinched defile that carried Turtle Creek on a horseshoe-shaped course into the Monongahela River. The trail down into the Narrows and back up out of it was steep and tree-lined, the road through it poor, but it would bring the army out to the northwest where the Monongahela meets the Allegheny River, an easy day's march south of Fort Duquesne.

On the final approach to Fort Duquesne, the rough trail squeezed between the Turtle Creek and high ground on the right. The creek's banks were too steep for the wagons. Hours of work would be needed to grade them, work that could be avoided, his scout Christopher Gist said, if the army marched across the horseshoe instead of around it. Gist told Braddock the river was low from a drought, its banks gentle. Braddock acceded to the change. Lieutenant Colonel Gage was to lead the advance party of some 600 men. The scouts, including Christopher Gist, a troop of mounted Virginians, and Scaroyady's handful of Indians, were to be followed by an engineer who was to hack the bark off trees that his detail of twenty pioneers were to chop down quickly to widen the narrow deer path to a twelve-foot roadway. Some 300 grenadiers, the best and biggest of the redcoats, along with the light infantry of the 44th Regiment, were to stay fifty yards back. They were followed by a work party to fill in holes for the guns and ammunition wagons. Still another work crew of Virginians and Royal Navy sailors would slope the riverbanks for the thirteen pieces of horse-drawn artillery and the thirty wagons full of shot, shell, and supplies. One hundred yards farther back would come the main contingent of Gage's advance force. Riding out in front was Captain Robert Stewart, a veteran of Fort Necessity, with twenty-nine mounted Virginia light infantry and more pioneers, one hundred yards back, Braddock and his aides leading 500 regulars flanking the wagons, cattle, horses, servants, soldiers' wives, settlers, teamsters (including young Daniel Boone), and then, finally, a rear guard of 100 Virginians. Some 200 more Virginia militia were to be broken up into twenty-four squads to patrol the woods on the flanks to guard against Indian attack. Braddock expected the French to remain in their fort until he began to besiege it or, if they came out, to face off against him in open-field formation and blast away at close range, just as they would have in Europe. General St. Clair had worried aloud outside the general's tent just before the council of war that the column was too strung out and exposed, but he had recently been dressed down by Braddock for menacing the Pennsylvanians. Inside Braddock's tent, he kept silent. So, evidently, did Washington, who was totally engrossed in this lesson in tactics. He had reason to be proud; after all, the commander in chief was following his advice.

Just before two the next morning, July 9, 1755, Washington and the rest of Braddock's staff got up and dressed in their best parade-ground uniforms. He had laid out his morning duties as carefully as his uniform. He would ride at Braddock's side, ready to carry orders to the unit commanders to fine-tune the advance. Still unable to stand the jarring of a horse over the rough road, Washington tied pillows to his saddle. Gage got going promptly with the first 350 men and two six-pounders to cover the vanguard as it crossed the river. By 4 A.M., St. Clair and the pioneers and carpenters and their wagons marched out. One hour later, Braddock's main force stepped off: 750 men in bright crimson uniforms, about 400 wagons, 1,000 pack animals, a large herd of cattle, and more artillery, all stretching out over five miles. George Washington sat gingerly on his horse at Braddock's side. Each unit marched briskly past them in review, their uniforms immaculate, their muskets gleaming. He was moved. He would later say that it was the most thrilling sight of his life. He watched with Braddock and all his resplendently uniformed staff officers as the crimson column crossed the river, climbed up the embankment, and disappeared into the dark, majestic forest.

At 9:30 A.M., Braddock sent Washington ahead with the order for the main force to halt while pioneers graded the riverbanks. His scout, Gist, apparently had crossed the river only on one side of the horseshoe. The banks at the second ford were sheer twelve-foot bluffs. Many of the soldiers had gone hungry the day before. If they had anything to eat, they should have it now, but only one in twenty did. They gnawed on dried biscuits and watched as the officers' batmen milked cows and made rum punch and served it with Gloucester cheese to their masters. Benjamin

Franklin had prevailed on Philadelphia merchants to make a gift of a good horse, some meat, and cheese for each of Braddock's twenty staff officers. After a ninety-minute delay, at eleven o'clock, they stepped off again. By 2:30 in the afternoon, the 1,500-man vanguard was within seven miles of Fort Duquesne. Crossing a ravine, the British and their Virginia guides marched through thick woods. They passed the ruins of John Frazier's trading post. Here Washington could see the spot where he had first held a winter parley with the French nearly two years ago. As the advance guard marched along Turtle Creek, they passed a heavily wooded slope on their right. Just beyond it, the Indian scouts saw something moving. Men, stripped to the waist, ran straight toward them.

The French inside Fort Duquesne had been up early, too. Contrecoeur, the commandant, was still waiting for a promised reinforcement of regulars from Quebec. He had only about 125 professionals, plus 146 Canadian militiamen and some 650 Indians. He decided to risk everything in an attempt to stop Braddock before the Englishman could bring up his heavy guns and batter the fort. It was his only hope. He dispatched Captain Daniel Lienard de Beaujeu with 900 men, all but the few who were left behind to guard the fort.

Suddenly, Gage's scouts saw a French officer wearing a gleaming silver gorget on his otherwise bare breast. The British scouts fired immediately, then retreated. The crews of two field guns, Royal Navy gunners, swung them around, loaded, and fired grapeshot at point-blank range. The front rank of Frenchmen dropped as the British grenadiers opened fire in an orderly volley. Some French soldiers turned and ran, but Captain Beaujeu coolly gestured with his left hand and then his right for his Canadians and the Indians to divide and go around the British flanks. They ran up the slope above the English, raced along both sides of the red-coated column, and took cover. Dashing from tree to tree, they became invisible to the British. As the Virginia scouts and pioneers pelted back past them, the British grenadiers steadied themselves under the command to "fix bayonets." They formed line of battle, the front rank kneeling, and fired in orderly volleys. The third volley cut down the French commander Beaujeu. He died at the side of the deer path with a musketball through his brain. Many of the French Canadians now fled, but a platoon of French regulars held firm. Their volleys repelled the British grenadiers as they made a bayonet charge.

A mile back, Washington was riding beside Braddock when they heard the first sounds of firing, scattered at first, then a volley, then more light, scattered fire, then another volley and another. Washington and every officer stiffened. The men clutched their muskets and turned toward Braddock. He was the only officer present who could tell most of them what they were hearing. The firing, he said, was by large parties heavily engaged. He ordered his column halted. Washington shouted the command, other officers passed it back from unit to unit. Braddock ordered his secretary, Captain Shirley, to ride ahead and find out what was happening.

By the time Shirley covered the mile, the French and Indians had already seized the high ground and the ravine and had driven in the British flanking parties, their murderously accurate fire picking off the mounted red-coated officers and killing their horses. Slowly at first, Gage and his grenadiers gave ground, making an orderly retreat of 150 yards. They reloaded and fired in volleys at targets they could not see. But the bark of sergeants' orders could not drown out the war cries of the Indians. The heaviest fire came slicing into the red-coated ranks from the wooded hillside Gage had neglected to take. Backing up hurriedly now, not waiting for orders, Gage's troops ran smack into the advancing quick-marching detachment of reinforcements Braddock had hurriedly sent forward. Washington later found Gage a mile and a half to the rear. The reinforcements tried to keep their formation instead of parting and letting the retreating men through, and the two units collided. Soon, amid the heavy firing down on them, there was a tangle of redcoats huddling twelve abreast in the road. The British soldiers began to panic as they saw Indians jump up, scalp the dead and wounded, then dive for cover. All the redcoats could aim at was puffs of smoke where an Indian had fired; they, on the other hand, offered close-packed, bright red targets with white crosshatches to sight in on.

As the gunsmoke thickened, the red ranks of the regulars became an undifferentiated mass, no longer fighting units but terrified men, loading and firing at the men in front of them. Time after time, British line officers yelled orders, threatened, tried to get the men into formation to charge that hill. More officers fell. The few men who ran up the hill ran back down into the road. The Virginians, who had fanned out to the flanks on either side of the redcoats to shield them, had taken cover in the trees. They held their ground. Captain Thomas Waggener, a veteran of Fort Necessity, had coolly kept his men together. Some 170 of them began to work their way up the hill, squirming on their bellies toward a great fallen tree he intended to use as a parapet to protect his marksmen. He lost only three men to French fire during the ascent, only to have his men cut down from behind by British fire. Seeing the smoke from the Virginians' position, the British officers in the road mistook the buckskin-clad Virginians for French Canadians and ordered volley after volley, and shot many of the Virginians in their backs. Captain William Polson, who had also survived his wounds from Fort Necessity, stood up and yelled, "We are English." An English soldier yelled back that they had no choice, they were under orders to fire. In the next volley, a British ball hit Polson in the heart, lifting him off the ground. All of his officers and noncoms died. Only five men in his company of fifty survived. Washington later reported that "the Virginia troops showed a good deal of courage" and were nearly all killed in the crossfire. "Captain La Péyronie and all his officers down to a corporal was killed," he wrote. What remained of the Virginians fanned out behind trees to form a rear guard and fought on stubbornly for more than two hours.[10]

French fire came from three sides by this time. A rumor started down the broken red line that the French and Indians had gotten around behind the British and were attacking their baggage wagons. If the enemy was behind them, the men reasoned, they would all be killed and scalped. The redcoats turned and ran. In a wild surge that gathered up Braddock's troops as well as the laborers, many of the redcoats dropped their guns and ran as fast as they could toward the rear and across the river. Braddock and Washington galloped up and down the road trying to rally them. They had to dodge teams of horses charging at them. The teamsters, including twenty-one-year-old Daniel Boone, cut the tackle of the wagon teams and clung to the terrified animals as they spurred them along the crowded roadway as fast as they could away from the screaming Indians. By this time Washington was Braddock's only aide. Shirley had been shot through the head and scalped; Morris was disabled by a wound; Orme crippled by a thigh wound.

Washington's first reaction remained with him for years. The Virginians had nearly all died because of the "dastardly behavior" of the regulars, who ran off without trying to rescue any of the wounded or even attempting a counterattack. The vaunted redcoats "were immediately struck with such a deadly panic that nothing but confusion and disobedience of orders prevailed among them" while "the officers in general behaved with incomparable bravery." The artillery was useless. Gun crews, unprotected by infantry, were killed by the Indians "very fast." Some of the officers killed the men for running away; some of the men shot the officers for trying to rally them. Washington never forgot Braddock's gallantry as he rode back and forth, flailing at men with the flat of his sword, trying to rally them. But he refused to fight Indian fashion. He cursed and slashed at men who crouched down to fire from cover, and when he spied La Péyronie's surviving Virginians on the hillside, he ordered them back down into the road, where more died.

Braddock and Washington found themselves the only officers left in the saddle. Attempting to stop the stampede, they exposed themselves "to almost certain death," Washington later reported. He wrote with disgust that the redcoats "were as sheep pursued by dogs, they broke and ran with more cowardice than it is possible to conceive." Still, Washington thought that he could pull together enough Virginia troops to take the high ground and drive back the enemy. He asked permission to make an assault. He did not know how many Virginians had already been killed. Braddock, dazed, only shook his head. Washington later recalled that

Braddock was too slow to allow him to help; all his years of British by-the-book training made him balk at the "impropriety" of Washington's offer until it was too late.[11]

When fresh British reserves arrived, their officers begged them to charge the hill. When these officers, too, were picked off by Indian sharp-shooters, it unnerved their men. Redcoats "dropped like leaves in autumn," as one survivor put it. The reinforcements joined the "deadly panic," adding their own disorganized mass to what Washington termed "the general confusion and disobedience of orders." Braddock managed to rally the troops briefly. He had five horses shot from under him. He finally sent Washington galloping off with the orders Washington wanted. Find some officers. Tell them to organize 150 men to charge the hill, a like number to retake the cannon. As Washington rode off in search of surviving British officers, he, too, twice had his mounts killed. One horse rolled over and briefly pinned him under it. Each time, he grabbed another riderless horse. With so many British officers dead, there were empty-saddled horses running all over the battlefield. Washington's weakness evidently had been banished by adrenaline. He rode off again, dodging his way through the smoke-filled woods toward the Virginians, his tall form a conspicuous target for Indian marksmen. Captain Orme later praised Washington's courage—"the greatest courage and resolution"—as he dashed back and forth under heavy fire trying to organize a counterattack. He later found one bullet hole through his hat and wrote to his mother, "I had four bullet holes through my coat."[12]

He had little luck finding officers. General St. Clair had been shot; Colonel Halkett was dead. Then he received the worst possible news. Braddock, who had been trying valiantly to lead the charge up the hill himself, had been shot. The bullet crashed through his right arm and chest into his lungs. As his men laid Braddock on the ground, the officer now his second-in-command, Colonel Burton, appealed to his men to follow him. One hundred did. Up the hill toward the hidden enemy they raced—until Burton fell dead. Then they all fled back down into the huddling red mass again. The last attempt at counterattack was over.

Now only sporadic resistance by a few officers who, like the Virginians, had posted their men behind trees held back the Indians. Orders ceased to mean anything. Adam Stephen, also a veteran of Fort Necessity, wrote "you might as well send a cow in pursuit of a hare as an English soldier loaded (down) in their way after naked Indians accustomed to the woods." The Virginia rear guard kept up a steady fire from behind trees and high tufts of grass. Washington was the only officer who had not been killed or wounded. Braddock lay mortally wounded, but, according to one Virginia burgess cowering nearby, cried out, "'My dear blues (which was the colors the Virginians wore) give 'm tother fire, you fight like men and will die like soldiers.' During that time he could not bear the sight of a red coat. Whenever one came in his sight, he raved, but when one of the blues, he said he hoped to live to reward 'em."[13]

As the sun sank, the firing from the red mounds of men ceased. They were all dead, wounded, or out of ammunition. The incessant howling of the Indians did not stop until, suddenly, they broke into barrels of rum they found in the supply wagons. The Virginians screened the retreating British as they dragged themselves toward the river. Washington rode among them, slashing at them furiously with his saber, trying one last time to turn around this herd of cowards "with as much success as if we had attempted to stop the wild boars of the mountains." All his hope was gone. Washington was one of the last to cross the river. He found a small covered cart and he got Braddock into it along with some of the general's baggage. He somehow organized a company of men to protect the wounded. Under heavy fire he conveyed the dying general across the river, even as Indians plunged in to the water and killed exhausted stragglers near him. Most of the Indians stayed behind on the battlefield, preoccupied with scalping and stripping the 450 dead and wounded, including eight women. With the help of two wounded officers and with Braddock's approval, Washington gathered the survivors on high ground 200 yards east of the river. Before losing consciousness, Braddock sent Washington to find Colonel Dunbar in the rear and tell him to bring up the other regiment. At this moment, the British still had more troops than the entire force of French and Indians. Braddock still thought victory possible. On his forty-two-mile way back along the line of march, Washington was to rally any men he could.

An exhausted Washington and two guides picked their way all night through a darkened scene of horror he still remembered vividly thirty years later. "The shocking scenes are not to be described," he wrote. "The dead, the dying, the groans, lamentations and cries along the road of the wounded for help were enough to pierce a heart of adamant." But he could not stop to help. The "gloom and horror" of the ride, Washington told biographer Humphreys, "was not a little increased by the impervious darkness" created by "the close shade of thick woods." Time after time, the guides could not tell "when they were in or out of the track but by groping on the ground with their hands." Somehow holding himself upright, Washington rode on for twelve hours. He must find Dunbar, bring back reinforcements.[14]

Late on the morning of July 10, Washington found Dunbar's wagon train at Rock Fort, as the British had renamed the spot where Washington had attacked Jumonville. Rumors had arrived before him that Braddock's force had been wiped out. After reassuring Dunbar that Braddock wanted him to bring his troops forward, Washington collapsed into a tent. He slept for twenty-four hours. When he awoke late the morning of the eleventh, to his astonishment he found that Colonel Dunbar was still there. He had gathered only a few companies of men—100 out of his entire regiment—to send back to Braddock with wagons to evacuate the wounded. Hundreds of other redcoats were fleeing south toward Fort Cumberland, nearly one hundred miles from Braddock's little knot of survivors. But Braddock himself had managed to mount a horse and ride toward Rock Fort. He was still giving orders as he led a column of 387 wounded officers and men. He had decided to give up his expedition and lead the retreat. Everything was to be destroyed—ammunition, powder, flour, 150 wagons, all but two small cannon to protect the wounded. The work of destruction took two full days. Washington rode back and forth between Dunbar and Braddock, Braddock and Dunbar, shuttling the orders. After ordering the burning of his supplies, Braddock rode one more mile toward Fort Necessity. Then he collapsed. He was in terrible pain, wheezing with each whistling breath as he jolted along in the covered cart. Yet he was clearheaded until his death. "Who would have thought it?" he asked his young friend, Washington. No one recorded the answer. A little later, Braddock told Orme to put it in his report of the disaster that "nothing could equal the gallantry of the officers nor the bad behavior of the men." Three days after the Battle of the Monongahela, Braddock ordered his cart halted two miles west of Fort Necessity and turned the command over to Colonel Dunbar. "We shall know better how to deal with them next time," he said. Just before he died at dusk on July 13, he gave one last set of detailed orders: Captain Washington was to bury him. Early the next morning, Washington chose a spot in the road and ordered a squad to dig a deep trench where the Indians could not find the body. Washington made the arrangements to bury Braddock with full military honors. He recited the prayers for the dead as he had for his father, and then he gave the command for a squad to fire a salute. He had Braddock in his best uniform lowered into the ground and then he ordered every wagon to be driven over the grave to pack down the dirt. What was left of his defeated army passed over Braddock as it retreated to Fort Cumberland. While the bodies of many others were dug up and mutilated by the Indians, Braddock's corpse was never discovered. And George Washington, who had learned so much about how, and how not, to be an officer, from Edward Braddock, never uttered in public or wrote a word against him.[15]

Eight

"OBSERVE THE
STRICTEST DISCIPLINE"

It was another three days before Washington staggered into Fort Cumberland, now a crowded hospital with barracks full of the wounded. Washington learned that he had been reported dead. It was the first time in weeks that he was able to laugh. He dashed off a message to his brother Jack that he was "in the land of the living by the miraculous care of Providence that protected me beyond all human expectation." Then he rode on to the British camp at Frederick, Maryland, where he bought a mattress and slept. When he awoke, he wrote a long letter to his mother. She must have heard, too, that he was dead. "I doubt not, but you have heard of our defeat and perhaps have had it represented in a worse light if possible than it deserves," he began. Washington still believed that the British had been routed by a mere 300 French-led Indians and that only the panic and cowardice of British enlisted men had caused their slaughter. There were "many" brave English officers, but he was especially proud of the courageous stand of the Virginia troops. Of 300 Virginians in the advance guard, only 30 survived; every Virginia officer but Washington had been killed or wounded. In all, 63 of 86 British officers had died or were wounded; 914 of 1,373 enlisted men were killed or wounded. With two-thirds casualties, it was the worst disaster in British military history. "I luckily escaped without a wound," he reassured his mother, "though I had four bullets through my coat and two horses shot under me." The early deaths and wounds of Braddock's other aides had left him

> the only person then left to distribute the General's orders, which I was scarcely able to do. I was not half recovered from a violent illness that had confined me to my bed and a wagon for above ten days. I am still in a weak and a feeble condition

which induces me to halt here two or three days in hopes of [gaining] a little strength to enable me to proceed homewards.[1]

He would not have time to stop off at Ferry Farm, he wrote. He must get home to Mount Vernon and bring in the harvest. Once again as in the aftermath of Fort Necessity, he was anxious about money. So much of what he had owned—his horses, papers, clothing, weapons—had, along with his prospects of a military career, been left behind in ruins at the Monongahela.

George Washington was surprised by his own popularity. He had every reason to be disenchanted when he rode home to Mount Vernon in the late summer of 1755. He believed he was a failure. His two years of hardship and defeat on the frontier seemed to have yielded nothing. With Braddock dead and the remnants of the British army retreating toward Philadelphia, his service as a volunteer had come to an abrupt end. Braddock's promise to secure a royal commission as a regular had died with him. His health was damaged. He had neglected his farms. As he wrote to his half-brother Augustine, he had "suffered much in my private fortune besides impairing one of the best of constitutions." After five weeks, he still had not recovered. But there was little time for bitterness. No sooner did he arrive at Mount Vernon than he discovered, to his immense surprise, that his valor as Braddock's aide had made him the only hero of the Fort Duquesne debacle. People must have their heroes as well as their scapegoats. Braddock was being blamed for everything; Dinwiddie and the other lying royal governors and corrupt contractors for nothing. Washington was the talk of Williamsburg. He was credited with stout resistance and bravery under fire. His bad advice on battle strategy was a secret that had died with Braddock. Even the British officers were commending him publicly.

A harbinger of this reversal of fortune awaited him at Mount Vernon. He instantly recognized the handwriting of Sally Fairfax on an envelope and tore it open. Sally was overjoyed at his return. If he was up to it, could he come over to Belvoir the next day? Was he up to it! The next afternoon, ignoring his debilitated condition and enlisting the help of his faithful manservant Thomas Bishop, Washington bought some watermelons and rode as fast as he could over to Belvoir.

One week later, after daily exchanges of visits by Sally and her friends, Washington began to write letters about the disaster in the Ohio Valley. He was prodded into action by messages from visitors to Williamsburg who reported that Virginia's legislative leaders wanted him to serve once more to defend the colony's exposed 350-mile frontier. Only privately in a letter to Augustine from Mount Vernon on August 2 did he express in writing his personal anger and frustration at what he considered his ill-usage by the governor:

> I was employed to go a journey in the winter (when I believe few or none would have undertaken it) and what did I get by it? My expenses borne! I then was appointed with trifling pay to conduct a handful of men to the Ohio. What did I get by this? Why, after putting myself to considerable expense in equipment and providing necessaries for the campaign—I went out, was soundly beaten, lost them all—came in, had my commission taken from me or, in other words, my commission reduced under *pretense* of an order from home [England]. I then went out a volunteer with General Braddock and lost all my horses and many other things. I have been upon the losing order ever since I entered the service.

Augustine had wanted to come see him. Washington rebuked him for considering leaving his seat in the House of Burgesses to make the journey. And "I am not able, were I ever so willing, to meet you in town." He bluntly reported the "shameful defeat" on the Monongahela. "It is easily told. We lost all that we carried out." All twenty-one pieces of artillery had either been captured, or destroyed "to expedite flight." Obviously Augustine's politically well-connected friends had asked him to sound out George's willingness to accept a new command and lead a fresh expedition into the Ohio country. Without artillery and supply bases, "I think it is impossible," George answered bluntly. Nothing could dislodge the French short of starvation.[2]

The flight of the remnants of the British army from Fort Cumberland, in western Maryland, all the way across Pennsylvania to Philadelphia left the Allegheny Mountains frontier, including all the back settlements of Virginia, Maryland, and Pennsylvania, exposed to ever more frequent Indian raids. By autumn 1755 the attacks by unusually large bands of up to 150 Shawnees left seventy settlers dead in Virginia alone. In Pennsylvania, Shawnee and Delaware Indians struck within one hundred miles of Philadelphia by October, within fifty miles by November. As soon as the last of Braddock's forces withdrew from Fort Cumberland, the 256 Virginia troops left behind began to desert, sometimes as many as a dozen a day, to protect their families. Virginia lay defenseless. There was no coherent militia system to fall back on after Governor Dinwiddie had set up and then dissolved the Virginia Regiment in favor of his latest unrealized scheme of independent companies. Even if there were willing and able militiamen, there were no guns left in the magazine at Williamsburg. He'd sent them all off to the north to aid other British offensives.

An outcry of public opinion made it clear to Governor Dinwiddie that as much as he disliked the idea, he had to recall Washington to reorganize the original Virginia Regiment. Dinwiddie considered Washington both an opportunist and an ingrate. He believed he had been a generous patron, yet the young man was always caviling and whining and making absurd demands. But Dinwiddie was an astute politician. Once he accepted the fact that Braddock's army was defeated and found another assault on Fort Duquesne, he wasted little time in trying to mend fences with Washington, but only after making another alarming discovery. Calling up militia companies in the Shenandoah Valley, he learned that most would-be recruits had already abandoned their homes and fled eastward with their families.

When the General Assembly convened in emergency session on August 5, it was obvious to the burgesses that the Virginia Regiment not only must be resuscitated but must be given plenty of money and weapons and a respected leader, one who would accept sole responsibility for stopping the headlong flight of settlers. Only one name cropped up. Washington's brother Augustine urged him to ride to Williamsburg to advance his candidacy, but George believed he was still too ill. While he recuperated at Mount Vernon, his cousin, Burgess Warner Lewis, kept him posted. At first, he seemed not at all interested. He had lost too much in the past two years. And he was sure he would not be offered the new command on terms he would accept. As the Indian attacks worsened, the Shenandoah Valley emptied out. The Blue Ridge effectively became the western border of Virginia. Washington felt compelled to reconsider. If for no more patriotic reason, he had land and farms in the west that could fall into French hands.

At this moment Warner Lewis wrote him that the assembly had voted a generous £40,000 for defense and wanted to raise the largest army in Virginia's 150-year history. Some 4,000 Virginia troops were to mount a fresh expedition to oust the French. Everyone in Williamsburg wanted Washington to take "command of the men now to be raised." Yet Washington felt he was still too weak to make a 150-mile-long ride. He kept Lewis's servant waiting overnight while he wrote Lewis a crucial letter.

He'd had plenty of time to ponder what "ignorance and inexperience made me overlook before." From this trusted kinsman he did not conceal his pride. If he turned down a new command, "I should lose what at present constitutes the chief part of my happiness, i.e., the esteem and notice the country has been pleased to honor me with." He hesitated to volunteer for fear of appearing presumptuous. "If the command should be offered," he would feel free to suggest what "my reason and my small experience have pointed out." He left no doubt that he was willing to accept a new command if the terms suited him.

After the courier left, Washington summoned his courage to write to his mother. He resented her latest intrusion but was less than candid with her. His letter to his cousin made it clear that he would lead a new expedition to the west in a minute. Yet to his mother he wrote: "Honored Madam, If it is in my power to avoid going to the Ohio again, I shall." But

> if the command is pressed upon me by the general voice of the country and offered on such terms as cannot be objected against, it would reflect eternal dishonor on me to refuse it and that, I am sure, must, or ought, to give you greater cause of uneasiness than my going in an honorable command.[3]

She would not like it if he accepted; she would not like it if he didn't. Washington had heard his mother object to his military aspirations since he was fourteen and he did not now begin to consider her point of view. Could she not simply want to save her son from being killed like so many other mothers' sons on the frontier in recent years? Equally sadly, Mary Ball Washington seemed utterly unable to take pride in his honors, so hard-won and so important to him. Protesting every step of his attempt to create a military career for himself, she probably only succeeded in pushing him toward one.

Ironically, it was at this moment that Washington heard from his mother's brother Joseph, the uncle who had advised her to prevent George from pursuing a military career. In its August number, the *Gentleman's Magazine* of London had reported that, while Braddock's regulars "fled with the utmost terror and precipitation," the Virginians who formed the rear guard "still stood unbroken and continued the engagement on very unequal terms near three hours." After a silence of thirteen years, his uncle saluted George as "Good cousin" and asked his nephew "to give me a short account how you proceed. As I am your mother's brother, I hope you can't deny my request." George could not help feeling a touch of pride when he read that "it is a sensible pleasure to me to hear that you have behaved yourself with such a martial spirit in all your engagements with the French nigh Ohio. Go on as you have begun, and God prosper you." People can change their minds and admit they have been wrong. Washington saved the letter. These were probably the first words of praise he had ever read from a family member.[4]

W ashington arrived in Williamsburg on August 27, 1755, to find that the General Assembly had voted him £300 compensation—a handsome sum roughly equivalent to $12,000 today—for personal property he had lost on the march with Braddock. He also learned that the Assembly had whittled down its 4,000-man army to a total authorization of only 1,200 troops, including the three already funded 50-man companies of rangers supposedly protecting the entire Shenandoah Valley and the 50-man Virginia company at Fort Cumberland. That left only a reconstituted 1,000-man Virginia Regiment, which was to be made up of volunteers or, if recruiting fell short, by drafting unmarried militiamen. The new militia law left intact a provision that a draftee could avoid conscription by paying a £10 fee, something many Virginians could afford. Dinwiddie had already appointed most of the sixteen new captains by the time Washington arrived. In Washington's private letter spelling out his demands to Warner Lewis, his number-one stipulation had been that the governor consult him on appointments: "having the officers in some measure appointed with *my* advice and with my concurrence." Washington had given the governor too much time to organize the new military units before he arrived. As Washington feared, some of Dinwiddie's choices were dreadful. He later called Peter Hog, commissioned captain at half-finished Fort Dinwiddie, "the most unfit person in the world to raise and command a company of rangers." Eventually, Washington dismissed him. Dinwiddie's latest brainstorm was to appoint rangers to patrol the frontier. He had wasted fully half the commissions on amateurs who claimed they knew all about rangers. By the time the governor formally offered the command, Washington felt his hands were already tied. Unless Dinwiddie met his other demands, he would reject the appointment. It was the first time Washington publicly displayed his ability to put everything in which he believed unflinchingly on the line.[5]

For five tense days Washington and Dinwiddie negotiated so acrimoniously that the bargaining had to be carried on through go-betweens. Dinwiddie was not to be refused. He enlisted a large part of the Assembly to bring influence to bear individually on young Washington. Burgesses took Washington off to this tavern or that. He had never been so flattered, but he would not budge. In the end, rather than lose Washington Dinwiddie gave in on nearly everything he wanted, and Washington, rather than lose the command, compromised, something new for him. He accepted all he could get, which happened to be just about all of his demands. He not only would have the rank of colonel and full command of the Virginia Regiment or any other troops raised in Virginia but he could appoint his lieutenant colonel and major, a telling point for Washington. He wanted to avoid any more challenges over his rank. He commissioned two veterans he trusted as his key subordinates: Adam Stephen, his second in command at Fort Necessity, and Andrew Lewis, Washington's cousin. He could appoint his own aide-de-camp, secretary, adjutant, commissary, quartermaster, "and such other inferior officers as you shall find necessary." He also would receive a military war chest to "use as you see the nature and good of the service requires." He could design a regimental uniform. He came up with a blue coat trimmed in scarlet and silver with a red waistband and silver-edged tricornered hat. His financial worries seemed to be over. He was to receive 30 shillings a day pay (about £500 a year or some $50,000 a year today) plus generous expenses that included £100 (about $10,000) for his table and an allowance for batmen. He was to act as regimental commissary officer and paymaster and receive a 2 percent commission on all the money he handled. Washington had studied an officer's prerogatives in Braddock's camp and now he drove a hard bargain with the Scottish governor. He realized how important an expense account and perquisites were to his prestige as well as to his financial well-being. In September 1755, at age twenty-three, Washington became commander in chief of the tiny Virginia army he had designed himself. It is hard to imagine how he could have struck a more successful deal in his first bargaining session with politicians.[6]

Washington's shrewd decision to serve Braddock without pay had paid handsome dividends. In the public view, he had metamorphosed from soldier of fortune, a man on the make, to public-spirited defender of his home country. His transition to professional soldier complete, Washington plunged eagerly into his new duties. He applied the principles of total personal control he had learned as a young planter and owner of a surveying business to micromanaging his little army—which happened to be the largest permanent military establishment in the British-American colonies. He set up supply and recruitment bases at Winchester, Fredericksburg, and Alexandria; he issued orders to recruiting officers to come meet him in Williamsburg. Instinctively, he tackled his worst problem first. Only 256 men volunteered during that autumn of conflagration on the frontier. Of these, many were vagrants and ex-convicts deported from England and northern Ireland. In Fredericksburg, they mutinied and had to be locked in the county jail to prevent their desertion en masse. This produced a riot. The prisoners' friends broke into the jail and freed the reluctant warriors. Washington reacted swiftly. He transferred his cousin, Captain Lewis, to Fredericksburg and ordered him to impose strict military discipline. Washington had no notion of nepotism. He often chose family members to serve under him because he trusted them more than strangers. Soon, Lewis had the recalcitrants broken up into platoons and shooting at targets.

Washington had studied discipline closely under Braddock. He had borrowed a copy of Humphrey Bland's *Treatise of Military Discipline* from one of Braddock's officers. He now required his officers to follow "the book." Beginning a tour of inspection at Alexandria in mid-September, he rode to Winchester, his intended headquarters. He stopped only long enough to order an accounting of supplies left behind by the British and to issue strict orders to his officers about how to deal with drunkenness and desertions. By October 17, riding fast, he reached Fort Cumberland at Wills Creek, Maryland. This sprawling, poorly placed wooden fort was still incomplete. It lay exposed to easy enemy fire and was garrisoned by fewer than fifty survivors of his old Virginia Regiment plus a Maryland contingent of about 130 men. There were almost daily desertions. He found discipline so lax that one private was openly peddling liquor to the hard-drinking soldiers around him.

Ordering his commanding officer's commission read aloud to the assembled troops at Fort Cumberland, he summoned all the officers to a five o'clock briefing. Denouncing the fort's "disorderly and riotous assembly," he announced a new command structure and put Adam Stephen in command. He read aloud the orders he had just written. The officers were to complete the stockade, construct a below-ground powder magazine, and "have the barracks well cleaned and sweetened as soon as the hospital is removed." Officers and soldiers "are to be regularly and constantly exercised twice a day." Officers were to order, pay for, and wear the new blue Virginia uniform. They were to treat any Indians who joined them "in the most familiar manner." He overlooked nothing. When coopers arrived to make barrels for the gunpowder he was going to distribute to the other frontier forts, they were told to "make their casks so small that a horse may carry two of them." There would be none of Braddock's slow-moving wagon trains. Gunsmiths were to be put to work "repairing the arms"; the fort's carpenters were "to make ram-rods for them." The officers were to assemble the troops and read out the roll three times a day to discourage desertion, and they were to hunt down any would-be deserters for trial. They were to deal sternly with drunkenness, swearing, and obscene language. They must shut down liquor trafficking. In short, they were to crack down on infractions of all kinds. Washington revealed himself to be a stickler for discipline who had seen what the lack of it could do at the Monongahela. He also devised a daily camp routine:

> The Guard is to be regularly relieved every morning at ten o'clock. The drummer must observe the beat. At the appointed times, the following beats [will be]: revelé [sic] at daybreak; troop, at ten o'clock, retreat, at sunset; and tattoo at nine o'clock at night. An officer is to see that the above orders are duly executed. The tour of duty [is] to begin with the eldest captain and to continue through the rest of the officers according to seniority. The Officer of the Day is to make a report of the Guard as soon as he is relieved.

Washington was determined to eliminate corrupt military practices. He was aware that some officers were lining their purses at the expense of their men. Officers were no longer allowed to require their men to buy supplies or clothing from them and then to debit their pay: "They are for the future to receive their pay without deduction." Washington, surprised at the greed of officers and civilians who tried to profit from the common danger, understood the reluctance of civilians to enlist. He instructed his officers to supervise the work of the gunsmiths and keep them on the job. After the meeting he fired off written orders to distant outposts. He warned Captain Hog at Fort Dinwiddie to be "very circumspect" about the physician at Fort Dinwiddie. "See that he has no more opportunities than what are absolutely necessary to enhance a bill."[7]

After shaping up Fort Cumberland, Washington dashed off to the southern end of the Shenandoah Valley, where there were rich new farms and badly needed cattle. Riding west over the Allegheny Mountains, he found nearly all the farms deserted. After five days in the saddle he reached Fort Dinwiddie, a wretched stockade still unfinished because its garrison was constantly responding to Indian attacks. He read aloud written orders to Captain Hog "to add bastions to and build barracks in the fort and to fell all the woods within musket shot." Washington feared another disaster, like the recent attack on a stockade twenty miles farther west where sixty settlers had taken refuge. Indians had killed twenty-five of them before they were frightened off by reinforcements. The Shawnees had burned eleven houses and led off some five hundred horses and cattle and two young girls. Washington urged vigilance. Patrols were to range woods at least twice every day. Before riding off he issued contracts to ship 620 beef cattle up the Shenandoah to Fort Cumberland by November first, for salt to pickle the beef, and for hired coopers to make the barrels to ship it.

Washington fired off orders for supplies in all directions, advancing the money the governor had given him. Virginians could supply suits, stockings, shirts, and hats but a contractor had to go to Philadelphia to buy shoes, white yarn stockings, kettles, tomahawks, cartridge paper, blankets, and tents. Washington ordered rum from the West Indies. He expected no man to fight without his daily rum. He ordered strict accountings, then parceled out the supplies left behind by the British. When enlistment lagged, he sent recruiters to Maryland and Pennsylvania. One of the ranger captains he commissioned was his old friend Christopher Gist, who promptly reported that "your name is more talked of in Pennsylvania than any other person of the army. Everybody seems willing to venture under your command. If you could send some discreet person [I] doubt not but they will enlist . . . especially to be irregulars. . . . All their talk is of fighting in the Indian way." Gist passed along a message from Benjamin Franklin, chairman of the Pennsylvania Assembly's defense committee: "If you was to write [a] pressing letter to them informing them of the damage and murders and desire their assistance you would now get it sooner than anyone in America."[8]

So much of what Colonel Washington did during these harried months he had learned from recent bitter experiences. Not yet twenty-four years old, he had devoted his mind and talents for more than three years to the military, much of it on a frontier largely at war. Probably no Virginian had more military knowledge or experience. He had seen combat three times and had actively studied tactics, artillery, fortifications, logistics, discipline—all the military skills of his time. His mastery showed up in each day's orders. In September, he instructed his captains to cut firewood so it would be cured by winter. Buy horses, wagons, flour, and feed for the horses from farmers if you can; if not, commandeer them. Sometimes he joined in the unpleasant near-raids on settlements. Many farmers had not yet been reimbursed for requisitions of their draught animals by Braddock's quartermasters. One uncooperative farmer threatened to "blow out my brains," Washington reported, adding that he drew his sword to persuade the crowd of his seriousness. As if heedless of the danger, he rode off with an aged horse in tow.[9]

Working hard at the virtually impossible, Washington was trying to defend Virginia's vast borderlands with only a few hundred men, a feat that meant answering constant alarms. He was heading home for a brief visit on October 7 when an express rider brought an urgent message from Adam Stephen at Winchester. Communications with Fort Cumberland had been cut off. Indians were raiding deep into the Shenandoah Valley:

> They go about and commit their outrages at all hours of the day. Nothing is to be seen and heard but desolation and murder and unheard of instances of cruelty. The smoke of the burning plantations darken the day and hide the neighboring mountains from our sight.[10]

Washington rode pell-mell across northern Virginia to Winchester with thirty recruits. He found the town packed with refugees, many with their livestock and wagons bulging with all they could drag away. That night, an express rider alarmed the town: the Indians were only twelve miles away! Another rider arrived the next morning: the Indians were only *four* miles away! He had heard their yells and heard gunfire himself. Washington rounded up forty horsemen and rode out to scour the woods. He soon heard yelling and shooting. He ordered his men to spread out and move in. He found three drunken Virginia troopers hallooing and firing off their guns. The "Indians" from the day before turned out to be two slaves trying to round up stray cattle.

The Indian raiders had gone home, dissuaded by Washington's quick action. To Dinwiddie, he reported that reinforcements had difficulty crossing the Blue Ridge "for the crowds of people who were flying as if every minute was death." Washington sent express riders to tell the settlers to return to their homes, keep the roads free for his reinforcements. He ordered a formal warning read in every town throughout the region:

> Whereas diverse timorous persons run through the country and alarm its inhabitants by false reports of the Indians having attacked and destroyed the country, even Winchester itself. This is to give notice to all people that I have great reason to believe that the Indians who committed the late cruelties are returned home. I do advise all my countrymen not to be alarmed on

every false report they hear, keep to their homes and take care of their crops. In a short time the frontiers will be so well guarded that no mischief can be done.

Washington managed to stem the panic. He then siphoned off the thirty recruits to march northward to reinforce Fort Cumberland.[11]

On their three-day march, Washington and his men passed deserted houses, barns filled with oats and grain abandoned, horses and cattle wandering around. Yet the settlers had not imagined the Indian attack. A Shawnee war party of 150 repeatedly raided the region from its base at Fort Duquesne. Near Patterson's Creek, Washington passed a homestead where the farmer had been killed, the farmhouse burned, the cornfield destroyed. Within gunshot of Fort Cumberland, Washington saw the unburied bodies of a scalped woman, a little boy, and a young man. Soldiers he sent to harvest corn found more scalped, half-burned bodies. As soon as he reached the fort, he began to send out patrols to prevail on the farmers to harvest their corn crop. Six weeks after he had become Virginia commander, Washington was still riding from wilderness county to wilderness county in southwestern Virginia. At least once he narrowly escaped an Indian ambush. As he rode toward Fort Dinwiddie on a narrow horse trail in dense woods, he galloped past the spot where several Shawnees had prepared an ambush. The Indians had gone off to relieve themselves just before Washington rode by. They killed the next soldier who came down the path.

*C*olonel Washington soon realized that his chances of stopping Indian raids altogether were slim. At first, Governor Dinwiddie was sympathetic. "I cannot expect you can do much this fall," Dinwiddie wrote to Washington, "but to keep the (provincial troops) together, to have them taught their exercises, and to teach them as much as possible bush fighting." Without the support of Indians to fight at their sides, Virginians must fight like Indians. The defeat of Braddock made a reevaluation of military tactics imperative. Americans were gradually developing a new style of warfare that blended Indian and colonial tactics with textbook British methods. One British observer had foreseen the failure of Braddock's orthodox tactics against Indians: "They [redcoats] are only of use to defend a fort or to support *Indian* forces against regular troops." Another critic argued that "regular troops, in this wilderness country, are just the same [as] irregular ones would be in Flanders. American irregulars would easily be confounded by regular troops in the open fields of Europe and regular troops would be as easily reduced to the like confusion by American irregulars in the woods here."[12]

Benjamin Franklin supported Washington's advocacy of a revolution in American military tactics. Militia was useless, he argued. As Washington went to the relief of Virginia and Maryland frontier families, Franklin organized militia and lobbied for tax money to build a line of forts, within a day's march of one another along the Pennsylvania frontier, to act as bases for special ranger forces. But Franklin denounced sole reliance on militia: "The manual exercise and evolutions taught [to] a militia are known by experience to be of little or no use in the woods." The news that flashed through the settlements of Virginia at Braddock's defeat—"The British are beaten! The British are beaten!"—carried with it a note of excitement along with horror. The British army *could* be beaten unless it drastically changed its habits.[13]

But no one was addressing one problem. Washington ran smack into his old bugbear again that fall: any royal-commissioned officer still outranked any colonial officer. To Washington, no coherent reform of the militia to meet a new kind of threat from the French could be achieved until American colonial officers were given equal footing with British officers. That English subjects lost their equal status as free Englishmen as soon as they settled in America outraged them. When he arrived at Fort Cumberland, he encountered Captain John Dagworthy, who commanded Maryland militia there. Dagworthy had once held a royal commission to lead Maryland troops in Braddock's army and refused to take orders from any colonial. Nor would Colonel Washington take orders from a captain. So angry was Washington that he left his troops at the fort and rode all the way to Williamsburg, some 200 miles. There, he demanded to see Governor Dinwiddie and then John Robinson, Speaker of the House of Burgesses. The governor agreed to write to Massachusetts governor William Shirley, who had been acting as commander in chief of British troops in North America since Braddock's death. Dinwiddie agreed with Washington that Captain Dagworthy could outrank Colonel Washington only if the king had specifically ordered Dagworthy to Fort Cumberland. Dinwiddie also asked Governor Shirley to issue Washington a new brevet (temporary) commission in the British army.

Washington agreed to return to his duties while he awaited a ruling. He received no answer for months. Finally, he learned that Governor Shirley had passed the buck to Governor Sharpe of Maryland, who controlled Maryland militia and posts. Washington may have been surprised to know that Governor Sharpe had ruled that Captain Dagworthy could not give orders to Virginia troops and that Dagworthy concealed his new orders and continued to command the garrison at Fort Cumberland. Washington was not alone in his frustration: his officers threatened to resign en masse unless they received royal commissions. As winter approached, Washington got Dinwiddie's permission to leave his troops and ride north to Massachusetts to appeal personally to Governor Shirley.

Wearing his brand-new blue uniform, Colonel Washington left Virginia in February 1756, accompanied by his aide, Captain George Mercer, and two slaves. It was the second time Washington had made a thousand-mile winter trek. This time there was a growing number of critics who insisted the mission was personal and that his place was at the front with his men.

No doubt he had to resolve the rank-of-command problem, but couldn't he write a letter? Wasn't it hard to justify leaving the panicky frontier in such danger for two full months? Instead, he decided to storm the citadel where he believed British power over America resided. He had a pretext to pay a call on Governor Shirley. Shirley's son had befriended him on Braddock's expedition and Washington wanted to tell him in person how valiantly his son had died. Washington had also met Shirley once at the governor's conference in Alexandria. Washington considered the risk of attack somewhat diminished in winter and he was no longer willing to tolerate such a challenge to his authority. And here was a chance to make a personal pitch for a British officer's permanent commission, something he had wanted for so many years.

Riding through deepening snow in eastern Maryland and Pennsylvania, Washington stopped off in Philadelphia to introduce himself to the proprietary governor, Robert Hunter Morris, whose son, Braddock's secretary, had been so kind to him. Morris briefed him on the state of Pennsylvania's defenses. For seventy-five years, Pennsylvania had been ruled by pacifist Quakers who did not believe in war. Their dealings with Indians had at first been exemplary, making the colony a haven against Indian attack. In all the Indian wars between the English and the French in the past century, there had never been any killing in the Penns' colony. But sharp land dealings in recent years had forced most of the native Shawnees and Delawares off their lands and driven them west to the Ohio Valley, where they now fought beside the French. Vengeful Shawnees had carried out raids as far east as Allentown and Easton, within fifty miles from Philadelphia, and were threatening the defenseless Quaker City itself. When Washington arrived, an extralegal militia led by Benjamin Franklin and his son, Captain William Franklin, was fortifying frontier towns and building a chain of forts in Northampton County. Washington was anxious to learn all about Franklin's bold actions. He was coming to believe, like Franklin, that the underlying problem of defending against the French and Indians was the method of settlement. Newly arrived immigrants in search of cheap land scattered as far as they could from existing settlements. They assured their isolation by staking out as much land as they possibly could. This fact alone made them easy prey for Indian raiding parties.

Wherever he went that winter, Washington discovered that he was known as the hero of the Monongahela campaign. Washington's visit in uniform gave Governor Morris the idea of a well-qualified candidate for commander in chief of Pennsylvania militia. Washington seems to have encouraged the idea. If he could not win the support he needed for the defense of Virginia he might be willing to become Pennsylvania's commander in chief. Gossip quickly circulated that Washington had met with Morris to discuss plans for a joint Virginia-Pennsylvania assault on Fort Duquesne that Washington would lead.

Washington did not spend all his time politicking. He went shopping. His service with dapper young British officers had whetted his taste for fine clothes. His visit to the Quaker City stretched out to five days as tailors fitted and finished new suits for him and handed him the bill for a hefty £60. Packing up his purchases against the mud and slush of the road, Washington crossed the Delaware River for the first time and hurried along the Post Road through Burlington and Allentown to Perth Amboy and sailed to New York City. He stayed with native Virginian Beverly Robinson, the brother of John Robinson, Speaker of the House of Burgesses. Robinson had married Susannah Philipse, heiress of a vast Hudson Valley manor. Washington's visit with Robinson revealed his ever-closer ties with Speaker Robinson, the mortal political enemy of Governor Dinwiddie, who grasped its significance as soon as he learned of it.

The pleasure of arriving in New York City for the first time at the peak of its winter social season multiplied when Mrs. Robinson introduced the tall, elegant young Virginian to her younger and still unmarried sister. He felt he had to pay a courtesy call on the ladies of New York society. Mary Eliza Philipse, known as Polly, was rich. A wide mouth and dimples only emphasized her large nose. But Polly Philipse exuded self-confidence; she possessed a stubborn drive to dominate everyone around her that made her resemble Washington's mother. Yet even if she owned 50,000 acres of valuable New York real estate, she was not exactly the woman George Washington had in mind. After the obligatory bows and curtsies, Washington escorted her to a popular exhibit at the News Exchange, a museum of sorts, called "The Microcosm or World in Miniature." He nodded appreciatively when he saw a mechanical tableau of Orpheus playing his lyre and then nine muses playing their instruments and windup birds that flew around and sang in a simulated grove. More interesting to him were models of a gunpowder mill and ships sailing across waves. George liked the exhibit well enough to take the ladies back a second time.

He left Polly Philipse behind when he visited several taverns and men's clubs. He shopped for shoes, played cards and lost. He hired a horse trader to find him three good horses and gave his friend George Mercer the best horse. This heavy £75 outlay took most of his remaining cash. He so much overspent his budget he had to borrow £100—his adjutant's salary for a year—from Beverley Robinson to get him home. His purse refilled, he pushed off for New England on February 20, 1756. In New London, Connecticut, he visited Joseph Chew, an old friend of his parents. He sailed on to Newport, Rhode Island, where he visited another old Virginia friend, Godfrey Malbone. As winter weather worsened, he sailed on a British man-of-war to Boston. The *Boston Gazette* announced his arrival, introducing to its readers "the Hon. Col. Washington, a gentleman who has deservedly a high reputation for military skill and valor though success has not always attended his undertakings." Unofficially, there was gossip he was meeting Governor Shirley to discuss a strategy for dealing with the southern Indians. He had to wait to be received by Shirley. He played cards at the governor's house—and lost again. By now, he was counting his change.[14]

Finally summoned to pass through the iron gates of Province House at the head of Milk Street, he rode past rows of bare trees, then climbed the twenty red sandstone steps that led to the imposing three-story brick building. In his elegant new uniform, Washington bowed deeply to Governor Shirley, the royal official he had found so kind when he had met him at Alexandria. He presented Shirley with the petition he and his officers had signed asking to be put on the royal military establishment and a copy of Dinwiddie's letter about Dagworthy. Shirley was surprised. Hadn't he already asked Governor Sharpe to deal with the matter? Washington was stunned to learn that Dagworthy had already been told he was not in command at Fort Cumberland. The governor said he would need some time to consider Washington's requests. An aide then ushered Washington out.

On March 5, 1756, Governor Shirley called him back to Province House. He could not issue royal commissions. He had just learned from London that he was to turn over his duties as head of all British troops in America to Governor Sharpe of Maryland. Furthermore, he lacked the power to grant Washington even a brevet regular army commission. That had to come from London. He handed Washington a document that forbade Dagworthy to attempt to give orders to Virginia troops. If he stayed at Fort Cumberland or went anywhere in Virginia, Dagworthy was to follow Washington's orders. There was nothing else Shirley could do for him, so Washington left Boston immediately. He overtook Benjamin and William Franklin on the road and they exchanged ideas about breaking the stalemate with the French. He reached Williamsburg exactly sixty days after he had left Mount Vernon.[15]

*T*he carnage on the frontier resumed with springtime. Washington's little army, no matter what he did, was largely ineffectual. He wrote bluntly about his helplessness in his April 7, 1756, report to Governor Dinwiddie:

> The enemy have returned in greater numbers, committed several murders not far from Winchester and even are so daring as to attack our forts in open day. Five hundred Indians have it more in their power to annoy the inhabitants than ten times their number of Regulars. For, besides the advantage they have of fighting in the woods, their cunning and craft are not to be equaled neither [are] their activity and indefatigable sufferings. They prowl about like wolves and, like them, do their mischief by stealth. They depend upon their dexterity in hunting and upon the cattle of the inhabitants for provisions.[16]

As the war continued to expand, Washington urged that the settlers be compelled to live in towns, driving their cattle into "the thick settled parts" and "working at each others' farms by turn." They could only be protected by soldiers drawn not from the dregs of English society, but from the American mainstream: "As I apprehend you will be obliged to draft men, I hope care will be taken that none are chosen but active, resolute men—men who are practiced to arms and are marksmen." Washington began to beat his drum for a professional soldiery in America to replace the militia, which he considered an undisciplined mob of one-afternoon-a-week warriors who did as little as they could but drink and desert and were utterly unreliable under attack. "Such men as are drafted should be taken only for a time," he argued. "We shall get better men [who] will in all probability stay with us." In a letter to Speaker of the House Robinson he was more specific: "They should only serve eighteen or twenty months and then be discharged. Twenty months will produce two full campaigns." His letter to Dinwiddie, he knew, would go to the executive council; that to Dinwiddie's rival, Robinson, to the Assembly. He was learning that a military commander must besiege politicians as well as fight and he was becoming fearless in his paper battles with the royal governor, knowing he had growing support in the House of Burgesses. To Dinwiddie's consternation, he carried his campaign personally to Williamsburg. Back at Winchester, he wrote Pennsylvania governor Morris, "Our Assembly have voted £20,000 more and [our] forces will be increased to 2,000 men."[17]

Washington had convinced the Assembly that, at the bare minimum, he needed two full regiments and a string of forts within easy reach of settlers. After visiting Pennsylvania and talking with the Franklins, he submitted a comprehensive defensive plan to Governor Dinwiddie that called for construction of twenty-two forts on a line from Fort Cumberland along Patterson Creek then down the south branch of the Potomac to its headwaters and following the tributaries of the James to the Roanoke River and then its tributaries to the North Carolina border. The forts were to be from ten to thirty miles apart. Their garrisons were to be made up of a core of trained members of Washington's Virginia Regiment augmented by militia garrisons of twenty to five hundred men. The largest fort was to be built at Winchester and would be strong enough to serve as the depot for all the frontier forts and be the natural place of refuge for all the settlers of the lower Shenandoah Valley. Washington and his troops built it during the summer of 1756. Washington used some of his own money for the effort.

The work on four of the forts began, but the governor ignored Washington's strategic plan. The ranks of his regiment remained a thin 1,000, far too few to garrison such a large number of posts. Washington believed that his only recourse was to enlist the aid of natives. Braddock had scoffed at the aid of Delawares sent him by the Six Nations, and many of them had gone over to the French. Yet Washington had come to believe that Indians "are the only match for Indians." "Without these, we shall ever fight upon unequal terms." He complained that there was no coordinated attempt by the royal governors to persuade the natives to support his efforts.[18]

Forced to work with the 1,000 men he already commanded, Washington vowed to whip them into an effective fighting force. He imposed British army discipline so far as the laws of Virginia permitted and argued for even harsher sanctions against desertion and drunkenness. He ordered brutal floggings not only for these, but for swearing, looting, and a long list of offenses. Gambling and dereliction of duty brought five hundred lashes. Washington made all his troops line up to watch the whippings, which sometimes continued until the onlookers were in tears. When desertions continued, he lobbied the Assembly for the death penalty. His letters to officials in Williamsburg brimmed over with complaints about poorly paid, inadequately fed and clad troops who had no respect for their officers and whose terms of enlistment were too short. If the government stopped wasting money, he maintained, and used it to increase soldier's pay, he could attract better soldiers. His pleas for more forts, more tools to build them, and more men to guard them began to irk the budget-minded burgesses, who were also the same planters who did not want to pay more taxes. Some of them were even willing to believe that Washington was making up atrocity stories just to get more money.

Amid his constant complaining, Washington was probably the only soldier in America who was trying to puzzle out how to build a new model army that suited frontier warfare. Since settlers were strung out over vast distances, his idea of closely placed stockades with small, highly trained garrisons of fast-moving rangers to carry out constant patrols and periodic surprise sweeps of the frontier could have at least retarded Indian attacks. He knew that nothing could end the attacks entirely until the Indian base at Fort Duquesne was destroyed once and for all, but the legislators would not spend the money to raise a large enough professional force, and the British government, which had taken over the war, gave priority to other campaigns. Washington had to be content with fighting a defensive war with a skeleton force. As his troops responded to ceaseless alarms they sustained heavy casualties. In the course of the year 1756 nearly one-third of his men were killed or wounded.

The mounting casualty toll and the absence of a single demonstrable success left some Virginians looking for a scapegoat. They turned on Washington. His mentor, Colonel Fairfax, had warned him to tone down his constant grousing. Shortly after Washington submitted his fort-building plan to the governor and his council, Fairfax reported "some jealousies" among the councillors over Washington's appointment of an aide-de-camp and secretary, and among burgesses there were rumblings of an investigation of Washington's recruiting practices and his cashiering of men "at pleasure." The *Virginia Gazette* ran a long letter essay signed "Virginia Centinel," which attacked Washington without mentioning his name. Its author accused him of abusing his men and claimed his officers were engaging in "all manner of debauchery, vice and idleness" while frontiersmen suffered and died. Washington was unfit for command. More attacks soon found print. Washington was away from the front too much. He lived in high style in a fine headquarters in Winchester while settlers starved and their cabins burned. It did not help that there was some small grain of truth in each charge. In addition to his long sojourn to the north Washington rode to Williamsburg to politick for his army and took side trips to Mount Vernon, Belvoir, and his farm at Bullskin Creek. He had not yet learned to live without interruption with his troops and to suffer conspicuously with them.[19]

Stung, Washington wrote a rebuttal to "Centinel" and sent it to his brother Augustine for advice. Should he print it? Augustine did him a big favor and destroyed it. But no one could dissuade George Washington from once again threatening to resign—this was his sixth threat—but then once again he reconsidered, unaware that each time he rendered it the threat was more meaningless. His officers could quit, however. When Washington went undefended in the pages of the *Gazette*, all sixteen company commanders signed a pledge to resign unless Governor Dinwiddie published a public defense of his commander in chief. Their threat compromised Washington, who would be forced to resign if they did. He promised them he would ride into Williamsburg and negotiate their demands with Dinwiddie. In time, fresh Indian raids distracted the captains and he did not have to make good his promise, but he decided to confront Dinwiddie anyway. He stopped off at Belvoir, where Sally Fairfax gave him several shirts she'd had made for him, and then he followed the groove he had worn to the governor's palace.

There, even before he could see the governor, he received quite a shock. Dinwiddie, he was told, believed "Centinel's" censures were true. He ordered Washington to go back to the front at once. He was to move his headquarters from the comforts of Winchester to Fort Cumberland Gap, which Dinwiddie correctly believed sat astride the main Indian invasion route into Virginia. Washington was to take 100 of the 160-man Winchester garrison to Fort Cumberland, and he was to stay there. Furious, Washington did not try to see the governor. He rode straight back to Winchester. For once, he did not threaten to resign, even if he was never more justified. He, the commanding officer of Virginia's only armed force, believed that he must obey the orders of the civilian governor.

Back at Winchester, he got himself under control and wrote the governor. His tone seemed polite; his style self-criticizing. He began with an apology. Dinwiddie must have been momentarily disarmed as he read:

If my open and disinterested way of writing and speaking has the *air* of pertness and freedom, I shall redress my error by acting reservedly and shall take care to obey my orders without offering it more.

But then Washington became sarcastic: "So, to comply with my order (which I shall do literally if I can) not a man will be left [at Winchester] to secure the works or defend the King's stores, which are almost wholly removed to that place."[20]

Washington no doubt knew what the governor did not: the enlistments of the sixty men left at Winchester expired in two weeks. If he followed the governor's order, no one would be left to defend the largest town in the west. Washington waited a few more days at Winchester while he cooled down. He realized that he had enemies in the capital who wanted him to quit or be intemperate enough to provoke the governor, who had the backing of many influential Virginians. Without disobeying his orders, Washington listed all the shortages that made the move to Fort Cumberland impracticable. Hardly able to bridle his anger, he lashed out at critics: "I am tired of this place, the inhabitants and the life I lead here."[21]

In the end Washington won a partial victory. Dinwiddie rescinded his order to go to Fort Cumberland and Washington gained new support in Williamsburg. But Speaker Robinson urged him to "allow your ruling passion, the love of your country, to stifle your resentments." And Dinwiddie would no longer be giving Washington military orders. The British army was taking control of every detail of the war for America and the new commander in chief, Lord Loudoun, was counting on Washington's services. Loudoun needed him to hold Fort Cumberland until he himself could reinforce it.[22]

Gathering up all his belongings, including a new puppy he had just bought, Washington rode off to the Cumberland Gap, but he could not resist firing a parting shot at his cowardly unseen critics:

All my sincerest endeavors for the service of my country [are] perverted to the worst purpose. My orders are [considered] dark, doubtful and uncertain, today approved, tomorrow condemned. Left to act and proceed at hazard, accountable for the consequence and blamed without benefit of defense, I am determined to bear up under all the embarrassments some time longer.[23]

*M*iserably unhappy because he was incapable of making any successful move against the far more mobile enemy, Washington hung on. At a time when advancement in a military career usually depended on birth and patronage, he continued his untiring search for the right patron.

At no time in his life was he more abject. His original patron, Colonel Fairfax, could do nothing more for him. His next patron, Governor Dinwiddie, he now considered a spent bullet. Old and sick, Dinwiddie considered Washington a rank opportunist. When Washington reported to Dinwiddie that he had shifted his headquarters to Fort Cumberland, Dinwiddie said scornfully: "It gives me great pleasure that your going to Fort Cumberland is so agreeable to you, as without doubt it's the proper place for the commanding officer."[24]

Now Washington was about to switch allegiance again. When he learned that the new British commander in chief was John Campbell, Earl of Loudoun, he wrote His Lordship probably the most obsequious letter of his life. Washington criticized almost everyone involved in the Virginia frontier stalemate. In the recitation, only he was blameless. Soon after Loudoun arrived in America in March 1757, Washington wrote what started out as a long list of complaints Dinwiddie had ignored over the years. The missive soon descended to a new and groveling level: "Hence it [is] that I draw my hopes and fondly pronounce your Lordship our patron. Do not think, my Lord, that I am going to flatter. Notwithstanding I have exalted sentiments of your Lordship's character and respect your rank it is not my intention to adulate. My nature is open and honest and free from guile."[25]

Washington informed Lord Loudoun that just before he died General Braddock had personally promised to promote him. "Had his Excellency General Braddock survived his unfortunate defeat, I should have met with preferment."[26]

As if this letter were not enough, Washington wanted to leave his post at the Cumberland Gap on a second midwinter trip to deliver it in person. If his latest putative father figure could not come to Washington, Washington would go to him. Dinwiddie begrudgingly let him go. "I can't possibly conceive what service you can be of in going there." But since Washington was determined to go, "I now give you leave as you will be able to give him a good account of our backcountry." Washington was unaware that he could not even get an interview with Lord Loudoun unless fellow Scot Dinwiddie put in a good word for him. Off again to Philadelphia, this time at Dinwiddie's side, Washington had to cool his heels in an expensive inn for four weeks before Loudoun would see him; meanwhile, Dinwiddie briefed Loudoun thoroughly.[27]

To Washington, Lord Loudoun was a highly placed, well-educated, experienced soldier who would at last advance his military career; to Loudoun, Washington was a troublesome young provincial with little or nothing to offer. The squat, fifty-two-year-old general made short work of the lanky young Virginian. He did not let Washington speak. Instead, he peppered him with orders that sounded almost identical to Dinwiddie's. There was only one new item: move the command back to Winchester. After he briefly questioned Washington, Loudoun turned his back on him. The meeting obviously was over. An aide gestured to Washington to leave the room.

Shunned, stunned, his search for patronage and promotion at an end, Washington rushed back to Virginia. Lord Loudoun had no intention of launching another expedition against Fort Duquesne. There was nothing more he could do but his job and he would do that with a vengeance. Whenever he felt rejected—by the governor, Sally Fairfax, Governor Shirley, or Lord Loudoun—Washington rushed to the frontier, often reacting angrily. He introduced harsher discipline at his frontier outposts. He had a young ensign who had been caught cheating at cards (he concealed two cards under his thigh) cashiered for "acting inconsistently with the character of a gentleman." He used the episode as a pretext for assembling his officers and reading them a lecture on honor that is probably his most succinct utterance on the subject of an officer's duty. In his dress uniform, he pointed out that too many of them, still wearing buckskin, were remiss for not wearing the prescribed uniform: "I am determined as far as my small experience in service, my abilities and interest of the service dictate, to observe the strictest discipline through the whole economy of my behavior!"[28]

Only the unexpected arrival of southern Indians after a series of Indian conferences finally stopped the raids from the Forks of the Ohio. But after more than two years of uninterrupted warfare, by early 1757 Washington seemed unable to draw comfort from the sudden slackening of what he called the "horrid devastation." Two hammer blows in quick succession had only added to his frustration. Governor Dinwiddie had launched a bitter personal attack on him. "You know I had reason to suspect you of ingratitude, which I'm convinced your own conscience and reflection must allow," he wrote Washington. When Washington asked Dinwiddie permission to come to Williamsburg to defend himself, Dinwiddie flatly refused it. Washington had been absent from his duty too frequently. "Surely the commanding officer should not be absent when daily alarmed with the enemy's intent to invade our borders."[29]

Cooped up at backwater Fort Cumberland far from the British army's vast counterattack against the French, George Washington was wretched. When he received the news in the autumn of 1757 that his oldest friend and mentor, Colonel Fairfax, had died, Washington, unable to attend the funeral, became so depressed he became physically ill. His chronic dysentery returned, sapping his strength. Washington later described this "inveterate disorder in [my] bowels" as the worst bout since the Braddock fiasco. By November, he could no longer walk. He was also suffering from "violent pleuritic pain"—recurrent pleurisy in the drafty, smoky fort—and thought that he, like his brother Lawrence, was dying of tuberculosis. Dr. James Craik, his University of Edinburgh–trained neighbor from the Northern Neck and his closest comrade-in-arms since the days of Fort Necessity, bled Washington three times and then ordered him home for a long rest, not waiting for permission from Governor Dinwid-die. George Washington, heartily sick of the frontier war, his military career obviously going nowhere, went home at the end of 1757 to his sanctuary at Mount Vernon. It was the lowest point of his life.[30]

*E*ven at the times when it seemed to him that he had wasted nearly four years on the frontier, George Washington learned to his surprise that he had won a new kind of support from his officers and from many of the planters he had protected. Away from the frontier in December 1755, Washington had his first brush with politics. He served as an election official on behalf of his friend and neighbor George William Fairfax. On election day, he sat by the poll where Fairfax voters lined up and, as Fairfax poured them punch, Washington recorded the names of some 674 men from the Northern Neck who got to see him and shake the hand of their young military hero. It was a close race for a seat in the House of Burgesses. His friend Fairfax lost by only two votes. Tempers ran high and one account says a supporter of another losing candidate knocked Colonel Washington to the ground with a club. But Washington had had his first tantalizing taste of rough-and-tumble Virginia politics. He came away believing he could count on strong support from veterans as well as from many planters interested in speculating in the western lands he was fighting to keep out of the hands of the French.

Washington's first successful harvests at Mount Vernon also gave him a fresh reason to reconsider his military ambitions. He yearned for the life of a planter by late 1757, for the days of riding through the fields and woods and afternoons of ease, and for all the little day-to-day luxuries that contrasted so sharply with the raw confined life of a frontier fort. When his first crop came in, he went on a long-distance shopping spree. He shipped three hogsheads of tobacco (about 3,000 pounds) to a cousin in London to sell. He asked him to use some of the proceeds to buy, among other things, fine cloth and have it made up into livery for two manservants. He also ordered "one set horse furniture with livery lace and the Washington crest on the housing." He ordered silk stockings, cambric for ruffles, "three gold and scarlet sword knots" to drape from his saber, and "one fashionable gold laced hat." At this point he was still contemplating the possibility of a British officer's career. He also now ordered his own copy of Bland's *Military Discipline*. The next crop, a year of hardships and rebuffs later, was four times larger. This time, Washington bought slaves.[31]

He had obviously given up his aspirations for a military career and was laying the groundwork for a civilian career. During the summer of 1757 he entered his name as a candidate for a seat in the House of Burgesses from Frederick County. While he did not reside there, he worked a farm at Bullskin Creek. He was well known to the county's electorate. For three years he had defended their frontier farms. But many farmers were still bristling at his confiscations of livestock for Braddock's expedition, and a majority of his natural constituency, the veterans, were scattered in Virginia units from Maryland to South Carolina. Washington still might have won over enough votes, but he did not campaign and refused to provide the customary refreshments at the polls. He lost.

Nine

"THE OBJECT OF MY LOVE"

For the more than two and a half years since he had eaten rotten meat during Braddock's march to the Monongahela, George Washington had suffered from a chronic intestinal ailment that at age twenty-six had left him an emaciated six foot four inches in a baggy blue uniform. Winter months in the mountains of western Virginia in a drafty log stockade kept half-warm only by a smoky fireplace had contributed to his exhaustion from a second source, a severe case of pleurisy that he worried was tuberculosis. Added to his cough and general debilitated condition, his long confrontation with Governor Dinwiddie had worn Washington out.

One bright spot in a gloomy winter came when he learned that Dinwiddie was resigning and going home to Glasgow. His parting letter was bitter and added to George's pain. "My conduct to you from the beginning was always friendly but you know I had good reason to suspect you of ingratitude," wrote Dinwiddie, himself worn out by the long war. "I am convinced your own conscience and reflection must allow I had reason to be angry." Washington sent off a last letter to the receding Scot:

> I do not know that I ever gave your honor cause to suspect me of ingratitude, a crime I detest and would most carefully avoid. If an open, disinterested behavior carries offense, I may have offended because I have always laid it down as a maxim to represent facts freely and impartially, but no more to others than I have to you, sir.[1]

Washington was no longer the sycophant. He was speaking as an equal to a man he no longer held in awe. He was not only ill, he was sick and tired of toadying to royal officials. His quick response coupled with a request for leave left Dinwiddie time for one last insult. He turned down the request. Robert Dinwiddie's last words to George Washington were: "You have been frequently indulged with leave of absence. You know the fort is to be finished. Surely the commanding officer should not be absent when daily alarmed with the enemy's intentions to invade our frontiers."[2]

By June 1757 Colonel Washington had become sufficiently alarmed to write confidentially to Speaker Robinson, "I am convinced it would give pleasure to the Governor to hear I am involved in trouble, however undeservedly, such are his dispositions to me." By July 1758 Dinwiddie began to complain that Washington was building Fort Loudoun too slowly. He also accused Washington of passing along information too slowly from Colonel Stanwyx, the British officer in charge of the regional war effort. On August 13, 1758, Dinwiddie sharply rebuked Washington for being lax in sending in his accounts. This offended Washington perhaps more than any other charge because he was scrupulous in his financial dealings and had almost a fetish about accurate and timely record-keeping and reporting. Such an accusation implied Dinwiddie did not completely trust Washington. Dinwiddie also chastised Washington for not telling him how many men he had sent off to Augusta County, for failing to acknowledge a shipment of arms, and for omitting to keep him posted on the latest Indian raids. "You must allow this is a loose way of writing and is your duty to be more particular to me," Dinwiddie chivied him. Washington reported more promptly in September. On the seventeenth the Indians killed twenty settlers only twelve miles from Fort Loudoun; a few days later, fifteen more died. Once again the Shenandoah emptied out. The settlers were "terrified beyond expression." In October Washington pleaded for permission to come to Williamsburg to present his arguments to the Assembly for a fresh expedition against Fort Duquesne. But weeks passed and no answer came.[3]

Washington's anxiety from the running feud was heightened by his deteriorating health. Suffering a new bout of dysentery on November 5, he sent off what proved to be his last words to Dinwiddie. He would not admit to Dinwiddie that he was too ill to stay at the fort any longer. Growing weaker since July, he still refused to relax his pace. He became much weaker after November 1, so wracked by cramps he could hardly walk. Dr. James Craik, Washington's neighbor and the regimental physician since Fort Necessity, had done all he could according to the barbarous medical practices of the time, including bleeding Washington three times within two days. But his advice was sound. Washington was in such pain by November 7 that Dr. Craik warned him that if he did not go home for a long rest he might well die. Without asking the departing royal governor's permission for a leave, on November 9, 1757, Washington turned over his command to Captain Robert Stewart at Fort Loudoun and went home.

Stewart had been his trusted subordinate since Fort Necessity. He wrote Governor Dinwiddie an ominous letter:

For upwards of three months past Colonel Washington has labored under a bloody flux. About a week ago his disorders greatly increased attended with bad fevers. The day before yesterday he was seized with stitches and violent pleuritic pains upon which the doctor bled him and yesterday he twice repeated the same operation. The doctor has strongly recommended his immediately changing his air and going some place where he can be kept quiet (a thing impossible here) being the best chance that now remains for his recovery. The Colonel objected to following this advice before he could procure Your Honor's liberty but the doctor gave him such reasons as convinced him it might be too late and he has at length with reluctance agreed to it.[4]

Washington was well on his way in an army wagon to Alexandria for examination by another physician by the time Governor Dinwiddie wrote to Captain Stewart at Fort Loudoun and expressed his dismay that Washington, in all these months, had never hinted to him that he was ill. The "violent complaint" was "completely unknown to me or he should have had leave of absence sooner." He wished his contentious protégé "a speedy recovery." The conciliatory letter, which might have helped Washington's spirits, took weeks to reach him. In Alexandria he went to the home of his friend John Carlyle and his wife, Sally Fairfax's sister Sarah. They nursed him while he waited for the return of Dr. Charles Green, his Mount Vernon physician, who was visiting patients on the Eastern Shore. That physician was also the Anglican pastor of Washington's parish. When he returned he gave Washington welcome news. He was not suffering from tuberculosis. He only needed a long rest and good food in his own warm dry house.[5]

The Mount Vernon that he returned to was empty except for his sister-in-law's servants. His brother Jack, who had agreed to manage the farm while George was on active duty, had married recently, but the newlyweds were away. At least the place had more the look of home because they were living in it. Over the past two years Washington had begun to remodel and refurnish it. In exchange for his April 1757 shipment of tobacco to his London factor he had ordered wallpaper for five rooms, a marble mantel, papier-mâché cornices for the living room and dining room, 250 panes of glass, two mahogany tables that could be joined for large gatherings, and a dozen matching chairs. The word he always specified in ordering was "fashionable."

For a few weeks Washington's condition continued to deteriorate, but then around Christmas he began to get better. One reason may have been the almost daily visits of Sally Fairfax—whether alone or with her usual coterie of women friends is unknowable. A few days after Washington reached Mount Vernon he wrote to Sally. For once he could speak frankly.

There was no danger of her husband intercepting the letter and taking umbrage at his intimate tone. Fairfax had gone to England after his father died to settle his estate and would not be back for months:

> I have labored under an indisposition for more than three months and finding no relief [at Fort Loudoun] on the contrary that I daily grew worse I have followed my surgeon's advice to leave the place and try what effects fresh air and water may have upon my disorder.[6]

The day before Washington sat up to write this letter Dr. Green had "prescribed to me":

> He forbids the use of meats and substitutes jellies and such kind of food. Now as my sister is from home and I have no person that has been used to making these kinds of things and no directions, I find myself under a necessity of applying to you for your recipe book for a little while and, indeed, for such materials to make jellies as you think I may not just at this time have, for I can't get hartshorn shavings anywhere. I must also beg the favor of you to lend me a pound or a smaller quantity if you can't spare that of hyson tea. I am quite out and cannot get a supply anywhere in these parts. Please also lend me a bottle or two of mountain [sweet wine from Malaga] or Canary [Islands] wine. Mr. Green directs me to drink a glass or two of this every day mixed with water of gum arabic [from the sap of acacia trees].[7]

Sally Fairfax's visits, her nursing, and the long hours they spent together all began to have their effects. Probably they did nothing more than play endless rounds of cards, but Washington's state of mental health improved with each week in her company. By the day after Christmas he was writing to chide a London merchant for omitting hoes, axes, and nails he had badly needed for spring planting and repairs at Mount Vernon. Shortly after New Year's 1758, he began to talk about going to Williamsburg.[8]

Soon Washington felt well enough to begin to talk about going back to the war. He felt he could not stay away from his troops any longer because he had heard that all discipline had broken down at Fort Loudoun in his absence. According to Major John Baylis, who was in command on Christmas night, his men had started a brawl with the local militia. Washington's soldiers beat up a man they thought was Baylis and threatened Lord Fairfax, who was recruiting tenant farmers in the area. Several soldiers went to jail and at least one duel resulted. Only the insistent advice of Washington's friends and neighbors dissuaded him from riding back to the mountains in midwinter to quell the disturbance. His friend and neighbor George Mason told Washington his premature return to duty would be self-indulgent:

> I hope you will comply with the opinion and advice of all your friends and not risk a journey to Winchester till a more favorable season of the year or a better state of health will permit you to do it safely. And give me leave, sir, to mention another consideration which I am sure will have weight with you. In attempting to attend the duty of your post at a season of the year when there is no room to expect an alarm or anything extraordinary to require your presence you will in all probability bring on a relapse and render yourself incapable of serving the public at a time when there may be the utmost occasion. There is nothing more certain than that a gentleman in your station owes the care of his health and life not only to himself and his friends but to his country.

Washington found it difficult to ignore such well-meaning advice and gave himself over to the ministrations of Sally Fairfax and Dr. Green. In mid-February, after nearly three months of convalescence, Washington tried to travel to Williamsburg to meet with acting governor John Blair, who had taken over when Dinwiddie resigned. Washington started out on horseback but suffered severe abdominal pain and developed a fever and returned to Mount Vernon for three more weeks.[9] By March 4, 1758, shortly after he turned twenty-six, he felt well enough to begin to correspond about the war. Lord Loudoun had forwarded to Colonel John Stanwyx, his deputy commander of British troops from Pennsylvania to South Carolina, a proposal by a British officer just arrived from England to assault the French fort at Detroit after capturing Fort Duquesne with only 1,000 men. Stanwyx sent the plan to Washington for his comments. Washington was still in command of nine frontier forts garrisoned by the Virginia Regiment. By now he had lost all illusions about the abilities of British officers sent to America and felt free to criticize the plan frankly. He heaped sarcasm on the would-be expedition's commander: "Surely, he intended to provide [the men] with wings to facilitate their passage over so mountainous and extensive a country." He had nothing personal against this latest British officer who expected to take command of Washington and his Virginia troops. Colonel Stanwyx wrote how sorry he was to hear Washington was too indisposed to ride from Mount Vernon to Winchester to meet him. He proposed, instead, as Washington wrote sarcastically, that Washington "attend him at his house in Augusta, about 200 miles further away, when, I suppose, he intends to honor me with his orders." Disgusted, Washington wrote back to Colonel Stanwyx that he was pessimistic about his ability to return to the frontier any time soon:

I have never been able to return to my command, my disorder at times returning obstinately upon me in spite of the efforts of all the sons of Aesculapius. At certain times, I have been reduced to great extremity. I am now under a strict regimen and shall set out tomorrow for Williamsburg to receive the advice of the best physicians there. My constitution is certainly greatly impaired. As nothing can retrieve [my health] but the greatest care and the most circumspect conduct, as I now have no prospect left of preferment in the military way and as I despair of rendering that immediate service which my country may require from the person commanding their troops, I have some thoughts of quitting my command and retiring from all public business.[10]

But Washington was only making excuses; in fact, his thinking had strayed so far from military matters that he sent off to England for a new saddle and bridle, a new wardrobe, some Gloucester cheese and beer for his guests, some coffee and chocolate for himself. To aid his recovery he ordered "6 lb. best Hyson." There were also hints in his planning that he expected to be well soon enough to begin to have dinner guests at Mount Vernon. He ordered "six dozen fancy China dinner plates, pray let them be neat and fashionable." A second order indicated he planned to entertain on a grand scale: "two dozen deep plates, four dozen shallow."[11]

If Washington wanted to see Sally at Mount Vernon now, he would have to invite her with her husband and her friends. Fairfax had returned unexpectedly from England. The visits from Belvoir were bound to become less frequent and Washington was bound to miss them terribly. George and Sally had spent many days together that winter. She had, he was convinced, brought him back to life more than any tea or soup or change of air. She made him want to be alive again—and being with her made him want to marry her. But their predicament was hopeless and Washington knew he must not do anything to jeopardize her reputation. George Fairfax and Sally's sister were all too aware of Washington's devotion to Sally. Sally's husband evidently had warned her to be discreet while he was away—which was often and for long periods. There was no possibility of divorce in colonial Virginia or any English colony. Only a special bill passed by Parliament in London could dissolve a marriage. Only a scandalous affair could lead to a court trial and an annulment in Virginia, but such cases were rare and Tidewater society would disapprove. Unless Fairfax wished to seek an annulment, and there was no hint he did, Sally must protect his name from gossip. There can be no doubt that George Washington loved Sally Fairfax, whether or not she reciprocated that love or felt she was even free to express it. Whatever passed between them during those three months when she cooked for him and nursed him, it had to stop now that Colonel Fairfax was home.

*B*y the time Colonel Fairfax returned, Washington was well enough to begin to entertain with the help of his servants. But he was still housebound. He ordered a mahogany card table and two dozen packs of playing cards from London and "two pair of worked ruffles at a guinea each" to wear at his cuffs and fifty pounds each of raisins, currants, and almonds "in the shell" to serve in a "1/2 dozen fashionable china bowls." He longed for Sally's visits "when you are at leisure to favor us with a visit." He was bored after four months of self-imposed house arrest, but Dr. Green warned him that there were definite indications of some "decay"—the term for consumption.[12]

When spring came at last, he vowed to go to Williamsburg to seek the verdict of the best physicians in Virginia. He was in an agitated state in early March when he had to decide whether to "retire from all public business." He was not willing to believe his years at war had permanently ruined his health. On April 5, he rode slowly south in pain to visit his mother at Ferry Farm where he rested for several days before going on to Pleasant Hill, where he asked Speaker John Robinson to approve his regimental expense accounts. He took the gentlest route to Williamsburg and there consulted Dr. John Amson, an expert on dysentery who finally was able to convince Washington that he was not going to die. Despite all his symptoms he did not have tuberculosis and he would eventually recover.[13]

In the capital he learned the latest British plans for the coming season of war against the French. Prime Minister William Pitt had fired Lord Loudoun and as part of a new policy of dealing with the American colonies, Pitt promised that England would provide all arms, ammunition, and equipment while the colonists would only have to raise and pay their own soldiers. Pitt had removed the grievance that had so long angered Washington. Colonial troops serving with the British would no longer be subservient to British officers of the same grade. Furthermore, Virginia's Assembly was about to respond to double its forces and call up its militia for a fresh assault on Fort Duquesne. In all, some 4,000 troops, including battle-seasoned Scottish Highlanders, a newly formed Royal American Regiment, and provincial regiments from Virginia, Maryland, Pennsylvania, and North Carolina, were to join in the new Ohio Valley expedition. The news electrified Washington. As if miraculously cured, he rode out of Williamsburg by a new and shorter route, only stopping on his way home long enough to pay a call at the White House, the home of the recently widowed Martha Dandridge Custis.

*I*n the small, close-knit society of Tidewater Virginia where only 130 families dominated the economic and social life of the largest British American province it is unlikely that George Washington had not met

Martha Dandridge Custis before the spring of 1758. He no doubt had seen her with her husband, Daniel Parke Custis, at assembly balls that punctuated the intense winter social season of Williamsburg, which was only thirty-three miles south of the Custis plantation. He could hardly have escaped hearing that her husband had died and he must have known that she was the wealthiest widow in Virginia. He already knew she was attractive, a poised, mature woman with dark hair and beautiful skin, hazel eyes, and the kind of refined manners that entranced him. Everything about her was in sharp contrast to the roughness and crudeness he had seen on the frontier and in British army camps. Chesapeake society, which thrived on gossip, considered Martha Custis one of its most eligible candidates for a quick, strategic remarriage.

Since she had been a very young girl, Martha had heard Tidewater gossip about bloodlines and fortunes that was the very basis of its fireside-and-veranda society. She was the oldest child of Colonel John Dandridge and his wife, Francis Jones, of New Kent. They were not in the front rank of Virginia's landed gentry. The colonel, one of four sons of an immigrant merchant, owned a modest plantation. The highest office he ever held was that of county clerk. His wife, like Washington, was descended from a line of scholars and churchmen. Their plantation lay on the banks of the tidal Pamunkey, a tributary of the York River. Many of their neighbors lived in brick mansions that in essence were self-contained villages made up of manor house, stables, shops, mills, storehouses, smokehouses, and slave quarters surrounded by extensive fields of tobacco, grain, and forage to feed the livestock. A young woman whose parents wanted her to marry advantageously in this society had to learn to manage a plantation. Born on the first day of summer of 1731, eight months before Washington was born fifty miles to the north, Martha Dandridge had to learn early the rituals of maintaining a facade of elegance and civilization superimposed over a system short on cash and supported by brutal, hard slave labor.

Like all the women of her family, Martha was small. She measured under five feet tall when she was fully grown, nearly a foot and a half shorter than Washington. In a primitive painting made a year before her first husband's death, John Wollaston, the same man who painted Sally Fairfax and Lawrence Washington, gave Martha bright, almond-shaped eyes, a small pursed mouth, a high, domed forehead, and a trim figure. She radiated a calm, poised self-confidence. The portrait does not show her perfect white teeth, a rarity at the time, her tiny delicate hands, or her gentle manner. After giving birth four times, by the time Washington met her she was plump. She was always elegantly dressed and bejeweled. Everything in her manner said that she had grown accustomed to wealth and was at ease with her own authority.

Her education was fairly typical of Virginia's more fortunate daughters.

Schooled at home, she had learned to read the Bible, sermons, and tracts, and how to ride and dance. According to Virginia legend, itself a masterpiece of embroidery, she learned great adeptness at weaving and sewing at an early age. Taught how to cook by her mother from recipes passed down in writing in her family, she became a famous cook. She learned how to supervise the growing, harvesting, and preserving of large quantities of foods as well as how to furnish and decorate a house and keep its accounts. She was also expected to take charge of hygiene and health care for her family and her slaves. Martha was taught that her privileges brought commensurate responsibilities. In effect, she had to learn to be a town manager, supervising every detail of the lives of a growing number of people, especially when her husband was away for months on end. She was expected to master all of this by the time she made her debut in Williamsburg at age fifteen. From then on, the wide, tree-lined streets and spacious townhouses of the Virginia capital were to be her second home in a public life where she was always on display and always watched. Here she made her first curtsies at a series of assembly balls, dances, and concerts at the governor's palace. Martha Dandridge made an immediate good impression as she moved quietly and gracefully through the company. Over the next few years of attracting a suitable husband, she became known as kind, thoughtful, loyal to friends, and extremely modest.

Among the eligible suitors she attracted was Daniel Parke Custis, a bachelor thirteen years her senior. He was the son of a notorious miser, Colonel John Custis, one of the wealthiest men in Virginia and owner of the White House on the Pumankey and Six-Chimney House, a Williamsburg mansion. Colonel Custis wanted his son to marry Evelyn Byrd, daughter of arguably the wealthiest Virginian, William Byrd of Westover. She was considerably older than young Custis, who managed to drag both feet until she died. A son dared thwart his father's matrimonial wishes even if a daughter did not. Daniel Custis was then free to court Martha Dandridge. A Dandridge would be Colonel Custis's least likely choice, he made it known. They did not even warrant a coat of arms on their gravestones and were of too low a rank in Virginia society to expect a marriage settlement from him for their daughter. Before he would give Martha any of the family silver and jewelry he offered it to a farmer's wife. In an affidavit the woman swore that Custis had threatened to "throw them into the street for anybody to pick up" before he would give them to "any Dandridge's daughter or any Dandridge that wore a head." His only explanation for his wrath was that "Mr. Dandridge's daughter [is] much inferior to his son in point of fortune." The old colonel was living with a young black boy he had made his sole heir. He was not prepared for Martha's patience and tact. She made a charming speech, presented the colonel's young black heir a pony and saddle, and won him over. He made out a new will in his son's favor and would die before he could change it again. Martha and Daniel fell in love and, after a brief courtship, Colonel Custis grudgingly gave them permission to marry.[14]

Martha Dandridge was seventeen in June 1749 when she married. A few months later, when Colonel Custis died, Martha became the mistress of a great estate at age eighteen. Attending and giving balls and dinners, the Custises lived amid a constant round of social visits and obligations. Martha lived near her parents and she stayed close to them. She made especially long visits home at Christmas time. At one of these, the throng of houseguests included young Thomas Jefferson, who was on his way to classes at William and Mary; another was the gifted young fiddler and storyteller Patrick Henry. In her first five years of marriage the fecund Martha gave birth to four children, a boy and a girl who died in infancy and two children who survived, John, called Jacky, and Martha, nicknamed Patcy. Shortly after Patcy's birth Daniel Custis died of heart failure in the spring of 1757. He left Martha a twenty-five-year-old widow.

During the year-long official period of mourning, Martha was besieged by visitors whose grief was sometimes indistinguishable from courtship. The richest widow in Virginia, she inherited 17,438 acres of tobacco-growing lands appraised at £23,632 (about $1 million today) as well as £9,000 in cash, nearly $500,000 today. One-third of the Custis estate, the widow's portion, became hers until she remarried. She could charge the expenses of raising her children against their shares of the estate. Whoever married her would instantly receive one-third of the estate—her third—and have the management and income of the rest. The line of suitors was so long that Martha fled to neighbors' houses where, as a guest, she had more privacy than in her own home.

According to an account written seventy-five years later by her grandson, Daniel Parke Custis, she was visiting Major William Chamberlayne on the estate next door when Colonel Washington, who was going out of his usual way home to Mount Vernon after visiting his doctor in Williamsburg, arrived at Williams Ferry over the Pamunkey:

> It was in vain the soldier urged his [press of] business. Mr. Chamberlayne, on whose domain the [colonel] had just landed, would hear of no excuse. Passing by one of the old castles of the commonwealth without calling and partaking of the hospitalities of the host was entirely out of the question.

As Custis told it, Washington agreed to stop "on condition that he should dine, only dine." Washington instructed his servant, Thomas Bishop, to wait with the horses. Inside, Washington met Widow Custis:

> The lady was fair to behold, of fascinating manners and splendidly endowed with worldly benefits. The morning passed

pleasantly away. Evening came with Bishop true to his orders and firm at his post. The sun sank in the horizon and yet the colonel appeared not.

Eventually, presumably after talking alone by the fire for hours with Martha, Washington sent out word toward midnight that he was spending the night. In the morning, according to Custis's 1835 account (at least part of which came from his grandmother Martha), "the sun rode high in the heavens" by the time Washington emerged.[15]

*T*he man who captivated Martha during a single social call was, as his best friend, Lieutenant Colonel George Mercer, described him that spring, "straight as an Indian" and very thin, at six feet four weighing only 175 pounds:

> His frame is padded with well-developed muscles indicating great strength. His bones and joints are large as are his hands and feet. He is wide shouldered but has not a deep or round chest, is neat waisted but is broad across the hips and has rather long legs and arms. His head is well shaped though not large but is gracefully poised on a superb neck. His face is long rather than broad with high round cheek bones and terminates in a good firm chin. He has a clear though colorless pale skin which burns with the sun. [He has] a pleasing and benevolent though a commanding countenance [and] dark brown hair which he wears in a cue. His mouth is large and generally firmly closed but which from time to time discloses some defective teeth. [Washington had just had one tooth extracted at Winchester and he suffered from chronic gum disease.] His features are regular and placid with all the muscles of his face under perfect control though flexible and expressive of deep feeling when moved by emotions. In conversation he looks you full in the face, is deliberate, deferential and engaging. His demeanor [is] at all times composed and dignified. His movements and gestures are graceful, his walk majestic and he is a splendid horseman.[16]

What was it about Martha that attracted the young hero? Certainly her newly inherited wealth does not completely explain the attraction. In the open-book society of colonial Virginia he could easily have discovered that Daniel Custis had died intestate and that she and therefore he would have only the use of one-third of Daniel Custis's estate and that every penny of her children's two-thirds must be sequestered and invested for them until they came of age. He would have to take on the burden of acting as their legal guardian and twice a year submit meticulous records to the general court to which they were wards. Moreover, much of Martha's land was played-out tobacco fields on scattered farms that must be managed by paid overseers. All of this added up to a chronic headache for any would-be suitor.

But there was something quiet, deep, and gentle about the tiny woman with whom Washington no doubt had danced at parties in Williamsburg over the years. Most of all, she was the woman he expected to marry. He did not want an outspoken, domineering, all-controlling yet quaveringly insecure woman like his mother and he had grown weary of the coquettish, constantly teasing sophistication of a Sally Fairfax. Martha, shy and refined and content with him, would be his partner and his companion. She would bring order and stability to his life after all the years of struggle and anxiety. Long ago he had copied out the lines of "True Happiness" in his boyhood commonplace book so that he would remember them. That night at the White House on the Pamunkey they came to life for him:

> These are the things which once possess'd
> Will make a life that's truly blessed:
> A good estate on healthy soil
> Not got by vice, nor yet by toil.
> Round a warm fire, a pleasant joke
> With chimney ever free from smoke:
> A strength entire, a sparkling bowl,
> A quiet wife, a quiet soul.[17]

*L*ittle is more frustrating in studying George and Martha Washington's lives than the almost complete lack of surviving correspondence between them. According to several sources, they frequently wrote to each other, but why fewer than a handful of letters survive is that Martha destroyed as many as she could find after he died. His letters to Sally Fairfax eluded Martha, who never knew of them. Only two or three letters between the Washingtons—and one of them of doubtful authenticity—remain. There are a few fleeting glances that survive in the form of postscripts that Martha appended to the letters other people around her wrote to Washington, and there are letters she wrote to other people. These combine to give her the appearance of a happy, affectionate woman who was very close to her family and to his, someone who hated to be away from her home and her children. She once described herself as "a fine, healthy girl" who was "cheerful as a cricket and busy as a bee."[18]

In 1762, when she was barely thirty-one and her two children were under seven, she wrote this brief letter to her youngest sister:

> *My dear Nancy,*
> I had the pleasure to receive your kind letter of the 25 of July just as I was setting out on a visit to Mr. Washington in

Westmoreland where I spent a weak very agreeably I carred [carried] my little Patt [Patcy] with me and left Jacky at home for a trial to see how well I could stay without him though we ware gon but won fortnight I was quite impatient to get home. If I at aney time heard the doggs barke or a noise out, I thought thair was a person sent for me.

Her homespun spelling and lack of consistent punctuation were not unusual for a woman of her time who had not enjoyed formal schooling. They bothered Washington more as time went on, until he was disturbed enough to begin to write out letters for her to copy and sign as if they were her own.[19]

If ever there was one in writing, Washington's reaction to meeting Martha does not survive, but other women took note of her amiability and kindness. In 1776, when Martha visited Massachusetts for the first time, Mercy Otis Warren wrote of her "sweetness of manner." Abigail Adams, not given to flattery, wrote of Martha's "great ease and politeness," her "modest and unassuming" manners, the pleasantness of her expression. And Martha had another attribute that was important to George: she was never happier than when she was nursing someone— children, servants, soldiers—back to health.[20]

Whatever his exact first reaction, George Washington could not get Martha out of his mind. Only one week later, after taking remarkably little time to follow his doctor's orders to rest at Mount Vernon, he was back on his horse for the three-day ride to the Pamunkey, this time to visit Martha as an invited guest at her own plantation, the White House. Here he ignored his doctor's advice to eat cautiously. He feasted on lavish meals she prepared in his honor. Then Martha gave him a tour of the mansion. He visited her children in their nursery and he strolled the grounds with her, the two of them deep in conversation. By the time George departed the next day, they were engaged to be married. In all, he had spent fewer than twenty-four waking hours with her, but then, this was not unusual in Virginia society at the time. As events turned out he would get to see her only once more in the next nine months. And then they married.

Rushing resolutely back to his frontier command at Winchester, Washington took the first spare minutes to dash off an order to his cousin in London to send him "by the first ship bound to any port of Virginia" as much of "the best superfine blue cotton velvet as will make a coat, waistcoat and breeches for a tall man with fine silk buttons to suit it, six pairs of the very neatest shoes [and] six pair gloves." George Washington was going to be married, and not in the officer's uniform he would be expected to wear if he remained in the service. At the White House, Martha, too, was preparing an order for the next ship to London for "one genteel suit of clothes for myself, to be grave but not to be extravagant and not to be mourning."[21]

*I*n their few days together, George and Martha must have talked over many things, including where they would live and whether he should return to his regiment. During his brief visit to Williamsburg Washington had come to believe that the war with the French would be won at last that year. The British ministry was now headed by the vigorous and brilliant William Pitt and was preparing an all-out campaign that would combine attacks on Fort Duquesne on the Ohio, Fort Ticonderoga on Lake Champlain, and the key fortress of Louisbourg in the Cape Breton Highlands of Nova Scotia. All would make use of large numbers of American troops for the first time. The commander assigned to the Fort Duquesne prong of the offensive, General John Forbes, had made it known that Virginia forces were to be built up to division strength with the creation of a second regiment. All of Virginia's army was to be under the command of George Washington if he wanted it. Washington, furthermore, would have command of all American troops on the Forbes expedition and they would, as he had recommended, be allowed to fight Indian style in new units and uniforms suitable for forest warfare.

In what he probably considered the capstone of his military career after five years of frustrating frontier fits and starts, Washington wanted to be in at the kill. His betrothal and choice of marriage attire indicate that he had given up all hope of a British army career, yet as a man obsessed by honor he could not desert his command until the Virginia frontier was safe from attack. He had long believed that only the elimination of Fort Duquesne as the base of Indian attacks would bring enduring peace to Virginia. His marriage would have to wait until the war was over. (Apparently a hastier wedding was out of the question, although why he never made clear.)

Before riding off to the west again, Washington hired a master builder and left behind instructions and plans for making Mount Vernon a suitable home for Martha. In many ways he imitated the designs of Belvoir, the Fairfax estate next door. Basically this meant nearly tearing apart and rebuilding all of his brother's house. There seemed to be no question where they would live. If Washington changed counties, he might lose his adjutancy, which was his political base. Eventually, when a seat in Fairfax County became vacant, he could expect to be elected to the House of Burgesses from his home district. Mount Vernon was also close to his friends the Fairfaxes. Martha probably welcomed an escape from the house where her first husband had died. That summer, Washington, drawing heavily on the income of his tobacco crops, in absentia shelled out a whopping £325 for renovations to Mount Vernon (about $13,000 today excluding slave labor). This was three times his full salary as adjutant of the Northern Neck and thirteen times what the foreman overseeing the work made in a year. Washington entrusted overall supervision of the reconstruction work to George Fairfax. Washington's engagement to Martha had eased the tension with his old friend. Fairfax was confident enough of their friendship that with Sally at his side he took to visiting the worksite in the gutted Mount Vernon mansion. He wrote George that he had "taken the liberty" to make modifications to Washington's plans. He had ordered the old upstairs floors torn up and new ones put down:

> Undoubtedly they may do with a little planing but that can't bring them even or make them of a piece with the rest of the house. If you prefer a new floor there must be new doors also. I took the liberty to hire a hand to paint the house which is suffering for want of it. I think the chimneys upstairs are much too contracted and would be better if they were enlarged.[22]

By July, a month after Washington left Martha to join Forbes's expedition, Fairfax was reporting that the new expanded edition of Mount Vernon was under roof; by August, he sent along the good news that Washington's overseers and field slaves had grown "some of the finest tobacco and corn I have seen this year." He passed along the "best wishes" of Sally and her friends, one of whom was sewing shirts for George.[23]

Now that Washington was engaged to marry Martha, Sally Fairfax felt free to write to Washington and to tell her husband that she was doing it. Her letter of September 1, 1758, has disappeared but Washington at once wrote back from Fort Cumberland to Belvoir. He undoubtedly knew that Colonel Fairfax was away in Williamsburg for the regular Assembly session. It was the first word George had heard from Sally in the six months since he had become betrothed, and he fairly exploded with excitement. His answer was hardly in the tone of a man engaged to marry someone else:

> How joyfully I catch at the happy occasion of renewing a correspondence which I feared was disrelished on your part I leave to time, that never-failing expositor of all things, and to a Monitor equally faithful in my own breast to testify. In silence I now express my joy, silence which, in some cases—I wish the present—speaks more intelligibly than the sweetest eloquence.

In her lost letter to him, Sally Fairfax evidently teased Washington about being anxious over his impending marriage. He now contended that his unease was solely over the "present system of management" of the Forbes expedition to the Ohio. As the British once again dragged themselves and everything they owned slowly west, Washington was becoming for the first time openly critical of their tactics in letters to British commanders and Virginia politicians as well as to Sally: "You destroy the merit of it entirely in me by attributing my anxiety to the animating prospect of possessing Mrs. Custis. Should not my own honor and country's welfare be the excitement?"

This bold letter surfaced only after historians and biographers had overlooked it for two centuries. It materialized in the Houghton Library at Harvard in 1958 after it was sold at auction nearly a century earlier for only a few dollars because it was considered a hoax. Modern Washington scholars have authenticated the handwriting as unmistakably his. Affecting the eighteenth-century drawing room literary style as his cover, Washington went on to confess that he was in love. He used no names but his meaning undoubtedly was clear enough to Sally Fairfax:

> Tis true, I confess myself a votary of love. I acknowledge that a Lady is in the case—and further I confess that this lady is known to you. Yes, Madam, as well as she is to one who is too sensible of her charms to deny the power whose influence he feels and must ever submit to. I feel the force of her amiable beauties in the recollection of a thousand tender passages that I could wish to obliterate till I am bid to revive them. But experience, Alas! sadly reminds me how impossible this is and evinces an opinion which I have long entertained that there is a destiny which has the sovereign control of our actions, not to be resisted by the strongest efforts of human nature.

George Washington's experience with Sally, his recollection of a "thousand tender passages," and his fatalistic allusion to a controlling destiny all must have made it perfectly clear that he was still in love with Sally Fairfax, even if he was resigned to marriage without excitement to Martha Custis. No wonder Sally, who had known him for fully ten years, since he was a sixteen-year-old boy, had detected his anxiety; no wonder his answer was, at first reflex, so defensive.

But now, in an already reckless letter that could have cast a shadow over so many close relationships, Washington, about to risk death again on the Allegheny frontier, plunged on. He was trying desperately after all these tantalizing years to get Sally, just once, to admit that she, no matter how hopeless was their case, reciprocated his feelings for her:

> You have drawn me, my dear Madam, or rather I have drawn myself, into an honest confession of a simple fact. Misconstrue not my meaning—'tis obvious—doubt it not nor expose it. The world has no business to know the object of my love, declared in this manner to you when I want to conceal it. One thing above all things in this world I wish to know and only one person of your acquaintance can solve me that or guess my

meaning. But adieu to this, 'til happier times, if ever I shall see them.[24]

*T*he correspondence George Washington had so long sought with Sally Fairfax blossomed briefly in the summer and fall of 1758 as the Virginia colonel chafed and waited for action that would end America's longest war and release him at last to begin his new life as a Tidewater planter. Less than two weeks after he sent Sally Fairfax his remarkably passionate confession of love, an answer came back from Sally. At first blush, it was not the answer he wanted to hear. Once again, her letter was discreet, at least on the surface. She refused to spell out any feelings she had for him. He wrote to her with a touch of exasperation on September 25 from Raystown (now Bedford), Pennsylvania, advance base of the Forbes expedition, to ask whether "we still misunderstand the true meaning of each other's letters."

Sally's reply had come at a particularly bad moment. Washington had just been called on the carpet for his outspoken objections to the British taking the time to build a road across the Pennsylvania mountains instead of following the route that he and his men had built, the path of Braddock's 1755 expedition. Completely disenchanted with British tactics and once again ignored whenever he argued for more speed as another winter in the mountains approached, Washington made a bleak prediction that "so miserably has this expedition been managed" that after "the loss of many men by the sword, cold and perhaps famine we shall give the expedition [up] as impracticable this season." In that case, he and his men would come home "condemned by the world and derided by our friends."

In her letter to him, Sally had evidently chatted about an amateur stage play she and her friends had mounted recently. It was Joseph Addison's *Cato: A Tragedy*, Washington's favorite play. Sally had played Marcia, the daughter of Cato, who sends away her secret lover, Juba, in the first act. He must keep hidden his forbidden love as he goes off to war against Caesar. In the second act, Marcia, believing Juba has been killed, proclaims her love for him while he is hiding nearby. In the only two scenes they have together, Juba says:

> O Marcia, let me hope thy kind concerns
> and gentle wishes follow me to battle!
> The thought will give new vigor to my arms.
> Add strength and might to my descending sword,
> And drive it in a tempest on the foe.

In the second scene with Marcia, Juba ends his speech:

> Juba will never at his fate repine;
> Let Caesar have the world if Marcia's mine.

Both George and Sally knew these roles and lines so well that, despite the surface breeziness, Sally's mention of the play, if indeed it was produced at all that summer at Belvoir, could only have been a signal to Washington. Tucked away in Washington's dolorous recitation of news from the war front, apropos of nothing he wrote: "I should think my time more agreeably spent, believe me, in playing a part in Cato with the company you mention, and myself doubly happy in being the Juba to such a Marcia as you must make." All the war news was a mask. A favorite technique in coded messages is to surround the essence with unrelated details. Washington knew that Sally understood, after all, his true meaning. He knew that, in Marcia's words, his marriage to Martha Custis followed the *Cato* script. Juba was fated to make "any of womankind but Marcia happy." This was his controlling destiny. In their silent, secret wordplay, George William Fairfax, Sally's husband, was Cato; Sally was his "daughter." It is Marcia who says at the end,

> While Cato lives, his daughter has no right
> To love or hate but as his choice directs.

Washington promised he would not write to Sally Fairfax anymore. He had only to write "one thing more and then have done":

> You ask if I am not tired at the length of your letter? No, Madam, I am not, nor never can be while the lines are an inch asunder to bring you in haste to the end of the paper. You may be tired of mine by this [time]. Adieu, my dear madam, you possibly will hear something of me, or from me before we shall meet.

It was his last letter to her before he married Martha.[25]

*R*esuming his command after an absence of five months, twenty-six-year-old George Washington was eager to shake off the longest period of illness of his life. He had nearly died and he would not be completely rid of his symptoms for another four years, but he had no intention of staying out of the climactic struggle between the French and the English that was now taking shape. The average life expectancy of a British commander in chief seemed to be about two years. After Braddock and Shirley the arrogant Lord Loudoun had already proven ineffectual and was being recalled by London. Loudoun had dismissed Washington as a country bumpkin, but his second in command, Colonel Stanwyx, appreciated Washington's soldierly qualities and had treated him with a respect that Washington warmly reciprocated. Stanwyx had just been promoted to brigadier and assigned to serve under the new commander, General John Forbes, in the fresh assault on Fort Duquesne. Only five days after

Washington returned to his troops he began to lobby again for promotion. He wrote Stanwyx:

> Permit me at the same time I congratulate you to express my concern at the prospect of parting with you. I can truly say it is a matter of no small regret to me! I should have thought myself happy in serving this campaign under your immediate command. I beg that you will add one more kindness and that is to mention me in favorable terms to General Forbes not as a person who would depend upon him for recommendation to military preferment, for I have long conquered all such expectations, but as a person who would be gladly distinguished in some measure from the *common run* of provincial officers as I understand there will be a motley herd of us.[26]

General Forbes had already heard all about Washington. Shortly after he assumed command he wrote to Washington's superior, John Blair, who was now Virginia's acting governor. Blair forwarded Forbes's comments to Washington, who responded immediately with a flowery demonstration that he had assimilated the English officer's epistolary style:

> Permit me to return my sincere thanks for the honor you were pleased to do me. [I] assure you that, to merit a continuance of the good opinion you have expressed therein for me shall be one of my principal studies. I have no higher ambition than to act my part well during the campaign and if I should *thereby* merit your approbation it would be the most pleasing reward for the toils I shall undergo.[27]

On April 27, 1758, the Virginia Regiment became part of Forbes's command. It was among his fellow officers of the Virginia Regiment that Washington had found the comradeship and camaraderie of camp life that pulled so hard all his life against his strong instinct to stay home at Mount Vernon. He was very close to his brother Jack and was growing closer to his older half brother, Augustine, called Austin, but in the regiment he acquired close friends for the first time. They were loyal to him as he was to them. There were the mutually shared hardships and risks, but there were also the long relaxing hours after dinner around the officers' table, where Washington learned to tell stories and crack jokes and hickory nuts in a ritual of family-style dining that later would amaze French officers with its leisurely intimacy. His closest friend was the talkative George Mercer, his aide since Fort Necessity and now a lieutenant colonel. They had traveled from Virginia to Boston and played cards together and daydreamed about western lands they intended to claim under Governor Dinwiddie's recruiting bounty once the war was over. They also talked about women. If Washington confided in anyone about his love for Sally Fairfax, he would have told Mercer of his predicament. When General Forbes detached part of the Virginia Regiment and ordered it to march to Charleston, South Carolina, Mercer wrote Washington frank letters including one in which he complained about the "bad shape of the ladies" of Charleston: "Many of them are crooked and have a very bad air and not those enticing heaving throbbing alluring plump breasts common with our [Virginia] belles." But then Mercer felt compelled to apologize to Washington for using such language. Was it because Washington was his superior officer, or because no one used such language to George Washington?[28]

For many years the men who were close to Washington during the five-year frontier war were closest to him, with the possible exception of his brother Jack. And when any of them needed help it was Washington who always lent them money without charging interest. Sometimes, as in the case of Robert Stewart, he waited patiently for five years or more without pressing them for payment. Sometimes he knew he would never see his money again. He allowed old comrades to impose on him and even defraud him as he adhered to a stoical personal philosophy that he later summed up as "we must make the best use of mankind as they are as we cannot have them as we wish." He helped George Mercer time after time, even when the man seemed fated to fail. When Mercer couldn't win a commission as a British officer but came back from England proud that he was the Virginia commissioner of the hated stamp tax, Washington rescued him from an irate mob. And when Mercer failed to win his veteran's land bonus to begin life over again on the Ohio frontier, Washington arranged to back him financially for five years of expensive living and lobbying in London. Washington had learned to put personal loyalty above every other virtue.[29]

It took all of Washington's loyalty to his friends and to his duty as a British colonial officer to pull him back to a rude frontier fort in the spring of 1758. While the new British commander worked to win the support of southern Indians, Washington was sent back and forth from Fort Loudoun to Williamsburg to line up pay and supplies for his men. He had time for only a brief stopover at Martha's house in early June. By June 24 he was back at Fort Loudoun in time to ride north at the head of his buckskin-clad Virginia Regiment on their march to Fort Cumberland. He had won a minor victory by persuading Forbes that buckskin should be the American uniform. Washington arrived at the post where his military duties had begun fully four years earlier and began another summer of frustration, once again chronically complaining while he awaited the latest British slow march to the Monongahela. This time Washington was in a rebellious mood.

*E*ver since he had first assisted his neighbor George Fairfax at the polls in 1755, Washington had been lining up support for a seat in the House of Burgesses. As a burgess he could see how the government dealt with the province's defense and have a voice in expediting it. George Fairfax's incumbency blocked any chance of Washington winning a seat from Fairfax County, but his exploits on the frontier qualified him to stand for one of the two seats from Frederick County on the frontier. In Washington's first bid for office in 1757 he had lost because he had no organization and had spent no money. His decision to resign from the military as soon as he could prompted him in the summer of 1758 to listen when his friends urged him to run again. While he would have to campaign in absentia, a long-distance campaign might alleviate some of his frustration at the slow British preparations. The prospect of political office excited him. He had taken orders for nearly five years from the burgesses. Now he served notice; he wanted to be one of them. He found himself aligned with the Fairfax faction, although it is unlikely he had sought or particularly wanted its support. Frederick County was represented by Hugh West and Thomas Swearingen. A young nephew of Lord Fairfax, Colonel Thomas Martin, who was an incumbent burgess from Hampshire County, decided to shift his seat to Frederick County where his uncle had just given him 9,000 acres of land. Martin targeted incumbent West. This meant Washington had to run against Swearingen. Washington was at an early disadvantage because the writs of election did not arrive from Williamsburg at Winchester, the county seat, until July 4. By this time Washington had already marched north to Fort Cumberland. Once the writs arrived, Washington had only twenty days for a campaign before the election.

George Fairfax and John Carlyle rolled up their sleeves to help the absent Washington. They rode over from Alexandria to the Shenandoah and whipped up the support of their tenant farmers. Washington also received the backing of two of the most influential men who lived in the Shenandoah Valley, John Wood and Gabriel Jones. Jones was himself a burgess and the leading lawyer in neighboring Augusta County. He wholeheartedly campaigned for Washington, to the point of neglecting his own reelection. But Washington's most enthusiastic and effective campaign workers were his own officers. At Fort Loudoun, Lieutenant Charles Smith, the commandant, arranged with Washington to pay the fiddlers and the bills at the taverns and grog shops of Winchester so that there would be no hungry or thirsty would-be Washington voters on election day. At first, it looked like an easy victory, but when General Forbes turned down Washington's request for a leave to make an election-eve appearance in Winchester, Fairfax wrote Washington that he feared Washington would be "very hard pushed." But many of the voters, especially soldiers and veterans, understood. One of Washington's campaign workers wrote him that they "entertain a notion of the inconvenience you lie under of attending the Assembly [election] and of defending them at the same time." Even if Washington could have gotten permission, he had learned that he dared not leave his post during a campaign. If an emergency arose, he would be criticized for abandoning his troops and he would lose the election anyway. All he could do was to wait, hope, and outspend his opponent.[30]

The vote in Winchester on July 24 was unusually heavy. Soldiers and settlers streamed into the taverns and then staggered off to the polls to call off their names. When the count was tallied that night, Washington led the four-man field. The vote was: Washington, 309; Martin, 239; West, 199; and Swearingen, 45. Washington learned two days later that he had drubbed the incumbent, Swearingen, by an overwhelming seven-to-one margin. To win, Washington had laid out a considerable £40 to ply the voters with rum, beer, and wine at what one observer called "dull barbecues and yet duller dances." Washington by age twenty-six had emerged from the frontier warfare a popular, confident leader who inspired other men. They would fight under him, endure hardships and harsh discipline, and then vote for him.[31]

Far from doing cartwheels, Washington only allowed his gloom to dissipate momentarily as the British offensive dragged along. He remained pessimistic about his chances to come home to Mount Vernon and Martha. He could not see that Forbes was correcting Braddock's worst failure by wooing the support of the Indians. Now that Washington had two good reasons to be impatient, his new status as a soon-to-be-wealthy member of the House of Burgesses encouraged him to speak out with a new frankness. Even in his thank-you letters to his campaign managers he grumbled: "Our expedition seems overcast with too many ills. God knows what's intended, for nothing seems ripe for execution. Backwardness and I would (if I dared) say more appears in all things."[32]

Washington was growing increasingly irate at the British command's decision to build a new road from Shippensburg, Pennsylvania, due west to the Forks of the Ohio, rather than to improve the old Virginia Company road northwest from Cumberland Gap. By late July, advance redcoat units had reached Raystown, Pennsylvania, on the east slope of the Alleghenies. Washington fumed at "Pennsylvania artifice" when he learned that General Forbes planned to build another eighty miles of roadway over the Alleghenies (the present route of the Pennsylvania Turnpike) when he could more quickly have made repairs to Braddock's route over Laurel Hill and Chestnut Ridge. If Forbes went ahead with the new Pennsylvania highway more time would be lost. All the Virginia troops and their supplies would have to be transported from Fort Cumberland to Raystown, another long and costly delay. The line of supply from

Virginia to the Cumberland Gap—and all postwar trade—would be shifted north to Pennsylvania. Not only were Virginia and Pennsylvania interests clashing but the Virginia Company stood to lose heavily. Settlers would pour into the Ohio Valley as soon as the French were cleared out and they would come through Philadelphia, not Alexandria. Was Washington oblivious to his obvious conflict of interest as he pressured the British command to improve the road that passed close to his lands at Bullskin Creek? Or was the new burgess from Frederick County justifiably plumping for British gold to improve his district's economy in the short and long term?[33]

In any event, Colonel Washington argued that it was foolish to take the time to build another road. He railed to an old friend from Braddock's staff who was now serving at Forbes's headquarters that if Forbes did not follow the Virginia route, "All is lost! All is lost by heavens! Our enterprise [will be] ruined." Forbes reconsidered but remained adamant. When Washington learned that Forbes had decided to press on across Pennsylvania, he lamented to Speaker Robinson, "Poor Virginia."[34]

When Washington still continued to criticize Forbes's decision, the general summoned him to his headquarters at Shippensburg, Pennsylvania. Forbes told Washington "plainly" that, whatever he thought, the British command had "proceeded from the best intelligence that could be got for the good and convenience of the army" and that had not been actuated by any preference for "one province or another." He accused Washington of showing "weakness" in his "attachment" to Virginia "having never heard from any Pennsylvania person one word." It was the sternest rebuke Washington had ever received and it was not unwarranted. Forbes called him on the carpet for provincialism. If he knew of Washington's financial interest in the opening up of Virginia Company lands, he ignored it. Other critics close to Forbes were less diplomatic. "Colonel Washington has been a good deal sanguine and obstinate," wrote one gloating Pennsylvanian trader.[35]

Forbes's dressing-down came at exactly the time when Washington was writing "adieu" to Sally Fairfax. He also had more bad news to pass along to the Fairfaxes. Several companies of Washington's Virginians had been detached to cross the Alleghenies with a British reconnaissance-in-force of 750 white men and a handful of southern Indians. The joint Anglo-American force failed to find any Indians and marched up close to the silent Fort Duquesne. Suddenly the big gates swung open and the French and Indians poured out. They worked through the woods from tree to tree, firing and loading and firing again. The Braddock debacle unfolded again in miniature. All the Scottish officers were quickly shot down; the soldiers broke and ran. The Virginians tried to rescue the British and then fought a dogged rearguard action as the redcoats fled. In all, 300 men died, were wounded, or were captured, nearly half of them from Washington's regiment. No wonder Washington's letters to Sally, her husband, and friends in Washington were filled with a sense of impending doom.

He was not consoled when Forbes complimented him on the bravery of his men. He had come to believe that American courage was as axiomatic as British cowardice and bungling. In a private letter to his brother Austin he observed with "infinite pleasure" that "Virginian officers and men distinguished themselves in the most eminent manner," but he kept silent from that moment on around British officers. He turned his mind to the carpets and furniture he was ordering from England for Mount Vernon.[36]

It was not that Washington was sulking. When the British sought his advice, he gave it. When Forbes's colonels asked him to draw up plans for forming a wagon train into line of battle quickly and quietly in the forest, he complied. He allowed for every detail for a force equal to Forbes's 4,000 men. But his enthusiasm was gone. By early November Virginia's shivering buckskinned troops were slogging through cold slashing rains over Laurel Hill, "encountering every hardship that an advanced season, want of clothing and no great stock of provisions will expose us to." But there was a new fatalism in Washington's tone. "It is no longer a time for pointing out difficulties and I hope my next [letter] will run in a more agreeable strain."[37]

Finally, Washington saw some action—and wished he had not. When Forbes finally did allow his restless Virginia colonel his head, Washington marched off to the most embarrassing blunder in his whole frustrating frontier career. On November 12, 1758, as the British force pressed northwest in a desperate effort to reach Fort Duquesne before winter, Indian scouts rushed back word to Forbes that French and Indians were approaching their forward observation post at Loyal Hannon and appeared determined to seize vital British horses and cattle. Forbes sent Washington's friend and second in command, Lieutenant Colonel George Mercer, with a detachment of Virginia troops to deter the French attack. Mercer engaged the enemy in a prolonged skirmish. When Forbes heard that Mercer was losing ground, he gave Washington permission to reinforce Mercer with five hundred Virginians. It was nearly nightfall on a "remarkably dark and foggy day." Dog-trotting with his men within half a mile of the shooting, Washington, as he wrote in his memoirs near thirty years later,

> detached scouts to communicate his approach to his friend Colonel Mercer, advancing slowly in the meantime. But being near dusk and the intelligence not having been fully disseminated among Colonel Mercer's corps and they taking us for the enemy who had retreated . . . commenced a heavy fire upon [our] relieving party which drew fire in return in spite of all the exertions of the officers one of whom and several privates were

killed and many wounded before a stop could be put to it. To accomplish which George Washington never was in more imminent danger by being between two fires, knocking up with his sword the presented pieces.

What Washington seems to have forgotten was that, as his men fell all around him, amid their screaming he could make out that the officers of the opposing force were shouting in English. It was George Mercer's men, who were killing their own compatriots; his own men were shooting other Virginians. By the time Washington could run between the lines of fire swinging his saber and yelling for them to cease firing, fourteen Virginians were dead and twenty-six lay writhing and moaning on the forest floor. Only thirty years later could he bring himself to write that he had put his life "in as much jeopardy as it had ever been before or since."[38]

Washington's timely capture of a British deserter as he rushed to reinforce Mercer spared him the full official weight of this latest humiliation. The prisoner brought Forbes the astonishing news that the Ohio Indians had abandoned the French and gone home, severely weakening the French post. Forbes believed the man—and that the right moment had come. He split his force into three brigades and assigned one to Washington. Forbes gave Washington the brevet rank of brigadier (brigadier general to later generations of Americans). Brigadier Washington was now, for a while, what he had always dreamed of becoming—a British general. He commanded an all-American force, his own Virginia Regiment, as well as three companies of Virginia pioneers and troops from Maryland and North Carolina and Delaware. With their axes, their knapsacks and muskets, and nothing else they set off to hack down the last few miles of trees that stood between the British and the French.

Now Washington threw himself into the fray with all his great strength and energy. At dawn on November 16, he and his men began felling trees and building bridges and roads over streams and marshy ground. They cleared a roadway six miles long in a single day. The next day, after seeing to it that his men ate a hot breakfast, he drove his work parties ahead eight more miles. After a third day of brutal hard work he began to wonder how far away the French fort must be. Had their Indian scouts sent them in the wrong direction? On the morning of November 19, he led a 1,000-man advance force as Forbes's main army overtook him. They followed what was left of Braddock's route along Turtle Creek. Washington guarded the artillery. He gave orders for the strictest silence. Any man who fired off his gun would receive two hundred lashes on his bare back on the spot. All dogs were to be tied up and muzzled or sent back to Loyal Hannon, or they would be hanged on the spot. At night, the soldiers slept on the frozen ground with their weapons cradled in their arms. On the fourth day of the march, Washington climbed a hill with Forbes and his staff. From the high ground they stared off at—smoke! A great column of it was spreading into the sky above the evergreen forest. Only minutes later, the scouts came racing back. The French were gone. They had burned Fort Duquesne and gone up the Allegheny in their canoes.

For George Washington, five years of frustrating frontier warfare were finally over. There was no battle, no surrender, no booty, no captured flags, no lasting honors. With the end of the campaign he would revert to the rank of Virginia colonel again. But he only cared now about going home and beginning a new life as a planter, a politician, and head of a family. He lingered at the Forks of the Ohio—so long his lodestone— only long enough for a solemn march to the field where Braddock's army had been slaughtered. Quietly, grimly, Washington and his men collected 450 skulls and buried them with military honors. The wolves had long ago scattered the rest of the remains. And then, sick of war and exhausted, Washington started the long journey home to Mount Vernon.

George Washington's first war formed him. He learned to endure terrible hardships and he suffered serious illness. He came close to dying from disease and was shot at on at least five occasions. He was the only British officer who survived Braddock's debacle on the Monongahela without a wound. Indians who were usually deadly marksmen somehow missed his tall and conspicuous figure time after time. Except when he surprised a patrol of half-asleep Frenchmen, he never won more than a skirmish. He lost a fort. He surrendered a regiment. He failed in his mission to protect the Virginia frontier, and he went home before the war was over and missed out on the final defeat of the French. Yet even when his own men attacked one another and inflicted heavy casualties all around him, he received one promotion after another.

He was tremendously lucky. He not only survived five years of appalling hardship and many serious mistakes, but he escaped blame for most of the fiascos in which he found himself involved. Yet in his own mind he was a failure who could not achieve what he most coveted—to become a career officer in the British navy or army. He rose briefly to brevet brigadier general at the remarkable age of twenty-six, but many British officers considered him a provincial bumpkin, or worse. In his first armed engagement, when he killed a French officer who may have been on a diplomatic mission, he was accused by many of touching off a worldwide war. Horace Walpole, an influential member of the British Parliament, declared that "the volley fired by a young Virginian in the backwoods of America set the world on fire."[39]

During the first three years of his five years and three months as a Virginia officer, Washington had failed to undertake a single major attack. Instead he complained constantly about shortages of gunpowder, food and clothing, the worthless Virginia currency, and the abysmal pay of officers as well as the cowardice, drunkenness, and insubordination of his troops. He had lost Fort Necessity by selecting an indefensible position and then building a useless stockade. When Braddock had followed Washington's advice by dividing his forces and stringing out his best troops in a five-mile line, a few French and a few hundred Indian and Canadian auxiliaries cut to pieces the vastly superior British force. Washington came away vilifying the enlisted men and admiring the vainglorious British officers. Given pay and rank under Forbes, he had been completely wrong in his prognosis for the British war effort. When Forbes ignored Washington's irate advice and refused to follow the disastrous route Braddock had followed, Washington descended to intercolonial rivalry, antagonizing not only his British superior officers but Pennsylvania officials. He seemed incapable of grasping that the British were inexorably driving the French and Indians before them and winning by logistics rather than bloody combat.

By the time he resigned his commission effective the last day of 1758, Washington was thoroughly disgusted not only with the British but with himself. In his eyes he had lost money, neglected his farms, and possibly destroyed his health. He had a chance now to begin a new life and to prove himself adequate in his own eyes and in those of his family and friends as a husband, a stepfather, and that most revered of figures in Virginia, a planter.

It came as a complete surprise when, shortly after he arrived at Martha Custis's White House plantation, he received a petition signed by all of the twenty-seven officers remaining on duty with the Virginia Regiment pleading with him not to resign. They also sent their appeal to the governor and the *Virginia Gazette:*

> The happiness we have enjoyed and the honor we have acquired together with the mutual regard that has always subsisted between you and your officers have implanted so sensible an affection in the minds of us all that we cannot be silent on this critical occasion. . . .
>
> Judge then how sensibly we must be affected with the loss of such an excellent commander, such a sincere friend and so affable a companion. How rare it is to find these amiable qualities blended together in one man! How great the loss of such a man. We with the greatest deference presume to entreat you to suspend those thoughts for another year. . . . Your presence only will cause a steady firmness and vigor to activate in every breast despising the greatest dangers and thinking light of toils and hardship while led on by the man we know and love.[40]

Washington was moved, but not enough to ride back into the war. He sat down to write farewell to his "dear gentlemen." He had "almost despaired" of proving himself "the smallest ingredient of a character you have been pleased to celebrate." With absolutely no presentiment of his future success, Washington called his Virginia command "the greatest happiness of my life." He was proud of only one other thing—"a steady honesty: this I made the invariable rule of my actions." He left his comrades sadly. Reflections on his military career "fill me with grief. I must strive to forget them." Thirty years later when he edited David Humphreys's draft biography after so much more praise had been heaped on him, Washington still remembered the plea of his comrades in the Virginia Regiment. But now he had other promises to keep.[41]

*C*hristmas Day of 1758 was George Washington's last as a bachelor and he spent it with George and Sally Fairfax at Belvoir. The threesome drove over to Mount Vernon to inspect the nearly completed renovations. His half-brother Lawrence had already raised the roof to transform an ordinary low-browed Virginia farmhouse into a handsome Georgian manor house. Now craftsmen followed Washington's plan to encase the house of his memories within a more stylish home suitable for Martha and the Custis heirs. One and a half stories had grown to two and a half, yet he had kept the familiar informal corner fireplaces that sat askew and did not follow the latest formal symmetrical English style. Now there were four rooms up and four rooms down, bisected by wide dark-paneled hallways. George and Sally picked their way over the construction debris and ascended an elegantly plain stairway with slender balustrades that doubled back toward the front of the house and led them to a second story, where high-ceilinged bedrooms flanked the dark wood hallway. The upstairs rooms were whitewashed and bare, awaiting Martha's taste in wallpaperings. Washington was proud of his Spartan amendments to his ancestral home but was aware that it would have the look and feel of bachelor officers' quarters until Martha arrived.

The three then rattled off in the Fairfax carriage for the chilly two-day journey to the White House on the Pamunkey where Martha awaited. They followed a sandy roadway that cut through ninety miles of bare scrub oak and winter-dark slash pine, arriving half-frozen at the Custis plantation ten days before the other wedding guests.

Nearly six months had passed since Washington and his fiancée had seen each other. As the White House filled with the frenzied sounds of preparations for the wedding and the invited guests assembled with their slaves, their luggage, and their presents, George and Martha had plenty to do. Under Virginia law, Martha's estate and all her chattel, including slaves and household furnishings, must be turned over to George. English common law did not allow a married woman to exercise control over any property. Martha's one-third of the Custis estate would become George's as soon as they pronounced the marriage vows. Her children and their two-thirds would pass into the guardianship of their new stepfather once he prepared a formal petition and took it to the general court during its spring term in Williamsburg. While Martha supervised all the cleaning and cooking and decorating, George Washington bent over Daniel Custis's desk and drew up the necessary papers and wrote headings in new account ledgers. After dinner and in the evenings, George spent time getting acquainted with Martha's chubby, timid children. Patcy was nearly two and could not remember having a father; Jacky was four and could barely see the top of George Washington until he sat down.

Nearly forty guests, including the new royal governor, the decadent Francis Fauquier, braved bitter-cold winds to come from all over Virginia to the White House in time for the days and nights of celebration. On the evening before the wedding, candlelight shimmered from all the frosted windows as George and Martha and their families and best friends danced country dances and minuets far into the night. By one o'clock the next afternoon, they were all sufficiently revived to dress in their finest clothes and crowd into the long high-ceilinged drawing room. The flames leaped in the great fireplace and twin chandeliers cast down warm soft haloes as George Washington and Martha Dandridge Custis marched in slowly and tentatively. Martha's wedding gown of stylish grosgrain silk with shiny pink silk ribbons and an aigrette of white and deep red contrasted sharply with George's dark blue coat and breeches and pure white silk stockings. The fine blue Manchester velvet suit he had ordered from England nine months earlier did not arrive until three months later. The Reverend David Mossom from nearby St. Peter's Church intoned the brief Anglican ceremony, and then they were married. They had become George and Martha Washington. On Twelfth Night, 1759, they began forty years together with a daylong feast and another night of dancing, laughter, and toasts. After three more days and nights of celebrating, the guests finally rattled off in their unheated carriages. The Washingtons could begin to get to know each other.

*M*artha Washington loved few things more than nursing the sick back to health. For nearly all of the first three months of their marriage at the White House and in Williamsburg she administered to her enfeebled bridegroom, applying a combination of gentle attentiveness and well-thought-out cooking and herbal remedies. It was one of the rare times in George Washington's life when he did not rise at four in the morning and start to write letters. A few days after his marriage he did sit down to pen a long and emotional response to the petition of the Virginia Regiment. He promised as a new member of the House of Burgesses to promote the "reputation and interest" of his former comrades in arms "though the fates have disjoined me from [the regiment]." Between January 10 and April 5, 1759, there ensued an uncharacteristic gap in his correspondence, the longest of his epistolary life. Martha had ruled absolutely that he should make a complete break with military affairs, stop worrying about the soldiers, rest, and eat. Her obedient husband eagerly obliged her and he began to put on, in all, forty pounds as he settled into an unfamiliar security and serenity. By mid-February, Martha thought George was strong enough to travel. The newlyweds wrapped themselves in carriage robes and drove into Williamsburg in Martha's post chaise—with Braddock's former batman, Thomas Bishop, on the lead horse cracking the whip, and a wagonload of slaves and baggage behind them. For the next ten weeks they lived in old Colonel Custis's Six Chimney House.[42]

On February 22, 1759, George Washington, twenty-seven, began his fifteen-year career in the Virginia House of Burgesses. He took his seat beside his friend George Fairfax. Both of them were called "Colonel" as they filed into their dark oak bench, but it was the tall young redhead from Fairfax County who caught the attention of the few older members who did not already know who George Washington was. He was the tall young man with the majestic bearing and weatherbeaten face. Speaker of the House John Robinson paid rare tribute to the newest burgess. He appointed Washington to the key Committee of Propositions and Grievances, one of only two standing committees of the House. From this vantage point he could create and support legislation that benefited Virginia's soldiers and could monitor the use of the funds. On Washington's third day as a lawmaker, Speaker Robinson called for Burgess Washington to rise and stand in his place while he read aloud a resolution:

> That the thanks of this house be given to George Washington, Esq., a member of this House, late colonel of the first Virginia Regiment for his faithful services to his Majesty and this colony and for his brave and steady behavior from the first encroachments and hostilities of the French and their Indians to his resignation after the happy reduction of Fort Duquesne.

Robinson then called on the House to vote. The burgesses unanimously chanted their "ayes" and thumped their canes in applause.[43]

Washington was still too weak to enjoy the crowded calendar of parties and assembly balls in the opulent taverns and drawing rooms of Williamsburg that winter term, but he did attend committee meetings and plenary sessions of the House until he was satisfied that his shoeless former comrades would be well fed and clothed when they marched off to take part in the next British offensive against the French in Canada. He began to make himself known as someone who spoke little and then only about legislation that touched directly on his constituents' interests. Many years later he wrote to a nephew to give advice on how to comport oneself in a public assembly. His hints explain why he seemed timid beside more firebrand colleagues, but also why he won the respect of quieter and more thoughtful delegates:

Speak seldom but to important subjects [which] particularly re-
late to your constituents. . . . Make yourself *perfectly* master of
the subject. Never exceed a *decent* warmth, and submit your
sentiments with diffidence. A dictatorial style, though it may
carry conviction, is always accompanied with disgust.

A fellow burgess described Washington more succinctly: "He is a modest man but sensible and speaks little—in action cool, like a bishop at his
prayers." Thomas Jefferson later served for five years with Washington in
the House of Burgesses and then closely observed Benjamin Franklin
in the Continental Congress during the Revolution. He found they shared
the ability to use a few well-chosen words at the right moment. "I never
heard either of them speak ten minutes at a time nor to any but the main
point which was to decide the question," Jefferson later recalled. "They
laid their shoulders to the great points, knowing that the little ones would
follow of themselves."[44]

The only point that seriously concerned Washington during his first
session was the replenishment of the Virginia Regiment and appointment
of a new commander whom he found acceptable. Colonel William Byrd
rode off toward Winchester with a fresh commission and orders to bring
the regiment back up to 1,000-man strength. Washington pushed through
a few minor bills affecting Fairfax County and then received permission
from the House to go home early. As his strength returned in March, he
began to take care of business again. The general court approved his
guardianship over the Custis estate. He bought a young racehorse, "a fine
English colt," for £7. He took Martha to a ball—tickets cost £1. He wrote
it all down. The newlyweds gave a party at their townhouse for members
of the Assembly. George and Sally Fairfax came, and the two couples
danced together. Washington had little cash of his own at the moment.
He borrowed a substantial £200 from his one-third share of the Custis estate. Other people, especially his former subordinates, owed him money.
As it dribbled in, he repaid the estate, with interest.[45]

By April 5, the Washingtons were ready for the jarring four-day, 160-
mile journey over spring-sodden roads from Williamsburg to Mount Vernon. They rolled out of the capital in a long train of wagons that grew
even longer when they stopped at the White House. By early April the
roadsides were festooned with white laurel blossoms visible through the
diaphanous tracery of oaks and shrubs. George had prepared for the annual Combined Kent County Inventory a careful list of goods "in the estate used by Martha Custis" that they were taking to Mount Vernon. It
ran to 247 headings. It included Martha's "chariot and harness," 15
horses, 60 gallons of rum, "a little brandy and some old cyder," 22 loaves
of sugar, barrels of sugar and saltpeter, three pots of raisins, 50 bushels of
oats, 141 yards of Irish linen, 49 yards of white flannel, and pieces of cal-
ico and sagathy. There were 11 pairs of "men's stockings," five pairs

"men's gloves," two jockey caps, money scales, and weights. George selected an array of tools and materials to flesh out the workbenches of his barebones plantation: "3 small barrels paint . . . 5 paint brushes . . . four [barrels] small nails . . . 80 lb. sheet lead . . . 6 sides of leather . . . 7 skins . . . a few small barrels lamp black . . . a parcel old window glass . . . some old casements."

There were wagons full of furniture—10 beds and bolsters, counterpanes and bedspreads for them all—blankets and rugs, 24 pair of sheets, 49 tablecloths, 99 napkins and towels, five diaper tablecloths. Mount Vernon would soon be crowded with furniture. The slaves gingerly wrapped and loaded a mahogany desk, a large mahogany dining table, and 24 cane-bottom chairs, two bureaus, and two dressing mirrors. There were bowls and vases and the "old cabinet" (how old must it have been?) that housed them. Washington selected for the ten fireplaces of Mount Vernon brass plate warmers, shovels and tongs, plate baskets, andirons, fenders, and bellows. For informal meals, George and Martha brought along 134 pewter plates; for fancier dinners, "8 dozen and 8 China plates & 15 [serving] dishes . . . 1 set gilt China and Coffee Mill . . . a parcel China tea cups, saucers, tea pot, milk pot, bowls, etc." The dining room would be graced by Martha's tea chest. Family members would sip from "30 wine and beer glasses" and the "dozen wine glasses" would be reserved for guests. How important the kitchen was to Martha and the way of life she was transplanting to Mount Vernon can be gleaned from the array of 13 copper kettles and pots, two iron pots, "two bell metal skillets and 18 pattipans," the stew pan and frying pans, the dripping pan, ladles, and tongs. All of these George listed meticulously as she described them for him.

At least he got around to the tools he would need in his new profession of gentleman farmer. In addition to the maintenance materials and the King William workhorses, he helped himself to

> 2 whipsaws
> 1 currying knife and 1 fleshing ditto
> 1 hatchet, 2 taper bits and 1 [branding] iron
> 5 dozen and 8 files of several sorts
> 60 awl blades[46]

When he had listed everything in his Custis account book and placed a value beside it he supervised the slaves as they packed the wagons. All his years of managing and supplying and transporting a small army served him well now. He forgot nothing. At the last moment he sent ahead his servant Miles Richardson with a note for John Alton at Mount Vernon. He was to "get the key from Colonel Fairfax's." His orders were paramilitary and emphatic: "You must have the house very well cleaned." He was to "make fires in the rooms" to dry them out and air them. "You must get two of the best bedsteads put up—one in the hall room and the other in the little dining room" downstairs. Here, off the dining room, the newlyweds would make their bedroom just as it had been in his parents' Epsewasson. "You must also get out the china and tables and have them very well rubbed and cleaned." Everything must be ready for Washington's white-glove inspection. "The stair case ought to be polished in order to make it look well." George Washington wanted to show off to his bride not only his overall design but the details he was so proud of. And they would be hungry: "Enquire about in the neighborhood and get some eggs and chickens and prepare them in the best manner you can for our coming." [47]

George Washington might have remained quietly at Mount Vernon enjoying the life of ease of an English country squire after his ordeal of a dozen hard years on the frontier had the British not systematically threatened everything he had worked for all those years. He enjoyed presiding over his dinner table, the fields, the county courts, the parish workhouse, and the Anglican vestry. He provided endless hospitality and generous alms. He liked nothing better than to chase after foxes at breakneck speed on horses he bred through woods and fields he enjoyed acquiring, fencing, and surveying. He was content with Martha, but a bit mystified why, year after year, he and Martha could produce no Washington heir. Soon after their marriage, Martha suffered a perilous bout of measles, probably severe enough to make further pregnancies impossible. He was unambitious as a politician. He eventually won a Fairfax County seat in the House of Burgesses and he kept it by paying more and more for the fiddlers and the beer, but he had no wish to govern beyond his own and his near neighbors' farms. Eventually, he became proud of his youthful efforts in driving off the French and ending the Indian raids.

If he was at all restless, the form it took was in a determined quest to gain vast tracts of western land that he considered his both by right of discovery as a surveyor and right of conquest as the Virginian who had held on to the frontier backcountry through years of bloody battles and raids. Here his appetite was unquenchable. He really expected one day to own something like 100,000 acres of rich riverfront land in the Ohio Valley, all those "beautiful groves" through which he had dragged a surveyor's chain and paddled and fought. Only when the British government began to question his right to all he had struggled for did Washington pull himself away from his sybaritic life as a wealthy American businessman and decide to put on his old brigadier's uniform. He would risk everything rather than go on bending his knee to Englishmen whom he now believed considered him their inferior, their chattel, someone they could exploit as if he were a slave.

And then George Washington came out swinging.

Ten

"NO LAW CAN COMPEL US"

At the end of October in 1765, thirty-three-year-old burgess George Washington, deeply tanned from a summer in the saddle supervising his plantations and slightly paunchy from Martha's cooking, rode into Williamsburg for the semiannual ritual of presenting his accounts as guardian of the Custis estate to the general court of Virginia. As Washington knew, the royal governor, Francis Fauquier, had refused to call the fall session of the House of Burgesses. A shrewd if decadent old aristocrat, Fauquier had dissolved the Assembly after it had passed Patrick Henry's explosive resolutions condemning a new British tax, the stamp tax. Protests against the tax were spreading throughout the American colonies and delegates from the colonial assemblies were gathering for a Stamp Act Congress in New York City. Governor Fauquier reasoned correctly that to convene a new Virginia Assembly would allow the burgesses to vote for delegates to send as Virginia's representatives. Virginia's participation would greatly strengthen the anti-British movement.

The hated new tax was to take effect only a few days after Washington arrived in Williamsburg. He had left the fall plantings to his overseers and slaves and driven to Williamsburg on roads crowded with horses and carriages. The tax would hit hard almost every Virginian at a time when the British had banned colonial currency even as the end of the long war with France had dried up Britain's subsidies. All over British America, there was a great depression. Any new tax meant suffering for the cash-poor colonists. Even wealthy planters like Washington lived on credit and had little cash. He would have to part with scarce silver or gold coins for virtually every financial dealing as well as most of his pleasurable activities. Every time he recorded a deed or executed a lease, sent his crops aboard a ship or insured its cargo, filed a document with the courts—including this semiannual probate filing for his stepchildren—he would have to come up with four shillings hard money for a stamp. This was equivalent to what he paid one of his farm managers for a week's wages.

Another tax on his leisure hours annoyed Washington almost as much as one on necessities. After five hours in the saddle each day directing his workers and several hours each day hunched over the account books and the correspondence, Washington liked to play cards or roll the dice with guests at his Mount Vernon gaming table. Now, every new pair of dice or pack of cards would require a ten-shilling stamp—enough to buy a barrel of fine Madeira or a pair of workhorses. For weeks, Virginia's two newspapers had been printing scores of essays and letters protesting the new tax. Now every page of those printed arguments would have to bear the detested one-penny stamp.

As Washington rode down dusty Duke of Gloucester Street between rows of handsome white clapboard houses and shops and taverns toward the courthouse, he had to coax his horse through knots of rough-hewn farmers who had come from as far away as the Shenandoah Valley. These were the men in the colony who had helped him to drive out the French and the Indians, and it was they who would be most affected by the new English tax. These men suffered from any tax. They rarely had any cash. They bartered for everything they could not hunt for or pay for with their tobacco crops. Where were they supposed to get cash? Every loan for seed money, every lease and every lien against their future harvests, already required gold or silver for the courthouse fees. And now they would somehow have to come up with hard money for the stamp man. Washington could plainly see that these upcountry farmers in buckskin leggings and hunting shirts were in an ugly mood. They'd had to ride one hundred miles or more over bad roads, pay for blacksmiths, and be away from their farms and families for weeks to serve on juries or act as witnesses in the general court while they would have to pay cash to stay in vermin-infested taverns and buy execrable and expensive food. Washington rode past grim evidence of their mood: from the gallows in front of the courthouse hung the bodies of three black slaves condemned to death for stealing one hundred pence.

In the four months since a British ship had arrived bearing news from London that Parliament had passed the odious new tax despite a year of petitions and objections from the American colonies, Washington had stayed on the margin of Virginia politics. But privately he was growing more and more agitated at the imperial system that tightly bound Americans to England. For all of the six years since he had married Martha and taken over the management of her Pamunkey and York River farms as well as his own on the Potomac, Washington had grappled with ways to free himself from what obviously had, to him at least, become a suffocating way of carrying out business. He was going to great lengths to break out of the Virginia way of life and debt. During frequent visits to Mount Vernon by his wealthy next-door neighbor George Mason, the two men had talked about sponsoring a bill in the House of Burgesses that would ban further importation of slaves from Africa. Mason had convinced him that, so long as there was slavery, there would never be enough white laborers emigrating from Europe with the incentive of buying farmland to produce crops that would make Americans economically independent of the mother country.

Mason was one of the most influential Virginia planters. He had gout and believed he was unable to travel to government sessions in Williamsburg. Washington had become his spokesman as well as his political partner. Together they had talked about organizing a legislative assault on the British "policy of encouraging the importation of free people and discouraging that of slaves." Mason wrote only a month later that it was the first time that a debate on the abolition of slavery had ever been proposed for the House of Burgesses. The highly charged question

> has never been duly considered in this colony or we should not at this day see one half of our best lands in most parts of the country remain unsettled and the other cultivated with slaves, not to mention the ill effect such a practice has upon the morals and manners of our people. One of the first signs of the decay and perhaps the primary cause of the destruction of the most flourishing government that ever existed [the Roman republic] was the introduction of great numbers of slaves.[1]

Washington and Mason had obviously been talking at length about the paradox created by Americans who were arguing for equal rights with Englishmen "at home" even as they spread slavery throughout the American colonies. But that autumn Washington was facing an economic crisis that precluded any further discussions of freeing his slaves. Only a month before he rode off to Williamsburg that autumn, Washington had protested the stamp tax to the London commission merchants who sold his crops and bought all the goods he was not able or allowed to produce. The words he used were well thought out and obviously he intended them to be passed along to pro-American members of Parliament. The letters show his anger at being constantly at the mercy of an import-export economy "clogged with too much difficulty and expense." He felt he was first of all being robbed by merchant middlemen and then by customs agents and now by stampmen commissioned by Parliament and sent out from England:

> What may be the result of this (I think I may add) ill judged measure and the late restrictions [on] our trade and other acts to burden us I will not undertake to determine. But this I think may be said—that the advantages accruing to the Mother Country will fall far short of the expectations of the Ministry. For

certain it is that the whole produce of our labor hitherto has centered in Great Britain. What more can they desire? All taxes which contribute to lessen our importation of British goods must be hurtful to the manufacturers of them and to the common weal. The eyes of our people, already beginning to open, will perceive that many of the luxuries, which we have hitherto lavished our substance to Great Britain for, can well be disposed with while the necessaries of life are to be procured for the most part within ourselves. This consequently will introduce frugality and be a necessary stimulation to [our] industry.

After six years of study and experimentation, after years of watching his profits decline, even after he bought more land and more slaves and shouldered his way into the front rank of Virginia's aristocratic planters, George Washington was ready to emerge as a leading critic of the time-honored tobacco trade. In private at first, he was declaring his own independence from the tobacco culture that had built the mansions of the south and then locked it through debt into what he had come to consider a master-slave relationship with English merchants.

In 1765 Washington planted no tobacco on his Potomac plantations. Over the past few years he had gradually switched to wheat and corn that he could market in the American colonies. As a pioneer in diversified farming in America, he was now in a position to predict that punitive British levies would only drive other Americans to make themselves less dependent on imported English goods by developing their own crops and manufacturing goods for their own markets:

Great Britain may then load her exports with as heavy taxes as she pleases but where will the consumption be? I am apt to think no law or usage can compel us to barter our money or staple commodities for their manufactures if we can be supplied within ourselves upon better terms. . . . Where then lies the utility of these measures?[2]

Not only did Washington for the first time publicly criticize British trade policy, but he fired a volley from Virginia at the Stamp Act at exactly the time a specially summoned Stamp Act Congress was denouncing it in New York City. By this time there had been riots in Boston, New York, and Philadelphia, and in virtually every American seaport town. Every farmer and planter, every shipowner and investor, was threatened by the new levy. What Washington termed the "speculative part of the colonists"—anyone with any risk about his business—talked of nothing else. Washington was not one to join in a riot, but he complained bitterly from his paneled study at Mount Vernon to Robert Cary, his London agent, his official and only representative in England. Washington himself was one of those "speculative" Americans "who look upon this un-constitutional method of taxation as a direful attack upon their liberties and loudly exclaim against the violation."[3]

Washington went even further. In his own "single and distinct view" he predicted the Stamp Act would cause as much damage to the British as to Americans:

> The first bad consequence attending it I take to be this. Our courts of judicature will be shut up. It is morally impossible under our present circumstances that the Act of Parliament can be complied with were we willing to enforce [it]. . . .There is not [any] money to pay the stamp. If a stop be put on our judi-cial proceedings, it may be left to yourselves, who have such large demands upon the colonies, to determine who is to suffer most in this event—the merchant or the planter.[4]

In other words, if protesting Virginians shut down the courts, how could British merchants hope to collect the debts that Virginia planters had run up over so many years? Few men in all the south were as free to challenge the century-and-a-half-old system. Washington had, in little more than ten years, become a wealthy planter and then a major debtor and freed himself from the vicious cycle of dependency. Now he was emerging that rarest of men: a critic who could offer a solution.

*I*n the years after Washington resigned from the Virginia Regi-ment and took his seat in the House of Burgesses, he completely re-shaped his way of life into that of a Tidewater planter. His way of life, but not his methods. As the head of a small frontier army he had chosen to be a micromanager rather than to delegate. He had selected, whenever he could, his own officers and then he had made them his subordinates rather than delegating authority to them. They reported everything to him and deferred to him and enforced his decisions. But he made all the orders and all the decisions, large and small. As a planter, he merely shifted over the same system to agriculture. He chose the overseers, his farm managers. He told them exactly and in great detail what he wanted and expected and then he inspected the next day to see that his instruc-tions had been carried out. As a planter he was a good general and a busi-nessman. That still left him plenty of time to study, to experiment, and to innovate on both small and large scales. He took full responsibility for what he knew and could control, and what he did not understand he tended to blame on some higher authority. For many years he attributed his failures to the royal governor. Later, it was the British merchant and the British home government who were at fault. Yet his attempts at re-form are noteworthy. They led him to work out a new system. He tried to break out of the old Tidewater tobacco-and-slave culture into the over-the-mountains west, where he would sell land to thousands of new farmers. When these efforts were frustrated by faraway British bureaucrats, he decided to risk everything to create a new form of government, one he could personally arrange and control. The colonel became a successful businessman, and when his business schemes were stymied he became a general and a revolutionary.

While Martha Custis Washington settled into Mount Vernon and crowded it with the furniture from her first marriage, her husband developed a routine he broke only when he traveled to Williamsburg or to inspect distant landholdings. Up at four o'clock in the morning, he retreated into his small dark-paneled office and wrote letters, posted accounts, and studied until six. In the early years of marriage he mostly studied agriculture, as an inventory of his copious library shows. He kept careful records of everything imaginable, including his library holdings. Over the years he ordered four inventories and kept separate the books Martha had brought with her, which had once belonged to her late father-in-law Custis. By sorting out these books Washington left a good accounting of which books he purchased between 1759 when he married and 1764 when he ordered the next inventory. His books on farming included Henri Louis Duhamel's *Practical Treatise of Husbandry*, Langley's *Gardening*, Thomas Hale's four-volume *Compleat Body of Husbandry*, Edward Lisle's two-volume *Observations in Husbandry*, John Ball's *Farmer's Compleat Guide*, Robert Maxwell's *Practical Husbandmen*, Jacques de Solleysell's *The Compleat Horseman*, and Gibson's *Farriery*. He studied systematically the farmer, the field, the animal, and even the horseshoe. This was Washington's period of greatest self-education. He ordered the latest books on his favorite subjects from England and France as soon as he learned about their publication from conversations with his neighbors, his relatives, or his contacts in England. But he also read widely on other subjects. He read the Bible and a book about Mohammed—Humphrey Prideaux's *True Nature of Imposture Fully Displayed in the Life of Mahomet*—even before Thomas Jefferson acquired and read a translation of the Koran. The early morning hours were sacred to Washington, and his inventories give only scant hint of all the pamphlets, newspapers, and London magazines he devoured. He subscribed to Dodsley's *Annual Register* and to *Gentleman's Magazine*, as well as to *Merchants Magazine*.

All was not work and study. While there were standard reference works on medicine and chemistry and venereal disease he also made a special study of gardening. His neighbor George Mason brought him seeds, plantings, and advice. Washington continued to buy and read the latest novels—anything by Smollett or Defoe—and he bought Smollett's eleven-volume *History of England* as it was issued.[5]

From his books and from long talks with trusted friends and the best overseers he could hire, Washington tried to master the principles of the tobacco culture. His manor house was modest by Tidewater standards, but he had enough acreage to become a major planter. Before his marriage he leased or owned more than 4,700 acres and owned or rented fifty slaves who worked on his five separate Potomac farms. In addition, he still maintained his Bullskin farm. With his marriage he assumed the administration of 18,000 Custis acres on the York River, where the sweetest tobacco in Virginia grew. From the day he settled in at Mount Vernon with Martha he began to acquire nearby lands and dreamed of great tracts farther away.

While Washington was serving on the frontier he had entrusted the farming to his younger brother, Jack. His brother-in-law, Fielding Lewis, and Sally Fairfax's brother-in-law, John Carlyle of Alexandria, had marketed Washington's crops for him. But now he insisted on learning every fact of the tobacco trade. It was a practical science that had changed little since the early seventeenth century. Planting began early each year, traditionally twelve days after Christmas. Slaves planted the seeds in beds that they manured and then covered with oak leaves or straw to keep off frost. So many plants died that Washington, like his neighbors, sometimes set out ten plants for every one he expected to harvest. Four months later, in May, the slaves transplanted the survivors into mounds about three feet apart. Within a week the hoeing of the cloying red clay soil had to begin. Every five or six days the slaves had to repeat this endless backbreaking handwork to make sure air and rainwater penetrated to the roots. By mid- or late June, the field slaves, in their drooping felt hats and baggy overalls, had to top the plants. They pinched off the tops and left five to nine leaves to mature. The plant, stunted, sent all its nutriments to the broadening bright green leaves. For eight more weeks in the searing sunlight of a Chesapeake summer the slaves hoed the rows and bent low hour after hour to pull off any unwanted young leaves.

By September the crop was ready to be cut. The slaves chopped off the rich heavy leaves and left them in the rows to sun-dry for several hours and then gathered them in mule-drawn wagons that traversed the row ends to transport the sweet-smelling leaves to slit-windowed barns, where they hung on pegged sticks to dry and cure for several weeks. When the leaves were just dry enough so they would not rot and crumble, the crucial step of "prizing," packing them down tightly into hogsheads—barrels four feet high and three feet across crafted on the farm by slave coopers—could begin. By the time the slaves carefully crammed one thousand pounds of tobacco into each hogshead and carted it off in a wagon to the Fairfax County warehouse for inspection, grading, and weighing before spring shipment to England, fully fifteen months had elapsed since planting time. Washington was there every day supervising every step. He ate a hearty breakfast with Martha and the children at six, was on his horse by seven, and on his way on a fifteen-mile daily round of inspections.

*E*arly in his recuperation at Mount Vernon from Braddock's march in 1755, Washington began to trade his tobacco for the luxury goods from England that turned his farmhouse into a great manor. He sent his first two hogsheads of tobacco to Richard Washington (no relation) in London. Over the next three years he sent off to England more and more tobacco, which his brother Jack had raised while Washington was at the front. On his behalf, his friend John Carlyle opened up a commercial correspondence in 1756 by shipping a few hogsheads of Washington's tobacco to Thomas Knox, a factor in the western England port of Bristol. Washington ordered some goods from Knox so that he could compare the price he received for his crop and the prices he had to pay for English goods.

One of the functions of the British tobacco factor was to send out his own agent to shop for whatever goods the American client requested, whether it was a fine carriage, seeds, or a hoe. At every step of the way the planter bore the costs and paid commissions and assumed all of the risks. Few Virginians owned their ships. English factors dispatched their own ships to the Tidewater to sail upriver to take on the cargo of hogsheads that were rolled down the docks by gangs of sweating, struggling slaves. The planters paid for the cartage to the ship, paid a per barrel freight charge, and paid insurance in case the ship sank in a storm or was captured by the French. The ship captains advanced all the fees, especially the customs duties assessed by the British. These could amount to as much as 80 percent of the sale price of the tobacco.

It was understood that once the tobacco arrived in England and was unloaded (more fees) and carted to the warehouse (even more charges) the factor would seek the best price for good-quality leaves in exchange for a per-hogshead commission. After all fees and taxes, Washington probably received no more than 25 percent of the price his tobacco fetched on the London market. The consignment merchant then offered a variety of other services for additional fees. Their agents could buy the latest fashions in London, hunt up Washington's favorite cheeses—double Gloucester and Cheshire—or hyssop to treat his digestive ailment, or anything that could not by law be produced in the colonies, such as a felt hat. The merchant usually extended credit if the goods cost more than the value of the crop and charged 5 percent interest, the highest allowed by law. Three percent commissions on all of these purchases further reduced the profits. The merchants also acted as bankers, allowing their planter-clients to draw bills of exchange that served as certified checks against the proceeds of tobacco sales or in expectation of future shipments. To land-hungry tobacco planters such as Washington this ability to pay with what amounted to a certified check was crucial. The bills had become the principal medium of exchange in Virginia, as well as a source of credit. An important reason to use a large mercantile firm rather than a small one was that the great London factors could obtain discounts on customs duties because they could pay them in cash. In his first modest dealings in 1755, Washington was trying to gain access to British luxury goods. Ordering two suits of livery for his servants and personal furnishings such as a monogrammed saddle, he asked the merchant to "choose agreeable to the present taste and send things good of their kind." This became his constant refrain: the goods should be fashionable and of the best quality. Tidewater gentry expected to wear the latest London fashions within a few months of their appearance in the shops on the Strand.[6]

When Washington decided to turn Mount Vernon into a showcase, he began to exchange his increased tobacco production for the kind of British luxury goods found in the best Virginia plantation houses. His orders document his decision to leave the raw frontier army life and lead a life of English-style refinement and taste one month before he paid his first visit to Martha at the White House. He had ordered papier-mâché ceiling ornaments and Wilton carpets for the renovated Mount Vernon as well as a "neat" landscape that still hangs today over the mantel in the west parlor. In London, Richard Washington's agent bought him a selection of mahogany furniture—including a four-poster bed at auction for £25. He also sent along coarse cloth for the slaves, cheap stoneware, grubbing hoes, and large quantities of nails for the reconstruction work. The colonists were barred from making iron or steel. By the time he married, George Washington, like every other Virginia planter, depended on his London factor for nearly everything.

Marriage to Martha provided Washington with great new opportunities for getting and spending, not the least important of which was her London factor. Now he could sell and buy with the same few great mercantile houses who corresponded with the most opulent of Tidewater planters. He also gained a discernible voice in London. Readers of London magazines who had heard of Washington the intrepid young officer now learned that he had money to spend—and that he was proud of it. He closed out his accounts with Thomas Knox and curtailed his orders to Richard Washington and made Robert Cary & Co., a major mercantile firm that corresponded with many of the wealthiest Tidewater planters and was already agent for the Custis farms on the York River, his own agent in England:

> The enclosed is the minister's certificate of my marriage with Mrs. Martha Custis. . . . You will therefore for the future please to address all your letters which relate to the affairs of the late Daniel Parke Custis, Esq., to me as by marriage I am entitled to a third part of that estate and [I am] invested likewise with the care of the other two thirds by a decree of our General Court.[7]

Each spring now, the Cary ship picked up tobacco from Washington's York River farms, and Washington found ships on the Potomac that would carry his Mount Vernon crop to the Cary wharves in London. In this way, he began to study at close hand all the charges and inequities involved for an American trading with England. He learned the long list of customs duties. For each hogshead of tobacco he exported from Virginia he paid a two shillings export duty. The ship's captain advanced this hard-money duty and then charged it to Washington's London account. Once the ship arrived in England, the merchant paid the duties under a complicated formula. The Crown had repeatedly increased the original duty of one penny in the pound of tobacco. But the big London merchant houses never paid this amount in full because they received a discount for cash payments that was not available to faraway American planters. They then received a further discount for making payments with bonds on the remaining customs duties. In addition, Cary and other large brokers received even deeper discounts because they had accumulated sufficient reserves to pay all the duties in cash. The firm also paid the freight charges, which were double during the Seven Years' War, dropping after the Peace of Paris of 1763 from £16 to £8 per ton. Washington noticed that Cary charged more per ton, as large as the firm was, than the rate he could negotiate on his own with ship captains on the Potomac. He also discovered that the captains did not bother to weigh the hogsheads, but regardless of weight calculated that four barrels equaled one ton. He ordered his overseers to see that more than one thousand pounds of tobacco was prized into each barrel, cutting his freight costs in half. He then began to shop around for better rates for his tobacco and lower prices for staple goods. Sending test shipments to merchants in Liverpool and Bristol, he found that salt from Liverpool was much cheaper than from London.

But it was to Cary of London that the Washingtons sent their orders for luxury goods that the agent forwarded to as many as forty-five tradesmen and artisans. Cary bought the goods on credit and included the credit charge along with his 3 percent commission in the price he charged Washington. The broker made a further profit by paying off the charge early, but he did not pass this saving along to Washington. A whole range of new charges accumulated as the order went from merchant to warehouse to dockside to ship and through customs and insurance brokers' hands. Often a full year after Washington had sent off the big annual order with his crop, he received word that his order had arrived—somewhere in Virginia. Often it was dropped beside the wrong river and when he finally learned of it he had to pay a teamster to go fetch it with his horse and wagon.

Despite all these difficulties, the Washingtons flourished. Their long-distance buying and selling spree in the first two years after they married transformed Mount Vernon into a Tidewater gem. In 1760 and 1761 he produced 93,000 pounds of tobacco each year on his Mount Vernon farms. He cleared approximately £1,200 in each of these peak years, but that didn't include his production costs and excluded his investments in more land and slaves so that he could increase his production. Against the credit for tobacco on his London account, he ordered the blue-and-white wallpaper Martha had chosen for the upstairs rooms, the fine china and the silver, the latest in fashionable clothes, more furniture, books, porcelains, busts, and paintings. What they received often did not dovetail with what he thought he had ordered. When he ordered a series of martial busts for his library, Washington received instead the supposed likenesses of Roman philosophers. He complained but scoffed at the London merchant's suggestion that he return them for a credit.

Among the merchandise he ordered were slaves. As he plowed back his profits to expand his farms, he sent off orders to an agent in the West Indies for more slave laborers. Slavery had been expanding exponentially in Virginia for fifty years. The supply of white indentured servants had dried up as peace came to Europe and conditions in English towns and cities improved and the miserable chance of surviving the first five years of servitude in the heat and disease of the Chesapeake Tidewater—one in two—became widely known in Europe. Washington was no more racist than most Americans of his time. Only a few northern Quakers were troubled by the traffic in humans who were clearing the land and building the houses and the profits of the white ruling class. Washington accepted the institution he had always known and did not question it until he began to consider its financial consequences.

In his first fifteen years as a planter, he bought and sold slaves with a clear conscience. Sending off a shipment of tobacco to the Islands, he told his Caribbean agent to buy "Negroes if choice ones can be had under 40 pounds Sterling" and "if not, then [buy] rum and sugar." He seems to have sold slaves only when they attempted to run away: to him this was an unforgivable form of theft of his valuable property. He ordered one slave exchanged for molasses, rum, limes, tamarinds, and sweetmeats for Martha's kitchen and table. Other slaves, possibly even relatives of the bartered man, would serve these delicacies to Washington, his family, and friends.

When four of Washington's slaves escaped at once late in the summer of 1761, he wrote out a long, detailed description for inclusion in Virginia and Maryland newspapers and offered a hefty forty-shilling reward for their recapture. While planter and slaves were in church, the four young men "went off without the least suspicion, provocation or difference with anybody or the least angry word or abuse from their overseers." His descriptions were so vivid that it is no wonder that all four were eventually tracked down and returned to him in irons for severe floggings:

Ran away from a plantation of the subscriber's on Dogue Run in Fairfax on Sunday the 9th instant the following slaves viz.

Peros, 35 or 40 years of age, a well-set fellow of about 5 feet 8 inches high, yellowish complexion with a very full round face and full black beard. His speech is something slow and broke but not in so great a degree as to render him remarkable. He had on when he went away a dark colour'd cloth coat, a white linen waistcoat, white breeches and white stockings.

None of this, if it ever occurred to a man of his time and place, bothered him. In his diary, he wrote of "my Negroes" and "a wench of mine." They were valuable, productive, and sometimes troublesome property, nothing more and nothing less.[8]

The slave overseers Washington employed to manage his farms partially screened his view of the harsh conditions of servitude of his black chattel. On one farm a slave received only one shirt a year. One winter an overseer told Washington that he needed more money because the "little Negroes" were virtually without clothing in the poorly heated slave cabins, which had dirt floors and no glass over the windows. The same overseer reminded Washington that he had forgotten to provide blankets on the farm and reported that he was improvising with some "Negro cotton" he had found and distributed among pregnant women and small children. The reports of Washington's managers reveal frequent illness among slaves. One field hand was forced to work, even though he had measles and suffered from a "violent pox and vomiting." Usually it was the fault of the overseers, who did not bother to call a doctor and hesitated to trouble their master. No wonder that some slaves ran away despite their certain knowledge that they would be hunted down with dogs, severely flogged in front of the entire farm family, and, if they dared a second escape attempt and were caught, sold away from their families to the West Indies, where conditions were even harsher and life shorter.[9]

There is no indication Washington was any harsher than his white neighbors and, in fact, there is evidence he was beginning to call the slave system into question purely on economic if not humanitarian grounds. By the mid-eighteenth century there were as many white bond servants in America as black slaves, most of them in the north. Washington's first teacher had been an indentured servant at Ferry Farm, and in his surveying and military forays over the mountains Washington had encountered many former bond servants who had worked off their ship's passage in five to seven years and received 50-acre freeholds of Virginia land. Washington began to hire indentured white servants at Mount Vernon. He did not need more unskilled labor—he had black slaves for that—but he purchased the bonds of skilled white artisans. He employed a joiner and a gardener in this fashion and used white skilled laborers as carpenters, millers, bricklayers, weavers, and metal workers. He paid good wages for the time and demanded six days a week of hard work. Any sick time had to be made up. As he expanded his real estate speculations he explored the idea of importing shiploads of German farmworkers from the Rhine to work off their ship passage for five years clearing and cultivating his wilderness acres. He rewarded his plantation overseers with contract renewals. John Alton managed a Mount Vernon farm and worked for Washington for thirty years until his death in 1785. Lund Washington, a distant younger cousin, went to work managing Washington's home farm in 1764 and operated it in Washington's absence through the Revolution.

By 1764, when Lund took the reins at Mount Vernon under Washington's watchful eye, the master of Mount Vernon was calling much of the traditional tobacco culture into question and blaming its failures on the British. He had become a businessman who no longer relied on the traditional assumptions of the tobacco planter's way of life. One reason was that, after his first two bountiful harvests, his crop yields had declined. At the same time he discovered by talking to Northern Neck neighbors that they were receiving higher rates for their tobacco, often twelve pence a pound when he received eleven and a half. He later discovered that some planters on the York River received as much as 30 percent more per hogshead than he was paid. He never did realize that the York River plantations had alluvial soil far superior to his thin shale Potomac ledge soil. No one knew at the time that tobacco was the most devastating crop, one that depleted the soil in only a few years.

Almost as soon as Washington became a full-time farmer he began to conduct experiments that closely followed his readings. In March 1760, he planted alfalfa after reading "what [Jethro] Tull says." That same year he sowed clover, rye, grass, hops, trefoil, timothy, a variety of wheat called spelt, and several other grasses and vegetables, many of them unknown to other Virginia farmers. He also began to experiment ahead of his time with compost. On April 14, 1760, he recorded in his diary:

> *Mixed my composts in a box with the apartments in the following*
> *manner:*
> *No. 1 is three pecks of earth brought from below the hill out of the 46-acre*
> *field without any mixture;*
> *No. 2 is two pecks of sand earth and one of marl taken out of the said*
> *field;*
> *No. 3 has 2 pecks of sand earth and one of river sand;*
> *No. 4 has a peck of horse dung;*
> *No. 5 has mud taken out of creek;*
> *No. 6 has cow dung;*
> *No. 7 has marl from the gulleys on the hillside which seemed to be purer*
> *than the other;*
> *No. 8 Sheep dung;*
> *No. 9 Black mould from the gulleys on the hill side which seem to be purer*
> *than the other;*
> *No. 10 Clay got just below the garden.*

He ordered "all mixed with the same quality and soil of earth" and had each specimen broken up "to a tolerable degree of fineness" on a cloth. In each section he planted "three grains of wheat, three of oats, and as many barley, all of equal distances in rows and of equal depth by a machine [I] made for the purpose." He was systematic about watering "two or three hours after sowing" and "about an hour before sunset" with equal amounts of water left standing in a tub for "two hours exposed to the sun." Three weeks later he found that sections number 8 and 9 gave the best results.

That same spring he also experimented with a plow he designed, using his carriage horses to pull it. On the second attempt, after he "spent the greater part of the day in making a new plow of my own invention," he "found she worked very well." By adding more teeth to a drag harrow, he was able to break up the soil more finely "for harrowing in grain." Some of his experiments failed. He tried to grow oats in wintertime. Any experienced Virginia farmer could have told him the climate was too cold—the crop failed. But Washington had to try out everything for himself.

In his first full season of agriculture he also began to experiment with livestock. He kept a stallion for breeding both his own stables and those of neighbors. Eventually he introduced six stallions. The most famous was Magnolia, a full-blooded Arabian. He advertised in newspapers for other breeders to bring their mares to his pastures and guaranteed they would produce foals. It was another matter to collect the stud fees from the cash-poor country gentry. By 1785, shortly after he retired from the Revolutionary army, he had 130 horses grazing and switching in the lush grass outside Mount Vernon, including his old warhorses Nelson and Blueskin. Twenty-seven of them were worn-out army mares. He also introduced Narragansett pacing horses, one of which threw him for the only recorded fall of his adulthood when he was past sixty-five. Washington mounted the horse again and rode home. Thomas Jefferson, a master horseman and breeder of thoroughbreds, called Washington the greatest horseman of his age. The French Marquis de Chastellux noted that it was Washington "himself who breaks all his own horses and he is a very excellent and bold horseman, leaping the highest fences and going extremely quick without standing upon his stirrups, bearing on the bridle or letting his horse run wild."[10]

He had less success with raising sheep—which require the same skilled hand in constant attendance—but good luck with beef cattle and dairy cows. By the end of this first term as president he had 101 dairy cows producing milk and butter for the local market and more than three hundred Black Angus cattle branded with his *GW*. He also raised oxen to do much of the hard work on his farms. He was more successful in keeping track of his cattle than his hogs, little more than razorbacks that roamed free at Mount Vernon. He estimated that half of them disappeared into the pots of his slaves. Eventually he closed the pigs in modern pens with plank floors, roofs, running water, and troughs. Until his death he experimented with new breeds, including red Chinese pigs and Guinea swine he imported from West Africa. He also raised chickens, turkeys, swans, ducks, and geese. His former officers sent him specimens as presents: he was especially delighted by golden pheasants brought by an American ship captain from China.

His wide readings and his restless need to test out old ideas and introduce new ones led to constant hustle and bustle at Mount Vernon. He could not stand to see men idle. He even experimented with having gangs of slaves scoop up silt from the bottom of the Potomac and spread it on his fields. If the silt had not been the runoff of played-out tobacco fields, this would have been a wonderful idea. In the end, Washington was baffled. But he blamed his British factors, not his own self-taught farming or his poor soil. "Certain I am no person in Virginia takes more pains to make their tobacco fine than I do and 'tis hard then [to understand why] I should not be well rewarded for it." He finally conceded that tobacco raising might be "an art beyond my skill."[11]

*B*y 1765, when the Stamp Act crisis broke like a tidal wave over colonial America, Washington had all but abandoned tobacco planting at Mount Vernon. He only continued it on Custis lands along the York and Pamunkey Rivers, using the proceeds from his third of the estate to retire his debt with Cary. Even after peace with France returned in 1763 and the capture of English ships ended, he found tobacco sales disappointing. So he bought more land, more slaves, following the conventional wisdom. He used bills of credit drawn on Robert Cary's firm to buy it. In June 1760, he drew two bills totaling £669 to help pay for nearly 2,000 acres across Little Hunting Creek from the original Mount Vernon farm. Three months later he drew another £200 to buy 238 acres adjoining Mount Vernon. In 1761 he drew £259 on the Cary account to buy slaves. These drafts reached Cary about the same time Washington presented Cary with four bills of exchange paid to Washington by people who owed him money. They were protested—in modern terms, they were bad checks. Suddenly, Washington found himself £1,900 in debt to Cary. Just another debt-ridden Virginian like so many of his neighbors, he was stunned. He redoubled his efforts to produce tobacco efficiently, assuring Cary he was "more anxious about the quality than the quantity of tobacco I ship."

Mystified and frustrated, Washington fumed at having to pay interest on his debt. He cut back the consumption of luxury goods at Mount Vernon. What he ordered he now inspected with a gimlet eye, complaining whenever the goods weren't the best. He compared the prices Cary in London charged with prices he researched in Virginia stores and prices paid in other English ports. Cary's prices were running 25 percent higher than his research had led him to project. Linens, woolens, and even nails were of poor quality. Instead of being in the latest London fashion, some clothes Martha received "could only have been used," as Washington put it, "by our forefathers in days of yore." Nothing seemed to fit. Martha wound up wearing a nightgown intended for six-year-old Patcy. Washington concluded that London tradesmen were dumping inferior and out-of-fashion goods on the Americans at huge profits. When he ordered a post chaise for his sister Betty and her husband Fielding Lewis, he sent Cary orders not to tell the carriage maker it was to be shipped to Virginia. After five years of driving Martha's rattle-trap buggy, Washington had saved up enough to order a luxurious green carriage sporting his coat of arms on its doors. It began to fall apart at the dock.

Then Cary put pressure on Washington to pay off his debt all at once. Washington responded by sending him his entire crop and ordering only necessities until the debt was paid. But he deeply resented the high-handed treatment. He expected a firm that received most of his business to be patient about a temporary debt. He thought he should have time to collect what was owed him and retire the obligation to Cary "without distressing myself too much." He became more scrupulous about his credit, but he was clearly annoyed. When another large firm mistakenly protested a bill he had drawn on the account of Jackie Custis, Washington closed out the account and would not allow the firm to explain the error.

At first he focused his wrath on his British brokers because they refused to send their ships up the Potomac to his dock at Mount Vernon and forced him to waste his time hunting down isolated cargo ships to send off his Mount Vernon crops. For ten years he hounded Cary to accommodate him and stop dumping his deliveries anywhere his ships touched Virginia. He complained bitterly when he discovered that linens and woolens he ordered from Cary cost just as much as comparable goods in Virginia stores, despite all the shipping and insurance costs. Did not Robert Cary & Co. buy goods in sufficient quantities to receive a wholesaler's discount? Shouldn't that be passed along, in part at least, to such an important client? "The heavy charges upon our tobacco and the ample and uncommon commissions which are drawn upon the sales of it" ought to entitle the planter "every advantage which can be procured in the purchase of our goods. Otherwise I should be glad to know to what end we import them."[12]

This had, in fact, become the paramount question to Washington.

As his production and his profits declined in the 1760s, even as political tensions increased, George Washington came to view his problems in the tobacco trade as part of a larger problem: Virginia's total economic dependence on Great Britain. Poor soil, his own inexperience, the changing world tobacco market—none of these factors sufficiently explained the problem to him. He may have been the first Virginian who realized that the colony's complete reliance on a single export to England

and the virtual absence of any other alternative crop or manufacturing or source of credit created a hideous cycle of overproduction, expansion into even more unsuitable lands, falling prices, and even heavier indebtedness. Gradually, between 1760 and 1765, Washington decided to break his own dependence on England by diversifying his crops and developing his own alternative supplies of basic manufactured goods.

He began by investing in improvements to his flour mill, then decided to plant wheat; he increased the plantings each year until he crowded out all tobacco production at Mount Vernon by 1765. He built a sawmill and then built a fishing schooner to harvest shad and herring in the Potomac. When his sales of wheat and fish in the Alexandria market burgeoned, he bought an even larger ship for a whopping £275, a brigantine, to seine the waters of the Potomac and deliver catches quickly to local markets. He covered his hillsides with peach and apple orchards, introducing the hard, tart Newton pippin from Long Island, New York. He talked of buying an iron furnace in the Shenandoah Valley. When the Crown offered the American colonies a subsidy for growing flax and hemp, which the Royal Navy needed to make rope, he wrote to Robert Cary for instructions on how to cure the hemp. He ordered the equipment to turn flax into rough linen, which he then sold not in England but on the local markets. As his wheat crops outgrew the Alexandria market he began selling them in Philadelphia and to the West Indies.

His ventures flourished. By September 1765, when he wrote to warn Robert Cary of the consequences of further tax increases, Washington was in a position not only to predict but to profit from a buy-American campaign. He was systematically paying off his debt in England, had stanched the hemorrhage of buying luxury goods, and had become a net exporter of tobacco and wheat. He was also becoming the leading advocate of the domestic marketplace. He had taught his tenant farmers to sell their tobacco to Scottish merchants who took the trouble and expense to set up shop in Virginia and were paying cash for crops. Now the tenants were paying him his rents in cash. And if he needed to buy anything, he first tried to buy it for cash in Virginia or Maryland or Philadelphia. He knew he was on solid ground when he predicted that Britain's demands for even more tax revenue would only further weaken the mother country's commercial stranglehold on the colonies. All that the English would succeed in doing would be to force more Americans to do as he had done—"introduce frugality and a necessary stimulant to industry." Washington intended to be ready when that happened.

*L*earning by reading, by observation, by experience, George Washington had mastered the business of tobacco planting if not the act. Everything imaginable—glutted markets, rising costs, damages in shipping, too much rain or too little—had befallen his harvests. At first he practiced stoicism. When swarms of bugs and worms damaged his crop, he wondered why Noah ever "suffered such a brood of vermin to get a berth in the ark." What Washington did not for a long time grasp was that the world tobacco market was rapidly and radically changing. Once high, predictable prices in England had been sustained artificially by scarcity when the French captured English trading ships. Washington expanded his plantings just as Virginia tobacco production returned to full capacity after the defeat of the French. Now that virtually all the tobacco-laden ships got through to England, oversupply sent prices tumbling. London merchants re-exported their surplus tobacco to Europe. Peace brought an eager market in France but the additional costs for reshipping and customs left barely any profit for planters like Washington.[13]

Worse, European tastes were changing. The French did not like Washington's sweet tobacco but preferred the harsher Orinoco leaf—which was cheaper but also less profitable to Washington. Instead of adjusting his plantings he complained to his English agents. Yet he could plainly see that small-scale farmers in Virginia had no trouble selling their crops of the new Orinoco brand. The last straw in his dealings with his London factors came when Scottish merchants began to open hundreds of stores in Virginia and Maryland to buy tobacco directly from smaller planters who were not interested in access to luxury goods in England. Not only was the sweet tobacco crop of the rich Tidewater estate becoming unfashionable but the price of slaves to produce it was making the cost of labor insupportable. By the time the British added their latest obnoxious stamp tax to his expenses, Washington was ready to rethink the whole tobacco business. If small backcountry farmers were eager to grow the new tobacco and settle for smaller profits, he would cut his losses, curtail his planting, and provide them with what they wanted—land. He would either sell it or rent it to them. More and more he was becoming a land speculator, substituting the buying and selling of land for slaves. Instead of a slave trader he became a landlord. He was ready to listen when his friend George Mason talked about abolishing further imports of slaves so that more white immigrants would be attracted to Virginia to buy and rent his land. As it was, there was no work for white immigrant laborers and no incentive for them to migrate. While tensions with the British government increased and hundreds of Virginia planters continued down the road of escalating debt to English merchants, Washington planted his last tobacco crop at Mount Vernon in 1765 and once again turned to face west for his economic future. In the ten years before the Revolution he pursued land grants that would yield him tens of thousands of acres of rich saleable farmland from the Canadian border to Florida, from Virginia to the Mississippi.

As long ago as 1753, when the young Washington had tramped on snowshoes into the Ohio Valley for the first time to deliver an ultimatum to the French, he had grasped the possibilities of staking out a great landed estate in the rich soil of the interior river valleys. In a 1767 letter to one of the men who had fought at his side against the French, he summed up the philosophy that had made him persevere through five years of hardships on the frontier and now impelled him to push hard for what he considered the veterans' fair share of the rewards for driving out the French:

> There is a large field before you, an opening prospect in the back country for adventurers ... where an enterprising man with very little money may lay the foundation of a noble estate in the new settlements upon Monongahela for himself and posterity. The surplus money which you might save after discharging your debts would possibly secure you as much land as in the course of twenty years [with] five times your present estate.

In this remarkable letter to a friend who owed him money, Washington revealed the thinking that was making him turn his back on the Tidewater and plan a future in over-the-mountain America, now that the French had withdrawn and their Indian allies were more subdued. He told Captain Robert Posey "only look to Frederick" (Maryland), where he had bought his Bullskin farm and where settlers Washington had first met as a fifteen-year-old surveyor's assistant now owned vast plantations:

> See what fortunes were made by the first takers up of those lands. Nay, how the greatest estates we have in this colony were made. Was it not by taking up and purchasing at very low rates the rich back lands which were thought nothing of in those days but are now the most valuable lands we possess? Undoubtedly it was. . . . Disengage yourself of these incumbrances and vexations. Abiding where you are if you can save your land and have a prospect of reaping future advantages from it or [removing] back where there is a moral certainty of laying the foundations of good estates [for] your children—I say I would but ask which of these two is the best.[14]

Washington was reminding Posey of the amazing success of Jost Hite, whom Washington had visited on his first long-ago surveying trip and who now owned some 100,000 acres on the Virginia frontier. But such numbers no longer seemed grandiose as he advised a young man to go west.

Under the terms of the Ohio Company's 1749 grant, Lawrence Washington and his colleagues were to receive 200,000 acres of Ohio Valley land if they built a fort and settled one hundred people near the Forks of the Ohio; if they met the seven-year deadline they would receive a further 300,000 acres. At Lawrence's death, Washington had assumed his shares. Governor Dinwiddie had dangled 5,000 more acres—or so Washington had thought—for officers who enlisted in 1754 to march over the mountains to confront the French. During the nine-year-long French and Indian War, all the claims of the Ohio Company had expired. War had made fulfilling the terms of the grant impossible. Washington and his fellow officers had to start all over. In 1760, Washington helped to revive the company and prevailed on his partners to send his former second in command, Major George Mercer, to London as its agent to lobby Parliament to revive the grant.

In the aftermath of the French and Indian War, the British ministry decided that the only way to keep peace with Indians who had withdrawn to the west was to draw a line along the ridge of the Alleghenies and make it the boundary for western settlement by whites. Everything west of the mountains would be an Indian reserve. At first, Washington scoffed. The line was only to appease the Indians and was only temporary, he predicted. Land speculators could ignore it and, in fact, anyone who "neglects the present opportunity of hunting out good lands will never again regain it."[15]

This was a race Washington did not intend to lose. In 1763 he invested in a land company that proposed, if granted a royal charter, to drain the Great Dismal Swamp of southern Virginia, which he had first visited as a young adjutant at age twenty. After a few years of struggling with his own soil at Mount Vernon, Washington became intrigued by the idea of forming a company to drain this remote tangle of thickets and bogs that spread from the Chesapeake into North Carolina. Once, Governor Dinwiddie had fobbed him off with this adjutant's region. Now he willingly ventured in and found that all around the margins of the swamp settlers were draining the spongy land. They had turned it into rich, dark soil excellent for farming, and they were harvesting cypress and cedar. During his inspection tour early in 1763 Washington concluded that the deep rivers that cut in from the Atlantic could make the stands of timber and the alluvial soil highly profitable—if only the swamp could be drained. With his brothers-in-law Fielding Lewis and Burwell Bassett (married to Martha's youngest sister, Betty) he helped to organize the Adventurers for Draining the Dismal Swamp. Each shareholder pledged ten laborers to drain the land in exchange for a claim on 1,000 acres. In four subsequent visits, Washington and Lewis bought 1,100 acres on the swamp's southern rim. By 1768 Washington was marketing cypress shingles from these lands.

In June 1763, Washington and eighteen other planters from the Northern Neck met at the Stafford County plantation of Thomas Ludwell Lee to form yet another company, the Mississippi Land Company, that was to yield each of fifty prospective shareholders 50,000 acres each. The shareholders included Washington's brother Jack and four members of the Lee family. Two other Washingtons, Charles and Samuel, later bought shares. Washington wrote out the articles of agreement himself. The company sought 2.5 million acres at the confluence of the Ohio and Mississippi Rivers along 210 miles of Mississippi riverfront. They asked the Crown to build a fort to protect the settlement "from the insults of the savages." They asked for twelve years to settle the lands "if not interrupted by the savages." The company voted to hire an English agent, Thomas Cummings of London, and offer him one share. He was to find nine other influential English shareholders. Washington dangled the prospect of royal subsidies to grow hemp on the land. The lower Ohio, he wrote to Cummings, was peculiarly suited to hemp cultivation "because that plant so greatly and quickly impoverishes ground that to make it in many quantities not only a soil uncommonly fertile is requisite but there must be a prodigious quantity." Washington added some real estate boilerplate about "the fineness of the climate" and the "goodness of the navigation" that would offer "powerful inducements [that] cannot fail to effect a speedy settlement" and which "render the share of each adventurer extremely valuable."

The grant was supposed to open up lands extending along the Mississippi from the Ohio to the Tennessee Rivers. He wrote that it would not irritate the pro-English Cherokee and Choctaw neighbors. That it might violate the 1758 Treaty of Easton that guaranteed all lands west of the Alleghenies to the Indians was no problem, he contended, because the treaty only applied to Indians some 600 miles farther north. If further argument for settling on Indian lands was needed, Washington in his petition to the king pointed to Indian behavior during the recent war:

> By the common principles of reason and the laws of nations, that treaty is vacated by the Indians themselves who for the slightest causes have attacked his Majesty's fortifications and most barbarously murdered in cold blood the King's officers and troops. . . . They have also invaded most of the colonies east of the Alleghenies, murdering multitudes of his Majesty's subjects and destroying the country before them with fire and sword. This insult now puts it in the power of the Crown consistent with justice to pursue the political plan of getting that country settled as quickly as possible.

The settlement the Washingtons and the Lees proposed would not only offer a supply of hemp for the Royal Navy but would provide a new market for British goods and a buffer zone to thwart an alliance between French settlers on the west bank of the Mississippi and their former Indian allies east of the river.

Beneath the surface, the document reveals Washington's emerging philosophy that land acquisition should be pursued not by individuals but by corporations of stockholders. He had found that it was just too costly and ruinous for individuals:

> Large tracts of land taken up by companies may be retailed by them to individuals much cheaper than they can obtain them immediately from the Crown.[16]

The "poorer sort" of individuals also lacked the capital to cover the costs of soliciting land patents and surveys, even if they knew how to obtain them. To attract settlers and transport them to the site, Washington and his friends agreed to "sacrifice" one-third of the value of each share.

Only weeks after Washington sent off the Mississippi Company's petition to King George III, the royal proclamation of 1763 declared illegal any further white migration west of the Alleghenies. The shareholders continued to meet annually, but their petition was hopeless. Washington shrugged off the news. He considered the Proclamation Line unconstitutional, one more blunder by the postwar British cabinet. "I can never," he wrote to his Ohio Valley land agent, William Crawford, "look upon that proclamation in any other light (but this I say between ourselves) than as a temporary expedient to quiet the minds of the Indians." If he only waited a little while, Washington believed he could acquire vast holdings "in the King's part." The boundary line "must fall of course in a few years." Washington instructed Crawford to pose as a hunter as he searched out prime acreage "in the King's part" beyond the line in the Ohio Valley. He urged Crawford to keep the business—as well as his political views—"a profound secret." As a burgess, "I might be censured for the opinion I have given in respect to the King's proclamation."[17]

*I*t took George Washington, so recently so proud to be a brigadier and the highest-ranking American colonist in the British army, a long time to begin to question British policies toward the American colonies. For years he believed the problem was that there *was* no policy. Not until the Stamp Act crisis broke suddenly over English America did he suspect any hint of a deeper conflict with the Mother Country. Only a few years earlier the British had won a 75-year-long struggle to oust the French from Canada, so long the source of so much suffering by Anglo-American settlers. Americans generally regarded themselves as fortunate to be citizens of what they considered the most benevolent empire on earth, the largest since the Roman empire had collapsed eleven hundred years earlier.

But many British taxpayers at home were appalled by the accumulated costs of acquiring this empire and the virtual tax-free status of American colonists. The bill had been run up to £137,000,000—about $15 billion today—and ten thousand British army regulars and the squadrons of

Royal Navy ships on the American station drove the debt higher every day. Reports of American reluctance to fill troop quotas during the French and Indian War and widespread smuggling to avoid British duties fed English suspicions that the Americans were only waiting to be rid of the French before they turned and revolted against the British government. The English had to pay the taxes that Americans complained loudly about. They had paid a stamp tax for fifty years. They rejected the argument of Washington and other American colonial leaders that the British reaped most of the benefit from their raw materials and their consumer markets. According to mercantile theory, the colonies existed for the benefit of the parent country. A succession of British ministries reflected this public opinion and followed a hardening anti-American line.

As early as the late 1740s the British government had been quietly shifting from a policy of "salutary neglect," as the Dukes of Newcastle had styled their administration of the American colonies, to a tougher imperial policy. The gradual shift tightened the enforcement of trade laws to eliminate competition with the colonies, imposed new taxes on colonists, and set up separate administration of territories taken from the French and Spanish. The frontier-closing Proclamation of 1763 was followed quickly by the Sugar Act of 1764, which for the first time sought to raise revenue in the American colonies from duties on foreign sugar imports and cracked down on the smuggling of sugar from the Caribbean by wealthy New Englanders. But when the Stamp Act, which would affect all regions and all classes of people, was proposed, a firestorm of protest flared up in every colony. American colonial leaders complained that no one had any money in the postwar slump. Several northern colonies echoed Patrick Henry's angry Resolves of May 1765 and passed their own official legislative resolutions of protest. When Parliament ignored American petitions and protests, riots broke out in many coastal towns where there was high unemployment.

No one foresaw the ferocity of the popular reaction. Benjamin Franklin had favored the Stamp Act and encouraged personal friends to accept the post of stamp tax collector. Rumors of his support triggered a riot in Philadelphia in which a mob besieged his house until his armed supporters manned barricades inside it. His son, New Jersey governor William Franklin, refused to allow the stamps to be unloaded from a Royal Navy warship as a mob chased that colony's collector all the way to Philadelphia and coerced him into forfeiting a £3,000 bond. In Boston, mobs pulled down the houses of the stamp commissioner and the lieutenant governor; in New York City, a drunken throng sacked the house of the British major who had tried to prevent them from seizing the stamps inside Fort George.

George Washington's first inkling that there might be anything more than Patrick Henry's resolutions in the House of Burgesses may have come from his former second in command, Captain Robert Stewart. Washington had made Stewart a generous loan to go to London to seek a royal commission at Court. There he frequently saw George Mercer, another ex-Washington aide, who was being supported by the revived Ohio Company of Virginia to seek land bounties for the former Virginia officers. From London, Stewart wrote to Washington:

> Here the whole political frame has for some time been strangely agitated by the most unexpected revolutions. . . . People are so much and generally divided in their opinions that time can alone discover the rectitude or fallacy of their different sentiments which are maintained with such heat on both sides.

For news Washington was to speak to "the bearer, Col. Mercer, who returns to collect a tax upon his native land." Mercer was coming back from London not with the land grant he had been paid to obtain but as the stamp commissioner for Virginia. In faraway London, Captain Stewart believed Mercer must be oblivious to the news from America: "We are told [that] the people of America in general and the Virginians in particular look on [the tax] as an infringement of their liberties." Even in London, Patrick Henry's "very warm and bold resolves" were being printed "and handed about."[18]

While George Washington as burgess had no business in Williamsburg at the end of October 1765, as court-appointed guardian of Martha's children and administrator of the Custis estate, he had to be there to present his accounts to the general court. Stewart's letter of August 18 from London certainly must have reached him by this time with its ominous warning that Mercer was ignoring the reports in London and coming to Williamsburg with the hated stamps. By this time, too, the protests had spread to Westmoreland County, where so much of Washington's holdings and family still resided—Washington's mother still lived on Ferry Farm and his sister lived in Fredericksburg. As the day when all court business would require the tax stamps, the Westmoreland County magistrates, who included Washington's business partners, the Lees, moved faster than other county court judges throughout Virginia, cleared their dockets, and on September 24 ordered that the courts be closed. They refused to be agents of the new tax:

> We the undersigned magistrates of Westmoreland find ourselves compelled by the strongest motives of honor and virtue to decline acting in that capacity. . . . [The Stamp] Act will impose on us a necessity, in consequence of the judicial oath we take [of becoming] instrumental in the destruction of our country's most essential rights and liberties.[19]

Washington turned over to his managers his experiments with hemp and his fall plantings of turnips and hurried to Williamsburg to file his court papers before the general court could join the legal protest. The trip would also allow him to talk to Mercer and learn the exact status of the Ohio Company grant.

Colonel George Mercer arrived on October 30, 1765, two days before the Stamp Act was to take effect. Not only had he ignored the reports of violence in other colonies, but he seemed unaware of the calendar: the end of October meant court days and a Williamsburg teeming with people from all over the colony. He also seemed ignorant of the fact that among the leading citizens opposed to the new levy were his own father and brother, who had been writing letters against it to the Virginia newspapers. Mercer rode into town in midafternoon. He left onboard the *Leeds* the strongbox of stamps. He had just come from his father's lodgings and was on his way to find the governor when a crowd surrounded him in the street and demanded his resignation at once.

Governor Fauquier had gone to Mrs. Campbell's Virginia Coffeehouse near the Capitol and was sitting on the porch with Speaker Robinson and several burgesses and members of the governor's council when Mercer arrived, pursued closely by the shouting crowd that could have been considered a mob if it had not been so well dressed. Mercer hurried up onto the porch. The governor heard the chant, "One and all, one and all." He stood up as the crowd surged toward Mercer, who later reported to the Board of Trade in London, "I immediately heard a cry, 'See the Governor. Take care of him.' Those who were pushing up the steps immediately fell back and left a small space between me and them."

Governor Fauquier was popular. Even though someone shouted "Let us rush in," after a few seconds' faceoff the crowd backed away and allowed him to step down off the porch and, holding the stamp collector by the arm, walk "side by side through the thickest of the people." The two tried to ignore "the murmurs of the people" as they hurried toward the governor's palace. That night George Mercer met with his father and brother—"two lawyers attending the court who were both frightened out of their senses for him." The next morning Mercer resigned, reboarded the *Leeds*, and sailed back to England with the stamps. The next day, when the general court convened, not a single litigant or lawyer showed up.[20]

Whether George Washington was in the street or on the porch, he was careful to leave no record. From this time forward except to his closest friends and associates he did not expose or document his views on the gathering colonial crisis. He did, however, instruct Thomas Cummings in London not to let Mercer know he was pursuing a separate western land grant, and he also told William Crawford to keep his views "a profound secret." Close friends and relatives undoubtedly knew his opinions. He was learning not all of them sympathized with the colonial protests. And he had land grant applications pending before the royal governor and the Crown. He became very tight-lipped, even to the point of retrospectively recording Mount Vernon plantings made by his slaves in his farm diary while he was absent. It was, after all, only an agricultural diary at this point:

> *[October] 26. Sowed the remaining part of the turnips ...*
> *28. Sowed the residue of peach orchard.*
> *31. Finished sowing wheat ... plowed in a good deal*
> *of scattered hemp seed—27 bushels in all.*

As a soldier dealing with French spies and Indians of dubious allegiance on the frontier, Washington had learned stealth, subterfuge, the art of the bluff. And now as an American businessman determined to make himself rich and independent of England's contradictory policies and unenforceable laws, he honed his skills as a master of discretion and deception. The time was fast approaching when he would need both.[21]

*T*he Mount Vernon of the late 1760s was a handsome white house bookended by tall brick chimneys with a high-pitched slate roof. As yet, there was no veranda, no cupola, no porticoes connecting outbuildings to the main house. Martha was content with the house for fifteen years after their marriage and Washington did not think of expanding it again until 1774. What there was around this English-style manor house was an eighteenth-century English village that, ironically, demonstrated Washington's break with the traditional Tidewater tobacco culture. From the dooryard of Mount Vernon, Washington could see flax and hemp growing and champagne fields of wheat that had replaced the troublesome tobacco plants. Horses and slaves connected the house in constant traffic with fields that ran along the west bank of the Potomac from Hunting Creek to Dogue Run. Washington had hired white indentured weavers to turn his flax into homespun cloth that all his employees wore, as did, more and more, the tenant farmers of Fairfax County and the townspeople of burgeoning Alexandria, twelve miles to the north. He was repairing his father's sawmill and expanding it to accommodate other Fairfax planters who were following his lead and cultivating wheat and corn. The corn, fine-ground, and the applejack made by fermenting his pippin apples were staples of the Mount Vernon diet. The turnips he planted in larger quantities every year nourished the white workers and the livestock. He rotated the cattle and horses through his pastures to fertilize them; he cured hams in his new smokehouse and provided butter from his new dairy barn. The fish his growing fleet dredged up from the Potomac brought cash from the Alexandria market sheds and variety to Martha's cooking at Mount Vernon. Washington loved the fresh shad of spring, and one day it would save his army. As a result of his years of study and close observation on neighbors' farms, Washington had built stables at Mount Vernon where he bred and sold horses—tall, strong hunters that he field-tested in breakneck days of riding over fields and jumping fences. Washington was a thoroughly English country squire when it came to his passion for riding and hunting, and he liked nothing so much as galloping along on crisp fall days when the leaves were down and he could see the fox that was trying to elude him. More often than not he was accompanied on these rides by English-born Bryan Fairfax, George William's madcap younger brother, who liked to keep Washington laughing. Sometimes Sally and her husband joined in the hunts. There is no hint that Martha ever hunted with George, although she did go along on long rides.

After horse and rider worked up a sweat and the mocking sound of the hunting horn died away, Washington and his friends gathered before the corner fireplace in the center hall for silver cups of Madeira before joining Martha and the children in the parlor. Patcy was becoming adept at playing the fine Plenius London-made spinet he had bought for her in 1761 when she started lessons at age four. Washington could coax her into giving a demonstration. He had encouraged Martha to take lessons when they were first married—a songbook with her new name *Martha Washington 1759* written in his large bold hand bore mute testimony of the early experiment. Washington loved music. In 1766, when John Stadler, a German music teacher, came to Mount Vernon for four-hour sessions of lessons and dinner with the family, Martha resumed the lessons with her children as Washington beamed approvingly from the sidelines. In a letter to Francis Hopkinson, a well-known Philadelphia composer, he confided, "I can neither sing one of the songs nor raise a single note on any instrument." He liked the music of Joseph Haydn and Johann Christian Bach, of Ignaz Pleyel and Johann Baptist Vanhall, as well as country fiddle music and the eerie sounds of the armonica, a musical instrument made of turned goblets worked by a footpedal and perfected by his friend Benjamin Franklin.[22]

His requests for music had become part of the daily routine at Mount Vernon. After Martha summoned the house slaves to fetch the tea and poured it into the English bone china for her guests, Washington requested anyone with the slightest ability to play. Among the pleasures he shared with Martha were the theater, dancing, and music. As his stepdaughter or a guest played for them, the group sang lyrics they could find, if they needed, on the music stand in the pages of *The Bullfinch, Being a Collection of the Newest and Most Favourite English Songs*. Patcy was slender and beautiful and playful. Her vitality contrasted with the indolence of her four-years-older brother, Jack, who needed ample flattery before he could be coaxed to play the "good violin" or the "neat and good German flute," made of boxwood and tipped with silver, that his stepfather had bought for him when he turned twelve. The impromptu recitals that accompanied music master Stadler's visits sometimes drew the Carlyles from Alexandria. Washington's old friend John Carlyle wrote to relatives in Scotland in 1766 that his daughter Sally was learning the spinet. "She meets the master at Colonel Washington's where he attends the Colonel's two children. He is so kind as to let Sally stay two days." For Patcy Custis, the lessons and the little recitals were hard work. In her own letter, she wrote at age twelve in 1769 that "I have entered into [thorough] bass but find it very difficult."

Patcy and Jack liked it much better when Washington, a famous dancer, convened the monthly dancing classes in the large drawing room at Mount Vernon. The children of several prominent Northern Neck families—Washingtons, Masons, Carters, and Lees—gathered with their carriages and servants one month at the Washingtons', one month next door at Gunston Hall, manor house of Washington's friend, George Mason. Dancing was deadly serious business in the ritual-conscious Tidewater society. A young Princeton-educated tutor was amazed at how strict was the dancing master, John Christian:

> Mr. Christian is punctual and rigid in his discipline, so strict indeed that he struck two of the young misses for a fault in the course of their performance, even in the presence of the mother of one of them! And he rebuked one of the young fellows so highly as to tell him he must alter his manner, which he had observed to be insolent and wanton, or absent himself from the school.[23]

There can be little doubt that the culprit was Jack Custis.

The lessons continued for two, three, even four days in a swirl of children and their parents that lasted for hours as the young Virginians worked hard to learn the intricate patterns of the minuet and the allemande. When the formalities ended, an impromptu ball invariably broke out and the court dancers dissolved into high-spirited country dances—reels and jigs accompanied only by the playful sounds of the fiddlers. In the minuets, in the country dancing, George Washington, tall, elegant, at his most relaxed, stood out above the others—and, year after year, as long as he could, made the music go on.[24]

As year after year slid by and George and Martha Washington had no children of their own, Washington came to the conclusion that Martha was no longer capable of becoming pregnant. Martha had given birth four times. Washington had no acknowledged child but until he was in his sixties many years later he was still telling friends that he could have an heir if Martha died and he married a young girl, but that he had no desire to do that. He never discussed the possibility that he was unable to father a child. He had suffered a variety of illnesses that could have rendered him sterile. He had suffered from a severe bout of the mumps as a young man, and he had contracted smallpox and malaria simultaneously as a nineteen-year-old in Barbados. Either one of these events could have minimized his chances of becoming a father. But he took himself seriously as a step-father and came to consider himself the father of Martha's children.

Especially Patcy: he loved this young girl more each year, at least in part for her courage. Patcy had never been a strong child. Born only a few months before her father died of heart disease, she seems to have always worried Martha, who clung to her as much as the baby did to its mother. Martha would go nowhere without her children for several years, and as a result rarely left Mount Vernon except sometimes to accompany Washington to Williamsburg, to make long Christmas visits to her family, and take a family vacation to the mountains each summer. The family visited Williamsburg together so infrequently that Washington sold their house there: Martha and the children often stayed at Mount Vernon or stopped at the White House on the Pamunkey. Jack was seven years old before she left him behind at Mount Vernon for the first time.

Washington's mother never visited Mount Vernon after George and Martha married and Washington repelled several hints from her about visiting. He went to see her and he usually went alone. When Patcy was five, Martha went on a family visit while Washington was visiting his mother and sister in Fredericksburg. "I carried my little [Patcy] with me," she wrote to her younger sister Nancy, "and left Jackey at home for a trial to see how well I could stay without him. Though we were gone but [two weeks] I was impatient to get home. If I at any time heard the dogs bark or a noise outside, I thought there was a person sent for me. I often fancied he was sick or some accident had happened to him so that I think it is impossible for me to leave him as long as Mr. Washington must stay when he comes down [to the Pamunkey]." It was Martha who was afraid to be away from her little boy: she was so timorous she was begging out of a visit to her own favorite sister, as she must get home to Mount Vernon. She was anxious whenever George was away very long from Mount Vernon. When he went to Williamsburg for the spring 1767 session of the Assembly she wrote a postscript on a letter his cousin Lund Washington, an overseer at Mount Vernon, was sending him:

> *My Dearest.*
> It was with very great pleasure I see in your letter that you got safely down we are all very well at this time but it still is raining.

The postscript is her only surviving letter to Washington.[25]

When George and Martha did get away from Mount Vernon and the usual houseful of guests, they took the children and a handful of servants. They visited the Bassetts on the Pamunkey whenever they went to

Williamsburg, and several times they escaped the summer heat by making a four-day drive across the mountains to the baths at Berkeley Springs. There, they borrowed a cottage from their next-door neighbors, the Masons. Washington slipped away from his family and the servants and found a mountain stream to do a little fishing or went shooting. He used his field dogs—he gave them whimsical names like Sweetlips and Truelove—to flush pheasant and duck and went fishing. Martha stayed behind with the children. There is no evidence that she ever spent a night away from Patcy.

Martha fussed over both her children. She bedecked Patcy in fine clothes and jewels and shopped avidly for both children. One order to Cary's in London is fairly typical:

> Tea set ... toys ... a bird on bellows ... a cuckoo ... a neat dressed wax baby ... an aviary ... a stiffened coat made of fashionable silk ... 6 handsome egrets, different sorts ... 1 pair little scissors ... 1 fashionable dressed doll ... a box gingerbread toys and sugar images and comfits.

When Jack was eight and Patcy four, Washington hired Walter Magowan as their tutor. The order that spring to Cary's reflects the teacher's great expectations: "two copies of the Rudiments of the Latin; 2 Phaedrus's Fables, 2 Salust, Horace, the Grammatical Exercises Erasmus & [one] English Dictionary." Magowan was the first tutor to despair of teaching Jack, who only seemed to study how to do less work.[26]

As it turned out, Martha had ample reason to fret about her daughter. One summer day in 1768 when she was eleven Patcy fell to the floor while George and Martha were having tea. Washington's diary entry for June 14 records the shock: "Sent for Dr. Rumney to Patcy Custis who was seized with fits." A slave rushed the eight miles to Alexandria and brought a doctor. The English-born former British army surgeon bled Patcy and prescribed valerian drops for her "nerves." A month later he came back and dosed her with more valerian drops and some musk oil, thought to be an antispasmodic drug. When she had another attack five months later, Dr. Rumney prescribed purges, mercury tablets, and a warm vegetable decoction laced with herbs. When yet another seizure came on, he ordered an iron ring installed on one finger. "Joshua Evans, who came here last, put an iron ring upon Patcy [for fits]," Washington noted in his diary.[27]

Patcy's epilepsy (as it would be called today) grounded the Washingtons for months on end and especially terrified Martha. When the family tried a brief excursion, "Patcy being taken with a fit on the road by the mill, we turned back." In the summer of 1769 when the family attempted its usual vacation trip to Berkeley Springs, Patcy seemed better at first. Washington's diary reveals how her illness haunted him:

> *[August]   6—Arrived at the Springs about one o'clock, and dined with*
> *Col. [and Mrs.] Fairfax.*
> *19—Rode with Mrs. Washington and others to the*
> *Cacapehon Mountain to see the prospect from*
> *thence.*
> *20—Went to church in the fore and afternoon.*
> *23—Dined alone—Patcy unwell.[28]*

By late 1769, Washington had found a new Dutch-trained doctor. He examined her frequently over the next year, but by July 1770 she was suffering from seizures and fevers. Her doctors tried cinchona (Peruvian
bark) that was used to treat malaria as well as epilepsy. A third, Edinburgh-
trained physician was called in. He prescribed oral doses of ether for the
unhappy thirteen-year-old. Washington rode back and forth to Alexandria
to search for the vials.

But nothing worked. Patcy, now a lovely young girl with dark hair and
dark eyes, high brows and a delicate nose, showed some of her fatalistic
melancholy as she sat for portraitists who came to Mount Vernon. But on
good days she so charmed Washington and made Martha so happy that
Martha's apprehension momentarily died down. Washington drew close
to this young girl with the sad eyes. He loved to see her with her young
cousins as, each spring and fall, the entire family visited relatives en route
to General Assembly sessions. They liked to eat oysters with the Bassetts
at Campbell's Coffeehouse in Williamsburg. At home, her playing of
"Psalms and Hymns Set for the Spinet" delighted him, and he took her
to balls and to the theater in Alexandria. He lavished presents on her like
a suitor. He set aside his self-restraint when he ordered clothes and presents from London:

> A handsome set of Brussels lace for a young lady . . . a garnet
> comb for the hair . . . a set of necklace & earrings . . . a tambour
> frame to work muslin in with proper needles and thread . . . a
> string of amber beads . . . quadrille [a Spanish game] counters
> made of mother of pearl . . . a large family Bible with silver
> clasps . . . a small and very neat prayer book . . . Lady's Maga-
> zine.[29]

When Patcy was nine, Martha wrote a letter to a milliner ordering
"such things as misses of her age usually wear"—actually, Washington
helped her rough-draft the letter and Martha copied it out. The clothes
should be "genteel and proper" and "done with frugality for as she is
only nine years old a superfluity or expense in dress would be altogether
unnecessary." Martha ordered a corset for herself for the first time "with a
pair of stays which I beg may be very good, easy made and very thin."
She also hoped there was still time to change an order: instead of "a

French necklace and earrings" George had ordered for her, Martha wanted "a blue Turkey stone necklace and earrings sent in their place if the price does not exceed two guineas."[30]

In these years when Martha rarely left Mount Vernon, and Washington was away so much, Martha managed the mansion, superintending its kitchens and its house servants, and attending to all the logistics of a manor house while raising her children. She also supervised the spinning of yarn, the weaving of homespun, and the tailoring of clothing for the family and upward of 160 Mount Vernon slaves. She presided over the workers in a simple dress and apron. Sometimes there were sixteen spinning wheels turning at once in the spinning house: other artisans and slaves followed her directions at the looms, at the reels and flaxbrakes. In 1768 Martha's team of one white male weaver and four slave girls produced 815 yards of linen, 365 yards of woolens, 144 yards of homespun linsey-woolsey, and 40 yards of cotton cloth.

He seemed at a loss what to do about Patcy's brother Jack. From the time Jack was eight Washington's orders to London carry the reminder that his clothing must be "suited to the arms of the Custis family." By the time he was fourteen he was "tolerably well grown" and wearing a "silver laced hat." Washington ordered him "two strong pocket knives and one handsome fowling piece" and was careful to charge it to the Custis estate account. Washington had to raise his stepson as the English aristocrat he was born, but it would be with a practical American accent. He taught Jack the gentlemanly sport of fox hunting, but he also insisted that he learn surveying and he ordered the boy his own "case [of] surveyor's plotting instrument." Jack must learn to survey his own lands. When Jack turned fourteen, Washington convinced Martha that the boy needed more than a home tutor. He needed to break away from her apron strings and go to a boarding school.[31]

Just who should teach the Custis heir Martha left entirely to Washington. He chose an Anglican priest, the Reverend Jonathan Boucher, who had come out from the north country of England to open a school near Fredericksburg, a day's ride from Mount Vernon. Washington introduced the boy as "a boy of good genius" who remained "untainted in his morals and of innocent manners." He had been reading Virgil and "a Greek Testament" even if he was "a little rusty in both." Jack would be accompanied by a slave boy and "two horses to furnish him with the means of getting to church." Jack was "the last of his family and will possess a very large fortune." Washington told the dominie of "my anxiety to make him fit for more useful purposes than a horse racer."[32]

Washington's letters to and from Jonathan Boucher show his attempts to be a good husband to Martha and good father for her son. He admonished Boucher to write him frequently. "We should be very glad to hear how he is reconciled to an absence from home, unusual to him 'til now."

He did not ask "any peculiar indulgence." Jack was "healthy and of good constitution":

> I rather wish that he might lead a life of as little indulgence and dissipation as should be thought necessary to relax and keep his spirits. . . . [He is to be] restrained from the practice of those follies and vices which youth and inexperience but too naturally lead into.[33]

On August 2, 1768, Boucher wrote to reassure the anxious Washington:

> Master Custis is a boy of so exceedingly mild and meek a temper. . . . Possibly he might be made uneasy by ye rougher manners of some of his school fellows. . . . I have not seen a youth that I think promises fairer to be a good and useful man than John Custis!

Boucher knew how to flatter a rich new client. He told Washington what he wanted to hear. He added in passing that Jack "is far of being a brilliant genius."[34]

When Jack came home for summer vacations, Washington always wound up writing Boucher an excuse for late return to school. On September 4, 1768, Washington wrote Boucher that Jack had run a fever and was vomiting during their visit to Washington's sister, Betty, "which induced his Momma to take him home with us 'til he is perfectly restored." That apparently took four months. On January 29, 1769, Washington sent Jack back to school with a note. "After so long a vacation we hope Jacky will apply close to his studies and retrieve the hours he has lost from his books." In the heat of a Chesapeake summer, Martha worried that her son might swim too often. "Mrs. Washington [requests] that you will restrain Jacky from going too frequently into the water or staying too long in it." And when Jack returned to school a week later than the other boys, Boucher complained of "Jack's laziness which, however, I now hope is not incurable." Like many boys in boarding school, Jack could find little time to write home. "I have nothing new to tell you," he wrote Washington. "My love to Mama and sister. With the greatest respect, Your obedient servant."[35]

Whatever Boucher was doing to educate Jack, it was only exasperating Washington by December 1770, when the boy was sixteen:

> His mind is a good deal released from study and more than ever turned to dogs, horses and guns, indeed upon dress and equipage. . . . Keep him close to those useful branches of learning which he ought now to be acquainted with. . . . The time of

life he is now advancing into requires the most friendly aid and council (especially in such a place as Annapolis). Otherwise the warmth of his own passions assisted by the bad example of other youth may prompt him to actions derogatory of virtue.

Boucher was to keep the youth "under your own eye" and not "allow him to be rambling about of nights in company with those who do not care how debauched and vicious his conduct may be."[36]

By now, Boucher and Washington were commiserating. Boucher wrote that their "sentiments of this young gentleman" were the same. Boucher wrote, "I never did in my life know a youth so exceedingly indolent or so surprisingly voluptuous. One would suppose nature had intended him for some Asiatic prince."[37]

As Martha worried more and more about Patcy's epilepsy, Washington protected her. He instructed Boucher to have Jack sent to Baltimore and secretly inoculated for smallpox. Washington was keeping his wife "in total ignorance of his having been there 'til I hear of his return or perfect recovery." He instructed Boucher to write him under cover to Lund Washington, his trusted cousin and the overseer at Mount Vernon, "in a hand not your own. Martha's anxiety and uneasiness are great." He felt he had to justify his deception to the clergyman-schoolmaster. Martha had "often wished that Jack would take and go through the disorder without her knowing of it that she might escape those tortures which suspense would throw her into." Soon, Boucher reassured Washington that "Jack is out of all danger." Boucher was annoyed that Jack himself had not written.[38]

By the time Jack was sixteen Washington was completely disillusioned with him. His educational progress was "trifling." He "knows [little] arithmetic and is quite ignorant of the Greek." Washington had tired of his guardianship. He had all the responsibility but none of the pleasure of being the boy's father. "Every farthing which is expended in behalf of this gentleman must undergo the inspection of the General Court." "There is much greater circumspection [required] by a guardian than a natural parent." Jack filled Washington "with a sincere concern not because of the expense but on account of the lost time."[39]

Eleven

Shortly before sunrise on April 5, 1769, George Washington bent over his writing desk in the plain pine-paneled study at Mount Vernon and wrote the most important letter of his life. For nearly five years since the outbreak of the Stamp Act crisis he had been quietly observing the deepening rift with England over a host of imperial policies. He had kept himself mostly on the sidelines, confiding only in a few close friends. Instead of taking to the streets in the style of the northern patriots he had been systematically and quite radically altering his entire way of life. By now he was virtually independent of trade with the mother country. His cottage industries in the thirty buildings clustered around Mount Vernon and the profits from the sales of his crops and products, fishing boats, and 1,000 head of livestock made it possible for him to survive with very little intercourse with England. He only exported enough tobacco to retire his debt to his London agent; he had already reduced it by half, and with his increasing frugality it would soon be only a poignant reminder of a newly-wed's shopping binge.

Elected burgess from Fairfax County by an overwhelming margin in 1765 when a seat became available, he had become part of an independent-minded circle of wealthy planters on the Northern Neck who were increasingly alarmed by British actions. At first he had been inclined to believe that there was no fixed British policy of repressing American trade and industry, only understandable chaos in the wake of winning a long, worldwide struggle and with little previous experience trying to administer a far-flung empire acquired by default. But restrictions had continued to flow from Whitehall in London. It had become apparent to Washington and other leading Americans that many Englishmen had seen the Stamp Act crisis as a challenge to Parliament's authority. In the very next breath after repealing the stamp tax, Parliament the same day

231

had overwhelmingly passed the Declaratory Act, asserting the absolute authority of Parliament over its empire "in all cases whatsoever."

Under the young King George III, cabinet shuffles of the same handful of amateur ministers had become so frequent that they were becoming a repertory theater of the absurd. Benjamin Franklin, agent in London for several American colonies, reported in the autumn of 1766 "such continual changes here that it is very discouraging to all applications to be made to the Ministry: I thought the last [cabinet] established but they are gone. God only knows whom we are to have next." The Earl of Bute's government had closed the Appalachian frontier and passed the Sugar Act and then after a series of mob actions in London had resigned. His cousin George Grenville succeeded him, bored the king with long dull lectures, and after thoroughly bungling the Stamp Act crisis, resigned at the king's insistence. The Earl of Shelburne, a self-appointed expert on American affairs, had been bent on reorganizing the system governing the empire and wanted to tax Americans for the first time to pay for their own defense. He believed in chartering new self-supporting colonies as defensive buffers in the unsettled lands west of the Proclamation Line. Land-hungry colonists like Washington and Franklin had formed rival companies and were scrambling to apply for huge land grants. But so far nothing had come of them. Amid all the confusion and indecision, American commerce was stagnating.[1]

The land rush had triggered a strong reaction among British landowners. The imperious Lord Hillsborough, leading member of the Board of Trade and Plantations, took a hard-line view of Americans. He was one of the largest absentee landowners in Ireland. With hundreds of poor Scottish-Irish cottagers on his lands to provide cheap labor and abundant crops of flax, he was deeply involved in developing the Irish linen industry. Understandably he was alarmed at the number of his tenant farmers who were leaving for America. George Washington's fields and looms— staffed by skilled immigrant labor—were unwanted competition. His Lordship had no desire to foster any further movement to cheap lands in the American west. Consequently, Washington's various land schemes ran into a solid wall of red tape when they reached the Board of Trade and Plantations. Amid the official confusion, some royal governors accepted the Proclamation Line and some did not; colonial legislatures picked and chose which Indian treaties to respect and which to ignore. Several colonial boundary lines from present-day Vermont to Florida remained in dispute, and settlers raided and burned out rival claimants. The British government could not even determine the western boundary of Pennsylvania.

By 1769 the British government had not decided whether it wanted to create new colonies west of the Alleghenies, let alone which company to charter. Lord Shelburne had seemed on the point of deciding the question when the king's attorneys general ruled that all land in the western

Indian reserve belonged to the king. Just when Washington and his fellow Virginia officers appeared on the verge of prevailing upon the ministry to honor the recruiting bounties promised by Governor Dinwiddie, rumors began to circulate that a rival Illinois Company, organized by Benjamin Franklin and his illegitimate son, royal governor of New Jersey William Franklin, had numerous stockholders in Parliament and was about to receive a charter to settle the same lands in West Virginia and Kentucky claimed by Washington and his colleagues. An alarmed Washington protested to Virginia's governor Francis Fauquier that the Philadelphia-based company's enterprise would be a fatal blow to Virginia's westward expansion.

The colonial crisis had flared anew with the latest cabinet reshuffling, in June 1767. Charles "Champagne Charlie" Townshend, as chancellor of the exchequer under the new prime minister, attacked the age-old distinction that the Americans—and his predecessors—had made between internal and external taxation of the colonies. Until this time British taxes stopped at the American shoreline: they consisted mostly of customs duties. The American colonies under their royal charters were left to tax themselves to pay their own internal expenses. Townshend announced that he was preparing a new internal tax for America. At the same time, opposition leaders in Parliament were pushing through a reduction in the British land tax at home that created a whopping £500,000 deficit in Crown revenues. The Townshend Acts decreed import duties on glass, lead, paint, paper, and tea. While their estimated yield was only £40,000 annually the new revenues could be spent not only to pay for British army and navy units based in the colonies but also to defray "the charge of the administration of justice and the support of civil government" in the American colonies. Administering the courts and deciding how much to pay royal officials were ancient charter rights, which Washington considered sacred. To collect the new duties Parliament affirmed the right of superior or supreme court justices to issue writs of assistance—blanket search warrants. New admiralty courts would take the prosecution of colonists away from the colonial courts, ending local trial by jury—as old as Magna Carta. Accused smugglers and antigovernment protesters would be shipped to England for trial and punishment. A new American Board of Commissioners of the Customs was to be created in Boston with branches in every American coastal seaport responsible directly to the Board of Trade in London. Soon America would be swarming with new British tax and customs agents.

By the end of 1767, angry town meetings from Boston to New York City had condemned the broad-based assault on colonists' rights. In Philadelphia, Quaker lawyer John Dickinson in his "Letters from a Farmer in Pennsylvania" denied the right of Parliament to tax in order to raise revenue in the American colonies. He declared the Townshend duties unconstitutional. A boycott of British luxury goods by Boston merchants took effect on January 1, 1768; Newport, Providence, and New York City followed suit. Boston tightened the ban to include most British imports early in 1769. New York merchants canceled all orders sent to England after August 15, 1768, and boycotted all British imports until Parliament repealed the Townshend Acts. Philadelphia merchants banned British goods on February 6, 1769, and Baltimore merchants joined the embargo on March 30. Dr. David Ross of Bladensburg, Maryland, forwarded to Washington a copy of the letter to Maryland merchants forwarded by the Philadelphia Association, the nonimportation committee. He also sent Colonel Washington copies of the response of Annapolis merchants to the Philadelphia merchants organizing the nonimportation agreement, as well as a copy of the letter to Virginia merchants from Annapolis merchants.

That the papers came first in all Virginia to Mount Vernon was not only fortuitous but appropriate. Even if Washington had kept out of the fray stirred up in the past year by the Quartering Act, another Townshend measure, he was on the House grievances committee. To protect the western frontiers, Major General Thomas Gage, Washington's old companion-in-arms against the French, decided in his capacity as commander in chief of all British land forces in North America that the number of garrisons must be reduced and a mobile force concentrated in New York City. The New York Assembly was to come up with a new appropriation to build and maintain barracks—which it refused to do. The Quartering Act touched off riots in New York City at the same time the Bostonians marched to protest the arrival of the new customs commission. The Massachusetts House of Representatives asked all the other colonial assemblies to endorse its petition to the king in a circular letter disputing the constitutionality of the new laws. When the Virginia House of Burgesses convened on March 28, 1768, to take up the petition, Washington was not in his seat. While the House debated, Patcy Custis was enduring another seizure and a visit from Dr. Rumney, who administered "numerous powders." A distracted Washington had taken his stepson Jack and Washington's cousin, Lund, foxhunting. "Catched a fox after three hours chase," Washington recorded.[2]

Washington had a second reason for missing the spring session of the burgesses. Originally it had been scheduled for early May, as usual, when the Washingtons made their customary pilgrimage to meet with Martha's lawyer, present records to the general court, and engage in the round of dinners and balls crowned by the Queen's Birthday Party. But Washington had long ago scheduled an urgent meeting with William Crawford, his land agent, who was negotiating the purchase of 2,700 acres of land from Colonel Charles Carter. Washington had concluded that because the surveying of the Mason-Dixon Line between Maryland and Pennsylvania had been completed, westward expansion would soon resume. He had arranged for Crawford to come from his farm on the Youghiogheny

River in Pennsylvania to Mount Vernon, where they could confer at length. Crawford arrived on April first and stayed six days. Money changed hands. Washington summoned Matthew Campbell of the Alexandria firm that bought much of Washington's fine-grade wheat. The agent paid Washington a handsome £121 11s. 9½d. for wheat Washington had delivered in the past six months. Washington turned over £20 of it to Crawford to reimburse the agent for his expenses while finding good land for him "in the King's part." When Crawford rode off to search out "rich and level" lands in western Pennsylvania, the Washingtons "went up to Alexandria to a ball."[3]

For the past year as he had traveled widely in Virginia in his restless quest for land, Washington had been thinking over the confrontation with the British. There is no evidence whether or not he read widely on current political philosophy, as Jefferson and Franklin did, but he kept up with the arguments printed and reprinted from other colonies in the Virginia press and argued them with his neighbors, especially George Mason, the Fairfaxes, and the Lees. He traveled on horseback all over Virginia and saw the hardship in its towns. He plunged into the forests as he had virtually every year since he was fifteen in search of good land, but this time he was reexamining basic propositions of changing American life. Sixteen years of hope, investment, and effort in the Virginia Company had so far come to nothing. Since he was the only former Virginia Regiment officer or enlisted man who had consistently pressed for the recruitment land bounty, virtually all of the expenses for fees, agents, surveys, documents, even George Mercer's living expenses in London, had devolved on him. When the Crown decreed that all lands west of the mountains belonged to the king, an infuriated Washington realized that all the expense had been for nought. Instead of the 500 percent profit he had expected from the wilderness venture, so far he had earned nothing.

He had nearly died as a young officer, had let his surveying business wither away, and had lost out on every land speculation so far. He had a hundred slaves who were idle at any given moment due to contradictory Crown policies and now the shutdown of the colonial courts made it virtually impossible for him to get clear title on any new land. George Mason's bill to end the slave trade had died stillborn when the royal governor refused to call the Assembly after the Stamp Act protests. Washington wanted to import German indentured servants, not slaves, but the Germans would not come to a colony where there was no freedom of religion and where the state Church of England was established. He had become frustrated at every turn by England's refusal to rationalize and reform its imperial system and deal with the American colonists on an equal footing with British subjects at home. Washington was ready for drastic action when, by chance, the trade boycott papers arrived at Mount Vernon to be forwarded to Virginia's Committee of Correspondence.

For at least five years, Washington and Mason, also a major investor in land speculations, had grumbled about British bureaucratic bungling and what seemed to be a developing anti-American agenda in London. Washington considered Mason an expert on the English constitution and Virginia law, and he deferred to his "better mind than mine." Mason would know what to do. Now Washington took up his pen and at the first stroke leapt into the imperial dispute in a way totally atypical of his usual studied reserve. Sarcasm mingled with powerful reasoning now flowed through his pen:

> At a time when our lordly Masters in Great Britain will be satisfied with nothing less than the deprivation of American freedom, it seems highly necessary that something should be done to avert the stroke and maintain the liberty which we have derived from our ancestors.

Washington considered himself an Englishman who happened to live in the colony of Virginia. There was still no such notion as an American other than when used to describe a native or as a geographical description. There was no question left in Washington's mind that the British government was mounting a broad-based assault on the civil liberties of the American colonists. Only concerted and immediate action—"something should be done"—could prevent the devastating effects of this British campaign of anti-American suppression of the rights of English citizens whose ancestors came from England and who inherited their rights as freeborn Englishmen. What to do "is the point in question." The answer was so dangerous that to spell out every word would be considered treason and subject to criminal prosecution if his letter ever fell into British hands. He was after all a government official in a Crown territory:

> That no man should scruple or hesitate a moment to a-ms in defense of so valuable a blessing on which all the good and evil of life depends is clearly my opinion. Yet a-ms I would beg leave to add should be the last resource, the *denier* [*sic*] *resort.* [Yet] addresses to the throne and remonstrances to Parliament, we have already, it is said, proved the inefficacy of. How far, then, their attention to our rights & privileges is to be awakened or alarmed by starving their trade and manufactures remains to be tried. The Northern colonies, it appears, are endeavoring to adopt this scheme. In my opinion it is a good one . . . provided it can be carried pretty generally into execution.

Washington was putting his trust, indeed his life, in the hands of Mason. The letter in the wrong hands was plainly seditious on the face of it. Washington was suggesting a concerted plan to strike a severe blow by boycotting British trade. Worse, he was doing so in collusion with other colonies. The House of Burgesses in April had informed the Massachusetts Assembly that it intended to act in concert "with other colonies in their application for redress." As Virginia and other colonies rallied to support the Massachusetts circular letter, the imperial government angrily ordered all royal governors to treat the letter as subversive and dissolve any assembly that joined the protest against the Townshend duties. When the British colonial office ordered the Massachusetts House to rescind its circular letter, Massachusetts refused. The new colonial secretary was Lord Hillsborough, the same man who as secretary of the Board of Trade and Plantations had sealed off the frontier with the Proclamation Line. In a letter to Massachusetts Speaker Thomas Cushing, Franklin described Hillsborough as "proud, supercilious, extremely conceited (moderate as they are) of his political knowledge and abilities and inimical to all who dare to tell him disagreeable truths."[4] Washington was pointedly referring to Hillsborough when he wrote Mason derisively of "our lordly Masters."

To put teeth in Hillsborough's order, Parliament, a few months before Washington wrote his impassioned manifesto to Mason, voted both to approve Hillsborough's heavy-handed colonial policy and to revive an ancient law that permitted the British government to arrest and transport to Westminster for trial any person accused of treason outside the kingdom, a clear reference to the supposed traitors in American assemblies from Massachusetts to Virginia. The word *treason* was not an empty one for subjects of England of the time. Washington had been a newspaper-reading fifteen-year-old boy when three Scottish lords had been executed in London after the Rising of 1745. Their skulls still graced spikes at the gates of London. The British government had already shut down the Massachusetts House of Representatives and ordered two regiments of redcoats into Boston when Massachusetts radicals called on other colonial legislators to set up standing committees of correspondence to orchestrate American resistance to British policies. But Washington was advocating going further than any other American at this time or for another five years. Not only was a boycott in order but, if it failed, Americans must be prepared to take up arms in a civil war against a tyrannical Parliament to protect their civil rights. Washington's family had once before fought—and lost everything—in a civil war with Parliament. He was, as every American knew, the most visible symbol of an armed solution to Virginia's problems. He knew what he risked even if he did not dot his "i"s and fill in the blank when he twice wrote "arms." Was such a boycott possible or practicable?

> There will be difficulties attending the execution of it everywhere from clashing interests and selfish designing men ever attentive to their own gain and watchful of every turn that can assist their lucrative views.

In the tobacco-producing colonies, where trade was both diffused and wholly dependent on English brokers, "these difficulties are certainly enhanced." But Washington believed that the "gentlemen" of the House of Burgesses could explain to the people and "stimulate them" not to purchase anything but essential goods from the English factors or the British-owned stores spreading throughout the colonies. Anyone refusing to cooperate "ought to be stigmatized and made objects of public reproach. The more I consider a scheme of this sort the more ardently I wish success to it."

There could be, he knew, "private" as well as "public advantages" from such a boycott. The same power of Parliament that assumed the right of taxation over the colonies "may at least attempt to restrain our manufactories." England could just as easily "forbid my manufacturing" as "order me to buy goods," which Parliament "loaded with duties for the express purpose of raising a revenue." As it was, Parliament had banned so much manufacturing in the colonies that planters like Washington could forgo all luxuries and still be dependent on England for much that they needed to run a plantation. Parliamentary law banned American iron manufacturing, something Washington's father had been allowed to do. Washington wanted to restart his family's Principio Iron Works, but could not under current English law. In a typical year he had to buy many essentials that his own artisans could have been trained to produce at Mount Vernon. One order included nails, saddler's tacks, blacksmith's files, axes, hoes, keys, adzes, bungborers, locks, screws, scythes, iron, wire, sieves, fishing seines, and lead sinkers.

Such an "exertion of arbitrary power" as this latest insult by Parliament would only further anger the colonists:

> We cannot be worsted I think in putting it to the test. On the other hand that the colonies are considerably indebted to Great Britain is a truth universally acknowledged. Many families are reduced almost if not quite to penury and want from the low ebb of their fortunes. Estates [are] daily selling for the discharge of debts. The public papers furnish too many melancholy proofs.

A boycott of products that only enhanced the debts of Americans could help the country to emerge "from the distress it at present labors under." Washington knew that fully one-third of all England's exports were sold to the American colonies and tens of thousands of jobs depended on this transatlantic trade. In Virginia, only the merchants could object to a trade boycott:

> As to the penurious man, he saves his money and he saves his credit, having the best plea for doing [what] before perhaps he

had the most violent struggles to refrain from doing. The extravagant and expensive man has the same good plea to retrench his expenses. He is thereby furnished with a pretext to live within bounds and embraces it. Prudence dictated economy to him before but his resolution was too weak to put it into practice. For how can I, says he, who have lived in such and such a manner, change my method? I am ashamed to do it.

Washington ended by endorsing a continent-wide boycott of British goods. He called on Mason to help him arrange a private meeting of influential Tidewater politicians to come up with a "uniform plan" to submit to the Assembly when it convened for the May 1769 session.[5]

George Washington's diary for April 1769 gives no hint of his political activities. The whitefish were running. He planted corn, sold clover. On the river, his fishing schooner plowed the waters: "The herrings ran in great abundance." But in actuality Washington and Mason spent most of the month huddled at Mount Vernon or talking as they rode into Alexandria together to preside over the Fairfax County Court. Mason returned to Mount Vernon on April 18 for a visit that lasted four days. As John Stadler cracked his baton over the neighborhood dancing school, Washington, Mason, Richard Henry Lee, Middlesex County planter Augustine Smith, and Colchester merchants James Dennistone and Dr. David Ross of Bladensburg, Maryland, worked on a rough draft of a plan for a nonimportation agreement. For the next two days, Washington and Mason rode the lines between their farms and, on horseback, talked safely all day. Two days after he returned home, Mason sent from his home, Gunston Hall, some suggested changes in "the Association." When Washington left for Williamsburg for the May Assembly session he took the proposal with him in an inside pocket.

Williamsburg was never more glittering. On May 3 the Washingtons checked in as usual at Mrs. Campbell's Tavern and dined with members of the governor's council. They spent the evening "in the Daphne," the ornate upstairs gaming rooms at the Raleigh Tavern on Duke of Gloucester Street. He bought subscription tickets to three purse races—the prize was £100 (about $4,000 today)—and amused himself by gambling at the card tables. He won £4 17s ($165 today). The next day the Washingtons dined with distinguished old Speaker of the House Peyton Randolph and spent the evening with Washington's sister and brother-in-law, the Lewises. Washington borrowed a thumping £50 (about $2,000) from Fielding Lewis to buy ten tickets in a land lottery.

On May 5, George and Martha dined with the new royal governor. The latest appointee from England was Norborne Burkeley, Baron de Botetourt, a cultured, genial, and diplomatic old man rumored to have accepted the Virginia post to escape his many creditors in England. He was the first English nobleman to govern Virginia in nearly a century, and he ruled in viceregal splendor. He carried secret instructions to use the first opportunity to call new elections. He was to meet with the "principal persons of influence and credit" and try to win them away from the "erroneous and dangerous principles which they appear to have adopted." If this failed, he was to dissolve the Assembly. At first Virginians were flattered by their noble governor and they wined and dined him.

On Monday, May 8, His Lordship left the turreted redbrick governor's palace at noon wearing a brilliant red coat faced with gold and drove the half-mile to the Capitol in a handsome carriage pulled by six cream white horses with harnesses studded with silver. He took his seat at the head of the council table and received the newly elected burgesses. Washington, the Lees, Fairfax—all of the radical faction stood tensely as Lord Botetourt intoned a brief welcoming address: "I have nothing to ask but that you consider well and follow exactly without passion or prejudices the real interests of those you have the honor to represent."[6]

The House reassembled in its own chambers. Speaker Randolph wasted no time. He had written the Speakers of the other American colonial assemblies for their views on the Townshend duties. Their replies were on the clerk's table for examination. So was five years' correspondence with the House's London agent. For a week, as individual members took turns paging through the documents, the burgesses carried on routine business. Randolph appointed Washington to two key standing committees on oversight, which entitled him to study legitimately the intercolonial protests. Then, on the afternoon of May 15, 1769, the Speaker announced that the next day the House would convene as a committee of the whole to "consider the present state of the colony." When the House reconvened, George Washington took the floor and led the arguments for fewer words and sterner actions, especially for a tough economic boycott of England's exports. He was strongly supported by Richard Henry Lee, of Chantilly in Westmoreland County, who was Washington's partner in the Mississippi Company and who had lost his awe of the English as a law student in London. Washington was widely quoted for his succinct summary of the colonists' position: "They should not have their hands in my pockets." He urged the burgesses to take up Parliament's challenge and to declare that Virginia's elected representatives alone and not members of England's faraway Parliament had the right to lay taxes on Virginians. The colonists should also have the right to petition the king over the head of Parliament and be entitled by right to seek the concurrence of other colonial legislatures.

The suave new royal governor had hoped for submission and silence; the militant Washington and the fiery Lee complained loudly about the "dangers" that they would suffer if they were transported to England for trial. Four strongly worded unequivocal resolutions passed the House *nemine contradicente*—no one contradicting them. When word reached Lord

Botetourt he rushed angrily to the Capitol and dispatched a clerk to summon the burgesses into his council chamber at once. The burgesses found that the governor had already dispersed his council. Once again dressed in official scarlet, he was sitting all alone at the council table. "I have heard your resolves and augur ill of the effect. You have made it my duty to dissolve you and you are accordingly dissolved."[7]

Lord Botetourt dismissed the Assembly before it could vote its support for the other colonies' boycott and before it could consider the Washington-Mason Articles of Association, but Washington's analysis was correct: no one could forbid them to discuss it. That Tuesday noon, May 16, 1769, when Governor Botetourt dissolved Virginia's 150-year-old representative government, the government just got up and marched down the street and reconstituted itself half a block away in a rump session in the crowded Apollo Room at the Raleigh Tavern. The former burgesses noisily elected Peyton Randolph as their moderator. Randolph named a special committee to study the embargo. He appointed Washington its chairman and adjourned the meeting until the next day.

In his diary, Washington tersely noted only that he dined with the influential burgess Robert Carter Nicholas that night and "was upon a committee at Hay's [Raleigh Tavern] until 10 o'clock." There were no other committee members, only Chairman Washington, and he was busy writing. The next morning the extralegal burgesses reassembled at the Raleigh. The committee of one pulled a folded document from his breast pocket. In effect, he had lightly rewritten the set of resolutions voted by the merchants of Philadelphia a month earlier, adding a list of banned imports. The list was long and would make life difficult for anyone who heeded it conscientiously. Washington read off the embargoed goods: further import of slaves, wine, liquor, foods, including fruit, meat, cheese, sugar, pickles, and candy, oil and candles, tables and chairs, watches and clocks, mirrors, carriages, cabinets and upholstery fabrics, jewelry, gold and silver, "ribbon and millinery of all sorts," lace, East Indian "goods of all sorts" (including tea), silken robes, woolens and linens (except fabrics for sewing at home), shoes, boots, saddles, and all manufactured goods. It was a sweeping ban on most British imports and, when it took effect on September 1, 1769, life in Virginia would become far more austere. It would also take a historic turn. The nonimportation agreement specified that its subscribers "will not import any slaves or purchase any imported after the first day of November next until the said Acts of Parliament are repealed."

When moderator Randolph called for a vote, an overwhelming 94 of 116 former burgesses adopted the Association. Several others were in favor but had already gone home. The ninety-four lined up and signed. Washington was number seven in the line. And then they ordered the drinks to flow. House of Burgesses records show toasts to the king, to the queen and royal family and royal governor, for "prosperity to Virginia," a "speedy and lasting union between Great Britain and her colonies," "the British liberty in America," and to "true patriots" in England and Virginia.[8]

The next day, George and Martha and Patcy Washington joined the former burgesses and their families at the governor's palace for the Queen's Birthday Party, the highlight of Virginia's social season. But Washington and all the others who had signed the document and authorized its printing and distribution would now be considered by Lord Hillsborough and his cabinet as traitors and rebels.

*S*ometime during those tumultuous two weeks in May 1769, probably the evening that Washington dined with the new governor, Washington asked Lord Botetourt if he could present to the governor and his council a new petition from the officers and men of the former Virginia Regiment. Washington had grown adamant that the colonial government reward him and his men with "some of those lands we have labored and toiled so hard to conquer," as he had put it to Colonel John Armstrong, who was in charge of Pennsylvania's land office in Carlisle. Washington's agent, William Crawford, had located 2,000 flat, well-timbered riverfront acres in a single tract about twenty-five miles from Fort Pitt. Five years after the royal proclamation of 1763 had closed the trans-Allegheny west to further settlement, the Crown had called together Indian and colonial leaders at Fort Stanwyx in New York in the summer of 1768 to negotiate treaties for the cession of land in the over-the-mountain west by Iroquois and Cherokee. Washington thought it high time that the royal government make good on Dinwiddie's fifteen-year-old promise of bounty lands for his troops. On December 8, 1769, Washington at Mount Vernon sent the petition to the most recent royal governor. He alluded to their "cursory" discussion in May in Williamsburg. The area around Fort Pitt was "settling very fast" and nothing but "barren hills and rugged mountains" would be left for "those who have toiled and bled for the country." The Proclamation Line was unenforceable.

> Unavailing is it to say that the settlements of individuals, illegal
> in their nature, are not to be respected. To remove them would
> prove a work of great difficulty, perhaps of equal cruelty as most
> of these people are poor [and] swarming with large families.

Washington's petition requested that the bounty grant finally be made, that the offer of land include officers as well as enlisted men, that the lands be located either on the Monongahela, the New River, the Great Ranaroha, or Sandy Creek—farther west and south of the original Ohio Company grant and beyond the illegal new settlements of squatters near Fort Pitt. The governor and his councillors agreed on all points. Washington and his officers were to choose 200,000 acres either in a single tract or in twenty separate parcels. Each field officer was to receive 15,000 acres; lower-ranking officers and enlisted men proportionately less, down to 400 acres for a private.[9]

By 1769, Washington was turning his back on the politics and the economic stagnation of the Virginia Tidewater. He had just sent Robert Cary in London his latest shipment of Custis tobacco with an angry complaint about "dear bought" goods and his "considerable disappointment" with "the chariot." He was furious about the condition of a custom-made carriage he had saved up for, a green-and-gilt, leather-lined "chariot" with his coat of arms for which he had paid £133 (about $5,000 today), a considerable portion of a year's profits.

> I begged [it] might be made of well-seasoned materials and by a masterly workman instead of which it was made of wood so exceedingly green that the [door] panels slipped out of the moldings before it was two months old—split from one end to the other.

The new carriage had started to fall apart as the Washingtons drove it into Williamsburg to propose the embargo on British goods.

For the next three years Washington took the lead in securing the grant for himself and his comrades-in-arms. He personally oversaw the appointment of an official surveyor—his agent, William Crawford—and the selection, surveying, and division of the land among the men entitled to it. En route to his annual vacation at Berkeley Springs on August 2, 1770, he met in Fredericksburg with several survivors of the long-ago campaign. As Washington had requested, the governor's council had ruled that the officers should find unoccupied western lands and that no one who enlisted after the fall of Fort Necessity in July 1754 was eligible for the grant. It was especially galling to Washington that one of the veterans who appeared at the meeting was George Muse, the former British officer who as his second in command had ignored Washington's positive order to hold the outer works and keep the Indians out of musket range of the stockade. Now they were to share a 7,276-acre tract land grant. For years Washington had borne all the costs of keeping the veteran's claim alive. Now he insisted Muse sign over one-third of his share to him and exchange 2,000 acres of land he owned nearby rather than be his neighbor. Eventually, Muse would accuse Washington of trying to pressure the veterans into selling their lands cheaply to him. Washington rarely if ever wrote so angry a letter as his response to the accusation:

> As I am not accustomed to receive such from any man nor would have taken the same language from you personally without letting you feel some marks of my resentment I would advise you to be cautious in writing me a second of the same tenor. For

though I understand you were drunk when you did it yet give me leave to tell you that drunkenness is no excuse for rudeness and that, but for your stupidity and pettishness you might have known by attending to the public gazettes . . . that you had your full quantity of ten thousand acres of land allowed you. Do you think your superlative merit entitles you to greater indulgences than others? Or that I was to make it good to you if it did?

Muse was justified in complaining, and that may be why Washington reacted so hotly. On January 31, 1770, he had written his brother Charles to try to find out if any of his fellow officers wanted to sell out their claims cheaply for cash. One lieutenant, sure he would never see an acre of bounty land, sold his share for £2. Washington instructed his brother to buy all he could under his own name. "Show no part of this letter," he warned.[10]

As early as 1770, Washington was becoming disgusted with all things English. He was focusing more and more of his time and energy on opening up a vast western estate where he could plant new settlements and sell products he manufactured at Mount Vernon. As early as his road-building expedition of 1754, he had daydreamed of linking the Potomac to the Ohio Valley by highway and canal. Since then a celebrated thirty-mile canal had been built by the Duke of Bridgewater in the English Midlands that linked the coalfields of the Pennine Hills with the mills of Birmingham and Manchester. Washington paid to send an observer to study and make drawings of it. The Industrial Revolution had begun. In towns all over America, men like Washington and Franklin were talking of canals to cut the travel time of crops from the interior to seaports from which they could be shipped to Europe or other American markets. But in the English colonies, Washington was not free to make such a giant step.

In fact, in October 1770, ten months after Governor Botetourt and his councilors approved the veteran's grant, Washington received a terrible shock. He began to hear rumors that the Crown had granted "a large tract of country on the Ohio" to an English company—Benjamin and William Franklin's Illinois Company—and was going to make it a separate colony. If this new grant passed the royal seals, all the Virginia officers' grant lands would be subsumed in it and go to rival claimants. The Virginians would get nothing—again. Washington felt especially betrayed when he learned that George Mercer was applying to become the proposed colony's first royal governor. Washington had subsidized Mercer, paying his expenses on the understanding that he was helping to lobby for the veterans' grant. Washington beseeched Botetourt to help him in his "predicament." He received the disquieting news just as he set out on an expedition to select and survey his own Ohio Valley lands.

Washington badly needed to get away from Mount Vernon. The boycott of British goods was not going well. At a meeting of the twenty-member Association's steering committee, he had been assigned to revise the agreement. The committee had split. Some members wanted to abolish the boycott because Parliament had rescinded all the Townshend duties except three pence on the pound duty on tea. Others, including Washington, did not want to compromise so long as one unconstitutional tax remained. Washington finally had to compromise. He wrote a more "relaxed" plan that exempted several types of food, silver, gold, and pewter, bridles and saddles, and cheap clothing. It was a typical political compromise and he detested the brokering behind each exemption, but he held out for tighter enforcement; as a result, committees of inspection in each county were appointed to assure "better effects."[11]

He was also worried about his stepdaughter Patcy's deteriorating health. In one 86-day period between June and September she had epileptic seizures on twenty-six days, sometimes twice a day. The Washingtons had been on their way to the Berkeley Springs spa when Patcy collapsed. Under the care of Fredericksburg physician Hugh Mercer she stayed for nine days at Ferry Farm at her grandmother's. The family tried again to take their vacation in August. Martha and Patcy visited his sister Betty in Fredericksburg while Washington rode to an all-day meeting with his former comrades. The officers agreed to Crawford's appointment as official surveyor and voted to send Washington, his old friend and fellow veteran Dr. James Craik, and Crawford on a journey to the Ohio Valley to stake out for them the best possible lands. Washington convinced them that they could wait no longer to lay claim to their lands. As he had just written Governor Botetourt:

> Any considerable delay in the prosecution of our plan would amount to an absolute defeat of the grant inasmuch as immigrants are daily sealing the choice spots of land and waiting for an opportunity of soliciting a legal title under the advantages of possession and improvement—two powerful pleas in an infant country.[12]

George Washington was bent on possessing and improving as much of the Ohio Valley as he possibly could, and he was no longer willing to rely on anyone else. He packed up his theodolite and chains and began a 1,164-mile, 64-day adventure. It was his longest absence from Martha and Mount Vernon in twelve years.

With Dr. Craik and two slave boys, Billy Lee and Giles, Washington rode on October 6, 1770, west through Snicker's Gap in the Blue Ridge near present-day Bluemont. He spent the night at his younger brother Samuel's house at Harewood and then rode ten miles to Casper Rinker's house on the Winchester-Cumberland Road. Washington as a youth had surveyed Rinker's land. After the midday dinner Washington and Craik rode on to Samuel Pritchard's. They covered forty miles in the saddle on that beautiful fall day. It took two new horses and eight days to follow the tortuous old Braddock route through Cumberland Gap to Redstone Creek and Crawford's farm on the Youghiogheny River at present-day Connellville, Pennsylvania. After so many years of futilely fighting the French and Indians based at Fort Duquesne, it is curious that Washington recorded no emotion as he followed Braddock's road through Great Meadows and past the mouth of the Turtle Creek massacre site and up to the fort built on the ruins of the ancient bête noir. He did eventually buy Great Meadows and, because Fort Necessity had been built on rough ground, thought it would be suitable only for a tavern, which at the end of that fateful day in 1754 it had become. After a day of meetings they rode to present-day Perryopolis in Fayette County, where Crawford had selected 1,600 prime acres for Washington. Washington would soon have Crawford build a mill on the site and begin leasing the land. The party next crossed the Monongahela River to Fort Pitt.

Instead of the smoldering ruins of Fort Duquesne he had found with the Forbes expedition, Washington could now see a pentagonal fort, two sides of brick, the others log stockades, all surrounded by a moat. The British garrison consisted of two companies of Royal Irish commanded by Captain Charles Edmonstone. About 300 yards from the fort was the raw new town of Pittsburgh—about twenty log houses inhabited by Indian traders on muddy unpaved streets branching off the Monongahela. Here Washington lodged in Samuel Sample's "very good house of publick entertainment." The night they arrived he dined at the Widow Myer's tavern at Sixth and Sycamore Streets, surrounded by frontiersmen and Indians in town to trade their pelts. On October 18, Captain Edmonstone gave Washington and Craik a tour of the fort. Washington noted that he "dined in the fort at the Officers Club." It was an occasion calling for Washington's best uniform. They also rode out about four miles to Croghan Hall on the Allegheny to meet trader and land speculator George Croghan. Captain Edmonstone had arranged to mediate a sixteen-year-old rift between Washington and Croghan over supplies for Fort Necessity. Croghan was eager to patch things up. On paper he owned 430,000 acres of Pennsylvania and New York wilderness and he wanted to sell some land to the Virginians. Washington dickered with him over a 15,000-acre tract but was not satisfied that Croghan could give him clear title to the land. The Indian trader had also arranged a parley with "the White Mingo and other chiefs of the Six Nations." They passed around the calumet and Washington received a belt of white wampum and a speech that welcomed him to the Ohio Valley. He in turn assured the Indians "that all the injuries and affronts" of the past were forgotten.[13]

Washington's buckskin-clad expedition set off in a pair of canoes on October 20, 1770, Indians in one canoe, whites in the other: Washington sent the slave boys back to Crawford's with the horses. The party spent whole days kneeling in the canoes, gliding through dense forests in "remarkably clear and pleasant" weather. At night they camped in tents at the mouths of rivers and creeks and in the daytime Washington took sightings and drew maps of desirable riverfront land. He used his sextant to take accurate measurements of the distance they covered to assist in directing settlers. According to his calculations they canoed 266 miles down the Ohio; a modern measurement by the U.S. Army Corps of Engineers says the distance was 266 and three-quarters miles. In eleven days they passed not a single white man and only one small Mingo village (at present-day Steubenville). They fished and hunted for their meals. As they neared the mouth of the Great Kanawha, Washington paused to parley with Chief Kiashuta, who gave him "a quarter of very fine buffalo." When the party reached the Great Bend of the Ohio, Washington "went out hunting"—for buffalo. On a five-mile side trip up the Great Kanawha River, Washington carefully surveyed the land he wanted near present-day Wheeling, West Virginia. He marked off the corners of "the soldiers land if we can get it." It was snowing by the time the little expedition turned back, arriving at Pittsburgh by mid-November.[14]

Soon after he got home after an absence of nine weeks, Washington authorized Crawford to survey individual tracts. He also asked his brother Charles, who lived near Winchester, to offer to buy out soldiers who might be strapped for cash. He was to emphasize that some of their land might be "very hilly and broken" and suggest that they could lose everything if the British government chartered the Vandalia grant, which would include "every inch of the land we are expecting." Charles was to pay visits on some of the men without letting Washington's involvement be known. Washington had no qualms about using such tactics on his old comrades: "If it had not been for my unremitting attention to every circumstance not a single acre of land would have been obtained." In addition to his 15,000-acre grant, he was able to buy up some 5,147 acres. Five years later, a bureaucrat in Williamsburg discovered that Crawford had failed to swear the necessary oaths of allegiance to the king required of every surveyor. His surveys were disallowed by Lord Dunmore, the last royal governor. It was not until the middle of the Revolutionary War that the revolutionary Virginia House of Delegates, no longer pledging allegiance to the Crown, voted that the original surveys were valid. Whether Washington ever got his coveted western lands depended on the outcome of the Revolution.[15]

*I*n the early 1770s, as the colonial protests against increasingly stringent British regulations sputtered on, Washington was busy consolidating his business ventures. This included selling off Ferry Farm after dislodging his mother. Their relationship never improved. He visited her sometimes as he passed through Fredericksburg, but he usually stayed with his sister in town and paid a brief visit to the farm. Martha infrequently visited Ferry Farm with him—usually as they passed by en route on their summer vacation—but Washington never invited his mother to Mount Vernon after he married. The poor soil of Ferry Farm had been long ago exhausted and the harvests were meager; Mary Ball Washington asked her son for money four times between 1765 and 1771, and each time he gave her cash, in all, about £25. When he went to pay her money he took along his sister Betty for a witness. In 1771, Washington, his sister, and his brother Charles agreed that their mother should move into a townhouse and give up the run-down farm. A dry-eyed Washington sold the place—virtually his entire birthright inheritance from his father—for £2,000 but out of that he paid to build her a house behind Betty's home in Fredericksburg. It was a spacious one-and-a-half-story house very much like Wakefield, which Washington's father had built for her, and it had a sizable garden. The indomitable old lady drove a hard bargain before she would leave her son's land. In addition to the house and town lot and moving expenses, George was to pay her basic bills plus a £30 annual annuity. So much of Washington's shrewdness—like so many of his other qualities—came from his mother. Sixty-three years old when Washington sent his wagons and slaves to move her, she lived another twenty-five years, frequently pestering him for more money.

*I*n the summer of 1771 Washington gathered the surviving soldiers of his first command for yet another meeting in Fredericksburg. They drafted a new petition to a new governor, Lord Dunmore and his council. In November Dunmore and his councillors had ignored the Proclamation Line and ordered the bounty lands distributed. Yet Washington was still so worried that the rival Philadelphia claimants might win the lobbying battle in London that his anxiety prompted him to explore whether he could buy shares in the Franklins' Grand Ohio Company. At the same time, he pushed William Crawford to complete the surveys. In October 1772, Crawford came to Mount Vernon with detailed plans for the settlement. By this time Washington was ready to tackle Lord Dunmore for the final distribution of the lands. On November 6, 1772, Dunmore and the council approved the bounty land distribution, including Washington's patent for 20,147 acres. The long-awaited news brought some grumbling from one former officer that Washington and Dr. Craik had reserved the best lands for themselves. Washington reacted hotly. His "shoulders had supported the whole weight" of pressing the land claims for ten years: "I might add without much arrogance that if it had not been for my unremitted attention to every favorable circumstance not a single acre of land would ever have been obtained."

Washington thought that he had all but won his long battle to confirm the veterans' grant by the summer of 1773. He was preparing to leave with Dunmore for Fort Pitt when, in summer 1773, he received a shock that made it unthinkable for him to leave Martha and Mount Vernon for some time to come.[16]

*B*y the time Jack Custis turned sixteen, George Washington wondered whether his diffident stepson would ever learn anything useful. He wrote to schoolmaster Jonathan Boucher, who had transplanted his small school to Annapolis, Maryland, that Jack's progress seemed "trifling." Boucher replied defensively that the boy's academic attainments were "not inferior to those of any other young man so circumstanced." In other words, the boy was rich and saw no reason to push himself. In his own defense, young Custis pleaded "that I am one of those who put off everything to the last," a trait that obviously infuriated his punctual stepfather. The opportunistic Reverend Boucher thought it might help to take the lordly young man on a grand tour of England and the Continent with himself as the tutor, paid £250 plus all expenses. Ever conscious of criticism, Washington answered that the constitution had placed him as Jack's guardian and that "every farthing which is expended in behalf of this gentleman must undergo the inspection of the General Court." Washington said he had polled his stepson's relatives and several were opposed because "being almost the last of a family they think he should run no risks that are to be avoided."[17]

The proposal did prompt Washington to think of sending Jack off to college. Washington first consulted the Rev. John Witherspoon, president of the Presbyterian college at Princeton, New Jersey. Two of Washington's nephews, the sons of Fielding and Betty Lewis, boarded there. Reverend Boucher, an Anglican, shrieked at the thought of a young English aristocrat going to this Scottish Presbyterian school. Boucher wrote to Washington: "Dr. Witherspoon, it seems, said I ought to have put [Jack] into Greek. Had Dr. Witherspoon examined this young gentleman he would not, indeed, have found him possessed of much of that dry, useless and disgusting schoolboy kind of learning." But Jack was not "illy accomplished" in "liberal, manly and necessary knowledge befitting a gentleman."[18]

George Washington was just as helpless in the role of parental guide when it came to choosing a college as anyone since then. He decided to check out several schools, weigh their strengths and deficiencies, seek recommendations, and then rely on his own judgment. Reverend Boucher kept up a stream of advice. If Washington insisted on removing Jack from his school, "all I have to add is a request that it may not be Princeton. Your own college [William and Mary] is a better one." That failing, he recommended King's College (now Columbia University in New York City). This new college was at least Church of England. The Academy at Philadelphia (now Penn) was closer and, as a consequence, Washington wrote that it was "more agreeable to his mother."[19]

By January 1773 Boucher wrote that the sooner Washington took Jack off to some college—any college—the better. Jack had fallen in love with sixteen-year-old Nelly Calvert, one of ten children of Benedict Calvert of Mount Airy, Maryland, just across the Potomac from Mount Vernon. Washington promptly wrote to Calvert:

> I am now set down to write you on a subject of importance and of no small embarrassment to me. [Miss Nelly had] amiable qualifications [but Jack's] youth, inexperience and unripened education is and will be inseparable obstacles in my eye to the completion of the marriage.

Washington did not doubt "the warmth of his affections" nor did he fear "of a change in them," but he did not possess "due attention" to anything, especially "the important consequences of a marriage state." Washington wanted the young couple to wait—two years. His reasoning was self-revealing: "If the affection which they avowed for each other is fixed upon a solid basis it will receive no diminution in the course of the years." Poor Jack—his elders had decided he should wait two years. Under Washington's personal escort, Jack Custis hugged his mother and sister and rode off in May 1773 to New York City. Along the way they visited Governor William Franklin in Burlington, New Jersey, where the two men undoubtedly discussed their explorations in the Ohio Valley.[20]

Two weeks after Washington's return to Mount Vernon, the family was gathered on July 19, 1773, for a long Saturday afternoon dinner—Washington's favorite brother, Jack, and his family, and Jack Custis's fiancée Nelly Calvert and a girlfriend who had come from Maryland for a visit. Martha was still dressed in black, still mourning her young niece, Betsy, daughter of her youngest sister of the same name, who had died a few months earlier. But in recent months Patcy had seemed much better. She had attended balls in Alexandria and Mr. Stedlar's dancing classes and was making slow progress with her music lessons. It had been a fine early summer day and Patcy was happy that they had so much company, so many young people. As dinner ended, Patcy fell from her chair to the floor. Washington lunged to help her as the family and guests shrieked and sobbed. But Patcy had suffered her last seizure, and in less than two minutes she was dead.

Nothing ever could erase those last few horrible moments when Washington helplessly struggled to save the beautiful young girl who had come to mean so much to him. In his diary he could only write, "At home all day. About five o'clock poor Patcy Custis died suddenly." He was only able to write a single letter in the next three weeks. The day after Patcy died he wrote to the Bassetts. Martha was unable to write her sister; Washington wrote for her:

She rose from dinner about four o'clock in better health and spirits than she appeared to have been in for some time. Soon after . . . she was seized with one of her usual fits and expired in it in less than two minutes without uttering a word, a groan or scarce a sigh. This sudden and unexpected blow I scarce need add has almost reduced my poor wife to the lowest ebb of misery which is increased by the absence of her son.

Washington's brother Jack and his family and George and Sally Fairfax came to Patcy's funeral at Pohick Church. Washington stayed close to Martha at Mount Vernon for weeks, and they went for long, silent carriage rides. He did not leave her alone. His diary was even terser than usual. "I continued at home all day. . . . Went with Mrs. Washington and dined at Belvoir. . . . Rid with Mrs. Washington to the Ferry [Farm] plantation [to visit his mother]. Rid with Mrs. Washington to Muddy Hole, Dogue Run and Mill Plantations. . . . Mrs. Washington and self went to Belvoir to see [the Fairfaxes] take shipping."

Washington's brief, numb notation belies the stark realization that the charmed circle of the Washingtons and the Fairfaxes had also been shattered. Sally Fairfax and her husband were going to England. Washington had known for two years that Sally was in ill health. He may also have known that the continuing colonial crisis had frightened off his timorous old friend George Fairfax. Not until Fairfax reached England did he reveal to Washington that it could be many years, if ever, before they returned to America. Washington was in shock. He began to take long walks alone in the woods near Mount Vernon. In three months he left overnight only once, to accompany Nelly Calvert home. The sixteen-year-old girl had stayed at Mount Vernon when her parents went home after Patcy's death, attempting to substitute in some way for her lost friend.[21]

When a letter came from Jack at college, Martha devoured it. He told first how hard he was working, going to classes punctually and making progress, and then that he had sold one of his horses. Finally, he got around to his "well-beloved sister." He was a seventeen-year-old college freshman—egotistical, immature, spoiled—but he was terribly worried about his mother. He urged her to come visit him in New York City, "for everything at Mount Vernon must put her in mind of her late loss. I beg you to write me immediately," he wrote to Washington, "as I am extremely anxious to hear how my mother bears this misfortune. . . . We ought to submit with patience to the divine will." But who ever knows what to say when his only sister dies?[22]

A few weeks later, Jack came home. Nelly Calvert was waiting for him. On December 15, Washington wrote to Jack's tutor at King's College that his hopes for his stepson's education "are at an end." Washington had wished so much that his stepson would have a better education than he had but now there was no way to persuade him to complete his schooling. Contrary to his judgment, he had yielded to Jack's wish to quit college so that he could marry Nelly. He did not think the boy would be ready "for some years hence," but Jack's determination and "the desires of his mother" had made him reluctant "to push my opposition too far and therefore have submitted to a kind of necessity."

On February 3, 1774, Washington set out in his patched-together green carriage for the barge ride to the Maryland shore and the Calverts with nineteen-year-old Jack and cousin Lund. Martha did not attend her son's wedding. She was still mourning Patcy and stayed behind at Mount Vernon.[23]

*U*nable to travel far from his bereaved Martha, Washington immersed himself in his dreams of opening up the west. On his voyage home from the Ohio Valley expedition of 1770, Washington visited Fort Pitt again. He also met again with George Croghan and his cousin, the trader John Connolly, who told him about the status of the rival Illinois Company land grant application at a dinner Washington gave at Sample's tavern for the officers at Fort Pitt and the traders. While Washington was getting one version from the Pennsylvanians, George Mason had learned that their representative Benjamin Franklin in London had given shares to leading members of Parliament who now were supporting their petition for a two-million-acre grant. All the duplicity and murky land titles left Washington "gloomy" at "the prospect of getting any land at all."[24]

Time after time Washington had to start all over with the veterans' claims. The governor and council had ordered 200,000 acres distributed to the veterans, but early in 1772 when a new royal governor, Lord Dunmore, arrived, he ignored the earlier order and declared he was unable to make any outright grant because of the proclamation of 1763, but he agreed to listen. Once again Washington argued the urgency of the case. New immigrants were crowding through the narrow Cumberland Gap and following Daniel Boone into Kentucky and staking out all the good lands along the rivers throughout the rich Ohio Valley region. They were, Washington pointed out, "daily and hourly settling on the choice spots waiting a favorable opportunity to solicit legal titles on the ground of pre-occupancy." The squatters expected to get clear title when the Crown finally opened up a land office in the region. Washington deeply resented that the government's dawdling had put "the soldiers upon a worse footing than the meanest individual in the community." He also criticized the Crown's refusal to reward enterprising adventurers who were helping to open up the western lands deserted by the defeated French:

> It is a fact well known, and every age evinces it, that no country ever was or ever will be settled without some indulgences.

What inducements do men have to explore uninhabited wilds but the prospect of getting good lands? Would any man waste his time, expose his fortune, nay his life in such a search if he was to share the good and the bad with those who come after him? Surely not.[25]

Squatters by the thousands were pouring across the mountains and driving settlers from their cabins. Others did not wait for such legal niceties as deeds and clear titles. Crawford reported to Washington:

The man that is strong and able to make others afraid of him seems to have the best chance. . . . I do not find I can get you the quantity of land [unless] I could stay all summer and be on the spot as people crowd out in such numbers the like was never seen.

Crawford wrote Washington that armed squatters had taken Washington's land on Miller's Run. Washington probably believed that the arrival of the former colonel of the Virginia Regiment on the scene would sway the claim-jumping settlers, but Crawford warned:

They took your land and say they will keep it. I could drive them away but they will come back immediately as soon as my back is turned. The man I put on [your] land they drove away or built a house so close to his door he cannot get into the house. There is no getting them off without force of arms.[26]

Washington's answer was to advertise his 20,000 acres of Kanawha lands for sale in the *Baltimore Advertiser* for August 20, 1775:

None can exceed them for luxuriance of soil or convenience . . . all of them lying upon the banks of the Ohio or the Kanawha and abounding with fine fish and wildfowl of various kinds . . . Most excellent meadows are in their present state almost fit for the scythe.

Washington did not mention the legal nicety that he still did not have title to the western lands.[27] By this time he was ready to use any means to settle them.

As early as his military road-building days in early 1754, George Washington had thought about making the Potomac River navigable and constructing a combination of roads and a canal to link the Chesapeake Bay with the Ohio Valley. Navigation was only possible as far inland as the natural barrier of the fall line, and then a slow and costly twenty-mile portage was necessary to transport goods around the falls. During the Forbes expedition of 1758, Colonel Washington had made himself unpopular at British headquarters by urging the improvement of Braddock's route; instead Forbes cut a new route across western Pennsylvania. But the persistent Washington dusted off his plan in 1762 and began to enlist support for a water route from the Cumberland Gap to the Great Falls. After the Treaty of Fort Stanwyx cleared the way for development of former Indian lands in western Virginia and Maryland, Washington and Richard Henry Lee, his partner in the Mississippi Company, introduced a bill in the House of Burgesses on December 8, 1769, "for clearing and making navigable the River Potomac" up to Fort Cumberland. The bill died in committee for lack of support—Washington was too far ahead of his time. He did succeed in getting House permission to form a private Potomac Company. If he succeeded he would dredge and build a 172-mile toll route to inland America that would link the Chesapeake with the Ohio and the Mississippi Rivers.

By this time Washington knew of the successful experiments of the Duke of Bridgewater in opening a canal to Manchester and Birmingham. Bridgewater's canal made it possible to bring large quantities of coal and iron ore from inland mines to factory towns at a fraction of the cost and time of the mule trains that had plodded down from the hills for centuries. Washington's observer returned from England in 1774 with plans essentially copied from Bridgewater's canal. To carry out the scheme Washington needed the cooperation of the Maryland legislature. It soon became apparent he would not receive official cooperation despite the efforts of many leading Marylanders. Reverend Boucher acted as a go-between from Washington to Thomas Johnson, a prime supporter of the scheme in Maryland. While Washington and the Virginians had envisioned a system of locks, Johnson and his Maryland friends proposed blasting out rock impediments to navigation. Johnson wrote enthusiastically to Washington in June 1770 that the cost of hauling wheat from Cumberland Gap to Alexandria could be cut in half. "The Europeans have grown fond of our flour," Johnson wrote to wheat farmer Washington, who needed no persuasion about the quality of good soil he had staked out in the Ohio Valley. By November 1774 the canal-building scheme was poised to begin construction. But George Washington was absent from the meeting. Washington and Lee and most of the Virginia trustees of the Potomac Company had gone to Philadelphia as the colonial crisis with England flared to new and dangerous heights. It would be ten years before Washington could turn his mind again to his grand design.[28]

*T*he death of Patcy Custis, the marriage of Jack, and the departure of Washington's oldest friends the Fairfaxes for England completed a transformation that had been gaining momentum for years. No longer a tobacco planter, Washington presided over more than thirty buildings, including workshops and mills that lined the roads that connected the 8,000 acres he had assembled in his five home farms, where 3,500 acres were under cultivation. Cousin Lund lived in Mount Vernon and took his meals as a member of the family, but Washington also paid him about $3,600 in 1997 dollars to manage the farms. Most of Washington's attention had turned to diversifying his business interests. His small fleet of fishing vessels plied the Potomac and brought in rich harvests of perch, shad, carp, and the herring that swarmed in the river. His flour mill turned his wheat harvests into a fine grade of flour that was snapped up by the Alexandria and Norfolk markets; his second-grade flour went aboard his own ship for the Canary Islands and the Caribbean and was exchanged for butts of Madeira and crates of delicacies. The farms produced milk, butter, and cheese from his dairy herds and beef from herds of Aberdeen Angus steers for the northern Virginia market. Smokehouses prepared hams from the free-ranging hogs. Ducks and geese seemed to be everywhere. He became a master horse breeder but had less luck with sheep. In all, about 1,000 head of livestock dotted his fields.

The result of all this was small by today's standards—about $19,000 a year on average—and that was before his expenses. He paid about $12,000 to $16,000 to care for and feed about two hundred slave workers and his livestock, and he had to buy seeds and fertilizers and tools. His gross farm and fishing receipts rose from $73,560 in 1759 to $128,520 by 1772, yet after paying these costs and Lund's salary he only netted between $4,800 and $13,000 a year from agriculture.

He had long ago stopped buying slaves. The first three years after he married he bought as many as eleven slaves a year at an average price of $3,000 in today's money, but by 1762 he had as many slaves as he could keep busy and he was running into debt. It was not difficult to see that the heavy cost of buying slaves was one reason. From that time on the slave population on his farms burgeoned, and by the late 1760s he calculated he had one hundred slaves idle at any given moment. He had begun to question slavery on purely economic grounds, but by the mid-1770s was beginning to speak of it as tyranny.

By 1774 his greatest income came from the rents tenants paid him for his farmlands. Even as he sought more land in what would become six states, he raked in £8,000 a year—in 1997 terms about $320,000—in his peak year of 1774. His lands and the idea of concentrating on making cash from them instead of foreign credits from tobacco had made him rich and virtually independent of English factors by 1774. Patcy's death provided more lands and an infusion of Bank of England stock. Her half-share of the Custis estate passed to Martha, which meant to him. Yet even this inheritance led to more frustration. When he tried to sell the shares to pay his last remaining debt to Robert Cary, he encountered one more round of aggravation as Cary protested the great difficulty of unloading the shares. Yet Washington considered himself debt-free, and in fact he was.

Among the handful of most successful businessmen in America before the Revolution, he seems never to have forgotten his near-poverty status as a boy on a second-rate backwoods farm. In part he expressed this in his insistence on only furnishing his house and dressing in the very latest and most expensive taste. Both Martha and George came from threadbare gentry families, and while they would wait to buy whatever they wanted, it was always the best. Yet a second part of Washington's well-worked-out philosophy of wealth was his purposeful generosity. He was not a deeply religious man. Once he left his Bible-thumping mother's household he may never have taken Anglican communion again, yet he went to church frequently and gave heavily to the Pohick Anglican Church near Mount Vernon, which he had helped to build. He had tipped heavily as a young traveler. Anyone who fed and groomed and cooled down his horses shared in his largesse. But his charities had metamorphosed into a set policy. When he rode off to war, he gave instructions to Lund to keep the level of giving at Mount Vernon to his customary £50 or so a year—about $2,000 today in cash—and to feed and shelter anyone who came to his door. He had accepted election as a vestryman at Pohick Church in 1765, which meant he became a guardian of the parish's poorhouse and any luckless indigents in Fairfax County. When he was reelected to the House of Burgesses time after time, it is hard to untangle whether it was because of all his benefactions, or because he spent more on the victory celebration than he earned as a burgess. But he believed in a public image and he spent openhandedly to maintain his. Not all of his charity was conspicuous. He gave his old army buddies large interest-free loans that he never expected to see repaid; he gave his weaver a loan to bring his wife and children from England, even though the man could never possibly afford to repay him. And he quietly paid for the schooling of cash-poor relatives and friends.

As his house sat astride the main north-south route through Virginia and there were few towns or taverns, Washington felt the obligation to provide southern hospitality to all strangers. By 1774 Mount Vernon was crowded with uninvited visitors as well as the guests of what had become the first family of Fairfax County. With cash rolling in, Washington decided to expand Mount Vernon. Martha had been content with the house as it was for fifteen years, but Washington saw the project as one more way to engage Martha's attention and pull her away from her terrible grief. He designed two wings that would add a large new library and a banqueting room on the ground floor and more sleeping rooms upstairs for guests. He also planned a gentler-sloping copper roof with a cupola. The house would spread its wings to porticoes that connected it to ensembles of kitchen, storage rooms, artisan shops. To provide shade and a spectacular vista, he planned a 90-foot veranda where he could rock and talk with Martha and his guests as they gazed out over the soothing waters of the Potomac.

In the distance, in winter when the leaves were down, he had once been able to look off toward Belvoir with its beckoning lights. But these had gone out now. At first George Fairfax had given out the story that they were only going to England for a while, for Sally's health and for him to pursue his claim to a lordship. Sally had become ill on the passage: she barely survived smallpox and now her pale skin must have become as pockmarked as just about everyone elses. From the safety of the walled city of York came a letter to Washington in early 1774 that Fairfax wanted him to sell off the furniture at Belvoir and rent it. It was no good to keep a damp, unheated house that could be closed up for years. His legal business was only a pretext. Fairfax was one of the first Loyalists to flee to England as the crisis with England deepened. Sally had no voice and no choice. She never saw her family or George Washington again, although she wrote to him from this safe distance until she died.

It was Washington's grim duty to write the ad for the *Virginia Gazette* that embalmed in printer's ink so many of his earliest and most romantic memories. When the auction took place—on one of the longest afternoons of Washington's life—he stood by as the auctioneer gaveled down the Fairfaxes' possessions. Washington took Jack and Nelly Custis with him to buy furniture for their new home. As strangers handled and carted away pieces of his memories, Washington spent freely for an elegant sideboard and dining room chairs, a mahogany chest of drawers, a carpet, and a mirror, in all paying a handsome £170 (about $6,800 today). He also bought a few more intimate articles: the bedspread, pillows, and bolsters from Sally Fairfax's bed.

Twelve

"THE CRISIS IS ARRIVED"

One warm day in January 1774 a courier spurred his horse up the steep grade from Johnson's Ferry on the Potomac to Mount Vernon with startling news from Massachusetts. Boston merchants, lawyers, and artisans posing as Mohawk Indians had wrapped themselves in blankets and painted their faces and boarded the Royal East Indian *Dartmouth*. They had used their tomahawks to smash open 342 black-lacquered chests and dumped £10,000 worth of tea into Boston Harbor. News of the unexpected sacking of a British ship was already racing across the Atlantic to an already anti-American ministry. Reprisals could certainly be expected. Washington's initial reaction was predictable. He disapproved of the inflammatory destruction of British property, even if he quite understood the exasperation behind it.

Even when Parliament had rescinded all of the Townshend duties on all goods but tea, Washington refused to buy what he considered an unconstitutional tax. He had switched from tea to coffee and made a point of serving it when he won reelection to the House of Burgesses. But few Americans remained as adamant on the subject. The anti-tax association had all but collapsed and merchants in Philadelphia had abandoned it. In Virginia tea imports were running 80,000 pounds a year. It was such a small thing, a penny in the pound. But when the ministry of Lord North early in 1773 moved to rescue the foundering East India Company by pushing through Parliament a new Tea Act, he was not only trying to dispose of a glut of 17 million pounds of tea in England, he was undercutting every American merchant who imported tea. Americans sometimes drank fifteen or sixteen cups in an afternoon. Now they would have to buy direct from one English importer. The East India Company, whose shareholders include many members of Parliament, was granted the monopoly. American merchants, earlier forced to buy their tea at auctions in

258

England through middlemen, were left with costly, overpriced inventories on their hands. At a stroke, American merchants who had been indifferent or opposed earlier boycotts became committed protestors. Radicals no longer had to use coercion to gain the cooperation of merchants. The "Mohawks" who stormed the *Dartmouth* on December 23, 1773, included importers whose economic survival was now threatened. In Virginia, Washington argued at first that the East India Company must be reimbursed. He had emerged in the past two years as an advocate of strict economic measures against the British, but he also by far was the first to suggest that if the English government failed to respond the colonies would be forced to resort to arms. As each British governor tried to coerce the Virginia Assembly to pass its own laws that made British taxation heavier and more odious, Washington became more radical. In early 1772, Governor Dunmore had pressed the House of Burgesses to impose customs duties on the purchase of slaves. The governor's initiative backfired. A House committee authorized a petition to the king to end altogether the imperial slave trade:

> The importation of slaves into the colonies from the coast of Africa hath long been considered as a trade of great inhumanity and under its present encouragement we have too much reason to fear will endanger the very existence of your Majesty's American dominions. . . . Your Majesty's subjects in Great Britain may reap emoluments from this sort of traffic but when we consider that it greatly retards the settlements of the colonies with more useful inhabitants [we hope] the interest of a few will be disregarded.

The largest slave trading company in the world at the time was the Royal African Company of Liverpool. The bill that Washington and Mason had hoped to sponsor in 1765 had seven years later borne the fruit of consensus.[1]

By 1774 Washington was writing to a more conservative friend, his neighbor Bryan Fairfax, that there was a close analogy between Parliament's treatment of Americans and the master-slave relationship. The slaves must revolt:

> The crisis is arrived when we must assert our rights or submit to every imposition that can be heaped upon us till custom and use shall make us as tame and abject slaves as the blacks we rule over with such arbitrary sway.[2]

What provoked Washington to enunciate his evolving philosophy of resistance to Parliament was a series of British measures that was escalating in pace and severity, until he now believed there was a set British agenda to strip Americans of their rights as English citizens. In March 1773, Governor Dunmore called the General Assembly into emergency session to try to push through a law to crack down on counterfeiters. The burgesses had something they considered more important on their agenda. A recent royal proclamation declared that henceforth suspected American radicals were to be shipped to England for trial. The prospect of transporting accused colonials to England offended the burgesses. Younger members of the House, led by Thomas Jefferson, drew up a series of resolves protesting the loss of "ancient legal and constitutional rights" and authorizing creation of an eleven-man standing committee of intercolonial correspondence. Washington thumpingly endorsed and voted for the measure. By February 1774 ten other colonies had followed Virginia's lead.[3]

By May 1774, when the Washingtons drove into Williamsburg in their battered green carriage, all of Virginia was in turmoil over the latest news forwarded by the Committee of Correspondence in Massachusetts. Parliament had passed a series of harsh new laws that closed the port of Boston. The Boston Port Bill prohibited the loading or unloading of any ships in New England's leading port. Parliament followed up with a second act that authorized the royal governor of Massachusetts to ship political prisoners or rioters to England for trial.

On May 19, 1774, Purdie and Dixon's *Virginia Gazette* printed the Boston Port Act just as the House of Burgesses began its session. Five days later the burgesses—declaring Parliament's action a "hostile" invasion—responded by passing a resolution which on June first, the day the British navy was to shut up Boston, set aside a colony-wide

> Day of Fasting, Humiliation and Prayer devoutly to implore the divine interposition for averting the heavy calamity which threatens destruction to our civil rights and the evils of civil war [and] to give us one heart and mind firmly to oppose by all just and proper means every injury to American rights.

Such a fasting would have special significance in "suffering Boston," where days of fasting were an old tradition in times of threatened invasion by the French or the Indians; in London, it would be recognized as a reminder of the English civil wars of the 1640s, when Puritans used the same device to whip up public opinion against Crown measures that suppressed civil liberties.[4]

The next morning, the fast-day proclamation appeared in the *Virginia Gazette*, where the red-faced royal governor read it. At 3 P.M. that same day Lord Dunmore summoned the House of Burgesses to the council chamber. He particularly objected to the phrase "sister colonies." This smacked of forming an American government without the approval of

Parliament, connecting colony to colony by cutting across the lines that connected each colony with the home government.

> I have in my hand a paper published by order of the House conceived in such terms as reflect highly upon His Majesty and the Parliament of Great Britain which makes it necessary for me to dissolve you and you are dissolved accordingly.[5]

It had become a ritual dance by now of protest, dissolution, and election of even more radical burgesses. Again stripped of its legal status, the House of Burgesses paraded down Duke of Gloucester Street and reconvened at the Raleigh Tavern. This time was different, however. They could not be put off any longer by the arbitrary decisions of royal appointees. The ex-burgesses voted to declare an embargo on all imports from England and, furthermore, to call a colony-wide extralegal convention—in effect, to set up a provisional government. Of eighty-nine burgesses who lined up to sign, Washington was number eight. He had cast his lot with Virginia's leading radical, Thomas Jefferson, who was the author of the fast-day resolution—and he would not turn back, even if his signature put him on a list for transportation to England and trial as a traitor.

History is replete with alternate possibilities, the "what ifs." If Lord Dunmore had not acted heatedly and dissolved the burgesses that day, the burgesses would have ridden home and the whole affair might have died down as surely as earlier protests. Until the Boston Port Act was announced in America, the colonial protests against the Townshend duties had—except in Boston—all but died out. By 1774 protest had collapsed in New York and Philadelphia. Many merchants had found it impossible to resist the temptation to take up the slack in sales created by competitors who honored the boycott. Because Boston merchants had been opportunistic and reaped large profits during the embargo, the complaints of Boston radicals were long considered suspect by other colonies. But the shock of the British government's decree that the leading port in all New England, where almost all trade and most jobs depended on shipping and fishing, jolted merchants throughout the colonies to join a concerted protest movement. Rich merchants now joined threadbare radicals in the streets, in town meetings, and, in Virginia, in church—the Church of England of Bruton Parish in Williamsburg.[6]

The morning after Lord Dunmore dissolved the burgesses, George Washington and more than one hundred ex-burgesses crowded into the Apollo Room of the Raleigh Tavern to continue the debate over an appropriate response to the intolerable Boston Port Act. Jefferson recalled years later the unforgettable excitement in the room. The radicals had taken over Virginia politics just as surely as any of Boston's tea dumpers.

"The lead in the House," he wrote, "being no longer left to the old members," a new generation of leaders agreed "that we must boldly take an unequivocal stand in the line with Massachusetts." The assemblage on May 27, 1774, enunciated a new and revolutionary doctrine: an attack on one was an attack on all. There was no such thing any longer as an impingement on the liberties of Massachusetts citizens: it was an attack on *American* rights. The Virginia burgesses that day took a long and bold step toward independence. Washington crystallized their sentiments when he called British taxation without American consent "an invasion of our rights and privileges."[7] When the day of public prayer, the day that Boston closed, came, Washington recorded in his diary that he "went to church and fasted all day." At the service, the usual "God Save the King" was omitted. In Williamsburg that week Washington went to church more than ever and he gambled for higher stakes.

He would not go so far as burgesses in the room. One Norfolk burgess described "some violent debate" about the extent of reprisals against the British. George Mason, Patrick Henry, Richard Henry Lee, and a few other influential speakers favored "paying no debts to Britain, no exportation or importation and no courts." Washington considered it ignominious and opportunistic to halt debt payments, but he favored a complete ban on trade—even if it meant great hardship for tobacco growers. More moderate Assembly leaders prevailed. Only imports from England would be banned and then not for six more months. All talk of an export ban was postponed for a year.

Exasperated at the pettifogging debaters who blunted what he considered necessary severe measures, Washington said little in the public debates. But the presence of Virginia's highest-ranking military officer in his old blue-and-buff regimentals signaled not only his support but his determined opinion. In an exchange of letters later that summer with his close friend and neighbor Bryan Fairfax (Sally's brother-in-law) he showed his impatience with any more talk of humble petitions and unenforceable trade sanctions. One week later, even before he returned to Mount Vernon, an agitated Washington wrote to his old friend George Fairfax, who, although he now resided in York, England, was strongly pro-American.

> The Ministry may rely on it that Americans will never be taxed without their own consent. . . . The cause of Boston [and] the despotic measures in respect to it I mean now is and ever will be considered as the cause of America (not that we approve their conduct in destroying the tea) and that we shall not suffer ourselves to be sacrificed by piece meals though God only knows what is to become of us threatened as we are with so many hovering evils hang over us at present. Those from whom we have a right to seek protection are endeavoring by every piece of art and despotism to fix the shackles of slavery upon us.

> Since the first settlement of this colony the minds of people in
> it never were more disturbed.[8]

And when Lord Dunmore called for new elections Washington urged
Fairfax's younger brother, Bryan, to run for a vacated seat. Washington
was no longer willing to wait for the Crown to respond to humble petitions. He'd had more than two decades of bending the knee to his "lordly
masters." Washington had carefully thought out the colonial crisis for five
years now, and when he returned to Mount Vernon he spelled out his
views in a series of letters to Bryan. In the half-darkened study at Mount
Vernon on the morning of July 4, 1774, he began a debate with the
younger Fairfax, who was English-schooled but had a quick mind and
had been Washington's riding, gambling, and raconteuring companion for
several years. Above all Washington wanted to keep Fairfax from slipping
off to England as so many Loyalists were doing these days. Better yet, he
hoped to coax his friend into the House of Burgesses with him. On Sunday mornings Washington met with other Fairfax County leaders in the
Pohick churchyard for safe and effective parleys on politics. Washington
had just learned that Fairfax had refused to stand for the House because
he favored petitioning the king once again to imposing a fresh and much
stricter boycott:

> As to your political sentiments I would heartily join you in them
> so far as relates to a humble and dutiful petition to the throne—
> provided there was the most distant hope of success. But have
> we not tried this already? Have we not addressed the Lords and
> remonstrated to the Commons? And to what end? Did they de-
> sign to look at our petitions? Does it not appear as clear as the
> sun in its meridian brightness that there is a regular, systematic
> plan formed to fix the right and practice of taxation upon us?
> Does not the uniform conduct of Parliament for some years past
> confirm this? Do not all the debates, especially those just
> brought us [from London] in the House of Commons on the
> side of the government expressly declare that America must be
> taxed in aid of the British. . . . Is there anything to be expected
> from petitioning after this?

Virginians had just learned that Parliament had passed the Administration of Justice Act, which offered encouragement to royal officials to crack
down on radical leaders by exempting them from being prosecuted in
colonial courts, even if the death of a citizen resulted. A royal governor
only had to swear an affidavit that the action on which the colonial indictment was based had been committed while putting down a riot or collecting revenues. On affirming that a royal official could not obtain a fair trial
in the colonies the trial would be transferred to Britain. The decision

would have held blameless British redcoats for the five deaths known as the Boston Massacre of 1770 and would allow British navy officers pursuing smugglers to kill them with impunity.

Washington was equally outraged at another new act of Parliament passed on May 20, which in effect annulled Massachusetts's century-old charter. Henceforth all members of the royal governor's council, the upper house of the Massachusetts Assembly, were to be appointed by the king. The attorney general, inferior judges, sheriffs, and justices of the peace, all were to be appointed and removed not by the elected House of Representatives but by the royal governor. The royal governor would nominate the chief justice and superior judges; the king would appoint, pay, and dismiss them at his pleasure. The Crown-appointed sheriff would choose and summon juries. No longer would jurors be elected by the people. Any shred of power flowing upward from the people was to be destroyed when the town meeting—the ancient bulwark of New England government and the most effective forum for legally sanctioned protest—was barred except without the express written permission of the royal governor after he approved its agenda.

As if the parliamentary assault on Massachusetts were not devastating enough, the House of Commons had passed on the same day a new frame of government for Quebec Province that extended its borders south all the way to the Ohio River. Washington and his 1754 veterans now could come under the jurisdiction of a powerful governor-general of Canada. All the years of expense and defense of the frontier could well be swept away as the vast Great Lakes and Ohio Valley region (including much of the present-day Midwest) became part of a new and enlarged British government-controlled Quebec that had few remnants of the rights of freeborn Englishmen like Washington.

For fourteen years since the British defeated the French, Canada had been ruled by martial law. At this exquisitely inopportune moment the English prime minister Lord North and his cabinet decided that since they were overhauling American colonial policy anyway they would draft a new charter for the province of Quebec. Intended as a model that would sound a cautionary note for other more restive colonies, the Quebec Act set off alarm bells throughout colonial America. The Quebec charter created a highly centralized royal government. It was to be ruled by a governor and a council entirely appointed by and serving at the pleasure of the king and with *no* representative-elected lower house. Parliament in London would set the taxes. All laws were to be subject to the king's veto. The rights, religious and civil, of the French majority were to be guaranteed. Since most Canadians were Catholic, this guarantee effectively made Catholicism the state religion. The courts were to follow French law, which did not admit trial by jury. Moreover the French-Canadian fur traders were rewarded by the extension of the provincial borders to the Ohio River, thus wiping out all the land grants not only of

Washington but of the Franklins and other land-hungry speculators from Massachusetts to South Carolina. As Benjamin Franklin described it, the British in secret and without consulting any of the American colonists had suddenly created "an arbitrary government on the backs of our settlements dangerous to us all." It was obvious to Washington that England intended to subdue Puritan New England and bring it under a Parliament-controlled government. There had never been such an extension of parliamentary power since Cromwell had deposed Charles I and nullified all American charters, except the new ones he had granted nearly 125 years ago.

In his first long letter to Bryan Fairfax in July 1774 Washington expressed in private his complete disenchantment with American attempts to appease and conciliate the power-grabbing British ministry: "Is there anything to be expected from petitioning after this?" After such an onslaught against the people of Massachusetts, what was the point of further knee-bending? Parliament had passed the punitive laws even "before restitution of the loss to the India Company was demanded—a plain and self-evident truth of what they are aiming at." The Tea Party had only provided a pretext to push through an irate Parliament bills to chastise Americans for ten years of resisting anti-American extremists in the British ministry. Should not these new laws "convince us that the Administration is determined to stick at nothing to carry its point? Ought we not then put our virtue and fortitude to the severest test?"

Fairfax had objected to further economic sanctions against England in part because he considered them unenforceable. Washington agreed to some extent: "With you I think it a folly to attempt more than we can execute as that will not only bring disgrace on us but weaken our cause. Yet I think we may do more than is generally believed." He did not consider it just to withhold payments from English creditors: "Whilst we are accusing others of injustice we should be just ourselves. Nothing but the last extremity, I think, can justify it. Whether this is now come is the question."

If Washington harbored any lingering doubts about British intentions, they evaporated when he learned late in July about a royal proclamation ordering Boston's Committee of Correspondence to disband and threatening criminal prosecution against anyone who sought to disrupt trade with Great Britain. The king's decree made Washington and all other Associators, as the signers of the trade boycott called themselves, liable to prison and, under the new Administration of Justice Act, subject at the discretion of the royal governor to extradition for trial in England, "where it is impossible from the nature of the thing," he told Fairfax, "that justice shall be done."[9]

Washington hoped to see Fairfax the next day in Alexandria, where "a meeting of the inhabitants of this county" had been called to sound out citizens before the burgesses attended the colony-wide convention. It was two more weeks before the meeting took place and then Washington led the way in drawing up the Fairfax County resolves. In the crowded, steamy Fairfax County Court House Washington chaired the all-day meeting that presented twenty-four strongly worded resolutions George Mason had drawn up. In the interim Washington was easily reelected to the House of Burgesses. No tea was served at the victory celebration. Washington plunked down £8 for coffee, chocolate, and cakes. On July 18 Washington and his friend Mason rode together from Mount Vernon into Alexandria. Washington and his fellow committeemen took their places behind the judge's bench. A courier immediately handed him a thick letter. Bryan Fairfax had written out his reasons for preferring a fresh petition to the king seeking reconciliation with England rather than retaliation. Washington scanned the paper and passed it to the others. Only one committeeman favored Fairfax's pleas. Washington and all the others decided they would not even present to the full House an opinion at odds with Mason's.

There was little new to the Fairfax resolves, only that they were so thorough an indictment of British policy by so distinguished a group of Americans, who resented being "considered as a conquered country. The present inhabitants are the descendants not of the conquered but of the conquerors. . . . Our ancestors when they left their native land and settled in America brought with them (even if the same had not been confirmed by charters) the civil constitution and form of government of the country they came from." Americans were as entitled to all the "rights, advantages and immunities" of other British subjects as if they had remained in England. Only freely chosen representatives of the people could govern them: this was the basis of the English constitution. Since Americans were not represented in Parliament they could only exercise their rights through their own elected assemblies. The key Fifteenth Resolve provided for reprisals against the ministry's recent high-handedness. "Until American grievances be redressed by restoration of our just rights and privileges," no goods "whatsoever" could be imported from England except for a few basic commodities like cheap cloth, nails, papers, and medicines—and these would be halted within two years. Washington obviously believed Americans could follow his lead and set up their own basic industries in short order. So confident was Washington by this time that he wrote to his brother Jack that even if Boston "gave way" after "being immediately under the lash" Virginia would not yield until Parliament rescinded its intolerable new laws.[10]

The electrifying Fairfax Resolves were to serve as the prototype for an intercolonial boycott of English trade. Part of the commerce they explicitly banned was the slave trade. The seventeenth resolution read:

> During our present difficulties and distress no slaves ought to be imported into any of the British colonies on this continent.

And we take this opportunity of declaring our most earnest wishes to see an entire stop forever put to such a wicked, cruel and unnatural trade.[11]

The penultimate resolve named Washington as a Fairfax County representative to the colony-wide convention on August first at Williamsburg. His name was also first on the list of a standing emergency committee that in effect had taken over the government of the county. Thirty Virginia counties passed resolves that month, but none were more influential. Mason had forged the gauntlet: Washington now hurled it down.

When he returned to Mount Vernon, Washington wrote again to Bryan Fairfax. He explained that it would have been pointless to read his long letter to the meeting.

What further proofs are wanted to satisfy [you] of the designs of the ministry than their own acts? Shall we after this, whine and cry for relief when we have already tried it in vain? Or shall we supinely sit and see one province after another fall a prey to despotism?[12]

Once more late that summer, in the sad days after Washington supervised the auction at Belvoir, he wrote to Bryan. The last of the Fairfax line in Virginia had shied away from running for his older brother's seat in the House of Burgesses and apparently had feared to attend the mass meeting in Alexandria on July 17. Washington was hurrying to prepare for the August convention, yet he wrote another long letter in which he said he had refrained from reading Fairfax's opinions at the Alexandria mass meeting because he feared it would be "repugnant to the very principle we are contending for" and inflammatory to the throng. "That I differ very widely from you in respect to the mode of obtaining a repeal," he began, in a 1,500-word final attempt to win over his friend, "I shall not hesitate to acknowledge."

But I see nothing on the one hand to induce a belief that Parliament would embrace a favorable opportunity of repealing Acts which they go on with great rapidity to pass in order to enforce their tyrannical system. I think I observe that government is pursuing a regular plan at the expense of law and justice to overthrow our constitutional rights and liberties.

For, Sir, what is it we are contending against? Is it against paying the duty of three pence per pound on tea because burdensome? No, it is the Right only we have all along disputed, and to this end we have already petitioned his Majesty in as humble and dutiful a manner as subjects could do.

Further petitions to England were pointless, even dangerous: "Why should we suppose an assertion of this power would be less obnoxious now." The people of Boston were being treated with uncalled-for harshness, their harbor filled with blockading British warships, their streets with hostile redcoats, their ships and warehouses and ropewalks idled, and their families cut off from work and food.

The threat of deportation to England for trial for treason cast a shadow across another Washington letter. The actions of the British general Gage—a coward under Braddock, a "Turkish bashaw" now in Boston—infuriated Washington. Taken collectively, England's high-handed assault on American civil liberties was all the evidence Washington needed of "the most despotic system of tyranny that ever was practiced in a free government." To his old friend, Washington spoke plainly. Never mind that this man had so long sat quietly in public deferring to "better minds than mine"—it was only a disclaimer. His letters to Bryan Fairfax reveal how thoroughly he had thought out the implications of British oppression. On Fairfax he used the crowd-pleasing aphorism he had developed to sum up the American position: "I think the Parliament of Great Britain hath no more right to put their hands into my pocket without my consent than I have to put my hands into yours for money."

But all of this had already been urged "in a firm but decent manner by all the colonies. . . . What reason is there to expect anything from their justice?" Washington only hoped that there was enough "public virtue" left among Americans "to deny ourselves everything but the bare necessities of life." If Americans resisted British tyranny together, "no power on earth can compel us." Washington "recoil[ed] at the thought of submitting to measures which I think subversive of everything that I ought to hold dear." He admitted to his old friend that there were moments when he was not so sure he was right, but he drew courage when he saw how many other leading Americans agreed with him: "the voice of mankind is with me."[13]

All through July 1774 Virginians were shaken repeatedly by news of the British crackdown in Boston as well as a rash of illegal actions. Without calling the Assembly, Lord Dunmore illegally called up the Virginia militia and declared an unauthorized war on Indians along the western Virginia frontier. At the same time the law setting court fees expired—closing the courts for land, lease, debt or apprenticeship filings as well as criminal procedures—and the Militia Act expired. Royalists and conservatives gathered around Lord Dunmore and nervously hoped for British men-of-war. In the absence of any legal authority, county committees sprang up. Burgesses like George Washington became county rulers and raised their own militia companies. Washington recruited and trained militia in Alexandria: he paid to equip them himself. Suddenly as the prospect of civil war loomed, Washington put on his old blue-and-buff uniform and strapped on his sword.

On August 4, 1774, the Washingtons drove to Williamsburg in their battered carriage to join other members of the Virginia Committee of Correspondence. In strictest secrecy, the 108 delegates, most of them burgesses, met in the Capitol and prepared resolutions that called for a Continental Congress of deputies sent from every colony. Calling for the emergency meeting, Virginia sent dispatch riders off to Annapolis, Maryland, and Philadelphia but kept the details of their proceedings behind closed doors. It was, after all, an illegal gathering and under the new laws all the county delegates were subject to criminal prosecution by the royal governor. But rumors of what was said that day leaked out. One of them was that George Washington made a dramatic speech in which he called for mobilization of militia units in every county. "I will raise one thousand men," he was quoted as saying, "subsist them at my own expense and march myself at their head for the relief of Boston." The *Virginia Gazette* broke the story of the outcome of the secret session:

> *Friday, August 5th.* This day the commissioners on behalf of this colony to attend the General Congress at Philadelphia the 5th of next month were appointed by ballot.... The Honourable Peyton Randolph [Speaker of the House of Burgesses], Richard Henry Lee, George Washington, Patrick Henry [etc.].

The committed pledged £1,000 and asked each of the sixty-one counties to contribute £15 each to support the delegates. George Washington was to receive his first federal expense money—£90 13s, today about $3,600—when he arrived in Philadelphia.[14]

*T*he last three weeks of August were crowded. George and Martha had only four days when there was not a house full of guests. As he wrote to his canal-building colleague Thomas Johnson in Annapolis, he was not keen on going away, especially so far as Philadelphia, at this time. Martha had just shed her mourning clothes, but she was still too frail for the trip and all the strangers they would have to meet. They had come back from Williamsburg slowly, so that they had time to visit relatives on both sides. Jack and his bride, Nelly, frequently visited Mount Vernon, but Martha's mother, the Widow Dandridge, had not yielded to Washington's practical argument that she should come to live at Mount Vernon with Martha instead of living alone. In those last days together before he went off to the congress, Washington took Martha to a barbecue, to church. They spent many hours planning the new wings on the house. There would be a wide new "piazza," as they were calling the deep, ninety-foot-wide veranda that would enable them to sit in the shade and rock and gaze out over the Potomac. And there would be a large new library and a master bedroom over it, where Martha would have privacy and could work at her desk planning the myriad details of running the great house and its kitchens. Those last days in August were "clear and very pleasant," Washington noted in his diary.[15]

On August 30 it became "very warm" with only a "stifling south wind." Patrick Henry arrived on time with another delegate, the august Williamsburg lawyer Edmund Pendleton. Over from Gunston Hall rode George Mason—the colonial crisis had vastly improved the old hypochondriac's health. They spent the evening talking and making plans, these four leaders, of what so quickly had become a vast and unpredictable political movement. From Georgia to Massachusetts delegates were riding in the "exceeding hot" weather toward Philadelphia. In a New York City tavern, Boston lawyer John Adams read with awe the resolutions Mason and Washington had introduced in Alexandria and then taken to Williamsburg and then sent to the compass points—some 2,000 copies of them. At Mount Vernon, George Mason was still talking and George Washington said little. The time for arguing was past. It was time now to act. After a midday dinner, he bade good-bye to Martha. Local legend, with an assist from Edmund Pendleton, records that she said to the departing delegates, "I hope you will stand firm—I know George will."[16]

*B*y late in the afternoon of September 4, 1774, the Virginia delegates arrived in Philadelphia and went to the brick mansion on South Second Street of Dr. William Shippen and his wife, Alice, the sister of Virginia delegate Richard Henry Lee. They spent the evening at the nearby City Tavern, a stylish new evocation of the best London taverns with several ample club rooms ideally suited for delegates' informal meetings. Here the next morning Peyton Randolph was elected president of the First Continental Congress, which then moved to a nearby union headquarters called Carpenters Hall. Boston's delegates had rejected use of the Pennsylvania State House, where the duly-established provincial government held its sessions. Washington was appointed to neither of the key congressional committees, leaving him free to make the acquaintance of delegates after congressional hours. Washington found rooms for himself and his black manservant, William Lee, at the Harp and Crown on North Third Street near Arch—just across from the city's open common lands where horses were in his view.[17]

In a constant round of dinner invitations he visited the home of Andrew Allen, the Pennsylvania attorney general who would shortly organize the First Troop of Philadelphia City Cavalry. The next day he dined with James Tilghman, secretary of the Pennsylvania Land Office: they had much to discuss. He dined with former governor Richard Penn and, on September 13, with Thomas Mifflin, a wealthy young merchant and delegate. He rode out to Fairhill, the country estate of the famous lawyer John Dickinson, the "farmer" whose 1767 essays had galvanized Americans against parliamentary taxation without representation. He rode through much of the redbrick white-shuttered town—America's largest—whose 23,000 citizens mostly lived within two square miles between the crowded wharves along the Delaware River and the slums along the Schuylkill. He visited the first American hospital—Pennsylvania Hospital—a great Georgian pile where the insane and would-be mentally ill were kept behind bars in the basement. For someone who had so recently witnessed years of epileptic seizures the spectacle of sight-seers poking the mentally ill through window grates with their canes must have been disturbing.

When finally the Grand Committee reported out of its secret meetings, the Congress began four weeks of six-day-a-week sessions. Washington lent his silent assent to adoption of a declaration of rights that emulated Virginia's 1769 resolves. The boycott on imports he had first heard hammered out in Alexandria and then in Williamsburg now became continent-wide until Parliament revoked the Tea Act and the Coercive Acts closing the port of Boston. Washington wanted to see a ban on exports as well, but congressional factions split and the decision was deferred for a year until southern planters could send off another year's tobacco crop. To enforce the ban on imports, an intercolonial Continental Association was created; local committees of inspection would enforce the boycott. It went without discussion that there were 10,000 Sons of Liberty in loose-knit cells throughout the colonies who would pay visits with tar and feathers on merchants who violated the sanctions. Benedict Arnold of New Haven, Connecticut, had arrived with his colony's delegates and while he had no seat in Carpenters Hall he was busy conferring with leaders of the Sons of Liberty from other colonies.

After the General Congress drafted a placatory letter to the people of Great Britain and dissolved itself on October 26, Washington rode home a day and a half faster than he had come, arriving at Mount Vernon after being away for two months. He had no way of assessing how he had been viewed by other delegates, but his dignified bearing, his military reputation, and his silence were appreciated by delegates after weeks of heated debating in hot, fly-infested Carpenters Hall, where the windows and doors had been kept closed to assure secrecy. He had learned much— about the rivalries and suspicions of the colonies even in a common cause. Washington even more than usual was happy to ride the rounds of inspection with his cousin Lund. He hunted almost every day and hosted a house full of guests almost every meal.

*B*ut the crisis would not go away. When Washington arrived home in late October he found Virginians in a martial mood, militia drilling in every town. Young men practiced the manual of arms, old men hunted for violators of the nonimportation agreements, and women struggled to adapt to new shortages in the kitchen, in wearing apparel, in the garden. Lamb's wool and mutton were in short supply; the Continental Association called for a ban on exports to England and other British colonies. Few sheep would be killed that winter. Englishmen without mutton must be fed more turnips, more grains. A tantalizing shipment of the proscribed imported linen was seized and sold at auction. The proceeds would be sent to the relief of the poor of Boston. Washington was busier than ever from early morning to midafternoon. In addition to his businesses he was Anglican vestryman, burgess, county court judge, chairman of the Association's county board, and he was now colonel of the Fairfax Militia. George Mason had found a legal way to form all men from sixteen to fifty into militia companies, "provide themselves with good firelocks and use their utmost endeavors to make themselves masters of the military exercise." Washington organized companies of riflemen—to be outfitted in tasseled hunting shirts—and he paid regular visits to Alexandria to train and drill the raw militia. He still believed that "discipline is the soul of an army."[18]

All that winter the drift toward war continued. In November, Parliament convened in London and Lord North laid before it the First Continental Congress's petition as King George III gave a belligerent opening speech from the throne in which he denounced Congress's "most daring spirit of resistance and disobedience to law." Even an impassioned pro-American speech by the aged Lord Chatham—the brilliant William Pitt, who as prime minister had engineered the great British victory over the French only a decade earlier—could not stem the anti-American tide. Chatham's bill to recall the troops from Boston was noisily defeated, 68–18. When the ailing Chatham in February called for a repeal of all the acts that had inflamed Americans in exchange for American acknowledgment of Parliamentary supremacy he was shouted down again, losing the vote 61 to 31. In Virginia, Washington and his fellow delegates were wary even before they learned of these fiery debates. Peyton Randolph consulted Committee of Correspondence members and summoned a new Virginia Convention to meet in the new town of Richmond—out of range of Lord Dunmore and English men-of-war. Fairfax County electors on February 20 once again chose Washington.

Riding along present-day U.S. Route 1 to Fredericksburg and then Route 2 to Richmond, Washington passed peach orchards in blossom and paused to inspect the Dumfries County militia. At the Richmond Convention, delegates crowded into the plain white St. John's Church and the crowd craned to get a better look when Washington on behalf of Fairfax County issued a "call to arm for defense." Patrick Henry of Hanover County introduced a motion of calling for new militia units, urging "the officers and men of each county of Virginia to make themselves masters of the military exercise." Washington opposed the motion. Defense was one thing: to form new and extralegal militia was a thinly disguised provocation and a threat of war that would place Virginia in the position of appearing not to resist armed conflict while actually inviting it. Independent militia companies were already being formed—why publicize them? Other moderate voices added that they must wait to hear from London the answer to the congress's olive-branch petition.[19]

This was too much for fiery Patrick Henry. In a dazzling speech, he excoriated the idea of nonresistance to British tyranny. In a speech that made some listeners faint, he urged the delegates not to "deceive ourselves longer":

> I repeat it, sir, we must fight. An appeal to arms and to the God of Hosts is all that is left to us. They tell us, sir, that we are weak, unable to cope with so formidable an adversary. But when shall we be stronger? Will it be the next week or the next year?

Going down on one knee, his wrists crossed as if locked in chains and his head down, the red-haired, chisel-sharp frontier lawyer in his twanging Celtic country accent half-moaned his words in a fire-and-brimstone call to arms:

> There is no retreat but in submission and slavery. Our chains are forged. Their clanking may be heard on the plains of Boston. The war is inevitable. And let it come! I repeat it, sir, let it come! It is in vain, sir, to extenuate the matter. Gentlemen may cry, peace, peace—but there is no peace. The war is actually begun. The next gale that surveys from the north will bring to our ears the clash of resounding arms. Our brethren are already in the field! Why stand idle here? Is life so dark or peace so sweet as to be purchased at the price of chains—and slavery? Forbid it, Almighty God!

And then he sprang up, pulling apart his imaginary shackles:

> I know not what course others may take but as for me give me liberty or give me death.

Sinking an imaginary dagger into his chest, he sank down into his seat.

When the pandemonium died down, Lee and Jefferson supported Henry's speech with a resolution calling for mobilizing all Virginia "into a posture of defense." George Washington was placed in charge of the committee. The convention ended with an appointment of a new Virginia delegation to a second Continental Congress called for May of 1775.[20]

While militant Patrick Henry supporters packed the new Virginia defense committee, it was plain that Washington was the commanding figure in the colony's extralegal mobilization. The night of his appointment his diary shows Washington forgoing a dinner visit across the James to his friend Archibald Cary. Instead he stayed in his room drafting a military plan to submit to the convention when it reconvened the next day. His former French and Indian War aide Adam Stephen and his cousin Andrew Lewis assisted him as he brushed up a plan he obviously had worked up before the convention. In sharp contrast to his earlier detestation of militia, Washington now called for a force of volunteers. The fervor of the cause must have led him to believe that good men and not the dregs of backwoods society would now come forward. Each county east of the fall line of the James River was to raise one or more troops of cavalry of thirty men each. Other counties were to raise at least one company of foot soldiers of sixty-eight rank and file. The county militia commander was to appoint his own officers. Washington's plan was sharply innovative: it not only minimized a political tug-of-war with the governor over officers' appointments, but it relied heavily on the use of cavalry, adding maximum maneuverability to overcome shortages of arms and ammunition in any given area of the colony. The convention adopted Washington's plan the next day, March 25, and appointed him to a three-man committee to develop the colony's pitiful military resources.

But the delegates had an even more important assignment in mind now that Washington had asserted himself. He was reelected to the Virginia delegation to the next Continental Congress with the second highest vote. This meant that if the health of the aged Speaker of the House Peyton Randolph continued to decline, Washington would succeed him as head of the seven-man Virginia delegation. Before he left Richmond and rode home, Washington finished a telltale letter to his brother Jack, praising him for "the laudable pursuit you are engaged in of training an independent company" and adding that Washington had "promised to review the independent company of Richmond [County] this summer they having made me a tender of the command of it. At the same time I could review yours." Washington was clearly planning to take a very active and conspicuous role in raising Virginia's troops. On his way home to Mount Vernon, Washington stopped off to pay his mother "part of her income"—and he took along his sister Betty as a witness.[21]

Washington arrived home at the most beautiful time of year at Mount Vernon. Fields of spring-green grasses and wheat waved beckoningly as he passed through the white plank gate and rode up to the rear entrance past the piles of brick and lumber and mounds of sand and gravel. Every flower bed bristled with firm young flowers. The house, too, was a growing thing now. From the front, when the new veranda had been marked out, he could survey the noisy scene below of his ships and fishermen hauling in the seines that bulged with shad and herring—the annual run was on! George and Martha had little time alone for him to tell her all the urgent news of his two latest weeks away before another round of visitors arrived.

For five days Washington played host to the garrulous, self-described general Charles Lee. This tall, unkempt British-born officer had come to Mount Vernon to seek a favor—or several—from Washington, who had last seen him during the Braddock expedition. Retiring as a half-pay major at the end of the French and Indian War, the tall, poodle-faced Lee had found work as a mercenary under the king of Poland, who promoted him to major-general. Lee had just come back to Virginia to buy land near Berkeley Springs. He had instantly launched into the political pamphlet wars by writing an attack on the conciliatory efforts of Dr. Myles Cooper, the president of King's College in New York City and Jack Custis's one-time mentor. A measure of George Washington's rising influence was that the haughty Lee knew where to offer his services for hire. He expected Washington to recommend him for the post of American commander in chief should the next Continental Congress be in the market for one. He finally left after borrowing £15 of Washington's scarce cash. He always considered himself a better officer than Washington, but he didn't mind accepting his money.

Washington did not stay long at Mount Vernon. There is a hint in a letter he wrote a few months later to Martha that, in her grief and loneliness, she had begun to complain incessantly when Washington was home. But she still would not travel far outside her normal sphere, even if Washington had hoped Patcy's death would liberate her. She "would not spread" so far as Annapolis, he wrote when she broke their travel plans. As demands for Washington's political and military services multiplied, he spent almost as much time away from Mount Vernon as at home. His absences and the constant noise and dirt of the renovations only gave her more grounds for discontent. George Washington had a history of riding off for long periods and once again the Continental Congress in Philadelphia was fast approaching, which promised more absences.

Both of the Washingtons received fresh reasons for anxiety just after Washington returned from reviewing the Alexandria militia on April 26. An express rider hurried his horse toward Mount Vernon with a message from Dr. Hugh Mercer in Fredericksburg. Early on the morning of April 21, the captain of an armed British schooner, *Magdalen*, had landed with fifteen marines and, on orders from Lord Dunmore, had seized all twenty barrels of the colony's meager store of gunpowder from the brick magazine and taken it aboard H.M.S. *Fowey*, anchored in the James River. Mercer wanted Washington's authorization to assemble the Fredericksburg Independent Company and call for other companies from adjacent counties to "support the honor of Virginia [and] secure the military stores yet remaining in the magazine"—in others words, to march on Williamsburg. An express rider came shortly from Dumfries, where the officers had voted to lead their troops to join Mercer on the Rappahannock. Meanwhile, a crowd in Williamsburg had agreed to wait before marching to the governor's palace while the town council asked Dunmore to return the powder, which they insisted was for their own defense in case of a slave uprising or Indian attack. Dunmore refused and issued weapons to his household and some navy officers visiting the town as the townspeople clamored outside for their gunpowder.[22]

As the possibility of an armed clash in Williamsburg loomed, the next day another rider charged up the lane to Mount Vernon. He reported sketchy details of fighting in Massachusetts to Washington. In the early hours of April 19 a crack force of 1,000 British grenadiers and light infantry marched from Boston to seize radical leaders and munitions reported to be in Concord. Warned of their approach, a volunteer company of Minutemen mustered on Lexington Green, about ten miles from Boston, and refused the British commander's order to disperse; eight died and ten lay wounded when he ordered the redcoats to fire. As the British marched on, more provincials gathered, and when the British set fires in Concord, attacked a contingent holding Concord Bridge. As the British retreated toward Boston, American riflemen firing from behind stone walls along the road inflicted heavy casualties. Only a British relief force firing field artillery had saved the attackers from complete destruction. Boston in effect was now under siege.

The news that Americans had stood and fought the British thrilled Washington, but he also felt caught between two fires. Should he stay in Virginia in case military action against Lord Dunmore became unavoidable, or go to Philadelphia where obviously the Continental Congress would be deciding how to respond to a far more serious and widespread challenge? The first Congress had warned that if any American colony were attacked, all the colonies would make common cause and would resist further aggression by force of arms. The British commander in Boston, obviously responding to new orders from London, had accepted the gauntlet and fired the first shot. Reassured by Peyton Randolph in Williamsburg that Dunmore was backing down and had said privately that he would surrender the keys to the powder magazine, Washington made last-minute arrangements to leave for Philadelphia. At this tremendously inopportune time he also received a haughty letter from Lord Dunmore declaring that he was nullifying the 1754 Ohio grant because Captain Crawford, the veteran's surveyor, had not sworn the correct oath. Infuriated, Washington decided to do nothing further about Dunmore. Washington's place was with the continental resistance movement—his own private interests would have to wait. Packing his red-and-blue British brigadier's uniform in his portmanteau, he turned over his business affairs to his brother-in-law, Fielding Lewis, his Mount Vernon farms and the renovations of the house to his cousin Lund. He sent off some cash to his mother. His brother Jack would supervise his fishing vessels and his flour exports.

There were so many visitors to Mount Vernon in the last days of April that there was little time left to talk privately with Martha; there was little he could say—his mind was made up that he must go. Washington hoped that Jack and Nelly would continue their frequent visits, that Martha's relatives would visit her more while he was away. Their farewell was not only sober but undoubtedly sad, yet both tried to put on a brave face. Washington would be in Philadelphia, a city he always enjoyed. He estimated he would be home by July. It would be just another slightly longer than usual trip. He would be back at Mount Vernon before harvest time.

When Washington had written to Jack in late March that "it is my full intention to devote my life and fortune in the cause we are engaged in," he did not exaggerate. Neither George nor Martha needed to enunciate their fears. They both knew that they had very little to gain from a revolution. They were established members and conspicuous leaders of Tidewater Virginia society, the "haves," not the "have-nots." They could lose everything in a war. As rebels in a revolution their properties and all their families owned could be seized by the Crown. They could be tainted as traitors, their family coat of arms suppressed, and all they owned, all they had worked for, made a part of the royal family's hereditary estate. Twice in the previous sixty years Scottish earls had resisted the Crown and suffered exactly this fate. If George Washington became a leader of the intercontinental revolt that had now taken shape, he could be hunted down by British commanders and transported to England in chains for trial and certain execution. Even if Washington played no prominent role, war would bring a drastic diminution in their way of life. The Washingtons ordered most of their clothing, furniture, tools, and household goods from England. All trade with England had come to a halt: all exports of crops could be stopped by an inevitable Royal Navy blockade. Mount Vernon would be an obvious target for British navy raiding parties—especially if Washington became a military leader. Everything they owned could be confiscated or destroyed. The Washingtons did not have to discuss the fact that they were risking everything: both of them knew that they were risking not just their wealth but their lives. With Richard Henry Lee and his brother Thomas and Charles Carter, Washington climbed into the green chariot and headed north.[23]

As militia drilled all over America, many loyal subjects decided to leave the British colonies rather than be caught in a civil war. As Washington's carriage rolled north the morning of May 4, 1775, he passed a post chaise carrying the Reverend Jonathan Boucher, the Anglican clergyman who had taught Jack Custis until only eighteen months ago and had been a frequent visitor at Mount Vernon. Boucher had dared to speak out against the Continental Association in sermons from his Annapolis pulpit—where he displayed two cocked pistols. No word passed, neither man waved as their carriages slowly forded a stream in opposite directions. For both men it was too late to turn back: Boucher was returning to England.

*T*he Washington carriage provided privacy for the Virginia delegates to discuss the latest dispatches from Boston, but the news from New England soon made the arrival of the delegates an occasion for parades and militia reviews all along the route. Twenty years ago Washington had been unable to rouse Marylanders to defend their colony from the French and Indian onslaught; on May 6, 1775, three Baltimore militia companies turned out in force to see the Virginians and North Carolina delegates who arrived that day. Young men stood at attention and slid their eyes to get a glimpse at the hero of Braddock's campaign in his splendid general's uniform. As they approached Philadelphia, some five hundred horsemen—all the officers of militia companies and Philadelphia leaders—met the party six miles out near present-day Darby and escorted the southerners through crowds of spectators. At noon the next day the New England delegates joined an equally enthusiastic cavalcade. British bayonets had dissipated last year's sectional rivalries—at least for a moment. The delegates assembled on May 10 at the Pennsylvania State House (now Independence Hall) and sat by colony around green gauze-covered tables in the bright-paneled hall. Peyton Randolph was reelected president and the doors and windows were ordered closed in an attempt at secrecy. Congress set about business at once. Massachusetts reported mobilizing 13,600 men but had a terrible gunpowder shortage; New Yorkers wanted to know what to do if redcoats inside Fort George on the Battery came out.

In that opening week, Washington wore his brigadier's uniform to make the statement that the time for reconciliation and rhetoric were past and that at least someone in the chamber was prepared for firmer measures. He had not been appointed to any committee in 1774. Now Peyton Randolph and a majority elected him to a committee to plan New York City's defenses. The importance of that post became apparent only a few days later when Congress received word that colonists from Massachusetts, Connecticut, and Vermont had seized the strategically important Fort Ticonderoga at the foot of Lake Champlain. A few days later Vermonters seized Fort Amherst at Crown Point. Washington at once grasped the significance of these attacks. They not only put the Americans on the offensive, but if any one of the forts could be held, would seal off the traditional invasion route from Canada down the Hudson. From the courier he learned that Ethan Allen and his 1,000 Green Mountain Boys—the largest mobile force in the colonies—had raced a spit-and-polish Massachusetts colonel named Benedict Arnold for control of the Lake Champlain forts. As more reports galloped in, Washington was intrigued by Arnold, whom he had met during the First Continental Congress.

Thirty-four and thickset, Arnold had little military experience and, like Washington, little formal education. Apprenticed to a cousin to learn the apothecary trade, he owned a general store in New Haven and a fleet of ships engaging in the mahogany trade with the Caribbean. He also imported and exported horses, an interest Washington shared. A smuggler, he was an early and open leader of the Sons of Liberty, personally flogging one informer and boasting of it in the newspaper. As the colonial crisis deepened, Arnold had organized and outfitted a New Haven militia organization, the Second Connecticut Company of Foot. After seizing the town's powder magazine at gunpoint, he marched to Boston within hours of the opening shots of the conflict.

Leading his column of scarlet-coated Foot Guards, Arnold had scarcely left New Haven before he came upon Samuel Holden Parsons, a New London land speculator who had led his company of Connecticut militia to Boston at the Lexington alarm and was now on his way back to Hartford for a meeting of the Connecticut Committee of Correspondence. Parsons told Arnold that the patriot army assembling around Boston had neither supplies nor ammunition and, worst of all, no cannon to besiege the heavily armed British. Arnold told Parsons that there were hundreds of good cannon at the dilapidated and weakly held British forts at Ticonderoga and Crown Point at the southern end of Lake Champlain, on the northern New York frontier.

When Arnold arrived at the American camp at Cambridge, he told the same story to the Massachusetts Committee of Safety. The full Provincial Congress of Massachusetts quickly approved Arnold's appointment as colonel and commissioned him to raise a regiment of four hundred men in the Berkshires, and then to seize the forts at Ticonderoga and Crown Point. Arnold soon learned that Samuel Parsons had taken Arnold's idea to the Connecticut authorities and organized a rival expedition that was now under the command of Ethan Allen. Furious at what he saw as Parsons's opportunism, Arnold left behind his recruits and dashed northwest with only an orderly sergeant to overtake Allen and assert his command.

At Shoreham, fifty miles north of Bennington, Arnold found Allen. Marching directly up to the green-uniformed commander, Arnold presented his written orders and said his rival officer had no legitimate authority. Daunted, Allen told his men that Arnold would lead them, but they would still receive their two-dollars-a-day pay. "Damn the pay," someone muttered, and several announced they would walk home if they couldn't serve under their own officers. Eager to press the attack, Arnold offered a compromise: Allen would be in charge of his Green Mountain Boys, Arnold of all the Massachusetts troops he could raise. They would lead the first American offensive of the Revolution in a joint command.

That night, 230 men, including 50 from Massachusetts, gathered in the woods across the lake from Ticonderoga, but by the time dawn broke on May 10, 1775, only two 30-foot scows had arrived and the initial attack was made by 83 men. Arnold and Allen led the troops, primarily composed of French and Indian War veterans, to the south side of Fort Ticonderoga, where the wall lay ruptured and the main gate would no longer close tight. Just inside, a single sentry dozed. Arnold, on the left, sprinted ahead of Allen and squeezed through the narrow opening and, sword drawn, rushed the guard. The startled redcoat woke, aimed, pulled the trigger. His damp gunpowder misfired. Americans surged into the fort, and four years later, when he published his memoirs, Allen claimed he and he alone had captured the works "in the name of the Great Jehovah and the Continental Congress."

Four hundred more Green Mountain Boys arrived from across the cove to crowd into the fort, and Arnold reported to the Massachusetts Provincial Congress that "the greatest confusion and anarchy" broke out. The Boys found a cellar housing ninety gallons of rum, then set about "destroying and plundering private property, committing every enormity and paying no attention to public service." When Arnold protested, an infuriated Ethan Allen stripped him of his joint command at gunpoint. Confining himself to the officers' quarters, Arnold wrote to Massachusetts authorities that inasmuch as he had been "the first person who entered and took possession of the Fort, I shall keep it, at every hazard." For four days, "often insulted by Allen and his officers and often threatened with my life," Arnold coolly studied the fort, surveyed its guns—nearly eighty usable cannon, six mortars, three howitzers—and waited for more of his own men.

On May 14 Arnold's regiment arrived with a schooner commandeered at nearby Skenesboro. Arnold named it *Liberty*, fitted it with four carriage and six swivel guns, and, leaving Ethan Allen and his troops behind, sailed north with fifty Massachusetts men to attack the British base at St. Johns (present-day St. Jean) on the Richelieu River just inside Quebec Province. In a matter of days he took St. Johns, scuttled five British vessels, and came home with four others; he now commanded the first American naval squadron. Arnold's raid rendered a British counterattack in 1776 impossible and left him master of the hundred-mile lake.

*M*any conservative members of Congress were horrified at Ethan Allen and Benedict Arnold, however. Until now they had preserved the appearance of acting only on the defensive. Seizing £2 million worth of Crown forts and taking 85 redcoats prisoner complicated affairs. Lamely, Congress voted only to remove the two hundred cannon—the reason for the attack—to Fort Edward at the southern end of Lake George and take an "exact inventory" so that they could later be "safely returned." The report by Washington's committee emerged from the back council chamber ready for the whole Congress on May 19—exactly one month after Lexington. Six days of often heated debate began over general defense preparations, recruitment bounties, garrison duties, a final attempt at reconciliation with England. By May 25 six resolutions emerged that were intended to prepare New York City for the inevitable British attack. Washington's plan to fortify King's Bridge on the Harlem

River, erect batteries on either bank of the Hudson, and enlist 3,000 men was approved.[24]

Washington's obvious experience as a military logician led next to his appointment as chairman of the key committee on military supply. He was to work with Philip Schuyler of Albany, Samuel Adams of Boston, Thomas Mifflin of Philadelphia, Silas Deane of Connecticut, and Lewis Morris of New York. Few meetings were necessary at first: there was little ammunition to collect. With no night meetings Washington was free to dine in the afternoons with other delegates, making more and more connections and becoming better known. As the only congressman in uniform, he made a vivid impression. At his first Congress, Washington had done little more than enlarge his acquaintance. John Adams, John Jay, and Joseph Reed were names that would play significant roles in his next few years. Some delegates had approved—as Silas Deane of Connecticut put it—of his "easy, soldier-like air and gestures: he spoke very modestly and in a cool but determined style and accent." But at least one other Yankee had seen him as a comic figure in that first pacific session. Rhode Islander Solomon Drowne wrote home a bit of doggerel about the Congress that ended: "With manly gait/His faithful steel suspended at his side/Pass'd W-shi-gt-n along, Virginia's hero." Drowne fantasized that George Washington of Mount Vernon and George III of England could settle the imperial crisis by engaging each other in single combat. But this Congress faced daily reports of troop movements and approaching British reprisals. A martial figure was no longer a laughing matter. "Colonel Washington appears in Congress in his uniform," John Adams wrote to his wife, Abigail, "and by his experience and abilities in military matters is of much service to us."[25]

Arousing confidence in a disheartened Congress, Washington found encouragement that others could not see when he studied all the accounts of the clashes at Lexington and Concord:

> I believe that if the retreat [of the British] had not been as precipitate as it was (and God knows it could not well have been more so) the ministerial troops must have surrendered or been totally cut off . . .

Washington had seen British regulars panic and run; he was enormously encouraged to see that tough American militiamen, sailors, and fishermen had rushed in from Marblehead and Salem and nearly cut off the British retreat into Boston, inflicting galling casualties.[26]

Each day he had more gloom to counteract. The latest dispatches from London showed that Parliament had denied the New England colonies fishing rights on the Grand Banks, the source of so much of the region's commerce, jobs, and food supply, and restricted all American trade to British territories, sealing off lucrative trade with the Caribbean, France, and the Mediterranean that represented more than half of American shipping. Each week brought more duties for Washington. The new president, John Hancock, appointed him to a board of financial estimate: the other members were all merchants. The work piled up and few solutions emerged. All that Washington could do to aid Massachusetts's defense, for example, was to ask interior towns to give some gunpowder to the ill-equipped volunteers barricading the British inside Boston.

As the effect of speeches faded, the Continental Congress turned to prayers, declaring a fast day for July 20. Washington was among those who believed prayer was not enough: he urged, and Congress agreed, formation of ten companies of "expert riflemen" from the backwoods of Virginia, Maryland, and Pennsylvania.

That piece of legislation provided that when the riflemen reached Boston they should be placed "under the command of the chief officer in that army." Congress had been receiving warnings that the siege of Boston would collapse unless supported by the united colonies. Men from other colonies would have to join the fight. Week after week Congress forestalled the obvious while conservatives argued for one more attempt at reconciliation. But the sticking point was just who could command a continental army and from which colony should he come. Most of the field-grade officers were old, left over from the French wars. John Adams had been working after hours to win support for his idea that unless such a leader came from outside Massachusetts other colonies would fear New England's domination.

The obvious choice was a Virginian. Virginia outnumbered Massachusetts and New York by five to one. Its troops, crops, and money were vital to intercolonial success. And one after another delegate considered Washington the right choice. Washington did not. Even when he agreed to take a seat in Congress he had marked his appointment "pro tem." At most he had considered taking command of Virginia's militia. He reacted soberly to the rumors he was about to be chosen to lead Congress forces. He asked Edmund Pendleton to draw up his will and he stopped mentioning the month he was coming home in his letters to Martha. On May 14 he sat in his uniform and listened as John Adams lectured Congress on the need for keeping New England's army in front of Boston and giving it support from other colonies. What better way than under the command of a seasoned veteran who represented Congress and all the colonies? At the Queen Anne desk on the dais where he presided, John Hancock, colonel and chief benefactor of Boston's Train Band of Artillery, brightened when Adams said he had one man in mind, then reddened when Adams said the man he had in mind was from Virginia. As if struck, Washington stood up and practically ran out of the room to the adjoining library. When he was ushered back in, he was informed that "all America" wanted him. In fact, a few New England delegates dissented but only mildly.

George Washington stayed away the next day, June 15. He asked the master trial lawyer Edmund Pendleton to help him draw up his acceptance speech. At the State House the debate over command moved quickly. Congress as a committee of the whole resolved that "a general be appointed to command all the continental forces raised or to be raised for the defense of American liberty." Washington's friend and Potomac Canal colleague Thomas Johnson of Maryland placed his name in nomination. There was little need for further debate. Washington was so obviously the outstanding American-born soldier available. Others of equal experience who could be considered—Horatio Gates, Charles Lee, or Richard Montgomery—were all ex-British officers, but that had become a liability. New Englanders could argue in favor of local heroes of the French and Indian War like Israel Putnam and Artemus Ward, who was now in command at Boston, but they were a generation older, their stamina in the field a question: Washington was the perfect age, forty-three, and in such obvious and vigorous good health. And he had more experience of command—five years under trying conditions—than any other American field officer, even if he had never won an engagement. Equally important, he brought the south into the fray.

Yet these were all reasons that made Washington appear reticent. With his stock so high he told Patrick Henry that to accept command of such an overmatched army could bring about his downfall. Henry later recalled that Washington had tears in his eyes when he confided his misgivings. "Remember, Mr. Henry, what I now tell you: from the day I enter upon the command of the American armies I date my fall and the ruin of my reputation." At moments of crisis this resourceful man who usually won respect for his can-do attitude dissolved in private into gloom and self-doubt. He led a busy useful life in Virginia and was in love with his home at Mount Vernon as much as his wife, whom he had described as "an agreeable consort." He was a proud man, even sometimes a little vain, but he knew his shortcomings as a soldier, even if he had managed to blame many of them on superior officers, governors, and subordinates. Yet here was the greatest opportunity of his lifetime and he was determined to resist the haughty British ministers and brutally incompetent officers now threatening America. He must resist these "lordly masters" or sink back into the groveling obsequiousness of his impecunious youth. He would accept.[27]

When Thomas Johnson proposed Washington, no other name was placed in nomination. The vote was unanimous. Charles Thomson, secretary of Congress, sent a messenger to summon Washington. He was to accept the next day. All that day, Washington, overwhelmed, kept busy. In his diary he only noted where he went to dinner and that he attended a committee meeting in the evening. The "committee" must have been with Pendleton, who had to know what to include in Washington's will and helped him with his speech.

The next morning John Hancock intoned the formulaic announcement that he had the order of Congress to inform Washington of his unanimous choice as commander in chief and would the gentleman accept. Washington in his red-and-blue general's uniform rose in his place at the Virginia table, bowed, and pulled a paper from his inside coat pocket:

> *Mr. President:*
> Though I am truly sensible of the high honor done me in this appointment yet I feel great distress from a consciousness that my abilities and military experience may not be equal to the extensive and important trust. However, as the Congress desires I will enter upon the momentous duty and exert every power I possess in their service for the support of the glorious cause. I beg they will accept my most cordial thanks for this distinguished testimony of their approbation.
>
> But lest some unlucky event should happen unfavorable to my reputation, I beg it may be remembered by every gentleman in the room that I this day declare with the utmost sincerity I do not think myself equal to the command I am honored with.
>
> As to pay, Sir, I beg leave to assure the Congress that as no pecuniary consideration could have tempted me to have accepted this arduous employment [at the expense of my domestic ease and happiness] I do not wish to make any profit from it. I will keep an exact account of my expenses. Those I doubt not they will discharge and that is all I desire.[28]

At least in some small part the applause was for Washington's generous gesture in refusing the $500 a month salary Congress proffered. Whether he would have refused it if he could see that the war would last more than eight years is a question Washington may have answered the next time he was offered a high government office: he insisted on a salary.

The next day, Sunday, Washington faced a task he relished even less than organizing a continental army. He wrote Martha his longest surviving letter to her:

> *My Dearest:*
> I am now set down to write you on a subject which fills me with inexpressible concern and this concern is greatly aggravated and increased when I reflect upon the uneasiness I know it will cause you. . . . You may believe me, my dear Patsy, when I assure you in the most solemn manner that so far from seeking this appointment I have used every endeavor in my power to avoid it not only from my unwillingness to part from you and

the family but from a consciousness of its being a trust too great for my capacity and that I should find more real happiness in one month with you at home than I have the most distant prospect of finding abroad if my stay were to be seven times seven years. But as it has been a kind destiny that has thrown me upon this service, I shall hope that my undertaking it is designed to answer some good purpose.

In recent letters to her, he pointed out, he had refrained from telling her when he thought he would come home. He had been "apprehensive" he might be appointed:

It was utterly out of my power to refuse this appointment without exposing my character to such censure as would have reflected dishonor upon myself and given pain to my friends. This, I am sure, could not and ought not to be pleasing to you and must have lessened me considerably in my own esteem. . . . My unhappiness will flow from the uneasiness I know you will feel from being left alone. I therefore beg that you will summon your whole fortitude and pass your time as agreeably as possible. Nothing will give me so much sincere satisfaction as to hear this and to hear it from your own pen.

Washington urged Martha to move into a townhouse they owned in Alexandria. Lund could add a kitchen building. But if she chose to stay at Mount Vernon, he hoped she would find "a tolerable degree of tranquility as it must add greatly to my uneasy feelings to hear that you are dissatisfied or complaining at what I really could not avoid."

Next Washington wrote to his stepson. He confessed to twenty-year-old Jack Custis his "very anxious feelings" and urged him to move with his bride of fifteen months to Mount Vernon until he returned. Just before he left for Massachusetts he wrote Martha again to tell her of his "unalterable affection for you which neither time nor distance can alter."[29] To his brother Jack, for so many years his closest friend and confidant, he wrote a letter without any demurrer about seeking the honor: "I am now to bid adieu to you and every kind of domestic ease for a while. I am embarked on a wide ocean, boundless in its prospect, and from whence, perhaps, no safe harbor is to be found." Jack knew him better. Washington urged Jack to visit Martha often and keep up her spirits.[30]

The next morning Washington was caught up in planning for his departure. Congress chose four major generals. Artemus Ward received the senior appointment, the ingratiating Charles Lee the second. That meant one major general from Massachusetts. Already Congress was semiconsciously steering a course between the shoals of regional interests. The next two appointments were Philip Schuyler of New York, a veteran logician from the French and Indian War, old and rich, and that old Indian fighter from Connecticut, the corpulent Israel Putnam. The debate over the major generals stirred up Congress into "dismal bugbears" of discord, wrote John Adams. "Nothing has given me more torment than the scuffle we have had in appointing the general officers."[31] But Adams wrote to James Warren, president of the Massachusetts provincial congress, nothing but praise for the "sage," the "modest," and "amiable" Washington, and John Hancock seconded the motion. The man who had beaten him out for command was "a fine man—a gentleman you will all like."[32]

Washington was too busy preparing to join his army to hear any accolades. He sent the green carriage back to Mount Vernon and bought five new horses and a lightweight phaeton. Then he asked two young Philadelphians, merchant Thomas Mifflin and lawyer Joseph Reed, to accompany him temporarily as his staff aides. Charles Lee and Philip Schuyler would also depart with him. On June 22, as he packed his papers and his portmanteau, a messenger arrived with news that added fresh urgency to his departure.

Thirteen

"A NEW MODELLED ARMY"

When the Massachusetts provincial congress learned from informants inside besieged Boston that the British were planning to seize the high ground overlooking the town, the talk of civil war in America ceased to be a matter of abstract possibility. The British plan was to take the hilly Charlestown peninsula, fortify it, and free enough troops to march to the provisional capital of Cambridge to arrest the entire Massachusetts provincial congress. At a secret meeting on the night of June 15, 1775, the very day that the Continental Congress appointed Washington as the commander in chief, Dr. Joseph Warren, a Boston physician who was president of the Provincial Congress, won the approval of militia leaders from Connecticut and New Hampshire for an immediate and fateful offensive. The rebel leaders voted unanimously to occupy Bunker Hill, the highest of three hills on the Charlestown peninsula opposite Boston, before the British could. For some odd reason, the small force dispatched to begin digging entrenchments marched past Bunker Hill and instead fortified Breed's Hill, which was lower.

Like so many battles that followed it, what became known as the Battle of Bunker Hill did not have to happen. The Americans were ill prepared, had few cannon, no skilled artilleryman or military engineer, little ammunition, poor communications, no chain of command, no reinforcements, no escape plan. They were an army of zealots, many of them veterans of the French and Indian War prepared to take on the British who had bullied them for so many years and now were trying to silence their protests in an all-out invasion of Massachusetts. For all their handicaps, the Americans had officers seasoned by many of the same battles in which the British leaders had learned their tactics in two wars against the French. And they had surprise on their side.

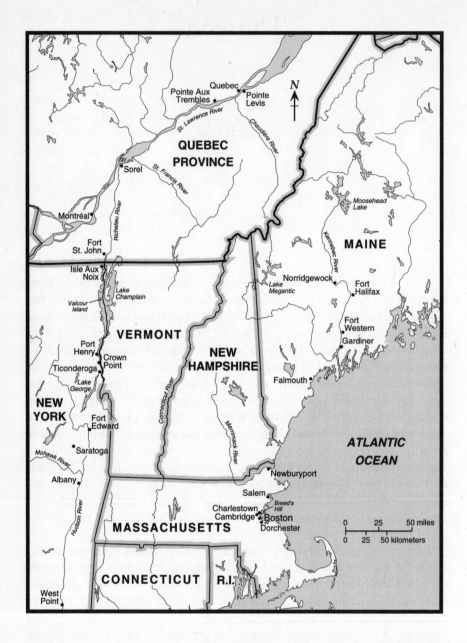

Washington's army besieged Boston, while Arnold marched up the Kennebec through Maine to attack Quebec and then retreated to Lake Champlain, where Arnold fought the key naval battle of Valcour Island in October 1776.

Only one day after George Washington was appointed their new commanding officer and two weeks before he could arrive at Cambridge, the Massachusetts leaders set off from Cambridge with approximately one thousand men from all over New England on the night of June 16 and marched on the double to Breed's Hill. As he drove north toward Boston, Washington would learn the details of the ill-timed battle too late. The hill was seventy-five feet high and flanked on the east by an impassable swamp. From its summit, shells could be lobbed down into Boston harbor and into the town of Boston itself. The Americans marked out a small redoubt roughly 130 feet on each side. At midnight they began digging and ran the east wall, a breastwork, one hundred yards down the hill to the swamp. Expecting the British would try to outflank them, they deployed two hundred Connecticut frontiersmen and two small cannon behind a stone fence two hundred yards behind the redoubt on a line running down to the Mystic River. In front of this they quickly constructed a zigzag rail fence and covered the space between the fence and the wall with fresh hay taken from a nearby field. Then, joined by four companies of riflemen from the New Hampshire frontier, they ran a high stone wall down across the beach to the water's edge. At the same time, eight hundred rugged farmers were busy digging a square hole five feet deep, piling the excavated dirt into a six-foot-high wall around it. They laid wooden shooting platforms along the insides of the redoubt. Then they pierced the front parapet and the side walls with six gunports for their small cannon.

At dawn, the British forward observers were startled to find that the rebels had fortified the entire hill overnight. General Gage summoned a hasty council of war. There was to be an immediate attack before the Americans could entrench the other hills and cut off Boston from the mainland. Major General Sir William Howe would lead the best troops. The British officers decided on a quick and classic textbook assault on the rebel positions. Their decision showed their scorn for the lessons of Lexington and Concord, and for the Americans facing them.

As Bostonians scurried onto rooftops for a better view, British men-of-war maneuvered closer to the Charlestown shore, anchored, and sent flatboats loaded with redcoats ashore even as their cannon began sending shells crashing into the hillside in front of the redoubt. Bothered by midday heat and erratic sniper fire from the deserted houses of Charlestown, British grenadiers marched down to the bank of the Charles River to board the landing craft. Within an hour British naval gunners had set the town ablaze. Soon, smoke could be seen twenty miles away. Delayed by the tide the British landing boats thumped up onto the riverbank at about two in the afternoon, where the temperature approached 100 degrees. The regulars wore their only uniforms, of heavy wool, and carried 125 pounds of weapons and gear, including a week's rations and cooking implements, on their backs. Their orders were to roll over the rebels on the peninsula and march right on to Cambridge and beyond if necessary to break up the rebellion before it could spread any further.

From the start, things went badly for the British. Their field artillery mired down in the muddy fields. The advance grenadier guard, trotting down the beach on the right, stumbled into the new rail fence and a withering fire. According to all the military textbooks, now was the time for a bayonet charge. But the Connecticut sharpshooters were firing in rotation. There was no pause in which to rush them as they reloaded. Row on row of redcoats—most of them shot in the legs and groin at close range with buckshot so they would never fight again—pitched into the fresh-mown hay as they tried to clamber across the fence, their heavy gear throwing them off balance.

When the first flanking effort faltered, General Howe called for reinforcements, this time unleashing 1,200 men up the steep rough hillside over fallen trees, tangles of blackberry and blueberry, through tall grass toward the strangely silent earthworks. Behind the long, low breastwork, an old man thanked God for sparing him to fight this day. Colonel Israel Putnam of Connecticut, cutlass in hand, lectured his sharpshooters: "Men, you are all good marksmen. Don't one of you fire until you see the whites of their eyes." This was the American secret weapon. Englishmen did not believe in aiming at a specific man: they laid down a field of fire impersonally. To aim was, in the view of British officers and gentlemen, to commit murder.[1]

At one hundred yards the redcoats fired a volley. Too high, too far away. At fifty yards, they fired again. Again, too high. Up they trudged, their bayonets glimmering, until the Americans could make out the brass matchboxes on their coats. At fifteen yards, the earthworks roared, flashed. Three long scarlet ranks of Britain's best troops crumbled, pitched into the tall grass, thrashing and screaming. Only the best American marksmen had fired. They sighted in on the crossed white sashes of the redcoats where they intersected at the belly. Behind the earthworks, young boys rammed home rusty nails and double charges of buckshot, bits of glass, lead balls, and cloth wadding, and handed them up to the sharpshooters on the parapet. Wave on wave of British died—casualties reached 95 percent in some companies—before the British commander allowed them to strip off their heavy gear and charge over the low breastworks and get at these vicious bloody rebel bastards with their bayonets.

By now, British artillery had pounded holes in the crude fort, sending shells through the useless little sally port and killing defenders with iron bombs that detonated as they skittered along the ground, shearing off arms and legs. Suddenly, the little fort had turned into a death trap. As careful as the sharpshooters had been to conserve their precious powder, it had been wasted by untrained artillerymen and was almost gone. The last two cannonballs were cut open, the gunpowder divided among the marksmen. Sensing victory, the decimated British ranks now regrouped, charged through the ragged fire, surrounded the ramparts, stormed over them. There was no way out. No escape route had been provided. The British fired down into the mass of stumbling, running, yelling Americans. Dr. Warren, thirty-five-year-old archdeacon of Massachusetts radicals, was shot in the head twice as he fled. A British grenadier, refusing to spare him, ran him through with his twisting bayonet. In the crossfire, 100 fleeing Americans died; 150 more were wounded and taken prisoner.

By late afternoon, the British held all of the Charlestown peninsula, but proportionately it was the most costly victory in all British military history: 1,054 killed and wounded out of 2,000 troops engaged. Yet both sides claimed victory. The Americans were certain now that, given enough gunpowder, time, and men, they were the match of the best soldiers in the world. Inside barricaded Boston, even as carts of moaning wounded rumbled over the rough rutted streets, the British high command declared that they had fallen short of totally destroying the rebellion only because they lacked adequate manpower. General Gage wrote to demand thirty thousand fresh troops from London. The Revolution, as John Adams put it, was now complete. The Revolutionary War had begun.

General Washington learned more details of the battle at Bunker Hill with each courier who dashed into Philadelphia. The grim news cut short his preparations. On June 23 at dawn he mounted a horse beside Lee and Schuyler and ahead of Mifflin and Reed, his aides-de-camp. They fell in behind several mounted militia units and the escort of congressmen who had gotten up to see them off. A band played as they rode up the cobbled Second Street past still-shuttered stores. As they followed the Old York Road toward the Bristol ferry crossing of the Delaware River, the hot summer sun added to the oppressive June heat. The militia turned back, but Washington and his staff rode on—for ten days. When they crossed over into heavily Loyalist New Jersey, Washington put a purple general's sack over his navy blue uniform and put on a hat with a tall plume. Ferried across the Hudson River, he passed through New York City. A crowd turned out at Whitehall to cheer him; one hour later, a crowd including many of the same people hailed the British royal governor, Sir William Tryon, just returned from England, with equal enthusiasm.

Nearly five hundred soldiers escorted Washington now. He spent only one day in New York City going over plans with General Schuyler. He appointed General David Wooster to defend the city of 22,000; he wanted Schuyler to carry out a more ambitious plan. New York State would not be safe so long as the British could counterattack down the Hudson. Schuyler was to lead a full-scale American invasion of Canada and seize Montreal and Quebec before they could be reinforced by the British. Only two days later Congress voted unanimously to authorize a preemptive invasion of Quebec Province if the intrusion was "not disagreeable to the Canadians." Before leaving New York City, Washington conferred with General Wooster only long enough to learn of an old familiar form of complaint: Wooster had been demoted from major general in the Connecticut militia to brigadier general in the new Continental service. But Washington had no time for such grousing. He drove on toward Massachusetts, only pausing long enough to review a New Haven volunteer company made up of Yale College students.[2]

During a midafternoon rainstorm and without any fanfare Washington arrived in Cambridge on Sunday, July 2. A sentry escorted him to his temporary headquarters at the home of the Harvard College president. In cramped quarters in a single spare room, he found it difficult to concentrate for the noise of brawling soldiers outside. At one point he called out the window for quiet and when the raucous shouting continued, he went outside and knocked a startled soldier to the ground. Inside two weeks he moved to the more commodious Vassall house—its wealthy Loyalist owner had taken refuge inside British lines in Boston. There he worked long days in a spare white room adjoining a small bedroom.

Each morning, as he did at Mount Vernon, he got up early to read and write letters. Then he rode the rounds of inspection. It took a full week to find out how many men he had—16,000 present; 14,000 fit for duty. But on the first day he realized how weak his army was for all its four-to-one numerical advantage over the bottled-up British in Boston. He had no cannon, no military engineers, only thirty-six barrels of gunpowder. Short on munitions, he decided to reorganize his forces while he extended his defensive works. On July 4 he took all the militia into the Connecticut Army with enlistments to run until December 31. "All distinctions of colonies would be laid aside," his general order of the day decreed. Distinctions of rank were not. Officers were to wear colored sashes indicating their rank. "New lords, new laws," commented Concord minister William Emerson.[3]

Washington deplored the conditions he saw in the camp. Eighteen thousand men were living in a shantytown of huts made of sod, planks, and fence rails or tents made of linen or sailcloth. Most men wore the clothes they had on when they left home—homespun breeches, rough linen shirts, and leather vests. They carried the family firelock and were as worried about food for their families back home as about fighting the British. Much of his time Washington spent throwing up more defenses. Where scores of men had been digging trenches and earthworks, hauling timbers, and planting sharpened and pointed trees, thousands now were put to work. Washington discovered that there were no trained sergeants and few experienced officers to teach his troops the myriad details and routines of military life and impose discipline and order. He not only ordered his officers to crack down on unsoldierly practices but made courts-martial, cashierings, drummings out of camp, and public floggings the

grim commonplaces of daily life until he purged the camps of all the officers and men he considered unsoldierly.

Washington was shocked to find officers shaving enlisted men, shocked
to find British and American officers and soldiers talking to each other
across the lines, shocked to learn of instances of cowardice by American
officers under fire at Bunker Hill. He insisted on precise discipline, forbade cursing, swearing, and drunkenness, required punctual attendance
at daily worship, neatness among enlisted men and officers, and the best
possible sanitation. He imposed severe sanctions for infractions, especially for theft and straggling from camp. Each day, the men were formed
up to witness floggings of wrongdoers, from a commonplace thirty-nine
lashes to as many as five hundred. Malefactors were required to ride "the
horse," a high wooden horse with a crude crossbeam that caught the men
in the groin while their hands were tied behind them and a sandbag
pulled their hobbled legs beneath them. Soon, the stockades were filled
as Washington fumed about the "exceedingly dirty and nasty" New Englanders he was supposed to pit against the spit-and-polish British professionals nearby. He blamed the "unaccountable kind of stupidity" he
often found among the soldiers on "the levelling spirit," the "principles
of democracy [which] so universally prevail." In a letter to his brother
Jack he betrayed his apprehensiveness. He had found a "numerous army
of provincials under very little command, discipline or order. I found an
enemy who had drove our people from Bunker's Hill strongly entrenching [and] had reason to expect before this another from them. . . . We have
been incessantly (Sundays not excepted) employed in throwing up works
of defense. I rather begin to believe now that I think it rather a dangerous
experiment and that we shall remain sometime watching the motions of
each other at the distance of little more than a mile and in full view." The
American Revolution had quickly settled down in trench warfare.[4]

The greatest problem facing Washington was finding officers to lead
his men. As he told the Massachusetts congress, he firmly believed that
all the deficiencies of his troops could be made up by the activity and zeal
of his officers. He struggled to put together a Continental general staff to
replace the haphazard militia system. The officers closest to him were of
the patrician breed he knew and trusted. He immediately ran into serious
difficulties with the New England officers he and his staff superseded.
The "stupidity" he found in "the lower class of these people" prevailed
"too generally among the officers." Washington saw himself—and the
British saw him—as the Oliver Cromwell of the American Revolution.
Like Cromwell he saw the struggle as a civil war with the virtuous American colonies oppressed by a corrupt ministry in the service of an errant
king. He was a member of the aggrieved squirearchy, like Cromwell, and
also of the Continental Congress, which, like Cromwell's Parliament, opposed the wicked ministry and its army by putting its own powerful army

in the field to force reforms. But also like Cromwell, this descendant of royalists now saw that the army, including its generals, must be subservient to the wishes of the elected politicians. The people voted for the congressional delegates, not for him as general. As one of those representatives he had helped to create Congress's Continental Army, and he never failed to remember his own subordination to that Congress.[5]

*I*n a democratic army in New England all problems eventually crossed Washington's desk and all curious his threshold. Abigail Adams, wife of Congressman Adams, came to welcome him—and was smitten. "I was struck," she wrote to John in violation of the congressional ban on personal correspondence, by his combination of "dignity with ease and complacency." She found the tall, courtly Virginian worth describing over and over: the "gentleman and soldier looked agreeably blended in him.... Modesty marks every line and feature of his face." She contrasted him to Washington's second in command, the "careless hardy veteran" Charles Lee, who in turn was so taken with Abigail that he called one of his huge shaggy dogs and had him perform tricks for her. As they sipped wine together—Washington spent £35 (about $1,400) a month for drinks for his staff and his guests—the beast sat and shook hands with her.[6]

While there was no shortage of interruptions, there was a paucity of nearly everything else: uniforms, muskets, gunpowder, cannon, picks, shovels, tents—and manpower. By the end of his first month of command Washington confided to a friend, "Between you and me, I think we are in an exceedingly dangerous situation." At first, Washington refused to allow the recruitment of Indians—although Stockbridge Indians had fought at Bunker Hill—and blacks, even though mulattoes had served in his Virginia Regiment. At his first council of war in Cambridge his officers informed him that it was becoming hard to find any new recruits other than "boys, deserters and negroes." Each New England colony forbade black men, indentured white servants, or apprentice boys to serve in its militia. Washington had preached an end to the importation of slaves in Virginia but only gradually did he get used to the sight of the freed blacks who enlisted outside Boston.[7]

*W*ashington did find time to micromanage his affairs at Mount Vernon. Lund kept him informed in almost weekly letters. By August 20 Washington was overseeing the harvest from afar: "I would not have you sell a single bushel of wheat till you can see with some kind of certainty what market flour is to go to." And Lund was to see that "spinning should go forward with all possible dispatch." He was, after all the work orders, worried about Martha. Lund had passed along a rumor of a royalist plot to kidnap her. Washington gave detailed instructions in diplomatically oblique language he knew Lund would relay to her:

I can hardly think that Lord Dunmore can act so low and unmanly a part as to think of seizing Mrs. Washington by way of revenge upon me. However, as I suppose she is before this time gone over to Mr. Calvert's [Jack's father-in-law in Maryland] and will soon after returning go down to New Kent [to the Bassetts] she will be out of his reach for two or three months to come in which time matters may and probably will take a turn as to render her removal either absolutely unnecessary or quite useless.[8]

It was not long before Washington received a reassuring answer from Martha through Lund:

'Tis true that many people made a stir about Mrs. Washington continuing at Mount Vernon but I cannot think her in any kind of danger. She does not believe herself in danger. Ten minutes' notice would be sufficient for her to get out of the way. She has often declared that she would go to [your] camp if you permit her.[9]

Despite the press of duties Washington kept his family posted. To his brother Jack: "We are all well and in no fear or dread of the enemy. . . . Very securely entrenched and wishing for nothing more than to see the enemy out of their strongholds that the dispute may come to an issue." By September 20, he told Jack that "seeing no prospect of returning to my family and friends this winter I have sent an invitation to Mrs. Washington to come to me." He had warned her "of the difficulties of the journey and left it to her own choice."[10]

When no more attacks came from the British inside Boston, Washington reasoned correctly that the British commander Gage was waiting for reinforcements and further instructions from London. In the meantime Washington turned his thoughts to using his superiority in manpower to go on the offensive. In his first days of command he had urged Philip Schuyler, general in chief of the Northern Department, to organize an invasion of Canada before British reinforcements could arrive. It was August 30 before Schuyler's forces disembarked on Canadian soil and waited for him—he was suffering from an attack of rheumatic gout. Another full month was lost while Connecticut troops at Fort Ticonderoga refused to fight under New York officers and a promised Vermont regiment failed to materialize. The delays also set back Washington's plans for a second attack—by Benedict Arnold.

George Washington and Benedict Arnold had much in common. Both men were virtually self-educated; both had made a thorough study of modern European warfare. They had observed the British army at close range and understood its weaknesses in fighting a war thousands of transatlantic miles from supply bases in an age of wooden ships, slow communications, widespread political corruption, and erratic logistics. They displayed familiarity with the latest European battle theories, which called for rigid discipline that enabled the use of massed firepower at close range. Both understood, too, the relationship of the highest technology to the aristocratic code of their times, a patrician order governed by the elite, ruled in war by an officer class that insisted on rank, order, and discipline and emphasized leadership by personal example. Above all, both men were daring soldiers by inclination and they sensed and admired this trait in others. Arnold had helped to seize Fort Ticonderoga and Crown Point to give the primitive American army a large supply of state-of-the-art weapons: heavy artillery. He had seized Lake Champlain with a squadron of British vessels he had captured along with a Canadian fort on the Richelieu River. And now he personally wanted to lead a surprise attack on Quebec from the rear.

When Arnold arrived in Cambridge during the dog days of early August, he told Washington's adjutant general Horatio Gates that he had come to offer his services to Washington and had a plan he would reveal only to the commander in chief. Gates kept him cooling his heels for about a week until he would grant him an appointment. Finally ushered in to the small white office, Arnold showed Washington a captured journal of a British engineer who had mapped the Kennebec River region of Maine. Arnold's bold plan called for a surprise attack on Quebec City through a pathless wilderness where only a few men in canoes had ever been before. Arnold assured Washington that there was still time to strike before the early Canadian winter set in. The lateness of the season, he asserted, was even an advantage: it would dissuade the British from attempting to send reinforcements from Boston on ships that could become icebound. If they moved quickly there were still only 775 British regulars in all of Quebec Province. An area one-third the size of modern Canada, large enough to double the size of the new American nation, could be conquered with a small number of men.

On August 20, Washington endorsed Arnold's plan. It would be necessary to tell Philip Schuyler that it was only a diversion in force from his attack from the south. Washington appointed Arnold a colonel in the Continental Army to shield him from the vagaries of provincial politics and offered him his pick of 1,100 enlisted men and officers from Continental forces blockading Boston. He told Gates to give Arnold whatever he needed. To Schuyler, Washington wrote to ascertain when they would attack. He sent the note "express to communicate to you a plan of an expedition which has engaged my thoughts for several days; it is to penetrate into Canada by way of Kennebec River." If Schuyler still planned to attack this season, he was to inform Washington immediately. No answer came for nearly two weeks.[11]

On the hot gray Sunday morning of September 3, 1775, the 16,000-man Continental Army formed up for Washington's inspection of the ten-mile cordon of fortifications that were now investing the British. Washington, his aides and brigade commanders, and Benedict Arnold in a red Connecticut Foot Guards uniform appeared to study every man, every musket. One regimental chaplain later wrote:

> The drum beat in every regiment for an instant and a general parade of the whole army, as for a review, was ordered. All was bustle . . . the whole army was paraded in continued line of companies. With one continued roll of drums, the general-in-chief with his staff passed along the whole line, regiment after regiment, presenting arms.[12]

Many of Washington's soldiers had grown tired of the heat, the boredom, and the grind of camp life. The prospect of action, especially in a cooler place, excited men who, at most, had fought only once in nearly five months in the army. After the review, Arnold rode to each regimental camp and ordered the men to form up again: "Officers to the front ten paces, march! Officers to the center, face! Officers to the center—march! Form hollow squares." Arnold advised the men that "volunteers were called for." When an aide intoned, "volunteers step on step in advance," the entire regiment stepped forward. All along the line, entire units volunteered. By noon, Arnold had nearly 6,000 volunteers, five times what he needed. Both Washington and Arnold were exuberant. Arnold made his selection by choosing men under thirty and taller than average. He asked each man, "Are you an active woodsman? Are you well acquainted with bateaux?" Today, every man was an expert woodsman *and* boatman. By nightfall, 747 men were chosen; with the riflemen under Daniel Morgan, Arnold now had 1,050 men.[13]

Washington was one of many officers happy to see the riflemen go. They and their hunting shirt and moccasin uniform were his creations, but since they arrived in camp they had been robbing farms and fellow soldiers and violating military etiquette by sniping at British officers at long range against Washington's express orders. Their guns, capable of hitting a man in the head at half a mile or in the nose at 150 yards, outraged the British, who were already calling the American riflemen "these shirt-tailmen with their twisted guns the worst widow—and orphan—makers in the world." Washington finished penning Arnold's orders quickly. He arranged for a fleet of eleven fishing vessels to take the regiment from Newburyport, Massachusetts, to the mouth of the Kennebec in present-day Maine. Washington supervised every step of the amphibious operation. The little army would march overland and sail up the Kennebec as far as Gardinerstown, where two hundred shallow-draft bateaux were being built to carry the men and their supplies all the way to

Quebec Province, where they would portage to the Chaudière River and float one hundred miles north to Quebec City.[14]

It was September 24 before enough blankets and equipment could be gathered so the musketmen could march off: an entire month had been lost awaiting the formality of Schuyler's approval. No matter how much time was lost, Washington was sure that once the army got moving the men could make it up on the march. With Arnold, he believed the men could make the march to Quebec in only twenty days once they reached Gardinerstown. Washington reviewed Arnold's troops and sent them off without waiting for the manifesto he was writing for the Canadians; a courier would bring that along later.

So confident was Washington that the expedition would succeed that when he finally informed Congress of it he grossly underestimated the distance and the difficulty of the march. In his written orders, Washington emphasized that the American invaders were to "consider yourselves as marching not through an enemy's country but that of our friends and brethren for such the inhabitants of Canada and the Indian nations have proved themselves." Washington ordered strict "punishment [for] every attempt to plunder or insult any of the inhabitants." And he gave Arnold a strongbox of gold and silver coins. They were to buy everything for cash, steal nothing. Washington told Arnold to ask the French and the Indians to stand aside while the Americans and the British fought over the future of Canada.[15]

Three days after he sent off Arnold, Washington proposed a second offensive. He wanted to attack Boston and drive the British out. In a council of war, each general officer had a vote. The commander in chief could override their decision but rarely did. Washington, according to his aide Joseph Reed, was "very serious" about the attack. With winter looming and shortages of tents, housing, firewood, and enlistments drawing to an end, Washington argued the necessity of seizing the town of Boston before it could be reinforced. Washington was aware that British morale was suffering from shortages of food. Some 1,100 Massachusetts Loyalists were draining British resources. And his army was ready—if he waited he would have to train a whole new army in the spring. Unless his men saw action he did not expect many reenlistments. Especially if Arnold succeeded in Canada, an all-out assault on Boston now could prove decisive and end the war by Christmas. But most of the generals chose safety. They preferred to wait until news of American resistance reached England and a new Parliament saw the wisdom of avoiding a long and costly war against resolute American resistance. Only Charles Lee supported Washington. He thought the Americans were ready now and the British besieged in Boston dispirited. Washington bowed to the majority.

The first year of war he had worked out his own philosophy, which he made American military policy. A later aide, Alexander Hamilton, said that Washington opposed fighting a war of posts European style; he preferred mobility, especially if it meant keeping his army intact in the field where it lent strength to congressional policy:

> Our hopes are not placed in any particular city or spot of ground but in preserving a good army to take advantage of favorable opportunities and waste and defeat the enemy by piece meal.[16]

*U*nleashing a two-pronged attack on Canada and seizing British ships changed the nature of the confrontation with England. Congress could no longer claim that Americans were only fielding an army to prevent the British from further violating the liberties of freeborn Englishmen. Organizing an army and fighting the British turned a political protest movement into a war with its own logic and momentum. And Washington's aggressive prosecution of the war was now pushing the politicians. He also yearned to unleash a *coup de main* against the British in Boston before the enlistments of his men expired on December 31. When recruitment lagged, producing only one thousand enlistees in the six months after Bunker Hill, Washington lamented the "death of public spirit and want of virtue."[17]

He received only one important new recruit as the year neared an end. Martha arrived at Cambridge on December 11, bringing with her a quiet tranquillity that reassured her husband, whose morale was beginning to sag. She arrived at Vassall House while he was wrestling with his worst problem: keeping an army in the field. By January first his recruiters had managed to persuade 8,212 men—including "the free negroes who have enlisted in this army"—to reenlist for the new year. Some five thousand new recruits were expected in the spring. Martha not only supervised the cooking for her husband and fellow officers but organized a salon for the wives of other officers who joined their spouses. Together the officers' wives followed her example and ministered to the sick soldiers and made bandages for the wounded.

All her adult life Martha had felt compelled to stay at home with her sick child. With her nephew, George Bassett (Betty's son), and a maid she had climbed into the green carriage in late November and set out toward Massachusetts, braving her first New England winter. Jack and Nelly Custis decided to come along, too: Jack had found a useful purpose bearing Fairfax County funds to the troops. The Washington carriage with its coat of arms on the doors, a coachman and postilion guiding the four horses, and Jack's valet riding behind made a regal stir as Martha and her entourage began an annual ritual. Martha had never made such a long trip; she had never been farther north than Alexandria, certainly not in winter. After a week on the road she was greeted warmly in Philadelphia. "You have seen the figure our arrival made in Philadelphia," she wrote, "and I left in as great pomp as if I had been a very great somebody." After several days' rest in Philadelphia they set out again, reaching Cambridge in another week.[18]

Mercy Otis Warren, widow of the slain hero of Bunker Hill and Abigail Adams's closest friend, bestowed her approval on Martha when she received Massachusetts's literary doge at headquarters "with that politeness and respect shown in a first interview among the well bred. . . . The complacency of her manners speaks at once the benevolence of her heart and her affability, candor and gentleness qualify her to soften the hours of private life or to sweeten the cares of the hero and smooth the rugged scenes of war." Warren also proclaimed Jacky "a sensible modest agreeable young man" and his bride Nelly "engaging" but "of so extreme delicate a constitution—a want of health a little clouds her spirits." But by now Mercy Warren was used to the pounding of artillery jarring the teacups. It took Martha and her family a little more time.[19]

But it would take more than Martha's soothing presence to overcome the critical shortage of muskets and gunpowder. Washington was proud of his achievements as he replaced one army with another under the British guns.

> Search the vast volume of history through and I much question whether a case similar to ours is to be found, to wit to maintain a post against the flower of the British troops for six months together without powder and at the end of them to have one army disbanded and another to raise within the same distance of a reinforced army.[20]

That was the only good news. Congress had expected the fall of Lord North when news of Bunker Hill hit London. Instead, in October, the king, in his annual speech from the throne, declared the American colonies in open rebellion and subject to all the military punishment at the command of Great Britain. More armies and fleets would be sent to crush the rebellion. From Canada came word that Richard Montgomery, who had taken over command from Schuyler and had captured Montreal with Arnold, had been killed in a winter attack on Quebec City on the last day of 1775.

So many things had gone wrong. Washington had refused the aid of Penobscot Abenaki guides and the expedition had gotten lost. The captured British map turned out to be a fraud. The two hundred bateaux had been made of green wood and had all sunk before the expedition reached Canada, not in twenty days but, nearly starved, in sixty days. Fully a third of the men died or deserted. The entire rear guard had mutinied and returned to Cambridge. Washington had court-martialed Major Robert Enos but all the witnesses were in Canada. Washington's cold fury had driven Enos out of the camp in a week. Arnold had arrived at the St. Lawrence three days too late. Loyalists—Scottish Highlanders from New York and Newfoundland—had reinforced the city and thoroughly defeated Arnold's assault. Arnold had been critically wounded and all but 150 of his men had been killed or taken prisoner. He was besieging the reinforced city with only a few guns and a few hundred French-Canadian volunteers. The Canadian expedition could only be salvaged with massive and timely reinforcements, but winter made any further effort impossible until spring.[21] In the meantime, Washington had lost 1,000 men and his first offensive.

As the face-off across the lines outside Boston dragged on and still no new British attack came, Washington explored other ways to put pressure on the enemy and ease his own shortages. Early in September 1775 he issued letters of marque to six privateering ships crewed by soldiers recruited from the Massachusetts port towns. Unaware of this initiative, the Continental Congress directed him to commission two ships to interdict arms shipments from the British naval base at Halifax, Nova Scotia, to the besieged garrison at Boston. Two ships, the *Cabot* and the *Andrew Doria*, became the first official U.S. Navy vessels. In October, Congress authorized two more ships; by year's end, Washington's Navy, as it was dubbed, included seven ships and thirteen more were scheduled to be built. In addition, Congress appropriated funding for two battalions of marines and approved a schedule for prize money allotments for officers and crewmen. One-tenth of all money derived from auctioning off ships and cargoes the privateersmen captured was to go to Washington himself for his private use, a typical arrangement for an eighteenth-century commander. The infant navy quickly solved one of Washington's worst problems when it captured a British ordnance brig carrying 2,000 muskets, 100,000 flints, 20,000 rounds of shot, and 30 tons of musketballs.

Fortunately, the winter of 1775–1776 was a mild one, as both armies faced critical shortages of fuel. Each day Washington's army—huddling in sailcloth lean-tos until they completed their 108-foot-long log barracks with crude fireplaces—consumed some 117 cords of firewood, or about four acres of timber, which had to be cut and dragged by teams of oxen an increasing distance each day across icy roads. The smoky clouds from greenwood fires were the envy of the cooped-up British, who began to tear down the deserted wooden houses of rebels. Winter also brought diseases, especially devastating among soldiers who had come from isolated farms and had never been exposed to communicable diseases at close quarters. The malaria of warm weather gave way to dysentery and typhus, until by October nearly 15 percent of the soldiers were on sick call. Each wave of new recruits seemed to bring new viruses. So many sick refugees came out from Boston that Washington became convinced that Howe was deliberately sowing illness in his ranks. He decreed that any refugee found behind American lines without a pass was to be jailed—a unique form of quarantine. The draconian solution seemed to work: by year's end the number of men on sick call went down to 7 percent.

Increasingly as the winter went by the talk in Washington's camp reflected the mood in Congress. The nonimportation agreement was extended as the British tightened the coastal naval blockade. With spring the Americans expected an onslaught of fresh British armies. Many Americans began to believe it was high time to give up on reconciliation with England and declare American independence. This growing movement received a considerable boost when Washington's army suddenly acquired a large supply of modern artillery. In November 1775 Washington had dispatched his massive young artillerist, a tall, deep-voiced, 280-pound former bookseller named Henry Knox, to fetch the cannon Benedict Arnold had seized at Crown Point and Ticonderoga. Knox waited until the Hudson River froze over and then, with requisitioned teams of oxen scarcely bigger than himself, towed a long column of sledges bristling with fifty-nine French- and British-forged cannon over the Berkshire Mountains along the route of the present-day Massachusetts Turnpike. His arrival in Framingham heralded the birth of a state-of-the-art American army.

By February, Washington was ready to use his new weaponry, and when on March 8 he learned from a spy inside Boston that the British command had received orders to evacuate, he decided to make political capital out of their departure by seizing the high ground of Dorchester Heights and fortifying it overnight. Anything less than a careful and quick movement would court disaster and the loss not only of his new artillery but of his army. Colonel Rufus Putnam submitted a plan to Washington on which he decided to gamble everything. Thousands of men were put to work making large frames of timber in which gabions, fascines, and bales of hay could be hauled quickly up on Dorchester Heights. The woven gabions were to be filled with earth; the hay was to be covered with as much dirt as the men could dig. Large branches, cut from nearby orchards, were sharpened to act as protective abatis to slow and ensnare infantry. Barrels of earth were readied to roll down on attackers.

By the night of March first, everything was ready. Washington put "Old Put," Israel Putnam, the hero of Bunker Hill, in command and designated John Sullivan of New Hampshire and Nathanael Greene of Rhode Island in charge of the divisions. To cover the noise of thousands of men and their carts and draft animals Washington began an artillery barrage that night and resumed it the next night. On the night of March 4 the exchange of cannon fire was heavy. Around 7 P.M., 2,000 men headed for Dorchester Heights, 800 infantry screening 1,200 workmen who threw up breastworks and laid out the redoubts for the cannon as 300 ox-carts brought up the tools, the gabions, the fascines. A fresh work party relieved them toward dawn; by this time there were two redoubts lined with cannon infantry.

The British were stunned when dawn revealed the night's work. Washington's artillery could fire easily into Boston and sink any Royal Navy ship. Howe's first reaction was to attack. He assembled troops and barges, but a storm scattered his landing craft, giving him time to ponder the possibility of another Bunker Hill. He had already decided to abandon Boston. He decided another attack was impossible and ordered the evacuation to begin. On St. Patrick's Day, March 17, three weeks after Washington's cannon appeared on Dorchester Heights the last British transport crowded with the loyal English subjects of Massachusetts and everything Howe's army could carry off sailed from Boston harbor. Washington had his first great victory.

The British retreat made Washington a popular hero. Harvard College granted him an honorary degree, Doctor of Laws for *honoris causa,* and Congress struck him a gold medal. But the real effect of his success at holding an army of farm boys and fishermen together under the glower of the British army for nearly a year was to convince Americans that men like John Adams—considered radicals a year before—were behaving rationally when they said America was ready to become a self-supporting nation. Only six weeks after Howe's withdrawal to Nova Scotia, Richard Henry Lee of Virginia introduced a motion in Congress that "these states are and have right to be free and independent states." As members of Congress hurried home to obtain authorization to vote for—or against—independence, Washington prepared to ward off the powerful counterattack he expected any day from the British. On July 4, when Congress voted narrowly to declare American independence, John Adams could have been speaking for his friend Washington when he wrote to Abigail Adams, "The revolution is now complete: all that remains is a war."[22]

Washington's jubilation at the precipitous British evacuation was marred by several discordant notes. He began a long-smoldering feud with General Charles Lee, who had convinced Congress that he had vast military knowledge that entitled him to the command. In a letter to his brother Jack, Washington hinted that all was not going smoothly between them: "General Lee is the first officer in military knowledge and experience we have in the whole army. He is zealously attached to the cause, honest and well-meaning but rather fickle and violent I fear in his temper."

Lee was soon on his way south, where he arrived too late to make any significant contribution. The South Carolina militia succeeded in driving off a British naval assault with well-trained artillery protecting Charlestown harbor. More good news came from North Carolina, where militia using small swiveling cannon shattered wave on wave of Loyalist Scottish Highlanders at Moore's Creek Bridge. Lee's arrival came too late and soon he drifted back. When the British attacked Norfolk, Virginia, and set it afire with naval gunfire, Virginia and North Carolina militia beat back the attack. By May 1776 there was not one British soldier or sailor remaining in arms in the United States.[23]

The congressional vote for independence electrified Washington. On May 31, when he learned that Congress had sent the delegates home to poll the support for a vote on independence, he wrote to his brother Jack that he was eager for Congress "to declare the colonies free and independent states absolved from all allegiance to or dependence upon the Crown or Parliament of Great Britain." He had once believed it would take only a change of ministry to bring about reconciliation, but now he was ready to renounce king and Parliament as well. His personal revolution was now complete.[24]

While he waited to shift his army and artillery south, Washington watched in considerable awe another kind of metamorphosis. At the end of April he wrote his brother that "Mrs. Washington is still here." Smallpox was raging throughout New England that spring and Martha, rather than flee it, had announced that she intended to undergo inoculation. She "talks of taking the smallpox but I doubt her resolution." His stepson and his wife were not waiting for Martha—they fled south. A month passed before Washington informed his brother that "Mrs. Washington is now under inoculation. This is the 13th day and she has very few pustules. She would have [written] to my sister [Betty] but thought it prudent not to do so." Washington believed the disease was being spread by contamination of the paper used to write letters home. Martha agreed to avoid the "danger of conveying the infection." Five days later a relieved husband wrote to Martha's sister and brother-in-law, the Bassetts, that "Mrs. Washington got through the fever [not] more than a dozen pustules appearing." The mild dose was enough to protect her, an essential safeguard as she insisted on spending more and more time nursing the sick troops. Moreover her beautiful complexion had not been marred. Washington was about to decamp to prepare the defense of New York, and now Martha was insisting on accompanying him, too, "if matters there are in such a situation as to make it a fit place for her to remain." The year 1776 brought Washington many surprises, not the least of which was a thank-you letter from his stepson, who had finally realized how much Washington had done for him. Jacky still feared Washington and could not display his gratitude in person. From the safety of his father-in-law's Maryland house, he wrote: "I often wished to thank you but my resolution failed me."[25]

By July 9, the Washingtons had reached New York City and had just seen the Declaration of Independence. Washington ordered it read aloud from the balcony of City Hall at the foot of Broadway above the din of a huge crowd, which set to work at once tearing the royal coat-of-arms and any other symbol of British rule off public buildings. At night, every patriot's household was specially illuminated with candlelight to mark the break from British rule. There was little time to celebrate. On July 4, 1776, the first of 479 British ships had sailed into New York Harbor and begun to disgorge the largest British expeditionary force in English history on Staten Island. "We have a powerful [British] fleet within full view of us," Washington wrote to his brother. Martha had decided to go on to Philadelphia "with thoughts of returning home." She soon hurried there to see her first grandchild, born to Jack and Nelly Custis. Just when he would see her again, or his beloved Mount Vernon, was more than ever in doubt. To Betsy Bassett, Washington wrote a letter he knew she would show Martha: "I do, my dear sister, most religiously wish there was an end to the war."[26]

Fourteen

"A FINE FOX CHASE"

Within hours of declaring the United States independent of Great Britain on July 4, 1776, delegates to the Second Continental Congress turned to the somber business of prosecuting the war in which they were now irrevocably enmeshed and providing for the defense of Philadelphia, the new nation's capital. By unanimous resolution, Congress purchased its first piece of real estate for £600 Pennsylvania currency—a flat, 96-acre wedge of southern New Jersey riverfront twelve miles downriver from Philadelphia where Great Mantua Creek oozed into the Delaware. Congress purchased a peach orchard from Quaker widow Margaret Paul and named it Fort Billings. It was intended by the congressman who selected it, Board of War member Benjamin Franklin, to be Philadelphia's first line of defense against the expected invasion upriver by the British fleet. Five hundred New Jersey militiamen promptly cleared the site. Then they began to lay out earthworks according to plans drawn up by a recently arrived volunteer Polish military engineer, Captain Tadeusz Kosciuszko, who also would design smaller fortifications at Red Bank and Fort Island, eight miles upstream on either side of the river, and just four miles below the city.

By July 1776, the American rebels were confident they could defend the city against British attack. Indeed, the heady series of encounters with the British regulars in New England in the preceding months had encouraged Congress to declare openly for independence. American militiamen had slaughtered redcoats by the score at Concord and Bunker Hill; American forces had besieged Montreal and Quebec in a bold winter offensive that very nearly conquered Canada. While these invasions had ultimately been repelled, they had created the impression that the rebels were on the offensive. To the south, rebel forces had blunted a Loyalist uprising in North Carolina by cutting down the Scots Highlanders at the Battle of Moore's Creek Bridge. Then they had repulsed a major British naval force at Charleston, South Carolina. In Virginia, the attempt by the British royal governor, Lord Dunmore, to arm slaves and put down the rebellion had failed miserably, serving to make Virginia, the largest American colony, a hotbed of rebel militancy.

Yet every realistic American expected a counterattack by their British rulers, and they did not have to wait long. On the same day the Declaration of Independence was proclaimed in Philadelphia, an enormous British fleet arrived silently on the horizon of New York, as the first sails of the mightiest armada ever seen in the New World tacked majestically off Sandy Hook. The forest of tall masts floated through the narrows between New York and New Jersey into New York harbor. Inside two weeks, 52 men-of-war and 427 troop transports jammed with artillery, supplies, and 39,000 of the world's most feared soldiers crowded the anchorages. It was the largest expeditionary force ever launched by the British. Its mission was straightforward: to crush the American rebellion, to restore America to subjugation as a string of dutiful colonies subservient to the British Crown, and, especially, to carry out King George's command to punish America.

As if in defiance of the red-coated British regulars and blue-coated Hessian mercenaries disembarking on Staten Island, the Sons of Liberty across the harbor in Manhattan reacted wildly to the Declaration of Independence. They celebrated by throwing ropes around a large cast-iron equestrian statue of King George III, hauling it down, and shipping off the shattered pieces in wagons to Ridgefield in western Connecticut, to be melted down into 42,088 bullets to fire back at the invaders. Their celebration was short-lived.

In the sweltering weeks that followed, the British were to unleash a stunning series of amphibious assaults and overland quick-marches to shatter the main American army and drive it from New York City, hounding it as if it were a tired and frightened fox across northern New Jersey until the British threatened to capture the seat of the rebellion—Philadelphia.

*I*t took nearly six weeks before Washington was ready to move the major portion of his army south from Boston to respond to the arrival of the huge British fleet in early July. Long before being forced to evacuate Boston, the British commander, Gage, had decided that New York City, with its solid Loyalist support, should be his base. As early as June 12, 1775, even before Bunker Hill, he had begun his preparations in secret. When Sir William Howe succeeded Gage, he had agreed with his brother, Admiral Lord Howe, that the main army and naval forces should remain in Boston through the winter to await reinforcement from England. Washington's fortification of Dorchester Heights, while it had caught the British unprepared, had only caused a brief diversion to Halifax. When

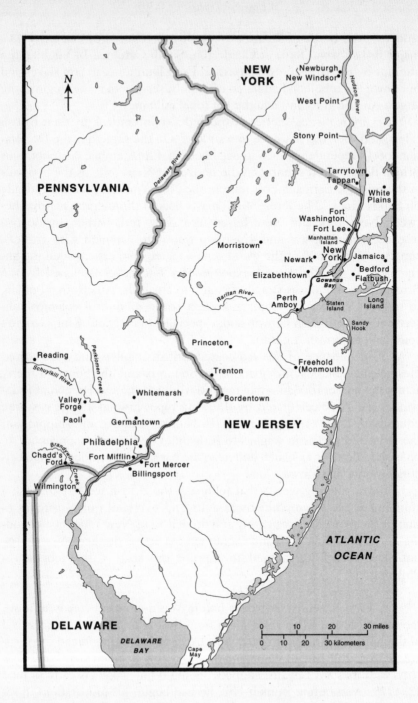

After the British attacked New York, Washington was routed at the Battle of Long Island, and he retreated through New Jersey to counterattack at Trenton at the end of 1776; when the British attacked Philadelphia in 1777, he fought doggedly at Brandywine, Germantown, and the Delaware River forts; in 1778 he fought to a draw at Monmouth Courthouse.

Howe had to reinforce Quebec to raise Arnold's siege, in May 1776, it further slowed Howe down, but by June, as the summer season of campaigning began, he began shifting his massive forces south to Staten Island. It was August before he had all the field equipment he wanted from England and was ready to attack the Americans on Manhattan Island.

As early as January 1776, Washington had decided to prepare for what he was sure would be a major British attack on New York from the south. He had detached his second in command, Charles Lee, to recruit volunteers in Connecticut. He could count on no help from the heavily Loyalist eastern counties of New York; in New Jersey, Governor William Franklin, an acute embarrassment to his father, was sitting tight at the helm of his Loyalist government in Perth Amboy waiting for a British relief force. Lee could expect little help from that quarter. And Washington could spare him no troops from the lines around Boston. When Lee arrived in New York City in early February, he found what he considered a nearly hopeless situation. On February 19, he wrote Washington, "It is so encircled with deep navigable waters that whoever commands the sea, must command the town."[1]

Lee's assessment, Washington knew, was correct. Bordered on the west by the Hudson River, Manhattan Island was not only a highway into the interior for Royal Navy ships but, at the same time, a barrier that made American troop movements from New Jersey and the south extremely difficult. The East River presented another ten-mile-long barrier to American reinforcements while it made amphibious attack by the British controlling the waterway easy. To counterattack the expected British landings, Lee decided to build strategic defenses on Long Island in Brooklyn Heights, where his guns could dominate the approaches to New York City. Lee believed that New York City could not be held, but he could slow down a British invasion that "might cost the enemy many thousands of men to get possession of it."[2]

When Washington arrived in the city on April 13 and set up his headquarters at 110 Maiden Lane he found little had been done. He hurried along the works that Lee had planned but discovered that little had been done. (In fact, Congress had yanked Lee out of New York City only a month after he had arrived and ordered him south to organize the defense of Charleston against a British fleet headed that way.) In the five-week hiatus before Washington's arrival, there had been two other commanders, first the self-styled Lord Stirling, William Alexander, a New Jersey iron manufacturer with no real experience at commanding more than his own workers, then Putnam, who had last held command at Bunker Hill, where he had demonstrated so clearly that he knew little about fortifications. Putnam had taken over when the first four brigades of New England veterans of the siege of Boston arrived. While Washington had ordered Heath, Sullivan, Greene, and Spencer's brigades to New

York City as early as March 18, the day after the British evacuated Boston, it had taken them nearly a month to move the 150 miles overland.

Under Washington's more rigorous discipline, the New England veterans had set to work like a legion of beavers, cutting down trees and throwing up defenses and digging lines all over lower Manhattan and Brooklyn for the next four months while they awaited the imminent attack. The arrival of clouds of sails on the East River in early July and the appearance of thousands of tents on Staten Island sent a thrill of fear followed by weeks of maddening tension until the British attack finally came in August.

At dawn on August 22, Washington received a dispatch from Colonel Edward Hand's outpost on the southwest shore of Long Island near Denyse Point (now Fort Hamilton) that the British were preparing a landing, ferrying troops over from Staten Island under the covering guns of four frigates (*Phoenix, Rose, Greyhound,* and *Rainbow*) and two bomb ketches (*Carcass* and *Thunder*) anchored in Gravesend Bay in The Narrows. By eight o'clock, some 4,000 men under Generals Cornwallis and Clinton, including von Donop's Hessian jaegers and grenadiers, started crossing to Denyse Point. Burning anything the enemy might use, Hand's 200 Pennsylvanian Continentals pulled back to Prospect Hill. Shuttling back and forth to Staten Island in seventy-five flatboats, eleven bateaux, and two row-galleys built for the day's operations, by noon the British had transported at least forty cannon and the horses of the dragoons in a flawless amphibious operation that put 15,000 well-supplied redcoats on Long Island in a single morning. Little happened for another three unnerving days, then the German general Heister landed with two more brigades of grenadiers, taking up a position slightly east of the earlier British right-flank landings. There was little American resistance as the Hessians quick-marched four miles inland to Flatbush, where Cornwallis had encamped ten battalions of men with von Donop's force.

The first skirmishing came on August 23, when Hand's Pennsylvanians attacked von Donop's Hessians and tried to drive them out of some houses, only to be counterattacked. By now, the British beachhead stretched all the way from Flatlands in the east through New Utrecht and south to Gravesend, and vast amounts of supplies were being ferried over. Between Howe's redcoats and Washington's forces on Brooklyn Heights lay a low, heavily wooded ridge known as the Heights of Gowanus. Rising sharply forty to eighty feet on the south and densely wooded, it made a British frontal attack by cavalry or artillery impossible and screened movements inside Washington's lines two miles to the north on Brooklyn Heights. This superb natural barrier commanding the plain where the British were encamped had only one drawback: it was cut by four roads. The man most familiar with this terrain was Nathanael Greene, Washington's ablest general on the scene: he had been the first to arrive on Long Island on April first and was thoroughly conversant with the region. But he was down with a fever. Washington turned to John Sullivan, who had little time to learn the lay of the land when Washington sent him over on August 20. Sullivan posted himself in the rear of Gowanus Heights with only a thin screen of outposts in the woods overlooking the plains. Four days later, Washington changed commanders again, putting Putnam (who knew even less of the terrain) over Sullivan.

On the eve of the battle, Putnam had only 2,750 men in four makeshift forts spread out over four miles of ridge, each fort blocking a pass through the heights. About 1,000 New England veterans were barricaded with four cannon in a crude fort made of felled trees at Flatbush. Isolated off to the east guarding Bedford Pass were only 400 Pennsylvania riflemen. Shortly after midnight on August 27, near the shore of Gowanus Bay, the vanguard of a 5,000-man British diversionary force under General James Grant slammed into the westernmost American defenses on Gowanus Road. Notified by 3 A.M., Putnam at Brooklyn Heights immediately ordered Stirling to take two regiments of Continentals, Smallwood's Marylanders, and Haslet's Delawares and counterattack. Stirling picked up more Pennsylvania and Connecticut troops along the way. Colors flying, Stirling took up his position on the American right flank. Meanwhile, John Sullivan had reached Flatbush in the middle of the American lines. He found only light shelling by the Hessians at his front and sent one of his battalions, roughly half his troops, west to reinforce Stirling. By the time Washington arrived on Long Island at eight o'clock, two-thirds of the Americans faced Grant's attack on the Gowanus end of the lines. Washington sent even more men to reinforce Stirling.

Washington could not have better played into Howe's hands. The day before, Cornwallis had moved from his Flatbush base camp to Flatlands on the east, on the weak American left flank. The Americans evidently didn't see or didn't understand this movement. When he finally arrived, Washington grasped at once that the main British attack was imminent and that it would be against Brooklyn. He called for more and more reinforcements from Manhattan. He had deployed 7,000 men now—but only five of them, a mounted patrol of five young militia officers, guarded Jamaica Pass.

At nine o'clock the evening of August 26, General Henry Clinton gave the signal to form up the main British force at Flatlands. Washington was outnumbered more than three to one. Nearly half the British stepped off with Howe—Clinton with the 17th Light Dragoons and a brigade of light infantry, Cornwallis with the First Brigade of Grenadiers, two regiments of infantry, the 71st (Fraser's Highlanders), Howe and Lord Percy with the Guards, and three brigades of infantry, a regiment of rear guards, plus artillery and wagons of supplies—in all 10,000 soldiers and 28 artillery pieces, marching stealthily to Washington's left, cautiously marching all night behind three Loyalist guides who deserted the main Jamaica road and led the British along a dirt track even farther east, reaching Halfway House near Jamaica Pass about three in the morning.

At eight that morning, on the opposite end of the line, the British general Grant, now leading 7,000 men, opened fire with his artillery and unleashed a strong infantry attack into Stirling's Americans, who stood, flags flying out in the open, British style, as gun crews dueled. Stirling was to hold his ground for four hours, even when British gunners opened fire from men-of-war maneuvering in close on Gowanus Bay. At nine, near Bedford Pass in the center of the line, the British fired two heavy guns, the signal for the main attack. By the time the Americans under Sullivan realized that the British had gotten behind him, British dragoons and light infantry were charging down on him from Bedford and his gunners were overrun. As the Americans tried to turn about and fight, von Donop's Hessian jaegers came rushing up the ridge at the Americans. The American riflemen had no time to reload before the Germans were on them. At the center of the long line, Heister and his Germans were now freed to move left, to the west, to join Grant in attacking Stirling, whose 950 men were holding off the 7,000 redcoats.

Cut off from retreat, Stirling had only one way out of the trap: behind him lay the wide Gowanus Creek, broad swamps lining both banks. To retreat across a swamp under heavy fire seemed a recipe for disaster. First, they would have to fight their way through. So Stirling decided to attack. He led off, first, some 250 Marylanders, ordering the Delaware Blues and then the rest of Smallwood's Marylanders to retreat across the creek. Stirling than pivoted and marched off with 256 men, "in perfect order" under their shot-shredded battle flags. Five times, Stirling's men charged as Cornwallis added canister and grapeshot to the barrage of artillery and musket fire. After a sixth attack, what was left of Stirling's forces scattered and tried to escape. Only ten men of the 250 made it. All the rest were killed in the fight, drowned in the swamp, or captured.[3]

All along the American line, the debacle was now complete. Colonel Miles at Flatbush, completely outflanked, tried to fight his way to join Sullivan but was captured with 159 men. A few of his men made it to Putnam at Brooklyn Heights to tell of the disaster. At Bedford Pass, the Americans broke and ran toward Brooklyn; so did the troops at Flatbush Pass. Sullivan and some of his men tried to fight their way to Brooklyn, bringing three guns to bear on a British light infantry battalion blocking their retreat, but the British, reinforced, captured the guns and drove Sullivan's force into the Hessian jaegers. Through woods, down slopes, and across open fields, the men fled, some singly, some in companies, toward the fortified camp on Brooklyn Heights. Washington watched through a telescope from a hilltop within the lines. "Good God," he said to Lord Sterling, "What brave fellows I must this day lose!"[4]

As the first European-style open field battle of the Revolutionary War, the clash at Long Island was vitally important, as it indicated what might come after it. The defeat of the Americans cast gloom over the entire American cause. On Lake Champlain, where Benedict Arnold and his makeshift navy were awaiting the northern prong of the attack, Horatio Gates, Arnold's commander at Fort Ticonderoga, refused to tell anyone when he learned the outcome. For Washington, the news was especially devastating. He had made a series of serious mistakes. He had replaced Greene with someone entirely unfamiliar with the terrain and had delayed personally taking charge of the forces until the British attack actually began. He had split his force, leaving the Americans on Long Island hopelessly outnumbered. He had poorly reconnoitered the terrain, leaving Jamaica Pass completely open. But, in fairness, Howe would have struck Manhattan and taken it if Washington had concentrated all his forces on Long Island and, with the support of the Royal Navy, then most certainly would have isolated and destroyed Washington's main army. Moreover, Howe's plan was brilliant. Only his failure to follow up his advantage and storm the Brooklyn fortifications while the Americans were in pandemonium kept the Revolution alive.

Howe's hesitation saved the American army, and then Washington saved it again. As Howe inexplicably ordered a formal siege of Brooklyn Heights, the north wind stiffened and kept British men-of-war out of the East River while Washington used Glover's and Hutchinson's Massachusetts regiments of fishermen first to bring over reinforcements, and then, as he saw Howe's trenches approaching, enabling him to evacuate his entire army from Long Island. All boats found along the East River joined Glover's whalers as they rowed all the foggy night of August 30. In one night, Washington removed 12,000 cold, sick, and demoralized troops across the East River with all their supplies, all but three of their precious cannon, and all of their horses. Only three men who stayed to loot the American camp were left behind.

*B*y early September 1776, it had become obvious to Washington that the British planned to take New York City quickly, then take advantage of unseasonably warm autumn weather to quick-march overland through New Jersey to surprise and seize Philadelphia. After a futile peace conference on Staten Island on September 11, the British resumed their offensive. It was Washington's inclination to follow Greene's suggestion to abandon and then burn New York City to the ground. To him it was not only a potential British winter encampment but was riddled with Loyalists as well. But the Continental Congress overruled him. As long as the city survived, it could be reoccupied. Reorganizing his 15,000 remaining effective troops, Washington decided to spread his forces over sixteen miles, leaving 5,000 men under Putnam in New York City while he deployed 9,000 to defend the line from Harlem to Kingsbridge. Greene, with five brigades, was to repel landings along the East River. The parchment-thin American defenses invited a British attack at its weakest point, which came in due course. Washington had already received permission from Congress to retreat northward. On September 14, he received a congressional resolution that he did not have to "remain in that city a moment longer than he shall think it proper." Washington was still trying to find enough horses and wagons to evacuate his supplies when the British attacked on September 15.[5]

Clinton, whose stock was high in British councils of war because of his brilliant flanking attack on Long Island, now urged a bold attack at Kings Bridge to cut off and destroy the Americans. Howe wanted to spare the housing in New York City and called for the attack at Kip's Bay (between present-day 30th and 34th Streets) and the East River. On the Sunday morning of the fifteenth, six British ships towed eighty-four flatboats of redcoats into shore while three men-of-war shelled Connecticut militia cowering behind low earthworks. A Continental private, Joseph Plumb Martin, said the American defenses consisted of "nothing more than a ditch dug along the bank of the river with the dirt thrown out towards the river." Concealed by the heavy smoke from the 70-gun British cannonade, some 4,000 British and German troops bumped ashore. Ambrose Serle, secretary to Admiral Howe, wrote in his journal that "so terrible and so incessant a roar of guns few even in the army and navy had ever heard before."[6]

As the British picked their way up the rocky shore, they found that the Americans had fled without firing a shot. Connecticut units under Colonels William Douglas and James Wadsworth had fled north. Supporting units stayed out of cannon range. According to tradition, George Washington, arriving on the scene and, waving his saber in an attempt to rally his troops, swore profusely in words no one recorded then. Throwing his hat on the ground, in his rage he exclaimed, "Good God, are these the men in which I am to defend America?" Other accounts say he fired his pistols at the runaways and cane-whipped privates, colonels, and brigadier generals with equal rancor. Whatever he did, camp gossip magnified it into American legend.[7]

He dispatched Putnam to gallop south and rescue Sullivan's leaderless brigade, Knox's artillery, and the other troops occupying the town. Leading them north along the Post Road (now Lexington Avenue), he was guided by his aide-de-camp, Aaron Burr, through a peach orchard on the Bloomingdale Road on the Hudson River side of Manhattan, at one point separated from the British by only a city block. Only Howe's orders for his troops to await his arrival saved the escaping Americans. Howe didn't arrive until 5 P.M. He got New York City, but again, the Americans got away.

The British celebration after taking New York City was short-lived. The next day, September 16, 1776, Washington retreated to the high natural plateau of Harlem Heights and ordered construction of three lines of defenses. Washington posted Greene with 3,300 men along the southern defensive line between modern-day Manhattan Avenue and the Hudson overlooking West 125th Street, Putnam with 2,500 men (including many who had bolted the day before) to Greene's rear, and Spencer with 4,200 Connecticut troops with Pennsylvanians to stiffen them in the rear. In the front lines, he ordered three redoubts dug overnight and connected by trenches. Three-quarters of a mile back, four more linked redoubts were thrown up. At King's Bridge and at Fort Washington, he posted a combined 8,500 men.

On the morning of September 16, he sent Lieutenant Colonel Thomas Knowlton with 150 Connecticut rangers on a predawn reconnaissance of the British lines, two miles to his south along 106th Street. Following a ravine called the Hollow Way (near West 125th Street), Knowlton scaled the heavily wooded, rocky Morningside Heights. He ran into the dreaded Black Watch regiment at West 106th Street and Broadway and, in a brisk skirmish, got off eight volleys before escaping with ten men wounded and the Highlanders in pursuit. Heavy fighting broke out between noon and 1 P.M. in a wheatfield at West 120th Street and Riverside Drive. British light infantry and Highlanders were reinforced by Hessians and light artillery dragged three miles just in time to rescue the Highlanders from a crushing defeat. Chased south by the Americans, the British finally received 5,000 reinforcements and turned and fought in an orchard at West 111th Street. Finally, Washington called off the attack, but his remarkable counterthrust the day after the humiliating rout at Kip's Bay was a psychological victory for the Americans. Twice in less than a month his army had absorbed British beatings and held together well enough to counterpunch. "This little advantage has inspired our troops prodigiously," Washington wrote to General Philip Schuyler at Albany. "They find that it only required resolution and good officers to make an enemy (that they stood in too much dread of) to give way."[8]

Only five days later, the British received another setback. As Howe paused for fully four weeks to build formidable defenses across northern Manhattan, someone set fire to New York City. The fire apparently broke out at midnight September 20 in a frame house along the waterfront near Whitehall Slip and was fanned by high winds. Only a shift in the wind kept the flames from engulfing the entire town—as it was, 493 houses between Broadway and the Hudson River were destroyed before British soldiers and sailors and the townspeople put out the flames. The British accused Washington of ordering the fire set, but no proof has ever been found. Forcing the British to crowd into basements and tents in the streets as cold weather arrived, the fire further slowed the reticent Howe's attack. All Washington would comment in a letter to his cousin Lund was, "Providence, or some good honest fellow, has done more for us than we were disposed to do for ourselves."[9]

It was late October before Howe was ready to attack again. By now, the British invasion from Canada had been fought to a standstill in the five-day naval Battle of Valcour Island on Lake Champlain, October 11–15.

Two-thirds of Arnold's makeshift flotilla had been destroyed or scuttled, but Arnold's fierce resistance and the months of delay he had imposed on the British to build a fleet had thwarted any British plan to link northern and southern New York invasions and cut off rebellious New England from the other colonies. Abandoning their march from Quebec at the walls of the key American fortress of Ticonderoga, the British stopped only long enough to rustle 150 cattle outside its walls and then sailed all the way back to Quebec as heavy snow fell.

At White Plains, New York, on October 28, Howe overtook Washington again. Still short of transport, Washington was busily trying to evacuate supplies. Howe had moved slowly north through Throg's Neck and Pell's Point in a slow race with Washington, who sent Stirling to hold White Plains. Howe's juggernaut passed through New Rochelle on October 21. With 13,000 men in two columns, he approached White Plains. Washington could have found better terrain father north, but he decided to hold the town. After an hour-long skirmish with a mixed force of American militia, Howe deployed his redcoats a mile in front of hastily built American fortifications, atop 180-foot-high Chatterton's Hill, their brilliant uniforms and glinting bayonets dazzling the Americans. The Hessians paused to build a pontoon bridge across the flooded Bronx River as the British unleashed a bayonet charge up the wooded slope. The assault was repulsed with heavy British and Hessian losses. Ultimately, Howe got his entire army across a ford downriver and marched north for an attack up the heights. Despite stout resistance by New York and Maryland troops, the British ignored American musket fire and grapeshot and finally routed the Americans after Massachusetts militia on the right flank were overrun by the Hessians under Colonel Johann Rall. Haslet's Delawares fought off two attacks before Washington ordered them to withdraw. Once again, the British claimed a technical victory by holding the field of battle; once again, protected by a storm, Washington slipped away. And, once again, the militia had run away and a complete rout had only been prevented by Continentals. Some of General Alexander McDougall's New York militia had not fired a shot.

As October ended, Howe gave up the chase and returned to the comforts of what remained of New York City, taking up residence at One Wall Street in the home of a rich Loyalist merchant. He turned over the task of mopping up pockets of American resistance to his subordinates. Plans for the 2,800-man American garrison of Fort Washington were sold to the British by a defecting young officer. The stronghold's crude earthworks at present-day West 184th Street at the northern tip of Manhattan had been held by two Pennsylvania regiments since July. The night of November 14, the British moved thirty flatboats of men upriver without the Americans taking notice. British and Hessian forces enveloped the fortress by midafternoon on the fifteenth. Washington made a personal reconnaissance from Fort Lee on the New Jersey shore with Putnam, Greene, and Hugh Mercer even as Lord Percy attacked the inner ring of defenses.

*T*he betrayal of the last American stronghold on Manhattan Island was the handiwork of William Demont, adjutant to Colonel Robert Magaw of the 5th Pennsylvania, in command at Fort Washington. Demont was English by birth. He had been appointed adjutant early in 1776 by the Pennsylvania Committee of Safety. On the night of November 2, 1776, Demont, described by a fellow officer Captain Alexander Graydon of Pennsylvania as "intelligent in point of duty," deserted the American lines and went to the camp of Lord Percy. As Demont attested in an attempt to win compensation from the British at war's end, "I sacrificed all I was worth in the world and brought with [me] the plans of Fort Washington. At the same time I may with justice affirm, from my knowledge of the works, I saved the lives of many of His Majesty's subjects." (The British government eventually allowed him £60, about the cost of his voyage back to England.) When the British assault came, the redcoats "must have had a perfect knowledge of the ground." Graydon suspected Demont, but it was too late. There was nothing Washington could do: he had to recross the river and watch in frustration through a telescope. The Hessians drove the Pennsylvanians inside the fort and then, despite heavy fire, they outflanked the fixed guns of the fort. As the Americans abandoned one battery after another under Hessian attack, Colonel Rall demanded the American surrender. By 4 P.M., the Americans marched out. Some 2,818 Americans were captured. Not only was the surrender a blow to morale but large quantities of equipment were lost. Four days later, the disaster repeated when a British-Hessian combined force crossed the Hudson and besieged Fort Lee on the New Jersey shore. This time, the Americans evacuated the fort, useless for controlling the Hudson without Fort Washington, but in their hasty withdrawal left behind 146 precious cannon, 2,800 muskets, and 400,000 cartridges.[10]

*B*y late November, British General Sir William Howe ordered a lightning British winter offensive, unleashing his boldest field commander, Earl Charles Cornwallis, with a handpicked force of 6,000 British grenadiers, light infantry, and Hessian grenadiers with heavy artillery. After descending on Fort Lee, Cornwallis quick-marched 4,000 men up the Raritan River Valley to cut off Washington's retreat from New York. For a month of sleepless nights and dogged, hungry days, the rebels were pursued from town to town across New Jersey. Washington had counted on Jerseymen to rise to his standard. But at the village of Newark, only 30 turned out to join the Americans. On that same day, 300 New Jerseyans joined the British.

As Cornwallis dispensed grapeshot to rebels and amnesty to Loyalists, the British occupied Hackensack, Newark, New Brunswick, Perth Amboy, Princeton, Trenton, and Bordentown; their skirmishers spread out ahead of the assault and reached the east bank of the Delaware River, within twelve miles of Philadelphia. "I tremble for Philadelphia," Washington wrote privately as he retreated across the Delaware into Bucks County with fewer than 3,000 men, all that remained of the confident 20,000-man force he had commanded only three months earlier. In a panic, Congress issued a series of pompous resolutions declaring that it wasn't really fleeing the capital, but then proceeded to bundle up its records and laundry and desert Philadelphia at the critical moment. All the signers of the Declaration of Independence were considered arch-traitors by the British, and while it would be another year before the signers made their names public, the Loyalists knew who they were. As the British moved forward they hunted the signers down.[11]

When the British occupied Princeton, they sacked all its houses. They saved especial wrath for Morven, the sprawling stone farmhouse of Declaration of Independence signer Richard Stockton. They burned its library, stole all of Stockton's furniture and belongings, then hauled Stockton himself off to the New York prison called the Provost, where they had fitted out a special section called Congress Hall for captured rebel leaders. Congress fled, first west, then south 110 miles to the town of Baltimore, and turned over dictatorial powers to Washington. Washington, who preferred to allow civilian control when there was a civil government to exert itself, now had his military duties compounded with civil responsibilities.

By now, though, much of the capital was deserted. As British troops tramped toward it on December 3, Philadelphia journalist Christopher Marshall scrawled tense entries in his notebook: "This city alarmed with the news of Howe's army . . . proceeding for this place. Drum beats a martial appearance; the shops shut, and all business except preparing to disappoint our enemies has been laid aside." Nine days later, Marshall noted that every able-bodied resident had been ordered "to go this day and assist in entrenching the city."[12]

*T*he overland attack could not have come at a worse time for Philadelphia. More than 3,000 of the city's best troops had been lost in the New York campaign, most of them having been captured at Fort Washington, a makeshift mud fort along the Hudson River in which they were bottled up. Nearly 1,500 more had contracted typhoid fever at the "flying camp," a reserve base in Perth Amboy, and had been brought back to Philadelphia to die. Among the sick and captured were many of the city's best artisans, shipwrights, carpenters, laborers, and apprentices, as well as the sons of many of the city's leading families. More than three out of four of the prisoners would die in filthy British prison ships and jails before the winter was over. Little revolutionary zeal remained in

Philadelphia by mid-December 1776. "Vigor and spirit alone can save us," clockmaker-turned-politician David Rittenhouse told his fellow members of Pennsylvania's hard-pressed Council of Safety. "There is no time for words. Exert yourselves like freemen."[13]

As Philadelphians loaded their wagons with bedding, furniture, and food and fled toward summer houses and relatives' farms and refugee camps as far west as Reading, Lancaster, and York, Washington tried to reassure the citizenry and stem the evacuation by sending in Major General Israel Putnam, the hero of the French and Indian War and, more recently, Bunker Hill, as military governor. The corpulent "Old Put," whose sneak march out of New York City had saved 5,000 Americans from capture, declared martial law in the city, ordered the execution of anyone caught setting fires, and rounded up all suspected Loyalists, whom he herded west along with the British prisoners in the area. Still, in a report dated December 12, Putnam had to report ruefully to Washington upriver at Bristol: "All things in this city remain in confusion."[14]

At his camp in Bucks County, Washington had to turn and face a threat from the rear. The Bucks County militia had turned out as ordered all right, but it turned Loyalist. Washington, still desperate for recruits, had to order it dismissed and dispersed. Writing to Virginia to his cousin Lund, in a letter he knew he would show to Martha, Washington said, "The game is pretty near up," but even so saying, he had begun to formulate one last bold turn of the cards. Weeks earlier, bottled up with the survivors of his routed army on Brooklyn Heights, Washington had detected a British flaw. Howe, he saw, had no trouble defeating him, but he did not follow up his battlefield victories. After a stunning victory, he would order his troops to stop, eat, rest, clean their weapons, and polish their brass—while the enemy slipped away. From this observation, the harried Washington stumbled onto an ingenious new strategy. By the time it became evident the British were aiming for Philadelphia, he wrote early in December, "Should they now really risk this undertaking, then there is a great probability that they will pay dearly for it, for I shall continue to retreat before them so as to lull them into security." After yielding all of New Jersey to the British, he would establish as formidable a line as possible along the western bank of the Delaware, and then rely on the puzzling lack of instinct for the jugular that characterized his enemy to give him more valuable time.[15]

Washington ordered all boats and barges along the Delaware for sixty miles seized and brought to the ferries near his Bucks County encampment; then he ranged his artillery along the western riverbanks and forced the British to extend their line of advance posts for thirty miles along the east bank of the river. The artillery repulsed British skirmishers with brisk fire if they ventured near the water. However, it would have been a relatively simple matter requiring scarcely another week for the British to gather wagons and haul their assault barges from the fleet in

New York overland for the attack on Philadelphia. Moreover, Loyalists pointed out a large supply of cut lumber at a lumberyard adjoining the British barracks in Trenton, but it was now mid-December, and the temperatures plummeted. The British decided to go into winter quarters and rest before the spring offensive to take Philadelphia.

For the Americans, it was an incredible piece of good fortune. Instead of imminent disaster, they could look ahead to several months of safety. What's more, Washington realized that despite the success the British had enjoyed in the campaign, they were now strung out along a 30-mile front—and vulnerable. In his official report to Lord George Germain, mastermind of the war effort, the British commander Howe said he had found the weather "too severe to keep the field," despite the fact that his men were far better clad, armed, and fed than the desperate Americans. "The troops will immediately march into quarters and hold themselves in readiness to assemble on the shortest notice," Howe assured Germain. But then he added a disquieting note, that "the chain [of outposts], I own, is too extensive."[16]

*C*ornwallis, eager to return to his wife in England for the winter, turned over the command in New Jersey to a cocky but thoroughly mediocre field officer, General James Grant. Grant sent the British troops back toward New York, and garrisoned the outposts with Hessians. The Hessian officer placed in command at Trenton, the British strongpoint nearest Washington's forces, was Colonel Johann Gottlieb Rall. It was his troops who slaughtered Americans as they tried to surrender on Long Island and again on the slopes around Fort Washington. A noisy, fastidious, hard-drinking gambler who spoke no English and scorned all Americans, Rall had trouble in Trenton from the outset. His 1,600 troops had a reputation for plunder and raping that worried even the British. Lord Howe's secretary, Ambrose Serle, had commented in his reports on their behavior during the fall offensive:

> It is impossible to express the devastations which [they] have made upon the houses & country seats of some of the rebels. All their furniture, glass, windows, and the very hangings of the rooms are demolished or defaced. This with the filth deposited in them makes them so offensive . . . that it is a penance to go into them."[17]

In mid-December, the Hessians in the 100-house village of Trenton, crowded into commandeered winter quarters, made the best of the monotony of winter garrison duty in the manner to which they were accustomed. One day an American patrol on the Pennsylvania riverbank heard a group of women calling for help. Rowing over, they learned that all of the women, including a fifteen-year-old girl, had been raped that morning by the invaders. Hessian brutality succeeded where all of Washington's appeals had failed. The fence-straddling Jersey farmers began to come over to the American side. Until now, they had refused to help the Americans, and had sought instead to protect their property by swearing allegiance to the king. They tacked red ribbons on their doors to mark their loyalty. Now, they angrily formed marauding militia bands that ambushed Hessian patrols and British scouting parties whenever they ventured outside the Trenton stronghold. Not a day passed that the Hessians didn't lose a few more men.

"We have not slept one night in peace since we came to this place," a Hessian officer bemoaned to his diary on Christmas Eve. So serious had the skirmishes become that Colonel Rall saw fit to send a 100-man escort with a letter to General Grant in which he complained that his position was "too much exposed." From his base camp at New Brunswick, Grant pooh-poohed the danger. He reassured Rall there were fewer than three hundred rebels in all New Jersey and that he had little to fear from Washington's men, who, according to his latest intelligence reports from Loyalists, were "almost naked, dying of cold, without blankets, and very ill-supplied with provisions."[18]

While Washington's tired army was anything but comfortable, its condition was not so dire as he had carefully led the British commander to believe. Indeed, for weeks Washington had shrewdly used spies to cultivate the myth of his army's impotence. One of the most effective members of Washington's fledgling secret service was a weaver named John Honeyman, who had been conscripted to serve with the British in the French and Indian Wars and had once been a bodyguard to General James Wolfe, conqueror of Quebec. He was eager to serve against the British now, though, and used their trust to provide vital information to Washington and misleading information to them. Posing as a cattle dealer and butcher, he lived in Griggstown, near Princeton, and, whenever he had information for Washington, he arranged to be captured by the Americans.

On December 22, he walked into a woods inside the American lines, cracking his bullwhip as if chasing cattle, attracting the attention of an American patrol that took him into custody. The patrol delivered its prisoner to Washington's headquarters. Washington excused the guards and closed the doors as Honeyman gave him detailed information on the Hessian forces and routines in Trenton. Washington then handed him a key to the guardhouse where he was to be locked up, and ordered him taken away. To pay for his spy network, Washington had appealed to one member of Congress, Robert Morris, who had not fled Philadelphia. Washington asked him to send him £150 in gold immediately on his own account and, if there was any way to raise it, $50,000 in the new Continental money to pay his troops a bounty to stay on past the expiration of their enlistments. Morris knew that the only people in Philadelphia with that kind of money were the rich Quaker merchants. They would not lend money directly to the war effort, but they would loan it to Morris personally. What he did with it, of course, was up to him. Soon canvas bags began to arrive at Washington's headquarters with the cash he needed to carry out his bold plan.

By now, Washington had decided to attempt what no one, British or American, believed possible. He would attack, and attack quickly, before the enlistments of his best Continental troops expired at midnight December 31. By this bold, almost foolhardy, stroke he hoped to keep his army from melting away. Perhaps he couldn't give them the pay, clothing, and equipment they needed, but he could give them what they had come for: a chance to attack the enemy. He may even have felt he was giving them more—a small but real opportunity to win.

On the morning of December 24, Dr. Benjamin Rush of Philadelphia, another member of Congress who had remained behind, rode out to William McKonkey's handsome three-story stone house on the Delaware to visit Washington, who appeared to be "much depressed." Rush reassured the general that Congress was behind him all the way, if at a considerable distance, and as Rush held forth, Washington kept scribbling on small pieces of paper. One fell to the floor. Rush picked it up and read, "Victory or Death."[19]

It was the watchword for Washington's boldest gamble: an all-out, do-or-die attack on Trenton while its garrison slept off the effects of its Christmas celebration. If he won, Washington foresaw that he would inspire the lagging Patriots, cow the Loyalists, encourage enlistments and reenlistments, drive back the British from the approaches to Philadelphia, and keep the Revolution alive. He had no illusions left. If he lost, Washington felt, the American cause was dead.

The suggestion for the surprise attack seems to have come from Benedict Arnold, whose brilliant battle against a British naval squadron on Lake Champlain in October had forced the British to abandon their march south from Canada for another year. When the British northern army retreated to winter quarters in Quebec Province, Arnold and Gates had quick-marched Pennsylvania troops freed from the defense at Fort Ticonderoga to reinforce Washington's decimated columns.

At the same time, Philadelphia's Brigadier General John Cadwalader had recruited 1,800 Pennsylvania militia to attack directly across the river at Trenton, and Brigadier General James Ewing was to strike Trenton from the south to cut off retreat by the Hessians. Washington had learned from bitter experience not to rely on militia. His principal reliance had to be on the main assault force, which he would lead himself. It was made up entirely of toughened American veterans—regulars from Virginia, Delaware, Maryland, and New England. And it was led by reliable officers: Henry Knox, Nathanael Greene, James Monroe, John Sullivan, John Glover, and William Washington. The future leaders of America's army and republic were huddled around McKonkey's Ferry that frigid afternoon of December 25, 1776, as Washington gave his marching orders. The men had eaten uncured beef the day before and repaired their shoes with strips of the raw hides. Many wore capes made out of their blankets and kept warm only by pounding their feet and slapping themselves with their crossed arms.

Washington had decided to fortify the resolve of his soldiers by an unusual method. He was counting on a splendid piece of oratory provided at exactly the right moment by journalist Thomas Paine, who had been writing essays for weeks on a drumhead in General Greene's tent as the American army retreated across New Jersey. Hurrying to Philadelphia in mid-December, Paine had the first copies of *The American Crisis* printed on December 19. Now, as the troops prepared to get in the boats to be rowed across the ice-clogged river in a swirling snow squall on Christmas night, Washington ordered his commanders to read the essay to his men.

> These are the times that try men's souls. The summer soldier and the sunshine patriot will, in this crisis, shrink from the service of their country; but he that stands it *now*, deserves the love and thanks of man and woman. Tyranny, like hell, is not easily conquered; yet we have this consolation with us, that the harder the conflict, the more glorious the triumph.

Solemnly, the men heaved the heavy artillery pieces into the nine-foot-wide, sixty-foot-long Durham iron-ore barges Washington had seized the week before. Silently, they pushed the horses aboard and waded through the freezing water, huddling for warmth as Massachusetts seamen under Colonel John Glover poled the encumbered craft carefully through the ice floes to the Jersey shore. A nineteen-year-old officer, Major James Wilkinson, would never forget the scene, noting in his journal that footprints down to the river were "tinged here and there with blood from the feet of the men who wore broken shoes."[20]

Jut-jawed Marblehead ship captain John Glover, who had managed the cool retreat of Washington's vanquished army by boat under the British guns at Long Island, ordered the first boatloads to push off from McKonkey's Ferry at two in the afternoon, into the storm. By evening a faint wintry moon overshadowed the operations, the wind was rising, and the ice floes could be heard crunching against the awkward barges. By eleven o'clock, snow and sleet slashed into the boatmen's eyes: "It was as severe a night as I ever saw," Delaware officer Thomas Rodney remembered later.[21]

On the Jersey side, General Washington, wrapped in his cape, sat grimly, quietly on a crate, talking softly from time to time to his men. By 4 A.M., after fourteen terrible hours, they were all across, and the commanders formed them into ranks. Washington personally urged them on, as they moved out down the River Road. The wind, howling by now, drove in from the northeast. "Press on, boys, press on," Washington urged from his tall chestnut horse. "Soldiers, keep by your officers, for God's sake, keep by your officers." Two men sat down by the roadside to rest—and froze to death. Tramping silently past darkened farmhouses, the force divided into two columns at Birmingham. Greene's division swung off to the east to skirt the town. Sullivan's men trudged due south along the River Road straight for the main Hessian barracks on King Street. A courier raced up to Washington, informing him that Sullivan had noticed his men's gunpowder was soaked and useless. Washington told his aide, Colonel Samuel Webb of Connecticut, "Tell General Sullivan to use the bayonet. I am resolved to take Trenton." Captain Rodney wrote his father, Congressman Caesar Rodney, "I have never seen Washington so determined as he is now."[22]

It was a cruel ten-mile march before they reached the outskirts of Trenton, where, incredibly, word of their approach had been ignored by the Hessian commander. As was his habit, Rall had eaten heartily and late, then adjourned for an evening of cards with a few aides and his host, a mysterious figure named Abraham Hunt, who had a way of getting along with both sides. When a uniformed servant answered the front door shortly after midnight and found a shivering Loyalist from Bucks County with a message for Rall, the Hessian refused to be disturbed. Before disappearing into the storm, the informer left a note that the American army was marching on Trenton. The servant gave it to Rall, who, without reading it, tucked it into his waistcoat pocket, and continued playing cards. Rall and all but a few Hessian pickets were asleep the next morning when the first American units, already an hour behind schedule, double-timed toward the town.

One mile north of Trenton, Washington ordered Greene to halt a few minutes to give Sullivan's column time to reach its target, the barracks. At precisely eight o'clock, Sullivan's advance guard arrived and rushed Hessian lieutenant Andreas Widerhold's ten pickets. At three minutes after eight, Washington heard the firing to his right, indicating Sullivan was attacking. He ordered his advance force to storm the town. The sun had been up for half an hour. Having difficulty making out the surging Americans through the wind-driven snow, the Hessian pickets, dropping their knapsacks, took up posts behind fences and returned the fire until they were overrun by a horde of Americans, who were now treated for the first time to the sight of Hessians turning and running for their lives.

By now the Americans were pouring into the town and driving back the Hessians with their bayonets. The Americans charged into houses, clambered upstairs, and watched as the groggy Hessians awoke. Some Hessian units threw on their coats and attempted to form up in the streets. Then the Americans opened fire. The mercenaries were cut down by shattering sheets of grapeshot sent slashing from both ends of the town by Henry Knox's batteries of six-pounders firing from the ends of Trenton's two main streets. The Hessians sought cover behind houses but were driven back from house to house by General Hugh Mercer's sharpshooters, now racing in from the west. Hessian artillerymen managed to get off thirteen rounds before the deadly American crossfire silenced them. Half the Hessian cannoneers were dead, along with most of their horses.

Running from the Hunt house, Rall jumped on his horse and lashed it down an alley toward his regiment, by now formed into ranks and marching down King Street into the hail of grapeshot. "Lord, Lord, what is it, what is it?" Rall kept shouting in German as he tried futilely to regroup his men and form them for a desperation bayonet charge. But the Hessians broke and ran even as the brigade band kept playing its fifes, bugles, and drums. Rall was hit twice. The first was only a slight wound in the side, but he was bleeding badly. His aides helped him off his horse and half-carried him into the sanctuary of the Queen Street Methodist Church.[23]

Completely demoralized, many of their officers killed or wounded, and almost totally disorganized, the Hessians' best regiments, the Rall and Lossberg, surrendered. The remaining officers put their hats on their swords, the corporals lowered their flags, and the infantry men grounded their arms. One more regiment, the Knyphausen, tried to fight its way out, even though its commander, Major von Dechow, also had been fatally wounded and, seeing the others surrender, had given the surrender order. His officers refused, however, and led their men across the shoulder-deep Assunpink Creek. On the far shore they were surrounded and shelled by artillery at point-blank range. General Arthur St. Clair shouted to a Hessian captain, "Tell your commanding officer that if you do not surrender immediately, I will blow you to pieces." The Hessians said they would—if they could keep their swords and their baggage. The two officers shook hands. The Battle of Trenton was over. Galloping off to find Washington, Major Wilkinson reported the capitulation. Washington gave him a rare smile and grasped his hand: "Major Wilkinson, this is a glorious day for our country!"[24]

Washington had little time to celebrate: a hasty council of war with his officers brought the sobering fact that a fourth Hessian regiment had escaped and would now alert Count Karl von Donop's force of Hessians at Princeton. It was painfully obvious to Washington that he either had to attack Princeton swiftly or turn around and, with 948 Hessian prisoners, slog back upriver and recross into Pennsylvania. Even though they had suffered only four casualities to the two hundred Hessians killed and wounded, Washington decided his men were in no shape to take on a fresh, angry, entrenched force of Hessians that day. He ordered his weary men to gather the Hessian supplies, weapons (including sixty howitzers), and prisoners—and head back to McKonkey's Ferry.

In the fading daylight, they began the twelve-hour process of recrossing the river. By now it was so cold the Hessians and Americans had to stamp their feet in time in the boats to break up the new ice that was forming and slowing down the boats. In the bitter cold, three more men froze to death. After forty-eight hours without food and twenty-five miles of marching, the Continental troops collapsed into their tents. The next day the Hessians were marched south toward Philadelphia to the tune of their own marching band. The sight of all those ranks of neatly groomed prisoners tramping in cadence under the guns of their ragtag, shambling guards did more for American morale than any sight in months.

Washington was not completely thrilled with the day's work. Philadelphia's militia had not shown up for the Battle of Trenton. Cadwalader and Ewing marched as far as the river, saw the ice floes, figured Washington wouldn't risk an attack in such a storm, and pitched camp. Cadwalader's failure to cut off the Hessian retreat at Trenton was a major factor in the events of the grim week that followed. Finally crossing the river when the storm abated on December 27, Cadwalader sent word to Washington that he was now in position with 1,500 men to join the attack—which was, of course, over. It was Cadwalader's absence that had forced Washington to recross the Delaware to protect the Pennsylvania and New Jersey militia or leave them to be slaughtered by the infuriated British and Hessians.

Stung by the Trenton attack, Cornwallis left his ship and his luggage and, with a picked force of battle-seasoned grenadiers and light infantry raced across New Jersey to join von Donop's Hessians in a retaliatory attack. Preparing to cross the Delaware once more to meet him, Washington also had to face the possibility that his army would evaporate. While he had offered a $10 bounty—almost two months' pay for a private—he was having little luck in getting the soldiers of his victorious army to reenlist. Almost half of Washington's 2,400 men had gone home by December 29. No bread and meat had been brought to feed the stalwart remnant of his army, now down to 6 percent of its strength the previous summer. Nor was that the only crisis. The ice was too thin to march across the river and Colonel Glover's Marblehead fishermen had marched home to find more lucrative jobs privateering.

With one day in the enlistments of his Continental soldiers remaining, Washington announced he was going to attack again, whether the regulars were with him or not. Lining up his men, he talked to them softly. One man said later that Washington spoke "in the most affectionate manner, entreating us to stay." When he was finished, he rode off to one side while the regimental commanders asked each man willing to reenlist to step forward. No one moved. Wheeling his horse around, the embarrassed Washington poured out one last appeal to his embarrassed men:

You have done all I asked you to do, and more than could be reasonably expected. But your country is at stake, your wives, your homes and all that you hold dear. You have worn yourselves out with fatigues and hardships, but we know not how to spare you. If you will consent to stay only one month longer, you will render that service to the cause of liberty and to your country which you probably never can do under any other circumstance.

He closed by saying the army that day faced "the crisis which is to decide our destiny," then rode off to one side again.[25]

At first, no one moved. Then a few men began to look at each other. One lone veteran stepped forward, then a few more, then others, until only the very sick held back. By the end of the day, 1,200 men had accepted the bounty and reenlisted.

Washington had taken a bolder step than most imagined: he had pledged a bounty without consent of Congress. But, as he wrote its president, John Hancock, "What could be done?" And the men wanted their money immediately. Fortunately and incredibly, Robert Morris kept the sacks of money coming from Quaker Philadelphia: 410 Spanish silver dollars, two English crowns, half a French crown, 1,072 English shillings, all the hard money he could find in the city, much of it plucked in fines from pacifist Quakers who refused to turn out and drill at the weekly musters and instead paid the equivalent of a day's wages in hard money. Fortunately, too, Congress from the safety of Baltimore agreed with Washington and sent along the necessary resolutions giving him authority to take "whatever he may want for the use of the Army." That gave him carte blanche to commandeer food, clothing, livestock, anything his men could find in their line of march, an open authorization to loot Loyalist and Quaker property.[26]

As the British army drew up its lines across from the Americans on a three-mile line along the south bank of Assunpink Creek just outside Trenton late on January 2, 1777, Washington saw that he had left himself no chance to retreat if things went badly for him the next day. He also saw that the British were about to make their characteristic mistake— resting before going into battle. Washington ordered a rear guard to continue noisily digging trenches within the hearing of Cornwallis's pickets all night and ordered them to pile firewood on the roaring campfires. But he formed the main body of his troops into three columns and sent them silently marching off under cover of darkness around the British right flank to attack the British rear guard in Princeton.

The effect of the news of the victory at Trenton was now also taking hold on the populace at large. Militia volunteers began to swarm to the American standard. In addition to Cadwalader's 1,600 troops, General Thomas Mifflin rounded up 1,600 more eager Pennsylvania and New

Jersey recruits. Washington ordered them to join him in Trenton to face the British. One more piece of good luck came Washington's way. As Colonel Joseph Reed led his small detachment of Philadelphia Light Horse toward Princeton and his rendezvous with Cadwalader, he followed a little-known local route called the Quaker Road. While on it, he stumbled upon twelve dismounted British dragoons looting a house. Reed took them prisoner. Interrogated separately, they gave up the information that 6,000 Hessians and British were marching on Princeton, and that Howe had dispatched another 1,000 men from New York several days before.[27]

The message arrived almost simultaneously with word that Cornwallis had led a forced one-day, 50-mile march by 1,000 redcoats from Perth Amboy to Princeton and was spending the night at Morven, the abandoned Princeton home of Declaration of Independence signer Richard Stockton, preparing "to bag the fox the next morning." The British quartermaster general, Sir William Erskine, argued that they should strike immediately. "If Washington is the general I take him to be," he told Cornwallis, "his army will not be found there in the morning." Cornwallis, however, dismissed this advice, again using his favorite metaphor: "We've got the old fox safe now," he assured Erskine. "We'll go over and bag him in the morning." Morning found Cornwallis wrong. The American trenches were empty, the fires smoldering low, the roads frozen, and Washington gone.[28]

Washington had split his force, sending the main column along the little-used Quaker Road, the wheels of the cannon wrapped in blankets to deaden the sound. In its vanguard was General Hugh Mercer, his close friend from Fredericksburg and partner in western land schemes, a tough 52-year-old doctor turned soldier, with 350 veterans from Virginia, Delaware, and Maryland. Just after dawn, the column ran into British lieutenant colonel Charles Mawhood's crack troops, the 17th and 55th Regiments, marching to reinforce Cornwallis at Trenton. The British were not expecting to meet the Americans. Henry Knox reported later, "I believe they were as much astonished as if an army had dropped perpendicularly upon them."

Mawhood, riding a pony and escorted by his pet dogs, reacted quickly, however. He sent the lead element of his troops running across Stony Brook Bridge after what appeared to be a small party of Americans. At the same moment, Mercer turned his men to engage them, cutting through an orchard on the William Clark farm. At forty yards, the British opened fire. The Americans answered with their rifles and canister shot fired from two cannons hastily lugged up a hillside through foot-deep snow. Though badly outnumbered, the Americans held off the British for about ten minutes. But the American rifles took much longer than British muskets to load, and Mawhood, seeing this, ordered a bayonet charge. Breaking into a run, the long line of red-coated regulars charged over the forty yards and, yelling and swearing, bayoneted their way through the orchard.

Mercer's horse was shot from under him. "Surrender, you damn rebel," the British soldiers yelled, mistaking Mercer for Washington. Instead, Mercer drew his sword and slashed about him until a British grenadier smashed him in the head with the butt of his musket, dropping Mercer to his knees. The redcoats bayoneted him in the stomach, legs, and arms seven times—and left him dead. Trying to rally the Americans, Colonel John Haslet, last of the 550 Delaware Blues who had marched off to New York six months before, was killed by a shot through the head.[29]

But now American reinforcements started to stream over the hill and through the field. General John Sullivan, who had been marching a parallel route toward Princeton, and who had been well beyond Mercer when news reached him of Mawhood's attack, turned back. As he did so, he ran hard into the 55th British Regiment, sent by Mawhood to intercept him. The two forces deadlocked. Cadwalader also came up with his raw militia, but as the militiamen came up beside the veterans under Sullivan and were met by the full force of British artillery firing at close range, the Philadelphia militia ran for their lives.

Still, back at the Clark farm it was a handful of the Philadelphia Associators, who were also militiamen, who prevented a rout from becoming a major American disaster. One Philadelphia artillery officer in Mercer's column, Captain Joseph Moulder, managed to swing two guns into position on the edge of the woods near the Clark farmhouse itself. He opened fire on four British guns and a company of British light infantry as they formed for a second bayonet charge at the reconstituted American position. Those two guns slamming grapeshot at close range stopped the British attack just long enough for Lieutenant Thomas Rodney to bring up a score of militiamen to support the gun emplacement whose fire kept the British on the defensive. The fire also afforded just enough time for Washington to arrive on the scene. He rode up and down in the woods among the panicked militia, "Parade with us, my brave fellows!" he shouted above the smoke and din. "There is but a handful of the enemy and we will have them directly."

Slowly, the militia men began to fall into line around him, joined by the remains of Mercer's men, who had fallen back. Soon New England troops came along and Washington himself led the small force in a bayonet charge, riding ahead, his hat in his hand, waving them onward. Forcing the British to shift to the left, he edged closer to their murderous fire with an ever-lengthening American line. Washington told the Americans to hold their fire until he gave the signal. Then he screamed his order: "Halt! . . . Fire!" Two thundering volleys followed, one from each side, and when the acrid blue-smoke rose, Washington's aides were amazed to see the American commander still on his horse and still waving his troops forward.

For the first time, American troops, mostly raw recruits, were charging from three sides against regular British troops and keeping up an incessant fire. The spectacle unnerved the British. They slowly gave way, then turned in panic and bolted from the field. The Americans, finally realizing what they had done, broke into a cheer and pursued them all the way into Princeton. "It's a fine fox chase, boys," Washington shouted over his shoulder. Falling in with the Philadelphia Light Horse, Washington led the chase momentarily, then ordered his men to take time to scoop up the gear the British had left in their wake.[30]

Mawhood was able to regroup some of his regulars, who were now trapped between what had originally been the Sullivan and Mercer columns. They turned and bayoneted their way through a portion of the American line and ran away over the hills nearby. When Sullivan's men stormed into the town, the British, including some of the best troops in the British army, fled their redoubts and barricaded themselves inside Nassau Hall at the College of New Jersey (now Princeton University). It was the largest building in America and solidly built of stone. It should have been easily defensible, but when Captain Moulder and Lieutenant Alexander Hamilton wheeled up their six-pound field guns to begin blasting away at the building and when an angry Princetonian named James Monroe (whose house had been looted by the British) led the storming of the front door and when a cannonball crashed through the hall, beheading the portrait of King George I, all at about the same time, the terrified British threw down their guns and surrendered.

The Battle of Princeton was over. It was a smashing success for Washington and a humiliating debacle for the British. More than that, the Revolution was alive again. Washington could safely march into winter camp. And could he dare to hope that he could recruit and train a permanent army? Now would the French stop their diplomatic flirtation with the Americans and openly send aid? In fact, when Benjamin Franklin, the new American emissary to the court of King Louis XVI at Versailles, announced the twin American victories at Trenton and Princeton, the French dispatched four shiploads of guns together with the best gunpowder in the world, developed by chemist Antoine Lavoisier. The campaign of 1776, which had begun in overconfidence, which had survived defeat, despair, and bitter experience, now came to a jubilant end. The United States of America now existed in fact as well as on paper.

A change in British strategy was immediate and obvious. Howe pulled back from the outposts in New Jersey all the way to New York, leaving only an outpost at Perth Amboy. Never again would the British try to hold large portions of the countryside. Their concept became to capture the coastal cities and, from these defensible bastions, try to dominate the countryside. Washington's bold do-or-die stroke had changed the conflict into a war of posts. The countryside, where the majority of Americans lived, was his.

Fifteen

As soon as news of Washington's victories at Trenton and Princeton reached England, the British government, at the zenith of its incompetence, set to work to compound its errors. By summer 1777 the beginnings of an even grander British strategy began to emanate from Lord George Germain's colonial ministry offices in Whitehall. The plan was as old as warfare: divide and conquer. General John Burgoyne, who had marched south with Carleton from Canada in 1776, had prepared a strategy that would divide the rebellious colonies by attacking down the Hudson River from Canada at the same time as striking northward from New York City and eastward through the Mohawk Valley from Fort Niagara. This would split off incendiary New England from the other colonies: without the head of the rattlesnake, the body would die. The armies would meet victoriously in Albany where, supposedly, America would surrender. It was a good plan when drawn on maps in London and seemed brilliant when frustrated playwright "Gentleman Johnny" Burgoyne performed it before the King's Privy Council. What neither Burgoyne nor Germain, in overall command of the Ministry's war effort, imagined was that a simple omission could destroy it. Germain didn't bother to send off a positive written order in time to Sir William Howe, in command of the expeditionary force in New York City, to cooperate with Burgoyne. This left Howe free, in his own mind at least, to act as he saw fit.

Not unlike the British high command in London, Washington could not really be sure what Howe had in mind when, on July 22, he crowded 17,000 of his best troops aboard 267 ships with their horses, artillery, and supplies and sailed from New York harbor. Howe's brother Richard, Lord Howe, admiral of the British fleet on the American station, gave orders to sail to Delaware Bay by a long, circuitous route, feinting first northward to confuse Washington into thinking they were attacking up the Hudson in support of Burgoyne. Washington had to worry which way the vast expeditionary force was heading. He already knew that Burgoyne had easily taken Ticonderoga on July 5 and was advancing southward. Should he keep his own army split or join Gates and the Northern Army? For six days, the huge British fleet disappeared from view while Washington waited in agony for intelligence reports. Then, on July 29, American lookouts in makeshift towers along the southern New Jersey coast spotted sails far at sea.

Long before they took ship, the Howe brothers had learned from their Loyalist spies that the Delaware River, the broad water route from the Atlantic to Philadelphia, the rebel capital and America's leading seaport, had been heavily fortified. The Howes sailed into the bay and then, in another surprise maneuver, led their armada out to sea again and south to the Chesapeake, finally depositing the army three weeks later at Head of Elk, Maryland, only sixty miles south of Philadelphia. There, thousands of Loyalists were supposed to be waiting to flock to the royal standard. Instead, Howe found that the "old fox," Washington, had quick-marched his 11,000-man army some 150 miles from the Watchung Mountains of northwestern New Jersey through Philadelphia and on south through Wilmington to face him. The soldiers had worn sprigs of hemlock in their hats to symbolize their hope of keeping the British out of the capital as they marched past Independence Hall.

By now, Washington was beginning to know his man. There was little chance that Howe would move north toward Philadelphia quickly. Indeed, many of Howe's men were in only slightly better condition than their dead horses, whose legs had been shattered in the holds of the ships. For five weeks the British army had roasted aboard the fetid ships in woolen uniforms: sick, exhausted, half-starved on salted sea rations, the redcoats and their Hessian auxiliaries needed rest before they could lug their gear north in the steamy late summer heat. There was also the need to commandeer hundreds of horses—at least enough for the officers to ride and to pull the heavy guns and hundreds of supply wagons. Two more weeks were lost. It was September before Howe finally began to move north through drenching downpours over rough hilly country that turned to muck underfoot. He decided to leave most of his supplies under heavy guard at Elkton so he could march quickly. He was harried all the way in a dogged retreating campaign by that master of the retrograde maneuver, George Washington.

Washington halted his retreat at Brandywine Creek, near the border between present-day Delaware and Pennsylvania. He intended to stop the British as he had at Trenton. Instead of the bold, surprising tactical sleight of hand he had practiced in the New Jersey counterattack, this time he intended to engage the British in a set-piece, European-style battle. The question of whether he really hoped to win at Brandywine is open to debate. Almost all Americans by late 1777 considered the fall of

Philadelphia inevitable. What he may have had in mind was to delay the British occupation of Philadelphia. To him, the capital was less important than keeping his army in the field to support Congress until aid could be enlisted from England's ancient rival, the French. Secondarily, Washington wished to engage Howe so that the British could not join forces on the Hudson. Reinforcing forts just south of the city along the Delaware River was part of Washington's overall strategy of pinning down Howe's army even if he didn't expect to be able to keep the British out of the capital. Once again, his goal was to keep the enemy divided, never risking an attack unless he was sure he could win.

Most important at the moment was to keep Howe from marching any farther inland. At least half of America's iron industry and much of its agriculture were in the hill counties to the west of Philadelphia. There were 250 mills along Darby and Ridley Creeks alone and scores of furnaces and forges in the rich hinterlands of Bucks, Delaware, Berks, and Lancaster counties. And there were major arm depots at Reading and Valley Forge bulging with munitions from France. A steady flow of arms including artillery and muskets culled from French arsenals had been arriving with tons of gunpowder and bales of cotton for uniforms since spring. Some eighty ships had cleared Bordeaux alone, bound for American ports or Caribbean islands where American ships waited to run through the leaky British navy blockade. Ultimately, when it came to a choice of defending these resources or Philadelphia, Washington had no trouble deciding to abandon the city. To Howe, there also was no choice involved. His main target was not only the rebel capital but the colonies' leading seaport. Washington surely would try to defend it. Howe could crush the main rebel army and end the war. Even Howe's severest critics later admired the speed and precision with which he went about his self-appointed mission.

The opposing forces at Brandywine Creek were about even in strength. Washington deployed Nathanael Greene's Continental division and "Mad Anthony" Wayne's Pennsylvania brigade at Chadd's Ford with most of Knox's artillery. Half a mile downstream, John Armstrong's Pennsylvania militia guarded his left flank. As soon as Washington retreated behind his strong, prepared works at Chadd's Ford at 4:30 the morning of September 11, Howe sent General Knyphausen and his 5,000 Hessian veterans straight against the center of the American line. The roar of the Hessians' guns fooled Washington into believing that this was the entire British force. Meanwhile, Howe and Cornwallis were leading 7,500 crack British troops up the Brandywine for fifteen miles. They crossed well beyond the American lines and, in a mirror image of the maneuver so successful at Long Island, marched around the American right flank. In fact, Washington had warned one of his best generals, John Sullivan of New Hampshire, who occupied the position of honor on the right flank, to watch for such a maneuver. But it was a foggy, rainy morning in those wooded hills and valleys, and even though Sullivan was tipped off by the locals that the British were coming around behind him, he ignored the warning, convinced that the Quaker farmers were all Loyalists on the side of the British. One of these farmers was a determined country gentleman, Squire Thomas Cheyney. After getting nowhere with Sullivan, he carried his warning on to Washington. Unfortunately, Washington had already received a message from Sullivan that the warning was a false alarm.

When the British advance guard of riflemen under Major Patrick Ferguson and Loyalists of the Queen's Rangers made contact with Washington's covering force at Chadd's Ford, the British were able to push Maxwell's New Jersey brigade across the ford and take up high ground in the woods. They fired down at reinforcements Washington sent to recross the creek—two Virginia regiments of riflemen—to buttress Maxwell. Oddly, by 11 o'clock, after nearly eight hours of cannonading, Knyphausen still was making no attempt to attack in force across the creek at the center of the lines. By this time, Washington had learned there was sufficient gunfire from the vicinity of Birmingham Meeting House to the west to explain why—and to confirm Cheyney's intelligence. Washington set off at once to meet what he was now convinced was the main British attack. He was almost too late.

Amazingly, once again the British blew their chance for total victory by hesitating at the pivotal moment. Cornwallis's flanking force was only one mile from enveloping the American right wing and was already firing from behind Washington's lines when the British stopped for a late lunch. This gave Washington a chance to reinforce the battered right wing under Sullivan. Setting out himself with Lafayette at his side and with Weedon's Virginians toward the Meeting House, Washington sent Greene ahead with Maxwell's and Stephen's regiments. In an incredible four-mile double-time march through thick underbrush and fog, they traveled from Chadd's Ford to Birmingham in only forty-five minutes and were lined up behind a stone wall and unlimbering their field artillery when the British lunch hour ended. The Americans now absorbed a terrible pounding from heavier British guns and withstood bayonet charges for more than an hour. When Washington arrived with newly minted Major General Lafayette and Weedon's Virginians at 5:30, he deployed them on his exposed right just in time to blunt a bayonet charge by the Grenadier Guards. Washington and the young Frenchman trotted up and down the line swinging their swords and cheering on the men. Once again, Washington proved bulletproof under intense fire but Lafayette fell from his horse, shot through the thigh. A bare-bones 170-man Virginia regiment under Colonel Thomas Marshall protected Washington's artillery while it kept up a murderously accurate point-blank fire at the charging British. Washington slowly and neatly disengaged and retreated at dusk.

By this time, after nearly fourteen hours of combat, even the diversionary Hessian attack at Chadd's Ford was beginning to succeed. Knyphausen drove across the creek and attacked Wayne's Pennsylvanians, pushing them back. Wayne fought back marvelously with the aid of a half-mad Polish cavalryman named Count Casimir Pulaski. Their rearguard tactics slowed the British drive across the ford until Washington arrived on the scene and reorganized his men. Then, in the darkness, the weary, hungry Americans marched fifteen miles to Chester Heights to the northwest. Some eight hundred Americans had been killed or wounded and four hundred captured in this all-day stand-up fight against the best British and Hessian troops. While the British were the technical victors because they held the field of battle at day's end, they had failed in Howe's main objective: to destroy Washington's army. Once again, Washington escaped and now successfully kept himself between Howe and the American supply bases. And once again, at this crucial moment, the British did not pursue him. It was another two weeks before Cornwallis and his chosen troops managed to slip between Washington and Philadelphia, crossing the Schuylkill River at night over a pontoon bridge. But by then Washington was insisting that he could march no more: 1,000 of his men were barefoot after 140 miles of hard marching in heavy rains that rotted shoe leather and exhausted his hungry men.

When British advance units marched into the capital, Washington began to come under fire of a different sort: criticism from Congress, which had fled west to Reading and then 110 miles to York, as well as from foreign observers. John Adams wrote in his diary that he was disgusted by Washington's "timorous defensive part which has involved us in so many disasters." Elias Boudinot, commissary of prisoners writing from Washington's camp to his brother in New Jersey, complained that the army had "never fired a gun" to defend the capital. A newly arrived French volunteer, the Baron de Kalb, reported to officials in Paris that Washington was "too slow, even indolent" and "much too weak: if he gains any brilliant action he will always owe it more to fortune or to the faults of his adversary than to his own capacity."[1]

While Washington withdrew his main force beyond reach of Howe to reequip and rest at Reading in the mountains of Berks County, he sent Wayne and his Pennsylvanians to harry Howe's rear as the British marched triumphantly toward Philadelphia. Constant skirmishes with Wayne led Howe to order Major General Charles "No Flint" Grey to turn and punish the Pennsylvanians. Grey was a twenty-year veteran who had fought in Scotland, at Minden and in the West Indies, had twice been wounded in the king's service, and had nothing but scorn for rebels, as his bayonet charges at Culloden had bloodily demonstrated. At Paoli, twenty miles west of Philadelphia, at one o'clock on the morning of September 20, Grey, with his aide Major John André at his side, ordered his troops to fix bayonets and remove the flints from their muskets. The British were to attack in three waves: light infantry—cavalry—first with sabers, then infantry with bayonets, and then the Black Watch with claymores, sabers, knives, and bayonets. André carried Grey's orders from company commander to company commander, telling the men to be absolutely silent and not to fire a shot. "Firing will discover us to the enemy. By not firing, we know the foe to be wherever fire happens."

The Americans were just waking up and preparing for their own dawn attack on the British rear. They had lit bonfires in front of makeshift huts and were cooking a quick breakfast before forming up. Wayne was dragging his guns across the camp when Grey's 2d Battalion of Light Infantry swept through the camp in a saber charge. Before the Americans could grab their guns the British infantry huzzahed and charged and then the Black Watch finished the job, methodically stabbing men who tried to surrender and setting fire to huts where some Americans cowered to escape the bayonets. André described the grisly scene accurately and matter-of-factly in his journal:

> The picket was surprised and most of them killed in endeavoring to retreat. On approaching the right of the camp, we perceived the line of fires, and the cavalry being ordered to form in the front, we rushed along the line, putting to the bayonet all they came up with and overtaking the main herd of the fugitives, stabbed great numbers. . . . Near 200 must have been killed and a great number wounded.

Occasionally brilliant but characteristically careless, Wayne had left weak pickets and blazing bonfires to guide the attacking British. In what became known as the Paoli Massacre, patriot propagandists attempted to portray the bloody commando raid as a horrible instance of British bestiality in combat. In fact, in retaliation, Wayne himself would carry out a night bayonet attack on the British at Stony Point in July 1779 in exactly the same manner and, only a few weeks after Paoli, refused to take prisoners when Washington counterattacked.[2]

*I*f Sir William Howe had hoped that he would now be free to dine and dance in snug winter quarters in the brick town houses of Philadelphia, Washington was not yet ready to leave him undisturbed in the capital. He first marched to Reading in mountains fifty miles west of the city and, at his main supply base, reoutfitted his men and refilled their cartridge boxes—400,000 cartridges had been ruined in the rain because of shoddy workmanship of the cartridge boxes. Then he was eager to fight again. While he kept his army out of reach, he sent out calls for help. Some 900 men rushed from the Hudson Highlands. Morgan's riflemen disengaged from the fighting at Saratoga and joined Washington at his new base at present-day Schwenksville. Two thousand raw recruits hurried from western Virginia under command of the troublesome Adam Stephen, Washington's nemesis since Fort Necessity. From New Jersey, William "Scotch Willie" Maxwell brought a brigade of the New Jersey Line and 1,000 Massachusetts men joined the replenished army around Pennypacker's Mill. Each man was ordered to make up forty cartridges. Fresh beef filled their bellies; hides covered bare feet. From all over eastern Pennsylvania and the Allegheny hills recruits, 1,000 of them, quickmarched to reinforce Wayne's battered Pennsylvania Line and avenge Paoli. Only three weeks after his failure at Brandywine, Washington was ready to counterattack.

He knew he must move quickly. On September 26th, as Cornwallis led his crack British grenadiers into Philadelphia, Washington learned from intercepted letters that Howe had sent off some 3,000 redcoats on the long march south to Head of Elk to bring up the supply wagons and that he was detaching a strong force to join a British navy attempt to take the American forts on the Delaware. The defenses on both shores coupled with the row galleys and gunboats of the Pennsylvania Navy were making British resupply difficult. With some 2,000 British also garrisoning Wilmington, Howe's forces were badly scattered, with only 8,500 available at the main encampment at Germantown, eight miles north of Philadelphia. Washington decided to pounce before British engineers could complete a protective line of forts and redoubts that would stretch from Kensington on the Delaware to Fairmount on the Schuylkill River. He correctly surmised that the British would leave the bulk of their force at Germantown while the fortifications were completed. Tired and weakened by six weeks of hard marching and fighting, the British were becoming further exhausted from short rations and hard labor preparing their lines for the winter. He saw an opportunity to repeat his crucial victory at Trenton. For several days at least he would outnumber the British two-to-one. If he struck quickly and succeeded, he just might dislodge the British from the capital after all.

For the first time in his more than three years in command, he ordered an attack by his entire army. It was Washington's greatest gamble. His blueprint, which depended on surprise and on cutting off reinforcements, bore a striking resemblance to the complicated tactics used more than two thousand years earlier by Scipio Africanus, the Roman general who crushed the armies of Hannibal. Washington's plan required high morale and good weather, well-coordinated movements, massed force, and clockwork precision. Morale could hardly have been higher. Washington and his army by now knew of Gates's repulse of the British attack from Canada on September 19 at Freeman's Farm near Saratoga. Washington now felt he could count on the total ruin of Burgoyne. The weather, too, appeared in his favor. After seven days of heavy rains out of fourteen had thwarted his maneuvers in late September, it was now clear and unseasonably warm. The temperature reached 69 degrees on October 3 as his men prepared to march off.

Washington's intricate plan called for five columns to strike the British at Germantown. The two center columns of battle-seasoned Continentals were to converge on the British camp after overrunning the outposts at dawn. Right and left wings made up of Pennsylvania, New Jersey, and Maryland militia were to attack the left and right flanks of the British line. Washington sent the fifth column down the west bank of the Schuylkill River toward the city to divert the grenadiers so they would not reinforce Germantown. The entire American army was to march at least twenty miles at night over unfamiliar roads in strict silence and strike the British before they could wake up.

No one slept in the American camp the night of October 3. The first units marched off by 6 P.M.; the entire army was on the move by nine in utter darkness. The moon was obscured by thick clouds. The balmy day gave way to chill damp night air. It was so dark the footsore men were issued slips of white paper to tuck into their hats so they could make out each other. Despite the fact that guides could not find landmarks in the dark and Washington's directions were even murkier, by 2 A.M. the first American patrol stumbled into an outpost of the 1st Battalion of British Light Infantry. The redcoats took a prisoner and sent him to their commander. The man, hoping to spare his life by claiming he was deserting to the British, promptly revealed the entire American plan. But when he was sent on to British headquarters in Philadelphia, the officer on duty put him into the guardhouse without interrogating him. Washington's secret plan was safe, but the British advance base at Germantown was ordered to "alert and accoutre." While redcoats inside Germantown rubbed their eyes and slung on their gear, staff officers somehow lost track of two exposed units, the 2d Light Infantry—the very troops who had charged and slashed through Paoli less than two weeks earlier—and the 40th Regiment of Foot, bivouacked on the grounds of Cliveden, the handsome granite country house of Pennsylvania chief justice Benjamin Chew.[3]

By 5:30 on October 4, the lead American regiment, the 6th Pennsylvania, under Irish soldier of fortune Thomas Conway, trotted with bayonets fixed into the advance post of the 350-man 2d Light Infantry. Pennsylvanians shouted, "Have at the bloodhounds! Avenge Wayne's affair!" as they fired a volley in the direction of makeshift British wigwams. The British fired back with muskets and with two six-pound artillery pieces. The two cannon shots they got off signaled the main British force in Germantown two miles south before the guns were overrun. One of the balls went high, hissing over the heads of the Pennsylvanians and ricocheting off a signpost before tearing the neck of the horse of North Carolina militia general Francis Nash. The ball slammed into Nash's thigh and then struck Major James Witherspoon, son of Declaration of Inde-

pendence signer John Witherspoon, in the head. Both Nash and Witherspoon died.

In bloody hand-to-hand fighting, the Pennsylvanians pushed back the
British. Twice the British drove back the Americans but finally the reinforced Pennsylvanians outflanked the British and overwhelmed them.
Wayne's men attacked with particular fury and refused to take prisoners.
While the officers yelled for them to give quarter, the Pennsylvanians
bayoneted every light infantryman they captured. For the first time in
the Revolution, Americans heard a British bugler sound retreat.

Hurrying up Germantown Pike with his staff, General Howe was
startled to see his crack light infantry—the unit was his pet creation—in
full flight. "For shame! For shame!" he shouted. "I never saw you retreat
before! Form! Form! It's only a scouting party!" But then a round of
American grapeshot—a sack of lead balls the size of grapes—slammed
into a tree nearby. Howe and his staff dived for cover. By now right and
left American wings were continuing to encircle the British even as the
Continentals in the center of the three-mile American line drove British
regulars through wheat fields and over fences. The British retreat was becoming a rout as Washington and his staff reached the Billmeyer farmhouse at what is now the intersection of Germantown Avenue and Upsal
Street. Through his spy glass, Washington could dimly make out Cliveden, the fortresslike house on a rise surrounded by broad lawns dotted
with classical statuary. Beyond it, he could see the tents of the 40th
Regiment.[4]

By this time Washington's advance troops were already firing volley
after volley into a dense smog of battle. The dank night air on the warm
ground had released a ground fog thickened now by gunsmoke. Neither
side could see the other clearly. Washington was worried that his men
would waste all their ammunition before the main British counterattack
he was sure was coming.

"I am afraid General Sullivan is throwing away his ammunition," he
told an aide. "Ride forward and tell him to preserve it." As the aide,
Colonel Timothy Pickering, rode back from delivering the message, he
came under fire from Cliveden. He found Colonel Thomas Proctor, an artillery officer, and told him to bombard the house, then hurried to inform
Washington. The main American attack had already swept past Cliveden.
A heated debate ensued inside Washington's headquarters. Captain
Alexander Hamilton and Colonel Pickering wanted to surround the
house with a regiment of reserves to keep the British from escaping and
press onward with the main army. Artillery chief Henry Knox objected: a
fortress in the rear was a real threat: by the logic of European warfare, it
must be reduced by artillery. Washington bowed to Knox's argument, as
he did so often. He insisted on sending an officer first with a flag of truce
but a sharpshooter inside Cliveden only saw a soldier's moving form and
shot him. The bombardment of Cliveden began. Four American light

field pieces opened fire from 120 yards while two captured British sixes blasted away ineffectually from 100 yards. They accomplished little more than shattering the statues, the shutters, and the doors. Deadly accurate British fire from inside the stone house kept the guns back and tore into infantry Washington ordered into the siege.[5]

In the first-wave infantry attack, the New Jersey Brigade stormed the massive oak front doors. As Maxwell's men tried to force the front doors, they were bayoneted by the British defenders. Eighteen Americans died in the doorway. Seventy-five Jerseymen lay dead or dying on the grounds by the time Maxwell ordered a retreat. Attempts to set fire to the doors and windows also failed. More American artillery opened fire from the opposite side of the house. In the smog, American gunners blasted away at each other, the cannonballs passing through the house and striking more Americans than Englishmen. The sounds of heavy fire halted Wayne, who ordered his men to about-face and quick-march back to Cliveden: they opened fire from the south. Now American guns blazed away from all four sides, hitting one-third of the British 40th Regiment marksmen inside. But Wayne's volte-face left a gaping hole in the American line, which now had run head-on into the main British force. Suddenly Adam Stephen's Virginia militia came under heavy fire. The Virginia officers ordered their men to pivot and fire a volley. (Stephen himself had fallen behind and was lying drunk in a barn.) The Virginians shot Wayne's countermarching Pennsylvanians: in the smog Virginians and Pennsylvanians blasted away at each other until they were out of ammunition. When they yelled for more ammunition, they gave away their positions to the British, who began to pour in their own deadly fire.

Washington never could find out who started the pell-mell retreat, but the American flanks disintegrated quickly. The men began to back away at first, then turned and ran as the British pursued them. Men around Washington shared his disbelief. By ten o'clock that morning the American offensive had collapsed. Only one column reached its target on time: it arrived in downtown Germantown after the battle was over and surrendered en masse to the British. All the others walked or ran the twenty miles back to Schwenksville. Washington would justifiably explain to a Congress also on the run that his attack had nearly succeeded. The British once again failed to pursue him: the British were stunned by the attack and equally surprised when the Americans ran away. For three hours, it had appeared that Washington was winning. The sheer boldness of his attempt only three weeks after losing at Brandywine bolstered the American cause. That Washington's troops, despite their lack of training in maneuvering under fire, should attempt and nearly carry off such a difficult feat drew the admiration of kings and generals in Europe and, combined with Gates's and Arnold's victories at Saratoga, won open support from France. It was George Washington's most impressive failure and, in the long run, it succeeded more than he could imagine.

*T*he gay social season the British had embarked on in Philadelphia was soon blighted further by the grim news that Burgoyne, forces drained and destroyed piecemeal, had surrendered after two humiliating battles at Saratoga. Clinton, left in command in New York City, had too late decided to sail up the Hudson to attempt a rendezvous. On October 18 an express rider from Albany reached Washington. At five that afternoon, regimental chaplains gave short thanksgiving "discourses" to the troops who had been drawn up in two lines. As thirteen cannon boomed, the soldiers fired two volleys into the air. Washington and his army were elated; he felt vindicated for taking the great risk of dividing his army. Burgoyne's surrender, he wrote, was not only glorious but important. Four days later, Howe sent his letter of resignation to London. The British had occupied Philadelphia but at a dreadful cost and now faced severe problems. Washington had stripped the city of every scrap of food he could find before turning it over to the British. Housewives were begging and stealing British provisions by late October. Some three hundred Loyalist merchants eventually assembled from as far away as New York City to sell goods and food at exorbitant prices.

The cause of the worsening shortages was the complicated set of defenses the Philadelphians had erected over, under, and on both banks of the Delaware River over the past fifteen months. The defenses prevented the British fleet from supplying the British army. After failing to dislodge Washington from the strong base he had taken up at the George Emlen farm at Whitemarsh sixteen miles upriver, Howe turned his army and navy loose to tear apart the string of river forts and underwater obstacles. Washington now put his mind to directing a defense of the river fortifications that was to frustrate the British for months. Every night Washington's dispatch boats—part of the Pennsylvania Navy—plied the Delaware from Whitemarsh to three mud forts guarding the southern approach to the capital. Thousands of Pennsylvania and New Jersey civilian volunteers had worked for nearly a year under the direction of a Polish-born, French-trained military engineer named Tadeusz Kosciuszko. He had laid out complicated river defenses that now slowed down the British invasion for two full months and made their occupation of the capital an uncomfortable interregnum.

A history of the Revolution based on evidence would present a rich ethnic tapestry, not an all-white, all-WASP pantheon. Revolutionary politics and the ranks of revolutionary soldiers included Czechs, Poles, Hungarians, Greeks, Danes, Swedes, Italians, Bohemians, Dutch, Germans, Scots, Irish, Scots-Irish, Swiss, French, Africans, Indians, Protestants, Catholics, and Jews from many countries.

The British army in America was preponderantly made up of Irish, Scottish, and German mercenaries, more Germans fighting on the English side than Englishmen. British major general James Robertson, who had served in the American colonies for a quarter-century, reported that half the rebels were Irish, an estimate that accords with the testimony that Joseph Galloway, Loyalist superintendent of police of Philadelphia during the British occupation, gave before the English Parliament. A modern Irish historian has concluded that 38 percent of the American soldiers were Irish. Yet Galloway and Robertson may not have been differentiating between Irish Catholics and Protestant Scots-Irish like Charles Thomson, secretary of the Continental Congress. His ancestors had settled in Ireland temporarily and remigrated to America in the first half of the eighteenth century after enduring frequent crop failures combined with increasingly repressive English laws and taxes.

After fitful migrations in the 1730s and 1750s, thousands of Scots-Irish came to America in the 1770s when the linen-weaving industry collapsed in Ulster. Many of them migrated first to Liverpool and London, where they worked for day wages and lived in slums before they left England in disgust and remigrated to America. By 1776, an estimated 300,000 had come to the mainland English colonies of America. Many Scots-Irish, like Patrick Henry, who became the first governor of Virginia, and Charles Thomson, who organized Philadelphia's Sons of Liberty, took active roles in the earliest protests against the British. Others, like John Rutledge, took part in the Continental Congress's debate over independence. Still others, like Henry Knox, Washington's chief of artillery, fought all through the eight-year-long war. The Scots-Irish were only slightly more numerous than German immigrants. By 1776, at least 225,000 Germans of at least 250 different Protestant sects migrated to America in the wake of European religious wars. Many of them left behind the constant warfare of Europe only to march off to the war for America, some with clergymen like Frederick Muhlenberg. Other Germans came not to settle but to fight beside the Americans, most notably the self-styled Baron von Steuben, a Prussian professional soldier who drilled the American troops at Valley Forge into a tightly disciplined, highly maneuverable army. Steuben stayed in the new United States after the Revolution. So did 12,562 of the 29,875 German mercenaries brought mostly against their wills to fight on the British side. These hated so-called Hessians were rented to the British to fight in America by their landgraves in Hesse-Hanau and Brunswick as they had been in Scotland when, under the Hessian Duke of Cumberland, they had bayoneted the clans at the bloody Battle of Culloden in 1745. Their presence accounted for widespread support of the American Revolution by Scots and Scots-Irish immigrants.

In virtually every military engagement, what would today be called ethnic Americans took part. Polish American sailors in the crew of the American ship *Bonhomme Richard*, fought under a famous Scottish American captain, John Paul Jones, lobbing grenades into a powder magazine of the British man-of-war *Serapis* until it struck its colors.

Thirteen-year-old Pascal de Angelis, an Italian-American, fought under Benedict Arnold in the naval Battle of Valcour Island on Lake Champlain that saved the new United States from being cut in two by British armies and navies in 1776. Twenty Hungarian hussars came to America to fight under their Polish friend, Casimir Pulaski, a dashing cavalry officer who did stunt riding outside Washington's headquarters at Morristown to attract the commander in chief's attention and then commanded four cavalry regiments in the south until he was killed. Greek knights journeyed to America and fought as volunteers under the French Marquis de Lafayette in Virginia; at least half a dozen Greek American patriots suffered the horrors of imprisonment on the disease-ridden British prison ship, the *Jersey*.

Two regiments of Italians recruited in their homeland fought under the French flag at Yorktown, while their countryman, Filippo Mazzei, Thomas Jefferson's next-door neighbor in Virginia, took a musket and marched off as a private in 1776. Then he went to Italy as Virginia's diplomatic agent to drum up financial and political support in Florence for the American cause by writing pamphlets and books published in Italy. Joseph Vigo, an Italian who left his Piedmont home, came to New Orleans with a Spanish regiment and became a leading Mississippi Valley fur trader. When George Rogers Clark captured Vincennes and British troops recaptured it, Vigo found himself caught between the lines. He carefully observed British troop strengths and gun positions. Released because of his Spanish citizenship, Vigo supplied vital information to Clark in time for the American counterattack—as well as badly needed money and excellent credit that helped the Americans recapture Vincennes. By pledging his entire fortune to help the American cause, Vigo helped to extend American territory into the modern-day Midwest.

North and south, blacks fought on both sides, both sides offering them freedom if they survived. An estimated 7,500 blacks fought under Washington, more than double that number on the British side. And, all through the war, Jewish Americans fought, suffered, and gave often all they had to keep the Revolution and its army and navies alive. Many revolutionary leaders had no income as they served in Congress, relying on the generosity of patriots. James Madison attested that when any member of Congress was short of cash, all that was necessary was to call on Haym Solomon. Bernard and Michael Gratz equipped the 150 Virginians under George Rogers Clark who made the original surprise attack on the Illinois country. Moses Levy, as partner of Robert Morris, built and hired crews for privateering warships that captured and destroyed British shipping. The Jews of Charleston, South Carolina, marched off in the Jews Company to defend their city against invading British and German forces. Colonel Mordecai Sheftall acted as commissary general for the southern Continental Army and was held prisoner on a British prison ship with his sixteen-year-old son for two years in horrible conditions and with very little food. Jacob Pinto of New Haven, Connecticut, a member of the town's revolutionary committee, and his brother, Benjamin, fought in the 7th Regiment of the elite Continental Line.

A leading American Jewish revolutionary was David Salisbury Franks. Only days after the fighting had started at Lexington in 1775, a crowd gathered in Montreal, where King George III's bust had been smeared with a coat of black paint. Young David Franks, who was to become Benedict Arnold's aide-de-camp, admitted his handiwork and was dragged off to jail. When Arnold led an American invasion of Canada later that year, Franks did everything he could to organize French Canadians to fight on the American side. When most of Arnold's force was killed, captured, or deserted, French-Canadian regiments maintained the siege all through a bitter winter. When the Americans retreated south, Franks went with them and enlisted in a Massachusetts regiment. Arnold's treason meant a court-martial for Major Franks, but he cleared his name. At war's end, Congress honored him by asking him to carry the signed treaty of peace to Paris.

And there was Tadeusz Kosciuszko, the impoverished son of Polish gentry who had fled his homeland after he tried to elope with the daughter of a nobleman who had ordered him arrested. Escaping to Paris, he studied at the French royal military academy, Ecole Militaire, and the royal artillery and engineering school at Mezieres. He specialized in river and harbor defenses, mastering the techniques of the great seventeenth-century French engineer Vauban. Kos, as the American officers called him (Washington misspelled his name eleven different ways), came to Philadelphia in 1776 as a volunteer military engineer. He quickly showed he had a genius for river fortifications and also was thoroughly grounded in European warfare. The Continental Congress commissioned him as colonel of engineers for the Northern Department, which primarily was armed and outfitted by the French. But before Kosciuszko could ride north, Benjamin Franklin, in charge of defending Pennsylvania, commandeered Kosciuszko's talents. Together, they planned the elaborate network that was supposed to impede the expected British naval attack on the American capital. More than 5,000 men—one in five Philadelphians, including many freed blacks—joined the gigantic defense-building effort that began in the summer of 1776 and lasted until the British attack came in October 1777.

*O*n the New Jersey shore opposite the present-day site of Philadelphia International Airport, Kosciuszko laid out two forts on the marshy banks of the Delaware River. Fort Billings, near present-day Paulsboro, was the first parcel of federal land. Purchased by Congress on July 5, 1776, it had been transformed by Kosciuszko into a 180-foot square redoubt with strong points at the corners, parapets for riflemen, the walls pierced for eighteen heavy guns. On the land side, he laid out earthen breastworks and a deep ditch, or *fosse*, filled with felled trees, their branches sharpened to impede infantry attack.

The main purpose of the fort was to protect the downstream end of a *chevaux de frise*, an ingenious underwater barricade designed to pierce the hulls of ships passing over it, and hold the ships while the fort poured cannon fire into it. Both Franklin and Kosciuszko were smitten with the idea of the *chevaux de frise*. To the assembly area at Gloucester they hauled 239 great hemlock timbers, 15 to 20 inches thick and extremely tough. Pine timbers were lashed together on the bottom and sides into giant caissons, or cribs, each 60 feet long. These were floated raftlike to the river, where the damaging iron-tipped prongs, or pikes—some of them 70 feet long—were attached, and braced with iron straps and angles. The cribs were then sunk by removing plugs from their sides and bottoms and filling each with 30 tons of rock brought down the Schuylkill on barges from the quarries of Conshohocken. Submerged six or seven feet below the waterline, the pikes spread out into a fan shape, each covering a 60-foot-wide arc. In all, there were 70 of them—24 under the guns of Fort Billings and 46, in three staggered rows, eight miles upstream between Fort Mercer and Fort Mifflin.

Fort Mercer, at Red Bank, on the New Jersey shore above present-day Woodbury, was named after Washington's friend Hugh Mercer, who had been slain at Princeton. Here, Kosciuszko was able to demonstrate his dual genius as engineer and artilleryman. The fort's guns could fire down from the 40-foot-high bluffs to cover both Fort Mifflin, across the mile-wide channel, and the approaches to the *chevaux de frise*. Because of its elevation, it was also beyond the reach of the British naval guns and was virtually impervious to amphibious assault because of its formidable landward defenses. To the north of the redoubt, a dirt road ran due west toward Deptford and Haddonfield. The road was flanked by heavy woods on the south and swamps to the north. Cutting down orchards to provide a clear field of fire, Kosciuszko had his men dig deep trenches around the walls, which ran from north to south slightly more than 350 yards. Long, low breastworks ran along the river for 200 yards. A moat filled with the standard abatis of sharpened trees and breastworks made up the outer works. The main body of the fort was a high earth-and-log redoubt with walls 12 feet thick and 15 feet high. The moat could be manned with sharpshooters to slow up any attack.

To this fortress in early October Washington dispatched Colonel Christopher Greene, a tough Rhode Islander, with two companies of Rhode Island Continentals, most of them blacks who had been promised their freedom—if they survived the war. When Washington sent a newly arrived French volunteer engineering officer, Chevalier Mauduit du Plessis, to inspect the fort with an eye to correcting any flaws in Kosciuszko's planning, they found the tattered black garrison waiting grimly behind eighteen heavy guns for the expected British attack.

Mauduit, a skilled engineer, recognized the fort's possibilities as the ideal place to spring a trap: inside the deep embankment between the inner and outer works on the north side, he suggested Greene build another embankment to screen an artillery battery.

The attack on the Delaware forts came soon enough. On October 11, one week after Germantown, Cornwallis and Lord Howe unleashed a combined land-sea attack, 2,000 of Cornwallis's best regulars encircling Fort Billings downriver. The weakest of the three forts, it was garrisoned by only 250 men and six cannon. All of the cannon faced the river and were quite useless against the land attack. During the night, its New Jersey militia garrison spiked the guns so they would blow up if the British tried to use them. Then they blew up the bakehouse, barracks, and stockade and retreated to Fort Mercer. On Mauduit's recommendation, the Pennsylvania Navy stationed galleys with 18-pound cannon on them at the foot of the bluffs of Fort Mercer. The row galleys of the Pennsylvania Navy were useless against British men-of-war, but might deter an amphibious landing. This they did: General Howe now ordered a land attack on Fort Mercer.

Cornwallis in turn entrusted the assault by three battalions of Hessians and 1,000 redcoats to Count Karl Emil von Donop, an able 37-year-old field commander still smarting from his defeat at Princeton. Ferried across the Delaware from Philadelphia to present-day Camden, they marched to Deptford and rested for the night. A fleet-footed American named Jonas Cattell, whipper-in for the Gloucester Hunt Club, ran nine miles from Deptford to Fort Mercer to warn Colonel Greene, who until then had been expecting a waterborne assault. That night, the largely black garrison, joined by the 250 Jersey militia from Fort Billings, sweated as they hauled the big guns around to the land side—and set their trap. After placing sharpshooters in the outer works, Greene placed two heavy guns, double-loaded with grapeshot and canisters, inside the hidden embankment, as Mauduit had suggested. Fallen trees and brush were set in front of them.

The Hessians marched down the Deptford Road at noon on October 22. Drums beating and bugles blaring, they fanned out and formed a cordon that extended from the swamp to the plain south of the fort. Swinging down from his brown stallion, von Donop handed the reins to an aide and told him to carry this message to Greene: "The King of England orders his rebellious subjects to lay down their arms, and they are warned that if they stand the battle, no quarters whatsoever will be given." Greene hurled back a loud reply: "We'll see King George damned first. We want no quarters and we'll give none." Von Donop ordered simultaneous attacks against both the north and south walls. From the south the Hessians hacked through the abatis and bayoneted their way through the thin line of skirmishers in the south ditch, ignoring the heavy, well-directed musket fire from the black garrison inside.

Then the attackers charged the walls. A few made it to the top before they were riddled by point-blank fire. On the north side the American trap was set. At the first volley, the American skirmishers fired one ragged salvo, and then dropped back. Charging and huzzahing wildly, the Hessians poured through the breastworks and into the outer fort, then on toward the tall north wall on the fort. Then the trap sprang. Yanking away trees and brush, the hidden gun crews fired—and fired again. The fort's cannon and the marksmen on the parapets poured in a brutal crossfire. Shot in the hip, chest, and face at such close range that a cannon's wadding was pounded into his face, blinding him, von Donop staggered and fell along with scores of his troops and fifteen officers. From below, the river gunboats opened up a crossfire against Hessians now attempting to climb the west wall, on the river side. The German grenadiers were mowed down.

Inside fifteen minutes, the battle was over. The surviving Hessians ran back to the woods, jettisoned their cannon in the creek, and after pausing to make stretchers for their wounded officers, fled back to Woodbury. They left 414 dead and dying on the field, in the ditches, sprawled all over the fort. Carried to the Whitall house nearby, von Donop died slowly and painfully. He told Mauduit, the architect of the trap, who now nursed him for nine days: "I am content. I die in the hands of honor itself. It is finishing a noble career early, but I die the victim of my own ambition and the avarice of my sovereign." It was, proportionately, the greatest American victory of the war: only twenty-four Americans had been killed or wounded, nineteen of them when a cannon carelessly swabbed by its crew exploded while being fired.

The British land attack had proven a fiasco; the naval assault by the infuriated Royal Navy turned into an even worse disaster for the British. To support von Donop's assault, Lord Howe had ordered six men-of-war to maneuver through the lower *chevaux de frise*, where they dueled all day with the Pennsylvania Navy's 75-foot heavily armed row galleys. By nightfall, the British squadron opened up a two-hour broadside bombardment of Fort Mercer. But between this flotilla and the Jersey shore lay a narrow, shoaled channel. When the British commander, Captain Francis Reynolds, aboard the 64-gun flagship *Augusta* ordered two ships up the channel to prevent the highly maneuverable Pennsylvania galleys from reinforcing Fort Mercer, high winds frustrated the British. Unable to warp upriver, the British vessels had no better luck slipping downriver again. In the darkness, *Augusta* and the sloop-of-war *Merlin* ran aground. At dawn, the remaining men-of-war and their longboats tried to tug the stranded men-of-war free under heavy fire from the Pennsylvania Navy and the gunners of Forts Mercer and Mifflin. Half of the British aboard the ships perished before they could be rescued. An American cannonball struck the *Augusta*'s powder magazine. Captain Francis and his crew jumped into the river. At noon, when the *Augusta* blew up, Washington could hear the blast at Whitemarsh and most if not all of the windows in Philadelphia, three miles away, shattered. Lord Howe ordered the *Merlin* scuttled. Tom Paine, at Washington's side, reported a "report as loud as a peal of one hundred cannon at once." Thick smoke rose "like a pillar" and spread "from the top like a tree."[6]

The stage was set for one of the most vicious engagements of the war, the battle for Fort Mifflin. For more than a month, the 18-pounders of Fort Mifflin had punished the British fleet. Howe now decided on a classic siege and he ordered the man who had built the fort five years earlier for the British to destroy it. He was Captain Joh Montresor, a Swiss-born military engineer who had retired from the British army and was living in New York City when the revolution broke out. He had been roused to reenlist after witnessing the excesses of the patriots in that city before the British invaded it. It was Montresor who had planted the false map of his explorations of the Maine backwoods on Benedict Arnold, and yet he had befriended Nathan Hale before the British hanged him as a spy. Montresor had paid Loyalists to retrieve the head of the equestrian statue of King George III from the spike outside a Bronx tavern where the rebels had displayed it and he had arranged to send it back to London to show Parliament the depth of the Americans' defiance of king and Crown. Now Montresor proceeded to reduce the fort with fierce cannonades from artillery batteries protected by earthworks that he built steadily closer to the fort, a crude affair of four blockhouses and log-and-mud ramparts on the marshy western banks of the Delaware.

Before the Americans inside Fort Mifflin could carry out the central point of Kosciuszko's scheme of defense—to break holes in the dikes along the river and flood the low-lying land and make the fort an island—the British stormed American positions on two marshy islands adjoining the fort, Carpenter's and Province. Montresor was now free to set up his heavy guns, which began an intermittent barrage, firing roughly every half hour.

At the outset of the forty-day siege on October 10—the day British troops marched on Fort Billings—the American garrison, now commanded by a Marylander, Colonel Samuel Smith, and a French artillerist-engineer, Major Andre de Fleury, was incredibly high-spirited. Even one month of artillery barrages later, as the noose of the British gun emplacements tightened, on November 10 Fleury confidently noted in his journal: "The 24 and 18-pound shot from the batteries Number 16 and 17 broke some of our palisades this morning, but this does not make us uneasy—they save us the trouble of cutting . . . [the fort walls] to the height of a man, which we should do." But Fleury could foresee problems. Fleury later complained in his journal about the useless blockhouses: "The fire of the loopholes is in itself not very dangerous, and our loopholes in particular are so badly contrived as to leave two-thirds of the [earthworks invisible]. . . . The wall of masonry is only ten feet high, and is not out of the reach of an escalade [assault by ladder], notwithstanding the ditches, pits and stakes with which we have endeavored to surround it."

The British barrages were becoming more troubling. Fleury closed his notation, saying, "I am interrupted by the bombs and balls, which fall thick." When Colonel Smith was wounded, he was rowed over to Fort Mercer at night. In the course of the siege, some 1,000 men would be rotated by night between the two forts. After November 10, the cannonade became so intense the men could not sleep. If they went into the shattered barracks, they were dead within minutes from the bombs that landed there with regularity. Most could only doze minutes at a time sitting upright against the walls. Sensing the approaching climax, Fleury made almost hourly entries in his journal.

> *At 2 o'clock: The direction of the fire is changed—our palisades suffer—a dozen of them are broke down.*
>
> *Eleven at night: The enemy keep up firing every half hour. General Varnum [now at Fort Mercer] promised us fascines [baskets filled with earth] and palisades [of logs to repair the damage] but they are not arrived and they are absolutely necessary.*
>
> *Nov. 14: Daylight discovers us a floating battery of the enemy, placed a little above their grand battery and near the shore. . . . The fire of the enemy will never take the fort. It may kill us men but this is the fortune of war, and all their bullets will never render them masters of this island. . . . We must have men to defend the ruins of the fort. Our ruins will serve us as breastworks. We will defend the ground inch by inch, and the enemy shall pay dearly for every step.*

The next day, November 15, the British plan when into its final phase. Lieutenant Samuel Lyons of the Pennsylvania Navy had deserted to the British. In Fleury's words, he gave "sufficient intimation of our weakness." The British now hauled the *Vigilant* off a mud bank downriver, cut off its masts to raise it in the shallow water, fitted it with four 24-pounders, and towed it within 40 yards of the fort, slipping it over a sandbar at Hog Island at high tide at night. With the light sloop-of-war *Fury,* armed with six 18-pounders and its rigging crowded with Royal Marine sharpshooters, the *Vigilant* began to bombard the fort from its weak west side at point-blank range. At the same time, the British fleet sailed up to the *chevaux de frise.* The 64-gun *Somerset,* along with the *Isis, Roebuck, Pearl,* and *Liverpool,* commenced a constant barrage day and night into the now flattened quagmire that had been Fort Mifflin. Americans who raised their heads above the parapets or attempted to return the fire were slaughtered by volleys from the royal marines or killed by grenadiers aboard *Fury* who continually hurled grenades from vantage points an easy lob from the fort. After four broadsides from the *Vigilant,* Fort Mifflin's remaining parapets and gun carriages were smashed. Even the iron of the guns was broken to bits and the gun platforms pulverized. The *Vigilant* moved within 20 yards, belching shot and canister, blasting big pieces of debris into smaller pieces of debris. Every twenty minutes, another thousand shots smashed into the ruins in one of the heaviest bombardments in American history. When the officers in the fort ordered the Stars and Stripes lowered so that a blue flag of distress could be hoisted, the British cheered loudly.[7]

While this wasn't intended as a surrender—it was meant as a signal to the other American forces in the area—the Stars and Stripes remained lowered. When a sergeant ran out to try to put the new American symbol back up, he was shot to death. Out of ammunition, its guns useless, exploding splinters in its blockhouses and palisades impaling the survivors, the fort was a death trap. That night, when the British halted their bombardment to figure out if there was anything left to shoot at, the American officers ordered it evacuated. A message brought boats from Fort Mercer and 250 wounded men were taken off while the other 200 set fire to the wreckage.

The next morning, when British grenadiers stormed the fort, a herd of sheep and some oxen were the only living creatures they found standing. Dead animals and men were piled around the fort. One man was found lying down drunk in the barracks. He maintained that he was a Loyalist and a prisoner, and he was drafted into the British army. For that, he received a bounty and a new uniform. But he had apparently not told the British the truth, for later that winter he deserted and rejoined the Americans at Valley Forge, giving Washington detailed information on the British defenses. In late November, Washington finally began an eleven-day, 30-mile march, safely moving his army into winter quarters at Valley Forge. Two weeks later, Fort Mercer, too, was evacuated, its garrison joining Washington in the hills twenty miles west of Philadelphia. The British made no attempt to follow.

George Washington's dogged battle for Philadelphia had, on paper, gone badly for the Americans, but, coupled with the news of Burgoyne's defeat at Saratoga and Howe's incredibly lethargic generalship, it became the turning point in the American Revolution. Washington's grinding rearguard effort had ruined the British spirit of victory at capturing the rebel capital, and his bold tactics and successful strategy of delay in large measure encouraged the French a few months later to take the ultimate step and officially sign a treaty of alliance with the United States, thus declaring war on England. Now the American Revolution became a world war in which Britain was outnumbered. If Washington could only keep an army in the field long enough, the United States could not lose.

It had taken the Howes four months, thousands of casualties, and the loss of two men-of-war to move the army and navy ninety miles, only to find that Washington's army, far from capitulating when the capital city fell, were only fighting more fiercely now that they had heard of the

American victory at Saratoga. Preferring to be entertained by his officers to attacking Washington in the wintertime, Howe only occasionally sent out detachments, but then it was not to fight but to scour the surrounding countryside for cattle, horses, grain, and firewood, all in short supply in the city.

The pain and suffering that Washington's troops suffered that winter at Valley Forge have become a cliché in American history. It has been estimated that three thousand men died in the American hospitals of typhoid and smallpox, which many of them contracted after coming to the hospital with wounds or other ailments. Two thousand more died as prisoners inside Philadelphia. The lack of food and clothing was acute. It was not an unusually cold winter: in fact, it was one of the warmest in memory. Still, there were heavy snows and the temperature rose above 40 only eight times between Christmas and mid-March. The privations suffered by the army did not reflect any shortages in the land. Instead, they reflected the inefficiency of the Congress in arranging for adequate logistical support for its army. It also reflected the reluctance of farmers in the area to accept the atrociously inflated Continental currency. Washington, as a result, was forced to resort to somewhat unconventional methods that winter to provide food for his troops. He detached General Wayne and about three hundred of his men to rustle cattle. Most of the farmers managed to hide their herds deep in the Pine Barrens, but in all some eight hundred cattle were seized from Loyalist farmers in Salem County in southwestern New Jersey. And when spring came, Washington the fisherman ordered his cavalry into the Schuylkill to stir up the shad run. His jubilant soldiers jumped into the shallows and caught the rich fish with their bare hands.

While some of the British generals inside Philadelphia fumed that they could end the war in ten days, Howe learned that France in February 1778 had signed two treaties with the United States, one granting reciprocal most favored nation trading status, the other a treaty of military alliance. In August 1777 when he landed in Maryland, he had written to London that he would be unable to subdue Pennsylvania in time to cooperate with Burgoyne on the Hudson. His dispatch calling for 35,000 more troops reached London one day before news that Burgoyne's army had surrendered. Two days later the prime minister, Lord North, anticipating French entry into the war, advocated to the king abandoning British efforts to destroy Washington's army and occupy the colonies and to shift instead to a series of expeditions from strong coastal bases, a tight naval blockade, direct negotiations with the rebels, and liberal expenditure of secret service funds to encourage discord and high-level defections. On March 8, 1778, the American secretary, Lord George Germain, sent instructions that the new British commander was to be General Sir Henry Clinton. He was authorized to abandon all offensive operations, to withdraw from Philadelphia, and to retire to New York. The French alliance had made the American Revolution a secondary consideration to war with France.

That winter Washington's intelligence service reached such a degree of sophistication that Washington was able to spoil the farewell party that Howe's officers had prepared for him. The date of departure—and Howe's send-off—were supposed to be secret. After a lavish cold supper was served for 430 British officers and their escorts at the commandeered Wharton estate, a band played "God Save the King" and everyone was singing along. Suddenly the north windows swung open. This was not part of the plan. In the distance, American cavalry, guided by spies inside Philadelphia, had slipped up to the British defense line of abatis at dusk and dumped buckets of whale oil over the dried branches. Now in unison they set them afire. The north sky blazed with light. Howe's officers tried to assure their shrieking escorts that it was all part of the show. But furious British officers jumped on their horses and dashed toward the front line. There Daniel Morgan's riflemen awaited them, picking off their silhouetted figures against the eerie skyline.

It was the high point of a gloomy season of suffering and deprivation for Washington's withering army. Between September 1777 and March 1778 fully one-half of Washington's troops were killed, captured, or wounded or froze to death on patrols, died of camp contagions, deserted, or resigned. Even Martha's arrival at the handsome brown fieldstone Dewees Mansion at Valley Forge did little at first to lift the gloom. Her sister Nancy Bassett, "the greatest favorite I had in the world," died in December just before Martha's scheduled departure for camp. Washington's correspondence had been full of his frustrations over congressional tardiness in providing everything—shoes, bread, meat, blankets, and pay for his barefoot, freezing soldiers. Martha's talk of family and babies and news from Mount Vernon over quiet cups of coffee eventually lifted Washington's spirits. Martha again organized the officers' wives into a nursing corps and sewing circles and arranged music and dancing and even a performance of his favorite play, *Cato: A Tragedy*. The theme of the play was timely: it was a homily against betrayal of a leader. A growing number of critics in Congress and the army were conspiring to oust Washington as commander in chief.[8]

*O*n October 28, 1777, James Wilkinson, scheming 21-year-old aide to Horatio Gates, stopped off at Reading on his way from Saratoga with a report to Congress on the great victory over Burgoyne. He told an aide to Lord Stirling of a remark about Washington he had heard before he left Gates. Gates by reporting to Congress was deliberately snubbing Washington, his commanding officer. Wilkinson revealed to Stirling's aide that Brigadier General Thomas Conway, serving under Washington, had written secretly to Gates. By this time, several members of Congress wanted to wrest control of the army away from Washington and vest it in a newly created Board of War to which Congress would appoint their chosen generals. Congress persisted in promoting politically well-connected officers out of turn without consulting Washington. Benedict Arnold was among the generals who had been passed over for promotion, had resigned, and had only reenlisted because Washington was engaged in a running battle with Congress to apportion promotion according to seniority and merit. When Congress appointed Conway, the most junior of twenty-four brigadier generals, a major general, Washington called the move "as unfortunate a measure as ever was adopted" in a letter to his old friend, president of Congress Richard Henry Lee: "Conway's merit as an officer and his importance in this army exists more in his own imagination than in reality. The brigadiers will not serve under him."

The constant wrangling over rank and preferment and regional interests—John Adams was always sure the Virginians were getting all the good-paying officers' commissions while New England was losing out—had wearied Washington beyond disgust. "I have been a slave to the service," he complained to Lee, not knowing that his old crony in western land companies had joined the ranks of his congressional critics. "I have undergone more than most men are aware of to harmonize so many discordant parts." But Congress's constant and inept interference, especially in Conway's case, were beyond his patience. "It will be impossible for me to be of any further service if such insuperable difficulties are thrown in my way." Amazingly, he was threatening to resign, putting his career on the line to block the scheming Conway and his backers.[9]

On January 2, 1778, Washington wrote to Congress that he could hardly cooperate with Conway: "My feelings will not permit me to make professions of friendship to a man I deem my enemy."[10]

As soon as he had heard of Conway's letter writing to Gates, he had confronted Conway in writing. Stirling, loyal to Washington, had written him, quoting Conway in these words: "In a letter from General Conway to General Gates he says, 'Heaven has been determined to save your country or a weak general and bad councillors would have ruined it.'" In ordinary times, Washington did not take criticism easily; in wartime such a written comment suggested that Conway believed Gates agreed with him. Gates had remained safely behind the lines during the critical stage at Saratoga while Benedict Arnold had actually decided the outcome of the pivotal battle with a dashing attack against the Hessians. Yet Gates had left Arnold's name out of official dispatches to Congress and had taken full credit for the victory. Only from New York governor George Clinton did Washington learn who had done what.[11]

To the alarmed Washington, the note Stirling had sent him gave Washington what he considered sound evidence that at least two of his generals were plotting to overthrow him, something that seemed not only disloyal but virtually treasonous. He had little regard for Conway, an Irishman married to a French countess who had fought well enough at

Germantown but then had personally lobbied Congress to be promoted over all the other brigadiers. Washington immediately sent Conway a stiff note, which began, "Sir, a letter which I received last night contained the following paragraph," and he copied out Stirling's note to him. By mailing his letter to Conway through normal channels in his headquarters, Washington made sure all of his general officers knew its contents. Conway wrote back to deny he had called Washington a "weak general." On November 14 Conway sent his resignation to Congress. What became known as the Conway Cabal would have ended but Congress sent it to the Board of War, whose chairman, Thomas Mifflin, was an active partner in the plot to unseat Washington.[12]

With an unacknowledged assist from Mifflin, several members of Congress now began to beat the drums to promote Conway to inspector general of the army. Pennsylvania radicals joined congressional critics to denounce Washington. Pennsylvania attorney general Jonathan Dickinson Sergeant wrote Congressman James Lovell that "thousands of lives and millions of property are yearly sacrificed to the inefficiency of the commander-in-chief. Two battles he has lost for us by two such blunders as might have disgraced a soldier of three months' standing." One week later, Lovell wrote Gates at Albany, "We want you in different places. Good God! What a situation we are in!" Lovell blamed all America's woes on Washington.[13]

Washington knew that Conway's weak spot was his service record: he had only been a staff officer in the French army and had no combat experience. Somehow he got the message across to friends in Congress that the only diplomatic solution was to make Conway a staff officer with no authority to give orders to other officers. When Conway appeared at Valley Forge to inspect Washington's troops, Washington treated him with "flawless, cold courtesy." After an exchange of formal notes, Conway complained to Congress that he could not do his job because "I can expect no support." That was too much for Washington: he turned over their correspondence to Congress, denying that he refused to cooperate with a congressional appointee. In the meantime the plot had coalesced in Congress, where Mifflin had accused Washington's aide-de-camp Alexander Hamilton of rifling Gates's files during a recent visit to Albany. Gates by now believed he could discredit Washington by disgracing his aide Hamilton. In early December Gates wrote Washington that Conway's letter had been "stealthily copied." By now Washington knew that his opponents and Gates supporters in Congress included Samuel Adams, Dr. Benjamin Rush, Richard Henry Lee, John Adams, and most of all, his own former aide, Mifflin, who had been working quietly with another former aide, Joseph Reed, a leading Pennsylvania politician.[14]

Now Washington was ready to spring his trap. Gates's revelation in a letter to Mifflin that he knew about the note from Washington to Conway was not only a serious breach of security but revealed that he had known all along that the disclosure had come from his own office *before* Washington told him where it had come from. When Gates feigned surprise and next accused Wilkinson of the theft, Wilkinson challenged Gates to a duel. Before they could prime their pistols, their aides intervened just as nine brigadier generals sent a written protest about Conway's incompetence to Congress. Gates brought the crisis to a head when he rode all the way from Albany to York, Pennsylvania, the latest hiding place of Congress and showed the new president of Congress, Henry Laurens, Conway's original letter. (He never did offer to show it to Washington.) Laurens said it was "ten times worse" than the small quote Wilkinson had leaked. Congress referred the matter back to Washington, who decided to go on trusting the thoroughly chastened Gates. But most of Washington's generals did not trust or forgive Conway for making a bad winter at Valley Forge so much worse. Pennsylvania general John Cadwalader challenged him to a duel and shot him in the face. Conway survived. He soon resigned and returned to France. Mifflin also resigned from the Board of War. The so-called Conway Cabal collapsed like a soufflé in a cold wind. Washington remained convinced there had been a plot against him among his generals and that it had failed. It was a long time before anyone challenged his command again, but the episode left Washington shaken with the knowledge that there were generals and congressmen he could not trust.

*D*espite his problems with the Irish Conway, Washington, with so few experienced American officers, had to rely heavily on foreign-born officers. Some, at least, proved helpful. They also brought a modicum of civilization to his headquarters. At first they were a mixed lot. The American ministry in Paris became an employment agency for "men who had already lost their reputations and replaced them with debts," as one chaplain with a French regiment put it. "They came with a great display of false titles and names, were given commissions in the Continental Army, sometimes received considerable advances in pay and then disappeared." In various ways: when Congress commissioned the Frenchman Tronson de Coudray, a major general with the title of General of Artillery and Ordnance, Knox, Greene, and Sullivan threatened to resign. Congress voted him "of the staff," as it had Conway. On his way to inspect the army, Coudray rode a skittish horse onto a ferry. The horse jumped into the river. None of the American officers nearby made a move to rescue him. He drowned. One of the few Frenchmen who came to volunteer and won many friends was nineteen-year-old Marie Joseph Paul Ives Roch Gilbert du Motier, Marquis de Lafayette. "The moment I heard of America I loved her; the moment I knew she was fighting for freedom I burnt with a desire to bleed for her," he later wrote. Defying the orders of the French king, Lafayette had chartered a ship, *La Victoire*, and sailed to Charleston, South Carolina, with an assortment of volunteer nobles. By the time he landed in the summer of 1777 he found to his chagrin that Congress had been overwhelmed with applications from unemployed European officers for commissions. "So many candidates appealed to Congress every day that finally the representatives listened to no one. I was received myself so coldly that it looked like a dismissal." Lafayette assured Congress he wanted to serve as a volunteer at his own expense. Congress accepted. Lafayette quickly demonstrated his bravery and was slightly wounded at the Battle of Brandywine. He recovered in time to help brighten the table talk at Washington's headquarters at Valley Forge. In some ways Washington must have found a resemblance to himself in the shy, awkward outsider at Braddock's side. Lafayette, to be sure, was brave and eager to learn, and he also worshiped Washington with a puppy-dog attentiveness that evoked some of his own years as sycophant at the feet of Lord Fairfax. Whatever mix of affection and mutual exploitation was involved, a sort of father-son relationship developed.[15]

No such attraction explained Washington's friendship for one of the last foreigners to enlist. Frederick Steuben, who called himself Frederick Wilhelm August Heinrich Ferdinand, Baron von Steuben, arrived at Valley Forge in the black February of 1778. His real name was Friedrich Wilhelm Rudolf Gerhard Augustin Steuben, without any "von" to denote noble birth, and his highest previous rank had been as a captain and aide-de-camp on the vast staff of Frederick the Great. Much of what he claimed about himself through his French-born interpreter, Chevalier Jean Baptiste de Ternant, was untrue. He had not been a lieutenant general in the army of the king of Prussia; he had never led troops in battle. He did not own a great estate in Swabia. But he did know how to train soldiers, and he arrived at a time when Washington was making a concerted effort to remodel his army and needed a drillmaster to teach his own officers how to maneuver after the tangled debacles at Brandywine and Germantown. Washington was still living in his tent while his men built their log huts in December 1777 when he informed Congress that he was undertaking major reforms "to rectify mistakes and bring things to order" before the fighting resumed in the spring. "We have not more than three months to prepare a great deal of business in," he wrote to Congress, "and if we let these slip or waste [them] we shall be laboring under the same difficulties all next campaign." Steuben's arrival could not have come at a more propitious moment. Morale in camp had hit an all-time low and even officers had gone for weeks without meat. By late January Washington's overhauling of the supply departments started to produce some food. Washington permitted the opening of a civilian market: those who could pay could improve their larder. Also in January, the British brig *Symmetry* ran aground and its cargo was seized by American forces. Its hold yielded cloth, hats, shoes, boots, and stockings. Once again only the officers had the money to buy it.[16]

By the second week of February there was no meat at all for four days. Washington called the situation "most melancholy." As he rode through camp he heard from the huts of enlisted men the chant, "No meat, no meat." Desertions averaged twelve a day; scores of officers resigned and went home. Washington warned Congress of "a general mutiny." He feared a "fatal crisis" had begun. Steuben's arrival and his parade-ground formations as he taught the fine points of how to maneuver under fire distracted the hungry men until Wayne returned from New Jersey with the rustled cattle. Spring, discipline, higher morale, and fresh beef saved the half of Washington's army that still remained with him.[17]

Washington's new inspector general, Steuben, spouting profanity in several languages, imposed a sense of military discipline, a new method of organizing the army, and a rigorous program of military training. The new organizational plan included the designation of light infantry companies that could fulfill the specialized need for skirmishers that warfare in the wilderness presented. Steuben's genius was in being able to distill and transmit the essential portions of the European military tradition. In the bloody snow of broken boots on a frozen landscape, Washington's army learned to maneuver as smoothly as any parade ground regiment of British regulars. It would soon change the nature of the war.

*T*he British decision to evacuate Philadelphia and consolidate their land forces at New York caught Washington by surprise. The evacuation, which began on June 16, 1778, was executed by the new British commander, General Sir Henry Clinton, who as a field officer had led the devastating flanking attacks at Long Island and Brandywine. Incredibly, it was two full days before Washington caught on to what the British were up to. When he did, the chase was on. Washington now had the superior force, with 13,000 well-trained regulars to Clinton's loot-encumbered 10,000 men. And Clinton had another worry—interception by the French fleet, a major factor in the choice of an overland route. Clinton wanted to avoid a battle with Washington at this time and Washington had to chase him hard for seven days in an early summer heat wave. The new British commander was slowed by the fact that his entourage included a huge, 1,500-wagon baggage caravan, 3,000 Loyalist refugees and their belongings, and a goodly number of camp followers. The heat also may have had more effect on his troops, who were wearing their heavy, red wool winter uniforms in the steamy 100-degree heat. Washington sent out Lafayette with 5,000 men who finally overtook Clinton's rear guard at a place called Monmouth Courthouse, not far from where his army had narrowly escaped annihilation at the hands of Cornwallis's quick-marching columns in 1776. And if it hadn't been for the loud-mouthed British officer turned American general Charles Lee, recently released from British captivity two years after his breakfast-table capture, he might have destroyed the main British army in North America. Lee had recently been repatriated in an exchange of prisoners and automatically by seniority of appointment became second in command under Washington.

Lee had long since ceased to be Washington's rival for the position of commander in chief. It was not until thirty years after the Revolution that documents were found establishing that during the time he was in British custody, Lee had turned traitor. He had drawn up a plan for the British military conquest of the colonies and submitted it to Howe, who chose not to act on it. But at the time Washington knew nothing of this. He had heard, somewhat to his dismay, Lee's vitriolic discourses on the quality of the American soldier, who, Lee maintained in his monologues, could not stand up to British bayonets. But that was the man's style.

Because Lee was the second-highest-ranking officer, he had to be placed in command of the American right wing in the American attack against the British rear guard at Monmouth, and he replaced the eager Lafayette. Washington gave the order on June 27 to attack in the morning but left the details of the maneuver up to Lee.

The next morning, the British rolled slowly out of Monmouth toward New York, with Knyphausen and his Hessians in the lead, the wagons in the middle, and Cornwallis, together with the main British force, guarding the rear. By 10 A.M., large bodies of American troops had come up on all sides of the British rear guard. Quickly, Clinton gave Cornwallis orders to attack, even though the British were outnumbered. Clinton hoped his bold move would delay or drive off the Americans. Clinton was surprised to see the Americans, after a few feeble efforts, begin to retreat. Quick to seize an advantage, Clinton promptly gave orders to pursue and destroy the enemy. The problem was not with the high-spirited American troops, but with Lee, who had issued a few halfhearted orders and then contradicted them. As these senseless orders passed down the chain of command, units found themselves advancing while adjacent units on their flanks were retreating. The general confusion may have pleased General Lee. If treachery was his goal, he was succeeding marvelously; if he was looking for evidence that Americans still couldn't fight head to head with Englishmen, he was creating it all around him. Soon Lee's whole division was in retreat, the men staggering in the searing heat.

The whole business was somewhat perplexing to Clinton, the first to notice an odd fact: the Americans, while clearly in a confused state, were not running in panic. There was no litter of packs and weapons in their wake. Unfortunately for Clinton, he was unable to make use of this perception in time. Suddenly, just after the British forded Middle Ravine, the Americans turned around smartly and fired a volley. The volley had a discouraging effect on a British bayonet charge. The abrupt about-face was due to the arrival of a very angry General Washington at about noon.

In a towering rage, Washington ordered Lee to the rear, and, according to some reports, continued cursing and swearing—for the first time anyone could remember since the rout at New York. He ordered Lee placed under arrest; he was ultimately court-martialed, convicted, and sentenced to be suspended from the army for twelve months. Before the year was over, after one last blast at Washington in a letter to Congress, he resigned.

Washington now put "Mad Anthony" Wayne in charge of the thin American vanguard, which hung on grimly against the swarming British bayonet attack, but was giving way slowly, foot by foot. Wayne halted them in front of Washington's hastily formed main army. All afternoon, as men on both sides dropped of sunstroke, the British attacked with infantry and artillery and cavalry. Only a year earlier, it would have been a rout, but the Americans now stood firm. Neither army yielded. Clinton decided that he could not halt the assault. It would look like a defeat. There was prudence as well as pride in Clinton's tactics. Certainly his chances of making good his escape were improving with each minute he could keep Washington on the defensive. And he could see an opportunity—the American left flank was still disorganized. He struck it. But Steuben's training now paid off. The troops in the American center swung smoothly to intercept the British charge and fought it out with the redcoats hand-to-hand for more than an hour. Then Washington mounted a counterattack that drove the British back.

In the intensifying late afternoon heat, Clinton ordered another attack against the other end of the American line. He failed to anticipate that this would put his troops into a brutal artillery crossfire. Now Washington's infantry tightened ranks in European fashion and sent volley after volley crashing into the attackers—just as Steuben had taught them to do. Even the vaunted British Grenadier Guards could not withstand such an attack. Still, Clinton demanded one more effort. Taking an hour to reorganize his troops, he hurled them at Wayne's men in the front and center of the American line in an all-out attack. Clinton's audacity almost succeeded. The roaring British were too numerous for Wayne to stop and he had to fall back, but only until he was supported by the main American force under Washington's personal command. The British, exhausted, finally broke off the attack. Reasoning that he had protected his wagons and given a good accounting, Clinton called off the fight at dark. The next day he was gone, leaving Washington the battlefield, technically the sign of a victory. This time it was the British who had gotten out of a potential disaster alive. Washington had inflicted heavier casualties than he sustained: 250 British and Germans died, only 72 Americans. The British suffered 59 dead of sunstroke, the Americans, 37.

The overall effect of the Battle of Monmouth was that the British were back in New York, where they had started two years before. The difference now was that they had failed to hold the American capital and were relinquishing the Middle States. Now they were the besieged. Washington's army of veterans and powerful French allies with a fleet equal to Great Britain's bottled them up inside New York City.

By the summer of 1778, the American Revolution had settled into a long stalemate; for the first time, as Washington waited to coordinate his campaigns with the French, he could turn to dealing with the Indian attacks ravaging the frontiers. His relations with the Indians had never been good and the war exacerbated them. The Six Nations Iroquois had aligned themselves with their old masters, the British. For sixty years since the Treaty of Utrecht they had considered themselves British subjects and their leaders were educated in England and were baptized as Anglicans. Loyalists from the Mohawk Valley in New York had escaped to Fort Niagara on Lake Erie at the beginning of the Revolution. With Loyalist rangers under Major John Butler and his son, Walter, the Iroquois raided white settlements along hundreds of miles of frontier, pillaging, burning, and scalping. Early in June 1778, a force out of Fort Niagara traveled more than three hundred miles and destroyed settlements in the Wyoming Valley near present-day Wilkes-Barre, Pennsylvania. Major Butler reported taking 227 scalps and only five prisoners. The so-called Wyoming Massacre shocked and terrified the frontier and spawned numerous atrocity stories. For example, a half-breed Seneca called Queen Esther, it was said, arranged fifteen prisoners in a ring and, circling them and singing a dirge, tomahawked them one by one.

When more joint Loyalist-Iroquois expeditions raided German Flats on the Mohawk River (below Utica) in September and struck Cherry Valley, only fifty miles west of the state capital of Albany, in November of 1778, Washington decided to detach a large force of Continentals to be bolstered by state militias in the summer of 1779 to invade the Iroquois homelands around the Finger Lakes and the Genesee Valley of western New York, destroy their homes and crops, and force the Iroquois to deplete the rations of the British at Fort Niagara. He chose a frontiersman, Major General Sullivan, and gave him terse, carefully formulated orders: "The immediate objects are the total destruction and devastation of their settlements. . . . [The Indian country] may not be merely overrun, but destroyed." Sullivan was to lead a three-pronged attack, assembling his main force of 2,500 Continentals at Easton, Pennsylvania, on the Delaware. General James Clinton of New York was to march from Albany with 1,500 New York Continentals to the headwaters of the Susquehanna River at Otsego Lake and then float his forces downriver to rendezvous with Sullivan at Tioga. A third column was to set out from Fort Pitt in southwestern Pennsylvania (the former Fort Duquesne) with 600 Continentals under Colonel Daniel Brodhead. In all, Washington detached 4,600 Continentals, nearly one-third of his regulars. Sullivan was also to take artillery—the Iroquois, in all of America's century-long wars with European colonists, had never faced cannon. Washington the experienced former Indian fighter also stipulated that Sullivan's men were to attack with bayonet and war whoop, "with as much impetuosity, shouting and noise as possible."[18]

The Sullivan expedition lost three months while waiting for supplies and building roads to pave the way for the 1,200 packhorses, 100 officers' mounts, and 700 cattle. Sullivan's main force did not reach Tioga until August 11, 1779. They found the Seneca stronghold, supposedly "Queen Esther's Palace," deserted. Loyalist Butler had been alerted by American deserters about Sullivan's expedition but his commanding officer at Quebec, the Swiss-born general Frederick Haldimand, shrugged off the report: "It is impossible the rebels can be in such force as has been represented by the deserters." But Butler's green-uniformed Loyalist rangers roused the Indians to prepare to defend their homeland.[19]

Meanwhile, general James Clinton assembled his 1,500 men at Canajoharie, forty miles west of Albany on the Mohawk, with 200 flat-bottomed bateaux. The New Yorkers cut a 25-mile road over a high ridge and downhill to Lake Otsego. Hauling his boats by wagon to the lake's northern tip and paddling them to present-day Cooperstown, Clinton camped and waited for Sullivan. Clinton was chagrined to find out how low the Susquehanna River was that dry summer as it flowed out of the lake. He ordered a temporary dam built. Six weeks later, on August 9, when a courier brought word from Sullivan to begin moving south, Clinton breached the dam. Enough water had accumulated behind it to carry the bateaux thirty miles downriver in one day.

All along their route, the New York troops burned the deserted Indian villages. At Onoquaga, a Loyalist settlement, they put to the torch an Anglican church and all the Indians' log houses, which had stone chimneys and glass windows. When the New Yorkers rendezvoused with Sullivan, a military band sent along by Washington "played beautiful" as artillery fired a salute.

The delays now proved fortuitous. The Indians' ripe crops awaited as the troops attacked Chemung two days later. Fields full of corn, beans, squashes, and pumpkins fed the New York troops before they were totally destroyed. The Indians fled, sniping from the woods while the white soldiers gorged. One soldier wrote that he ate ten ears of corn, a quart of beans, and seven squashes. The troops trudged off with pumpkins impaled on their bayonets.[20]

On August 27, 1779, Sullivan's 4,000-man combined expeditionary force finally moved north along the Delaware with nine fieldpieces, including four 6-pounders, four 3-pounders, and a cohorn, a small, portable mortar that was also called a "grasshopper." The packhorses hauled solid shot and canister shot, which was timed to explode in the air and shower the enemy with small projectiles. Many of Sullivan's officers blamed the artillery for slowing down the march. "The transportation," Major

Jeremiah Fogg recorded in his diary, "appears to the army in general as impractical, and [as] absurd as an attempt to level the Allegheny Mountains."[21]

But when Sullivan's army struggled up the narrow, steep Chemung Valley defile and approached the Indian village of Newtown on August 29, the artillery proved welcome. Sullivan had brought along several Oneida Indian scouts. One of them climbed a tree on a 700-foot high hill and could make out painted Indians crouching behind a log breastwork camouflaged with green branches. The Loyalist-Iroquois position was well chosen. In all, a thousand Indians, probably the largest force of Iroquois ever assembled for battle, under Chief Joseph Brant, as well as 250 of Butler's rangers and 15 British redcoats, silently awaited Sullivan's advance.

Sullivan halted his column and detached a strong flanking force to attack the hilltop position from the rear. He positioned his artillery and opened fire on the breastwork with solid shot, spraying the defenders with canisters loaded with grapeshot and iron spikes. The terrified Iroquois endured the cannonade for half an hour, but the shells bursting behind convinced them that the enemy had outflanked them. They ran, the Loyalists with them. On the hilltop, the Indians and Continentals seesawed in hand-to-hand combat until Brant signaled the Iroquois to withdraw. Sullivan lost only three men killed and thirty-six wounded; twelve Indian men and one woman died. The whites scalped all the Indians. One Continental officer skinned two Indians from the hips down in an attempt to make two pairs of leggings, one for himself, one for his major.

Casualties on both sides were light at what became known as the Battle of Newtown but the artillery barrage had been decisive. The terrified Iroquois never again stopped to put up a fight. Sullivan's army was unopposed as it burned a swath from Elmira—where his men cut down eighteen-foot stalks of corn—to the St. Lawrence River and then southwest into the Genesee country. Detachments raided and burned Indian settlements in the Mohawk Valley, on the west side of Seneca Lake, and on both sides of Cayuga Lake. Typically, in a principal Indian riverside village southwest of present-day Genesco, the army collected an immense amount of corn, packed it into more than a hundred well-furnished "very large and elegant" houses, and then burned them all. At Aurora, they girdled and destroyed 1,500 peach trees. In all, Sullivan's army of 4,000 (Brodhead's column had turned back for want of shoes) destroyed forty villages and an estimated 160,000 bushels of corn as well as immeasurable quantities of other vegetables and fruits.[22]

Marching back to Elmira, the army celebrated its 500-mile expedition to the roar of a triumphant fireworks display and an ox roast, with a bull and a barrel of rum allotted for each brigade. A few days later, back at Tioga, they put on war paint and, led by an Oneida sachem, joined in a war dance, each step ending with a whoop. Finally demolishing their stockades, they returned to the Wyoming Valley. They had lost only forty men and had virtually eliminated the centuries-old culture of the Iroquois confederacy. Its survivors crowded into Fort Niagara and, as Washington had hoped, consumed precious British supplies and wasted gunpowder shooting at birds all winter.

While Washington had relieved the threat to his rear guard and seemed to have little to fear from the lethargic British commander Clinton in New York City, he had to deal with a new threat in Philadelphia. Joseph Reed, a failed merchant who had ridden out of Philadelphia in May 1775 as one of Washington's aides, now was president of the Supreme Executive Council of Pennsylvania, and he seemed determined to challenge the growing power of the military. Next to the tyranny of a strong Congress, what the Pennsylvania radicals feared most was that generals such as Washington really wanted to perpetuate themselves in power as an American military aristocracy replacing the old British nobility. The Whigs resented any threat of subservience to a military order. In the year and a half after the British evacuated Philadelphia, Benedict Arnold, wounded in Canada and crippled at Saratoga, served as Washington's personally appointed military governor of Philadelphia. He was considered a Washington favorite and he was becoming a lightning rod for political opposition to a strong national military establishment. In effect, Arnold became the first target for critics of the far more popular but out-of-range Washington. Arnold was preaching a hard new doctrine to ruggedly individualistic militiamen who resisted his brand of monotonous military discipline. His absolute insistence on the discipline that prepared men for battle seemed hierarchical, undemocratic, and distinctively English. Washington had faced this same problem with democracy in New England and had broken resistance with the whip and the court-martial.

After a brief stint as Washington's private secretary, the impecunious Reed had returned to Philadelphia and quickly rose to become chief executive of Pennsylvania. Reed had come to power after running simultaneously for three offices—delegate to Congress, Pennsylvania assembly, and Pennsylvania council—and by switching parties. Brought to power by moderate men, he deserted them to lead the radical attack on his old comrades, including Robert Morris and Silas Deane, and the army officer most closely aligned with them, Benedict Arnold. Reed's change of sides eliminated the moderate element in Pennsylvania, creating, in modern terms, a left-wing party, the Radical Whigs, and a right-wing party, the Republicans, whose leaders all were attacked in print and by mobs in the city's streets.

After Reed resigned from Congress to take over in Pennsylvania, it was more difficult for him to attack his Federalist foes. Instead, he concentrated his fire on the visible symbol of a strong central government, military governor Benedict Arnold. He criticized Arnold for his friendships with Loyalist merchants, for his extravagant style of living, even for attempting to stay out of the infighting between moderates and hard-liners. General Cadwalader accurately wrote General Greene at Washington's headquarters that Arnold was becoming "unpopular among the men in power in Congress, and among those of this state in general." He considered the campaign against Arnold ill-founded and the charges circulating against him in the city "too absurd to deserve a serious answer."[23]

When Reed learned of Arnold's private use of Pennsylvania's publicly hired wagons to haul the cargo of *Charming Nancy* from New Jersey into Philadelphia, and of his attempt to issue a passport to help Hannah Levy, the daughter of a wealthy Jewish Loyalist merchant, to join her family in New York City despite the Pennsylvania council's objections, he began his main assault. The Council summoned Arnold and his adjutant, Major Clarkson, to testify, but Arnold replied in less than tactful terms that he and his staff were accountable only to Congress and his commander in chief. Reed immediately fired off a protest to Congress alleging that Arnold had insulted Pennsylvania, treating its government with "indignity." He demanded that Arnold be removed from command in Pennsylvania "until the charges against him are examined." Although no charges had yet been specified, Congress appointed a special committee to investigate. Such a committee, Reed realized, was at cross-purposes with the Pennsylvania Council's attempt to assert its own authority. If Pennsylvania had to present evidence to the Continental Congress, it would be a tacit admission of a higher federal power. But if Reed backed down and did not offer any evidence, Arnold would be acquitted. While Arnold was delighted at Reed's quandary, the Council decided to keep up the pressure by offering Congress evidence only on the affair of the rented wagons. Reed, in charge of raising Pennsylvania's troops and levying Pennsylvania's share of tax revenues, now added a new threat: if Congress refused to oust Arnold, allowing him "to affront us without feeling any marks of your displeasure," Pennsylvania would think long and hard about cooperating with Congress in the future. This would especially cause severe problems for Washington, who not only relied on the troops of the Pennsylvania Line but on Pennsylvania's precious Conestoga wagons for the bulk of his transport.[24]

Early in February 1779, Reed and his councillors somehow got wind of Arnold's plan to take a furlough to visit Washington at his winter headquarters in New Jersey and then to travel to New York State to confer with that state's revolutionary leaders. For months, Arnold had been corresponding secretly with General Philip Schuyler, commander of the Northern Department, and meeting with James Duane, William Duer, and Gouverneur Morris. Arnold's friends in New York's congressional delegation had suggested to Schuyler that "the gentlemen of the State of New York" give Arnold a reward for his services in defense of their state during the Canadian campaigns of 1775, 1776, and 1777. They proposed that he be given one of two large confiscated Loyalist manors, either at Skenesboro at the foot of Lake Champlain or Johnson Hall on the Mohawk, to colonize with his former troops as a buffer against attacks from Vermont or Canada. Arnold was agreeable: he preferred Skenesboro's forty thousand acres near Lake Champlain, which were suitable for "iron works, mills, etc." He expected to pay for the land but hoped the grateful legislature would sell it to him very cheaply. On February 3, he planned to ride north to Kingston to negotiate with New York legislative leaders. Despite the encouragement of his powerful friends in the New York delegation to Congress, his Philadelphia Loyalist friends, including his beloved future wife, Peggy, considered the lands tainted because they had been seized from other Loyalists. On February 3, as Arnold was preparing to go to New York, John Jay sat down to write a strong recommendation to Governor Clinton for Arnold, which reveals how far Arnold had gone in his plan to leave the army and found a major new settlement on the New York frontier:

> Major General Arnold had in contemplation to establish a settlement of officers and soldiers who have served with him . . . and to lay the foundation without loss of time. . . . He gives our state the preference. . . . The necessity of strengthening our frontiers is obvious. . . . To you, Sir, or to our State, General Arnold can require no recommendation. A series of distinguished services entitles him to respect and favor.[25]

Reed and the Pennsylvania council were outraged that Arnold should escape them at the very moment they were preparing formal charges against him. On February 2, the day before Arnold was due to leave the capital, Reed rushed to the printer's eight charges against Arnold. As Arnold's portmanteau was hoisted onto his carriage and Major Clarkson helped him up, a proclamation was issued charging that, among other misdemeanors, Arnold had granted illegal passes to Loyalists; had closed the shops of Philadelphia so that he could make sizable purchases of foreign goods; had imposed degrading services on militiamen; and had used public wagons to transport private property. Arnold's "discouragement and neglect" of patriotic persons and his "different conduct toward those of another character" were "too notorious to need proof or illustration." To put teeth in its charges, the council proclaimed that so long as Arnold remained in command in Pennsylvania, they would pay none of the army's costs and would call out the militia only in "the most urgent and pressing necessity." No more militia would do Arnold or his staff's bidding.

The charges were made public, Arnold's aide Clarkson testified later, before Arnold saw them or could respond to them, and hours after Arnold drove across the frozen Delaware and that Arnold recrossed the river at Bristol the next day when he learned there was an express rider with a message for him from Philadelphia. Reed dispatched copies of the charges to every state and its congressional delegation and to Washington's headquarters in New Jersey. But according to Arnold, the first he knew of them was when his aide Matthew Clarkson overtook him on the road with a copy of the *Pennsylvania Packet* carrying the proclamation. That day, the council further resolved that, except in "the most urgent" emergencies, it would no longer call out wagons or militia to serve under General Arnold—which meant under Washington, who had appointed Arnold. The council also ordered that the attorney general of Pennsylvania was to prosecute Arnold in the state's courts. Facing indictment by Pennsylvania, Arnold had only two choices—to return to Philadelphia immediately to submit to the state's authority or to ignore the risks and press on to the army's headquarters, hoping for Washington's support. He decided to go on. To many Philadelphians, however, it appeared that Arnold had fled north toward the British lines.[26]

Alarmed at Reed's thoroughgoing denunciation, Arnold rushed to Washington's camp at Morristown deep in the snow-covered northwest highlands of New Jersey. As soon as he arrived, Arnold fired back a statement to the Philadelphia newspapers, protesting that he was being "persecuted." Arnold would not, he declared, submit to the authority of Pennsylvania; he would request that Congress order a court-martial to prove the council's allegations "as gross a prostitution of power as ever disgraced a weak and wicked administration."[27]

No official report of Arnold's visit with Washington survives, but whatever happened at Morristown made Arnold decide to abandon his plans to press on to New York to negotiate for land. Instead, a few days later, he returned to Philadelphia. As Arnold explained privately to Peggy, Washington had been sympathetic to him, had expressed outrage at the charges against Arnold, and had bitterly excoriated Reed and the Council for "their villainous attempt to injure me." Washington had urged him to request a congressional inquiry to hear the charges after Arnold protested that he did not trust the Pennsylvania politicians and would feel safer if he were tried by his fellow officers in a court-martial. Arnold's letter to the press shows that he acceded to Washington's advice but passed it off as his own idea. Washington's account of their meeting, written immediately after Arnold's treason, was somewhat different. When President Reed demanded of Washington whether it was, as rumor had it, true that he had received Arnold cordially, Washington replied that he could not even remember the meeting, "the conversation made so little impression on me." Washington's cool politeness that day thoroughly rattled Arnold.

It was that unmistakable Washington civility that amounted to incivility, and Arnold got the message. He quickly abandoned his plans to go on to New York. Dashing off a letter to Philip Schuyler, he blamed the bad roads and the worst winter in anyone's memory for putting off his visits.[28]

Arnold returned to Philadelphia to face criminal charges that involved virtually every major political controversy dividing the new republic. The case set off a tumult of "great debates" in Congress. After one particularly vituperative session, Congress voted to table a motion that Arnold be tried by a military, not a civilian, court on the grounds that to give in to Arnold's request would give Reed and the radicals a chance to accuse Congress of putting the interests of the military over those of the nation. Next, a motion by Reed's adherents in Congress that Arnold be removed from his command was defeated in a roll-call vote. Only Pennsylvania had a majority in favor of suspending Arnold. On February 16, every other state congressional delegation but Pennsylvania voted in Congress to refer the charges against Arnold to the committee presided over by William Paca of Delaware, which was already investigating Arnold's conduct. For two weeks, Paca's panel was "repeatedly pressed by General Arnold for a hearing with all the sensibility of a soldier injured in his honor." Arnold was quick to forward his own evidence and explanation. On March 5, Arnold alighted from his carriage at Independence Hall for the Paca committee's hearing. Arnold's defense was concise and almost straightforward. He defended his authority, as military governor, to grant passes.[29]

Arnold's fate was decided quickly, or so it seemed: the Paca committee cleared him of six charges they considered it within their power to try and recommended a court-martial for the charges of misuse of militia and wagons. Arnold was elated. He was certain that Washington or a board of officers would dismiss these two trivial charges. Sure that he was about to be vindicated, Arnold decided to resign as military governor of Pennsylvania. But the contest had become bigger than one man. It was a confrontation between state and nation. If a state could disband its militia and refuse the authority of Continental generals, then the quotas of Congress and the reserves of the national army would be rendered unpredictable and unreliable. The confrontation between Arnold and the Pennsylvania authorities had the potential for not only forming political parties in one state but dividing Congress into factions that could lead to the dreaded formation of national political parties that would, it was widely feared, injure the war effort. The rupture had grown so serious that there was even talk of moving Congress out of Philadelphia. Considering Arnold's reputation to be less important than the danger of an open left-right split, the full Congress voted to set aside the Paca report and the findings of the March 5 hearing and create a new committee to attempt to reach a compromise with the powerful Reed and his Pennsylvania council. After a stormy all-night negotiation, Henry Laurens of South Carolina wrote, "I feel this morning as if my life was breaking."[30]

The new committee recommended ignoring the Paca report and, even if it meant putting Arnold in double jeopardy, ordering him tried by court-martial. According to Thomas Burke of North Carolina, the debate in the full Congress was "peevish and childish," four states supporting Arnold but the majority resolved that Arnold should be tried by court-martial. On April 3, Congress reached an agreement with Reed allowing the charges against Arnold to be turned over to Washington. Arnold must once again journey to Washington's headquarters, this time to face a court-martial. In early April 1779, he protested to Washington. The case, he argued, had become an affront to the entire army. "Every officer in the army must feel himself injured" by the way one of them was being persecuted. He received a swift answer from Washington, who set the trial date for May first.[31]

When Reed threatened to provide no more Pennsylvania wagons unless Washington took the charges seriously and allowed time to gather evidence and witnesses, Washington granted an indefinite postponement. When Washington informed Arnold of this latest postponement, Arnold dashed off another demand to Congress to dismiss all charges. Indeed, sympathy for Arnold had been building. Congress now wavered. But when Pennsylvania's delegates warned Reed that Congress was about to dismiss all charges against its wounded hero for lack of evidence, Reed blasted Congress and threatened "perpetual disunion between this and the other United States." Confronted with the possible secession of Pennsylvania from Congress and from the war, Congress backed down and ignored Arnold's appeal.[32]

It was at this very moment that Benedict Arnold tore open a letter from headquarters that bore the seal of the commander in chief:

> *Dear Sir,*
> I find myself under a necessity of postponing your trial to a later period than that for which I notified your attendance. I send this information in a hurry, lest you set out before it might arrive. . . . In a future letter, I shall communicate my reasons and inform you of the time which shall be finally appointed.[33]

Terse, polite, vague, Washington's note left Arnold shaken. Arnold's old mentor, the man on whom he relied when his ungrateful country and its Congress deserted him, had now left him awaiting an indefinite sentence. Washington's boldest field officer was out of the war at least for a season. When no further word came from Washington, Arnold wrote a drastic letter:

If your Excellency thinks me criminal, for heaven's sake let me be immediately tried and, if found guilty, executed. I want no favor; I ask only justice. If this be denied me by your Excellency, I have nowhere to seek it but from the candid public before whom I shall be under the necessity of laying the whole matter. Let me beg of you, Sir, to consider that a set of artful, unprincipled men in office may misrepresent the most innocent actions and, by raising the public clamor against your Excellency, place you in the same situation I am in. Having made every sacrifice of fortune and blood and become a cripple in the service of my country, I did not expect to meet the ungrateful returns I have received from my countrymen; but as Congress have stamped ingratitude as a current coin, I must take it. I wish, your Excellency, for your long and eminent services, may not be paid in the same coin. I have nothing left but the little reputation I have gained in the army. Delay in the present case is worse than death.[34]

This tortured letter to the man Arnold admired as a father, the man who had urged him back into the fight after so many rebuffs, being passed over for promotion three times and court-martialed twice, had a ring of farewell about it. Arnold had given up hope of ever being appreciated. He said he wished only that Washington would not meet a similar fate at the hands of an ungrateful people manipulated by a "set of artful, unprincipled men in office." He was probably telling the truth when he said he had now lost everything. He had never been paid his Continental Army salary in the three years and seven months since he had been commissioned to lead the expedition against Quebec, plus the expenses allowed for a colonel's, a general's, a governor's table for his officers and guests. On April 27, the day Washington notified him his court-martial had been postponed indefinitely, Arnold was also notified that his accounts, bucked from Massachusetts to the Northern Department to Congress to the Board of War, were now to be scrutinized again by a congressional committee. He still had money but he was eating up his capital even as Continental currency depreciated to one-sixtieth its 1777 value. Arnold was tired of waiting for the politicians to rescue the nation's economy. He had decided to turn his back on the people who had rejected him and make peace with the British. Sometime early in May 1779, with the full knowledge and consent of his wife, Peggy, Benedict Arnold secretly offered his service to the British.[35]

Sixteen

"WHO CAN I TRUST NOW?"

George Washington had come to think of West Point on the Hudson River as "the key to America."[1] As long as he held it, he could maneuver his army and neutralize the British base at New York City. The road along the Hudson's west bank and the ferry that crossed the wide river just below West Point were the vital lines of communication between the French army now based in Rhode Island and Washington's main army. Roughly equidistant from Washington's winter encampments in Morristown, New Jersey, and his supply bases at Albany, Hartford, and in northwestern Pennsylvania, the forts at West Point were at the heart of Washington's quadrilateral strategy of offensive as well as defensive warfare, and he would commit its command only to a skilled and trusted general.

On August 5, 1780, Benedict Arnold wrote to his wife, Peggy, that American preparations for attacking New York City were being shelved because so few Americans had responded to the latest call for recruits. The entire American army was, however, marching to Dobbs Ferry so the British would believe they were about to attack the city. To appear strong enough to ward off a British attack, Washington had stripped West Point of all its Continentals, having only raw militia and invalids for its garrison.

Privately, Washington was on the verge of despair. All through the year 1779, his main army in the north saw little action as the French used it in support of their own operations against the British. Except for a reprisal in force at Stony Point, a night bayonet attack by "Mad Anthony Wayne," Washington's Continentals were sidelined. The French at first limited their contribution to the allied war effort by seizing Rhode Island after a botched first attempt in which American general John Sullivan tried to give orders to a French admiral and the French treated Sullivan's Continentals like rude country militia. Finally Washington had peeled off a southern army that cooperated with the French navy in attacking Savannah, Georgia, a Loyalist stronghold, but for the most part the French seemed bent on seizing rich sugar islands in the Caribbean and avoiding combat on land. Inactivity always depressed Washington. His only outlet, which became an obsession, was to build up his West Point stronghold on the Hudson in case the British once again tried a pincers attack up and down the waterway between New York City and Canada. Another worry during the long lull was the daily problem of keeping his army fit and properly supplied. At the same time several of his generals and at least two Congressmen pressured him to restore Benedict Arnold to a field command: Arnold had cleared himself of all charges at a court-martial in December 1779 and Washington had given him only a mild official reprimand for improper personal use of military wagons and improperly issuing a pass to a Loyalist ship owner. But Arnold was furious that he was not completely exonerated.

Two of Arnold's influential friends, Congressman Robert L. Livingston of New York and General Philip Schuyler, especially were putting pressure on Washington to grant Arnold's request that he be placed in command at West Point on the grounds that the commandant, Major General Robert Howe of North Carolina, was incompetent, had neglected his duties and weakened West Point. Resorting to half-truths, Washington countered that there was no "danger to the post at West Point" and that, indeed, he was "so well-persuaded of the safety of West Point" that he had "dismissed all the militia that were called in for the defense of the posts on the [Hudson] river." The letter directly contradicted his own activities on the Hudson and written instructions he had sent to Howe at West Point.

Fearful about supplies and enlistments, Washington wrote his brother, Jack, on July 6, 1780, "It is to be lamented, bitterly lamented, and in the anguish of soul I do lament, that our fatal and accursed policy should bring the 6th [of July] upon us and not a single recruit to the Army." The army was "reduced almost to nothing by short enlistments," went "five or six days together without bread, then as many without meat, two or three times without either." The early summer harvests were plentiful but army commissaries were redirecting them along with herds of cattle paid for by Congress and destined for Washington's army to the French in Rhode Island, who paid in gold, not depreciated Continental paper money. When Benedict Arnold joined Washington's army on the Hudson in midsummer, he confirmed Washington's bleak analysis in a letter to his wife, Peggy. The army had been "three days without a mouthful of meat and [West Point] is very little better." He sent this latest morsel of treasonous intelligence on August 25, one day after Peggy finally got word through to him that Clinton was willing to meet his price for West Point and its garrison, a price roughly equal to Benedict Arnold's entire new worth, including all the debts, public and private, that were owed to him.[2]

At West Point the 200-foot-deep channel narrows and bends nearly ninety degrees, then immediately bends another ninety degrees, squeezing between high cliffs on the west bank and the rocky shores of Constitution Island to the east. Once the point was fortified, British men-of-war that dared to run the gauntlet against the river's strong tidal current would still have to come about twice past the lethal broadsides of scores of well-placed heavy cannon. In 1775 Arnold's friend, the military engineer Bernard Romans, had laid out redoubts and batteries on the east side of the Hudson and recommended that the west point of land overlooking the island also be fortified. The first fort at West Point, modeled after Ticonderoga, with high earth and log walls and four triangular ramparts on a bluff at the river's bend, was named Fort Arnold when it was built after Saratoga, and bristled with the heavy artillery Burgoyne surrendered. The fire of the guns from Fort Arnold and Constitution Island protected a 1,097-foot chain, each 12- by 18-inch link of 2-inch-thick bar iron weighing at least one hundred pounds, which floated on log pontoons just below the river's surface to block passage of the river.

When the Marquis de Chastellux visited the stronghold that autumn, he described West Point as a ring of forts perched on hills and cliffs in the shape of an amphitheater, protecting each other. In addition, there was, on the outer plateau behind Fort Arnold, a small city, including rows of wooden officers' barracks, a hospital and tents, a bakery, powder magazine, storehouses, a jail.

At the end of July 1780, after Clinton called off the British attack on Rhode Island and withdrew his armies from eastern Long Island and New Jersey into his heavily fortified defensive lines, Washington and the American army marched and countermarched, trying to entice Clinton into leaving New York City, leaving it vulnerable to a French naval attack. But Clinton was biding his time, waiting for Arnold to betray the Hudson forts. On the last day of July, Arnold overtook Washington on a high bluff opposite Peekskill, New York, where he was watching the last of the American brigades being rowed across the Hudson at King's Ferry. It was a sweltering midsummer day, and thousands of weary soldiers were taking all of it to march down the twisting dirt road to the landing below Fort Lafayette, cross the river, and tramp up the steep grade at Stony Point for a 25-mile march south to Tappan, the main American base camp.

As Washington sat on his tall bay charger, he could see long columns of tired Continentals, their flintlocks shouldered as they shambled along, saddle-weary dragoons and artillerymen trudging beside their horse-drawn cannons; groaning wagons full of wounded men suffering in the hot sun from dysentery, cholera, fever; more than two hundred creaking Conestoga wagons filled with barrels of wheat and salt pork, rolling along behind a thousand huge drayhorses.

Among George Washington's attributes as a general was his stubborn unpredictability. Off and on for weeks, as Arnold's friends in Congress prodded Washington to give Benedict Arnold the command at West Point, Washington not only resisted the pressure, but pointed out that he was short on good battle-seasoned major generals. Benjamin Lincoln was a prisoner in Charleston, South Carolina, which had fallen to the British after a long siege in May; Nathanael Greene had been removed from command in the Hudson Highlands and was going south with a detachment to replace Gates, who had been routed and disgraced at Camden, South Carolina, only a month before in August. Old William Heath of Massachusetts was coming out of semiretirement and Washington hoped to put him, not Arnold, in charge of the rear-area base at West Point. As Washington later explained to Joseph Reed, when he met with Arnold in June he had told him:

> As we had a prospect of an active and vigorous campaign, I should be glad of [his] aid and assistance, but saw little prospect of his obtaining such a command as [West Point]. . . . It was my intention to draw my whole force into the field . . . leaving West Point to the care of invalids and a small garrison of militia; but if, after his previous declaration, the command of the post, for the reasons he assigned, would be more convenient and agreeable to him than a command in the field, I should readily indulge him.[3]

Washington decided that he needed Arnold in command of the entire left wing of the army, three divisions of his best infantry. It was the post of honor, an appointment that would have resuscitated Arnold's reputation in a single stroke by making it apparent that he was back in Washington's favor. Washington, no doubt, expected Arnold to accept it, gratefully. So on that hot August afternoon in 1780, when Arnold rode up to Washington at King's Ferry, the commander in chief, turning from watching the loaded barges glide across the Hudson, nodded to him with his usual grave courtesy. In Washington's mind, Arnold's promotion to divisional commander was a settled issue. Washington later recalled that Arnold "asked me if I had thought of anything for him?" Washington was pleased to see the brave Arnold back on a horse, reporting for duty, back in the fight. Yes, yes, he answered, smiling. Arnold was to have "a post of honor." Arnold smiled, too: the post of West Point was now his, in his gift to deliver to the British. But Washington went on: Arnold was to be a divisional commander, in command of the left wing. "Upon this information," Washington remembered, Arnold's "countenance changed and he appeared to be quite fallen, and, instead of thanking me or expressing any pleasure at the appointment, never opened his mouth." Officers closer to Arnold that day said his face had turned dark red, almost purple, as if he were angry. Washington, perplexed, asked Arnold to ride on to his headquarters and wait for him.[4]

Arnold may have been the only high-ranking American officer who did not know that Washington had already restored him to a field command, and that the general orders for August first had already been written. As Washington rode back toward headquarters, he was sad that the years of political wrangling and inactivity seemed to have sapped Arnold's martial spirit so badly that he would now settle for such an inferior command. Washington rode on and patiently argued with Arnold, trying to prod him, embarrass him into fighting at his side. But Arnold was adamant, arguing passionately about his wound, his need for a rear-area assignment. Two days later, Washington issued new general orders. Arnold was to "proceed to West Point and take command of that post and its dependencies." To justify assigning such a senior officer to West Point, Washington expanded Arnold's duties to include not only all the Hudson River forts from West Point south to Dobbs Ferry on both sides of the river but also command of a corps of infantry and cavalry "advanced towards the enemy's lines." Washington himself was marching south to the New York–New Jersey border.[5]

*B*enedict Arnold lost little time at West Point, selecting head-quarters that were ideally situated for clandestine activities. With his staff and servants, he took over Beverley, the confiscated mansion of Colonel Beverley Robinson, commander of the Loyalist King's American Regiment and the man who had recently written to Arnold to persuade him to assume a leading role among the Loyalists. The sprawling white clapboard house was set back a mile from the Hudson on a bluff among dense trees at present-day Garrison, two miles south of the ferry crossing to West Point. The house and its approaches could not be seen by officers at forts across the river.

There was no respite to his preparations for selling out West Point. A former aide reporting to duty found that Arnold had changed since Saratoga, becoming "very tenacious of ordering and attending to everything himself."[6]

*A*s soon as Arnold learned in late August that Clinton had approved the £20,000 payment for his defection and the surrender of West Point and 3,000 men, he called for returns of troop strengths from all his posts and then added them up: they came to 3,086 men—86 more than the minimum. His problem was that he did not want to obtain more troops, but as inconspicuously as possible deploy those he had so that West Point could not be defended against the impending British attack. He went about his clever shell game in a way that made it appear he was carrying out Washington's orders to buttress West Point's incomplete defenses even as he crippled the fortress's garrison. Some of his task was easy: a French engineer had concluded that the pontoons supporting the great chain across the river were rotted and that the large iron staples holding either end needed to be reinforced. Arnold simply did nothing to repair them.

On August 12, Arnold began to systematically weaken the garrison by ordering 200 of the 1,500 soldiers up the river to cut firewood. Usually, Arnold would have taken care of this routinely, but to keep alive the myth of his own decrepitude, he began to pester Washington about all sorts of minor business. At first, he complained that there were no camp kettles at West Point for incoming recruits and not even enough tents. Arnold bombarded the new quartermaster general, Timothy Pickering, with complaints about "this poverty-struck place." On August 16 he wrote, "Everything is wanting." He claimed that he could not carry out badly needed repairs on the redoubts, the barracks, the provost, without harnesses for ten teams of horses. Since the barracks could house only 800 men, he needed tents for that number again, but could find none: his men were living in lean-tos. And there was only one camp kettle for "80 to 100 men." Without a rapid infusion of supplies, "the garrison will be in a wretched, uncomfortable situation next winter," and by the next spring, West Point would be "defenseless." Arnold may have deliberately been trying to drain supplies from the main army to weaken his new enemies further; at the very least he was papering files in Congress and at Washington's headquarters to explain why he was doing little or nothing to strengthen West Point.[7]

In all, Benedict Arnold was able to weaken West Point's garrison by one-half in less than two months. He did not raise a protest when Washington requisitioned four companies of artillery. He sent another two hundred men down the river to Haverstraw for outpost duty. He detached even more men, some of his precious artillerymen, to escort Loyalist prisoners all the way to Washington's camp at Tappan. There were wine and fruit and fresh vegetables, a result of Arnold's sharp trading with neighboring farmers from his well-stocked larder, but Arnold was selling off barrels of port and rum and hams for hard cash, repaying himself, he told Franks, for all the meals for which Congress never paid him. Franks and Varick compared notes and swore to each other, they later testified, that they would no longer cover for Arnold's black-market dealings. One day when a Loyalist ship's captain came to headquarters to buy three barrels of port from Arnold, Varick blurted out that every time Arnold sold provisions for gold or silver, it made it that much harder to induce farmers to sell provisions to the garrison for Continental paper money. Arnold ignored Varick. He dropped his voice to a whisper, apparently agreeing to the sale, and then waved the would-be buyer out of the room.

Arnold's sale of army provisions seems at least to have been provoked by the news that Congress on August 12 had turned down a petition for pay raises for general officers. Arnold could not grasp the fact that Congress had no money. A desperate Congress sent the generals not a raise but a sermonette that left Arnold livid:

Patience and self-denial, fortitude and perseverance, and the cheerful sacrifice of time, health and fortune are necessary virtues which both the citizen and soldier are called to exercise while struggling for the liberties of their country; and that moderation, frugality and temperance must be among the chief supports, as well as the brightest ornaments of that kind of civil government which is wisely instituted by the several states in this union.

Congress reiterated its two-year-old promise that Arnold, like other major generals, would receive a bonus of seven years' half-pay and 1,100 acres of land after the war. Furious, Arnold proposed that a "committee" of 1,000 or 1,500 soldiers march on Congress.[8]

Arnold had been forced to take a Loyalist, Squire Joshua Helt Smith, more and more into his confidence. Before the Arnolds left for the bateau ride up the river to West Point, they invited Smith and his wife to join them the following weekend at Beverley. If Clinton approved his latest proposal, Arnold would need Smith's house for his midnight meeting with Major John André, now head of Clinton's secret service in New York City and Arnold's chief contact in the plot for the past eighteen months.

On August 16 Arnold learned that Washington was coming north. He wrote in a letter with a confidential postscript:

> I shall be at Peekskill on Sunday evening, on my way to Hartford to meet the French admiral and general. You will be pleased to send down a guard of a captain and 50 at that time, and direct the quartermaster to have a night's forage for about 40 horses. You will keep this to yourself, as I want to make my journey a secret.[9]

Arnold knew how rarely Washington traveled without his army, how vulnerable he would be. Not only Washington but Marquis de Lafayette, chief of artillery Henry Knox, and their combined staffs would be crossing the Hudson en route to Hartford for secret talks with the French command at Hartford, Connecticut. Arnold put a terse footnote on his interrupted letter of September 10 and 15 and sent off his most trusted courier under an illegal flag of truce to Clinton with word that Washington was coming. If the message arrived in time and the British moved quickly, their warships on the Hudson with the help of a few hundred dragoons could capture Washington as he crossed the river Sunday night, the eighteenth. If they did not arrive in time to take him during the ferry crossing, he would be spending the night at Peekskill, within an easy ride of the nearest encampment of British dragoons. Washington's second in command, General Lee, had been captured in just such a raid in 1776.

Arnold then dispatched an express rider to Washington's camp. He had received a letter a week earlier from Washington, asking for details on West Point's defenses. At a September 6 council of war with his generals at Tappan, New York, Washington had asked a number of questions that no one but Arnold could answer about the fortress's ability to hold out under a major British attack. "My answers to the questions proposed by your Excellency to the council-of-war I will do myself the honor to deliver in person." Now, Arnold had the perfect excuse to gather up-to-the-minute intelligence for the British from the post's officers to turn over not only to Washington, but to André. He wrote down a complete inventory of the 120 cannon at West Point, the brigade major's detailed orders for the garrison "in case of an alarm," and the engineer's report of the minimum number of men needed to man the works, 2,438 (there were fewer than 1,500 now on duty).[10]

Arnold's covering letter to Washington was all duplicity: a British attack would not be "very dangerous," with "little probability of succeeding." Washington had asked if Fort Arnold, the main fort, could hold out if the British took the weaker outer redoubts. Arnold responded that Fort Arnold, with 1,000 men protected by bomb-proof casements and 1,200 yards from Fort Putnam, the nearest outwork, "of course would not" fall to the British. Arnold's tone was brusquely reassuring: it would take a British army of 20,000 a long and bloody siege to capture West Point. His words were ironic: "Everything could be changed by the fluctuating situation of our affairs." The outcome of the war "may be totally changed in a short time by a variety of circumstances which may happen." Arnold hemmed and hawed at Washington's request for strategic advice: "It appears extremely difficult for me to determine with any degree of precision the line of conduct proper to be observed." Arnold had learned of Gates's disastrous defeat in South Carolina. Arnold resisted the urge to volunteer for the now-vacant southern command, once again his, by right. He had already written to Nathanael Greene, calling Gates "that hero," suggesting his defeat would "blot his escutcheon with indelible infamy." Gates's cowardly retreat before the British at Camden had "in no wise disappointed my expectations or predictions on frequent occasions."[11]

*L*ate the afternoon of September 18, 1780, Arnold personally led his handpicked guards to King's Ferry, where he met Washington the commander in chief at Squire Smith's Belmont before accompanying him across the Hudson to Peekskill. With Washington rode young Marquis de Lafayette and his aide, Captain James HcHenry, Henry Knox, Washington's aide, Colonel Alexander Hamilton, and a squad of nineteen of Washington's Life Guards. As the ferryboat crossed the river, it came within spyglass range of the *Vulture*, but Arnold's message about Washington's crossing evidently had reached New York City too late for a British raid: the three-masted sloop-of-war *Vulture* floated silently in the distance.

Washington's twenty-year-old legal aide, Alexander Hamilton, joined the commander in chief and Arnold at Peekskill after supper and went over Robinson's letters. Riding along with Washington's party to its next stop, Arnold turned over his long, written answer on the state of the defenses at West Point to Washington, who was already worried about the weakened condition of the fortress. It was the last time Washington ever saw Benedict Arnold.

As they rode east, Washington had his own misgivings about West Point, if not about Arnold. He had received a warning from a trusted spy on Long Island that one of the American generals "high up" was in league with the British. But the vulnerability of an undermanned West Point to sudden British attack had worried him for months. In recent weeks, Washington had diverted an entire regiment of Continentals to Haverstraw Bay, their picket posts within shouting distance of Belmont. He had built up forward bases at Dobbs Ferry to keep pressure on Clinton in New York City and beefed them up with two regiments of Connecticut militia. Only two weeks ago, he had ordered Ethan Allen, now a Vermont militia major general, to be ready to support Benedict Arnold at West Point in case of a British attack up the Hudson.

Then Arnold sent a coded message to Sir Henry Clinton. The British would have a second chance to capture Washington and his generals when they came to West Point "to lodge here on Saturday night next," September 24. If Clinton wanted to bag Washington as well as capture West Point, there would be no better time. Arnold would arrange for Washington's party to make a leisurely afternoon inspection of West Point. Once again, delay was Arnold's weapon of choice. But Arnold's meeting with André must happen swiftly and smoothly. Washington and the French no doubt were making final plans for a joint attack on New York City. Clinton must strike first.[12]

When he sat down weeks later to write his version of the West Point conspiracy, Sir Henry Clinton summarized his strategy for exploiting Arnold's defection in very few words:

> General Arnold surrendering himself, the forts and garrisons, at this instant, would have given every advantage which could have been desired. Mr. Washington must have instantly retired from Kingsbridge [at the outskirts of New York City] and the French troops upon Rhode Island would have been consequently left unsupported and probably would have fallen into our hands. The consequent advantage of so great an event I need not explain.[13]

Washington would be sent reeling, and when the Hudson was brought under British control and New England was cut off from the south, the

Revolution would, at last, sputter out. Arnold's message that Washington would be crossing the Hudson at Peekskill with a corporal's guard and could easily be captured the night of the eighteenth did not reach Clinton in time, but by September 19, Clinton was so sure of the success of his plan that he asked that newly arrived admiral George Rodney's ships be ready to dash up the Hudson as soon as his spymaster, John André, returned from a secret meeting with Benedict Arnold. Sir Henry later explained to Lord Germain, in London, that he was "determined not to make the attempt" but under "particular security," that Arnold was not planning a counterplot, that his surrender of the forts and their garrisons was part of "a concerted plan between us [so] that the King's troops sent upon this expedition should be under no risk of surprise."[14]

*O*n the morning of September 25, 1780, Arnold's bride of one year, nineteen-year-old Peggy, had planned a breakfast reception for the commander in chief's arrival, but Washington sent ahead his aide, Captain Samuel Shaw, and Lafayette's aide, James McHenry, with word that he would be late and that breakfast should go ahead without him. The commander in chief had taken a longer route back from Hartford for reasons of security and had spent the night at Fishkill. Peggy Arnold stayed with the baby in the master bedroom with its big windows and balustraded porch, a sunny, quiet place. She was exhausted not only from nine days in an open wagon but from anxiety over the safety of her friend André. She planned to go downstairs later, when Washington arrived. Arnold had come to the table with a neighbor, Dr. Eustis, Alexander Hamilton, and McHenry. They had just been served when Lieutenant Joshua Allen, muddy and dripping from riding through a downpour, clambered into the foyer with an express message from Colonel Jameson, in command at North Castle.

> *Sir*
> I have sent Lieutenant Allen with a certain John Anderson taken going into New York. He had a pass signed with your name. He had a parcel of papers taken from under his stockings, which I think of a very dangerous tendency. The papers I have sent to General Washington.[15]

British spy John André's luck had run out as he approached Pine's Bridge over Clark's Kill, half a mile north of Tarrytown, between nine and ten o'clock on Saturday morning, September 23, 1780. Three young militiamen who were absent without leave from their unit had banded together into a gang to waylay and rob Loyalist travelers. They forced André into the woods beside the road and through a gate into a thicket, where they ordered him to strip. They searched every piece of clothing, finding his watch and some Continental dollars. By now, André was naked except for his boots and stockings. André's and the Americans' testimony about the strip search was quite different. To a sympathetic American, Dr. Isaac Bronson, who examined André late in the day, André confided what happened next. They had ripped up the housings of his saddle and the collar of his coat and, finding no money there, were upon the point of letting him go when one of the party said, "Damn him! He may have it in his boots!" They threw him down, drew off his boots, and discovered the papers. David Williams, one of the highwaymen, testified:

> We told him to pull off his boots, which he seemed indifferent about, but we got one boot off and searched in that boot, but could find nothing. . . . We found there were some papers in the bottom of his stocking, next to his foot, on which we made him pull his stocking off, and found three papers wrapped up.

As the naked André anxiously watched, John Paulding, leader of the gang, struggled to read the documents, finally shouting to the others, "This is a spy!" Ordered to get dressed, André listened as the men argued about what to do with him.[16]

*B*enedict Arnold did not take time to read Colonel Jameson's list of documents found in André's stocking: he knew them only too well. Excusing himself from the breakfast table, he hurried upstairs to Peggy, locked the bedroom door, whispered to her that André had been captured, the plot discovered, and incriminating papers were on their way to Washington, who was expected any minute. "In about two minutes," testified an aide, "General Washington's servant came to the [front] door and informed me that his Excellency was nigh at hand. I went immediately upstairs and informed Arnold of it. He came down in a great confusion and ordered a horse to be saddled, mounted him and told me to inform his Excellency that he was gone over to West Point and would return in about an hour." Arnold lashed his horse down a precipitous shortcut to the boat landing where the crew was eating breakfast. Life Guard Alpheus Parkhurst, on sentry duty, saw Arnold step into his bateau and draw his sword. He told his crewmen he would give them two gallons of rum if they would get him downriver to Stony Point and back in time to meet Washington. The bateau, according to Parkhurst, "started off in great speed" with Arnold sitting in its stern.[17]

At ten-thirty, Washington, Knox, Lafayette, and their 160-man entourage arrived at Beverley, opposite West Point. Washington had not planned to have breakfast until he had inspected West Point, but Marquis de Lafayette was eager to pay his respects to the beautiful Mrs. Arnold, who was noted, he told Washington, for her cooking and her hospitality. "Ah, Marquis," Washington chided him, "you young men are all in love with Mrs. Arnold. I see you are eager to be with her as soon as possible. Go and breakfast with her, and tell her not to wait for me." Lafayette, embarrassed, rode on with Washington and Knox, but Hamilton and Lafayette's aide, McHenry, rode up to Beverley, where a Major Franks apologized that breakfast was not ready and that Arnold was not there to greet him—he had gone over to West Point—and Mrs. Arnold as well as Colonel Varick were sick in their beds.[18]

As Washington crossed the river, he expected Arnold to have arranged a cannon salute, as much for the French officers as for himself, and he expected Arnold to be there to receive them properly. Washington later recorded in his diary, "The impropriety of his conduct when he knew I was to be there struck me very forcibly, and my mind misgave me, but I had not the least idea of the real cause." Much more shocking was the condition of the defenses at West Point: its garrison scattered, its barracks falling down, its earthworks half-completed. For two hours, Washington rode and walked over them, stunned by the neglect. Only days before, Arnold had assured him that West Point could withstand any British attack. It was the second blow Washington had sustained in a few days, the French informing him at Hartford that the British had them bottled up on Rhode Island and that they could not support his attack on New York City. Now, Washington realized that the American lifeline on the Hudson was vulnerable.[19]

Crossing back to Beverley, Washington went upstairs with Lafayette to the rooms reserved for their noonday meal. They had barely taken off their cloaks and gloves when a messenger arrived, this time from Colonel Jameson for the commander in chief. As Washington broke open the seal and paged through the documents, the terrible, incredible truth struck him: Benedict Arnold had sold out to the British. Remarkably clearheaded under fire, Washington was the only one at West Point that day to act calmly. He immediately ordered Alexander Hamilton and James McHenry to go after Arnold. Lafayette came into the dressing room where Washington was sitting, head down, hand trembling with its load of treasonous papers, murmuring to Henry Knox, "Arnold has betrayed me. Who can I trust now?"[20]

While Washington had been across the river at West Point, Peggy Arnold ran down the hallway in her dressing gown, her hair disheveled, shrieking. She had gone to Varick's room the day before, he testified at his court-martial, "while I lay in a high fever, made tea for me, and paid me the utmost attention in my illness." Still running a fever from a long bout of dysentery, Varick now rushed up the stairs, where he found Peggy screaming and struggling with two maids, who were trying to get her back into her room. "The miserable lady" was "raving." Peggy grabbed the young aide by one hand, cried, "Colonel Varick, have you ordered my child to be killed?" Varick testified that Peggy then "fell to her knees at my feet with prayers and entreaties to spare her innocent babe." Varick "attempted to raise her up, but in vain." Major Franks and Dr. Eustis, the fort's physician, "soon arrived, and we carried her to her bed, raving mad." Years later, Varick would say that Peggy was acting to protect herself and her baby, to buy time for her husband's escape. But on September 25, 1780, when she was twenty and he was twenty-seven and devoted to her, Varick was only the first to be taken in by what at least began as a brilliant piece of acting, but apparently developed into a true dementia fueled by her fear that she might never see her husband or her friend André again. Her world had been exploded by a plot she had encouraged, aided, and abetted, and the sheer nervous tension of the day of discovery completely fooled everyone around her. It would be the twentieth century before the opening of the British headquarters papers at the University of Michigan proved what the eighteenth century refused to believe—that a young and beautiful woman was capable of helping Benedict Arnold plot the greatest conspiracy of the American Revolution and then completely fooling the astute warriors around her. Varick, like the others, could see "no cause for all this." He still did not know of Arnold's treason.

When Peggy learned that Washington had come back from West Point without Arnold, she cried out to Varick again that "there was a hot iron on her head and no one but General Washington could take it off, and [she] wanted to see the general." After Dr. Eustis examined the hysterical woman, he left the room with Varick and Franks and told them that they must send for Arnold "or the woman would die." By now, her repeated insistence that Arnold was gone forever had made the two aides suspect that Arnold had indeed gone forever, over to the enemy. They confided their fear to Dr. Eustis, but added they were afraid to make such an unfounded charge about their commanding officer to Washington, who still had not told them by noontime that he already knew. The threesome decided they must make the first move by letting Washington "see her unhappy situation." Varick went to Washington's room and told him all he knew, then accompanied Washington to Peggy's bedside. Varick told her, "Here is General Washington." Clutching her baby at her breast, Peggy said it was not Washington:

> She said no, it was not. The General assured her he was, but she exclaimed: "No, this is not General Washington; that is the man who was going to assist Colonel Varick in killing my child." She repeated the same sad story about General Arnold.

Washington retreated from the room, certain Peggy Arnold was no conspirator.[21]

When Hamilton had come back from his chase after Arnold he brought Washington a letter from Arnold:

On the *Vulture*, 25 September, 1780

Sir;

The heart which is conscious of its own rectitude cannot attempt to palliate a step which the world may censure as wrong. I have ever acted from a principle of love to my country, since the commencement of the present unhappy contest between Great Britain and the Colonies. The same principle of love to my country actuates my present conduct, however it may appear inconsistent to the world, who very seldom judge right of any man's actions.

I have no favor to ask for myself. I have too often experienced the ingratitude of my country to attempt it. But from the known humanity of your Excellency, I am induced to ask your protection for Mrs. Arnold from every insult and injury that a mistaken vengeance of my country may expose her to. It ought to fall only on me. She is as good and as innocent as an angel, and is incapable of doing wrong. I beg she may be permitted to return to her friends in Philadelphia, or to come to me, as she may choose. From your Excellency I have no fears on her account, but she may suffer from the mistaken fury of the country.

I have to request that the enclosed letter may be delivered to Mrs. Arnold, and she be permitted to write to me.

I have also to ask that my clothes and baggage, which are of little consequence, may be sent to me. If required, their value shall be paid in money. I have the honor to be with great regard and esteem, your Excellency's most obedient humble servant.

Benedict Arnold[22]

Despite his surface calm, Washington knew better than anyone that this was the most serious crisis of the Revolution. He quickly shifted regiments, called his best battle-seasoned units in from New Jersey, Connecticut, and Massachusetts, units headed by men who had fought under Arnold—Scammell, Meigs, Dearborn, Lamb. He put West Point under Nathanael Greene's command. He gathered his army around him like a cloak, evidently expecting the British to attack, with Arnold as their guide. Years later, honest, angry John Lamb would describe the consternation at West Point in 1780. Had André "exhibited a presence of mind worthy of his reputation for sagacity, the die had been cast which [would have] sealed the fate of the Highland passes, and of the army." West Point, "weakened as it was by the contrivances of Arnold, could not have made a successful resistance." The formidable British forces gathering for the kill were "sufficiently numerous to assault it on all sides at once."[23]

Washington moved quickly, decisively, ordering André brought to West Point for interrogation and a speedy court-martial. André was questioned in the next room. It was one of the few times Washington let go of his temper. Washington exploded at Colonel Jameson for his "egregious folly." If it hadn't been for Jameson's "bewildered conception" of his duty to tell Arnold that he had captured André, "I should as certainly have got Arnold," Washington wrote to Lieutenant Colonel John Laurens in Philadelphia. Publicly, Washington refused to concede the possibility that the Arnold-André conspiracy had included their attempt to betray him to the British, a belief that spread quickly throughout the country and persisted, making Arnold's treason more personal, evil, Judas-like. "How far he meant to involve me in the catastrophe," Washington wrote Laurens, "does not appear by an indubitable evidence, and I am rather inclined to think he did not wish to hazard the more important object of his treachery by attempting to combine two events, the lesser of which [Washington's capture] might have marred the greater." To Joseph Reed in Pennsylvania, Washington confided there had been reasons for doubt: "I am far from thinking he intended to hazard a defeat of this important object by combining another risk, although there were circumstances which led to a contrary belief." One of these was Arnold's knowledge of Washington's movements. To Major General William Heath, Washington acknowledged that Arnold "knew of my approach and that I was visiting [Beverley] with the Marquis [de Lafayette]." Washington's aide-de-camp Alexander Hamilton wrote a full report to Congress, which concluded that, while Arnold would have been "unwise" to try to capture Washington at the same time he surrendered West Point, he admitted "there was some color for imagining it was a part of the plan to betray the General into the hands of the enemy. . . . Arnold was very anxious to ascertain from [Washington] the precise day of his return, and the enemy's movements seem to have corresponded to this point."[24]

If Washington chose not to believe that his capture at West Point was Arnold's real objective, there were others who did. Lafayette, with him that week and a member of John André's court-martial, apparently propagated the French view. "The plan was [for the British] to come up suddenly before West Point and to present all the appearance of an attack," Lafayette wrote to the Chevalier de La Luzerne, French minister to the United States. "Arnold intended to say that he had been surprised by a superior force. . . . After retreating to the redoubts at West Point across the river, [he was leaving] Washington, Lafayette, Knox and the rest to be captured while he stood wringing his hands." Colonel George Matthews of the 9th Virginia Regiment wrote that "General Arnold was immediately to send to General Washington for a reinforcement, and before that could arrive, was to surrender." Clinton was then "to surprise the reinforcement, which probably would have been commanded by General Washington in person. . . . Had this plan succeeded, it must have put an end to the war."

That Washington was Arnold's real quarry was beyond doubt to others close to him. From New Jersey, Governor William Livingston congratulated him on "the timely discovery of General Arnold's treasonable plot to captivate your person." President of Congress John Laurens, writing to Washington from Philadelphia on October 4, had no doubt of Arnold's intent. "I congratulate my country, whose safety is so intimately united with yours, and who may regard this miraculous rescue of her champion as an assurance that Heaven approves her choice of a defender."[25]

*I*f Washington could not catch Benedict Arnold and hang him for his treason, there was John André. Someone must die for so blatant a conspiracy. Hamilton, legal aide-de-camp to Washington, wrote to Colonel John Laurens on October 11 to explain why André was condemned to death by a court-martial within a few days of his capture. "There was, in truth, no way of saving him. Arnold or he must have been the victim, and Arnold was out of our power."[26]

On September 26, Arnold wrote a letter to Clinton to be sent on to Washington asserting that André had been operating legally under a flag of truce granted by Arnold and thus should be immediately released. Once again, Arnold took full responsibility:

> Thinking it much properer he should return by land, I directed him to make use of the feigned name of John Anderson under which he had by my direction come on shore. . . . This officer cannot fail of being immediately sent to New York, as he was invited to a conversation to me, for which I sent him a flag of truce.[27]

Washington was not swayed by Arnold's attempt to portray André's spying as a protected negotiation. Under the Articles of War, Washington could have hanged André outright as a spy without a trial. André had been caught in disguise with hidden papers, behind enemy lines, violating not only Clinton's advice to him but the Articles of War. Washington had already executed eight British spies in the war. He wanted to assert the sovereignty of the United States and he wanted a showcase trial, but not a lone one. He named fourteen high-ranking generals, presided over by Nathanael Greene, and charged John Laurens with cross-examining André. The generals were to weigh the evidence and make a recommendation of guilt or innocence to Washington, the final authority. The trial was to proceed immediately, to avoid dragged-out British appeals, the danger of reprisals, or attempts to rescue André.

The court-martial took one day. It was convened in the old Dutch church at Orangetown, New York, on September 29. Washington eavesdropped on the proceedings from an adjoining room. He did not believe in facing the accused for fear of relenting. Even before his interrogation, André did not deny the charges. Arnold had pressed the hidden papers on him. André considered himself a brave officer on a high-level mission for Clinton. The board of generals considered him a spy. The court-martial called no witnesses, and the same day the board, its opinion unanimous, reported to Washington that André "ought to be considered as a spy from the enemy and that, agreeable to the law and usage of nations, it is their opinion he ought to suffer death." The next day, on Saturday, September 30, Washington announced that André was to die on October 1, at 5 P.M. That night, Washington sent the dying man his last meal from his own table.[28]

Washington put off the execution until noon on October 2 and offered secretly to exchange André for Arnold. Under British rules, no deserter was ever exchanged; furthermore, Sir Henry Clinton had long ago guaranteed Arnold his personal protection if the plot failed. Far from agreeing to Washington's clandestine offer to exchange André for Arnold, Clinton had nominated Arnold as the man who would avenge anything that was done to André. While he tried for a week to arrange André's release, Washington would settle for nothing less than a trade. According to eyewitnesses, Washington's hand shook as he signed André's death warrant.

Eyewitnesses said the first great swing of the rope killed André. As thousands wept, his body was lowered to the ground and buried at the foot of the gallows. Forty-one years later, he was disinterred and reburied in Poets Corner at Westminster Abbey.

*B*enedict Arnold's letter threatening Washington did not reach him before André's execution. "The horrid deed is done," wrote Clinton to his family in England. "Washington has committed premeditated murder, he must answer for the dreadful consequences. Washington is become a murderer and a Jesuit."[29]

*T*he defection of the general Washington had so long admired could not be assuaged by the execution of André. When Arnold accepted a British general's commission and began to recruit a corps of Loyalists from refugee camps on Long Island and 212 deserters from the Continental Army, Washington decided he must be stopped. Light Horse Harry Lee suggested Arnold be assassinated, and Washington drew up secret orders. Lee selected the scion of a Tidewater Virginia family, Sergeant Major John Champe of Lee's Virginia Light Horse. On the moonless night of October 20, 1780, Champe spurred his horse past the Continental Army guard post at Totawa, New Jersey, and rode quickly toward Bergen. The British had so thoroughly fortified New York City that it was virtually impossible to desert to the British.

The twenty-three-year-old Champe, a tall, powerfully built man known for his "uncommon taciturnity and inflexible perseverance," had been dumbfounded when Lee called him into his tent and told him Washington wanted Arnold assassinated. He was to slip into New York

City, "insinuate himself" by posing as a deserter, join Arnold's American Legion, and kidnap the traitor. Lee would put him in touch with Washington's spies inside New York City. He was to bring him to Washington for hanging. Champe rode all night across northern New Jersey, barely outdistancing an American patrol, which hurried back to camp to report his desertion to Lee. Champe had no qualms about killing Arnold but did not want to be listed as a deserter: the punishment was instant death and he no doubt had seen more than one of the thirty-odd hangings for desertion that Washington used as examples at the Tappan camp. He wrote to Washington that he agreed to "the accomplishment of your Excellency's wishes" and would say nothing to link his task to Washington: "I have said little or nothing concerning your Excellency as I presume it would operate disagreeably should the issue prove disastrous." Champe worked with a secret agent named Baldwin from Newark who was paid "one hundred guineas, five hundred acres of land and three Negroes"; Champe was to be promoted to lieutenant if he succeeded. Washington personally approved the plan and provided the money from his own pocket, "with the express stipulation and printed injunction that he, A——d, is brought to me alive. No circumstance whatever shall attain my consent to his being put to death. My aim is to make a public example of him."[30]

As Lee's dragoons—his own comrades—chased him, Sergeant Champe struggled through a saltmarsh near Paulus Hook and, a heavy knapsack on his back, plunged into the water. A British patrol boat opened fire on the American patrol while another boat crew picked up Champe. After Champe spent the weekend in the provost jail, Sir Henry Clinton personally interrogated him for two hours before tipping him two gold guineas for deserting. Released, Champe strolled the streets of Manhattan in his uniform and caught the eye of Arnold. When Champe told Arnold his desertion had inspired his own, Arnold bought him a drink and signed him up in his American Legion.

Over the next several weeks Champe frequently visited Arnold's house and found that every night Arnold ended a stroll in his garden with a visit to a brick outhouse near an alley leading down to the Hudson. Champe sent a message to Lee that he would kidnap Arnold the night of December 11: everything was to be ready. That very night Arnold ordered his troops—including Champe—aboard transports to sail for Virginia. Champe had to go along or face charges of insubordination or desertion. For the next several months he marched through Virginia with Arnold, pillaging his neighbors and fighting his own troops. It was several months before he dared desert again and rejoin his unit. The assassination plot had failed.

As the American Revolution became a civil war within a revolution, the treatment of Loyalists was a question that increasingly demanded Washington's attention. His feelings were divided: some of his best friends—including the Fairfaxes, Reverend Boucher, even his own mother—were not sympathetic to the revolutionary cause and in one degree or another were considered Loyalists. At times, Washington was lenient. When the fighting broke out at Lexington many Americans—John Adams later estimated about one-third—tried to stay neutral, many of those who were able retreating to country houses. Judge Edward Shippen, a Philadelphia Quaker, moved first to New Jersey, where the revolutionaries menaced him. He moved back to Philadelphia, where his admiralty court job had been abolished. When the British army advanced across New Jersey in pursuit of Washington's army, Shippen's eighteen-year-old son Edward went for a ride with two young cousins. On the spur of the moment, all three decided to join other Loyalists and the Hessians for the Christmas holiday festivities. When Washington's army attacked, Neddy Shippen was captured. After several days, Washington, who had dined with the Shippens only a year earlier and remembered the boy, personally ordered him freed.

Such was not the fortune of another dinner-table acquaintance, William Franklin, son of Congressman Benjamin Franklin and the former royal governor of New Jersey. Washington had visited the younger Franklin at Strawberry Hill near Rancocas with his stepson on Jacky's way to college in New York City. They had rival interests in land schemes and much to discuss. But since then Governor Franklin had defied Congress by continuing royal rule in New Jersey until he had been ordered placed under house arrest in Connecticut. He had violated his parole by issuing royal "pardons" to an estimated three thousand Loyalists in Connecticut and New York City until Congress ordered him placed in solitary confinement in the Litchfield, Connecticut, jail.

Shortly after William Franklin's arrest, his wife fled behind British lines in New York City, where by June 1777, she lay dying. Another Loyalist refugee wrote to Franklin that she was so weak she could not hold a pen. A doctor who knew her said she had given up seeing her husband ever again, and for no other apparent reason was dying. Only a visit from her husband could save her. William Franklin was not allowed to receive mail: it must have been Connecticut governor Jonathan Trumbull who allowed a servant to bring a note to Litchfield, where the sheriff allowed him to write a letter to General Washington. Brushing aside the flies, ignoring the stink of his fetid cell (where he was allowed no furniture), the erstwhile royal governor, who had known Washington since he had brought gift horses and food to all Braddock's officers so long ago, wrote to plead for a furlough to go to his wife's bedside. But when he received the letter Washington was still angry at William Franklin for what he considered a blatant violation of his parole. For all the sympathy he might feel, he would not overrule a direct order from Congress:

However strong my inclination to comply with your request it is by no means in my power to supersede a positive resolution of Congress under which your present confinement took place.[31]

He dispatched this note to William Franklin and sent Franklin's appeal to Congress along with his personal recommendation that the appeal be granted. Franklin's

> situation is distressing and must interest all of our feelings as I have no doubt of the great indisposition of this lady. I should suppose that after his solemn assurances [and] such further assurances as Congress may judge necessary [that Franklin] might be indulged to see her.... Humanity and generosity plead powerfully in favor of his application.

But Washington knew how congressional committees could stall unpleasant decisions. Benjamin Franklin had refused to intercede to prevent the already harsh treatment of his son. By backing the decision to Congress, Washington knew how long the appeal could take.

> If it is granted, he should have the earliest notice or the end and views of Congress may be disappointed in the death of Mrs. Franklin before his arrival.

Washington's letter took another week to reach Congress. His personal endorsement made a debate unavoidable. On July 28, Congress denied the request. By the time the congressional decision reached Washington, Elizabeth Franklin, first lady of New Jersey for fifteen years, was dead.[32]

*F*rom the time the French had entered the Revolution on the side of the Americans, the British had bottled themselves up in New York City, concentrating their few operations in the south. Loyalist refugees to England had convinced the ministry that the British could win by appealing for Loyalist support. All a British army had to do was to march into a rebellious state and raise the royal standard—and Loyalists would flock to the king's colors. Charleston became the prize, and it fell on the third British attempt in 1780.

Not only did Washington lose many of his best Continentals and General Benjamin Lincoln but the morale of his armies was at its nadir. As the value of Continental currency plummeted, his men grew more mutinous.

At the Morristown winter encampment in May 1780, troops of the Connecticut Line who had not been paid for five months and had been on short rations for several weeks prepared to march home. When their commander, Colonel R. J. Meigs, tried to stop them, one of the men punched him. Meigs called in a regiment of the Pennsylvania Line to seize the leaders and confine the men to their huts. A more serious mutiny took place the next month when thirty-one men of the 1st New York Brigade deserted from Fort Stanwix at Oriskany and were assumed to be heading for the British lines. Lieutenant Abraham Hardenburgh led Oneida Indian auxiliaries in pursuit, and they shot thirteen of the mutineers. It was the only time in the history of the U.S. army that an officer employed Indians to kill white soldiers.

In January 1781, the inactivity of winter quarters and grievances about food, clothing, living conditions, pay, and terms of enlistment provoked the Pennsylvania Line at Morristown to mutiny. The eleven regiments under the martinet "Mad Anthony" Wayne, known for his brutal discipline, were living in squalid huts built the preceding winter. Enlisted "for three years or during the war," they took this to mean whichever came first. At ten o'clock on New Year's night, roughly half of the 2,500 Pennsylvania soldiers came out of their huts with their muskets primed, captured the cannon and ammunition, and started to march away. Wayne and about one hundred officers harangued them, arguing that there was nothing they could do but try to alleviate their grievances and present them to Congress. Two officers were shot trying to keep the men from assembling.

Marching to Princeton, they seized the village on January 3. A Board of Sergeants ensconced themselves in Nassau Hall at the College of New Jersey (now Princeton), and the men pitched camp on the campus. Wayne, under guard, took up quarters in a nearby tavern. A delegation of congressmen and members of the Pennsylvania Council headed by President Reed arrived in Trenton, ten miles away, on January 6 and sent representatives to negotiate with the sergeants. As several generals, including Lafayette, arrived to talk with Wayne and the sergeants, Washington, who was in New Windsor, New York, at the main cantonment, decided not to intervene personally but to allow Wayne to deal with his men. Washington did send eighty chosen men to support him, but the sergeants ordered them blocked outside town. Washington reasoned that he should stay with his main army in case the revolt spread. He sent Wayne orders to stay with his men, refrain from using force, and urge them to cross the Delaware into their native Pennsylvania. Wayne proposed that Congress first flee Philadelphia and stay out of reach. Washington refused to pass along this advice. By now, five hundred New Jersey Continentals had joined the mutiny.

When news of the mutiny reached New York City, Sir Henry Clinton tried to exploit the unrest. He sent two secret envoys to Princeton. The sergeants arrested them. They were quickly convicted of spying and hanged. After three weeks of negotiations, Wayne wrote Washington that 1,250 infantrymen and 67 artillerymen had been discharged from duty on their oaths that they had been tricked by recruiting officers. Wayne promised them their back pay with adjustment for inflation, which now had reached nine hundred times the 1776 value of the dollar. Two leaders of the New Jersey mutiny were shot by a firing squad made up of fellow mutineers. When a small mutiny broke out in Wayne's division, now ordered south to reinforce Lafayette in Virginia, Wayne executed four men on May 22. The mutinies stopped.

Most of all, Washington believed, the men were starved for action. When the French decided that Savannah, Georgia, was the best target of opportunity for a combined American army–French navy attack, Washington's main army, under congressional orders to pen up Clinton in New York City, saw no major action for nearly two years. It takes victories to encourage recruits and, once again, Washington's army dwindled. Washington waited and brooded that he had lost the initiative. In desperation, by late in the summer of 1781 he began to draw up plans to besiege New York City to speed an end to the war, now in its seventh year.

For months Washington had been watching events in Virginia, where the best British field commander, Earl Cornwallis, had marched to the edge of the Chesapeake. Washington expected that Cornwallis, whose army was depleted by months of fighting against the dogged Nathanael Greene's southern army, would take ship back to New York City. As summer dragged by and Cornwallis dug in on the York peninsula, Washington daydreamed of the arrival of a French fleet so that he could trap Cornwallis and make his reinforcement or escape impossible. On August 14 he received an exciting message at his headquarters on the Hudson: the French Admiral DeGrasse was sailing for the Chesapeake with twenty-eight ships of war and three thousand crack French veterans. He would remain off Virginia until mid-October before sailing to the Caribbean, his real target, for the winter.

Washington jumped into action, careful to maintain the greatest secrecy. Within five days, leaving only a skeleton army in front of New York, he was on the march toward Virginia with 2,500 of his best Continentals. Every French soldier in America converged on Virginia: from Newport, Rhode Island, which they had wrested from the British, they marched south, linking up with Washington. Clinton was completely fooled: he thought the movement was a diversion in favor of the main attack on New York City. Now he was sure he could not spare any reinforcements for Cornwallis. By August 31 Cornwallis could see the French fleur-de-lis flickering from a topmast of one of DeGrasse's flotilla. By September 8, Washington had reached Mount Vernon for his first visit in seven years. He wrote no word, but none could describe his emotions after so many years. Three days later he was on the road toward Yorktown. He had sent Lafayette south in the spring and now he urged him to keep pressure on Cornwallis. He "hope[d] you will keep Lord Cornwallis safe without provisions or forage until we arrive." But it was already too late for Cornwallis to fight his way out of the trap. By September 5 the

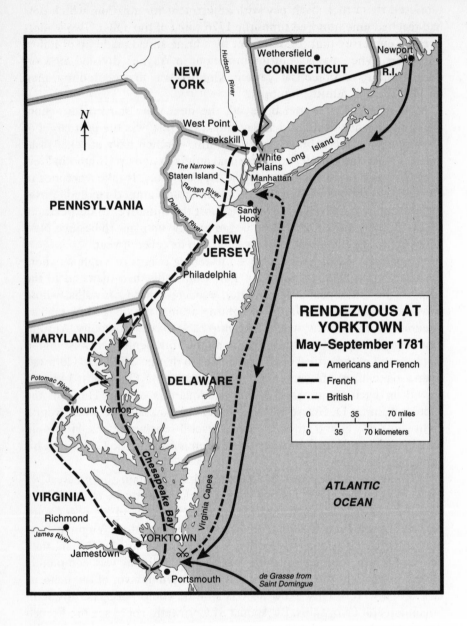

RENDEZVOUS AT
YORKTOWN
May–September 1781

- - - Americans and French
—— French
-·-·- British

0   35   70 miles
0   35   70 kilometers

As DeGrasse's French fleet sailed to Virginia from Saint Domingue, Rochambeau marched from Newport to meet Washington in mid-July. In late August, their combined armies marched toward Yorktown as Comte de Barras
sailed from Newport. DeGrasse reached the Chesapeake just before Hood
and Graves sailed in from Sandy Hook. The Battle of the Chesapeake Capes
sent the battered British back to New York while the siege of Yorktown began.

French had sailed into the Chesapeake and fought off the British fleet attempting to support Cornwallis. A second French fleet arrived with heavy artillery from the French base in Newport, Rhode Island, suitable for a siege. By the end of September the French and American armies had rendezvoused and were on the march to tiny Yorktown from Williamsburg. Washington took the right flank, the position of honor.[33]

By the end of the first week of October 1781 the French engineers and work crews had dug their first parallel trench close enough—only about 200 yards—to the British lines to begin round-the-clock bombardment by heavy guns. Washington was given the honor of touching a match to fire the first shot—from a French cannon. In the next five days Cornwallis lost 500 men to the murderous cannonade at close range: he himself lived in a cave to stay safe. He led only one fitful counterattack for form's sake. It was mostly a French affair. Washington allowed his favorite aide, Colonel Alexander Hamilton, to make a night bayonet attack on one British redoubt, but mostly French artillery and the impossibility of escape decided the outcome. On October 17, Cornwallis surrendered after only two weeks' feeble resistance. As the 7,241 British soldiers came out to lay down their arms, a British band played "The World Turned Upside Down." Many of the British veterans wept. Washington had no words to express his emotions. He lapsed into clichés about a "glorious event" and "an important success." It would be months before he knew that the British government had had enough. When word of Cornwallis's surrender reached King George III, he was talking to Lord North. All that the king could say was, "It is all over."[34]

Washington suffered an aftershock in the days after his final victory. All through the war, at Martha's pleading, he had kept Jack Custis out of the fighting. He was the last male of the Custis line, and he had a wife and small children. But Jack insisted on seeing the last battle: in a carriage behind the American lines he watched the siege of Yorktown. But more men died in the Revolution of disease than of wounds, and Jack Custis fell victim to a camp virus, probably malaria. Two weeks after Cornwallis's surrender, Jack Custis, Martha's last child, died at twenty-eight. To Lafayette, Washington wrote of his grief and of Martha's deep distress.

Five months had passed since Lord Cornwallis had surrendered at Yorktown before commissioners to negotiate the exchange of prisoners of war met for the first time in Elizabeth, New Jersey, in the spring of 1782. The Americans still held most of the 5,700 men who had surrendered at Saratoga nearly five years before. The issue of prisoners had finally reached the highest level of negotiations. Washington held more than 10,000 British prisoners as bargaining chips; the British held about half that number after the fall of Charleston (an estimated 10,000 Americans had perished in prison ships in New York and Charleston harbors). He did not let on that feeding and guarding so many men was a severe drain on already threadbare resources.

On the day the commissioners exchanged credentials, a schooner commissioned by William Franklin's Board of Associated Loyalists stood off Long Branch, thirty miles away, to pick up two of the Loyalist Associators. Ashore, a brief fight took place. The rebels captured Loyalist Philip White. He was never seen alive again. Rumors flew that White was cut down by sabers and his arms and legs hacked off. The story coincided with the Loyalists' growing anxiety over their fate at the hands of the British as well as the Americans. Cornwallis had refused to protect Loyalist prisoners at Yorktown and, as Washington had demanded, they were treated as prisoners of state, not war. This meant that they could be executed as traitors.

On April 8, 1782, as the prisoner talks dragged on at Elizabethtown, the Board of Associated Loyalists in New York City gave its permission to remove an American prisoner from the provost jail. Captain Joshua Huddy had been captured in a raid on New Jersey four days before Loyalist Philip White's disappearance. Huddy had admitted that he had pulled the rope that strangled Loyalist Stephen Edwards three years earlier. Huddy was taken out of the jail by Loyalist captain Richard Lippincott, who was the cousin of both Edwards and White. The removal papers were signed by William Franklin, president of the Board of Associated Loyalists, and countersigned by General Clinton. Lippincott was to exchange Huddy and two other prisoners for three rebels. Instead, with twenty-two other Loyalists, he took Huddy ashore and ordered him hanged from a makeshift gallows. A sign was pinned to his chest: it ended with the words, "Up goes Huddy for Philip White." Clinton learned of the lynching from General Washington.

George Washington had hanged many men throughout the long war, many of them Loyalists, but to him Captain Huddy—who had been captured while defending an American fort at Toms River, New Jersey—had committed no crime. As an officer and a prisoner of war he was entitled to the king's protection. Outraged, Washington demanded that Clinton send him the man responsible for execution. Clinton ordered Lippincott arrested but his four-month trial ended in acquittal. To Washington, Lippincott's guilt—and William Franklin's complicity— had been whitewashed. He flew into a rage. He ordered the hanging of a British prisoner of war of equal rank to Captain Huddy unless Clinton turned over William Franklin, the man he was sure was responsible. Washington ordered ten officers taken prisoner at Yorktown to draw lots. They refused and demanded an appeal to Clinton. Washington ordered that lots be drawn for them. The lot fell on Captain Asgill of the Grenadier Guards. Washington ordered him brought from Virginia to his headquarters at Morristown, New Jersey, and placed in solitary confinement.

The guardsman waited and watched as a huge gallows was erected outside his cell window. Congress studied the Lippincott court-martial record provided by Washington and decided that William Franklin was the culprit. As Washington prepared to carry out his threat and the prisoner talks remained stalled, the British prisoner's mother—the wife of a member of Parliament—wrote a personal letter to Queen Marie Antoinette of France appealing to her as a mother to intercede with King Louis XVI to ask Washington to relent. The French king and queen immediately complied. They wrote a letter to Washington that was "enough to move the heart of a savage" and instructed the French minister to intercede with Congress. In Paris, Benjamin Franklin, as American minister plenipotentiary the man in charge of all prisoner exchanges in Europe, was mortified by his son's involvement in the scandal. Amid the international uproar, Washington was stung that he had been made to appear the brute for ordering the execution of an innocent officer and gentleman. Reluctantly he bowed to the pressure from Congress and his French allies and freed Asgill. But he remained convinced that the British were covering up William Franklin's verbal orders to hang Huddy. William Franklin, the most notorious Loyalist after Benedict Arnold, sailed for England on a heavily guarded British convoy on August 13, 1782, some nine months after Arnold left the United States. George Washington's two greatest enemies never dared to return.

It was not until March 12, 1783, that the *Washington* brought news from France that on November 30, 1782, a peace treaty had been signed in Paris granting American independence. In that last year, as the war wound down, Congress was finally learning to do its job. It had finally given out civilian contracts to feed the army and had appointed a brilliant financier and merchant, Robert Morris, as superintendent of finance. Washington's second in command, Benjamin Lincoln, became the first secretary of war. As Washington prepared to turn over his army to Congress, he wrote another of what had become all-too-often beggar's letters for men and supplies. His last "Circular to the States" was different. This time he lectured the states:

> This is the time of their political probation. This is the moment when the eyes of the whole world are turned upon them. This is the moment to establish or ruin their national character forever. This is the favorable moment to give such a tone to our Federal government as will enable it to answer the ends of its institution. Or this may be the ill-fated moment for relaxing the powers of the Union, annihilating the cement of the Confederation and exposing us to become the sport of European politics which may play one state against another to prevent their growing importance. . . . According to the system of policy the states shall adopt at this moment they will stand or fall. . . . By their confirmation or lapse, it is yet to be decided whether the Revolution must ultimately be considered as a blessing or a curse: a

blessing or a curse not to the present age alone for with our fate
will the destiny of unborn millions be involved.

Circulated in newspapers all over America and Europe, this was called
"Washington's Legacy." Elias Boudinot, president of Congress, called it
the "finishing stroke to his inimitable character."

But even as Washington prophesied to Lafayette that "the winter will
be tranquil," the resentment of officers long underpaid and overpromised
by Congress boiled over at Newburgh in March of 1783. Washington got
wind that someone high up on his staff had anonymously circulated a
memo among his officers calling a secret meeting at New Windsor on
March 12. He moved quickly. Denouncing "such disorderly proceedings" and postponing the meeting for three days, he wrote what may
have been his most important speech.

*O*n March 15, Washington walked to the large new officers' barracks. His arrival was a surprise. He strode straight to the lectern, obviously
agitated, and pulling a paper from his pocket, began to read a stern lecture:

> Let me entreat you, gentlemen, on your part not to take any
> measures which, viewed in the calm light of reason, will lessen
> the dignity and sully the glory you have hitherto maintained.
> Let me request you to rely on the plighted faith of your country
> and place a full confidence in the purity of the intentions of
> Congress.

For five minutes he spoke, building to this point: it was his most powerful speech to his soldiers and they sat hushed.

> You will, by the dignity of your conduct, afford occasion for pos-
> terity to say, when speaking of the glorious example you have
> exhibited to mankind, "Had this day been wanting, the world
> had never seen the last stage of perfection to which human na-
> ture is capable of attaining."

He had finished his prepared speech, but his developed sense of theater
impelled him to add one more flourish. He took out a letter and then his
new eyeglasses, and slowly put them on: "Gentlemen, you must pardon
me. I have grown gray in your service and now find myself growing blind."
And then he walked from the hall. The Newburgh Conspiracy collapsed.[35]

*T*he devastation caused by one hundred heavy French cannon
at Yorktown and the defeat of a British fleet when the Royal Navy was
supposed to have naval superiority shattered the confidence of the English people. As news of one more British army surrendering reached

London, eight days of bloody rioting broke out and redcoats were ordered to shoot into crowds of looters. The news from Virginia combined with more bad news from India and Florida, until finally the British lost their nerve and began to negotiate independence seriously as part of a wider treaty with France and its allies. Until the ink was dry on a treaty, however, some three-fourths of the British forces remained undefeated and ready to go on fighting. A cautious Washington began to describe Yorktown as "an interesting event that may be productive of much good," yet he warned that "if it should be the means of relaxation it had better not have happened."[36]

By winter 1781–82, the Washingtons were in Philadelphia. While Washington negotiated over prisoner releases, distributed the spoils of Yorktown, and planned his next campaign, Martha set the style for a new republic. When she attended the opening ball of the new Assembly season she dressed all in black, as did her entourage of officers' wives; the American officers went wigless, the French officers dressed in white, and all the women wore black-and-white Union cockades. In March, Martha drove home to Mount Vernon and Washington went north to establish new headquarters at Newburgh, New York, on the Hudson near the New Windsor army encampment. There he waited—and waited—for the peace negotiations in Paris to conclude.

How George Washington brought the United States to victory in its war for independence was a mystery to the British, a wonder to the French, and a surprise to most Americans. As late as the autumn of 1780—only a year before the final victory at Yorktown—many Europeans regarded Benedict Arnold as the great military hero of the American revolutionaries and Washington as only the logician who supplied half a dozen better battlefield generals. When the American invasion of Canada collapsed and Arnold and its survivors fled, in 1776, the triumphant governor general of Canada, Sir Guy Carleton, trumpeted his success to London. A rebuke came sailing back: "I am sorry you did not get Arnold, for of all the Americans he is the most enterprising and dangerous." A French historian who had sat down to write a full history of the war put his pen aside late in 1780 after Arnold's defection. His first volume and a half were devoted to the exploits of Arnold—"the Hannibal of the North"—and Washington got only a footnote.[37]

Yet it was probably his penchant for avoiding the spotlight that helps to explain his amazing success. The British may have gotten him right. They, after all, had plenty of time to study him even if their leaders never seemed to learn. They called him "The Fox" and they played their hunting horns as they pursued him and his army. They meant it as an insult from fox hunters to a gentleman who understood their meaning. But they were right. He was smart, fast, elusive, familiar with the terrain, had great stamina, and most of all, had the capacity to strike isolated, fat, and complacent quarry when they least expected him.

And he could wear down the hunter.

Europeans still wonder why the American Revolution took so long. Revolutions are supposed to be quick. But eight years? Why couldn't the mighty British end it? They had a superb navy that blockaded the Americans from the start, cutting off their life-giving exports and their vital imports of arms, munitions, volunteers. But the British then and most Europeans now find the North American landmass, a vast countryside impossible to hold and pacify, incomprehensible: tens of thousands of miles of coastal caves and rivers were made for smuggling. And they totally underestimated the difficulty and expense of supplying the armies and navies it took to carry on such a war each year.

Some historians have tried to portray the outcome of a long struggle that included more than 1,200 armed clashes and the second-highest casualty rate in American history (second only to the Civil War) as a series of fumbling blunders by a blind giant. This red-coated minister staggered around until he bumped into another luckier leviathan, the French, who happened to be at the right place (Yorktown) at the right time. There is no denying the British did just about everything wrong. Their blockade failed. Their choice of generals was abysmal. They were inept at negotiating. They failed miserably at exploiting their natural allies, the one-third or so of the Americans who were willing to risk everything to oppose independence and remain in the proud British Empire—the Loyalists.

But these traditional explanations overlook two elements of the mystery: the entry of a monarchist France on the side of the colonists revolting against their king—and Washington. These two strands are intertwined, and that fact may help to explain why a weary England finally gave up most of its first empire. Not the least of the brilliant strokes of the Americans was to set aside a quite ardent and long-developed hatred of the French and seek their help. Astute Americans, such as Benjamin Franklin, who had studied the French at close range, knew how filled with humiliation and rage was the generation of younger French aristocrats, such as Lafayette, who had seen the English kill their fathers in the Seven Years' War and diminish their empire and their navy in the Treaty of Paris in 1763. George Washington, who had fought the French for so long on the Appalachian frontier, was perspicacious enough to trust French armies on American soil long enough to let them help him oust the haughty British. Even more important, Washington knew how to tempt his French allies with lost sugarplum islands in the Caribbean while keeping their armies away from what was to him the prize—the vast trans-Appalachian region and the old centerpiece of New France—Canada. Lafayette had coaxed the king of France to send Washington enough men and money to win back lost French possessions in America with the undoubted expectation that he, Lafayette, would lead a great Franco-American army to liberate Quebec. Instead, Washington distracted and diverted him with a small and hollow command in Virginia—and then he sent Von Steuben to watch him.

It was this capacity to fathom the motives of men and then to play off them to his own advantage that gave Washington power and enabled him to keep it in the face of the acknowledged enemy. Time after time Washington remodeled not only his army but his general staff until only fat, loyal Henry Knox and an equally elusive outsider, Nathanael Greene, of all the sunshine soldiers of 1776, were with him at the kill. Washington trusted only men as loyal to him as to the American cause. At war's end, he was surrounded by competitive, adoring young men who could imagine being George Washington one day but, in the meantime, basked in his words of praise and his every suggestion without resenting his totally obsessive control over every detail of American war and politics. The frontier post commander, the innovative Virginia farmer, the master land speculator, the breakneck rider—all had combined and metamorphosed into the first modern American corporate executive. The Americans won their revolution because Washington and his corporate family had introduced a new age that the British did not recognize or begin to understand and failed to adapt to. To win a modern war would now take more than great battlefield generals, which Washington was not; it also would take a creative, patient, micromanaging logistical genius, which George Washington certainly was.

He understood the importance of morale, terrain, and transport. He made political compromises to make sure his army was supplied, mobile, and flexible. Given the choice of guaranteeing the support of Pennsylvania's vital Conestoga wagons or placating his troublesome field commander, Benedict Arnold, he alienated Arnold. He was always short of good generals but he won the war without Arnold. He could not have won without wagons. Always a better commanding general than any of his British opponents, he was often hamstrung because his subordinates were not the equals of their opposite numbers. America, rebelling against aristocracy, had no hereditary officer class to draw upon.

Most of all, General George Washington was like Washington the farmer and Washington the frontier colonel—a master of improvisation, of trial and error. Stealthy, suspicious, elusive, and tenacious, he never attacked unless he thought he could win, putting the survival of his army—which was indistinguishable to him from that of the cause of independence—above every other consideration. Hard to catch, he was dangerous when cornered, either by plotters or by the Hessians at Trenton. And he was always wonderfully quick to react in a crisis, as he proved in the days after Arnold's treason, when only the traitor himself was lost to the American cause. As a general and in his private and public life, he was always moderate, always modest. A war was a job to be done. And when it was done, he wanted nothing more than to go home and rock on his porch.

Seventeen

"I HAVE HAD MY DAY"

Only nine days after Washington's victorious march into New York City on November 25, 1783, the last British troopship hoisted sail and slid silently through the cordon of French and American ships to head out to sea. Washington was already bored after a week of elaborate dinners and fireworks. He was ready to leave for home. He had personally written to thank and disband his troops in all but a few frontier and southern posts. He had a staff man, his aide-de-camp, Colonel David Humphreys, write all the appropriate speeches in answer to the paeans of churches, civic groups, and municipal officials who insisted on wining and dining him. But there was no escaping the embarrassing ritual of standing and listening to tributes that sounded as if he were already dead. Washington had never been very good at receiving praise.

Whenever he could interrupt the round of official receptions for a few hours, Washington went shopping with Martha, who had just joined him. For months she had been unwell at his last headquarters camp at Newburgh in upstate New York. Normally jovial, always smiling, her eyes quick and flashing, she had grown depressed and ill as they waited to go home until the last threat of armed clash sailed away with the British. In his first postwar letter to friends in England, he called her health "incompetent" and told of her frequent "bilious fevers and colics" that "reduce her low," so low that she had been unable to write letters for long periods. When the Continental Congress had moved briefly from Philadelphia to Princeton that autumn and summoned the general for conferences, Washington refused to drag her along. To move twice with all their accumulated baggage was too much to ask of her. Each year of the long war, she had moved north from Mount Vernon to join him at his headquarters, wherever it was. In September, she had recovered enough to drive to

Princeton with him. There, under a great marquee captured from the British, they had entertained all of Congress. The Washingtons returned to Newburgh early in November, and Martha, her spirits rising, kept busy packing off wagonloads of their wartime acquisitions homeward. Only in late November did she join him in Manhattan.[1]

Slipping away from his headquarters at Number One Broadway, they hunted for presents for Martha's four little grandchildren, orphaned when Washington's adopted (and only) son died at the very moment of final victory at Yorktown. Washington had vowed he would not buy anything from England that he could get anywhere else. Now he and Martha went to New York on a shopping spree. Martha bought herself hats and stockings, an umbrella, sashes, lockets for her little granddaughters. Washington bought them toys, books, a whirligig, a fiddle for their music lessons. Wherever the two alighted from their carriage—the tall thin general in his navy blue uniform and the round, less-than-five-foot-tall matron wrapped in her heavy cape—crowds gathered and mothers held up their children to see them.

As soon as the last British sail disappeared, Washington was ready to go. There was no question in *his* mind at least that he would stay in uniform to preside over a military government. He had resolved not to stay in New York City once the British left. He had precisely arranged every detail of his trip home. He summoned his officers to Fraunces Tavern, at the foot of Wall Street. At precisely four o'clock on November 25, they filed into a long, low-ceilinged room upstairs where only a few days earlier British officers had dined. The last four American generals in town plus a score of field officers crowded into the small, dark-paneled room. All rose when Washington entered. They were restless, subdued. They knew they were assembling for the last time. They knew that their lives were about to be altered radically. In all its simplicity, this was the last supper of the Revolution. The trays of bread, beef, and cheese, the bottles of claret and decanters of brandy must have seemed opulent to many of the men who had gone without meat for months in the darkest days of war. In the guttering candlelight of a late winter day, they picked halfheartedly at the plates of cold meats; they sipped the wine as if it were a communion. Few of them had appetites. Nobody got drunk. Everyone could see that Washington was not himself. Usually, he could be counted on, in the company of his official "family," as he called it, for some wordplay or a sophisticated barnyard joke, the coinage of eighteenth-century officers and gentlemen. Today, however, Washington was silent. After picking at his food, he poured himself a little brandy from a decanter, the signal for the others to take a glass with him. Then he rose. He did not fish out the customary prepared speech from a breast pocket or put on the spectacles that he had recently begun to wear in front of his officers. He stood up at his place and said, simply and softly, "With a heart full of love and gratitude, I now take leave of you. I most devoutly wish that your later days may be as prosperous and happy as your former ones have been glorious and honorable."[2]

He asked them to file up to him, one at a time, to say good-bye. Henry Knox, the onetime Boston bookseller who had brought him cannon and known how to use them so effectively, was first. He shook hands with Washington. Then Washington lost his customary reserve. He embraced Knox, kissed him lightly on one cheek. The others followed Knox's example, in a sad silent column filing up while Washington repeated the ritual. Many later recalled that Washington was weeping, something they had never seen him do before. Finally, he could stand it no longer. He left, leading a single aide out of the room. He left twenty battle-toughened veterans in tears. He only turned long enough to give his characteristic sweeping wave with his hat. Then he was gone. He hurried outside to a carriage where Martha was waiting. They drove quickly to a barge through a large cheering crowd. Their Hudson ferry-crossing to New Jersey began a four-week-long voyage south to Virginia, to Mount Vernon, to home, in peace.

*H*is mortal enemy all these years, King George III, had said that if George Washington could give up power, he would indeed be the greatest man of the eighteenth century. The most popular and powerful man in America, the man on horseback who had turned a mob of farmboys, sailors, and shopclerks into the well-disciplined soldiers who had humiliated the best army in the world, planned to carry out one more surprise attack. He would go to Annapolis, Maryland, latest seat of the Continental Congress, and resign his commander in chief's commission, turning over all his power to the feeble Confederation government. A serious student of the theater, he would make a dramatic appearance that would ring down the curtain on his public life. Few people alive at the time were prepared for such a bold gesture.

The king of England was, for once, in step with most Americans. English and Americans, subjects and former subjects, regarded the American Revolution as a replay of that earlier revolution, the English civil wars of the 1640s. That cataclysm, in which a country gentry member of Parliament had led an army that defeated the king, still haunted the eighteenth-century Anglo-American consciousness as much as the Civil War of the 1860s still affects Americans today. To Americans and the Englishmen, George Washington was Oliver Cromwell reborn. It was incomprehensible that he would willingly set aside his sword and relinquish power.

Only a few trusted members of Congress knew of his plan to resign utterly and return to civilian life, eschewing even his place as a delegate from Virginia. Washington had met privately with Thomas Jefferson at Princeton in October when Jefferson had rejoined the feeble Congress.

Both men agreed on the need to strengthen the weak national government, and Jefferson was already busy drawing up proposals for a federal capital on the Potomac. Jefferson had gone from Princeton south to Annapolis, the temporary capital; Washington went north to New York to disband his army. At Annapolis, Jefferson, the most distinguished member of Congress, was working secretly behind the scenes, stage-managing the important final tribute Washington was about to pay to a civilian government and, equally important, seeing to it that Congress responded with suitable dignity. Whether Congress won back any of the respect it had squandered during the Revolution depended on the perception, both in America and Europe, of Washington's grand public gesture of transforming his real power into the symbolism necessary for a democratic government.

Jefferson was personally crafting the resignation ceremonies, writing Washington's speech and Congress's reply, while Washington and his retinue traveled south at his customary five-mile-an-hour pace. The provost guard from West Point escorted the Washingtons as they rattled south along the Post Road. Two body servants and three aides accompanied them. Behind the carriage came two covered wagons, one with Martha's clothes and household appurtenances, the other, Washington's wartime gear, including a captured thirty-foot-long linen field tent, his well-worn field bed, a wooden chest of worn utensils. He had bought his kit out of his own pocket. Now he was about to give Congress the bill for eight years of out-of-pocket expenses, including Martha's outlays for travel. Throughout the long war, he had refused a salary but kept careful records.

*I*n financial terms George Washington badly miscalculated the length of the war. It was supposed to last only a few months, six at most. Instead it had lasted eight years and he gave up $48,000 in salary, in the currency of the times, or about $1.5 million today. He undoubtedly would not have given Congress such a bargain if he had known the war would drag on so long. But he was a man of honor and he refused to renegotiate his financial arrangements. He never discussed the fact that he was using up his personal wealth year after year without a salary. Away from Mount Vernon, he could nonetheless see its acres decline in productivity. Much of his profits had come from exports of wheat by ships to the West Indies and American coastal seaports, but this trade was disrupted by the British naval blockade. His tenant farmers could not sell their tobacco crops for cash and so they lagged years behind in their rents. And disreputable creditors paid him in depreciated Virginia paper currency. Meanwhile the costs of maintaining Mount Vernon and its nearly three hundred workers and slaves went on. Washington lost about $5,000 a year on the farms and another $50,000 in currency depreciation. In all Washington lost about one-half of his net worth during the Revolution. He made obvious financial sacrifices during the long war.

The $414,000 expense account Washington submitted to Congress in December of 1783 reflected the currency fluctuations Congress itself had allowed for. Yet, in what may be the greatest bargain anyone ever gave to Congress, Washington submitted a bill for only $88,000 in household expenses for eight years that included the entire headquarters costs of the commander in chief and his staff. It included meals for his staff officers and his aides-de-camp and his bodyguard, secretaries, servants, barbers, and tailors, as well as food and drink for "endless" visitors, foreign dignitaries, a free-grazing Congress, local officials, and would-be financial backers of the independence movement. The Father of His Country fed a large extended family. Still, his expense account amounted only to $1,000 a month for headquarters expenses.

About $100,000 of the bill was for "secret intelligence." Washington operated the secret service out of his own purse, personally handing out gold coins to spies for timely intelligence about the enemy: one example was John Honeyman and his advice on the capture of Trenton. Another $160,000 of the $414,000 was an adjustment to compensate for depreciation of the currency on a scale approved by Congress. If the currency had been stable, Washington's entire bill to Congress for eight years and eight months would have been only $250,000—about $2,600 per month ($100,000) for all expenses in today's terms of the commander in chief, his staff, his Secret Service, and the Central Intelligence Agency. It was one of history's best bargains and Congress paid it without question.

As the procession approached Philadelphia late on December 8, the First City Troop of Light Horse, in rich blue-and-red uniforms and towering shakos, rode out Old York Road to meet them, followed by the carriages of the once–Quaker City's revolutionary leaders. Long months of delays waiting for the peace treaty to be signed and the British to decamp had thwarted any organized national victory celebration. As the Washingtons hurried south, every town turned out in its own spontaneous, pent-up outburst of jubilation. How the war had transformed Philadelphia! Pacifist lawyer John Dickinson, once a Quaker, was now Pennsylvania's president. He and Robert Morris, both signers of the Declaration of Independence, had grown rich during the war. Church bells clanged as the cavalcade of carriages and wagons and cavalry with sabers drawn clattered down cobblestoned Second Street. A block away, in the Delaware River, a Dutch ship added its thirteen-round cannon salute to the tattoo of the city's shore batteries reverberating over the open water. Crowds surged toward them; wartime-precious candles illuminated every window. Arthur St. Clair, who had fled the great fortress at Ticonderoga, leaving it to the British without firing a shot, had the gall to ride out to honor Washington. Washington had so many conflicting memories of this city where he had been elected commander in chief. Twice, he'd had to return with armies to defend it. Now, standing victorious before the General Assembly of Pennsylvania in the same gray-paneled chamber of Independence Hall where he had once sat as a Virginia delegate to the First Continental Congress, he admitted in a short speech that the hero's welcome had overwhelmed him. "I consider the approbation of the representatives of a free and virtuous people as the most enviable reward that can ever be conferred on a public character."[3]

Before resuming their homeward journey, the Washingtons took a few more hours to shop. The general purchased a Pennsylvania hunting rifle, some books, a new pair of reading glasses, a case of good French wine, and other delicacies he could not hope to find in the Virginia countryside. Martha stocked up on imported delicacies for her famous kitchen: Brazil nuts, capers, olives, anchovies. And then they were off again. Washington dismissed his West Point guards and rode on with only his body servant and three aides: his pompous young secretary, Colonel David Humphreys; the verbose David Cobb; and the competent Massachusetts troop commander, Colonel David Walker. At Wilmington, Delaware, the next evening, leading citizens gave him "an elegant supper," lighted by blazing bonfires. "I return to a long meditated retirement," he assured the crowd, adding what was to become a set phrase: "I shall no more appear on the great theatre of action." At Baltimore, after another sumptuous dinner, the Washingtons were the guests of honor at a ball that lasted until 2 A.M. and then they were back on the road early the next morning. After covering only slightly more than two hundred miles in twenty-five days of near-constant celebration, they arrived in Annapolis, Maryland, on Friday, December 19. Washington knew that the Continental Congress was still in session but, a consummate master of drama, he had kept the delegates unaware that he had come to resign his commission as commander in chief. All they knew was that Washington was coming.[4]

Just west of town, a welcoming committee of Maryland officers and members of Congress awaited Washington. Another by now customary thirteen-gun salute greeted him as they all rode toward Mann's Tavern. Jefferson was among the dignitaries who welcomed the Washingtons, and the two old friends almost immediately went into a huddle. Both men were worried about the drift of the Continental Congress toward ineptitude and complete loss of respect both at home and in Europe. Earlier that year, Congress had fled Philadelphia when angry troops with fixed bayonets surrounded Independence Hall clamoring for back pay. Taking up temporary quarters in Princeton, the impecunious Congress had become the butt of jokes even as Washington's officers flirted with the idea of mutiny over their own arrears. In March, some of his senior officers had urged seizing Congress and setting up a military dictatorship. Washington, horrified, had confronted them. He urged them to "place a full confidence in the purity of the intentions of Congress." Again, at Princeton, he warned his departing troops that "unless the principles of the federal government [are] properly supported and the powers of the union increased, the honor, dignity and justice of the nation would be lost forever." But Washington sensed the need for a formal, dramatic farewell to underscore his fears and turned to Jefferson to orchestrate the event.[5]

That Congress could or would vote to receive Washington formally was not a foregone conclusion. When Washington's second in command, General Nathanael Greene, fresh from his victorious campaign in the south, had arrived in Princeton, Congress had voted to give him two cannon as mementoes, but the delegates did not formally receive or honor him. There was also the constant problem of a congressional quorum. Fewer than half the states had kept their delegations at full strength and able to cast votes. Only six states were properly represented when Washington rode into Annapolis; technically, it took nine to make up a quorum. When a single member went home ill, all business had to stop. Jefferson was haunted by the prospect of the definitive peace treaty arriving from Paris, where it had taken five years to negotiate, only to find insufficient congressmen on hand to ratify it. But, to Washington, Congress, with all its flaws, was Congress, and he would go ahead with his resignation.

Like Washington, Jefferson had great respect for the idea of Congress but little for the new breed of congressmen, so different from the men with whom they had first served. The Annapolis Congress, Jefferson wrote, was "little numerous but very contentious. Day after day was wasted on the most unimportant questions." Many members were "afflicted with the morbid rage of debate" who "heard with impatience any logic which was not [their] own."[6] Jefferson also considered many congressmen dishonorable for declaring that they could decide important questions without a quorum. He was taking no chance that such an important event as the transfer of Washington's military powers back to the civil Congress was carried off legally and with the necessary solemnity. He had arranged to be appointed chairman of the committee to receive Washington.

The next day, December 20, according to Washington and Jefferson's plan, Washington rode to the State House to inform the president of Congress in writing of his intentions. Washington's meeting with President Thomas Mifflin, his first aide-de-camp in the long-ago days of Bunker Hill, was perforce stiff and solemn. Washington had come to suspect Mifflin of plotting to overthrow him. Now his former aide was president of Congress, and Washington was, on the surface at least, coming to him for instructions. When the two men met, Washington handed him a brief note:

Sir:
I take the earliest opportunity to inform Congress of my arrival
in this city with the intention of asking leave to resign the commission I have the honor of holding in their service. It is essen-

tial for me to know their pleasure, and in what manner it will be most proper to offer my resignation, whether in writing or at an audience.[7]

Later that Saturday afternoon, Washington received an official answer. As Jefferson had arranged, Washington's letter had been read in Congress, which almost unanimously resolved that the delegates of only seven states were sufficient to act in this case. President Mifflin appointed Jefferson to chair the committee to devise the formalities of Washington's resignation and to write Congress's answer to Washington's resignation speech. In fact, Jefferson had already rehearsed every detail with Washington in a private meeting held immediately after Congress voted. Each man had spent several hours writing drafts of speeches. No aide would write this farewell speech for Washington, and Jefferson, likewise, did not trust such a state paper to the bombastic Mifflin.

Yet Mifflin was trusted to give the Washingtons a private dinner Saturday evening. After going to church on Sunday, Washington paid calls to Annapolis gentlemen, including his old second in command, Horatio Gates, hero of Saratoga. Then, on Monday night, Congress hosted a celebration that outshone anything the town of Annapolis had ever seen. More than two hundred guests, including all of Congress but Jefferson (who stayed in his boardinghouse with a migraine), arrived in a great traffic jam of carriages at Mann's Tavern. One Delaware delegate, James Tilton, wrote another, Gunning Bedford, that the "feast" was "the most extraordinary I ever attended":

> Between the two and three hundred gentlemen dined together in the ballroom. The number of cheerful voices with the clangor of knives and forks made a din of a very extraordinary nature and most delightful influence. Every man seemed to be in heaven or so absorbed in the pleasures of the imagination as to neglect the more sordid appetites, for not a soul got drunk.

After thirteen toasts, Washington was still able to stand up and speak. He offered a toast of his own: "Competent powers to Congress for general purposes." It was the succinct opening gun of Washington's long campaign to strengthen the central government.[8]

That evening, Maryland took its turn to honor Washington with a fancy dress ball at the new State House. Completed on the eve of the Revolution, the vast redbrick building's severe exterior and overpowering dome belied the warmth of its elegant interior. With Martha on his arm, Washington crossed the marble-floored portico, quickly bisecting the cheering citizenry, taking refuge in a wide arcaded hallway and seeing the shimmering Corinthian columns supporting the high central dome for the first time. The entire vaulted chamber was packed tonight with a jostling sea of invited guests. While Jefferson was too ill to be there, the fête was a tribute to his genius for behind-the-scenes organization, and Washington made the most of it. Tilton reported to Bedford, "To light the rooms every window was illuminated." The number of guests swelled to nearly six hundred, a "brilliant" assemblage, he added. George Washington, a famous dancer, astonished French officers with his skill and grace at the minuet. "The General danced every set," Tilton recounted, "that all the ladies might have the pleasure of dancing with him or, as it has since been handsomely expressed, get a touch of him."[9]

On Tuesday, December 23, at the prescribed noon hour, Washington's carriage rolled up the long hill above Annapolis Harbor and swung around to the portico of the State House amid the roar of a throng of well-wishers. With Martha at his side and two aides close behind, he stepped up to the heavy doors and halted. At a tap from an aide, the doors to the bright green Senate Chamber swung open. Charles Thomas, secretary of every Continental Congress since the first, led Washington and his aides to the front of the chamber past the twenty congressmen, all sitting with their tricornered hats on. Washington, his own hat in hand, sat down facing up to the speaker's platform where President Mifflin stood to welcome him. At a nod from Mifflin, the chamber's doors opened again and a surge of two hundred women spectators, led by Martha Washington, climbed the narrow stairs and found seats in the balustraded visitors' gallery. On the main floor, behind a low screen and on every window seat two hundred men who had fought under Washington and a few who had fought against him jostled for a place. Mifflin pounded his gravel for quiet. There was a moment when the only sound in the crowded room was the crackling of logs burning in the ornately fluted fireplace.

The hushed assemblage included Maryland's four signers of the Declaration of Independence, two future presidents, four Revolutionary generals, and several future cabinet members. Then President Mifflin gave the nod for Washington to speak. He rose and faced Congress, remaining in front of his assigned chair: he made no move toward the podium. Following Jefferson's lead, the delegates raised their hats, then lowered them, keeping them on. His hand visibly trembling, Washington drew a paper from his breast pocket and began to speak with great emotion. He was, he said, presenting himself "to surrender into their hands the trust committed to me." He was resigning to "a respectable nation" the "appointment I accepted with diffidence."

His voice broke as he neared the end of the three-and-a-half-minute talk, but by now many other people in the room were also choked up. Congressman James McHenry wrote to his fiancée, Margaret Caldwell, of the "solemn and affecting spectacle." The spectators all wept and there was hardly a member of Congress who did not drop tears. The general's

hand that held the address shook as he read. When he spoke of the officers who had composed his family, he was obliged to support the paper
with both hands. But when he commended the interests of his dearest
country to almighty God—his voice faltered and sunk. Washington
paused, recovered himself and went on:

> Having now finished the work assigned me, I retire from the
> greater theater of action and, bidding an affectionate farewell to
> this august body, under whose orders I have so long acted, I
> here offer my commission and take my leave of all the employ-
> ments of public office.[10]

With that, Washington folded the speech and, taking his commander in
chief's commission from his pocket, handed both up to Mifflin. He had
resigned.

*F*or most of the first year after he resigned as commander in
chief of the Continental Army, George Washington struggled to refill his
days with a sense of purpose. Through the decade of political struggles
and the hardships of the American Revolution, he had yearned for "the
walks of private life." He had wanted nothing more, he confided to his
young protégé, Marquis de Lafayette, than to be in "the shadow of my
own Vine and my own Fig-tree, free from the bustle of a camp and the
busy scenes of public life." Yet in his first restless months of peace, it only
gradually dawned on him that, for the first time in thirty years, he was a
common citizen again, even if America's most famous.[11]

As the postwar months slipped behind him, Washington turned fifty-
two and became convinced, as Martha hinted in her rare letters, that he
was growing old. His father had died before the age of fifty, as had many
of his family, but then, Washington had already outlived the average
southern male. He became subdued. Brooding, he tried to replace his
wartime habits with older, prewar routines. In February 1784, just before
his birthday, he wrote to Henry Knox, who had taken over his command
at West Point, "I am just beginning to experience that ease and freedom
from public cares which, however desirable, takes some time to realize."
After all the years in field tents and commandeered temporary headquarters, "for strange as it may tell it is nevertheless true," Washington was
having trouble readapting to his old country squire's way of life. "It was
not till lately," he confided to Knox, "I could get the better of my usual
custom of ruminating, as soon as I waked in the morning, on the business
of the ensuing day." It had been a "surprise," Washington added, "to find
that I was no longer a public man or had anything to do with public trans-
actions." Writing to Marquis de Lafayette, he went even further, as if to
convince himself:

I am not only retired from all public employments but I am retiring within myself, and shall be able to view the solitary walk
and tread the paths of private life with heartfelt satisfaction.
Envious of none, I am determined to be pleased with all; and
this, my dear friend, being the order for my march, I will move
gently down the stream of life, until I sleep with my fathers.[12]

At first the best he could do to compensate for the loss of the long-
accustomed companionship of his handpicked subordinate officers, their
businesslike behavior, their stimulating banter around his mess table, was
to formulate plans for new ventures. He began to plan for the first annual
meeting of the Society of the Cincinnati, a new order of veteran Revolutionary officers above the rank of colonel. He called the meeting for
Philadelphia for the following autumn. As if going off to war, couriers
rode out from Mount Vernon with detailed instructions to former officers.
Washington was having trouble beating his sword into a plowshare, he
confided to Knox. "I feel now like a wearied traveller" who, "after tread-
ing many a painful step with a heavy burden on his shoulders" had been
relieved of the weight. "From his housetop [he] is looking back and trac-
ing with a grateful eye the meanders by which he escaped the quicksands
and mires that lay in his way." He did not wish to seem ungrateful to "the
all-powerful guide" who had protected him in his wanderings, but now
he lacked any sense of direction.[13]

In that discontented first winter home, the more Washington began to
think of himself as old, the more he began to make excuses for giving up
old plans. To his friend the departing French ambassador Chevalier
LaLuzerne, he wrote that he was reluctant, as he had so long promised,
to visit Versailles to thank the French king in person for saving the American Revolution. Such plans no longer "comport with the years of a man
who is sliding down the stream of life as fast as I am." His letters show
that he especially missed the refined French officers who had paid court
to him for so many years. To Marquis de Chastellux, who had also gone
home to Paris, he wrote that he and Martha frequently and fondly remembered the Marquis's visits to Mount Vernon. "We talk of you often.
We wish in vain to have you [in] our party. We do not fail to drink your
health at dinner every day. I will not give up the hope of seeing you at
Mount Vernon before I quit the stage of human action. The idea would
be too painful." Washington's excuse for not leaving Mount Vernon long
enough to cross the Atlantic, he told LaLuzerne, was that his farms had
been "injured by war."[14]

During the past three years, when the fighting had swung north and
south and then settled in Virginia for a destructive final season, Mount
Vernon was visited by British raiders, but the house, at least, had been
spared. A British man-of-war had anchored in the Potomac within cannon
range and its captain, apparently ignorant of the fact that it was the home

of the rebel commander in chief, had sent a landing party to threaten it with destruction unless Washington's cousin Lund, the wartime farm manager, reprovisioned his ship. Lund had ransomed Mount Vernon, buying off the British captain with twenty slaves, some barrels of water, flour from Washington's mill, and hams from his smokehouse—only to have Washington fume at him that he would rather have seen Mount Vernon burned than give the British anything. Now that the war was over, Washington plunged himself into restoring his farms, finishing decorating and furnishing Mount Vernon's new wings, planting new meadows and a formal garden, breeding new herds of horses and cows, new flocks of sheep.

Only the rudest outline of his 1774 plan to renovate Mount Vernon had been completed by his return ten years later. The library wing was completed by late 1774 while he sat as a delegate to the first Continental Congress in Philadelphia. Two years later, as he led the retreat of his emaciated army across New Jersey, the exterior shell of the north wing, including the banquet hall, was roughed in: there were outer walls, windows, doors, and floors, but the walls remained unpainted, the fireplace unfinished, the rooms, unfurnished. By 1778, by the time the French joined the Americans in the war against the English, as Washington pursued the British army back across New Jersey toward New York City in a blistering heat wave, work on Mount Vernon ground almost to a standstill. Only two men, the master builder and one assistant, remained on the job. By 1784, when he resigned his command, Washington's most original design innovation, the 90-foot-long portico that was to become Mount Vernon's hallmark, was nearly finished, its thirty-foot-high roof supported by eight slender, square, fluted wooden pillars providing Washington, his family, and frequent guests a splendid view of the Potomac.

In his first year home, Washington, combining his eye for detail and his need to make decisions, set about researching stuccoes and interior paints for the banquet room, chose from among dozens of varieties of tiles, marbles, and flagstones for the rear piazza. (He finally decided on foot-square white flagstones.) Some of what had been built in his absence would have to be rebuilt, he decided: it was not good enough for him. The roof had to be replaced; there were endless leaks around the cupola. The shortage of skilled workers, always a problem in the Virginia Tidewater and worse since the war, exasperated Washington, who found he was completely at the mercy of would-be artisans. More and more, he was relying on skilled German workers emigrating to America after the war. They, in turn, found that they had a Prussian taskmaster who drew up his plans a year in advance so they would never for a moment run out of things to do. The vast grounds, long neglected and piled with construction debris, provided another time-consuming challenge. Washington wrote off to the Boudinots of Princeton, New Jersey, for a variety of timothy grass seed to sow ten new acres of lawn. He wrote to Maryland to dicker for a young bull. To establish a deer park, he wrote away to England for a buck, a doe, and six fawns. Eventually, he would add six American deer. He ordered an elaborate silver service from his friend the Marquis de Lafayette in Paris; it had to be French plate, not the English of pre-Revolutionary days. Then he abruptly countermanded the order.

By the summer of 1784, he had completely supplanted his wartime routines of daily inspections and meetings. Up early for a light breakfast on days when he did not have important houseguests, he rode a 24-mile daily circuit, closely inspecting his farms, forges, furnaces, construction projects. After a leisurely midday dinner with his family and guests, he rode off again, returning in late afternoon for tea. Then he excused himself to go to his study to write letters and work on accounts.

*B*y early February, as winter cut off the roads to Mount Vernon, Washington had more time to pick up the pieces of his old endeavors. On the first of February, he wrote to Lafayette, brave Duc de Lauzun, who had fought at his side at Yorktown, "I am now a private citizen on the banks of the Potomac, meditating amidst frost and snow, (which at present encompass me) upon the structure of walks for private life." That same day, he wrote to Thomas Lewis, the son of an old friend, "After an absence of almost nine years and nearly a total suspension of all my private concerns, I am at length set down at home and am endeavoring to recover my business from the confusion." He needed information: "My papers are so mixed [up] and in such disorder," he wrote, because of "frequent hasty removals of them out of the way of the enemy." His memory was not good enough to reconstruct the paper trail of a quarter century of land dealings west of the Appalachian Mountains.[15]

The endless stream of visitors had become a mixed blessing. The hero of the Revolution was expected to provide, at his own expense, hospitality to innumerable visitors. The code of civility he had followed all his adult life required him to spend many hours a day attending to guests. Washington enjoyed social gatherings, but he was having trouble adjusting to this steady stream of admirers and favor seekers. In a letter he wrote his aged mother, he made a rare and very private complaint about the day-to-day result of his fame. Mount Vernon "in truth" could "be compared to a well-restored tavern, as scarcely any strangers who are going from north to south, or from south to north, do not spend a day or two in it." There was no place where he could be completely "retired in any room of my house," because of the long hours of sitting up with company, "the noise and bustles of servants." Providing a key to how he himself was surviving in this resort-tavern atmosphere, he added that "happiness depends upon more the internal flame of a person's own mind than on the externals of the world."[16]

There were, to be sure, some welcome guests who actually helped Washington to recover from his postwar slump, none more so than the dashing young Marquis de Lafayette. It was understood between the two men that Lafayette would come to Mount Vernon whenever and as soon as he could. Their friendship had become one of Washington's most intimate. He had proved daring in a minor key, leading raids and skirmishes and a holding action in Virginia, but his real value to Washington and to the American cause was as the living symbol of French support for the Revolution. Before the Revolution was over, both men considered the younger man the childless Washington's second adopted son. Lafayette had gone home and named his firstborn son George Washington Lafayette, and Washington had agreed to be the boy's godfather.

For nearly a year, Washington at Mount Vernon had been expecting Lafayette, who now referred to himself in letters as "your adopted son." In May 1784, Lafayette finally wrote Washington from Paris that he was leaving for America immediately: "My course will be straight to [the] Potomac."[17]

On August 17, 1784, Lafayette arrived at Mount Vernon in a carriage accompanied by an entourage of young French aides and liveried servants. He wrote back to his wife, Adrienne, in Paris that, in his eagerness, he had crossed the countryside very quickly, arriving several days before Washington expected him:

> I found him in the routine of his estate. Our meeting was very tender. I am not just turning a phrase when I assure you that, in retirement, General Washington is even greater than he was during the Revolution. His simplicity is truly sublime. He is as completely involved with all the details of his lands and house as if he had always lived here.

Even with this young man he considered a surrogate son, Washington did not vary his routine, Lafayette noted:

> After thoroughly discussing the past, the present and the future, he withdraws to take care of his affairs and gives me things to read that have been written during my absence. Then we come down for dinner and find Mrs. Washington with visitors from the neighborhood. The conversation at table turns to the events of the war. . . . After tea, we resume our private conversations and pass the rest of the evening with the family.[18]

During their long talks, Lafayette brought Washington up to date on his own meteoric rise in French politics since they had last met. Because of the popularity of his American wartime adventures, he had been promoted by King Louis XVI over the heads of many older generals to the rank of *maréchal de camp*, making him a general officer in the French army before he reached twenty-five, the French age of majority. He had been scornfully dubbed *le Vassington français* by court rivals when he bought a splendid townhouse in the rue de Bourbon in Paris's fashionable faubourg St. Germain and then insisted on following the American style of family life, which meant spending his days and evenings with his wife and their ever-increasing children instead of taking up gambling and keeping a mistress, as many Frenchmen of his rank would have done.

As they rode around Washington's farms, Lafayette told his host that his brief tour of duty in Spain had brought to his attention at least one innovation that he now wanted to recommend to Washington: the Spanish mule. Lafayette insisted that as soon as he returned to Europe, he would personally prevail on the king of Spain, Charles III, to send Washington a Spanish jackass to breed with his American mares to introduce a new line of mules, strong, sure-footed beasts of burden that would be useful on the farm and in the American hill country. In his postwar attempts to cut costs and increase productivity, Washington wanted to replace farm horses with mules, which he preferred for "their longevity and cheap keeping," but most American mules were too small to pull heavy wagons or farm implements. Ordinarily, a royal edict prohibited the exportation of the large, strong Spanish work animals. The king of Spain eventually did take Lafayette's cue, sending Washington two jackasses (or jacks, as they were often called), but one died at sea. The other turned out to be a tall animal (fifteen hands high), which Washington found very large in proportion to its weight. Washington dubbed the jackass Royal Gift, but the animal refused for a long time to have anything to do with the common American broodmares he found in Washington's stables, where there were thirty-three mares and fillies to choose from.

After Royal Gift spurned all of the available mares, the patient Washington procured an attractive young jenny from a neighbor. Their progeny, named Compound, brought Washington considerable stud fees over the next decade. By June 1786, not losing the opportunity to mock an aging monarch, he was able to describe a favorable issue to a friend: "A female ass which I have obtained lately has excited desires in [Royal Gift] to which he almost seemed a stranger. Making use of her as an excitement, I have been able to get several mares served." Yet, as Washington explained to Lafayette, the royal jackass was still no Don Juan: "His late royal master, although past the grand climacteric, cannot be less moved by female allurements than he is. Or, when prompted, can proceed with more deliberation and majestic solemnity to the work of procreation." Lafayette would eventually try again to help Washington develop his international hybrid herd. "The Spanish jack seems calculated to breed heavy, slow draught [animals]; the [Maltese], for saddle or lighter carriage. From them, altogether, I hope to secure a race of extraordinary goodness, which will stock the country."

For the rest of his life, whenever Washington lapsed into "slothful humors," he liked to write notes about the proper handling of Lafayette's jackasses. The breed of American mule he created at Mount Vernon was to spread over the South and West, providing cheap cartage for farmers and teamsters for more than a century. By the time of his death, Washington had replaced two-thirds of the horses on his farms with the rugged mules, and when he traveled as president he proselytized the new breed.[19]

To Washington's intense surprise, Lafayette had suddenly made other plans. The French nobleman had been amazed at the warmth of his reception in every town as he paraded south with two other young French noblemen and his liveried servants. He had thrilled at the throngs of Revolutionary War veterans who turned out as he pranced by in his splendid white uniform on his tall white horse. It had been the first occasion since the end of the Revolution for the veterans, the politicians, the women, and children to celebrate, to add glory to the memories of suffering left by the long war. Lafayette's "canine appetite" for honor now bit him hard. Could Washington not go west later? No, he could not. His business affairs needed tending; he needed to collect money owed him. He had heard that squatters were laying claim to his lands, building houses and barns all over them. He had already waited several months for Lafayette's arrival and must go west and return before winter set in. Lafayette by this time had received scores of invitations to visit Philadelphia, New York, and the New England states and he was as stubborn as his adoptive father. A young man, he was sure there would always be enough time, another time. Before they parted for their separate expeditions, they rode into Alexandria one day to a reception being given in honor of Lafayette. There is a persistent rumor (apparently started by Lafayette) that, by the time they arrived, the two men were a bit tipsy. Finally, on September first, Washington declined once more to accompany Lafayette on his triumphal tour and the younger man still would not go west with him. They agreed to meet at Mount Vernon in six weeks.

Washington rode off to inspect his lands; Lafayette pranced north to bask in hard-pursued honors. They agreed to rendezvous at Mount Vernon in the fall. Young Lafayette wrote to his wife in Paris:

> It is not without anguish, that I resist the general's entreaties to go on a trip that he is obliged to make toward the Appalachians. He has delayed it so long for me that some of his property has become the prey of squatters. To get the general to go there without me, I had to promise to meet him again here.[20]

More and more, Washington's mind had been turning toward a great new undertaking. He had helped to organize the Potomac Company to develop an inland waterway to link the Potomac, by a series of roads, canals, and interior rivers, with the Ohio River, to open up the Old Northwest and bring the rich harvests of the American interior down the

Potomac to an expanded seaport at Alexandria, which he was also developing, en route to the Atlantic. Such a vast undertaking did not seem impossible to him. Had not the English Duke of Bridgewater in the early 1760s successfully staked his family fortune on digging the canal that now linked the Pennine coalfields with the furnaces and forges of Birmingham and Manchester? Ultimately, Washington's visionary plans would fizzle, and it would take another forty years before the construction of the Erie Canal, the grand canal that brought the riches of the American interior to the Atlantic seacoast. But in those heady post-Revolutionary days, as thousands of veterans and their families headed west to claim the lands they had fought to wrest from the British, Washington decided this would be his grand new venture, to open up the American west.

With his nephew, Bushrod Washington, and his longtime friend, Dr. James Craik and his son, William, Washington rode west followed by a string of packhorses carrying their camping gear and three servants. They would hardly be roughing it: his saddlebags included silver cups and spoons, a variety of libations including whiskey, Madeira, port, and a drink made of cherries soaked in brandy and sugar, called cherry bounce. For cooking, he brought mustard, oil, and vinegar, and took along "spices of all sorts." They would take tea whenever the occasion presented itself, and they brought along plenty of sugar. In addition to bedding, pots, and pans, they also brought fishing tackle. On nights when there were no roadside inns, Washington and his guests would sleep in the 30-foot-long marquee, the military tent that had been his home on the battlefields of the Revolution. (The tent, amazingly well preserved, is now on display in the National History Museum of the Smithsonian Institution in Washington, D.C.) Washington had daydreamed for years about making a long and dangerous western trip to follow up on his pre–Revolutionary War explorations in the Kanawha and Ohio Valleys. He had talked of going from Virginia north to Canada then west to the Mississippi and downriver all the way to the Gulf of Mexico, then across to Pensacola and back home by way of Georgia and the Carolinas. For now, he would have to content himself with inspecting his trans-Appalachian lands and putting pressure on squatters to pay up. His reduced farm income and loss from the British raid on Mount Vernon had left his finances in a "deranged state." (In today's terms his estate had dwindled by $400,000 during the war.) He especially wanted to collect the income from a gristmill he had built on the Youghiogheny River just before the Revolution, by all reports hugely prosperous and the most successful west of the mountains. "I expect something very handsome therefore from that quarter," he wrote to his partner, notifying him that he intended to auction off the mill during his visit.[21]

On September 1, 1784, he set out along the route he had taken so long ago with the British general Edward Braddock and his ill-fated redcoats.

He kept a careful record of his travels, conversations, and observations. The party covered twenty-five miles the first day, lodging that night at Shepherd's Tavern. Typically, they climbed on their horses at five o'clock the next morning while it was still relatively cold, leaving the servants and the baggage behind as they rode ahead and dined at the next wayside tavern. The second day they covered thirty-six miles, keeping up Washington's brisk pace of five miles an hour. By the end of the third day they reached the border of present-day West Virginia in time for a meeting with Washington's younger brother Charles. He had not seen Charles in more than the four years since he moved west. Once the proprietor of the Rising Sun Tavern in Fredericksburg, Charles had moved to the Shenandoah Valley during the Revolution and then on to found a settlement in West Virginia he named Charles Town after himself, its principal streets after other family members. After a brief if affectionate reunion, the elder Washington collected back rents from several tenants, pocketing about £96 (about one-fifth the amount due him).

Climbing into the hills toward Cumberland Gap, the party continued along the road hacked out of the wilderness by Braddock's troops. The horses were suffering "from the extreme heat of the weather [which] began to rub and gaul them," Washington recorded. To haul their baggage up to Warm Springs, they hired a wagon, covering only fourteen miles the fourth day. The road took him over the route he had taken to his first failure thirty years earlier at Fort Necessity. He was entirely unsentimental as he stood on the site of his first defeat. He wanted to own the land and he thought it would be a good spot for a roadside tavern. Great Meadows and the open fields around it, where the French and their Indian allies had once fired down on his makeshift stockade, would fetch good money one day as pastureland.

Despite an all-day drizzle, they covered thirty miles the fifth day, arriving at Warm Springs, where the next day, Washington met "the ingenious Mr. Rumsey." Working independently of the inventor Robert Fitch, James Rumsey was developing the steamboat and showed a model to Washington. "It might be turned to the greatest possible utility in inland navigation," Washington noted. To help materially in financing Rumsey's invention, Washington commissioned him to build a large shingled house, kitchen, and stable for him as a summer home for the Washingtons near the mineral baths. Together, they laid out the five-room house and a carriage house partially sunken into the hillside.

Ten days out, Washington reached his "exceedingly rich" lands near Fort Cumberland. At a neighbor's house, he "got a snack" and fed his horses, asking the man to rent out the lands for him with the express proviso that the virgin oaks and walnuts were not to be cut down. By this time, Washington was itching to strike out alone. He rode ahead with only his manservant, covering thirty-five miles of dirt road. Crossing over into Pennsylvania, he rode up the steep and "intolerably bad" road over

Allegheny Mountain in a heavy downpour. As he approached the spot where Braddock's army had come to grief nearly thirty years earlier, he recognized "what is called the Shades of Death." Here, where the road was always in the shadow of the mountains and under an umbrella of virgin forest, he had seen two-thirds of an army die in a three-hour ambush and realized for the first time that the British could be beaten. Suddenly, the trip began to feel "tedious and fatiguing." Notes of pessimism began to creep into Washington's diary. Still, he pushed his horse: "I endeavored to ride my usual travelling gait of five miles an hour." Creeks that he had hoped would be navigable were not; an "immense quantity of large stones" blocked the Cheat River that he had hoped would forge the main water link in his route from the Potomac to the Ohio Rivers.[22]

By the thirteenth day, he encountered another unexpected turn. There were reports from travelers along the wagon road he was following that Indians had attacked settlers along the north shore of the Ohio River. The "general dissatisfaction of the Indians" at whites intruding on lands they still claimed as their own "and our delay to hold a treaty with them made it dangerous and rather improper for me," Washington recorded, to proceed through Indian country as had been "my original intention." More and more, Washington was writing and speaking of the failure of the confederation of American states to cooperate with each other in such matters as making peace treaties with the Indians to further settlement on the western frontier. Disappointed, Washington turned instead to the business of the trip. His western partner, Gilbert Simpson, was heavily in debt to him and could not pay up. Instead of £600, he offered only £30, a female slave, and some wheat. (Washington was later to learn that the woman was not a slave at all and had to be released.) And the mill on which Washington had lavished £1,200, a fortune at the time, had been so poorly maintained during the war that now it was inoperable. No one bid on it at auction.[23]

Angrily, Washington called a meeting of the squatters who were trying to stall him by insisting that Sunday would not do for such business since they were all God-fearing, churchgoing folk. When he finally faced the Scots-Irish squatters, he flew into a rage made only worse when several insisted that they had only improved his lands by their hard work. The squatters, many of them pointing out that they were Revolutionary War veterans, said they wanted some credit for their years of effort. Washington, unused to anything but deference, brandished deeds to the land with pre-Revolutionary royal government seals on them. When the settlers offered to buy the lands, Washington at first refused. He refused to sell them individual plots. They would have to pool their resources and buy him out or rent from him the lands they lived on. When the settlers refused to pay him and said he would have to sue them, Washington said that was just what he would do. And he did. Leaving his heavy gear behind (after taking a careful inventory of it), he rode off to the courthouse in present-day Uniontown, Pennsylvania, and began the process of formally ejecting the squatters he found everywhere on his lands. Two years later, he won his suit.

*R*attling over the rutted Post Road in a borrowed carriage to Philadelphia with his outriders, Marquis de Lafayette had fallen in with another of Washington's young lieutenants, James Madison, who invited him to come along with him to an Indian conference at Fort Schuyler on the Mohawk River in New York State. Many of the northern Indians were faced with eviction by the new states. They still remembered the more fatherly treatment of the French and thronged now to meet the famous Lafayette. An amused Madison wrote to his friend, Thomas Jefferson, the American envoy in Paris, that Lafayette wore a gummed taffeta raincloak that had been covered in Paris newspapers that had stuck to it in his trunk at sea. As they rode the narrow trail through the New York rain forest, Madison could read the French news on Lafayette's back. Lafayette made himself a central figure in the talks with the Six Nations Iroquois, declaiming in French before a roaring fire on cold October nights and taking his turn sucking on the calumet as it was passed around. He rode away with two young Indians added to his retinue, an Oneida and an Onondaga who would follow him all the way to France and there, in full Iroquois regalia, become his couriers, running errands through the streets of Paris.

Wherever Lafayette went in America that autumn, there were jubilant receptions. It was as if he were Washington's stand-in. The town of Hartford, Connecticut, turned out en masse to honor him at Bull's Tavern. A cavalcade of former revolutionaries escorted him from Watertown, Massachusetts, all the way to Boston. Cannon on French ships in the harbor and in the American forts nearby pounded out a tattoo on the third anniversary of the great Franco-American victory at Yorktown. Lafayette was there to take the applause, but Washington wasn't. Three states along his triumphal route made Lafayette their citizen. Crowds everywhere Lafayette went turned out to make him the recipient of the greatest celebration since the war ended.

Arriving back in Virginia aboard a French frigate, Lafayette rendezvoused with Washington two weeks late in November. They had just two more weeks together and then it became time for Lafayette to head north to bid farewell to the Continental Congress and board a ship for France before winter set in. Washington was reluctant to let his young friend go. He rode with him in the carriage all the way to Annapolis, where the Maryland Assembly gave them both a reception. They lingered several more days until the snow began to fall. As Lafayette's carriage churned north, Washington still rode with him nearly to Baltimore. Then, finally, he said good-bye.

Washington once again drove home alone. On December 8, 1784, back in his study at Mount Vernon, he wrote his adopted son the Marquis one of his most emotion-filled letters:

Mount Vernon 8th, Decr. 1784

My dear Marquis,

In the moment of our separation upon the road as I travelled and every hour since I felt all that love, respect and attachment for you with which length of years, close connection and your merits have inspired me. I often asked myself, as our carriages distanced, whether that was the last sight I ever should have of you. And though I wished to say no, my fears answered yes.

I called to mind the days of my youth, and found they had long since fled to return no more, that I was now descending the hill I had been 52 years in climbing and that, although I was blessed with a good constitution, I was of a short lived family and might soon expect to be entombed in the dreary mansions of my fathers.

These things darkened the shades and gave a gloom to the picture, consequently to my prospects of seeing you again. But I will not repine. I have had my day. . . .[24]

G. Washington

Eighteen

"TO TASTE THE
FRUITS OF FREEDOM"

*O*n *March 25, 1785*, at General Washington's invitation, commissioners from Maryland and Virginia gathered in the new dining hall at Mount Vernon to try to iron out growing trade problems in the Chesapeake Bay region. Washington was not a delegate but, as president of the recently incorporated Potomac Company, he was the obvious choice to preside over the joint commission meeting, originally planned for Alexandria. The conference was a direct result of Washington's year-long efforts to gain public support for what he called his "grand design": a 190-mile combined Potomac waterway and canal to link the Ohio River Valley to the Atlantic Ocean. Reports that canal-building schemes were under way in New York and Pennsylvania added fresh urgency to the meeting, but lack of cooperation among the states had been thwarting Washington's efforts.

For thirty years now Washington had been aware of the riches of the American interior: no man was more the Apostle of American Improvement than Washington, and he saw the opening up of the over-the-mountain west as the key not only to prosperity but to survival as a nation. To establish better communication with the west was even more critical now than before the Revolution. Thousands of settlers were moving across the Alleghenies to farm the fertile lands of the Ohio and its tributaries, and the European rivals of the new nation were eager to alienate these pioneers from the United States.

As Washington saw it, on all sides the Confederation of American states was surrounded by enemies. The British, based in Canada, still had not relinquished seven of their forts along the Great Lakes, and many Indian tribes were still loyal to them. On the west bank of the Mississippi and in Florida, Spain was working through its Indian allies to woo away the trade of the settlers. And all along the eastern seaboard, the English once again dominated the seas while barring American shipping from her colonies in the Caribbean and Canada.

What was worse, from Washington's standpoint, was that the American states instead of cooperating with each other were competing and placing obstacles in each other's paths. No better example existed than Washington's renewed Potomac Waterway project.

Even before the war ended, Washington had turned his mind back to the project that had led him on the eve of revolution to send off work parties at his own expense to begin to clear a better roadway into his 33,000 acres of western lands. In January 1783, a recently migrated Irish engineer named Christopher Colles had written to Washington to offer his services in removing obstacles to navigating the upper Ohio River in western Pennsylvania. By blasting away only "two to three miles" of rapids, Colles claimed he could open the way for shipping all the way from Fort Pitt down the Ohio to the Mississippi. But after years of struggling with the states over troops and pay and supplies Washington was pessimistic that they would be willing to cooperate "for many years to come":

> From the present juvenile state of the country, the abundance
> of land, the scarcity of laborers and the want of resources, I say
> from these and many other circumstances it appears to me that
> this is too early a day for accomplishing such great undertakings.

Washington had tried to win over Colles to helping him in his Potomac River project, but Colles had found work rebuilding New York City's water system, and by the time of the March 1785 Mount Vernon conference had proposed a canal from the Hudson River to Lake Erie to a more receptive New York legislature.[1]

By war's end Washington was convinced that the Potomac River waterway was likely to succeed. But it would have to be a private venture: when Colles had approached Congress in the spring of 1783 with his Ohio River proposal, as Washington predicted the Congress stalled, not hearing his petition until July 4 and then declining to act on it. But by the spring of 1783 the Maryland Assembly was moving ahead with its own project, in direct competition to Washington's Virginia-based Potomac Company. Maryland authorized Charles Beatty of Montgomery County and Normand Bruce of Frederick County to study the costs of opening up the Potomac to navigation and they reported it would be less than $150,000 (about $6 million today). No wonder Washington could not wait to make his journey west once the war ended. Even as he waited for the definitive peace treaty to arrive from Paris in the summer of 1783 he made a sortie along the Mohawk River—the route to the interior proposed by Colles—with several of his generals. Just before disbanding his army in the autumn of 1783 he had written to Lafayette that he was preparing to make a grand tour of the west in 1784. He had confessed to Lafayette that "probably it will take place nowhere but in imagination." Only his shocking lack of cash and the dilapidated condition of his Mount Vernon farms seems to have made him abbreviate his travels. To Chevalier de Chastellux he confided that while his tangled "private concerns" beckoned him back to Mount Vernon, "I shall not rest contented till I have explored the western country and have traversed those lines [it was the old surveyor speaking] which have given bounds to a new empire."[2]

In Virginia Washington's partners in the waterway scheme had gone ahead without waiting for an end to hostilities. News that the British were ceding the vast territory between the Alleghenies and the Mississippi to the new nation had touched off a fever of speculation. The Virginians knew that if they could channel trade between the Chesapeake and Europe into the interior by way of the Potomac, Virginia could become the commercial capital of the nation. And, as early as the autumn of 1783, Congressman Thomas Jefferson was appointed head of a committee assigned to draw up plans to situate the capital of the Confederation's government. He proposed the shores of the Potomac.

Jefferson's plan to locate the nation's capital in Virginia was only one element in his plans to extend the influence of his native state, already the largest and by five times the most populous. On February 20, 1784, he wrote to James Madison, his ally in the reform party in the Virginia House of Delegates, that Virginia should press its claims to the west bank of the Kanawha River in present-day Ohio. There Jefferson proposed a densely populated buffer zone to protect Virginia from Indian attacks. In this same letter he urged Madison to support in the legislature the clearing of the Potomac. The waterway "between the Western waters and the Atlantic," Jefferson added almost as an aside, "of course promises us almost a monopoly of the Western and Indian trade." Jefferson pointed to a Pennsylvania plan to build a canal along the Schuylkill River from Philadelphia to Reading as an argument for Virginia to act quickly. Jefferson urged a "particular" Virginia tax of up to £10,000 a year to open up both the Potomac and James Rivers. To guarantee public support, Jefferson told Madison they must have a highly respected executive for the project:

> General Washington has [the] Potomac much at heart. The superintendence of it would be a noble amusement in his retirement and leave a monument of him as long as the waters should flow. I am of opinion he would accept of the direction as long as the money should be employed on the Potomac. The popularity of his name would carry it through the assembly.[3]

By March 1784, little more than two months after he had retired from the army, Washington heard from an excited Jefferson that plans were moving ahead quickly "on a subject I have much at heart," the "opening the navigation of the Ohio and Potomac." A long letter soon followed in which Jefferson banged away at an open door. Calling the rivers "the true doors to the western commerce," he told Washington, "I am sure its value and practicability are both well known to you. This is the moment however for seizing it if ever we mean to have it. All the world is becoming commercial." While the Hudson River or Mississippi routes to the interior could be used by western farmers to ship out their harvests, the Potomac route could provide by far the shorter distance for two-way commerce. A return trip up the Mississippi was still impossible; the Hudson route would be too costly for the European and domestic manufactures settlers craved. Jefferson urged Washington to join him in winning for Virginia "as large a portion as we can of this modern source of wealth and power."

Jefferson did not have to persuade Washington of the economic merits, and he knew exactly how to stroke Washington's ego. The grand project would not violate his declared intention to "quit all public employment." It would be "dignified amusement: What a monument of your retirement it would be!" Congressman Jefferson was quick to add that he himself did not own "one inch of land or any water either of Potomac or Ohio." His "zeal in this business is public and pure." Washington, it went without saying, was out of public office and was free to benefit handsomely.[4]

Responding quickly, Washington appeared skeptical. Interstate rivalries and problems of funding, especially the difficulty of wringing funds from debt-ridden state legislatures, made him doubt that a special tax for waterway improvements had a chance despite the "great and truly wise" nature of such a policy. Washington always drifted toward important decisions laden with doubts and then suddenly acted. On March 29, 1784, he agreed to superintend the Potomac project. His brief retirement was over.[5]

*T*hat spring of 1784, James Madison arranged to have himself appointed chairman of the commerce committee of the Virginia House of Delegates. He promptly sponsored a resolution that overcame one unpopular hurdle to the Assembly's approval of the Potomac scheme. In a moment of interstate cooperation in 1776, Virginia had granted Maryland jurisdiction over the Potomac. On June 20 Madison had himself appointed to a commission that also included George Mason and Edmund Randolph to negotiate with Maryland to pave the way for joint waterway jurisdiction. Washington's old friend Thomas Johnson pushed a similar resolution through the Maryland Assembly. All through the summer of 1784 Tidewater taverns and drawing rooms buzzed with excited rumors about the waterway. By fall, when Washington undoubtedly visited the site on his way west to inspect his Ohio Valley lands, workers were building huts on both sides of the Seneca Falls of the Potomac.

By October 4, 1784, Washington had carefully studied notes on proposed routes that he and Dr. Craik had compiled during their western tour and sent off a long report to Virginia governor Benjamin Harrison. With it he sent Harrison a formal petition for incorporation of the Potomac Company. Then on October 15 he sent Thomas Johnson incorporation papers to push through the Maryland legislature. In this letter for the first time he voiced his growing anxiety over problems he saw ahead for the new nation:

> The want of energy in the Federal government, the pulling of one state and party of states against another and the commotion amongst the Eastern people have sunk our national character much below par and has brought our politics and credit to the brink of a precipice. A step or two farther must plunge us into a sea of troubles, perhaps anarchy and confusion.[6]

By the end of 1784 Washington was lobbying influential friends. The more he wrote and talked about it, the better the Potomac waterway seemed to him, not just as a money-making scheme where the company could secure "a large portion" of the fur trade of the Great Lakes region and its commerce, but as a "necessary step for the well-being and strength of the Union also." Trade ties were essential to "bind that rising world" across the Alleghenies to the Atlantic states. The failure of the Confederation Congress to act forcefully when the British refused to vacate the northwest line of forts was damaging this east-west linkage. "It is by the cement of interest only," he wrote to Jacob Read, that "we can be held together." To counter criticism that he was directing a "utopian scheme," Washington argued that the national government should at least be surveying its vast new western territories, especially the tributaries of the Ohio River, so that the west could be opened up to even larger numbers of settlers and traders.[7]

Not content to press states and individuals into his cause, on December 14, 1784, Washington wrote to Richard Henry Lee, president of Congress (and his former partner in the Mississippi Company) to urge Congress "to have the western waters well explored, the navigation of them fully ascertained, accurately laid down and a complete and perfect map made of the country." If President Lee could persuade Congress to carry out this inexpensive survey, the nation would reap rewards in increased trade and taxes. But Washington's most powerful congressional ally, Thomas Jefferson, had already left for Paris as one of the new trade ministers to Europe, and Congress for the first time ignored Washington. Over the next four years Washington repeatedly circumvented Congress as he enlisted the aid of Richard Butler, U.S. Superintendent of Indian Affairs, to employ his "leisure hours" to explore waterways emptying into Lake Erie and measure portages between rivers in the proposed path of his waterway.[8]

On November 15, 1784, when the Virginia House of Delegates convened in Richmond, Washington appeared with a "numerous and respectable" group of Virginians and Marylanders who told anyone who would listen that their canal-building project was "one of the grandest chains for preserving the Federal Union." These same gentlemen helped to draft the requisite legislation and sent it on to Washington, who promptly forwarded it to James Madison, the commerce committee chairman. Washington stressed that he had grown impatient with the "limping behavior" of the two state legislatures to fund the project and had decided that the Potomac project "had better be placed in the hands of a corporate company." The company was to be capitalized at $1 million (about $40 million today) to be sold to shareholders. Washington's proposal sailed through the two legislatures in a single day. On January 25, 1785, Virginia and Maryland adopted identical bills. A triumphant if exhausted Washington related the news to President Lee in Congress, and Madison passed the word to Jefferson in Paris.[9]

So confident were lawmakers on both sides of the Potomac that each state bought fifty of the initial offering of 220 shares. Virginia also offered to grant fifty shares to Washington for his efforts—but here he drew the line. While he needed the money—he wrote to George Fairfax in England the stock would provide "the greatest and most certain" foundation for his income—he wanted to be "as free and independent as the air" and feared he would be accused by some of having "sinister motives." To Jefferson he wrote that he wanted public opinion to believe he was supervising the project "with no other motive for promoting it" than the good of two publics—Virginia first, the United States, second. Finally, Washington persuaded the Virginia Assembly to devote the profits from his shares to the education of the orphans of Revolutionary War soldiers.[10]

This public-spirited gesture did not hurt the sale of Potomac Company stock, and as Washington bought five shares he urged old friends and comrades to join him. He pressed financier Robert Morris, who held the franchise for American tobacco imports to France, to build a large warehouse at Alexandria. He wrote Morris that "had I inclination and talents to enter into the commercial line I have no idea of a better opening to make a fortune." Washington fairly exuded advertising copy in his letters. His scheme would inspire others and would eventually bring "navigation to almost everyone's door." Visitors to Mount Vernon found themselves captive audiences to a dinner-table sales pitch. One dazed German visitor reported that Washington bored him for two days with facts and figures.[11]

On May 17, 1785, a large number of Virginia and Maryland's wealthiest citizens gathered in Alexandria for the organization meeting of the Potomac Company. After a midday banquet at the old City Tavern, General Washington called the meeting to order and read a brief report on the commercial and political significance of the project; by now the two had become inextricable in his mind. He then called for the election of officers to preside over the meeting. Daniel Carroll of Maryland was chosen as chairman, Charles Lee as clerk. Representatives of the wealthiest family in each state guaranteed respect for the proceedings. The members passed around the share subscription books: 403 shares worth £40,300 (about $1.6 million) had been pledged. The enthusiastic members then moved on to elect a president and board of directors: Washington was unopposed for president.

Two weeks later, Washington called the first meeting of the board. A two-day-long affair, it was held in secret in a private room at City Tavern. Washington was keen to get the river clearing started. Two crews of fifty men each were to begin at once to clear stretches of river between Payne's Falls and Great Falls and between Shenandoah Falls and the height of navigation. The board also decided to begin collecting the money pledged for shares to cover the costs of the clearance. They also scheduled their first tour of inspection for the following August.

The negotiations between commissioners from Virginia and Maryland were scheduled for March of 1785 in Alexandria. Washington was not a member of the Virginia delegation so he saw fit to invite the commissioners to his newly renovated Mount Vernon, where in the mild early spring of the Tidewater they could rest from their deliberations in his new, two-story Prussian green banqueting room with spells of sitting and rocking on his 96-foot-long piazza, as he called the porch overlooking the river in question, between splendid meals directed by Martha. The conferees undoubtedly learned from Washington that Americans were snatching up the subscriptions to shares in the Potomac Company at double the expected rate. Two hundred fifty shares were needed to launch the project; five hundred sold that spring and Washington still expected to hear from foreign investors. He had asked Jefferson in Paris to sound out the markets in France, Holland, and England.

Against this roseate backdrop of fait accompli the Potomac commissioners had little choice but to iron out their differences. Maryland's delegates refused to discuss anything until Virginia agreed to forgo collection of tolls at the entrance to Chesapeake Bay. Toll collections for the waterway would be allowed only at the sites of the waterfalls removed from the river itself and along a toll road that was to replace the old Braddock Road. Virginia's delegates had instructions not to yield on the toll issue, but rather than see the talks collapse they huddled and decided to ignore their instructions. Access to the Chesapeake would remain free.

For eight days the negotiations went on with Washington the silent spectator. The commissioners worked out an agreement that allowed joint commercial and fishing rights in Potomac Tidewater. Maryland delegate Thomas Stone introduced a resolution that called for a joint application to Congress to request permission to organize a small independent navy in case the federal government (which had no navy until 1797) failed to protect the waterway. The conference had exposed many such weaknesses in the Confederation government, which the delegates believed needed repairing. Stone's second and bolder resolution suggested that the same application to Congress also seek approval for joint Virginia-Maryland regulation of state currencies, common import duties, and annual meetings to review commercial regulations.

Further, Stone proposed that delegates be invited from Pennsylvania and Delaware to attend their next meeting, which they scheduled for Annapolis in May 1786. The delegates agreed unanimously. Their agreement was to become known as the Mount Vernon Compact, the first serious critique of the Confederation government. In later years, James Madison regarded the talks as the first step on the road to creating a new Constitution for the United States and setting up a stronger national government.

*T*he heady conference at Mount Vernon turned Washington's attention more and more back toward what he perceived as the plight of his nation. On July 25, 1785, he wrote to Marquis de Lafayette for the first time in nearly a year since Lafayette's visit. He saw his role in opening up a route to the west by water in grand terms:

> I wish to see the sons and daughters of the world in peace and busily employed in the more agreeable amusement of fulfilling the first and great commandment—*"increase and multiply"*—as an encouragement to which we have opened the fertile plains of the Ohio to the poor, the needy and the oppressed of the Earth. Anyone therefore who is heavy laden or who wants land to cultivate may repair thither and abound as in the Land of Promise with milk and honey. The ways are preparing and the roads will be made easy.[12]

But not everyone applauded Washington's messianic devotion to his latest cause. Baltimore merchants laughed at him and he knew it. He told an English visitor that "they begin now to look a little serious," because "they know it must hurt their commerce amazingly." Washington revealed his pride in the project to anyone who stopped off at Mount Vernon, and his hospitality was even freer than usual. The Englishman reported that "the General sent the bottle about pretty freely after dinner and gave success to the navigation of the Potomac for his toast." But a side effect of his single-minded campaign was to remind the leaders of the Congress that he had not lost his edge as an organizer and inspirator of men, material, and money. President of Congress Richard Henry Lee wrote to a friend in Virginia, "You all know his persevering spirit and attentive character: these qualities promise success to the Potomac project."[13]

*B*efore Washington and the Potomac directors could visit the worksites along the river that summer, serious problems emerged and Washington began to impute them to what he considered worsening conditions in the fledgling nation. The company's supervisors had trouble finding workers. Most sober and able-bodied men in the region were busy with the hay and grain harvests. In August, Washington and the board rode along the Potomac and decided where the channel could be deepened by simply removing rocks and fallen trees and where the digging of canals would be necessary. They rode on to Thomas Johnson's farm at Frederick, Maryland, where the townspeople had prepared a dinner in Washington's honor. Washington disappointed them; he declined to attend. The time for the inspection tour was "short," he later explained, and they must not stop the work to celebrate. His loathing of public ceremonies was growing. After a three-day meeting at Shenandoah Falls, the board decided to concentrate all their workers on clearing—blasting away the larger rocks—Shenandoah and Seneca Falls. If more than one hundred men were needed, so be it. By September Johnson was writing Washington that there had been several successful blasts.

But finding willing workers was easier than getting subscribers to the company's shares to pay up. Even though Washington and the board issued repeated calls, many stockholders paid little or nothing on their pledges in 1786 and 1787, even after Washington threatened legal action. Washington professed no concern in public, but in private he laid the blame on a weak Confederation government and a resultant shortage of cash.

*T*he president and chief executive officer of the Potomac Company had as his corporate headquarters one of the finest mansions in America, which he had transformed for a second time by the mid-1780s. Its white wings spread toward porticoes that connected avenues of outbuildings to the manor house. A two-story columned veranda and large symmetrical Palladian-style windows trapped and funneled breezes into the ornate dining room, with its carved marble mantel, elaborate cornices, and the latest in smoke-eating whale oil lights accentuating the finest mahogany furniture. Presiding over his dinner table, Washington at home deferred to only one person—Martha. She had become in her early fifties a rotund, buoyant, and gracious hostess whose discretion and loyalty had won not only her husband's admiration but that of a generation of officers and politicians from Europe and all over America. Both Washingtons had returned to Mount Vernon exhausted by the war and they only gradually regained their full vigor.

Travelers' descriptions of the reticent mistress of Mount Vernon were understandably superficial. She was, one visitor wrote, "rather fleshy, of good complexion, has a large portly double chin and an open and engaging countenance on which a pleasing smile sits during conversation in which she bears an agreeable part." Others were less charitable: she was "small and fat" to one, "hearty, comely, discreet, affable," to another. Her orders from merchants show a conservative if expensive taste in dress: "fine thin handkerchiefs with striped or worked borders . . . very fine and pretty dimity muslin."[14]

Noted for her generosity, Martha studied the technique of inoculating against smallpox at Washington's Cambridge field hospital and then introduced inoculations first at Mount Vernon and then throughout her neighborhood. She sent shipments of her cured Virginia hams and homemade preserves great distances to friends—a barrel of hams followed Lafayette back to Paris. But most of all she was fond of adopting and raising the orphaned children of relatives. Mount Vernon swarmed with little children. When her sister Nancy Bassett died, her little Fanny came to live at Mount Vernon. She became Martha's replacement daughter: "She is a child to me," Martha wrote when Fanny went away on a brief visit. "I am very lonesome when she is absent." When Martha's stepmother and last remaining brother, Bartholomew, died on the same day, Martha brought daughter Patty to live at Mount Vernon. When Washington's brother Sam died, his nine-year-old Harriet joined her relatives at Mount Vernon. And since Jack Custis's death at Yorktown, Martha had the almost constant companionship of "charming" Nelly Custis and her four children. Nelly stayed close to Martha for years and soon stopped going to Alexandria's dances. The Washingtons were totally surprised when a family friend, Dr. David Stuart, married her. Two of Nelly's daughters went off with the bride and groom, but the other two, little Nelly and George Washington Parke Custis—Martha called him "Wash"—remained with their grandmother in the swirl of children and activity at Mount Vernon. Once again, George Washington arranged tutors and reported to relatives on "the little folks."[15]

An older, wiser Washington insisted that "Wash" Custis be prepared for a university and that he learn French. To that end he imported a recent Yale College graduate, Tobias Lear, as secretary-tutor. Washington spelled out his terms: Lear would "sit at my table, will live as I live, will mix with the company [and] be treated with civility." Recommended by General Benjamin Lincoln, young Lear arrived in midsummer 1786 and remained close to Washington for thirteen years, until Washington's death. Washington reported to Lincoln that his protégé was a "genteel, well-behaved young man." Lear waited two years before writing his appraisal of Washington to a friend. At first Washington was cold and reserved to him, but he had learned that this came from Washington's "caution and circumspection, striking traits in his character." Gradually Washington made Lear feel "a child" of the Washingtons. And to him "Mrs. Washington is everything that is benevolent and good."[16]

As Washington began to talk more of national affairs and prepared to attend a new political convention, Martha made it clear that, while she agreed with his views, she would not accompany him. "Mrs. Washington is become too domestic," wrote Washington to Robert Morris without any hint of criticism, "and too attentive to two little grandchildren to leave home." He did not wonder at her loss of all desire to leave her home. It was where he was happiest—beside her. "In my estimation more permanent and genuine happiness is to be found in the sequestered walks of connubial life than in the giddy rounds of promiscuous pleasure or the more tumultuous and imposing scenes of successful ambition."[17]

*Y*et Washington seemed helpless to resist the siren song of public life even as he coyly gave the appearance of resisting it. He held the presidency of the Potomac Company for four years, only resigning when it became evident that he was about to be drafted, despite all his protests of disinterestedness, to a much higher office. By the time he became president of the United States, boatmen, who included two company directors, were able to navigate to within twelve miles of Fort Cumberland on a boat loaded with thirty-five barrels of flour. They passed boats hauling tobacco and flour downriver from Cresap's Old Town on the Maryland-Pennsylvania border. They were part of a convoy of boats that were seventy feet long and carried 130 barrels of flour—on a river where it had once been dangerous for Washington to paddle a canoe. Thirty-five years before the Erie Canal opened a route from Lake Erie to the Hudson Valley, Washington had stolen a march into the American interior, opening the Ohio Valley he had once fought for to farmers and their families and merchants and their wares.

*W*hen the delegates to the Annapolis Convention of September 1786 gathered to continue their critique of the Confederation, there was no question where George Washington stood. He had become firmly convinced that "affairs seem to be drawing to an awful crisis." The British would not leave their posts in New York and the northwest because Congress lacked the power to force them. He ignored the fact that thousands of Americans were refusing to pay their debts to English merchants and to Loyalists who had been forced to flee or denied access to the courts. Until the Americans paid up and honored their treaty obligations, the English refused to leave their stockades. As long as they remained they lent support—and sold goods and weapons—to the Indians, the second of Washington's bugbears.

But Congress was not the nation any more than the Potomac Waterway was. Other Americans, such as Benjamin Franklin, saw the 1780s as a period of unparalleled growth and prosperity. Even in distressed areas the prospects seemed bright. Farmers lacked cash, but they had homes, abundant food, unlimited hunting and fishing rights, cash crops, and almost no taxes to pay. Life was crude but good for many, prosperous for thousands more. Washington and wealthy and powerful men he knew as strong nationalists objected to the United States having to take the last place in line at diplomatic receptions at Versailles and pouted that England sent no ambassador to its lost colonies. The United States had only the population and economic status of a Third World country, in today's terms, but it *was* a rapidly developing nation.

Many of the problems had to do with the honor and the impatience of a great but aging leader who found himself out of power and worried about his reputation. He did not like the way the next generation of leaders was running things: what had he risked everything for? He insisted that there needed to be drastic reforms and he left the door open to be drafted to do something about these largely unspecified feelings. A people accustomed to the rule of monarchs in an imperial system were uneasy without a bête noire to resist and Washington soon found many allies. Americans could not stand the light hand of an inexperienced ruling class of lawyers and merchants. Vague suspicions fueled a reform movement that had no specific substance to attack, only the loose form of the Confederation—and Washington once again emerged as the only possible leader the people could imagine.

When Maryland's and Virginia's delegates—this time including Washington—were joined at Annapolis late in 1786 they were joined only by the other middle states' delegates—not enough of a representative group to demand reforms. The delegates decided they could not solve any of the trade problems they had gathered to discuss but could issue a strongly worded report and send it to Congress. The Annapolis white paper declared that the middle states—the hub of commerce—believed the Union was suffering from serious problems that warranted a special convention of all the states in Philadelphia the next year. In addition to sending the resolution to Congress, the delegates sent the call for the convention directly to each state. It was generally assumed that, given his well-known views, Washington would attend the convention in Philadelphia. But it was not to be that simple for Washington to make up his mind. He had, after all, very publicly given up public office, even insisting on resigning his elective office as a vestryman of the Pohick Church. He believed his retirement barred him from *all* public office, even serving as a delegate elected by the Virginia Assembly. He would only reconsider if he could be sure of his country's "affection and confidence." The door back into public life seemed ajar.[18]

But an unforeseen obstacle suddenly cropped up. Washington had been invited to attend the first national meeting of the Society of the Cincinnati, a hereditary fraternity made up of ex–Continental Army officers. But many Americans objected to an aristocratic order of the elite. Washington had been active in arranging the meeting and had prepared reforms, which had been rejected by the state chapters. His honor wounded and his reputation, he believed, at stake, he tried to beg out of the Philadelphia meeting by claiming poor health and the press of personal business. How could he now accept an invitation to another meeting in Philadelphia without insulting his old comrades? Even his election as the head of Virginia's delegation left Washington in a quandary.

It took a nudge from faraway to the north to confirm all of Washington's fears of congressional weakness and send him packing to Philadelphia. In the Berkshire foothills of western Massachusetts, farmers, many of them veterans, led by Daniel Shays, a captain in the Revolutionary army, took down their flintlocks and resisted the collection of heavy state taxes. Congress seemed powerless to stop the spreading tax revolt. Shays and his followers soon shut down the courts and chased the sheriffs and stopped sheriff's sales. Numbering more than 1,200 men familiar with firearms, they set out to seize the United States arsenal at West Springfield. Shays was no general, however. He divided his force, and Secretary of War Henry Knox, his 300 pounds crowded into his general's uniform, ringed the arsenal with artillery, drove off one attacking column, and then crossed the Connecticut River and scattered Shays's force. The rebels fled to nearby hills of the Republic of Vermont, still a foreign country.

The fragmentary dispatches that reached Washington's veranda led him briefly to despair that Americans could govern themselves. But in February 1787, Congress approved the Philadelphia convention. The chances of a solid turnout of delegates from a majority of the states vastly encouraged Washington. He told himself that the convention was "the last peaceable mode of essaying the feasibility" of the Confederation form of government. The time had come for him to risk his reputation and align himself with this instrument of criticizing the government he had done so much to create and protect. He announced that he would accept his state's draft to head its delegation and furthermore promised "to adopt no temporizing expedient but probe the defects of the constitution to the bottom." He promised to "provide *radical cures*."[19]

*E*lected to preside over the Constitutional Convention of 1787, Washington said little in public in the four-month-long session. He didn't have to. His enormous prestige as he sat gravely each day on the dais overlooking the green-baize-covered tables where he had first come to represent Virginia eleven years before and where he had been chosen to lead the Continental Army and where he had come to receive the laurels of victory lent credibility to the extralegal proceedings and made its "radical cures" palatable to a majority of the people.

On Monday, May 14, he took his seat apprehensively. Delegates from only two states arrived on time. If there was anything Washington hated, it was tardiness. Once when he went to visit artist Charles Wilson Peale in Philadelphia—Peale had painted the Washingtons at Mount Vernon before the war and became his good friend—he arrived five minutes early according to his pocket watch and paced outside until the exact moment of his appointment. For states to send delegates late to such an important meeting only added to Washington's misgivings. In the two weeks before a quorum arrived, Washington did perhaps his most valuable work—socializing with old friends in the city and as they arrived. For a few weeks the real Capitol of the United States was City Tavern, where Washington held court.

Once the proceedings began Washington's role was mainly symbolic. He had made it known he would support any "tolerable compromise." He spoke from the floor only once, when he asked the delegates to reduce to 30,000 voters the minimum size of a congressional district to bring the new Congress closer to the people. The convention agreed unanimously. His silence about the convention's closed proceedings was so complete that he did not even enter a comment about it in his diary. He voted secretly and usually went along with his Virginia colleagues—or they with him. Yet Washington had strong and consistent opposition from an unexpected quarter: his next-door neighbor and old friend George Mason, who rallied the opposition to the new Constitution both in Philadelphia and, later, in Virginia. Mason, author of the revolutionary Virginia Constitution, disliked seeing Virginia give up any of its powers to a national government. It was Mason who had coached and confided in Washington in the early days of pre-Revolutionary protest. Mason had been one of the—if not *the*—much abler heads who had opposed the British from an understanding of natural rights law. Mason had acted as Washington's attorney in untangling Patcy Custis's estate. "I could think of no person in whose friendship, care and abilities I could so much confide," Washington had written at the time.[20]

Mason had returned to Virginia when Washington rode off to lead the army, but he had helped stem the ruinous wartime inflation that hurt Washington personally as well as causing such hardship to his army. Mason visited Mount Vernon frequently and rarely failed to bring some seeds, plants, or books to help Washington build his gardens. Mason quickly grew irritable at the Philadelphia convention. "I begin to grow heartily tired of the etiquette and nonsense so fashionable in this city," he wrote his son. He projected this distaste onto the entire process of replacing a small loose government with a larger, stronger national system. Mason seems never to have lost his affection for Washington, but the general cooled to anyone who opposed him and took Mason's opposition to a strong central government that would preserve the Union as a personal betrayal. For his part, Mason was stunned at Washington's new coldness toward him. "You know the friendship which has long existed (indeed from our early youth) between General Washington and myself," Mason wrote his son John. "I believe there are few men in whom he placed greater confidence. But it is possible my opposition to the new government [has] altered the case."[21]

Once again turning away from an old friend, Washington voted his principles. He voted for a strong central government at the expense of the state's rights. He voted for a single chief executive elected by the people, not secondhand by their state legislature. He wanted it to be all but impossible to override a presidential veto and so he voted for a three-fourths vote, not a two-thirds vote to overturn a veto. He was defeated on this issue.

And he kept silent when the cobra of slavery uncoiled amid the debates. Slavery had come up again and again in the Continental Congress. In his Land Ordinance of 1784, Jefferson had proposed a ban on the extension of slavery into the Northwest Territories and it had been abolished on federal lands. When he tried to have the ban extended to the existing thirteen states, he was defeated by a single vote. The Land Ordinance of 1787 also forbade slavery in the Northwest Territories. Yet Washington would not support anything that would jeopardize the proceedings, and when delegates to the Philadelphia convention deadlocked on the question of slavery, he supported a twenty-year moratorium on any further congressional debates over slavery. The Union must be preserved; it would be up to another generation to struggle with this divisive question. One million blacks and their children remained in bondage but the new Constitution, to benefit free white men, their property, and progeny, was saved.

Most of all, Washington's approving presence shaped the powerful new office of president of the United States. It became clear that Washington would once again accept a draft as head of the new government created in this convention. And because everyone believed he would be the first president, Congress left much of the president's functions unresolved. He would fill in the details; Congress would only rough in the outline in the constitutional document. No doubt no other president would have been trusted with such latitude.

*R*eturning to Mount Vernon, Washington conducted a discreet campaign from his study. He sent copies of the proposed Constitution to other Virginians with a covering letter that followed this basic form:

> I wish the Constitution which is offered had been more perfect but I sincerely believe it is the best that could be obtained at this time. . . . As a constitutional door is opened for amendment hereafter, the adoption of it under the present circumstances of the Union is in my opinion desirable.[22]

The letters found their way into the press, where a fierce war went on with old friends on both sides. Patrick Henry, George Mason, and Governor Benjamin Harrison led the fight against adoption. Thomas Jefferson, away in Paris, wrote to Washington's staunch ally James Madison that he was shocked that Washington had used Shays's brief rebellion as a pretext for replacing the Articles of Confederation with this much more conservative document. Had he been in Philadelphia in the summer of 1787, he wrote Madison, he would have fought against the new Constitution, but since Madison assured him that a Bill of Rights would soon be appended to it, he would now support it.

Throughout the bitter year-long battle over ratification Washington kept up his tacit support for the Constitution without publicly campaigning for it. He left the battle to his aides—Madison, Hamilton, John Jay. He let it be known he kept silent so that he did not appear to be running for the presidency of the new government. It was a foregone conclusion that his approval of the new form of government implied he would accept its leadership. His silence was construed as support for the document his presence had brought to life; his backing gave the Federalists—as the new Constitution's supporters became known—the margin of victory over those who would have given the Confederation more time to solve the adolescent nation's problems.

Two months less than a year after the Philadelphia convention disbanded, New York become the eleventh of the thirteen states to ratify: Governor Clinton, who had ridden into New York City at Washington's side only five years earlier, had led the anti-Federalists against him. In four states—New York, Massachusetts, Pennsylvania, and Virginia—the battle had been close and bitter and was only won with the promise of speedy amendments. The majority of Americans wanted a new government, as Washington had so intuitively sensed:

> When the people shall find themselves secure under an energetic government, when foreign nations shall be disposed to give us equal advantages in commerce from dread of retaliation, when the burdens of war shall be in a manner done away by the sale of western lands, when the seeds of happiness which are sown here shall begin to expand themselves and when every one (under his own vine and fig tree) shall begin to taste the fruits of freedom—then all those blessings (for all these blessings will come) will be referred to the fostering influence of the new government.[23]

At fifty-six years of age, General Washington had won his greatest victory. He had carried off a second American revolution without an army, without a shot. But then, who, possibly, could have opposed him?

While every American—friend or foe of the new federal government—seemed sure that George Washington wanted to be the first elected president of the United States, Washington himself was not so certain. He continued to be haunted by his fear that he would lose the good reputation built as the leader of the Revolutionary army and reinforced by his resignation from power. So many of his old friends had opposed the new form of government. Would they support the man who had renounced power so recently and now was breaking such a public and solemn promise? And what of the comfortable life he had made with Martha at his splendid estate overlooking the Potomac? What could be worth leaving it once again to its inevitable decline? And would the new government succeed?

The only conclusion Washington could reach to answer his own wracking misgivings was to fall back on his own highly developed sense of honor. How could he lead the fight to dismantle one government without risking failure at the helm of the new? It was, he told himself, his *duty* to accept the presidency. Nothing but his inescapable duty could make him again leave behind Mount Vernon

> unless it be a *conviction* that the partiality of my countrymen had made my services absolutely necessary joined to a *fear* that my refusal might induce a belief that I preferred the conservation of my own reputation and private ease to the good of my country.[24]

Once again Washington argued with himself as he drifted toward a momentous decision. As the end of his retirement neared, Washington insisted that he had only one wish, "which is to live and die on my own plantation." He told his would-be biographer David Humphreys:

> It is said that every man has his portion of ambition. I may have mine, I suppose, as well as the rest, but if I know my own heart my ambition would not lead me into public life. My only ambition is to do my duty in this world as well as I am capable of performing it and to merit the good opinion of all men.

And to another friend he confided, "My movements to the chair of government will be accompanied by feelings not unlike those of a culprit who is going to the place of execution. I greatly apprehend that my countrymen will expect too much from me."[25]

In the end, it was a side issue that forced him to take the fateful step. When Washington learned that the anti-Federalists were pushing George Clinton of New York as vice president, Washington announced that he considered John Adams better suited. But how could he choose the vice president if he were not willing to become president? Making no formal statement of acceptance, Washington began to settle his affairs at Mount Vernon. He hired his nephew, George Augustine Washington, to manage his farms and despatched Tobias Lear to New York City in early April 1788 to find the Washingtons a suitable residence. On April 14,

Washington learned that he had been unanimously elected president by the electoral college. Nobody was surprised at his acceptance. In his acceptance letter he acknowledged "this fresh proof of my country's esteem and confidence." The only surprise was how quickly he was ready to depart. Two days later President Washington left Mount Vernon for the new capital. To his diary he confided what few people could have guessed from his alacrity: he was, he confessed only to himself, "oppressed with more anxious and painful sensations than I have words to express."[26]

*C*areful to leave everything in good order at Mount Vernon, he left a detailed letter of "advisory hints" for his nephew George Steptoe, one of the two sons of his dead brother, Sam, whom Washington had "adopted." It shows his ideas for forming a young man:

Dear George:
As it is probable I shall soon be under the necessity of quitting this place and entering once more into the bustle of public life in conformity to the voice of my country and the earnest entreaties of my friends, however contrary it is to my own desires or inclinations, I think it incumbent on me as your uncle and friend to give you some advisory hints, which, if properly attended to, will, I conceive, be found very useful to you in regulating your conduct and giving you respectability, not only at present, but through every period of life. . . .

The first and great object with you at present is to acquire by industry and application such knowledge as your situation enables you to obtain as will be useful to you in life. . . . I do not mean by a close application to your studies that you should never enter into those amusements which are suited to your age and station. They can be made to go hand in hand with each other, and, used in their proper seasons, will ever be found to be a mutual assistance to one another. One thing, however, I would strongly impress upon you, namely that when you have leisure to go into company that it should always be of the best kind that the place you are in will afford. By this means you will be constantly improving your manners and cultivating your mind while you are relaxing from your books. Good company will always be found much less expensive than bad.

I cannot enjoin too strongly upon you a due observance of economy and frugality. As you well know yourself, the present state of your property and finances will not admit of any unnecessary expense. The article of clothing is now one of the chief expenses you will incur and in this, I fear, you are not so economical as you should be. Decency and cleanliness will always be the first object in the dress of a judicious and sensible man. A conformity to the prevailing fashion in a certain degree is necessary but it does not from thence follow that man should always get a new coat or other clothes upon every trifling charge in the mode when perhaps he has two or three very good ones by him. A person who is anxious to be a leader of the fashion or one of the first to follow it will certainly appear in the eyes of judicious men to have nothing better than a frequent change of dress to recommend him to notice.

Much more might be said to you, as a young man, upon the necessity of paying due attention to the moral virtues. But this may, perhaps, more properly be the subject of a future letter when you may be about to enter into the world. If you comply with the advice herein given to pay a diligent attention to your studies and employ your time of relaxation in proper company, you will find but few opportunities and little inclination, while you continue at an academy, to enter into those scenes of vice and dissipation which too often present themselves to youth in every place—and particularly in towns. If you are determined to neglect your books and plunge into extravagance and dissipation, nothing I could say now would prevent it; for you must be employed, and if it is not in pursuit of those things which are profitable, it must be in the pursuit of those which are destructive. . . .

Should you or Lawrence therefore behave in such a manner as to occasion any complaint being made to me, you may depend upon losing that place which you now have in my affections and any future hopes you may have from me. But if, on the contrary, your conduct is such as to merit my regard, you may always depend upon the warmest attachment and sincere affection of your friend and uncle.[27]

Before he left Virginia, President-elect Washington traveled to Fredericksburg to say good-bye to his mother. She was eighty-one now but still able to work each day in the garden that connected the back of the house, which Washington had bought and expanded for her at 1200 Charles Street, to Kenmore, her daughter Betty's house. Once a great horsewoman, now she no longer even kept a carriage: she was the only woman of her rank in town to walk everywhere. Relations between Washington and his mother—never good—had worsened over the years. She was discreet enough about their rift on most occasions, even gracious to strangers who came to sing her son's praises. When Lafayette visited her and heaped on the praise, she said she had always known he would do well because he was a good boy. As she said this, she poured mint julep and served tea cakes. There is no evidence that Washington wrote to her once during the Revolution, although he did see that she received an annuity and all her living expenses from Lund, his farm manager.

In the depths of the Revolution, Washington was acutely embarrassed to learn from Benjamin Harrison, then Speaker of the House of Delegates, successor to the House of Burgesses, that Mary Ball Washington had petitioned the Virginia government and claimed she was destitute, needed a state pension, and needed to have her taxes lowered. Outraged and mortified, Washington wrote back to Harrison that he regularly sent her money: "Whence her distresses arise therefore, I know not, never having received any complaint of inattention or neglect." All of her children were willing to provide for her, he had added, "to relieve her from real distress." Washington and all his siblings "would feel much hurt" if "our mother [were] a pensioner while we had the means of supporting her but in fact she has an ample income."[28]

His mother's avarice was only one cause of irritation to Washington. She was, according to French officers stationed in Virginia during the war, a Loyalist sympathizer who outspokenly opposed her son's revolutionary politics. Only Washington's stature protected her from being driven out of the community by resentful neighbors; many Loyalists had been imprisoned or tarred and feathered for their Tory views. When his brother Jack—"the intimate companion of my youth"—died in January 1787, Washington was left alone as the last son to deal with his mother. It was at this moment that his mother insisted that Washington bring her to Mount Vernon to live. In his longest, weariest, yet sharpest surviving letter to her he refused, concluding, "You would not be able to enjoy that calmness and serenity of mind which in my opinion you ought now to prefer to every other consideration."[29]

Washington predicted his visit to his mother in the spring of 1789 would be the last time he saw her. She was suffering from breast cancer and died less than six months later. The stopover in Fredericksburg, he wrote, was "to discharge the last act of personal duty I may ever have it in my power to pay my Mother." No one recorded the private scene, but according to local legend Mary Ball Washington did not receive him or invite anyone else who came with him into her house. As usual, she made her son come to her. She always believed that he owed her everything, that whatever he had become it was because of her. There, in the garden, the woman who had given him his visage, his stubbornness, his tenacity, his love of horsemanship and the outdoors, and his acquisitiveness and insecurity went on working on her flowers as her son, the president-elect, fumbled with his hat—and for the right words of farewell. He never did know what to say to her.[30]

*E*ven before he left Mount Vernon, Washington began to receive applications for federal jobs from old political colleagues, from the fathers of jobless immigrants from Europe, from old neighbors, from total strangers. He decided to work up an elegant form letter that ran this way:

> Should it inevitably prove my lot to hold the Chief Magistracy, I have determined to enter into the office without being under any pre-engagements to any person of any nature whatsoever. This answer I have already often given and especially for the——— office in the district of ———. And this line of conduct I have observed because I thought the justice I owed to my own reputation and the justice I owed to my country required that I should be perfectly free to act while in office with a supreme and undeviating regard for individual merit and the public good.
>
> Although I can easily conceive that the general principles on which nominations ought in good policy and equity to be made may be easily ascertained, still I cannot possibly form a conception of a more delicate and arduous task than the particular of those principles to practice. With the best possible intentions it will be impossible to give universal satisfaction.[31]

The letter not only shows Washington's dread and loathing of the task ahead but his stubborn insistence on micromanaging every step of forming a new government—from the clerk on up. It fell to his faithful amanuensis David Humphreys to put aside his biography of Washington and begin to write out longhand Washington's rejection letters. The document also reveals Washington's special resentment that erstwhile friends such as Virginia's Governor Harrison, who had opposed ratification of the new Constitution, felt they could now "importune" him for political appointments to the new federal government. Harrison had the nerve to ask Washington to appoint him to a lucrative customs office post. Washington left Virginia without acknowledging Harrison's letters and Harrison wrote again "to readily excuse your neglect of me," trying to explain away his anti-Federalist stance by adding that "if we could always be in such hands my fears would vanish." The battle over ratification had left lasting personal scars. Washington's only subsequent contact with his friend and neighbor George Mason was an exchange of stiff notes over a job for a carriage driver. Mason's employee had asked Washington for a job and Washington showed Mason that they could at least remain civil, that he would not steal away a worker, but it was the old Washington civility that was courtesy and nothing more. His friend since boyhood, his fellow co-conspirator in the early days of the Revolution, the friend who had even lent him the cash to attend the constitutional convention in Philadelphia in the summer of 1787—from now on Washington would refer to Mason only as "my quondam friend"; formerly, but no more. Washington never visited Gunston Hall again and after Mason opposed the Constitution there is no evidence that he was ever again welcomed at Mount Vernon.[32]

Few but his old comrade-in-arms remained trusted friends. To Henry Knox, the secretary of war under the old Congress, Washington could still confide his misgivings:

> My movements to the chair of government will be accompanied with feelings not unlike those of a culprit who is going to the place of his execution. So unwilling am I, in the evening of a life nearly consumed in public cares to quit a peaceful abode for an ocean of difficulties without that competency of political skill, abilities and inclination which is necessary to manage the helm. Integrity and firmness is all I can promise. These, be the voyage long or short, never shall forsake me although I may be deserted by all men.

Washington could always trust his oldest remaining comrade: soon he would call on him again.[33]

*L*eaving advice and instructions for one and all, Washington wrote a long and severe letter to Thomas Green, overseer of Mount Vernon's black carpenters. Washington had hired the man as a joiner when he had retired from the army in 1783 and only tolerated him because he was married to the daughter of Washington's old manservant Thomas Bishop, who had served him faithfully since the dying Braddock had asked Washington to take care of him in 1755. Now that Washington needed Bishop as chief groom at the new presidential stables under construction in New York City, Washington spelled out in strong language his understanding of the employer-employee relationship:

> First that all bargains are intended for the mutual benefit of and are equally binding on both parties and are either binding in all their parts or are of no use at all. If then a man received [pay] for his labor and he withholds or if he trifles away that time for which he is paid, it is a robbery—and a robbery of the worst kind because it is not only a fraud but a dishonorable, unmanly and a deceitful fraud.
>
> I advise you to keep always in remembrance [the] good name which common policy as well as common honesty makes necessary for every workman who wishes to pass through life with reputation and to secure employment. I have left strict orders with [my] nephew that if he should find you unfaithful to your engagements—either from the love of liquor [or] from a disposition to be running about—or from proneness to idle when at your work—to discard you immediately and to remove your

family from their present abode. The sure means to avoid this evil is first to refrain from drink which is the source of all evil and the ruin of half the workmen in this country and next to avoid bad company which is the base of good morals, economy and industry.[34]

The money wasted on providing the overseer's liquor was supposedly not the worst part. Washington went on (and on) that bad company led to dissipation and to the "ruin" of a "body debilitated" and to "an aching head and trembling limbs" which "disincline the hands from work." Washington wrote that he had taken the trouble of such a long letter at such a pressing time because "it has been a custom with me through life to give preference to those who have long lived with [me] and my wish to see them do well." In a parting shot, Washington added, "if you have gratitude or a mind capable of reflection it will make such an impression on it as may be serviceable to you through life." Thomas Green stayed on at Mount Vernon four more years, apparently sober. Washington left such strongly worded instructions to all three of his overseers, but he confided to his nephew George Augustine Washington that if they did their jobs properly, he should only have to take a morning horseback ride of inspection. He left detailed instructions to barter the fish caught in the river for such things as shingles, planks, nails, and rum for the field hands at harvest time. Cash realized from the crops and from stud fees from the mules should be paid to workmen for their wages and for the taxes. To his favorite nephew Washington gave orders quite different in tone and substance from the harangue he delivered to his overseers:

Nor is it my wish that you should live in too parsimonious and niggardly a manner. Frugality and economy are undoubtedly commendable and all that is required. Happily for this country, these virtues prevail more and more every day among all classes of citizens.

As he departed to take up his new post as president, Washington made a startling revelation to his nephew. He confided that he, too, would soon have been forced to economize, to cut back on his openhanded hospitality at Mount Vernon and his expensive remodeling and refurbishing, if the form of government had not changed and he had not been elected president. "Nothing but the event which I dreaded," he confessed privately to his nephew, "has prevented my following the example [of frugality]." With no army pension, with an aversion to trading with England, and British trade restrictions on his old Caribbean markets, and with tenants on thousands of acres who were as cash-poor as he was becoming, Washington had been bartering land for nearly everything. Even to buy a stud horse to raise badly needed cash from stud fees he had swapped land. Like most Americans five years after the Revolution's end, Washington was scraping. To no one else did he admit in writing what many of his old friends probably knew: that "necessity (if this [his election] had not happened) would have forced me into [frugality] as my means are not adequate to the expense at which I have lived since my retirement to what is called private life."[35]

In other words, the first president of the United States, George Washington, needed the job.

Nineteen

"I WALK ON UNTRODDEN GROUND"

At every town and ferry crossing in that warm April of 1789, multitudes thronged President-elect George Washington, cheering as if to ratify his unanimous selection by the electoral college. Militia marched, dragoons pranced, cannon fired (always thirteen times), and, at least in Trenton, New Jersey, young girls and women in long white gowns strewed flower petals at the feet of his horse. The bridge over Assumpink Creek where Washington's Continentals had fought off a bayonet charge by British grenadiers was now elaborately bedecked with garlands of greenery, and a sign on an arch bore the number 1776 and the anthem "The Defenders of the Mothers will also Defend the Daughters."

A line of matrons and maidens sang as an embarrassed Washington doffed his tricorn hat and waited:

> Welcome, mighty Chief once more!
> Welcome to this grateful shore;
> Now no mercenary foe
> Aims again the fatal blow;
> Aims at thee the fatal blow.
>
> Virgins fair to matrons grave
> These thy conquering arm did save
> Build for thee triumphal bowers
> Strew ye fair his way with flowers
> Strew your hero's way with flowers.[1]

The first of the ladies strewing flowers in Washington's path was his old friend Annis Boudinot Stockton. Sister of Elias Boudinot, the former president of the Continental Congress, she was the widow of Richard

445

"Signing Dick" Stockton, the only signer of the Declaration of Independence who had recanted. Taken a prisoner when the British overran Princeton in 1776, he had been held in New York City until he was released near death of cancer. So hated was he by many revolutionaries that his widow buried him in an unmarked grave and Congress refused to pause for even a moment to mark the former member's death. Washington had corresponded with Annis Stockton for several years and she had written several admiring poems to him during the Revolution. When he led his army south toward Yorktown he stopped off to visit her at Mowen, the Stockton residence in Princeton. Deeply touched, Annis had kissed his hand.

Just before he left Mount Vernon to travel to his inauguration, Washington received a long letter and a poem from Annis. She reminded him of

> the ardor which almost censured my delicacy—which impelled me to seize your hand and kiss it when you did me the honor to call on me in your way to Yorktown. . . . You will smile to see the sensations of that day, which I have never forgotten, thrown in the form of a [poetic] vision. . . . I have nourished it in my heart ever since.

Their platonic correspondence was to continue. Somehow Annis's poem with these lines later survived the flames of Martha's posthumous purge of private Washington papers:

> Rash mortal Stop, she cried with zeal
> One Secret more I must reveal
> That will renew your prime
> These storms will work the wishd for cure
> And for the state will health procure
> And last till latest time.

Washington was to have his share of adulation from both sexes as president. Ever discreet, Washington had sent her the "joint good wishes of Mrs. Washington and myself for yourself and your family" and a "grateful feeling" for "an elegant poem."[2]

At Princeton the new president spent the night at the home of John Witherspoon, president of the College of New Jersey. Washington had refused all other personal invitations and insisted on staying in hotels to remain "independent." Presbyterian Witherspoon, a signer of the Declaration of Independence, had educated the chaplains of seventy-seven regiments in Washington's revolutionary army, and Washington had contributed heavily to rebuild Nassau Hall, which had been seriously damaged by American artillery in the Battle of Princeton in 1777. On his way to his inauguration Washington paused to give a short speech to Princeton students. He spoke of his "grateful heart" as he went to take up "the first office in confederated America."[3]

Arriving in Elizabeth Town on April 22 Washington met with a joint delegation from the new U.S. House of Representatives and Senate at the home of Elias Boudinot. He was worried that it had taken six weeks to gather a congressional quorum to constitute the new government. Unless the new legislative body took power under the new Constitution before the spring fleets from Europe arrived in America, upward of $300,000 in customs duties, the bulk of the Federal budget for the year, would be lost. Washington set the date of April 30 for his inauguration; meanwhile, Vice President John Adams and the Congress would be sworn in so that government business could continue.

Able to relax now, Washington joined the congressmen, New York officials, and a crowd that had assembled at Elizabeth Town Point to escort him across the fifteen miles of open water to Manhattan Island. There, he boarded a large ceremonial barge with thirteen New York City dignitaries acting as the oarsmen. Thomas Randall, president of New York's Common Council, called the stroke. Another barge filled with musicians played alongside. Henry Knox provided an honor guard in a boat on the other side. They were surrounded by scores of vessels large and small. The Spanish man-of-war *Galviston* fired a fifteen-gun salute. In his diary, Washington recorded that the

> *display of boats which attended and joined us on this occasion, some with vocal and some with instrumental music on board—the decorations of the ships, the roar of cannon, and the loud acclamations of the people which rent the skies as I passed along the wharves filled my mind with sensations as painful (considering the reverse of this scene which may be the case after all my labors to do good) as they are pleasing.*

At this moment of public adulation, Washington realized that he had no political experience beyond a brief stint as a congressman and fifteen years of inattention to the office of Virginia burgess. He was worried that his long-fought public reputation would be tarnished and that he might fail at a new job no one understood or much less knew whether it would do any good.[4]

At the Battery, Governor Clinton the arch anti-Federalist put politics aside to escort Washington ashore. The crowd nearly crushed Washington as he was led to a borrowed house to prepare for his inauguration. Washington went over all the plans and approved the ceremony. The appointed day, April 30, was clear and bright. A crowd had been gathering outside the president's house since dawn. At nine, all the churches in the city were opened "and prayers offered up to the Great Ruler of the universe for the preservation of the President," wrote Tobias Lear,

Washington's secretary, whose room was under the eaves. "At twelve the troops of the city paraded before our door and, soon after, the committees of Congress and heads of departments came in their carriages to wait upon the President to Federal Hall."[5]

At half past noon a coach and four marching militia and a band led off and took Washington to Federal Hall, the recently converted City Hall. A long line of congressmen's and foreign ambassadors' coaches followed the white presidential coach of state, the first inaugural parade. The crowd strained to get a look at Washington. He was wearing a dark brown home-spun suit made at Hartford Manufacturing with eagles embossed on the buttons, white silk stockings, and a close-cropped brown tricorn beaver hat made in Philadelphia. He wore no wig; his hair was pulled back and powdered. Escorted into Federal Hall by four former aides-de-camp, Washington was introduced by Vice President Adams (who had already been sworn in) to Congress, which was packed into the second-floor Sen-ate chamber. Then Washington stepped out onto a balcony, where the crowd of ten thousand was cheering wildly. Robert R. Livingston, chan-cellor of New York State, administered the oath of office (there was still no federal judiciary). The instant Livingston declared him president of the United States, the crowd roared, "God bless our Washington! Long live our beloved President!" Church bells pealed and cannon fired the in-evitable thirteen-gun salute.

Back inside the Senate chamber Washington read a 1,200-word inau-gural speech. "Fellow Citizens of the Senate and of the House of Repre-sentatives," he began. He spoke of "inheriting inferior endowments," of being conscious of his "deficiencies." He asked the "Almighty Being" to bless "the important revolution" that he had just led "through tranquil deliberations and voluntary consent" by the people. He warned against "local attachments" and "separate views" and "party animosities" and recommended swift passage of the promised amendments that would grant Americans a written bill of rights. Then Washington left the hall.[6]

Some in the hall were deeply moved by Washington's modest perfor-mance. "It was a touching scene," wrote Fisher Ames, "and quite of the solemn kind. His aspect grave, almost to sadness; his modesty—[he was] actually shaking; his voice deep, a little tremulous and so low as to call for close attention." But not everyone was so impressed. Senator William Maclay of Pennsylvania was less charitable:

> This great man was agitated and embarrassed more than ever he was by the levelled cannon or pointed musket. He trembled and several times could scarce make out to read, though it must be supposed he had often read it before. When he came to the words *all the world*, he made a flourish with his right hand which left rather an ungainly impression. I sincerely, for my part, wish

all set ceremony in the hands of the dancing-masters and that this first of men had read off his address in the plainest manner.[7]

Following the inauguration Washington and the House and Senate walked 700 yards to St. Paul's Church for a thanksgiving service and the singing of a "Te Deum." Retiring to his house for a private dinner with his aides Lear and Humphreys, the president toured the town and watched fireworks displays on Bowling Green. Virtually every window in the city was illuminated by candlelight for the occasion. The French and Spanish embassies competed in lighted displays and taverns sported larger-than-life paintings of Washington.

Two male secretaries had accompanied Washington everywhere on his day of triumph—but Martha did not. It would be another month before the pilgrimage to the temporary capital by the First Lady. It began with tearful farewells at Mount Vernon six weeks after Washington left home. Washington had hired his nephew, Bob Lewis, as his personal secretary, and his first assignment was to escort Martha and her entourage to New York City. Lewis was on hand to report the emotional parting. "Servants of the house and a number of field Negroes [were] greatly affected [and] my aunt equally so." For the first time since her adoption Sam Washington's orphan, Harriet, was left behind with George Augustine, the new farm manager, and his wife, Fanny. Martha took Nelly along, her granddaughter, and eight-year-old Wash. They stopped overnight to say good-bye to their older sisters. At five the next morning, with "the family in tears [and] the children a-bawling," Martha and her two wards climbed into the carriage and crossed into Maryland.[8]

Martha and the children consumed two gallons of iced punch in fifteen minutes. The children, wrote Bob Lewis, were "very well and cheerful all the way." In Philadelphia crowds surrounded the First Lady and her entourage and church bells punctuated the usual thirteen-gun salute. Martha took time to shop for shoes, a doll for Fanny Stewart's youngest daughter, and artist's materials for two other Stewart granddaughters.

President Washington was waiting at Elizabeth Town Point with the same gaudy inaugural barge to escort the rest of his presidential family to New York City. A crowd of boats escorted the barge and "dear little Wash seemed to be lost in a maze at the great parade," Martha wrote Fanny. The first family took up temporary residence in a small house at Cherry and Queen Streets while renovations were rushed on the presidential mansion.[9]

Washington refused the loan of a finer house owned by Governor George Clinton, as he explained to Madison, because he did not want a house large enough for entertaining at first and because he wished "to be placed in an independent situation." He settled on renting the house of merchant Samuel Osgood, which had been the residence of the president of the old Congress. It was a handsome house—"square, five windows wide, and three stories high"—that faced Franklin Square. Congress had purchased much of the furniture for the use of its president. Senator William Maclay of Pennsylvania, who was to become an outspoken critic of the new government's spending, complained bitterly in September 1789 when Osgood billed Congress $8,000 (out of a $2 million federal budget) for repairs to the president's temporary quarters.[10]

*F*or nearly eight months the Washingtons lived on the second floor of a small house and the president's three aides crowded into the third floor while the city's grandest house at 39 Broadway was renovated at a cost of $10,000, about $400,000 in today's money. The house, built only three years earlier for merchant Alexander Macomber, had served as the residence of the French ambassador to the United States, the Comte de Moustier. The massive four-story honey-colored stone house overlooked the Hudson River. Washington himself added a new warehouse and stables for the six milk-white horses he had decided would pull the white presidential carriage.

At his own expense, Washington decorated the house with furnishings he purchased from Count Moustier. The ornate furniture and fine Turkish rugs would be displayed against scenic wallpaper in two large downstairs reception rooms. From Europe came gifts of vases and paintings from Washington's admirers. Marquis de Lafayette sent him the key to the Bastille— "a tribute which I owe as a son to my adoptive family, as an aide-de-camp to my general, as a missionary of liberty to its patriarch." The rooms and their elaborate furnishings glowed by day in the reflected light from the river, at night with the clear flames of fourteen new Argand whale-oil lamps sent by Gouverneur Morris, the American envoy in London.[11]

Just what Martha Washington thought of this temporary replacement to Mount Vernon came through in her letters to relatives. In the new air of formality she stopped referring to her husband as "Poppa" and started calling him "the General." Deeply depressed at first, she complained to relatives in Virginia that "I live a dull life here and know nothing that passes in the town. I never go to any public place. Indeed, I am more like a state prisoner than anything else. There are certain bounds set for me that I mustn't depart from—and as I cannot do as I like I am obstinate and stay at home a great deal." Gradually Martha's mood improved. She was, she wrote Mercy Otis Warren, pleased at their reception if a little tired from all the hustle and bustle of the people and the place. She would much rather be home at Mount Vernon:

> I do not say this because I feel dissatisfied with my present situation. No, God forbid: For everybody and everything conspire to make me as contented as possible in it yet I know too much from the splendid scenes of public life. I am still determined to be cheerful and to be happy in whatever situation I may be for I

have learned from experience that the greatest part of our happiness or misery depends upon our dispositions and not upon our circumstances. We carry the seeds of the one or the other about with us in our minds wherever we go.

Martha was one of the few people who impressed Mercy Warren, even if she gushed about many patriots in her writings, but Martha seemed to sense her respect and continued to write her honest letters: "I continue to be as happy here as I could at any place except Mount Vernon," she was writing by the spring of 1790. "My grandchildren have good opportunities for acquiring a useful and accomplished education. In their happiness my own is, in a great measure, involved."[12]

As the president found the time, Martha began to go frequently to the theater. Theater was Washington's abiding passion. The presidential theater party usually included three or four other invited couples. Wash later recalled that the audiences often called for the band to play "Washington's March." There were balls and dances where Martha, after a few rounds, could chat with friends while her husband danced hour after hour with every woman present. And on Sundays the first couple attended church services. Martha, a devout Anglican, invariably took communion; Washington never did.

If Martha was unhappy she managed to conceal it. She reported she was having her hair set and styled every day. "You would I fear think me a good deal in the fashion if you could but see me."[13] Abigail Adams, wife of Vice President Adams, found her

> a most friendly good lady, always pleasant and easy, dotingly fond of her grandchildren, to whom she is quite the Grandmama. . . . She is plain in her dress but that plainness is the best of every article. . . . Her manners are modest and unassuming, dignified and feminine . . . no lady can be more deservedly beloved and esteemed as she is.[14]

A good part of each of Martha's days revolved around her grandchildren's activities. "My first care," Martha wrote, "was to get the children to a good school—which they are both very much pleased at." Pudgy, unruly Wash began to study with seven other boys under a Mr. Murdoch. Martha saw to it that his sister Nelly was privately tutored in music and art: one art teacher—painter, historian, and playwright William Dunlop— was on his way to becoming famous. And her music teacher was Alexander Reinagle of Little Queen Street, a recent immigrant from England who was writing some of New York City's best music. She practiced on a new pianoforte the president had bought. Her teacher was demanding and, her brother later wrote, Nelly "played and cried and cried and played." There were certain advantages even then to being a ten-year-old child in the president's house, even if dark-haired Nelly was terribly homesick. For seven months, Nelly went to school at the fashionable establishment of Mrs. Graham of Maiden Lane where many prominent New Yorkers sent their daughters. Her studies included reading, English grammar, and embroidery, geography, dancing, and French lessons six days a week.

But on Sundays, after coming back from church, the Washingtons refused to let anyone penetrate their privacy. Martha had purchased "ball and marbles, a small cannon," and some "paints," Wash later recorded in his *Recollections*, and the children and their young friends performed *The Young Americans* in the attic for their grandparents. Nelly later recalled that Washington was "the most affectionate of fathers" and that he "laughed heartily at saucy descriptions of any scene in which [I] had taken part." She understood Washington better than her young friends did; she knew that he relished their pranks but her little friends saw a reserve that they "could not overcome."[15]

*F*or most of their first year in the president's house both Washingtons were busy devising the duties of a president and a First Lady, well aware that whatever they did established a precedent. There *was* no other president nor had there ever been in the Western world. The office was as new as the nation. A day at a time, Washington fashioned the presidency, often with his wife's help. Just as he had as commander in chief of the Revolutionary army, Washington turned for help to trusted advisors. Bombarding them with questions, he expected answers in a day or two at most. Should he seclude himself from the public? How often should he meet the public? Should he open his office for business at 8 A.M. each day? Should he periodically dine with members of Congress? And should he host state dinners? Would it be improper for him to call upon private acquaintances? Should he make a tour of the United States? In short, should he make the presidency resemble a monarchy or a more popular form of public office?

Establishing an English-style cabinet system with secretaries in charge of key departments—State, Treasury, War, the Attorney General's Office— he called infrequent meetings at first. He intended to act slowly and carefully the first year to establish a solid foundation for the government. There were two key offices. As secretary of state, his friend Thomas Jefferson must give up his idyllic life in the salons of Paris, where for five years he had been the leading American diplomat in Europe. For secretary of the treasury he had chosen Alexander Hamilton, lawyer, newspaper publisher, and Washington's former legal aide in the Revolution. Both men were redheads with nothing else in common.

Hamilton, the illegitimate son of a British admiral, considered the British government the world's best. To no one's surprise, he recommended George Washington behave like a king. His office should be wrapped in royal "dignity." He must distance himself from his subjects.

Only department heads, diplomats, and members of the Senate should have free access to the president. "Your Excellency," as he called George Washington, should conduct a "levee" only once a week, admit only invited guests, and make only a thirty-minute appearance, speaking only in the most concise and formal manner. He should give up to four state dinners each year, but the president should never call on anyone nor should he be entertained by anyone.[16]

While John Adams, the more democratically inclined vice president, also wanted a "dignified and respectable government," his recommendations were less courtly than Alexander Hamilton's. He wanted a more republican presidency so that the people would realize that the president was, like themselves, a citizen. He thought two levees a week would be better and that they should be open to the general public. He opposed state dinners. He told the president he should be free to entertain and call on anyone he pleased. President Washington took what he wanted of Hamilton's and Adams's advice and decided he would receive "visits of compliment" two afternoons each week for an hour each time. He would not go out of the president's house to be a dinner guest at any private residence. He would hold a public levee for suitably dressed men, but not women, for an hour every Tuesday afternoon; Martha would preside over a public tea party for ladies and gentlemen every Friday night. The two would host a small dinner by invitation at 4 P.M. every Wednesday. The Washingtons followed this routine for the next eight years.[17]

Just how to address the president at these gatherings or any other time was an important question that was not settled so quickly. Adams led a campaign in the Senate to coin an official title. For several days, the senators debated. Should he be "the Honourable," "His Elective Highness" or "Majesty," "His Exalted High Mightiness"? Adams favored "His Highness the President of the United States and Protector of the Rights of Same." This was all too much for Patrick Henry, who held out for something far plainer. Finally, it was simply, "The President of the United States." Washington decided how he should be addressed in person: "Mister President."

Washington was more concerned at the moment with a task he detested: hiring people. Benjamin Lincoln had warned him that "New York is now filled with a crowd of applicants." He had 1,000 offices to fill. He filled every job himself, right down to lighthouse keeper in Portland, Maine—and then he bought the oil for the lamp, quibbling over the price. He hated deciding who to hire or not hire because, he said, "a single disgust excited in a particular state [he meant New York or Georgia, for instance] might raise a flame of opposition that could not easily, if ever, be extinguished." But he also did not like turning people down who had sacrificed to make the new nation, even though he did not hesitate to reject the application of his nephew, Bushrod, for attorney general of Virginia on the grounds he still had too little experience as a lawyer.[18]

His major appointments to head government departments—State, War, and Treasury—all sailed through Congress, establishing a tradition that lasted until recent times. But when he appointed a naval officer to command the port of Savannah, Georgia's two senators yowled that this should be their prerogative. Washington backed down and withdrew his nomination. The tradition of "senatorial courtesy"—the nomination to all federal offices within a state having to come from a senator—was thus established. To settle how and how often he was to meet with his closest advisers, Washington turned to the British model and set up a cabinet that met once a week to advise the president, submit written answers to his questions and written reports on their branches of government, then debate the issues and vote. But Washington reserved the sole decision-making power.

Just how the president would live was a question that fascinated many in the early days of the American presidency. George Washington decided that the appearance of power and dignity was important. But he had never had any qualms about living well at public expense and he did not try to live within his salary. Congress rejected his offer to live on an expense account and settled on a $25,000-a-year salary—about $1 million in today's purchasing power—but that included all expenses, and he managed to run about $5,000 a year ($200,000 today) into the red some years, paying the deficit himself. He spent $3,000 of his own money ($120,000) to build a large stable for sixteen horses. These included two matched sets of six horses, one black set and one white set, to pull a large cream-colored carriage-of-state. He hired fourteen white servants and brought seven blacks from Mount Vernon. He kept the blacks out of public sight. He called his staff, as he had in the army, his "family." He paid quite a lot for medical care: $210 ($8,000 today) to remove a large carbuncle from a thigh; $200 (about $8,000) when he nearly died of influenza. He paid over and over for terrible dentures, including a set of teeth made of porous hippopotamus ivory that quickly turned black from port wine. He tried dentures made of cow's teeth and spring-loaded teeth he had to clench closed: all worked badly and must have hurt almost constantly. Perhaps this helps to explain why his liquor bill was staggering: 7 percent of his salary. Thomas Jefferson directed him to the best wine merchants in Burgundy and Bordeaux. Washington hired the best cook he could find. He bought a gaudy new saddle and draped his matched horses in leopardskin robes.

*M*artha Washington designed the role of First Lady and in many ways it has remained unchanged ever since. It went without saying that she presided over the kitchen and the dinner table, just as she had done at Mount Vernon. Washington considered her functions, even her letter writing, as important adjuncts of the presidency—too important for her informal spelling and grammar. He wrote out wishes for her, which became presidential orders to be followed with alacrity in the capital as well as Mount Vernon. The First Lady often drew on reserves at home to help her entertain the government and her obligatory guests in the capital:

> Mrs. Washington desires you will send her by the first vessel to this place one dozen of the best hams and half a dozen midlings of bacon. . . . Mrs. Washington requests that the gardener would send to her some artichoke seeds. . . . Mrs. Washington expected two barrels of *good* shad would have come round with the things which were sent from Mount Vernon. . . . Mrs. Washington desires you will direct [the slave] Old Doll to distill a good deal of rose and mint water. . . . We wish to know whether the linen for the people is all made up.[19]

Managing the president's house and directing the staff of a busy household, Martha poured tea at the Friday afternoon levees that were open to any ladies who had the nerve to appear and joined her husband at the table for the Tuesday night presidential soirees, usually reserved for the gentlemen. While she was a source of personal strength and comfort for him, she did not allow herself to participate or even speak up when social functions became government meetings. She stayed, she heard, but she did not comment or repeat what she heard and there is no hint that she ever asserted any opinion on any government or presidential business—except in the broadest sense of supporting whatever her husband said or did no matter the personal suffering or dislocation it caused her. She considered her role an honorable and worthy one, but she believed she should definitely stay in the background. She carried it all off with her usual grace, dignity, and charm for as long as she felt she had to. Her soft-spoken, pleasant, grandmotherly manner added greatly to the respect Americans and their foreign guests paid to the First Family of the United States.

George Washington was the head of the government, but Martha Washington became its heart. As Abigail Adams, the second First Lady, put it,

> Mrs. Washington is one of those unassuming characters [who] create love and esteem. Her manners are modest and unassuming, dignified and feminine—[there is] not the tincture of *hauteur* about her. A most becoming pleasantness sits upon her countenance and an unaffected deportment which renders her the object of veneration and respect.[20]

*F*rom the outset of his presidency, George Washington deferred to congressional authority, and in congressmen's eyes, the first problem to serve was revenue. A bill that exacted tariffs from all imports and a tonnage tax on all ships entering American ports was laid on the president's desk early in July of 1780. In its first draft, the bill would have discriminated against English goods and ships in retaliation for British restrictions on American trade with Caribbean ports, traditionally crucial to the American economy. The British had reimposed the Rule of 1756, which said British colonies could only trade with British merchants using British ships—"English goods in English bottoms." The British ruling was seriously hurting New England's maritime trade and southern planters like Washington who had for several years exported second-grade flour and corn to the islands. Washington wanted to flex the new government's muscles and wanted to retaliate against the British, but Congress had deleted the discriminatory language and sent the president a watered-down version. Washington had already decided that he would only use his veto on constitutional grounds. While he disliked the bill, he signed it on July 4.

By controlling salaries and budgets, Congress decided how the new government should be set up and authorized four executive departments. The Department of State was given charge of both domestic and foreign affairs under a secretary of state: there was no secretary of the interior or agriculture or commerce. A War Department would include the army and Indian affairs—there was no U.S. Navy until 1797. The army consisted of one regiment of 840 men and the War Department staff of five men under Henry Knox, the only holdover from the Confederation government. The Treasury Department was not only to collect customs duties and administer the post office but bring some kind of order to the new government's financial affairs. It would rapidly become the largest branch with some 2,000 customs agents and 1,000 postal workers. An attorney general rounded out the four-man cabinet. The government's legal department included the attorney general and a bare-bones system of federal courts with a six-man Supreme Court whose justices rode circuit to six circuit courts.

Congress had crafted the molds; Washington had to fill them. His easiest task was to appoint a secretary of war. No question, he would be Henry Knox, who had rarely peeled off his gigantic uniform except for a brief and unsuccessful stint as a land speculator in Maine. He had been called back into service in 1786 to crush Shays' Rebellion. The oversized former Boston bookseller, who was married to the beautiful Lucy Flucken—daughter of a leading Loyalist—had always been loyal only to Washington. The job was his along with a $3,500 salary and a generous expense budget. It never hurt Knox that Martha Washington and the vivacious and witty Lucy Knox were close friends. Lucy's gambling debts had pushed Knox into unsuccessful land deals and he was happy to accept Washington's War Department appointment. Within a year he would expand the military by 50 percent to 1,216 noncommissioned officers, privates, and musicians paid from $3.50 a month for privates to $60 for a lieutenant commander. Knox's salary seemed a fortune by comparison.

Knox had outranked Washington's second appointment. As secretary of the Treasury he chose Colonel Alexander Hamilton. Married into the rich and powerful Schuyler clan, from the balcony of his townhouse at 57 Wall Street he had been able to watch Washington sworn into office. Adams had called Hamilton "the bastard brat of a Scots peddler" because Hamilton had been born the illegitimate son of a Scottish merchant and his French Huguenot common-law wife on the West Indian island of Nevis. When his father abandoned his mother, she gave herself the name Madame Hamilton and moved to St. Croix in the now U.S. Virgin Islands, where Alexander went to work in the countinghouse of a firm that traded with New York City. When he was seventeen his employers sent him to the mainland to a school in Elizabeth Town, New Jersey, and at eighteen helped him to enroll at King's College, where he probably knew Washington's stepson, Jack Custis. When the Revolution came, he was appointed a captain of New York artillery and fought effectively at Trenton and Princeton. His pluck in combat made him a member of Washington's military "family" and by late 1777 he was Washington's personal secretary, legal adviser, and closest aide. Washington paid him his highest compliment by ordering him to lead the sole American attack on a heavily defended redoubt at Yorktown. Washington had, by then, begun to call him "my boy."

Small, red-haired, freckled, and pugnacious, Hamilton became a notorious womanizer who once confessed that his motto was "All for love." He married the wealthy Elizabeth Schuyler, daughter of Major General Philip Schuyler. They had eight children. And then he carried on an affair with her sister, Angelica. Admitted to the bar at the end of the Revolution, he made a fortune representing New York Loyalists, many of whom had fled into exile. From 1782 he served consistently in Congress and by 1786 was writing an appeal to Congress to authorize a reform convention. At the 1787 convention in Philadelphia he had championed a new form of government that would make the president the chief executive for life—an elective monarch—and the Senate appointive. He firmly believed that the United States government should adhere as closely as possible to the British model, and he shocked the convention by praising the English monarchy and demanding senators be chosen for life like members of the House of Lords. The convention adopted four of his ideas, but he worked hard for ratification of the Constitution by the states. Hamilton, Madison, and John Jay's letters to newspapers became known as the Federalist papers. His effusions in favor of a strong central government no doubt made Washington think he was the ideal choice for Treasury secretary. His harshest critic was anti-Federalist New York governor Clinton who called him "little Great Man."[21]

As his secretary of state, Washington could have been expected to appoint John Jay the incumbent secretary for foreign affairs of the old Congress. But Jay had recently proposed closing the Mississippi to Americans in a treaty with Spain. Washington rightly feared that Jay's appointment would incite western resentment toward the new government and would prevent Jay's effectiveness. He took Madison's advice to bring Jefferson into the cabinet to cement the loyalty of the west. Jefferson had fought to give farmers on the Virginia frontier an equal footing in the state's government and had championed the carving-out of Kentucky from Virginia territory as governor. He had launched the George Rogers Clark expedition to seize the Northwest Territories during the Revolution and had emerged as the champion of the yeoman farmer. After two terms in Congress and two terms as governor of Virginia he had served five years in Paris as a diplomat, replacing Benjamin Franklin as minister plenipotentiary to France, the highest-ranking American diplomatic post. Washington considered him the expert on European affairs and readily agreed to his appointment as secretary of state.

That did not mean that Jefferson was equally enamored of the post. He preferred to return to Paris. He had taken the embassy assignment after his beloved wife died and he could no longer be at his Monticello home without her. In Paris he had become Lafayette's close friend and had helped him draft the Declaration of the Rights of Man and Citizens. He was handsomely installed in a villa on the Champs Elysée and had fallen in love with a married English portraitist, Maria Cosway, who made long annual visits to Paris. He had only come home on leave to attend to the marriage of his daughter, Patsy, and then he intended to return to France. But he had been an eyewitness to the early events of the French Revolution and Washington considered his knowledge indispensable.

When Jefferson arrived at Norfolk, Virginia, on November 23, 1789, he learned from newspapers that Washington had appointed him secretary of state despite Jefferson's attempt to rebuff a feeler from Madison shortly after Washington's inauguration. That Jefferson would reject his appointment apparently never entered Washington's mind: he had thus held the post open for him all these months. As Jefferson visited relatives around Virginia, a formal letter from Washington overtook him. He responded quickly by telling Washington of his "gloomy forebodings" of "criticisms and censures" if he accepted. Unless Washington insisted, he preferred to return to Paris. Yet he conceded that "it is not for an individual to choose his post. You are to marshal us as may be best for the public good." After a second letter from Washington and two private meetings that left Washington annoyed that such an effort was necessary, Jefferson accepted conditionally. He wanted assurance that Washington would appoint someone to supervise affairs at home if he found foreign affairs a full-time job. And he could not join the government until after his daughter's marriage.[22]

It was not until mid-February of 1790 that Jefferson finally accepted the appointment to join what he told his Albemarle neighbors in a farewell speech was "the holy cause of freedom." He arrived in New York in March, nearly a year after Washington's inauguration. Jay had filled in in the meantime. Jefferson settled into a rented house at 57 Maiden Lane. Despite the fact that he was the ranking member of the cabinet, he was already the outsider—although he did not realize it at first. He was reunited with his old friends John and Abigail Adams, who had lived closely with him in France. And Washington had appointed Jefferson's cousin and former law clerk, Edmund Randolph, as attorney general, and Jefferson's closest friend, Madison, had joined the Virginia delegation in the House of Representatives. But Jefferson was the only cabinet secretary who had not served on Washington's military staff. In almost all appointments Washington gave preference to veterans, establishing an enduring precedent. Jefferson had never before been an official in a bureaucracy, and he hated his new job. He had been away from America for five critical years—which made him, he felt, a stranger. He was also shocked at the plain republican style of the new government. He stopped wearing a ruby ring and the bright-colored suits that were à la mode in Paris and ordered only navy blue or black from his tailor.[23]

He went to work immediately on creating a new currency and a new system of weights and measures. Proposing the rod as the standard unit of measure, he divided everything decimally, "bringing the calculation of the principal affairs of life within the arithmetic of every man who can multiply and divide plain numbers." But Congress had trouble with numbers from the beginning and ignored his report, allowing France to adopt the revolutionary metric system first. Jefferson began to have migraine headaches after his first encounter with the Senate. His headache got worse when the Senate, convinced that money spent abroad was wasted, followed the advice of the backwoods Senator Maclay of Pennsylvania; "I know not a single thing that we have for a minister to do in a single court in Europe; indeed, the less we have to do with them, the better." It would take Jefferson several years to realize that Maclay was expressing in crude terms what Washington believed was America's proper relationship with European powers. Meanwhile, Jefferson had orders from the Senate to scale down the foreign service that he had worked so hard to create. Only France was to keep a minister plenipotentiary; Madrid and Lisbon, chargés d'affaires; London and The Hague, a consular agent each; Morocco, a consul—all within a $40,000-a-year budget.[24]

If Jefferson had not known what to expect, Washington had a clear view from the outset of the role his cabinet secretaries were to play in his administration:

> The impossibility that one man should be able to perform all
> the great business of the state I take to have been the reason

for instituting the great departments and appointing officers therein to assist the supreme Magistrate in discharging the duties of his trust.

The secretaries were to be his assistants, his agents. They were to do whatever he needed them to do. In addition to supervising a department, a secretary was to give Washington timely advice. According to Jefferson, files were carried from 39 Broadway each day from the president to his secretaries for oral or written reports within only four hours. Each officer could also be called upon to write state papers (they would be given slightly more time for these).[25]

If the lines between departments and requests became blurred, Washington did not care. His cabinet resembled his military family. He saw his cabinet as a unit and his cabinet meetings, infrequent at first, like councils of war: communal advisory meetings. Washington called only five cabinet meetings during his first term. He tracked what was going on in each department by reading and approving all letters sent out over a secretary's signature as well as the letters they were answering. Usually, Washington did not interfere with each secretary's work, but he accepted full responsibility for it. And he made sure that each department had its authority acknowledged properly by anyone seeking to do business with the government. When the French ambassador, the Comte de Moustier, attempted to see Washington without going through the secretary of state, Moustier was told that Washington would follow the practice of "most polished nations that business should be digested and prepared by the heads [of departments]."[26]

While Vice President Adams did not attend most cabinet meetings, he was one of the men Washington regularly consulted for advice. The president was not to confine himself to his cabinet secretaries for advice: as he had during the Revolution, he cast the net wide. He instructed his personal secretary Tobias Lear to mingle with the public and bring him samplings of public opinion. And when he wished to operate outside of official channels or mask his participation in a matter, he wrote out letters and had Tobias Lear sign them with his own name: "The President wishes. . . . [signed] Tobias Lear."

Washington's carefully constructed cabinet system helped sustain the embryonic government through its first presidential crisis in the spring of 1790 when, shortly after the Washingtons moved into the Macomb mansion, Washington became seriously ill. As much as Washington liked the elegant new president's house, it was no place for a Virginia farmer to find rest. Outside his windows, the sounds of the city shattered his usual tranquillity day and night. Broadway was the main wagon route into the city and wagons clattered over its stones amid the clang of cowbells, the lowing of herds of cattle and sheep, the crack of teamsters' whips, the cry of vendors hawking firewood, hot corn, and scissor sharpening. At dawn the cacophony began with the boyish cry of the chimney sweeps: "Sweep ho! from the bottom to the top, with a ladder or a rope, sweep ho!"[27]

Scarcely two months after his inauguration the president had been seriously weakened by painful surgery to remove a large tumor on his thigh. At the time he had been convinced he was about to die. He told his aide Humphreys, "I know it is very doubtful whether I ever shall rise from this bed—and God knows it is perfectly indifferent to me whether I do or not." The autumn and winter had been exhausting. Washington had his first clash with the Senate in August of 1789 when he went with Secretary of War Knox to seek the senators' "advice and consent" on a treaty with the southern Indians. Knox wanted an army big enough to create a permanent frontier defense force, something Washington strongly favored but frontier senator Maclay, emerging as the gadfly of Washington's administration, strongly opposed. "Give Knox his army," Maclay had raged, "and he will soon have a war on his hands."[28]

That war loomed in the south. A half-Scot-half-Creek named Alexander McGillivray, a highly paid secret agent of the Spanish, had come to Philadelphia to protest the cession by the Georgia legislature of 25 million acres of Indian lands it did not own to land speculators in South Carolina, Tennessee, and Virginia. According to David Humphreys, he warned Washington that McGillivray combined "the good sense of an American, the shrewdness of a Scotchman and the cunning of an Indian." Just the sight of Knox and Washington striding into the Senate chamber in Federal Hall to seek special powers to negotiate a treaty with the Creeks—a Senate prerogative—was enough to raise the hackles of touchy senators such as Maclay. The Senate was utterly unable to carry on its deliberations with the president in the room. Senator Maclay urged that the question be referred to a special Senate committee. "This defeats every purpose of my coming here," stormed Washington. He said he had brought General Knox along precisely because he wanted the Indian commissioner's instructions ironed out quickly. But the Senate balked: the talks were adjourned over the weekend. Maclay had his blood up. He just "knew" that Washington had come only to intimidate the Senate with his physical presence. "Form only will be left to us. This will not do with Americans!" The president was equally unhappy as he left—with a discontented air. "Had it been any other man than the man whom I wish to regard as the first character in the world, I would have said, with sullen dignity." On Monday there was no progress. As Washington left, it is reported that he muttered that he would be "damned" if he ever went "there" again. No president has ever gone to the Senate since then, and the Senate ever since then has only been asked to ratify a treaty after it was negotiated by the executive branch.[29]

But Washington was not finished chipping away at the power of the Senate. Two months later he decided to send his own special envoy to London, skirting both the Senate and the secretary of state's office. He commissioned Gouverneur Morris, in Paris on private business, to go to England to sound out informally the British government's views of a number of issues unresolved by the 1783 peace treaty. By this time neither England nor the United States had exchanged official emissaries. Washington's unilateral commission to Morris undercut the Senate's constitutional power to approve all nominees to represent the country abroad. Yet Washington was unfazed and, in fact, was delighted when Morris's unofficial report enabled him to take a tough stance when the British finally sent an emissary late in 1790.

But by this time Washington had survived a far graver crisis than anything in the power of his senatorial critics. He had nearly died of pneumonia. For days he had lain seriously ill in a second-floor bedroom at 39 Broadway. Martha, now called by most "Lady Washington," had taken over many of his duties, including directing the president's five-man staff in its deliberations of medical decisions. Martha had seen Washington's five-year bout with pleurisy, which he considered tuberculosis. She now conferred with John Adams, who had to be ready to step in at any time. Abigail Adams reflected how "greatly distressed" the nation was at the word that the fifty-eight-year-old president was seriously ill. "It appears to me," she wrote, "that the union of the states depends under Providence upon his life; at this early day when neither our finances are arranged nor our government sufficiently cemented to promise duration, his death would I fear have the most disastrous consequences."[30]

On May 12, 1790, Major William Jackson, Washington's aide and unofficial bodyguard, secretly sent for Dr. John Jones, Benjamin Franklin's last physician and the nation's leading surgeon, to come at once from Pennsylvania Hospital in Philadelphia. Jones was known for his applications of laudanum, a combination of honey and opium that facilitated sleep. The substance was tricky to apply in the proper dose: Dr. Jones died later that year when he inadvertently mixed too strong a dose for himself. Martha lay awake night after night listening to Washington's labored, feverish breathing. She ordered the street outside roped off to traffic and the paving stones muted with straw. The president must sleep. In one year in office, the last chestnut traces in his hair had gone white.

For four long days and nights Dr. Jones and a team of consulting physicians wavered between hope and despondence. By May 15, one week after the onset of symptoms, Washington was in critical condition. Even irascible Senator Maclay came to call and went away shaken, recording in his diary that he found a household in tears. One doctor told Maclay to be prepared: death was expected momentarily. Thomas Jefferson rushed to 39 Broadway as the president's breathing grew faster, fainter. Jefferson, a homeopath who distrusted doctors, asked to see the patient. Suddenly, at four o'clock that Saturday afternoon, as Jefferson reported to his daughter Patsy at Monticello, "a copious sweat came on, his expectoration, which had been thin and ichorous, began to assume a well-digested form, his articulation became distinct and in the course of two hours he had gone through a favorable crisis." From "total despair" the president's house was transformed the next day to ecstatic hope. "Indeed, he is thought quite safe," Jefferson wrote. By May 24 Jefferson was reporting the president "perfectly well except weak." But, Jefferson noted, "You cannot conceive the public alarm on this occasion. It proves how much depends on his life."[31]

*T*he demands on Washington only increased after his first year of grace in office. Congress had commissioned Treasury Secretary Hamilton to draw up a plan to fund the debts of the old Congress, which included the unpaid Revolutionary War debts of foreign loans and several states as well. Hamilton submitted his "First Report on the Public Credit" in January of 1790. In it Hamilton proposed to retire the old debt—an estimated $80 million—by funding a national debt. The Constitution had been pushed through largely to pay off these old debts. Current holders of debt certificates would become the new bondholders. Hamilton ignored the possibility of scaling the debt down or favoring the original holders, many of them Revolutionary soldiers or their widows or orphans who had in many cases been compelled to sell their certificates for a fraction of face value.

Whatever options Hamilton overlooked to come up with his plan to have the new national government assume the old debts at par, it was more than agrarian politicians from states that had already paid off their war debts could bear. Virginians especially hated the idea of paying off the debts of northern states, which not only hadn't paid as they fought but would make a fortune from speculating in the discounted debt certificates. At a stroke Hamilton's plan brought to life a states-rights opposition party in Congress led by that formerly staunch Federalist, James Madison, who joined forces with his old friend Thomas Jefferson. Washington was careful to stay neutral as his lieutenants faced off against each other in their first political duel. He said nothing while Congress debated the issue, but many felt they already knew his mind. He favored giving special consideration to soldiers who had been forced to sell their pay warrants at discount in 1783, but in 1789 he had drawn up a plan that called for the federal government to collect all taxes: national, state, and local. He believed this would be more just and efficient and would build loyalty to the national government. He could find no constitutional objection to "assumption," as it was called, and therefore would have no ground in his own mind to veto it. But he regretted the sectional controversy Hamilton's plan had ignited and, blaming Virginians for opposing the proposed policy, called them "irritable, sour and discontented."

But Washington was hardly able to maintain the appearance of disinterestedness after Hamilton began to strike bargains to get assumption through Congress. Congressman Madison of Virginia introduced a bill in the House to distinguish between the original Continental bondholders and speculators, but it was voted down by the northern states. But then Hamilton's assumption bill was voted down by the southern states. With Congress deadlocked, Hamilton feared that if there were no compromise the funding bill would die. And Secretary of State Jefferson feared that the national credit would be damaged on European markets. One day Hamilton and Jefferson bumped into each other outside Washington's office door; Jefferson described Hamilton as looking "somber, haggard and dejected beyond description." Hamilton asked Jefferson to use his influence with southerners in Congress. While it was part of Jefferson's job to handle domestic as well as foreign diplomacy, he did not want to appear directly involved in Hamilton's scheme, but he did agree to invite Hamilton, Madison, and congressmen from Maryland and Pennsylvania to dinner at his house the next day to discuss the impasse. That night and the next day before the dinner meeting he worked out a compromise that led to congressional passage of Hamilton's debt-assumption bill in exchange for the location of the nation's new capital on the Potomac. In July of 1790, when the debt-funding, debt-assuming, and capital location bills came before Congress, all three sailed to quick passage. In exchange for the siting of the capital on the Potomac, two Maryland and two Virginia members changed their votes on assumption. Jefferson would later claim that Hamilton had duped him but the "dinner-table bargain," as it became known at the time, was thought to have saved the Union.[32]

Actually, Jefferson had been as opportunistic as Hamilton. The new capital was to be located on land Jefferson had staked out as early as December of 1783 when he was appointed to a committee of the old Congress to find a home for the national government. It also happened to be a short ride from Mount Vernon. And the Potomac region—and therefore indirectly the stockholders of the Potomac Company—would benefit from a city most observers expected would become an important new commercial center if not the commercial capital of the new nation. The Potomac would get a city—the first major city in the south—that would be linked with the interior of the country by Washington's improved Potomac waterway. Washington quietly signed the bill into law. The new capital would be called Washington City in a new District of Columbia built on swampland yielded by Virginia and Maryland.

The demands on Washington increased considerably in his second year as president. He attempted to build himself up by taking long horseback rides. He had lost weight; his hearing was failing him, he complained about his memory, and he felt himself growing old. But visitors could only notice any change in his trim physique by fixating on his dentures. His teeth were almost all gone and he still could not find effective, unobtrusive dentures no matter how hard he tried. He realized how important his appearance was to the well-being of the young nation, so he sat for frequent flattering portraits and he decided to take a long trip during the adjournment of Congress to allow himself to see and be seen. To get away from New York City with its filth and noise and a contentious Congress were secondary considerations. His pretext was to welcome the last holdout, Rhode Island, into the Union after it belatedly ratified the Constitution.

During his trip to Rhode Island that summer, a reinvigorated Washington, traveling with Jefferson and George Clinton at his side, made it a point to visit factories and demonstrate that he wanted legislation that discriminated in favor of American industry and commerce so that they might survive fierce competition from European goods and have time to grow and flourish. The Industrial Revolution would arrive in Rhode Island only months later when Samuel Slater, using plans he had drawn from memories of Richard Arkwright's cording and spinning machines, opened the first textile mill in America at Pawtucket on December 21, 1790. He used the trip as a pulpit to make other public statements. At Newport he accepted an invitation to address the representatives of the Jewish congregation:

> It is now no more that toleration is spoken of, as if it was by the indulgence of one class of people that another enjoyed the exercise of their inherent natural rights. For happily the government of the United States, which gives to bigotry no sanction, to persecution no assistance, requires only that they who live under its protection should demean themselves as good citizens in giving it on all occasions their effectual support.

To the King David's Lodge of Masons he made a rare public acknowledgment that he subscribed to the tenets of that order (he had been a Mason for more than thirty years). He was

> persuaded that a just application of the principles on which the Masonic order is founded must be promotive of private virtue and public prosperity. I shall always be happy to advance the interests of the society and be considered by them a deserving brother.[33]

After his New England junket, Washington drove south to Mount Vernon, where he made it his practice to spend the month of September. Here he could restore his strength on his daily fifteen-mile rides and here he could find tranquillity in seeing a well-ordered universe where more people labored more efficiently than in the entire executive branch of government. He could relish the familiar and remember the past. He stopped by the stable each day, where he offered a handful of grain to Nelson, his old warhorse from Yorktown. And he could look off toward the charred ruins of Belvoir, where Sally Fairfax had once lived: her husband was dead now and Washington still exchanged letters with her, but she was never coming back. At night he slept peacefully in his comfortable six-foot-six-inch bed and at his six o'clock breakfast, ate modestly: three pancakes covered with honey and three cups of tea. The midday dinners were quite different: there were invariably a table full of grandchildren, cousins, and houseguests. Martha's marvelous home cooking, one visitor recorded, included at a single meal "a small roasted pig, boiled leg of lamb, roasted fowls, beef, peas, lettuce, cucumbers, artichokes, puddings, tarts, etc., etc."[34]

Washington's daily rounds did not always leave him in the best of moods during his summer visits. Despite the fact that he had a large dairy herd, he found his nephew was purchasing butter. He continued his early morning study of agriculture, corresponding with English farming expert Arthur Young and poring over his *Annals of Agriculture:* could he have known that King George III, under the pseudonym Ralph Robinson, was a frequent contributor? He must have read the discourse on turnips and deep plowing by William Pitt, the English prime minister who was beginning to disturb his peace as war loomed between France and England.

Every courier now brought news of the rapid unfolding of the French Revolution and the hostile reactions of other European powers. The fulminating prose of Edmund Burke had just aroused all England with his *Reflections on the Revolution in France.* America had seemed safely distant until that summer. American trade with England now accounted for only one-sixth of British exports and imports and the United States relied mostly on British merchants for luxury goods. American ships now plied the oceans from China to Constantinople and less and less the young country seemed to depend on the old overlord England. But France was another matter—she took all the tobacco crop.

Washington was able to hide behind the great moat of the Atlantic at first as tensions mounted between England and France. Washington wrote confidently to Lafayette, now a leader of the moderate Constitutional Party in the French Revolution, that the United States was

> gradually recovering from the distresses in which the war left us, patiently advancing in our task of civil government, unentangled in the crooked politics of Europe, wanting anything but the free navigation of the Mississippi (which we must have and as certainly shall have as we remain a nation). I have supposed that, with the undeviating exercise of a just, steady and prudent national policy we shall be the garners whether the powers of the old world may be in peace or war but more especially in the latter case. In that case our importance will certainly increase and our friendship be courted.

That summer of 1790 a war scare at faraway Nootka Sound in the Pacific Northwest reminded Washington that Europe's rival powers would not be content to fight it out in the Old World but still coveted territory in the New World.[35]

That summer, before he left New York, Washington had intimated his lingering uneasiness about being barricaded along the Atlantic Seaboard by European powers, especially the British. "The consequences of having so formidable and enterprising a people as the British on both our flanks and rear with their navy in front," he wrote to his secretaries, "are too obvious to need enumeration." But could the United States remain out of the impending clash and should the United States allow British troops to cross American soil on their way to confront their enemy, which was not America's enemy? The questions were no longer hypothetical. The Spanish had seized British ships when the Royal Navy sought to take over Spanish bases on Vancouver Island. As the two European leviathans girded for battle, Washington faced the possibility that the British would conduct expeditions from their Canadian bases against Spanish possessions on American soil—Florida and Louisiana were likely targets.[36]

The Nootka Sound crisis bared the growing conflict within Washington's cabinet over foreign policy. Perhaps because Washington felt so powerless to oppose any British incursion, he revealed his lingering antipathy to the English. This came at a time when, at last, a British envoy was arriving and Washington's vice president was writing a long series of anonymous essays in Hamilton's house organ, *The Gazette of the United States*, in favor of closer trade ties with England. While the United States could do little else, Washington wanted to protest British designs in the Pacific Northwest as loudly as possible.

The second major clash between Secretaries Hamilton and Jefferson only widened the rift in the cabinet. Assumption of congressional and state debts had not posed any constitutional problem for Washington, but Hamilton's proposal to create a national bank along the order of the Bank of England did. In December of 1790 Hamilton urged Congress to charter a private national bank to serve as the government's depository and fiscal agent. It would, he argued, stimulate the economy and attract foreign investment. The Bank of the United States was to be capitalized at $10 million with 20 percent paid in by Congress from tax revenues, and Congress would have a 20 percent share in its management. Part of the bank's funding would come from issuance of bonds and its charter would run for the life of the bonds. While southern agrarians leapt into opposition to the very instance of a national bank, Washington was more worried about government's constitutional right to establish such an institution. At the Constitutional Convention of 1787, delegates had already voted down a proposal for the federal government to issue charters to corporation: that was strictly a state function. But now a majority in

Congress, after a fierce debate over the bank's constitutionality, only altered the length of the bank's charter, limiting it to twenty years. The issue was placed squarely on Washington's desk: would he veto it?

Washington had only ten days after receiving the bank bill on February 16, 1791, to veto Hamilton's bill or sign it into law: if he did nothing it became law without his signature. He had already sounded out his secretaries informally and he knew Attorney General Randolph and Secretary of State Jefferson opposed chartering the bank on the grounds that such a power was not expressly delegated to the government by the Constitution. Knox simply went along with Hamilton. Because he knew nothing about financial affairs, he usually deferred to Hamilton on such matters.

Until this time, Jefferson had been generally distracted studying relations with England by dealing with the problem of American sailors taken captive by Algerians for ransom. Only on December 30, 1790, had he reported his recommendations. He believed the British had no intention of evacuating the Great Lakes forts or of negotiating a commercial treaty. In his report to Congress he favored joining naval forces with other countries trading in the Mediterranean. A solidly pro-Hamilton Senate committee had quickly reacted to his careful recommendation that Congress choose "between war, tribute and ransom" by ruling that "the trade of the U.S. to the Mediterranean cannot be protected but by a naval force" and that the government could not afford it. When Congress finally appropriated $40,000 for ransom, Jefferson was furious. It was then that he opined that the bank bill was unconstitutional. One of the most important documents in American history, it carried Jefferson's arguments for strict adherence to the Constitution, which he was to follow all the rest of his political life and which laid the foundation for the states' rights doctrine.

Jefferson's brief was concise. He argued that to charter a national bank was unconstitutional because the still unratified Tenth Amendment held that

> the powers not delegated to the United States by the Constitution, nor prohibited by it to the States, are reserved to the States respectively, or to the people. . . . To take a single step beyond the boundaries thus specially drawn around the powers of Congress is to take possession of a boundless field of power.

The Constitution had not delegated incorporation of a bank to Congress, not under its powers to tax, to borrow, or to regulate commerce. Congress could not "*do anything they please.*" Jefferson feared that free interpretation of any aspect of congressional power would reduce the Constitution to "a single phrase, that of instituting a Congress with power to do whatever would be for the good of the United States and as they would be the sole judges of good or evil, it would be also a power to do whatever evil they pleased." Jefferson also anticipated Hamilton's argument of implied powers granted by the Constitution to Congress to make all laws necessary and proper to carry into execution the powers specifically enumerated in the Constitution. Congress could only do what was necessary. To form a national bank was not necessary but only convenient. Without his insistence on limiting the Congress to enacting necessary laws, there was nothing "which ingenuity may not torture into a convenience, in some way or other, to someone." With his opinion on the bank bill, Jefferson also gave the president his reasoning on using the presidential veto. Despite Jefferson's arguments, unless Washington was convinced that the bank was unconstitutional, "A just respect for the wisdom of the legislature would naturally decide the balance in favor of their opinion."[37]

With two opinions against the bank in his hands, Washington turned them over to Hamilton, who refuted Randolph and Jefferson point by point. He directed his main attack at Jefferson's interpretation of the "necessary and proper" clause. Jefferson insisted on using the word "necessary" as if it were prefixed by "absolutely" or "indispensably." What is constitutional or not, Hamilton countered,

> is the *end* to which the measure relates as a *mean*. If the end be clearly comprehended within any of the specified powers, and if the measure have an obvious relation to that end and is not forbidden by any particular provision of the constitution—it may safely be deemed to come within the compass of national authority.[38]

When Washington was persuaded by Hamilton's end-justified-the-means argument, Jefferson was truly alarmed. He now considered the door open to the incessant extension of what he considered a heresy concocted to serve the special moneyed interests, what he called the "stockjobbers," without the consent of the majority of people, who were yeomen farmers.

Hamilton's brilliant brief of 15,000 words relied on a liberal interpretation of Article I, Section 8 of the Constitution that granted Congress the authority "to make all laws necessary and proper for carrying into execution all the foregoing powers" already enumerated in the document. Hamilton contended that "necessary" included any means that were convenient and were not specifically ruled out by either the Constitution or moral law. He was enunciating the doctrine of "implied powers." Washington never enunciated his reaction to Hamilton's argument. Whether or not he was convinced the bank was constitutional, he signed the bill. Ironically, he may have been following Jefferson's advice to sign it out of respect for Congress if he harbored any lingering doubts. But Washington required little persuasion. He wanted to see a strong and fiscally sound national government and Hamilton had given him a powerful new weapon.

*I*t was by accident that the split in Washington's government became public. Jefferson had become alarmed that his old friend, Vice President Adams, had been writing in the pro-Hamilton *National Gazette* under a pen name. Jefferson, therefore, was elated when he received a copy of Thomas Paine's latest anti-British blast, *The Rights of Man*, just published in London. Jefferson wrote a note recommending publication and sent it off to a printer. He intended his comments to remain private. He was chagrined when the printer published his signed letter as the introduction to Paine's tract. That spring, scores of newspapers reprinted Jefferson's letter. Overnight, Jefferson became the spokesman for Americans disenchanted with Washington's policies. "I am sincerely mortified," he wrote Washington, "to be thus brought forward on the public stage against my love of silence and my abhorrence of disputes."[39]

Before leaving on a spring vacation tour of New York and New England with his friend Madison, Jefferson wrote to his son-in-law, Thomas Mann Randolph, at Monticello and sent him a copy of a Philadelphia newspaper, the *National Gazette*, which supported Hamilton. Its editorial policy was, Jefferson wrote,

> pure Tories, disseminating [Hamilton's] doctrine of monarchy, aristocracy and the exclusion of the people. . . . We have been trying to get another weekly or half-weekly [newspaper] excluding advertisements set up, so that it could go free through the states in the mails and furnish [our] vehicle of intelligence.

Jefferson here was admitting in a private letter what he had been denying in public: that he was involved in an opposition faction within Washington's government and was seeking to establish his own partisan publicity organ. He asked his son-in-law to forward Hamilton's paper each week via government mail to stops along his route. Jefferson and Madison most assuredly would have the latest political news to discuss in the long days on the road, where they would have strictest privacy. George Beckwith, the new British consul general to the United States, wrote to his superiors in London, "I am sorry to inform your Grace that the Secretary of State's party and politics gains ground here. [They] will have influence enough to cause acts and resolves which may be unfriendly to Great Britain to be passed early in the next session of Congress. The Secretary of State, together with Mr. Madison, are now gone to the Eastern States, there to proselyte as far as they are able a commercial war with Britain." Alexander Hamilton's son and biographer, John, had no doubt Jefferson was politicking. He flatly asserted the Virginians were meeting secretly in New York City with newly elected U.S. Senator Aaron Burr, Hamilton's enemy, before going on to huddle with Governor George Clinton, a leading anti-Federalist, in Albany, the state capital. Aaron Burr had just unseated Hamilton's father-in-law, Philip Schuyler, from the Senate.[40]

If Jefferson and Madison were merely on vacation, they had no reason to conceal *or* to comment on visits to New York politicians on their way north. But if they were engaged, as John Adams's son, John Quincy, later wrote, in "double dealing," there was good reason for silence. Jefferson liked to give the impression that he was always completely open about his political dealings. "When tempted to do anything in secret," he wrote, "ask yourself if you'd do it in public; if you would not, be sure it is wrong." But he had been a revolutionary and was a skilled diplomat and he left no clear trace of his movements during those days in New York City. It is entirely possible that Jefferson and Madison paid a call on Aaron Burr. Instead of using his own distinctive Monticello-made carriage, which was recognizable, Jefferson's expense records show he hired a coach for one day. Even the possibility of such an alliance clearly worried Hamilton's supporters. "They had better be quiet," wrote Hamilton supporter Robert Troup to Hamilton, "for if they succeed, they will tumble the fabric of the government in ruins to the ground."[41]

Twenty

"A FIRE NOT TO BE QUENCHED"

While Thomas Jefferson and James Madison rode north and visited the new state of Vermont in the late spring of 1791, George Washington set out on a bone-jarring 1,900-mile ten-week carriage ride—albeit in a posh coach-of-state pulled by six white horses—over dirt roads that took him throughout the south. He traveled without Martha, who remained in Philadelphia until travel became easier as sandy roads dried out. When he reached Richmond on his way south, he received a jolt: a letter from his secretary, Tobias Lear. Attorney General Randolph had just learned that he was in danger of losing the slaves he had brought north from Virginia to the capital at Philadelphia because of a Pennsylvania law that provided that adult slaves would be free six months after their owner moved into Pennsylvania and became a citizen. In order to practice law in the Philadelphia courts, Randolph had registered as a Pennsylvania citizen.

President Washington had not become a Pennsylvanian and now was glad he had no reason to. He felt someone might try to entice away his slaves and that they would become "insolent" if they thought they could become free. Washington increasingly had been in a quandary about slavery. His respect for black soldiers in the American Revolution had led him to begin to think about the fundamental contradiction between American slavery and the freedom they had fought for. He went to great lengths and expense to provide humane treatment for loyal slaves. All through the Revolution his huge slave body servant, William Lee, had traveled with him and been at his side under fire. Lee had accompanied him on his frontier trips as well. More than anything else Lee had wanted to be at Washington's side when he became president—even in family portraits Washington allowed Lee to be portrayed in livery. When Lee fell ill on the way to New York Washington had left him in Philadelphia with a friend who followed his instructions and saw that he got expensive medical care at Pennsylvania Hospital. Washington did not complain when the bills came in.

But Washington believed this was different. His belief in his first responsibility to Martha's inherited estate may have led him to write remarkable instructions to Lear. Since all of the slaves Washington had taken to the president's house when it moved to Philadelphia were Martha's "dower Negroes," he felt he must spirit them back to Mount Vernon. "It behooves me to prevent the emancipation of them," he told Lear. Not only would he lose the slaves if they were freed, but he might have to pay Martha's estate for them. Since Washington had not become a Pennsylvania citizen the slaves might be exempted, but he could not take the chance and he did not want to publicize his dilemma. If on checking further Lear found the law applied to the president, he was to send the slaves back to Mount Vernon surreptitiously. When Martha journeyed home in May, she

> would naturally bring her maid and Austin and Hercules [the presidential chefs] under the idea of coming home to cook whilst we remained there. [They] might be sent on in the stage. . . . I request that these sentiments and this advice may be known to none but yourself and Mrs. Washington.[1]

Philadelphia was the center of the Quaker-inspired abolition movement. Recent controversies inside his administration were troubling Washington deeply, and his private problems always intermingled with the complexities of public office. The day after he signed the bank bill into law he had signed a new excise tax on whiskey and rum. The new tax fell hardest on cash-poor frontier farmers who distilled their surplus corn and grain to whiskey and used it as an easily portable liquid medium of exchange for other products, and on sailors and workingmen who were accustomed to their grog to get through a hard day's work. Washington could not have approved a more unwelcome law. Both measures had aroused strong opposition from the growing faction of southerners and westerners around Madison and Jefferson in Congress. He had reason to fear that his popularity was sliding even in Philadelphia, where he was increasingly identified with the big-money financial interests represented by Hamilton. When he learned that the Pennsylvania government was planning to pass a special tax to build him a temporary president's house, he had opposed the plan as he only expected to serve one term as president.

In the meantime he had accepted the loan of the mansion of financier Robert Morris, an old friend from Revolutionary War days. But Morris became president of the new Bank of the United States: nothing could have more cemented Washington to the moneyed interests in the eyes of the

Madison-Jefferson republicans. Perhaps his growing unease about factional infighting explains why Washington would take nearly three months away from the capital. As he toured the south, he would not only receive the invigorating adulation of his supporters, but he could learn the depth of disenchantment with his administration. He already knew of one southerner who was less than happy with his presidency—his wife.

Where Washington lived—if it could not be at Mount Vernon—mattered much less to Washington than to his wife. After all, he had lived in more than 280 headquarters buildings as commander in chief: by comparison, Martha had visited him at only ten. But to move the entire presidential establishment was not only a great deal of work but a strain: it took months before the disruption died down. After moving into two temporary presidential houses in New York City in one year, Martha packed up again when, as the result of the "Dinner Table Bargain," the capital moved south to Philadelphia. Now the First Lady had to begin all over to organize and supervise daily operations at a temporary residence not of her choosing, and at age sixty she was now sick and tired of it all. And then no sooner did the Washingtons move into the great garish pile of Morris's mansion at Sixth and High Streets than Washington drove off again for his southern tour.

The latest move meant finding schools for Nelly Custis, now eleven, and nine-year-old Wash. Martha worried that she would not be able to "enjoy so many advantages to the point of education" as she had in New York. The president took part of the task out of her hands and ordered his secretary to "use your best endeavors to ascertain the characters" of schools that might be suitable for Wash. Eventually, Lear found tutors for the boy at the Academy of Philadelphia (the present-day University of Pennsylvania). Lear coordinated his efforts with Hamilton, Knox, and Randolph, and soon all of the administration's young sons were attending classes at the Academy. Lear, the boy's former tutor, was not in a position to complain to anyone but faraway David Humphreys, now minister to Portugal:

> Nelly and [Wash] have every advantage in point of instructors that this country can give them and they certainly make good progress in those things which are taught them. But I apprehend the worst consequences particularly to the boy from the unbounded indulgence of the grandmamma. The ideas which are insinuated to him at home . . . that he is born to such noble properties both in estate and otherwise . . . and the servile respect the servants are obliged to pay him . . . he is on the road to ruin.[2]

Lear also kept the children's mother informed of his views of their progress and Nelly Custis Stewart responded gratefully from Virginia. She told of her "unfeigned satisfaction" that Martha had "at least seen the necessity of making the dear children respect as well as love her." Yet she worried about her daughter Nelly's "dissipation," that in Philadelphia she would become "an affected, trifling Miss of the town."[3]

In fact Nelly could not have moved in more stylish circles than in Philadelphia. The Morrises had moved into a house they renovated next door to the president's house and Nelly's closest friend was the Morrises' daughter, Maria. In the circle of young girls she soon numbered Elizabeth Bordley, the daughter of the manager of stock subscriptions of the Bank of the United States. In Philadelphia Nelly was making lifelong friends. But not Martha. She worried about Nelly and her giddy round of activities—"At present she is I fear half crazy"—but worse, she missed Washington terribly. By June she was complaining, "I have never heard from the President since he left Mount Vernon." When Washington wrote it was to Lear: "Furnish Mrs. Washington with what only she may want and from time to time ask if she does want, as she is not fond of applying."[4]

But by the time Washington returned to Philadelphia on July 6, Martha had already gone to Mount Vernon for the summer with her grandchildren and her slaves. And it would be two more months before he could join her. After touring every southern state and hearing the never-ending din of thousands cheering and fireworks and thirteen-gun salutes, Washington returned to a capital overrun with 25,000 French refugees and a pile of crises on his desk. Louis XVI and Marie Antoinette had fled and been hauled back to Paris under Lafayette's orders as prisoners to the French revolutionaries after they had tried to raise foreign armies against their countrymen. The French revolutionary government had broken the 1778 treaty with the United States by putting duties on American tobacco and whale oil. In Philadelphia, speculators were paying $325 a share for $25 shares of the new national bank's stock and the republican faction around Jefferson and Madison were screaming that Washington had joined the "monocrats" in betraying the principles of the American Revolution. And on the frontier an American army in the Northwest Territories had been defeated by British-armed Indians operating out of forts that were supposed to have long ago been turned over to the United States.

Washington returned to work convinced that sectional unrest had been overstated by his republican critics and that further opposition to his policies in Congress or his cabinet only endangered the union. At the end of the First Congress in March 1791 he had written to Humphreys in Portugal that while "our public credit is restored, our resources are increasing and the general appearance of things at least equals the most sanguine expectation" of his government. "The line between the southern and eastern interests" in Congress "appeared more strongly marked than could have been wished." When they went before Congress on October 25 with a reminder list of programs he still wanted enacted he mentioned that he hoped that "misconceptions" held in some parts of the country about the new excise tax would soon be cleared up. He informed Congress that he had selected a site on the Potomac for the new capital and gave a report on its progress.[5]

Washington was in fact deeply involved in every detail of the planning and construction of the city that was to be his enduring monument. He had selected a site at the junction of the eastern branch and the main body of the Potomac at the southern edge of the ten-mile-square district recommended by Jefferson to the old Congress in 1783; the stakes from the earlier proposed site were still in place. Each time he passed north and south Washington made a visit. He decided how many workers (most rented slaves) would be employed; they were to receive a pound of meat a day and all the cornmeal they wanted. He appointed commissioners to oversee the ten-year project who followed all of his wishes. He hired as superintendent a French military engineer, Major Pierre L'Enfant, to lay out the city and design its Capitol and he approved or disapproved the plans for every street, the purchase of land, and the construction of every building. When L'Enfant resigned the next year because so many of his plans had been changed, Washington pushed the commissioners even harder to complete the project.

But Washington was increasingly distracted by events at home. His nephew George Augustine was too ill to go on managing Mount Vernon and Washington had to turn over his farms to an English head farmer, Andrew Whiting, a recent immigrant. Also newly arrived from England was George Hammond, the first British ambassador from the Court of St. James. He arrived in November. Only a month later Miami Indians based in the British forts in the Northwest defeated an American force under General Arthur St. Clair, endangering U.S.-British relations just as a major war loomed with the French revolutionaries. The loss of hundreds of American soldiers on the frontier triggered the first congressional investigation of the executive branch. Washington complied by ordering Knox to turn over the administration's papers to Congress, establishing a troublesome precedent.

The next crisis came from the floor of the Second Congress, busy reapportioning its seats in light of the numbers of eligible voters counted in the first census in 1790. The Constitution as Washington had wished provided one representative in the House for each 30,000 citizens. But the population was not that neat. Congress wanted to throw any votes in excess of that number into a pool and dicker politically for which state got how many additional members. Once again, the south would have been the loser. The Virginians, Jefferson and Randolph, asked Washington to veto the bill. The northerners, Hamilton and Knox, contended that since the Constitution was unclear on the point and Congress had proposed a sensible solution, Washington should sign it. This time Washington hesitated: his southern travels had convinced him of the touchiness of many rural and small-town Americans to what was being perceived as the large-state interest. Jefferson surprised him when he countered that the president should not bend over too far backward to avoid the appearance of favoritism: he should sign. Washington finally decided the issue and asked Jefferson, Randolph, and, for the first time, Congressman Madison to draft his first veto message. Nine days after he sent it over to Congress Hall, the House and Senate sent back a bill that divided the population proportionately into 33,000-man units.

*O*n February 22, 1792, President Washington turned sixty. To his great surprise, he had outlived all of his male ancestors for many generations and all of his brothers, and lived to be about fifteen years older than the average Virginian. Despite all of his illnesses he was in good health. Each year his hearing and his eyesight were weaker and that vexed him. His memory lapsed from time to time: he called Congress for one week and then realized as he prepared to ride north from Mount Vernon that he had forgotten which week and then was mortified as he had to send a string of couriers dashing off to Philadelphia. But there was nothing wrong with his memory when he put it to work on legislation or the complicated logistics of his administration. His reputation, so important to him, was still intact. He had spent thirty-four years, more than half of his life, in public employment: nearly six years as a Virginia officer, seventeen as a burgess, nearly nine as commander in chief, three as president—it was time to quit. He hated his office routine mostly because he could not be outdoors getting exercise every day. Most of all, he yearned for the freedom of life at Mount Vernon. His long junkets away from the capital offered no relief, but they engaged his mind and body as well as satisfying his ego that most Americans still had confidence in him.

By the spring of 1792, Martha was beginning to make plans to return permanently to Mount Vernon, and Washington had given no hint that he planned to seek a second term. Indeed, he had asked James Madison to prepare his valedictory, a farewell address to the nation. As usual, he put off any definite announcement of a decision because he had made none, but in the absence of any statement that he would stay on as president it was logical for everyone to assume he would not. Once again, it was circumstance more than plan that made a great decision for him and he drifted toward acquiescence.

What pushed Washington into even considering a second term of what had become misery for him was the growing rift in his administration. Hamilton and Jefferson could not have become more diametrically opposed to each other and neither gave any sign of ameliorating their differences. In a series of four reports to Congress between 1790 and 1792, Hamilton had laid down his program. His Federalist financial system rested on the funding of a national debt, a program of external and internal taxes—customs duties and excise taxes—as well as creation of a national bank and the encouragement of domestic manufacturing. Each of these elements, he insisted, was indispensable to establish national power. Washington almost always supported Hamilton, not only because he believed in the man, but because he believed in his business principles. But because he did not know as much about banking as he did about commerce and manufacturing, he deferred to Hamilton's judgment more than he might if Hamilton had held any other post. In Hamilton's words, by establishing the credit of the United States on a firm foundation, the federal government would restore the confidence of foreign and domestic lenders, which would enable the United States to borrow large sums for improvements. Hamilton had no direct knowledge of European financial markets, but Jefferson, who had personally gone to the Netherlands and Paris to renegotiate Revolutionary War loans, knew that on most days the United States had a credit rating second only to Great Britain. Hamilton did not consult Jefferson or his data.

As part of his program to create a large and important central government Hamilton meant to eliminate the shortage of hard money in the country. He believed that federal taxes should be levied to give power as well as revenue to the central government while binding taxpayers and creditors to supporting and stabilizing the government. To make the United States independent of European mercantilism it was essential to develop "an extensive domestic market" based on American manufacturing that could put to good use the profits of American farm surpluses. Here he had the unqualified personal support of Washington. As long as the economy depended mainly on agriculture the United States would not be able to "exchange with Europe on even terms." Hamilton told Congress, "'tis for the United States to consider by what means they can render themselves least dependent on the combinations, right or wrong, of foreign policy."

But that was what Washington wanted to hear and it was for public consumption. Privately, Hamilton had been meeting for more than a year with British emissaries and telling them the proceedings of confidential cabinet meetings, not only breaking national security and faith with Washington but usurping the diplomatic functions of Secretary of State Jefferson.

Hamilton's brand of pro-British isolationism was completely opposite to the thinking of Jefferson and Madison, who were working to create a radically republican system based on a different set of assumptions. Since before the Revolution, Jefferson had believed that Anglo-American commercial ties were inherently unequal and exploitative: here he saw exactly eye-to-eye with Washington. He contended that England actually depended on American commerce. That had been true in 1765 and had brought about the repeal of the Stamp Act, but it was no longer true in 1792 when United States trade accounted for only one-sixth of the burgeoning British economy. Jefferson apparently never consulted Hamilton on this point, so essential to the settling of a sound foreign policy. For the next twenty years he would go on mistakenly assuming that American commerce gave the government the decisive weapon in reforming foreign trade policy. As Madison put it so succinctly, England supplied Americans "chiefly with superfluities." In exchange, America employed a large portion of the English workforce, the grain to make their bread, the whale oil to light their lamps, the lumber to build her navy. It was only necessary to press these two pressure points to bring the British to their knees, Jefferson argued; in peacetime to persuade the British to open all their domestic and colonial ports to American goods and shipping and, in wartime, to force the British to respect American neutral trading rights. The threat of commercial coercion became the linchpin of Jefferson and Madison's republican foreign policy. But, Hamilton countered, Americans would feel the ill effects of a commercial war long before Great Britain.[6]

All of these philosophical differences might have remained abstractions had it not been for the real politics of Europe, and they were never more in turmoil than at this exact moment as the French Revolution reached its most chaotic stage. By the spring of 1792, King Louis XVI and Marie Antoinette had been executed at the guillotine and Lafayette's moderate Constitutionalists had been brushed aside by the radicals of the Gironde. An attempt by royalists and the armies of European monarchs to crush the revolution by force of arms had been defeated by a revolutionary army at Valmy, only hastening the royal executions. No longer a monarchy, France was now a republic appealing to the American republic for recognition and payment of its debts from the American Revolution. Once again Jefferson and Hamilton clashed, this time squarely in the arena of foreign affairs. Hamilton said that the United States had made its treaties with the king of France and therefore owed neither alliance nor recompense; Jefferson argued the treaties and loans were with the French nation. For once, Washington backed him up.

Foreign policy differences between Jefferson and Hamilton also became evident when the French protested Congress's failure to exempt France from Hamilton's higher tonnage duties levied on foreign vessels. France protested that the new duties contradicted the Franco-American Treaty of Amity and Commerce of 1778. While rejecting the French argument, Jefferson recommended to Washington that, considering the importance of Franco-American relations and the small amount of customs duties involved, a concession be made to France. Hamilton openly opposed Jefferson's proposal in the cabinet and it failed to win support in Congress, which had earlier rejected Madison's efforts to impose higher duties on ships of countries that did not have commercial treaties with the United States. Just as Hamilton sought to weaken the American links with France, Jefferson was intent on strengthening them. In his September 1792 report to President Washington, Jefferson wrote,

> In the case of two nations with which we have the most intimate connections—France and England—my system was to give some satisfactory distinctions to the former of little cost to us [in] return for the solid advantages yielded us by them . . . Yet the secretary of the Treasury, by his cabals with members of the legislature and by high-toned declamation on other occasions has forced his own system which was exactly the reverse.[7]

Jefferson and Hamilton were also clashing bitterly on domestic politics. Secretary of the Treasury Hamilton increasingly saw himself as something of the American prime minister. The Treasury Lord in England had long served as the prime minister, controlling Parliament and cabinet for the king. When Hamilton tried to impose the English model on the American cabinet, Jefferson stopped cooperating with him. And when Hamilton proposed a national bank to Congress, similar to the Bank of England, Jefferson privately began to voice his concerns about Hamilton's policies in general while Madison, his lieutenant, led open opposition in Congress to the bank bill.

The first semiconscious step Jefferson and Madison took toward organizing a political party to oppose Hamilton and the Federalists came when they persuaded the radical New Jersey poet and journalist Philip Freneau to set up a newspaper in Philadelphia. Jefferson and Madison wanted a fairer hearing for their views, a national newspaper to counteract John Fenno's pro-Hamilton *Gazette of the United States*. Freneau's Princeton classmate, Henry Lee, had told Madison, another Princetonian, of the poet's impecunious state and of his desire to leave a poorly paid journalist's job in New York City and move to the capital. Jefferson offered Freneau a $250-a-year part-time translator's job that "gave him so little to do as not to interfere with any other calling," but Freneau held out until Madison negotiated with a New York printing firm to take him into partnership to establish the *National Gazette* in Philadelphia with Freneau as editor. Jefferson actively, if secretly, participated in the venture, insisted on paying Freneau the translator's salary for a no-show job, and promised him "the perusal of all my letters of foreign intelligence and all foreign newspapers, the publication of all proclamations and other public notices within my department and the printing of the laws." Just the printing business was enough to ensure the newspaper's survival. Jefferson and Madison then set to work drumming up subscriptions, especially in Virginia. They were bent on making Freneau's paper truly national. All that Jefferson asked in return for this was that Freneau "would give free place to pieces written against the aristocratical and monarchical principles."[8]

Freneau needed no coaxing. He promptly attacked the Hamiltonians and their policies. Disingenuously, Jefferson insisted he had not expected Freneau to go so far. "My expectations looked only to the chastisement of the aristocratical and monarchical writers and not to any criticisms of the proceedings of the government,"[9] he told the president, defending his role as merely support for an artist. Washington eventually asked Jefferson to do what he could to tone down Freneau's paper, but not until a full-fledged newspaper war that helped to bring on, in the Second Congress, the formation of opposing blocs in Congress that eventually became the Federalist and Republican parties.

Nine months after Freneau broke into print and while Washington, Jefferson, and Madison were out of town, Hamilton personally wrote attacks against Jefferson and placed them in Fenno's paper, assuming Jefferson was writing for Freneau's. Hamilton first exposed Freneau's salary at the State Department and then charged that his paper had been "instituted with the public money," its editor "regularly pensioned with the public money in the disposal of that officer."[10] The war escalated rapidly, Hamilton writing under a variety of pen names, assuming Jefferson did likewise. Freneau called Fenno, who received the Treasury's printing business, "a vile sycophant" with "emoluments from government" who was "disseminating principles and sentiments utterly subversive of the true republican interests of this country."[11] Madison contributed eighteen unsigned articles in the two years before Freneau's paper folded. Jefferson denied flat-out to Washington that he ever wrote anything for Freneau's paper under any name, but he encouraged others to write for Freneau and gave him invaluable access to State Department papers he personally selected, careful to protect the confidentiality of reports and equally careful not to let him see what he didn't want him to see. When Washington asked Jefferson to find a way to curtail Freneau, Jefferson refused.

> The President, not sensible of the designs of the party, has not with his usual good sense and sangfroid looked on the efforts and effects of this free press and seen that, though some bad things had passed through it to the public, yet the good have preponderated immensely.[12]

By 1792, both factions were accusing each other of contributing to what Jefferson termed "the heats and tumults of conflicting parties." Founded in unanimity, only five years after the federal government was formed at Philadelphia, a two-party system had emerged in the United States, with Hamilton at the head of the Federalists and, in Hamilton's words to President Washington, "Mr. Madison cooperating with Mr.

Jefferson . . . at the head of a faction decidedly hostile to me and my administration. Jefferson and Madison were in my judgment subversive of the principles of good government and dangerous to the union, peace and happiness of the country."[13]

In late summer 1792, Washington wrote confidentially to Jefferson and Hamilton, urging reconciliation and regretting that "internal dissensions should be harrowing and tearing our vitals."[14] His letters to the two rivals differed. He urged Jefferson to have "more charity for the opinions and acts of one another." He cautioned Hamilton about his temper and mentioned "irritating charges" in the gazettes. He urged both to make "allowances, mutual forebearances and temporizing yieldings on *all sides*." Washington complained to Jefferson that "in condemning the administration of government they condemned him, for if there were measures pursued contrary to his sentiments they must conceive him too careless to attend to them or too stupid to understand them."[15] Washington warned Jefferson that Freneau's *National Gazette* was inciting the breakup of the Union. If Jefferson feared monarchy, what would bring it on faster than the chaos that came with the collapse of the federal government? As the exchange continued Jefferson denied he had a hand in Freneau's writings and declared his intention to retire in March of 1793. Jefferson was implacable, placing all the blame on Hamilton, calling his policies "adverse to liberty" and predicting they would "undermine and demolish the republic" by giving his Treasury Department too much influence over Congress. But he steadfastly denied that "I have ever intrigued" in Congress or the state legislatures to thwart the government's policies. Jefferson did not rule out the possibility of continuing his opposition from outside the administration.[16]

But Hamilton kept up the attack in the press. Jefferson's friends anonymously took up the cudgels against him. Hamilton, sarcastically referring to Jefferson as "the quiet, modest retiring philosopher," said it was time he should be revealed as "the intriguing incendiary." Under the pseudonym Catullus, Hamilton kept up the attack through six articles. Madison and Monroe openly defended Jefferson in a series of six essays in Dunlap's *American Daily Advertiser*, Monroe doing the bulk of the writing. Both Hamilton's attacks and their "Vindication of Mr. Jefferson" appeared in print during the presidential election of 1792. Washington wanted to retire, but Madison and Jefferson pleaded with him to make "one more sacrifice," as Madison put it. Jefferson told Washington he feared a "corrupt squadron" in Congress would take unlimited power and create an English-style monarchy. Hamilton, warning against republicanism, also asked Washington to run again.[17]

Since June 1792 Jefferson had urged Washington to serve a second term: "The confidence of the whole Union is centered in you. North and South will hang together if they have to hang with you." Washington began to seek opinions: for once everyone—Madison, Hamilton, Tobias

Lear—agreed. When Lear visited New England that summer he reported that everyone he spoke with wanted Washington to continue in office. Washington did not need to be convinced that the preservation of the Union was at stake. When he asked Madison to write what was supposed to be his farewell speech to the nation, he emphasized that Madison was to include the phrase, "We are *all* the children of the same country." He was deeply agitated about the persistent press criticism of his administration: "There ought to be limits to it for suspicions unfounded and jealousies too lively are irritating to honest feelings." While both factions criticized major elements of his administration, they were pleading with him to stay on.[18]

On November 6, 1792, Washington delivered what he had intended to be his last Annual Message to Congress—his fourth report on the state of the Union. He was worried about popular resistance in western Pennsylvania to the excise tax on whiskey; he had sent out a proclamation declaring he intended to enforce the hated tax. Would sterner measures, even the use of troops, be necessary? In his speech he assured Congress the law would be enforced. Mostly he dwelt on Indian affairs and the steps he had taken to defend the frontiers. But he sounded a new note. The chronic clashing between white settlers and Indians had made him think deeply on the subject, and he urged Congress to adopt just and humane policies for dealing with the natives. He had gone far in changing his thinking since his years on the Virginia frontier when he only considered Indians as barriers to progress. He also surprised Congress when, despite his resentment of newspaper attacks, he urged a reduction in postal rates for newspapers.

As late as his November 6 appearance before Congress his closest friends and advisers did not know if Washington had decided to seek a second term. But the electoral college was to meet on the first Monday of December. No other candidate had come forward. If Washington did not announce his candidacy, he would be reelected anyway. Could he possibly refuse? Once again he had backed into an important decision. Some time around November 6 the president sat down with Martha, who had assumed all along that they were going home to Mount Vernon in the spring. When he told her he had decided to accept a second term, she told him angrily—just this once—what she thought of the idea. But then she calmed down. She was sorry for the outburst. Of course she would abide by his decision. If he stayed on, so would she. She would go anywhere he asked her. Washington put his arms around Martha and put his head down on her shoulder. "Poor Patsy," he said. "Poor Patsy."[19]

When the electoral college reelected Washington in December no one voted against him. He received 132 votes; three delegates abstained. But Vice President John Adams, who considered himself Washington's heir apparent, was surprised to encounter strong opposition.

New York's perennial governor, George Clinton, spokesman for the anti-Federalists since the Constitutional Convention, came in a strong third in the polling. Adams won 77–50, but there was fresh evidence of a second political party emerging from the rift in Washington's administration.

In February of 1793 when he returned to Philadelphia after the Christmas holidays, Washington persuaded Jefferson to stay on until the end of the year. But Jefferson would not promise to mend fences with Hamilton. Washington had learned from Henry Lee that there was deep dissatisfaction in the south, especially in Virginia, because of planters' losses at the hands of northern business interests. When Jefferson protested that he, unlike Hamilton, had never plotted against a colleague, Washington could stand it no more. Did not Jefferson and Hamilton comprehend "the extreme wretchedness of [my] existence while in office?"[20]

Added to Washington's burdens as he passed sixty-one years of age was the death of his trusted nephew, George Augustine, of tuberculosis. Washington left the capital and went home to the funeral. But he could not easily find a new manager for Mount Vernon. Each Sunday now, the president of the United States sat down and wrote out long, detailed letters of instruction to Anthony Whiting, his head farmer. At least in his imagination every detail of his beloved Mount Vernon was alive and vivid. He left out nothing. His memory was keen and so, in a way, was his pleasure.

He should not have been surprised that his inauguration to a second term was another matter. His cabinet—Hamilton and Jefferson again—could not agree on the format. Finally Washington followed the advice of Knox and Randolph to take his oath in a brief ceremony in the Senate chamber in Congress Hall. There were no crowds, no fanfare, and certainly no surprises in Washington's almost perfunctory speech. It was more oath than inaugural address. Washington merely wanted to say

> that if it shall be found during my Administration of the government I have in any instance violated willingly or knowingly the injunction thereof, I may (besides incurring Constitutional punishment) be subject to the upbraidings of all who are now witnesses of the present solemn ceremony.

After four years of growing dissension in his cabinet and opposition in Congress, Washington made it clear he had no sense of exultation or idealism as he was sworn in for four more years: only a grim sense of duty. There was little to cheer him. Each ship arriving from Europe seemed to bring more bad news. The French Reign of Terror had began. Thousands, including many old friends from the American Revolution, were being carted off to places of execution. Like most Americans Washington had at first applauded the French struggle against an autocratic monarchy. He had assured his old friend La Luzerne that "nobody can wish more sincerely for the prosperity of the French nation than I do."[21] But Washington grew increasingly worried that the United States would become en-meshed in war between France and England. As Federalists lined up to support the English and the emerging Republicans favored the French, Washington attempted to remain aloof from the name-calling by "Monocrats" and "Jacobins."

Washington thought a "just, steady and prudent national policy" could make the United States the ultimate "gainer" in a European war, but how could he achieve neutrality with England still occupying seven forts inside United States territory and inciting Indian raids and the Spanish at New Orleans blocking American shipping down the Mississippi to Europe? By the time he left for Mount Vernon in March 1793 for his nephew's funeral he had the first hint that the European conflagration was about to become even more general. News of Louis XVI and Marie Antoinette's executions was accompanied by word of an English declara-tion of war on the new French Republic. Hamilton had brought the news from a back channel to London. Jefferson refused to believe it at first. It was more garbled rumor mongering. Washington left instructions for Jef-ferson to receive a new French ambassador civilly but without any great show of enthusiasm. When Hamilton, bypassing Jefferson, sent a courier off to Mount Vernon that the report of war was now official, Washington said he would return soon but in the meantime his cabinet officers were to be careful to observe a "strict neutrality."

On his arrival on April 17, 1793, Washington called an emergency cabi-net meeting and asked each secretary for a written report of his ideas for a proper policy. Jefferson was opposed to strict neutrality. France was an ally, and he certainly opposed any stated policy. He wrote very little. But Hamilton once again was ready with a long list of questions about Ameri-can treaty obligations to France. Washington made Hamilton's list the agenda for the emergency session. Over Jefferson's objections that a pre-mature written policy would remove any leverage to win any diplomatic concessions from the British, Washington took Hamilton's advice to issue a written proclamation of American neutrality. Instead of assigning the task to the secretary of state, Washington gave it to Attorney General Randolph, who had become an independent swing vote in the cabinet. The second decision that day was anticlimactic: not waiting for cabinet or Congress, the president instructed the new American minister in Paris, his old friend Gouverneur Morris, to tell the French Republic that the United States would grant it full diplomatic recognition. At an adjourned session the next Monday, the cabinet took up the thorny question of how, without a navy, the government could enforce a ban on French outfitting of privateering ships in American ports. When Randolph suggested using customs agents, Jefferson, furious at his cousin, objected to using Trea-sury Department officials—who reported to Hamilton. The British am-bassador had lodged a formal protest of the practice.

Declaring neutrality was one thing, enforcing it another. In early April,

Edmond Charles Genet, better known as Citizen Genet, landed in Charleston, South Carolina. More than a month later he arrived in Philadelphia to the salute of a French warship after a triumphal slow march from town to town to the cheers of French sympathizers. On April 18 Jefferson accompanied Genet as he presented his credentials to the president. Jefferson was effusive, Washington cool and laconic. Genet was surprised at Washington's standoffish reception: was not America a fellow republic that had, too, thrown off the yoke of monarchy with French help? Rebuffed officially, Genet made the mistake of appealing to the American public and then violated protocol by outfitting a privateer and seizing an English merchantman, the *Little Sarah*, and fitting it out, too, to prey on British commerce. Jefferson had quickly revised his original assessment of Genet from admiration to one who was "hotheaded, all imagination, no judgment, passionate"—and, worse, disrespectful and even indecent to President Washington. Still, Jefferson took Genet at his word when he promised to keep the *Little Sarah* moored in Philadelphia.

For several weeks that spring, Washington was ill with influenza and running a slight fever. His patience frayed, he lashed out at Jefferson in late May over Freneau's attacks in the *National Gazette*. When his steward, Whiting, at Mount Vernon became ill, Washington rushed to Mount Vernon only to find the man had died. It was well into July before Washington returned to Philadelphia and learned that Genet had broken his word and ordered the *Little Sarah*, armed and renamed *Democrate*, to sail. Angrily, he wrote to Jefferson. Why had he not told the president earlier?

"Is the minister of the French Republic to set the acts of this government at defiance with impunity?" he demanded of Jefferson. "What must the world think of such conduct and of the government of the United States for submitting to it?" In high dudgeon, Washington summoned his cabinet. A formal demand for Genet's recall went sailing off to Paris; *Rules Concerning Belligerents* soon was published. But no one could placate Washington's wrath as July turned into a Philadelphia August and Freneau's press kept churning out daily criticism of his government. At an early August cabinet meeting called to decide whether to publish Genet's correspondence, Washington lost his temper completely. In his diary, Jefferson recorded the scene:

> The President was much inflamed. [He] got into one of those passions when he cannot command himself; ran on much on the personal abuse which had been bestowed on him; defied any man on earth to produce one single act of his since he had been in the government which was not done on the purest motives. That he had never repented but once having [lost] the moment of resigning his office and that was every moment since. That by God he had rather be in his grave than in his present situation. That he had rather be on his farm than to be made

Emperor of the World. *And yet they were charging him with want-*
ing to be a King. That that rascal Freneau sent him three of his papers
every day as if he thought he would become the distributor of his papers.
That he could see in this nothing but an impudent design to insult
him.[22]

To Jefferson and everyone else in the room it was clear that Washington was directing his rage at the secretary of state as the leader of his
tormentors, yet a few days later he had cooled down enough to ask Jefferson to stay the rest of the year. Washington wanted his cabinet to be bipartisan, even if he could not be. He only railed at Freneau, never at
Hamilton's paper or at Hamilton himself, who was regularly writing anti-
Jefferson essays for it.

An unwanted respite in the partisan strife came in August 1793, when
yellow fever caused more than 6,000 deaths in the capital city of 30,000
population. Washington moved his family eight miles to a modest fieldstone house on Market Square in Germantown. Up to a hundred deaths a
day did not frighten away Martha, who refused to leave for Mount Vernon
until the usual time for her departure on September 10. As Washington
rode his Tidewater acres and surveyed the damages of his continued absence to his estate, he came to the conclusion that Citizen Genet had fo-
mented organized resistance to his administration. All over the country
Democratic-Republican Societies that were noisily pro-French and anti-
Hamilton had sprung up; the first was the Democratic Society of Pennsylvania, organized in July 1793. Washington refused to believe the
movement was spontaneous. He told Governor Henry Lee of Virginia
that he believed its aim was "nothing short of the subversion of the Government of these states, even at the expense of plunging this country
[into] the horrors of a disastrous war." When he returned to Philadelphia
to deliver his fifth Annual Message to Congress, he was blunt about his
neutrality proclamation. It was "my duty"; without it "our disposition of
peace" could be called into question by the combatant nations. In a series
of subsequent messages to Congress he explained his demand for
Genet's ouster and outlined his strong objections to the British remaining
in forts on American soil ten years after signing the Treaty of 1783. Washington, over Hamilton's objections, insisted on evenhandedly publishing
the correspondence of both the British and French ambassadors. For
once, Washington took Jefferson's advice. It was his swan song: at the end
of December 1793, Jefferson resigned.

But there was to be no peace. Shortly after Washington appointed
Randolph as secretary of state, he learned that the British navy was seizing American ships in the Caribbean in an attempt to stop Americans
from trading with the French. The captured crews were being impressed
into forced service in the British navy. An irate Congress declared a
thirty-day embargo on all commerce with England. At that very moment,

a letter from the governor-general of Canada to Indian leaders promising them aid in a war with the United States arrived on the floor of Congress at the same time as Jefferson's final report—a major report on British trade discrimination against Americans by British suppliers. As war fever raged, the House passed a bill extending trade sanctions against Britain until the forts were evacuated and damages paid for the seized ships. Only John Adams's tie-breaking vote in the Senate defeated the warlike measure. But there was no stopping a bill to build four frigates, the nucleus of the first United States Navy.

Only Washington's coolness prevented war. He kept his opinions to himself and affected a new bipartisan appearance. When the Federalists urged him to send Hamilton as a special envoy to London, he told Senator Oliver Ellsworth of Connecticut that the people did not trust Hamilton. Instead, he sent the pro-French James Monroe to Paris and sent the Federalist John Jay to London. As riots broke out in Philadelphia, the president dispatched Jay in mid-May of 1794 with detailed instructions to negotiate the evacuation of the forts and compensation for recent seizures of ships and slaves during the Revolution.

During the year-long negotiations in England, new troubles sprang up in western Pennsylvania where Hamilton's excise tax gatherers had issued arrest warrants for home brewers returnable 300 miles to the east and several weeks of arduous travel to Philadelphia. The servers of the warrants were repulsed and a crowd attacked a Treasury official's house: one man was killed and the house burned to the ground. Labeling the western protests "the first fruits of the Democratic Society," Washington decided that only force could stem further armed resistance. But Pennsylvania refused to call out its militia. Why not try the courts first? But U.S. Supreme Court Justice James Wilson, himself a Pennsylvania signer of the Declaration of Independence, supported Washington's view that the normal legal steps had failed to enforce the law and that the government was justified in nationalizing the state militia to put down the "rebellion." But now Secretary of State Randolph balked: "The strength of the government is in the affections of the people," he countered, infuriating Federalists.

Randolph's conciliatory argument swayed Washington. In August, he sent a federal commissioner west to offer amnesty in return for order—and to gather intelligence. By mid-September they sent word of a strong armed minority in western Pennsylvania that was refusing amnesty. Washington now decided to call out 12,000 men from the Pennsylvania, New Jersey, Virginia, and Maryland militias. As he issued a proclamation to justify the use of troops to put down the so-called Whiskey Rebellion, he squeezed into his old uniform and traveled west toward the place of rendezvous with Hamilton at his side—Secretary of War Knox was on home leave. It was to prove Washington's last outing as a soldier. As he rode west, he learned the welcome news that his old cut-and-thrust field commander, "Mad Anthony" Wayne, had won a major victory over the western Indians at Fallen Timbers, Ohio. Suffused with martial spirit, the sixty-three-year-old, white-haired Washington rode toward Bedford, Pennsylvania, where nearly forty years ago he had chafed for action during the Forbes expedition. The militia rallied round the old commander singing, "To arms once more, our hero cries/Sedition lives and order dies/To peace and race then bid adieu/And dash to the mountains, Jersey Blue."[23]

After gathering his troops at Bedford on October 28, Washington returned to Philadelphia and left Henry Lee at the head of his army. All resistance collapsed. Twenty would-be "rebels" were shipped back to Philadelphia and, after a trial that produced little evidence, all but two were released. One was a simpleton, the other insane; Washington pardoned both. The episode not only provided an outlet for a virulent war frenzy but left Washington unshaken in his belief that the "self-created" Democratic-Republican Societies "have been laboring to sow the seeds of distrust, jealousy and of course discontent" and still could trigger "some resolution in the government."[24]

He saw further evidence when a copy of the treaty negotiated by John Jay reached the capital in March 1795. The British had promised to give up their forts, but only small ships could trade with the British West Indies and the British had the right to buy all cargoes, thus blocking all exports to the French. Fresh riots broke out in Philadelphia and Jay was burned in effigy. Before the Senate could debate ratification, one senator leaked a copy to Benjamin Franklin Bache, grandson of Benjamin Franklin and editor of the virulently anti-Federalist paper, the *Aurora*. Bache published the treaty, creating the impression the administration was trying to keep the treaty secret until Washington ratified it. As Washington pondered the treaty he learned that the British were confiscating cargoes bound for France. He sent word through Randolph to the British ambassador that he would not sign the treaty until the seizures stopped.

Even at Mount Vernon that summer Washington could not find respite from the "most tortured representations" of his Republican critics. There was now a solidly Republican majority in the House of Representatives. He saw French influence everywhere. He was grateful to Hamilton for writing his "Catullus" essays in favor of the treaty. Washington himself was drifting into the Federalist ranks with other "friends of order and good government."

When he returned to Philadelphia in August, he met with Randolph to dismiss the treaty. Suddenly, Timothy Pickering, who had recently replaced the retiring Knox as secretary of war, burst into the president's office. Pickering had been active in Washington's intelligence service during the Revolution. At Mount Vernon, Washington had received a note from him marked "for your eyes alone." He wanted to see

Washington alone now; the president ushered him into another room. "That man is a traitor!" Pickering told Washington, explaining that he had received a captured French diplomatic dispatch detailing an offer of a large sum of money to the chronically strapped Randolph to influence foreign policy in favor of France. Washington resumed his meeting with Randolph and for days gave no hint he suspected him, but he studied the documents and concluded Pickering was right. The last member of his original cabinet, his aide in the Revolution, the last nonpartisan voice in his government, had betrayed him!

Infuriated, Washington reacted by signing the Jay Treaty—only Randolph had spoken against it in his cabinet. And then he confronted Randolph. Shaken, unable to clear himself, Randolph resigned. He was never able to clear himself or find the evidence—which existed—that he, the last critic of British policy in Washington's government, was the victim of a plot by British intelligence. Now Washington's cabinet was solidly Federalist. He reshuffled his secretaries, appointed Supreme Court justices, found solace in reorganization as he began his last year in office. Now he felt the full fury of Republican writers convinced that he was the arch-Federalist. The attacks in the *Aurora* poked fun at his education and intelligence. As the Republican press geared up to oppose his renomination to a third term, "A Calm Observer" charged that he had overdrawn his expense account. He had always treated his salary as an expense draw and the charge was true. It did not help when his aides countered that he was unaware of the error. The Republican editors only stepped up their attacks.

When Washington gave his last Annual Message, he ignored his tormentors and pointed only to his foreign policy successes: peace treaties with Indian tribes north and south, with the Barbary states, with Spain and England. He counseled "prudence and moderation on every side." But Congress was in no mood to accept his advice. When it learned that Washington had unilaterally ratified the Jay Treaty, the House, now that appropriations were required for commissions of arbitration established by the treaty, demanded that Washington turn over all Executive Branch correspondence relating to the negotiations. But Washington insisted that the House had no constitutional role in treaty-making. The House's assent but not its consent was sometimes politically desirable. While a three-week debate raged in the House, the motion demanding the papers finally passed, 62–37. Washington, on the advice of Hamilton and the cabinet, refused to comply. Washington wrote Congress:

> The nature of foreign negotiations requires caution and their success must depend on secrecy. . . . A full disclosure of all the measures, demands or eventual concessions would be extremely impolitic. . . . It is perfectly clear to my understanding

that the assent of the House is not necessary to the validity of a treaty.

Washington's stubborn refusal to bow to the Democratic-Republican majority in the House led to a six-week face-off, but in the end it was the House that yielded and voted on April 29, 1796, to accept the president's refusal. In the end, Washington's prudent silence won out. He had suspected the Democratic-Republicans were only trying to assert their newfound power. "My tongue, for the present, shall be silent," he said.[25]

*U*nable to silence his critics in Congress, Washington smarted under the daily lashings he received in the Democratic-Republican press. "If you read the *Aurora* of this city," he wrote to Benjamin Walker in Virginia, "you cannot but have perceived with what malignant industry and persevering falsehoods I am assailed." He believed that editor Bache intended "to weaken if not destroy the confidence of the public" in his presidency. He depicted opposition journalists as "discontented characters" motivated by "an opinion that the measures of the general government are impure." These journalists were "bad and (if I might be allowed to use so harsh an expression) diabolical."

Bache in turn lambasted Washington and his administration as "enemies of democracy." Washington was not the father of his country but "weak" and "inept." His victories at Trenton and Princeton during the Revolutionary War had been inconsequential. Such falsehoods, Washington complained in private, were "no stumbling block to the editors of these papers." Washington's imperial-style presidency provoked the special wrath of Freneau, who attacked him in his *Jersey Chronicle* after the *National Gazette* folded. "He holds levees like a king, makes treaties like a king, answers petitions like a king and employs old enemies like a king," wrote Freneau. Worst of all, Washington "swallows adulation like a king and vomits offensive truths in your face."

More and more, Washington came to regard the opposition press as an erosive and disuniting force. "It is well known that, when one side only of a story is heard and often repeated, the human mind becomes impressed with it insensibly." To Pickering he confided his despair at giving the public a "clear and comprehensive view of the facts." And to Henry Lee he wrote that "no man was ever more tired of public life." To Adams he told of his "disinclination to be longer buffeted in the public prints by a set of infamous scribblers."[26]

But he did not counterattack in public. Always the moderate, sometimes the only one, in his government, he had no more patience with political discord. With his retirement less than a year away, he was writing the first draft of his farewell address. His draft showed, first, how wounded he was by the years of infighting and character assassination by the press. He pointed out he had taken no salary during the war and had sustained financial losses during his years in office. He had never sought office and it stung even more when he was attacked as ambitious and greedy:

> It might be expected at the parting scene of my public life that I should take some notice of such virulent abuse. But, as heretofore, I shall pass them over in utter silence.

It was a deafening, verbose silence and Washington was aware of "egotisms." He asked his closest friend Hamilton to revise his comments. As they passed drafts back and forth, the message grew longer, but it was in essence entirely Washington's. Whenever Hamilton injected ideas that Washington did not agree with, he struck them out. The final draft of Washington's *Farewell Address* was all Washington's thought, all Hamilton's writing, put out over Washington's signature.

It could have been a Federalist reelection campaign speech, as it revealed more than any other document how far Washington had drifted into partisan Federalist ranks by 1796. Most partisan of all was Washington's advice for Americans to avoid "permanent alliances." His isolationist message came after the experience of only a single alliance: with France. He warned against the growth of political parties: they were dangerous vehicles that could easily lead to foreign influence of domestic policy, a clear reminder of the Citizen Genet affair, where a foreign emissary used the domestic American press to bring pressure on the government.

Washington's valedictory did not stop bipartisan politics, it fanned them. It was the opening gun of the 1796 elections in which he supported his vice president, John Adams. Washington summoned David Claypoole of the *American Daily Advertiser* on September 16 and asked him to "usher it into the world." The address was published September 19 as Washington left for Mount Vernon. He returned to the capital in time to write his last Annual Message to a packed session of Congress on December 7, 1796. It was the last time Washington was expected to make a presidential speech.

A woman in the audience recorded Washington's "extreme agitation" and the audience's strong emotion as he concluded his eighth and last state of the union message:

> The situation in which I now stand, for the last time, in the midst of the representative of the people of the United States, naturally recalls the period when the administration of the present form of government commenced. . . . I cannot omit the occasion to congratulate you and my country on the success of the experiment nor to repeat my fervent supplications to the

Supreme Ruler of the Universe and Sovereign Arbiter of Nations that his Providential care may still be extended to the United States; that the virtue and happiness of the people may be preserved and that the Government which they have instituted for the protection of their liberties may be perpetual.

As she watched and listened, she thought to herself: "There is a magic in his name more powerful than the abilities of any other man can ever acquire."[27]

*O*n Saturday, March 4, 1797, the inauguration of John Adams as the narrowly elected second president of the United States took place in Congress Hall, next door to Independence Hall, where Adams had nominated Washington for commander in chief of the Continental Army twenty-two years earlier. President Washington wore a plain black suit as he walked alone to the hall while Adams in a lavish new suit rode in a new resplendent carriage of state. After the brief ceremony, Washington congratulated Adams, who later recounted their last moment together:

He seemed to enjoy a triumph over me. Methought I heard him say, "Ay! I am fairly out and you fairly in! See which of us will be happiest!"[28]

Twenty-One

"MY GLASS IS ALMOST RUN"

The Washington family left Philadelphia for the last time in March 1797 amid a frenzy of activity that could not mask their happiness at finally escaping public life. The former president's mood was improving by the day. He complained good-naturedly to Tobias Lear that it was his duty to remember everything: "On one side I am called upon to remember the parrot; on the other to remember the dog: for my own part I should not pine much if both were forgot." But he had learned to tolerate the bird, named Snipe, and the dog, Frisk.

As they prepared for life in the country after so many years in the city, Nelly, now sixteen and beautiful, was grieving at the loss of her close friends. And her brother Wash had deserted her, going off to study at Princeton. She had spent seven years in the capital, where she had learned some French, Italian, and Spanish, but now she was happy to be going home, where most of her memories were of wonderful summer vacations with her grandparents. She had been separated by death from her father and by economic necessity from her mother. Her grandmother, she wrote, "has been even more than a mother to me and the President [the] most affectionate of fathers." Nelly, Washington's favorite grandchild, had learned her grandfather's love of horticulture. She hoped to become "a great farmer" someday like her grandfather.

Her grandmother had not been well. Martha had been plagued by recurring bouts of malaria that had felled her four times in the past year: no one could be happier to be going home at last. There she would be able to rest in her large new upstairs room over the library. There in the mornings she could write letters and plan the elaborate menu, sew, make quilts, and embroider in the evenings. The household routine was, to be sure, rigorous, and she began to feel it more now as she passed sixty-five: breakfast with her husband at seven and for the grandchildren and guests as they came down, dressing for dinner and assembling everyone for the main meal at noon, then assembling everyone again for midafternoon tea—supervising every step of each preparation and service by her servants. But at least at Mount Vernon she would be surrounded by friends and children, not diplomats' wives and the obsequious spouses of politicians and favor-seekers.

When the Washington caravan of carriages and wagons left for Mount Vernon in March, there was, in addition to the family, secretary Tobias Lear, and the servants, a new ward of the Washingtons': George Washington Motier Lafayette, sixteen-year-old son of Marquis de Lafayette and President Washington's godson. For four years since his former aide-de-camp's arrest during the Reign of Terror, Lafayette had been held in an Austrian prison. His wife and her mother, La Duchess de Noailles, had been condemned to death by a revolutionary tribunal. Only Washington's secret intervention through Jefferson had spared the women literally at the foot of the guillotine. Washington had risked compromising his otherwise strictly followed doctrine of neutrality by sending gold to support the Lafayette family on its estate east of Paris for the entire five years of Lafayette's imprisonment. In the fall of 1795 Lafayette's firstborn son had been spirited out of France and had arrived in Boston with a tutor. Washington insisted that the boy stay in Boston. He would pay all the expenses. Working quietly to overcome opposition, even as Congress angrily debated the Jay Treaty, Washington sent the boy to Mount Vernon in the spring of 1796.

Described by a visitor as a gentle and melancholy youth, young Lafayette lived in fear and expectation of any news of his father. Quietly, Washington alerted postmasters in all coastal towns to forward any letters addressed to the youth to Mount Vernon at once. Nelly found him charming and witty. Washington treated him as his own son; Martha, young Lafayette later wrote, was "a second mother." When finally a letter arrived with word of the Marquis's release from prison, young George left at once—carrying with him Washington's affectionate greeting and praise for his "exemplary" godson. By late 1797 the entire Lafayette family, Washington was delighted to learn, was safe on Danish soil.

While Washington did not record his emotions when he reached Mount Vernon and his second retirement, Nelly drew a picture of the family's peace and contentment in those first months at home. "We have spent our summer and autumn very happy here." Everyone was "in general blessed with good health." As usual the house was full of "many agreeable visitors." By winter the family was assembling in the evenings around the fireside, "often speaking of and wishing to see again our good friends in Philadelphia but never regretting its amusements or a life of ceremony." Nelly wrote that life at Mount Vernon was so lively that she had not even been to Alexandria for three months. "I have never a dull or lonesome hour, never find a day too long."

But the same incessant hospitality and conviviality began to wear on Washington by the end of his first summer of retirement. Washington hired a housekeeper to help Martha with the burdensome entertaining. In a letter to Tobias Lear, who had come for a visit with his wife and children, Washington half-good-naturedly complained,

> I am alone at *present* and shall be glad to see you this evening. Unless someone pops in unexpectedly, Mrs. Washington and myself will do what I believe has not been done within the last twenty years by us—that is to set down to dinner by ourselves.[1]

The flood of visitors ate, gawked, slept, and left, often after recording their impressions of the most famous couple in America. Martha now rated comment. She was variously described as "cheerful," "extremely pleasant," someone who "loves to talk and talks very well about times past." Mrs. Washington, wrote one woman visitor, knitted incessantly. Others found her wide knowledge of foreign affairs and customs made her an admirable hostess. She impressed guests with her keen memory for details of the history of the past half-century.

Both Washingtons enjoyed the leisure to write more letters—and both renewed their correspondence with Sally Fairfax, now a widow living in England. Washington had long nursed the hope that the Fairfaxes would return from exile to rebuild Belvoir, but George William had spent the last twenty years of his life vainly pursuing a hereditary lordship in England. Now that Sally's husband was dead he could at long last write to her directly about his "recollection of those happy moments, the happiest in my life, which I have enjoyed in your company. It is a matter of sore regret, when I cast my eyes toward Belvoir which I often do, to reflect that the former inhabitants of it, with whom we lived in such harmony and friendship, no longer reside there."[2]

At about this time Eliza Powell, a close friend in Philadelphia who had purchased a desk from the Washingtons, found in it a packet of letters Martha had written him. She returned them unopened, but teased Washington about their intimate contents. Washington wrote to her that she would probably have been disappointed. Their letters were "more fraught with friendship than enamored love."[3]

Fondly remembering old friends, the Washingtons were not, Martha reported to David Humphreys, eager "to enter into new friendships" despite the fact that "our circle of friends of course is contracted." Tobias Lear returned to Washington's employment as his private secretary. Soon Washington was busy not only supervising his estates but editing his massive correspondence. For both of the Washingtons, their enjoyments were increasingly *en famille*. When an invitation for an assembly ball came, Washington declined it. "Alas, our dancing days are no more." Even when his nephew Laurence Washington became engaged and invited the Washingtons to the wedding in Winchester, an overnight ride away, Washington refused politely to leave Mount Vernon. Weddings were for people starting life, not leaving it. "I think it not likely that either of us will ever be more than twenty-five miles from Mount Vernon again."[4]

He did not add that Martha had been increasingly "indisposed," as Washington confided to his nephew Samuel in the spring of 1799. Martha suffered from chronic gastric problems, which sometimes kept them both awake all night. In the middle of one night, he had to send for his old friend and family doctor, James Craik. She was, Washington wrote, "now better and taking the bark but low, weak and fatigued."[5]

Washington rarely dared to leave Martha alone at Mount Vernon but, late in 1798, an emergency arose that made him ride off to Philadelphia. Washington had kept up with the growing confrontation between the Adams administration and France as the Napoleonic Wars widened. Three U.S. envoys were shaken down for a $50,000 *douceur* by three French representatives—X, Y, and Z—sent to negotiate a bribe with them in Paris by the foreign minister, Prince de Talleyrand. When President Adams made the affair public, a fresh demand for war against the old ally led Adams to propose calling up a "New Army" to fight the French.

Restless at Mount Vernon, Washington found a pretext to write to Secretary of War James McHenry that "if a crisis should arrive [a] sense of duty or call from my country should become so imperious as to leave me no choice"—in a rambling fashion Washington offered to organize Adams's provisional "New Army." As the French seized more and more American ships in the Caribbean, Congress had authorized increasing the army from two to twelve regiments in anticipation of an expected French invasion. When Adams hinted that Washington would be chosen as its commander if he consented, he quickly responded he would choose an all-new general staff, ordered a new uniform, and rode off to Philadelphia to select his officers—with Martha's blessing. Adams meanwhile went ahead with the appointment without accepting Washington's conditions, and over the protests of many Federalists who wanted to commission Hamilton. On July 2, 1798, the Senate unanimously approved Washington's appointment as lieutenant general and commander in chief.

Washington was nonplussed that Adams had not met his conditions, and Hamilton played to his fears that Adams himself would appoint "the wrong sort" of officer. Washington wanted only officers with proven Federalist credentials. He believed that Democratic-Republican officers would be too pro-French. Washington also insisted that Hamilton be appointed inspector-general—number two to Washington. Finally, as the crisis passed and no French invasion came, an embarrassed Washington returned to Mount Vernon, commander in chief of an army that mostly only existed on paper. Adams had proven clever in the affair, remaining content to give the appearance of military readiness without the consequences of a real mobilization.

As the Adams administration ground on and passed the unpopular Alien and Sedition Laws that led to the silencing and imprisonment of the Federalists' press critics—twenty-five editors and printers were arrested, ten jailed—Washington remained silent, tacitly approving the muzzling of the press. As early as 1793 he had argued that Freneau and Bache's journals could discredit the government. Shortly after he retired he wrote to Rufus King that nothing could "change the sentiments or (which would perhaps be more correct) the conduct of some characters amongst us." He sincerely believed that seditious journalists could break up the United States and bring them once again under a foreign power. Far from condemning the arrests under the Sedition Act, he told Charles Carroll of Carrolltown, "I even wish they had been *more energetic.*" More and more over the years he had developed a theory that there was a radical plot among Democratic-Republicans loyal to Jefferson and Madison to bring the United States under French control.

Until the last year of his life, Washington kept himself aloof from partisan strife, but by April of 1799 he finally emerged as a Federalist. By this time, the Federalists held only four of Virginia's nineteen seats in the House of Representatives, so thorough had been the Jeffersonian sweep. By late summer, Washington was helping to scour the state for Federalist candidates. He was working to persuade talented men who eschewed public life to run for office. One of them was John Marshall, who had served under Washington in the Revolution, had endured the bitter winter of Valley Forge when many Virginia officers resigned the service, and had since studied law and served as an American emissary to Paris. When Marshall wrote that he would be attending court days in Frederick County in September and would like to drop in to visit Washington at Mount Vernon, Washington responded eagerly that he wanted to talk to him about politics. Washington also wrote to his nephew, Bushrod, who was practicing law in Richmond, to join them: "The crisis is most important. The temper of the people in this state is so violent and outrageous that I wish to converse with General Marshall and yourself on the elections which must come soon."

Marshall and Bushrod arrived at Mount Vernon on September 3 and stayed three days. In long conversations at the dinner table, on the portico, and on tours of the gardens, Washington urged the two younger men to stand for election to Congress to wrest two seats away from the Democratic-Republicans. Bushrod acquiesced to his uncle's "Bushrod, it must be done!" but Marshall was adamant that he wanted to return to private law practice. Washington was implacable. He arranged a dinner in

Marshall's honor in Alexandria and, after dinner, came very close to ordering Marshall to run for office. Marshall was gracious: he did not want to take offense or give it, but he was determined not to run. The next morning, he rose early and prepared to leave without another confrontation. At dawn, he stepped onto the piazza on his way to the stable. Washington was waiting for him, wearing his new lieutenant general's uniform. Once more, Washington, cloaked in his old authority of commander in chief, appealed to Marshall. The conversation was lively, "one of the most interesting I was ever engaged in." The gist of it was that Washington, so long determined never to return to public life, had put on his uniform once more to save his country in a time of crisis. "My resolution yielded to this representation and I became a candidate for Congress." No one, including the fiercely independent future Chief Justice, could, in the end, refuse George Washington.[6]

By late 1799, while Washington still refused to take any further public part in politics, in private letters he worried that the Adams administration was incapable of keeping peace with the French. When he heard that some Federalists were whispering that Washington should be brought back for a third term, he quickly quashed the rumors: "No eye, no tongue, no thought" should be given to his candidacy. By this time Washington was telling close friends that "my glass is almost run" as he composed his business affairs and sat down to write his will. His eight salaried years as president had helped him to stabilize his finances. He had lost no money as president and had time to bring about the restructuring of his various businesses. He had built a state-of-the-art, sixteen-sided threshing barn, similar to the latest model in France, that enabled horses to thresh grain in all weather, giving a boost to his fine-grade flour business. He also built a highly profitable whiskey distillery. He had been less successful in collecting rents for his western lands, even though as the result of his lifelong efforts to open up the over-the-mountains west more than one million Americans had crossed into the interior valleys and floated down rivers he had once explored to open up scores of new towns.

When he sat down to draw up his will—dated July 9, 1799—he was probably worth $2 million in today's dollars, but most of his assets were tied up in land and slaves, property his heirs could not easily liquidate. His attempts to sell 23,000 acres in twelve tracts of land on the Ohio and Kanawha Rivers and in Virginia, Maryland, and Pennsylvania to a speculator led to an agreement but no cash. On elegant 8⅛ x 6¼-inch paper, with the goddess of agriculture as its watermark, Washington meticulously wrote out twenty-eight pages. He gave mementoes and cash bequests to friends and all retainers, including an annuity and the gift of freedom for his crippled black manservant Billy Lee. He gave lifetime use of a farm to Tobias Lear. All his lands outside Mount Vernon he ordered sold and the proceeds distributed among his relatives. Everything he did not specifically bequeath, including his five home farms of 8,000 acres and one thousand head of livestock, he left to Martha during her lifetime. Then the main Mount Vernon farm and acreage and his private papers were to go to Bushrod Washington, the son of his favorite brother, Jack, who had tended it for him all through his years as a soldier on the frontier. Worried about growing sectional strife between North and South, he bequeathed his Potomac Canal stock to help build a national university where "youth of fortune and good talents" could meet and overcome "habitual jealousies."

He left all of his slaves, about two hundred people, to Martha with annuities to provide for them and instructions that she was to free them at her death; Martha had already agreed she would free her one hundred dower slaves. Washington had long considered freeing all his slaves, even though he took pains to prevent their escape or doing anything that would encourage them to clamor for their freedom. When his presidential chef Hercules ran away in Philadelphia rather than face going back to Mount Vernon, Washington did not pursue him. He had vowed by 1796 never "to hold another slave by purchase." But he still considered his slaves as property. When a young black woman, Oney Judge, whom Martha had raised as if she were white, had fled with a French lover to the freed-black sanctuary of Portsmouth, New Hampshire, President Washington pressured Joseph Whipple, U.S. customs collector for Portsmouth, to help him bring her back to Philadelphia. "I am sorry to give you or anyone else trouble on such a trifling occasion but the ingratitude of the girl ought not to escape with impunity." Told he would have to take the case to the courts of the anti-slavery state, Washington had backed off. In the end, Washington freed his slaves to spare his aged wife the headaches of supervising three hundred people and because he feared a slave revolt. But for whatever motive, free them he did.[7]

*O*n the morning of December 13, 1799, as the eighteenth century drew to a close, sixty-seven-year-old George Washington caught a cold. He went out riding on his usual rounds despite the fact that it was, as he wrote in his diary,

> *snowing and about three inches deep . . . wind at northeast and mercury at 30. . . . Continuing snowing till one o'clock and about four it became perfectly clear. Wind in the same place but not hard. Mercury at 28 at night.*[8]

These were the last words George Washington wrote.

When he came back from his long daily ride, his greatcoat was soaked through. His neck was wet and snow was hanging from his white hair. He went to the dinner table without changing his damp clothing. By evening, he admitted having a sore throat. That evening, his secretary Lear wrote to his mother that Washington was "very cheerful" and read parts of the newspaper "aloud as much as his hoarseness would permit." When he went to bed, Lear urged him to take some medicine.

"No," Washington answered. "You know I never take anything for a cold. Let it go as it came."

Between two and three in the morning after tossing and turning in the six-foot-six-inch bed, Washington woke Martha and complained he had a very sore throat and was feeling unwell. He could hardly talk and was having trouble breathing. Alarmed, Martha wanted to summon a servant. Washington didn't want her to: she might catch cold, too. When a maid came at dawn to light a fire, Washington sent her to fetch the overseer, Rawlins, who usually took care of sick slaves, and his secretary, Lear. He also sent for Dr. Craik, but he insisted Rawlins bleed him before the doctor arrived. Washington was shivering from chills and had developed what he called ague—in this case strep throat.

When the overseer came, Washington, baring his arm, told him not to be afraid. Rawlins made an incision, but Washington complained it was not wide enough. Martha begged her husband not to lose too much blood and asked Lear "to stop it." When Lear stepped closer, Washington raised his other hand as a sign not to interfere. "More," he ordered. Dr. Craik arrived, applied Spanish fly to Washington's throat to draw blood into a blister, and bled him again. When Washington tried to gargle sage tea and vinegar he nearly choked. Craik saw that Washington could not swallow, either; he sent for a second doctor and bled Washington again.

Between three and four in the afternoon, two other doctors, Gustavus Brown of Port Tobacco and Elisha Cullen Dick of Alexandria, arrived. The three conferred. Craik and Brown agreed on a diagnosis of quinsy (acute tonsillitis) and a course of treatment that included more bleedings and blisters, and purges with laxatives. But Dr. Dick, a thirty-seven-year-old graduate of the University of Edinburgh School of Medicine (Craik's alma mater), disagreed. Washington was suffering from "a violent inflammation of the membranes of the throat, which it had almost closed, and which, if not immediately arrested, would result in death." He urged a radical new procedure he had learned in Scotland for such cases—a tracheotomy below the infection to allow Washington to breathe. But Craik and Brown, the two senior men, would not agree.

At least, Dick pleaded, do not bleed him again. "He needs all his strength—bleeding will diminish it." But Craik and Brown ignored the younger man. They asked Washington's consent to bleed him a fourth time. This time "the blood ran very slowly." At about four, Washington rallied briefly and was able to swallow. Craik took the opportunity to give him calomel and other purges. At about half past four he asked Lear "to ask Mrs. Washington to come to his bedside." He asked her to go down to his office and get his two wills. He instructed her to burn the old one. Martha threw it into the fire. Then she took the other and put it into her closet.

Washington had convinced himself early in the day that he was going to die and he had deferred to the advice of Dr. Craik, the senior physician present, his companion in the French and Indian War and on frontier voyages of exploration. He refused the radical advice of a younger man. As the evening approached, Washington gave Lear his hand and whispered, "I find I am going. My breath cannot continue long." He gave Lear instructions to arrange all his military papers and accounts. Lear agreed. Then Washington, smiling, said that death "is the debt which we must all pay," and that he "looked on the event with perfect resignation." A little later, when Dr. Craik came in again, Washington whispered, "Doctor, I die hard, but I am not afraid to go. My breath cannot last long."

When the other doctors came and asked Washington to sit up, he asked to "be permitted to die without further interruptions." A stoic all his life, he did not now complain of his undoubtedly acute pain. Summoning all his strength, he told Lear, "I am just going. Have me decently buried and do not let my body be put into the vault in less than three days after I am dead." Too choked to speak, Lear nodded; Craik sat by the fire bowed in grief.

"Do you understand?" Washington rasped.

"Yes, sir."

"'Tis well." Those were Washington's last words. Five hours later, at ten on the night of December 14, 1799, with Martha at his side, George Washington died without uttering another word.[9]

KEY TO ABBREVIATIONS IN
NOTES AND BIBLIOGRAPHY

AA = Abigail Adams
AH = *American Heritage* magazine
AHI = *American History Illustrated*
AH = Alexander Hamilton
AHR = *American Historical Review*
Am. Arch. = Force, ed., *American Archives*
BA = Benedict Arnold
BF = Bryan Fairfax
BHQP = *British Headquarters Papers,* WLCL
DGW = *Diaries of George Washington*
DH = Humphreys, *Life of General Washington*
DM = Dartmouth Manuscripts
FCS = Frances Calvert Custis Stewart
GW = George Washington
GAW = George Augustine Washington
GM = George Mason
HC = Henry Clinton
HG = Horatio Gates
HGP = Horatio Gates Papers, NYHS
JA = John Adams
JAW = John Augustine Washington
JB = Jonathan Boucher
JC = Jack Custis
JCC = *Journals of the Continental Congress*
JHBV = *Journal of the House of Burgesses of Virginia*
JM = James Madison
JR = Joseph Reed
JSH = *Journal of Social History*
L&B = Lipscomb & Bergh, eds., *Writings of Thomas Jefferson*
LDC = Smith, *Letters of Delegates to Congress*
LW = Lund Washington
MBW = Mary Ball Washington
MHS = Massachusetts Historical Society

MOW = Mercy Otis Warren
MVLA = Mount Vernon Ladies Association
MW = Martha Washington
NEQ = *New England Quarterly*
NYHS = New-York Historical Society
NYHSQ = *New-York Historical Society Quarterly*
PA = Hazard, ed. *Pennsylvania Archives*
PAAS = *Proceedings of the American Antiquarian Society*
PAH = Hamilton, *Papers of Alexander Hamilton*
PBF = Labaree, ed., *Papers of Benjamin Franklin*
PGW = Abbot, ed., *Papers of George Washington*
PJM = Madison, *Papers of James Madison*
PMHB = *Pennsylvania Magazine of History and Biography*
PS = Philip Schuyler
PSA = Peggy Shippen Arnold
PTJ = Jefferson, *Papers of Thomas Jefferson*
PUL = Princeton University Library
RD = Robert Dinwiddie
RV = Van Schreeven, ed., *Revolutionary Virginia*
SF = Sally Fairfax
TJ = Thomas Jefferson
TL = Tobias Lear
VC = *Virginia Cavalcade*
VMHB = *Virginia Magazine of History and Biography*
WLCL = William L. Clements Library, University of Michigan
WMQ = *William & Mary Quarterly*
WW = Fitzpatrick, ed., *Writings of George Washington*

NOTES

Preceding the numbered notes in each chapter are background subjects, each with sources that were found especially valuable and pertinent. Full particulars of each work together with other readings carefully considered are listed in the bibliography on page 517.

INTRODUCTION

Triumphal Entry into New York City: *WW*, 27:255–59; Freeman, 5:451–68; Flexner, 2:511–28; Wertenbaker, 266–84.

1. *New Jersey Gazette*, Apr. 30, 1783, 3; *Massachusetts Spy*, May 29, 1783, 3; *Pennsylvania Gazette*, July 16, 1783, 2; *Maryland Journal*, May 3, 1783, 2; *Connecticut Journal*, May 3, 1783, 3; *Gazette of the State of South Carolina*, Dec. 18, 1783, 3; *New Hampshire Gazette*, Dec. 27, 1783, 2.
2. Irving, 4:440.

One. "A PROMPT AND LITERAL OBEDIENCE"

GW's English Ancestry: Quitt; Walne; DH; Waters; Longden; Pape; Hoppin; G. S. H. Lee Washington, "Washingtons of Sulgrave" and "Amphyllis Washington."
Virginia Forebears: Freeman, 1:15–47; Flexner, 1:9–17; Thomas; Ferling, *First of*

Men, 1–3; Weiner, "Washington and His Mother"; Glenn.

1. Fitzpatrick, *GW Himself*, 17.
2. DH, 5.
3. Quitt, 172.
4. Waters.
5. Carson, 41–42.
6. Morison, 21.
7. Truman, 138.
8. Freeman, 1:42.
9. Conkling, 44–45.
10. McBarron, 85.
11. Quoted in Freeman, 1:118–19.

Two. "TAKE ALL ADMONITIONS THANKFULLY"

Childhood of George Washington: *PGW*, Col. ser. 1:1–8; Freeman, 1:31–72; Flexner, 1:1–17; Ferling, *First of Men*, 1–6; Fitzpatrick, *GW Himself*, 3–38; Knollenberg, *GW: The Virginia Period*, 3–5; Morison; Alden, *GW*, 1–12; Thomas, 4–6; Weiner, "Washington and His Mother," 44–47; Glenn; Carson; McBarron; Morton; Wertenbaker; Wall, "Notes on the Early History of Mount Vernon."

1. DH, 5–6.
2. Fitzpatrick, *GW Himself*, 22.
3. Ibid., 30.
4. Lawrence Washington of Chotank, quoted in Conkling, 22.

5. DH, 7–8.

6. GM to GW, June 12, 1756, *PGW,* Col. ser., 3:202–3. GW's schoolmate was David Piper. They attended school at the Lower Church of Washington Parish.

7. Fitzpatrick, 25.

8. DH, 7.

9. Ibid.

10. Wm. Fairfax to Lawrence Washington, Sept. 9, 1746, quoted in Freeman, 1:193.

11. *Virginia Gazette,* Jan. 19, 1745.

12. Robert Jackson to Lawrence Washington, Sept. 18, 1746, quoted in Freeman, 1:195.

13. Freeman, 1:198–99.

Three. "WE WENT THROUGH MOST BEAUTIFUL GROVES"

Education of GW: *PGW,* Col. ser. 1:1–5; Flexner, 1:18–45; Freeman, 1:73–258; Ferling, *First of Men,* 6–17; Knollenberg, *GW: The Virginia Period,* 5–16; Addison, *Cato: A Tragedy;* Addison, *The Spectator,* vols. 1 and 2; Rhodehamel, ed., "Rules of Civility and Decent Behavior"; Wall, "Notes on the Early History of Mount Vernon"; Seneca.

GW as Surveyor: Phillips; *DGW,* 1:1–210; Andrist, 13–28.

1. *WW,* 3:447.

2. Addison, *Spectator,* 1:8.

3. Ibid., 10.

4. Ibid., 11.

5. Ibid.

6. Humphreys, 6.

7. Addison, *Cato: A Tragedy,* 1.

8. Ibid., 11.

9. Ibid., 10.

10. Ibid., 50.

11. Seneca, 268–69.

12. Ibid., 310–11.

13. Ibid., 100.

14. Ibid., 9.

15. Ibid., 269.

16. W. Leybourn, *The Compleat Surveyor,* in *PGW,* Col. ser., 1:3.

17. *DGW,* 1:6.

18. Ibid., 7–8.

19. Ibid., 9.

20. Ibid., 9–10.

21. Ibid., 13.

22. Ibid., 15.

23. Ibid., 18.

24. Ibid.

25. Ibid., 19.

26. Ibid.

27. Ibid.

28. Ibid., 23.

29. Quoted in Flexner, 1:40.

30. GW to SF, Sept. 12, 1785, *PGW,* Confed. ser., 3:221–22.

31. GW to Richard [?] [Nov. 1749], *PGW,* Col. ser., 1:43–44.

32. To Robin [?], [1749–1750], ibid., 40–41.

33. Ibid., 47.

34. Ibid., 46–47.

35. *DGW,* 1:45–46.

36. Ibid., 58.

37. Ibid., 59–66.

38. *DGW,* 1:21.

39. Freeman, 1:250–51.

40. Ibid., 250–53.

41. Ibid., 253.

42. Ibid., 255.

43. GW to Wm. Fauntleroy, May 20, 1752, *PGW,* Col. ser., 1:49–50.

44. Freeman, 1:263.

45. Ibid., 265.

Four. "I PUT MYSELF INTO INDIAN DRESS"

Mission to Fort LeBouef: *DGW,* 1:118–61; T. A. Lewis, 3–119; *PGW,* 1:1–179; Freeman, 1:259–376; Ferling, *First of Men,* 17–27; Flexner, 1:59–77; Draper, 72–161; Knollenberg, *GW: The Virginia Period,* 17–25; Hunter; Abernethy, 1–10; Parkman; Leach, 328–31; Ambler.

1. Quoted in Draper, 82.

2. Quoted in W. S. Randall, *A Little Revenge,* 56–57.

3. Leach, 327.

4. T. A. Lewis, 42.

5. Ibid., 43.

6. *DGW,* 1:6.

7. Ibid., 148.

8. Ibid., 149–51.

9. Ibid., 155–56.

10. Ibid., 158.

Five. "I HEARD BULLETS WHISTLE"

The Jumonville Affair: *DGW,* 1:162–73; *PGW,* Col. ser., 1:107–75; T. A. Lewis, 120–52; Ferling, *First of Men,* 26–27; Leach, 331–36; Leduc; Pound, 157–61; Cleland, 79–90; W. Johnson, 1:409; E. P. Hamilton, 147–48.

Fort Necessity: Harrington; Freeman, 1:377–445; DH, 10–13; Ferling, *First of Men*, 27–31; T. A. Lewis, 153–57; Leach, 337–50.

1. *DGW*, 1:155–58.
2. Freeman, 1:327.
3. *PGW*, Col. ser., 1:70–71; Freeman, 1:336.
4. RD to GW, Mar. 15, 1754, *PGW*, Col. ser., 1:75–76.
5. GW to RD, Mar. 20, 1754, *PGW*, Col. ser., 1:78.
6. Ibid., 65.
7. Quoted in T.A. Lewis, 333.
8. GW to Horatio Sharpe, Apr. 24, 1754, *PGW*, Col. ser., 1:85–86.
9. GW to Half King, Apr. 25, 1754, *PGW*, Col. ser., 1:88–89.
10. GW to Sharpe, Apr. 24, 1754, *PGW*, Col. ser., 1:85.
11. GW to RD, May 18, 1754, *PGW*, Col. ser., 1:99.
12. GW to RD, May 29, 1754, *PGW*, Col. ser., 1:110.
13. Ibid., 110–11.
14. Ibid., 112.
15. *DGW*, 1:194–95.
16. GW to RD, May 29, 1754, *PGW*, Col. ser., 1:116.
17. GW to JAW, *PGW*, Col. ser., 1:118.
18. GW to RD, June 10, 1754, *PGW*, Col. ser., 1:134.
19. RD to GW, May 25 and June 4, 1754, *PGW*, Col. ser., 1:102–4; GW to RD, May 29, 1754, *PGW*, Col. ser., 1:116–17.
20. *DGW*, 1:203.
21. *PGW*, Col. ser., 1:159–61.
22. DH, 12–13.
23. *PGW*, Col. ser., 1:165–67.
24. T. A. Lewis, 342.
25. Ibid.
26. GW to RD, Aug. 20, 1754, *PGW*, Col. ser., 1:189–91; GW to James Innes, Aug. 12, 1754, *PGW*, Col. ser., 1:189.
27. T. A. Lewis, 349.
28. Ibid., 349.
29. *DGW*, 1:172.
30. Freeman, 1:413.
31. T. A. Lewis, 349.
32. Ibid., 349 n. 75.

Six. "TO OBEY THE CALL OF HONOR"

Braddock Expedition: *PGW*, Col. ser., 1:232–364; Leach, 351–69; T. A. Lewis, 158–93; Kopperman; Cleland, 119–50; E. P. Hamilton, 151–59; DH, 10–18; Alden, *General Gage in America*, 121–31; Fitzpatrick, *GW Himself*, 74–83; Pargellis, "Braddock's Defeat"; Freeman, 2:64–102; Flexner, 1:119–31; Ferling, *First of Men*, 32–40.

1. See GW to Wm. Fairfax, Aug. 11, 1754, *PGW*, Col. ser., 1:183–87.
2. T. A. Lewis, 162; GW to Col. Wm. Fitzhugh, Nov. 15, 1754, *PGW*, Col. ser., 1:225–26.
3. GW to Robert Orme, Mar. 15, 1755, *PGW*, Col. ser., 1:242–45.
4. Orme to GW, Mar. 2, 1755, *PGW*, Col. ser., 1:241.
5. GW to Orme, Mar. 15, 1755, *PGW*, Col. ser., 1:244.
6. Orme to GW, Apr. 3, 1755, *PGW*, Col. ser., 1:249.
7. GW to Orme, Apr. 2, 1755, *PGW*, Col. ser., 1:246.
8. DH, 19.
9. John Carlyle to George Carlyle, Aug. 15, 1755, *VMHB* 97 (1989) 4:209.
10. *ABF*, 215.
11. GW to JAW, May 6, 1755, *PGW*, Col. ser., 1:266–67; GW to MBW, May 6, 1755, *PGW*, Col. ser., 1:268–69.
12. GW to JAW, May 14, 1755, *PGW*, Col. ser., 1:278.
13. GW to MBW, June 7, 1755, *PGW*, Col. ser., 1:304.
14. Sarah Carlyle to GW, June 17, 1754, *PGW*, Col. ser., 1:145.
15. GW to SF, Apr. 30, 1755, *PGW*, Col. ser., 1:261.
16. GW to JAW, May 14, 1755, *PGW*, Col. ser., 1:277; GW to SF, May 14, 1755, *PGW*, Col. ser., 1:276–77.
17. GW Memorandum, May 15–30, 1755, *PGW*, Col. ser., 1:282–83; GW to JAW, May 28, 1755, *PGW*, Col. ser., 1:289–92.
18. GW to John Carlyle, June 7, 1755, *PGW*, Col. ser., 1:306; GW to Sarah Carlyle, June 7, 1755, *PGW*, Col. ser., 1:307; GW to SF, June 7, 1755, *PGW*, Col. ser., 1:308–9.

Seven. "I HAD FOUR BULLETS THROUGH MY COAT"

Disgruntled Officer: *PGW*, Col. ser., vols. 2 and 3; Freeman, 2:103–68; Flexner, 1:132–75; T. A. Lewis, 194–240; Ferling, *First of Men*, 40–49; Leach, 369–73; Pargellis, *Lord Loudoun in North America*, 218–27; Fitzpatrick, *GW Himself*, 82–104.

1. T. A. Lewis, 357.
2. GW to John Carlyle, May 14, 1755, *PGW,* Col. ser., 1:274.
3. GW to Wm. Fairfax, June 7, 1755, *PGW,* Col. ser., 1:298–99.
4. Freeman, 2:57.
5. DH, 14.
6. GW to Wm. Fairfax, June 7, 1755, *PGW,* Col. ser., 1:298–300.
7. DH, 15–16.
8. GW to JAW, June 28–July 2, 1755, *PGW,* Col. ser., 1:319–24.
9. GW to Orme, June 30, 1755, *PGW,* Col. ser., 1:329; GW to JAW, *PGW,* Col. ser., 1:319–24.
10. GW to MBW, July 18, 1755, *PGW,* Col. ser., 1:336; DH, 5–6.
11. GW to RD, July 18, 1755, *PGW,* Col. ser., 1:339.
12. GW to MBW, July 18, 1755, *PGW,* Col. ser., 1:336.
13. Freeman, 2:79.
14. DH, 16–18.
15. Orme, quoted in *ABF,* 226.

Eight. "OBSERVE THE STRICTEST DISCIPLINE"

Frontier Commander: *PGW,* Col. ser., vols. 5 and 6; Freeman, 2:191–275; T. A. Lewis, 215–240; Ferling, *First of Men,* 46–51.

1. GW to MBW, July 18, 1755, *PGW,* Col. ser., 1:336–37.
2. GW to Augustine Washington, Aug. 2, 1755, *PGW,* Col. ser., 1:352, 354–55.
3. GW to MBW, Aug. 14, 1755, *PGW,* Col. ser., 1:359–60.
4. Joseph Ball to GW, Sept. 5, 1755, *PGW,* Col. ser., 2:15–16.
5. GW to Warner Lewis, Aug. 14, 1755, *PGW,* Col. ser., 1:360–63; GW to RD, Oct. 24, 1757, *PGW,* Col. ser., 2:18 n. 2.
6. "Instructions," Aug. 14, 1755, *PGW,* Col. ser., 2:4–6.
7. GW to Adam Stephen, Nov. 18, 1755, *PGW,* Col. ser., 2:171–73; GW to Peter Hog, Jan. 10, 1756, *PGW,* Col. ser., 2:272.
8. Christopher Gist to GW, Oct. 14, 1756, *PGW,* Col. ser., 1:114–15.
9. GW to RD, quoted in T. A. Lewis, 198.
10. Adam Stephen to GW, Oct. 4, 1755, *PGW,* Col. ser., 2:72–73.
11. GW, "Advertisement," Oct. 13, 1755, *PGW,* Col. ser., 2:109–10.
12. RD to GW, Sept. 17, 1755, *PGW,* Col. ser., 2:43; Lewis, 409 n. 40.
13. *PBF,* 6:219.

14. *Boston Gazette,* Feb. 27, 1756.
15. Freeman, 2:165 n. 70.
16. GW to RD, Apr. 7, 1756, *PGW,* Col. ser., 2:332–35.
17. GW to Robert Hunter Morris, Apr. 9, 1756, *PGW,* Col. ser., 2:345–46.
18. GW to John Robinson, Apr. 7, 1756, *PGW,* Col. ser., 2:337–39.
19. GW to RD, Dec. 5, 1755, *PGW,* Col. ser., 2:200–201; RD to GW, Apr. 8, 1756, *PGW,* Col. ser., 2:343–44.
20. GW to RD, Nov. 24, 1756, *PGW,* Col. ser., 4:29–32.
21. Ibid.
22. John Robinson to GW, Nov. 16, 1756, *PGW,* Col. ser., 4:28–29.
23. GW to Robinson, Dec. 19, 1756, *PGW,* Col. ser., 4:68.
24. RD to GW, Dec. 27, 1756, *PGW,* Col. ser., 4:70–71.
25. GW to Lord Loudoun, Jan. 10, 1757, *PGW,* Col. ser., 4:79–90.
26. Ibid.
27. RD to GW, Feb. 2, 1757, *PGW,* Col. ser., 4:107.
28. RD to GW, Oct. 19, 1757, *PGW,* Col. Ser., 5:21.
29. Robert Stewart to RD, Nov. 9, 1757, *PGW,* Col. ser., 5:46–47.
30. Ibid.
31. GW to Richard Washington, Apr. 15, 1757, *PGW,* Col. ser., 3:13.

Nine. "THE OBJECT OF MY LOVE"

Sally Fairfax: *PGW,* Col. ser., vols. 5 and 6; Flexner, 1:185–205; Fitzpatrick, *GW Himself,* 110–14.
Martha Dandridge Washington: Flexner, 1:188–96, 227–48; Freeman, 2:276–302; Fitzpatrick, *GW Himself,* 119–23; Engle, 209–35.
Forbes Expedition: Freeman, 2:303–67; Flexner, 1:206–223; Leach, 415–44; T. A. Lewis, 241–74.

1. GW to RD, Oct. 5, 1757, *PGW,* Col. ser., 5:3.
2. GW to RD, Oct. 24, 1757, *PGW,* Col. ser., 5:25–26.
3. Robert Stewart to RD, Nov. 9, 1757, *PGW,* Col. ser., 5:46.
4. Ibid.
5. Ibid.
6. GW to SF, Nov. 15, 1757, *PGW,* Col. ser., 5:56.
7. Ibid.
8. GW to Thomas Knox, Dec. 26, 1757, *PGW,* Col. ser., 5:72–73.

9. GM to GW, Jan. 4, 1758, *PGW,* Col. ser., 5:77.

10. GW to John Stanwyx, Mar. 4, 1758, *PGW,* Col. ser., 5:100–102.

11. GW to Richard Washington, Jan. 8, 1758, *PGW,* Col. ser., 5:80.

12. GW to Thomas Knox, Jan., 1758, *PGW,* Col. ser., 5:88; GW to SF, Feb. 13, 1758, *PGW,* Col. ser., 5:93.

13. GW to John Stanwyx, Mar. 4, 1758, *PGW,* Col. ser., 5:102.

14. Ibid.

15. Daniel Parke and George W. P. Custis, *Recollections,* quoted in Flexner, 1:191.

16. Ibid., 191–92.

17. Ibid., 21.

18. AA, "New Letter," in *PAAS* 40 (1947), 125.

19. MW to Nancy Bassett, Aug. 28, 1762, quoted in Knollenberg, *GW: The Virginia Period,* 173 n. 6.

20. Ibid., 173 n. 7.

21. Freeman, 2:301–2.

22. G. W. Fairfax to GW, July 25, 1758, *PGW,* Col. ser., 5:328.

23. Ibid., Sept. 1, 1758.

24. GW to SF, Sept. 12, 1758, *PGW,* Col. ser., 10–12.

25. Ibid.

26. GW to John Stanwyx, Apr. 10, 1758, *PGW,* Col. ser., 5:117.

27. GW to John Forbes, Apr. 23, 1758, *PGW,* Col. ser., 5:138–39.

28. George Mercer to GW, Nov. 2, 1757, *PGW,* Col. ser., 5:40–42.

29. Freeman, 1:257.

30. Ibid., 318.

31. Freeman, 2:319–20.

32. Ibid., 322.

33. Ibid., 324.

34. Ibid., 335.

35. John Armstrong to Richard Peters, Oct. 3, 1758, *PA,* 3:552.

36. DH, 21–22.

37. Ibid.

38. Ibid.

39. Quoted in T. A. Lewis, 147.

40. "Address from the Officers of the Virginia Regiment," Dec. 31, 1758, *PGW,* Col. ser., 6:178–81.

41. "GW to Officers of the Virginia Regiment," Jan. 10, 1759, *PGW,* Col. ser., 6:186–87.

42. Ibid., 187 n. 3.

43. Freeman, 3:6.

44. *WW,* 29:313–24; Flexner, *GW,* 1:250–51.

45. "Resolution of the House of Burgesses," Feb. 26, 1759, *PGW,* Col. ser., 6:192.

46. "Account of Items in the Estate Used by Martha Custis," 1759, *PGW,* Col. ser., 6:232–35.

47. GW to John Alton, Apr. 5, 1759, *PGW,* Col. ser., 6:35.

Ten. "NO LAW CAN COMPEL US"

GW, Tobacco Planter: *PGW,* Col. ser., vols. 6–9; *DGW,* vols. 1 and 2; Freeman, vol. 3; Flexner, 1:227–88; Ferling, *First of Men,* 61–85; *RV,* vols. 1–5; Gray; Kulikoff; Price, "The Rise of Glasgow in the Chesapeake Tobacco Trade," "Economic Function and the Growth of American Port Towns"; Rosenblatt; Horrell and Oram, "Marble colour'd folio Book"; Craven; Soltow; Ragsdale, "GW, the Tobacco Trade and Economic Opportunity in Prerevolutionary Virginia;" Bergstrom; Breen, Wall, "Housing and Family Life of the Mount Vernon Negro."

Life at Mount Vernon: *PGW,* 6–8; Wall, "Notes on the Early History of Mount Vernon"; Wilstach, *Mount Vernon;* Wall, *Mount Vernon;* Pogue; Freeman, 3:78–81; J. S. Britt, "Lessons for Martha's Children"; Bourne; Carroll and Meacham; Griffin; P. L. Ford.

Stamp Act Crisis in Virginia: *RV,* 1:1–26; E. S. and H. M. Morgan, *The Stamp Act Crisis,* 53, 160; W. S. Randall, *A Little Revenge,* 195–200; Griffith, 34–40, 156–48; Miller, 111–64; Maier; Henriques.

GW's Land Dealings: Ambler; Abernethy; Philbrick; Sosin; W. S. Randall, *A Little Revenge,* Chapter 9; Freeman, vol. 3; Flexner, 1:288–310; Ferling, *First of Men,* 61–85; Sturdevant; DeVorsey.

GW's Western Lands: *PGW,* Col. ser., vols. 7–9; Nordham, *GW and Money;* Ferling; Freeman, vols. 2 and 3; Flexner, vol. 1; "Washington and the Potomac," *AHR,* 28 (1923), 497–519, 705–722; Carter, "Documents Relating to the Mississippi Land Company"; Ambler.

1. GM to GW, Dec. 23, 1765, *PGW,* Col. ser., 7:424–25.

2. GW to Robert Cary & Co., Sept. 20, 1765, *PGW,* Col. ser., 7:400–401.

3. Ibid., 401.

4. Ibid., 402.

5. *PGW,* Col. ser., 7:343–50.

6. GW to R. Washington, Dec. 6, 1755, *PGW,* Col. ser., 2:207.

7. GW to Cary, May 1, 1759, *PGW,* Col. ser., 6:315.

8. GW, "Advertisement for Runaway Slaves," Aug. 11, 1761, *PGW*, Col. ser., 7:65–68.

9. GW to Cary, Apr. 3, 1761, *PGW*, Col. ser., 7:34; GW to Cary, May 28, 1762, *PGW*, Col. ser., 7:136.

10. Wilstach, 91.

11. GW to Cary, Aug. 20, 1771, *PGW*, Col. ser., 8:369–71.

12. Freeman, 2:46.

13. GW to John Posey, June 24, 1767, *PGW*, Col. ser., 8:1–4.

14. GW to W. Crawford, Sept. 21, 1767, *PGW*, Col. ser., 8:29.

15. GW, "Articles of Association," June 3, 1763, *PGW*, Col. ser., 7:219–25; [GW], Mississippi Co. to Thomas Cummings, Sept. 26, 1763, in *AHR* 16 (1911):314; Illinois Historical Coll., vol. 10, 26.

16. GW to Wm. Crawford, Sept. 17, 1767, *PGW*, Col. ser., 8:279.

17. Robert Stewart to GW, Aug. 18, 1765, *PGW*, Col. ser., 7:388–91.

18. *RV*, 1:19.

19. Fauquier to Bd. of Trade, Nov. 3, 1765, *JHBV, 1761–1765*, lxviii–lxxi.

20. *DGW*, 1:210–22.

21. Quoted in Britt, "Lessons for Martha's Children," 172.

22. Ibid., 177–78.

23. Ibid., 181–82.

24. MW to Nancy Dandridge Bassett, Aug. 28, 1762, quoted in Knollenberg, *GW: The Virginia Period*, 173 n. 6.

25. MW to GW, Mar. 30, 1767, *PGW*, Col. ser., 7:495.

26. GW to Cary, quoted in Bourne, 35–36.

27. *DGW*, 2:68; *DGW*, 2:128.

28. Ibid., 174–77.

29. Quoted in Bourne, 36.

30. MW to Mrs. Shelbury, Aug. 10, 1767, *PGW*, Col. ser., 7:328–29; Haworth, 229.

31. GW to Cary, quoted in Bourne, 39.

32. GW to Jonathan Boucher, May 30, 1768, *PGW*, Col. ser., 8: 89–90.

33. July 31, 1768, *PGW*, Col. ser., 8:120–21.

34. Boucher to GW, Aug. 2, 1768, *PGW*, Col. ser., 8:122–23.

35. GW to Boucher, Sept. 4, 1768, *PGW*, Col. ser., 8:128–29; GW to Boucher, Jan. 29, 1769, *PGW*, Col. ser., 8:166.

36. GW to Boucher, Dec. 16, 1770, *PGW*, Col. ser., 8:411.

37. Boucher to GW, Dec. 18, 1770, *PGW*, Col. ser., 8:413–17.

38. GW to Boucher, Apr. 20, 1771, *PGW*, Col. ser., 8:448–49.

39. GW to Boucher, June 5, 1771, *PGW*, Col. ser., 8:476–78.

Eleven. "ARMS SHOULD BE THE LAST RESORT"

GW and the Association: *RV*, vol. 1; Selby; *PGW*, Col. ser., vols. 8 and 9; Freeman, vol. 3; Flexner, 1:309–23; Henriques.

GW's Business Ventures: Ambler; *PGW*, Col. ser., vols. 8 and 9; *DGW*, vols. 2 and 3; Nordham, *GW and Money;* Haworth; Wilstach, 122–66.

GW and the Potomac Canal: *AHR*, 33 (1923), 497–519, 705–20; *PGW*, Col. ser., vols. 8 and 9.

1. Benjamin Franklin to William Franklin, Sept. 12, 1766, *PBF*, 13:416.

2. *DGW*, 2:47.

3. Ibid., 51–52.

4. Benjamin Franklin to Cushing, June 10, 1771, *PBF*, 18:121–22.

5. GW to GM, Apr. 5, 1769, *PGW*, Col. ser., 8:177–81.

6. *JHBV, 1766–1769*, May 15, 1769, 1:69.

7. *RV*, May 16, 1769, 1:70.

8. Ibid., May 18, 1769, 1:75.

9. GW to Armstrong, Sept. 21, 1767, *PGW*, Col. ser., 8:33.

10. GW to Botetourt, Dec. 8, 1769, *PGW*, Col. ser., 8:272–75.

11. GW to RC, Aug. 20, 1770, *PGW*, Col. ser., 8:368–71.

12. GW to CW, Jan. 31, 1770, *PGW*, Col. ser., 300–303.

13. GW to Botetourt, Oct. 5, 1770, *PGW*, Col. ser., 8:388–90.

14. Ibid.

15. *DGW*, 2:281–82; Ambler, 141–47.

16. GW to W. Crawford, quoted in Ambler, 147.

17. Crawford to GW, Nov. 12, 1773, quoted in Ferling, *First of Men*, 73 n. 5.

18. GW to Charles Mynn Thruston, Mar. 12, 1773, *PGW*, Col. ser., 9:194–95.

19. GW to JB, June 5, 1771, *PGW*, Col. ser., 8:476.

20. JB to GW, Nov. 19, 1771, *PGW*, Col. ser., 8:548–49.

21. GW to JB, Dec. 24, 1772, *PGW*, Col. ser., 8:212–13.

22. GW to Benedict Calvert, Apr. 3, 1773, *PGW*, Col. ser., 9:209.

23. GW to Burwell Bassett, June 20, 1773, *PGW,* Col. ser., 9:243–44.

24. JC to GW, July 5, 1773, *PGW,* Col. ser., 9:264–66.

25. GW to Myles Cooper, Dec. 15, 1773, *PGW,* Col. ser., 9:406–7.

26. GW, quoted in Ambler, 147.

27. GW to G. Mercer, Nov. 7, 1771, *PGW,* Col. ser., 8:543.

28. William Crawford to GW, Mar. 15, 1772, *PGW,* Col. ser., 8:25–26.

Twelve. "THE CRISIS IS ARRIVED"

Onset of Revolution: *RV,* vol. 1; *DGW,* vol. 3; J. Adams, 2:15–17; Freeman, vol. 3; *PGW,* Vol. 10; P. H. Smith, *Letters of Delegates to Congress,* vol. 1; Flexner, 1:324–45; W. S. Randall, *Thomas Jefferson,* 169–220; Benedict *Arnold,* 96–106; R. Jones; Ferling, *First of Men,* 86–110.

1. *RV,* 1:87.

2. GW to BF, July 4, 1774, *PGW,* Col. ser., 10:212.

3. *RV,* 1:90.

4. *RV,* 1:95.

5. *Autobiography of Thomas Jefferson,* 9.

6. *RV,* 1:93.

7. *DGW,* 3:254, quoted in Ferling, *First of Men,* 99.

8. GW to GF, June 19, 1774, in *RV,* 1:193.

9. GW to BF, July 4, 1774, *PGW,* Col. ser., 10:109–10.

10. GW to JAW, July 11, 1774, *PGW,* Col. ser., 10:112.

11. *RV,* 1:131–32.

12. GW to BF, July 20, 1774, *PGW,* Col. ser., 10:128–31.

13. GW to BF, Aug. 24, 1774, *PGW,* Col. ser., 10:154–55.

14. *DGW,* 3:268.

15. Ibid., 272.

16. Ibid., 276.

17. Freeman, 3:399–400.

18. Quoted in Fitzpatrick, *GW Himself,* 102.

19. *RV,* 2:366.

20. Wm. Wirt, 141–42; *RV,* 2:369.

21. GW to JAW, Mar. 25, 1775, *PGW,* Col. ser., 10:308.

22. Hugh Mercer to GW, Apr. 27, 1775, quoted in Freeman, 3:410.

23. GW to JAW, Mar. 25, 1775, *PGW,* Col. ser., 10:308.

24. W. S. Randall, *Benedict Arnold,* 96–106.

25. *JCC,* 2:56; Freeman, 3:424.

26. Ibid.

27. Ibid., 3:427.

28. Quoted in R. F. Jones, 43.

29. *PGW,* Rev. War ser., 1:1.

30. GW to MW, June 18, 1775, *PGW,* Rev. War ser., 1:3–5.

31. GW to JC, June 19, 1775, *PGW,* Rev. War ser., 1:15.

32. JA to James Warren, June 20, 1775, *LDC,* 1:518.

Thirteen. "A NEW MODELLED ARMY"

Reorganizing the Army: Ward; Higginbotham, *War of American Independence;* Lesser; Commager and Morris; Middlekauff; P. S. Foner, *Blacks in the American Revolution;* Quarles; *PGW,* Rev. War ser., vols. 1 and 2.

Attack on Quebec: W. S. Randall, *Benedict Arnold,* 133–237; *PGW,* Rev. War ser., 1:455–62.

1. Quoted in W. S. Randall, *A Little Revenge,* 343.

2. *JCC,* 2:109–10.

3. GW, "General Orders," July 4, 1775, *PGW,* Rev. War ser., 1:54–55; Wm. Emerson to his wife, July 17, 1775, Commager and Morris, 153.

4. GW to R. H. Lee, Aug. 29, 1775, *PGW,* Rev. War ser., 1:372.

5. GW to Samuel Washington, July 20, 1775, *PGW,* Rev. War ser., 1:135.

6. AA to JA, July 16, 1775, Butterfield, *Adams Family Correspondence,* 1:246–47.

7. GW to R. H. Lee, July 10, 1775, *PGW,* Rev. War ser., 1:98–100.

8. Quoted in P. S. Foner, *Blacks in the American Revolution,* 42–44.

9. GW to LW, Aug. 20, 1775, *PGW,* Rev. War ser., 1:334–37.

10. LW to GW, Oct. 5, 1775, *PGW,* Rev. War ser., 2:116.

11. GW to JAW, Oct. 13, 1775, *PGW,* Rev. War ser., 2:160–62.

12. GW to Philip Schuyler, Aug. 20, 1775, *PGW,* Rev. War ser., 1:332.

13. Quoted in W. S. Randall, *Benedict Arnold,* 158.

14. Ibid., 161.

15. GW to BA, Sept. 14, 1775, mss., Copley Library.

16. R. F. Jones, 47.

17. Quoted in ibid., 48.

18. GW to Joseph Reed, Nov. 28, 1775, *PGW,* Rev. War ser., 2:449.

19. GW to president of Congress, Dec. 31, 1775, *PGW,* Rev. War ser., 2:623; MW to GW, Dec. 1775, mss., MHS.

20. Quoted in Freeman, 4:77.

21. Quoted in R. F. Jones, 47.

22. JA to AA, July 4, 1776, *LDC,* 4:321–22.

23. GW to JAW, March 31, 1776.

24. Ibid., May 31, 1776.

25. GW to Betty Bassett, June 4, 1776; JC to GW, June 9, 1776.

26. GW to B. Bassett, Aug. 20, 1776.

Fourteen. "A FINE FOX CHASE"

British Invasion of New York: Ward, 1:202–84; Bliven, *The Battle for Manhattan* and *Under the Guns*; Middlekauff, 333–62; Gruber; Mackesy.

Battle for New Jersey: Dwyer, *The Day Is Ours;* Freeman, 4:303–79; Callahan, *Henry Knox,* 78–98; Scharf and Westcott, vol. 1; Boldt and W. S. Randall, 203–44.

1. C. Lee to GW, Feb. 19, 1776, *PGW,* Rev. War ser., 3:339.

2. Lee to GW, Feb. 14, 1776, *PGW,* Rev. War ser., 3:310–11.

3. Ward, *War of the Revolution,* 1:225.

4. Quoted in ibid., 226.

5. *JCC,* 5:749.

6. Serle, 103.

7. Ward, 1:243.

8. GW to PS, Sept. 20, 1776, *PGW,* Rev. War ser., 6:357.

9. GW to LW, Oct. 6, 1776, *PGW,* Rev. War ser., 6:495.

10. Van Doren, *Secret History of the American Revolution,* 17.

11. GW to president of Congress, Dec. 1776, *WW,* 6:346.

12. C. Marshall, *Diary,* Dec. 3, 1776, quoted in Boldt and Randall, 226–27.

13. Ibid., 226.

14. I. Putnam to GW, Dec. 12, 1776, *WW,* 6:204–5.

15. GW to LW, Dec. 17, 1776, *WW,* 6:346–47.

16. W. Howe to G. Germain, Dec. 20, 1776, Colonial Office Papers 5/94.

17. Serle, 110.

18. J. Grant to J. G. Rall, Dec. 1776, Force, *Am. Arch.* 5:11, 1317.

19. Quoted in Dwyer, 213.

20. J. Wilkinson, quoted in Stryker, *TP,* 32.

21. T. Rodney to Caesar Rodney, Dec. 30, 1776, Commager, 514–15.

22. Ward, 1: 295.

23. Dwyer, 265.

24. J. Wilkinson, *Memoirs,* 1:131.

25. Dwyer, 293–94.

26. Ward, 1:305.

27. Ibid., 304.

28. Ibid., 310.

29. Quoted in Dwyer, 342.

30. Ibid., 347.

Fifteen. "WE'LL SEE KING GEORGE DAMNED FIRST"

The Battle for Philadelphia: Weiner, "Military Occupation of Philadelphia"; Jackson, *With the British Army in Philadelphia;* Boldt and W. S. Randall, 224–41; Weigley, *Philadelphia;* C. Marshall, *Extracts from a Diary During the Revolution;* W. B. Clark, et al., *Naval Documents of the American Revolution,* vol. 5; Freeman, 4:443–633; Ward, 1:334–83, 2:543–69; Balderston; Jackson, *The Pennsylvania Navy;* Drinker; W. C. Ford, ed., *Defences of Philadelphia in 1777;* McGuire; Serle; Simcoe; Wister, *Journal;* Reed; Scharf and Westcott, vol. 1; Gruber, 224–303; Higginbotham, 175–221; Middlekauff, 384–428; W. S. Randall and N. Nahra.

Destroying the Iroquois Nation: Commager and Morris, 1011–33; Flick, "New Sources on the Sullivan Campaign" and *The Sullivan-Clinton Campaign of 1779;* Campbell; *WW,* vol. 11; Fogg; Parker; McAdams; New York (State), *The Sullivan-Clinton Campaign of 1779;* Russell; Stone; Stanley; Chalmers; Swiggert; Graymont; A. H. Wright.

1. Adams, 2:264; Elias Boudinot to Elisha Boudinot, Sept. 23, 1777, quoted in Knollenberg, *Growth of the Revolution,* 195; Baron de Kalb to Comte de Broglie, Sept. 24, 1777, in Stevens, 8:755.

2. André, 49–50.

3. Quoted in Freeman, 3:500.

4. McGuire, 46.

5. Ibid., 57.

6. Quoted in W. S. Randall and N. Nahra, *American Lives,* 1:76.

7. Vicomte de Fleury, quoted in Morris and Commager, 633–35.

8. Quoted in Bourne, 75.

9. GW to R. H. Lee, Oct. 17, 1777, *WW,* 9:387–89.

10. GW to Lee, Jan. 2, 1777, *WW,* 10:176.

11. GW to T. Conway, Nov. 9, 1777, *WW,* 10:30.

12. Quoted in Plumb, 27.

13. James Lovell to HG, Nov. 27, 1777, mss., HGP, NYHS.

14. HG to GW, Dec. 8, 1777, HG Papers, NYHS, microfilm reel 6, no. 111.

15. Plumb, 26.

16. GW to president of Congress, Dec. 23, 1777, *WW*, 10:197.

17. GW to Congress, Feb. 1, 1778, *WW*, 10:414.

18. GW to John Sullivan, Mar. 6, 1779, *WW*, 14:201.

19. Quoted in Randall and Nahra, 2:38.

20. Ibid., 39.

21. Ibid.

22. Ibid., 40.

23. John Cadwalader to Nathanael Greene, Dec. 5, 1778, Charles Lee Papers, NYHS *Collections*, 6, no. 3 (1887–1891): 270–71.

24. Pa. Council to GW, Jan. 31, 1779, mss., Joseph Reed Papers, NYHS.

25. John Jay to George Clinton, Feb. 3, 1779, *LDC*, 12:17–18.

26. Quoted in Van Doren, *Secret History*, 189.

27. BA, quoted in *Pennsylvania Packet*, Feb. 9, 1779.

28. GW to Joseph Reed, Oct. 18, 1780, *WW*, 20:370.

29. Wm. Paca to Pa. Council, Mar. 4, 1779, *LDC*, 12:152.

30. Henry Laurens, Mar. 6, 1779, quoted in Flexner, 251–52.

31. *JCC*, 13:417.

32. JR to Congress, Apr. 24, 1779, *PA*, 8:349–50.

33. GW to BA, Apr. 25, 1779, Sparks, 6:518–19.

34. BA to GW, May 5, 1779, Sparks, 6:523.

35. Ibid.

Sixteen. "WHO CAN I TRUST NOW?"

Benedict Arnold's Treason: Van Doren, *Secret History; PAH*, vol. 2; W. S. Randall, *Benedict Arnold;* H. Clinton, 209–18; Wallace, *Traitorous Hero*, 215–51; Hatch, 169–252; L. B. Walker; Barbé-Marbois; *WW*, vols. 19 and 20; Davies, vol. 18; Willcox, *Portrait of a General;* Varick, *Varick's Court of Inquiry.*

1. GW, quoted in Winsor, 1:165.

2. GW to R. Livingston, June 29, 1780, *WW*, 19:91; GW to JAW, June 6, 1780, *WW*, 19:135–36; BA to PSA, Aug. 25, 1780, mss., Clinton Papers, WLCL.

3. GW to JR, Oct. 18, 1780, *WW*, 20:214.

4. Quoted in Wallace, *Traitorous Hero*, 221.

5. GW, General Orders, Aug. 3, 1780, *WW*, 19:313.

6. Varick in Varick, 158.

7. BA to Col. Timothy Pickering, Aug. 16, mss., de Coppet Coll., PUL.

8. *JCC*, 17:722–73.

9. GW to BA, Sept. 14, 1780, *WW*, 20:48.

10. BA to GW, Sept. 14, 1780, Sparks, *Correspondence*, 3:85–7.

11. BA to Nathanael Greene, quoted in Van Doren, 310.

12. BA to Col. Beverley Robinson, Sept. 18, 1780, Van Doren, *Secret History*, 483.

13. H. Clinton to Germain, Oct. 11, 1780, Van Doren, 483.

14. Ibid.

15. Col. John Jameson to BA, Sept. 24, 1780, Sparks, 7:530–31.

16. Quoted in Hatch, 246.

17. Varick, 190; Dann, 58.

18. L. B. Walker, 24: 415.

19. GW to JR, Oct. 18, 1780, *WW*, 20:214.

20. Quoted in Wallace, *Traitorous Hero*, 251.

21. Varick, 189–93.

22. BA to GW, Sept. 25, 1780, *PAH*, 2:465.

23. Leake, 264.

24. Joshua Hett Smith, *Narrative*, 52–53.

25. Lafayette to Luzerne, Oct. 12, 1780, *Revue de la Révolution*, 5:546; George Mathew, "Narrative," *Historical Magazine*, April 1857.

26. AH to John Laurens, Oct. 11, 1780, *PAH*, 2:461.

27. BA to HC, Sept. 26, 1780, Mss., Clinton Papers, WLCL.

28. André court-martial board to GW, Sept. 29, 1780, Boynton, 139.

29. HC to his sisters, Oct. 9, 1780, Mss., Clinton Papers, WLCL.

30. Lee, 2:165–66.

31. GW to Wm. Franklin, quoted in W. S. Randall, *A Little Revenge*, 448.

32. GW to president of Congress, ibid., 449.

33. GW to Lafayette, quoted in R. F. Jones, 72.

34. Ibid., 74.

35. GW, Mar. 12, 1783, *WW*, 124–26.

36. Quoted in Mackesy, 435–36.

37. G. Germain to d'Auberteuil, quoted in Hilliard d'Auberteuil 2:39; John Burgoyne, Aug. 23, 1776, mss., Stopford-Sackville Papers, WLCL.

Seventeen. "I HAVE HAD MY DAY"

Resignation to Congress: *WW,* 27:265–285; Flexner, 2:527–28; Freeman, 5:472–77; W. S. Randall, *Thomas Jefferson,* 358–59; *PTJ,* 6:402–19.

Washington in Retirement: *LDC,* 21:217–39; Freeman, 5:450–77; Flexner, 3:5–38; Idzerda and Crout, 5:200–38; *WW,* vol. 27; Ferling, *First of Men,* 323–46.

1. *WW,* 27:340, 317–18.
2. Ibid., 264.
3. Ibid., 277.
4. Ibid., 286.
5. Ibid., 340, 317–18.
6. *LDC,* 21:221, 232.
7. *WW,* 27:340, 317–18.
8. Ibid., 340.
9. Ibid., 457.
10. Ibid., 460.
11. Ibid., 317–18.
12. Ibid., 161–62.
13. Idzerda and Crout, 5:208.
14. Ibid., 237–38.
15. Ibid., 238.
16. Ibid., 237–38.
17. *PGW,* Confed. ser., 2:175.
18. Idzerda and Crout, 5:237–38.
19. Ibid., 238.
20. Lafayette to Madame Lafayette, ibid., 239–40.
21. GW to Wm. Crawford, Sept., 1784, *WW,* 27:346.
22. Freeman, 6:15.
23. *DGW,* 286–87; Freeman, 6:18–19.
24. *PGW,* Confed. ser., 2:176.

Eighteen. "TO TASTE THE FRUITS OF FREEDOM"

Potomac Waterway: *PGW,* Rev. War and Confed. ser. vols. 1–6; *WW* vols. 26 and 27; *PTJ,* vols. 6 and 7; C. Bacon-Foster, "Early Chapters in the Development of the Potomac Route to the West," Ph.D. diss.

Constitutional Reform: Bradley; Holcombe; Rossiter; Bowen; R. F. Jones, 77–85; *PGW,* Confed. ser., vol. 5.

1. GW to Christopher Colles, Jan. 25, 1783, *WW,* 26:56–57.
2. GW to Lafayette, Oct. 12, 1783, *WW,* 27:185–88; GW to Chastellux, Oct. 12, 1783, *WW,* 27:188–90.
3. TJ to JM, Feb. 20, 1784, *PTJ,* 6:544–51.

4. TJ to GW, Mar. 15, 1784, *PTJ,* 7:25–27.
5. GW to TJ, Mar. 29, 1784, *PTJ,* 7:28.
6. GW to T. Johnson, Oct. 15, 1784, *PGW,* Confed. ser., 2:86.
7. GW to George Plater, Oct. 25, 1784, *PGW,* Confed. ser., 2:106–9; GW to Jacob Read, Nov. 3, 1784, *PGW,* Confed. ser., 2:118–23.
8. GW to R. H. Lee, Dec. 14, 1784, *PGW,* Confed. ser., 2:181–83.
9. *Virginia Gazette,* Dec. 4, 1784; GW to JM, Nov. 28, 1784, *PGW,* Confed. ser., 2:155–57.
10. GW to GWF, Feb. 27, 1785, *PGW,* Confed. ser., 2:386–90.
11. GW to Robt. Morris, Feb. 1, 1785, *PGW,* Confed. ser., 2:309–15.
12. GW to Lafayette, July 25, 1785, *WW,* 28:207.
13. R. H. Lee to Wm. Short, June 13, 1785, quoted in Sturdevant, 221.
14. Quoted in Bourne, 100.
15. Ibid.
16. GW to TL, *PGW,* Confed. ser., 4:314; TL, mss., MHS.
17. GW to Robt. Morris, Feb. 1, 1785, *WW,* 28.55.
18. GW quoted in R. F. Jones, *GW,* 81.
19. Ibid., 82.
20. GW to GM, May 10, 1776, Rutland, ed., *Mason Papers,* 1:94.
21. GM to Geo. Mason, Jr., May 27, 1787, *Mason Papers,* 3:884.
22. GW to B. Lincoln, Oct. 26, 1788, quoted in Freeman, 6:153.
23. Ibid., 84.
24. Ibid., 85.
25. GW to Benjamin Lincoln, Oct. 26, 1788, *PGW,* Confed. ser., 70–73.
26. *DGW,* 5:312.
27. GW to George Steptoe Washington, Mar. 23, 1789, *PGW,* Confed. ser., 1:438–41.
28. GW to Benj. Harrison, quoted in F. Weiner, "Washington and His Mother."
29. GW to MBW, Feb. 15, 1787, *PGW,* Confed. ser., 5:33–36.
30. GW to Richard Conway, *PGW,* Confed. ser., 1:368.
31. GW to John Clements, *PGW,* Pres. ser., 2:123–24.
32. Benj. Harrison to GW, Feb. 26, 1789, *PGW,* Pres. ser., 1:345–46.
33. GW to H. Knox, Mar. 1, 1789, *PGW,* Pres. ser., 1:356–57.
34. GW to Thomas Green, Mar. 31, 1789, *PGW,* Pres. ser., 1:467–69.

35. GW to GAW, Mar. 31, 1789, *PGW*, Pres. ser., 1:472–73; see also GW to Dr. James Craik, quoted in Freeman, 6:144.

Nineteen. "I WALK ON UNTRODDEN GROUND"

Washington's First Term: *PGW*, Pres. ser., vols. 1–6; Freeman, vol. 6; R. N. Smith, 1–177; *PTJ*, vols. 19–25; *PJM*, vols. 4–11; R. F. Jones, 86–108; Bourne, 127–37; W. S. Randall, *Thomas Jefferson*, 489–529.

1. Quoted in *PGW*, Pres. ser., 2:108–10.
2. Annis Boudinot Stockton to GW, Mar. 13, 1789, *PGW*, Pres. ser., 1:392–93; GW to Stockton, Mar. 21, 1789, *PGW*, Pres. ser., 1:423.
3. GW, *PGW*, Pres. ser., 2:110.
4. *DGW*, 5:477.
5. *PGW*, Pres. ser., 2:155.
6. Ibid., 2:175.
7. Wm. Maclay, quoted in ibid., 2:155.
8. Robt. Lewis, diary, mss., Mount Vernon Library.
9. MW to FCS, June 8, 1789, quoted in Bourne, 129.
10. GW to JM, Mar. 30, 1784, *PGW*, Pres. ser., 1:464–65; Wm. Maclay, *Journal*, 162.
11. Lafayette to GW, Mar. 17, 1790, *PGW*, Pres. ser., 5:242.
12. MW to MOW, quoted in Bourne, 131.
13. MW to FCS, quoted in Bourne, 128.
14. AA, *New Letters*, 19.
15. Nelly Custis, quoted in ibid.
16. R. F. Jones, 89.
17. Ibid.
18. Ibid., 92.
19. GW to GAW, quoted in Bourne, 132.
20. AA, quoted in Freeman, 6:213–14.
21. George Clinton, quoted in R. F. Jones, 91.
22. TJ to GW, Dec. 15, 1789, *PTJ*, 16:34–35.
23. TJ, "Holy Cause of Freedom," Feb. 12, 1790, *PTJ*, 16:178–79.
24. TJ, *PTJ*, 16:653–54; Wm. Maclay, *Diary*; *PTJ*, 16:381.
25. GW quoted in R. F. Jones, 92.
26. TJ to Moustier, May 25, 1789, quoted in Jones, 93.
27. R. N. Smith, xv.
28. Wm. Maclay, *Journal*, 125.
29. Ibid., 125–28.
30. MW, quoted in R. N. Smith, xvii.
31. TJ, May 24, 1790, quoted in ibid., xxi.

32. TJ to GW, Sept. 9, 1792, L&B, 7:137.
33. GW, Dec. 21, 1790, Freeman, 6:276.
34. Bourne, 115.
35. GW to Lafayette, Aug. 11, 1790, *WW*, 31:88–92.
36. GW to Cabinet, ibid.
37. TJ, "Report to the President," Feb. 15, 1791, *PTJ*, 19:275–80.
38. AH, quoted in N. Cunningham, 166–67.
39. TJ, quoted in W. S. Randall, "TJ Takes a Vacation," 45.
40. Ibid.
41. Ibid.

Twenty. "A FIRE NOT TO BE QUENCHED"

GW's Second Term: McDonald; GW, *Journal of the Proceedings of the Presidency, 1793–1797*; De Conde; R. F. Jones, *GW*; R. N. Smith, 178–361; N. Cunningham.

1. Freeman, 6:308–9.
2. TL to David Humphreys, quoted in Bourne, 135.
3. Quoted in Bourne, 133.
4. GW to David Humphreys, quoted in R. F. Jones, 102.
5. AH, "Report of the President," Jan. 28, 1791, *PAH*, 7:570.
6. Quoted in Peterson, 422.
7. TJ, "Report to the President," Jan. 18, 1791, *PTJ*, 18:570.
8. TJ to Freneau, Feb. 28, 1791, *PTJ*, 19:35.
9. TJ to GW, Sept. 9, 1792, L&B, 7:145.
10. Ibid.
11. "An American," *Gazette of the U.S.*, Aug. 4, 1792, *PAH*, 12:159.
12. TJ, May 23, 1793, L&B, 1:274.
13. *PAH*, 12:125.
14. GW to TJ and AH, quoted in N. Cunningham, 172.
15. GW to TJ, Apr. 23, 1792, *WW*, 32:128–34; TJ, Apr. 6, 1792, L&B, 1:310.
16. TJ to GW, Sept. 9, 1792, L&B, 7:137–38.
17. JM to GW, June 20, 1792, *PJM*, 14:321.
18. TJ, quoted in Peterson, 468.
19. Quoted in Nordham, *GW*, 102.
20. Ibid., 103.
21. GW to LaLuzerne, April 1790, quoted in R. F. Jones, 110.
22. Quoted in Nordham, *GW*, 109.
23. Ibid.

24. TJ, quoted in R. F. Jones, 123.

25. Bemis, 19.

26. GW to Henry Walker, quoted in R. N. Smith, 172; B. F. Bache, *Remarks Occasioned by the Late Conduct of Mr. Washington, President of the United States*; GW quoted in R. N. Smith, 289; Freneau, *Jersey Chronicle*, quoted in R. N. Smith, 252; GW to Pickering, quoted in R. N. Smith, 266; GW to H. Lee, quoted in R. N. Smith, 229; JA to Abigail Adams, Mar. 25, 1796, Charles Francis Adams, 2:214.

27. R. F. Jones, 123.

28. JA to AA, Mar. 5, 1797, *Adams' Letters to His Wife*, 244.

Twenty-One. "MY GLASS IS ALMOST RUN"

1. GW to TL, Bourne, 198.

2. GW to SF, Bourne, 197.

3. GW to Eliza Powell, Bourne, 198.

4. Ibid.

5. Ibid., 199.

6. Quoted in J. E. Smith, 240–41.

7. GW, *Last Will and Testament, WW*, 37:275–305.

8. *DGW*, 6:253.

9. TL, *Letters and Recollections*, 129–41.

BIBLIOGRAPHY

Abbatt, Wilbur C. *New York in the American Revolution.* New York: Scribner's, 1929.

Abbot, W. W. "General Edward Braddock in Alexandria." *VMHB* 97, no. 4 (1989): 205–15.

Abernethy, Thomas P. *Western Lands and the American Revolution.* New York: Russell & Russell, 1937.

Adams, Abigail. *New Letters.* Ed. Stewart Mitchell. Boston: Houghton Mifflin, 1947.

Adams, Charles F. "Washington and Cavalry." In *Studies Military and Diplomatic, 1775–1865,* 59–108. New York: Macmillan, 1911.

Adams, John. *Diary and Autobiography.* Ed. L. H. Butterfield. 4 vols. Cambridge, Mass.: Belknap Press, 1961.

Adams, Randolph G. *Political Ideas of the American Revolution.* New York: Barnes & Noble, 1958.

Addison, Joseph. *The Spectator.* Ed. D. F. Bond. 5 vols. Oxford: Clarendon Press, 1965.

———. *Cato: A Tragedy.* 7th ed. London: Jacob Tonsan, 1713.

———. "Cato." In *Eighteenth Century Plays,* ed. Ricardo Quintana. New York: Random House, 1952.

Akers, Charles W. *Abigail Adams: An American Woman.* Boston: Little, Brown, 1980.

Albanese, Catherine. "Newness Transcending: Civil Religion and the American Revolution." *Southern Quarterly* 14, no. 4 (1976): 307–31.

Alberts, Robert C. "The Cantankerous Mr. Maclay." *AH,* Oct. 1974, 48–50, 84–89.

Alden, John R. *The American Revolution.* New York: Harper, 1954.

———. *General Charles Lee: Traitor or Patriot?* Baton Rouge, La.: Louisiana State Univ. Press, 1951.

———. *General Gage in America.* Baton Rouge, La.: Louisiana State Univ. Press, 1948.

———. *George Washington: A Biography.* Charlottesville, Va: Univ. Press of Virginia, 1976.

———. *Robert Dinwiddie: Servant of the Crown.* Charlottesville, Va.: Univ. Press of Virginia, 1973.

Allen, Ethan. "A Narrative of the Captivity of Colonel Ethan." In *America Rebels,* ed. Richard M. Dorson. New York: Pantheon, 1953.

Allen, Gardner W. *Naval History of the American Revolution.* 2 vols. Boston: Houghton, 1913.

Alvord, Clarence W. *The Mississippi Valley in British Politics.* 2 vols. Cleveland: World, 1917.

Ambler, Charles H. *George Washington and the West.* Chapel Hill, N.C.: Univ. of North Carolina Press, 1936.

Anburey, Thomas. *Travels through the Interior Parts of America.* 2 vols. London: Lane, 1789.

André, Major John. *Journal of Operations of the British Army, June 1777 to November 1778.* New York: Macmillan, 1904. Repr. 1930.

Andrews, William Loring. *New York as Washington Knew It after the Revolution.* New York: Scribner's, 1905.

Andrist, Robert K., ed. *George Washington: A Biography in His Own Words*. 2 vols. New York: Newsweek, 1972.

Applegate, Howard L. "Constitutions Like Iron: The Life of the American Revolutionary War Soldiers in the Middle Department, 1775–1783." Ph.D. diss., Syracuse University, 1966.

Armstrong, William H. "Red Jacket's Medal: An American Badge of Nobility." *Niagara Frontier* 21, no. 2 (1974): 26–36.

Arnold, Benedict. "Journal of His Expedition to Canada." In *March to Quebec*, ed. Kenneth Roberts. New York: Doubleday, 1938.

————. "Letters Written While on an Expedition across the State of Maine to Attack Quebec in 1775." *Maine State Historical Society Collection* 1 (1831): 341–87.

"Arnold's March to Quebec: 11th September to 14th November, 1775." *Canadian Defence Quarterly* 7 (1929–30): 63–77.

Asonevich, Walter J. "George Washington's Speeches and Addresses: Origins of an American Presidential Rhetoric." Ph.D. diss., Univ. of Delaware, 1987.

Aspinall, A. *The Later Correspondence of George III*. Cambridge: Cambridge Univ. Press, 1962.

Atkinson, C. T. "British Forces in North America, 1774–1781: Their Distribution and Strength." *Journal of the Society of Army Historical Research* 14–15 (1936–37): 136–46; 16 (1937): 3–23; 19 (1940): 163–66.

Atwood, Rodney. *The Hessians*. Cambridge: Cambridge Univ. Press, 1980.

Augur, Helen. *Secret War of Independence*. New York, 1955.

Axelrad, Joseph. *Patrick Henry: The Voice of Freedom*. Westport: Greenwood, 1947.

Bache, Benjamin Franklin. *Remarks Occasioned by the Late Conduct of Mr. Washington, President of the United States*. Philadelphia: Benjamin Franklin Bache, 1797. Redex Microprint 31, no. 759.

Bacon-Foster, Cora. *Early Chapters in the Development of the Potomac Route to the West*. Washington, D.C.: Columbia Historical Society, 1912.

Bailyn, Bernard. *Ideological Origins of the American Revolution*. Cambridge, Mass.: Harvard Univ. Press, 1967.

————. *The Ordeal of Thomas Hutchinson*. Cambridge, Mass.: Harvard Univ. Press, 1974.

Bakeless, John E. *Turncoats, Traitors and Heroes*. Philadelphia: Lippincott, 1960.

Balch, Thomas Willing. *The Pennsylvania Assemblies*. Philadelphia: n.p., 1916.

Balderston, Marion. "Lord Howe Clears the Delaware." *PMHB* 96 (1972): 326–46.

Banning, Lance. *The Second Fire of Liberty: James Madison and the Founding of the Federal Republic*. Ithaca: Cornell Univ. Press, 1995.

————. *The Jeffersonian Persuasion: Evolution of a Party Ideology*. Ithaca: Cornell Univ. Press, 1978.

————. "Jeffersonian Ideology Revisited: Liberal and Classical Ideas in the New American Republic." *WMQ*, 3rd ser., 43 (1986): 3–19.

Barbé-Marbois, François de. *Conspiracy of Arnold and Sir Henry Clinton*. Paris, 1816. Repr. New York, 1972.

Barck, Oscar T. *New York City during the War for Independence*. New York: Columbia Univ. Press, 1931.

Barker, Creighton. "A Case Report." *Yale Journal of Biology and Medicine* 9 (1936–1937): 185–87.

Beers, H. P. *The French in North America*. Baton Rouge, La.: Louisiana State Univ. Press, 1957.

Bemis, Samuel F. *Pinckney's Treaty: America's Advantage from Europe's Distress, 1783–1800*. New Haven: Yale Press, 1960.

Bergstrom, Peter V. "Markets and Merchants: Economic Diversification in Colonial Virginia, 1700–1775." Ph.D. diss., Univ. of New Hampshire, 1980.

Bickford, Charlene B., and Helen E. Veit. *Documentary History of the First Federal Congress, 1789–1791*. Vols. 4–6. Reviewed *PMHB* 117 (1993): 363–64.

Bill, Alfred Hoyt. *The Campaign of Princeton, 1776–1777*. Princeton: Princeton Univ. Press, 1948.

————. *A House Called Morven*. Princeton: Princeton Univ. Press, 1954.

————. *Valley Forge*. New York: Harper, 1952.

Billias, George Allan. *General John Glover and His Marblehead Mariners*. New York: Holt, 1960.

————, ed. *George Washington's Opponents.* New York: Morrow, 1969.

————, ed. *George Washington's Generals.* New York: Morrow, 1964.

Bishop, Morris. "The End of the Iroquois." *AH* 20 (1969): 28–33, 77–81.

Blake, J. B. "The Inoculation Controversy in Boston." *NEQ* 25 (1952): 489–506.

Blanton, Wyndham B. *Medicine in Virginia in the Eighteenth Century.* Richmond: Garrett and Massie, 1931.

Bliven, Bruce. *Battle for Manhattan.* New York: Henry Holt, 1956.

————. *Under the Guns: New York, 1775–1776.* New York: Harper & Row, 1972.

Blumenthal, Walter H. *Women Camp Followers of the American Revolution.* Philadelphia: Mac Manus, 1952.

Bodle, Wayne Kenneth. "The Vortex of Small Fortunes: The Continental Army at Valley Forge." Ph.D. diss., Columbia Univ., 1990.

Boldt, David R., and Willard Sterne Randall, eds. *The Founding City.* Philadelphia: Inquirer/Chilton Books, 1976.

Boller, Paul F. *GW and Religion.* Dallas: Southern Methodist Univ. Press, 1963.

————. "Washington and Civilian Supremacy." *Southwest Review* 39, no. 4 (1954): 9–23.

Bolles, Albert S. *The Financial History of the U.S. from 1774 to 1789.* 4th ed. New York: D. Appleton & Co., 1896.

Bolton, C. K. *Private Soldier under Washington.* New York: C. Scribners, 1902.

Bonsal, Stephen. *When the French Were Here.* New York: Doubleday, 1945.

Bowler, R. Arthur. *Logistics and the Failure of the British Army in America, 1775–1783.* Princeton: Princeton Univ. Press, 1975.

Boucher, Jonathan. *Reminiscences of an American Loyalist, 1738–1789.* Boston: Riverside Press, 1925.

————. *A View of the Causes and Consequences of the American Revolution in Thirteen Discourses.* New York: Atheneum, 1967.

Bourne, Miriam Anne. *First Family: George Washington and His Intimate Relations.* New York: Norton, 1982.

Bowen, Catherine Drinker. *Miracle at Philadelphia: The Story of the Constitutional Convention.* Boston: Atlantic–Little, Brown, 1967.

Bowling, Kenneth P. *Politics in the First Congress, 1789–1791.* New York: Garland, 1990.

————. "Dinner at Jefferson's: A Note on Jacob E. Cooke's 'The Compromise of 1790.'" *WMQ,* 3d ser., 28 (1971): 607–28.

Bowman, Allen. *The Morale of the American Revolutionary Army.* Intro. by Arthur Pope. Washington, D.C.: American Council on Public Affairs, 1943, repr. Kennikat Press, 1964.

Bowman, Larry G. *Captive Americans: Prisoners during the American Revolution.* Athens, Ohio: Ohio Univ. Press, 1976.

————. "The Court-Martial of Captain Richard Lippincott." *New Jersey History* 89 (1971): 23–36.

————. "Pennsylvania Prisoner Exchange Conferences, 1778." *Pennsylvania History* 45, no. 3 (1978): 257–69.

Boyd, George A. *Elias Boudinot, Patriot and Statesman, 1746–1821.* Princeton: Princeton Univ. Press, 1952.

Boynton, Edward C. *History of West Point.* Freeport, N.Y.: Books for Libraries Press, 1970.

Bradford, S. S. "Hunger Menaces the Revolution," *Maryland Historical Magazine* 61 (1966): 1–23.

Bradley, Harold W. "The Political Thinking of George Washington." *JSH* 11 (1945): 469–486.

Breen, T. H. *Tobacco Culture: The Mentality of the Great Tobacco Planters on the Eve of the Revolution.* Princeton: Princeton Univ. Press, 1985.

Brissot de Warville, J. P. *New Travels in the United States of America, 1792.* M. S. Vamos and Durand Echeverria, trans. Cambridge, Mass.: Harvard Univ. Press, 1964.

British Headquarters Papers. mss., WLCL, University of Michigan, Ann Arbor.

Britt, Judith S. *Nothing More Agreeable: Music in George Washington's Family.* Mount Vernon, Va.: Mount Vernon Ladies' Association, 1984.

————. "Lessons for Martha's Children." *VC,* spring 1986, 172.

Brooke, John. *George III.* New York: McGraw-Hill, 1972.

Brown, Gerald Saxon. *American Secretary: The Colonial Policy of Lord George Germain, 1775–1778.* Ann Arbor, Mich.: Univ. of Michigan Press, 1963.

Brown, Wallace. *The Good Americans: Loyalists in the American Revolution.* New York: Morrow, 1969.

———. *The King's Friends: The Composition and Motives of the American Loyalist Claimants.* Providence, R.I.: Brown Univ. Press, 1966.

Brunhouse, Robert L. *The Counter-Revolution in Pennsylvania, 1776–1790.* Harrisburg, Pa.: Pennsylvania Historical Commission, 1942.

Buel, Richard. *Dear Liberty: Connecticut Mobilization for the Revolutionary War.* Middletown, Conn.: Wesleyan Univ. Press, 1980.

Burnaby, Andrew. *Travels through the Middle Settlements in North America, 1759–1760.* London: Payne, 1798.

Burnett, Edmund C. "Ciphers of the Revolutionary Period." *AHR* 22 (1917): 329–74.

Busch, Noel F. *Winter Quarters: George Washington and the Continental Army at Valley Forge.* New York: Liveright, 1974.

Bush, Martin H. *Revolutionary Enigma: A Reappraisal of General Philip Schuyler of New York.* Port Washington, N.Y.: Kennikat, 1969.

Butterfield, Lyman H. *Adams Family Correspondence.* 2 vols. Cambridge, Mass: Belknap Press of Harvard Univ. Press, 1963.

Calderhead, William L. "Prelude to Yorktown: A Critical Week in a Major Campaign." *Maryland History* 77, no. 2 (1982): 123–35.

Calhoon, R. M. *The Loyalists in Revolutionary America, 1760–1781.* New York: Harcourt, Brace, 1973.

Callahan, North. *Flight from the Republic: The Tories of the American Revolution.* New York: Morrow, 1967.

———. *George Washington: Soldier and Man.* New York: Morrow, 1972.

———. *Henry Knox: General Washington's General.* New York: Reinhart, 1958.

Calloway, Colin G. *The American Revolution in Indian Country: Crisis and Diversity in Native American Communities.* Cambridge: Cambridge Univ. Press, 1995.

Campbell, Dr. Jabez. *Diary.* In NYHS *Proceedings,* 2d ser., 3, no. 3 (1873): 115–36.

Carp, E. Wayne. *To Starve the Army at Pleasure.* Chapel Hill, N.C.: Univ. of North Carolina Press, 1984.

Carr, Lois Green, Philip D. Morgan, and Jean B. Russo, eds. *Colonial Chesapeake Society.* Chapel Hill: Univ. of North Carolina Press, 1988.

Carrall, Peter N., comp. *Religion and the Coming of the American Revolution.* Waltham, Mass.: Ginn-Blaisdell, 1970.

Carrington, Henry B. *Battles of the American Revolution.* New York: A. S. Barnes, 1876.

Carroll, Frances L. and Mary Meacham. *Mount Vernon Library.* Pittsburgh: Mount Vernon Library, 1977.

Carson, Paul. "The Growth and Evolution of Interpretation at George Washington's Birthplace." *Northern Neck of Virginia Hist. Magazine* 36, no. 1 (1986): 4110–25.

Carter, Clarence E. *Great Britain and the Illinois Country, 1763–1774.* Port Washington, N.Y.: Kennikat, 1970.

———. "Documents Relating to the Mississippi Land Company, 1763–1769." *AHR* 16 (1910–11): 311–19.

Catlin, George B. "George Washington Looks Westward." *Michigan History Magazine* 16, no. 1 (1932): 127–42.

Cavendish, Sir Henry. *Debates of the House of Commons.* London: Ridgway, 1839.

Chalmers, Harvey. *Joseph Brant: Mohawk.* East Lansing, Mich.: Michigan State Univ. Press, 1955.

Chambers, William N. *Political Parties in a New Nation.* New York: Oxford Univ. Press, 1963.

Chastellux, Francois Jean, Marquis de. *Travels in North America, 1780–1782.* Chapel Hill, N.C.: Univ. of North Carolina Press, 1963.

Christensen, Lois E. "Washington's Experience and the Creation of the Presidency." Ph.D. diss., Univ. of Nebraska, 1957.

Clark, William Bell. *George Washington's Navy.* Baton Rouge, La.: Louisiana State Univ. Press, 1960.

———. "American Naval Policy, 1775–76." *American Neptune* 1 (1941): 26–41.

———. ed. *Naval Documents of the American Revolution.* 10 vols. Washington, D.C.: Government Printing Office, 1964–1973.

Cleland, Hugh. *George Washington in the Ohio Valley*. Pittsburgh: Univ. of Pittsburgh Press, 1955.

Clifford, John Garry. "A Muddy Middle of the Road: The Politics of Edmund Randolph, 170–1795." *VMHB* 80, no. 3 (1972): 286–311.

Clinton, Sir Henry. *The American Rebellion: A Narrative of His Campaigns, 1775–1782*. New Haven: Yale Univ. Press, 1954.

———. Papers. WLCL.

Coatsworth, John H. "American Trade with European Colonies in the Caribbean and South America, 1790–1812." *WMQ*, 3d ser., 24 (1967): 243–66.

Cobbett, William, *Peter Porcupine in America*. David A. Wilson, ed. Ithaca, N.Y.: Cornell Univ. Press, 1994.

Commager, Henry Steele, and Richard B. Morris. *The Spirit of 'Seventy-Six*. New York: Harper & Row, 1967.

Conkling, Margaret C. *Memoirs of the Mother and Wife of Washington*. 2d ed. Auburn, N.Y.: Derby, Miller, 1850.

Corwin, Edward S. *The President: Office and Powers, 1787–1948*. New York: New York Univ. Press, 1948.

Cousins, Norman, ed. *In God We Trust: The Religious Beliefs and Ideas of the American Founding Fathers*. New York: Harper, 1958.

Crary, Catherine. *The Price of Loyalty*. New York: McGraw-Hill, 1973.

Craven, A. O. *Soil Exhaustion as a Factor in the Agricultural History of Virginia and Maryland*. Urbana, Ill.: Univ. of Illinois, 1926.

Crevecoeur, J. Hector St. John de. *Letters from an American Farmer and Sketches of Eighteenth-Century America*. New Haven: Yale Univ. Press, 1925.

Cronin, Thomas F. *Inventing the American Presidency*. Lawrence, Kansas: Univ. Press of Kansas, 1989.

Crout, Robert R. "The Diplomacy of Trade: The Influence of Commercial Considerations on French Involvement in the Anglo-American War of Independence, 1775–1778." Ph.D. diss., Univ. of Georgia, 1977.

Cummings, Hubertis M. "The Villefranche Map for the Defence of the Delaware." *PMHB* 84 (1960) 4: 424–434.

Cunliffe, Marcus. *George Washington, Man and Monument*. Boston: Little, Brown, 1958.

Cunningham, Noble. *In Pursuit of Reason: The Life of Thomas Jefferson*. Baton Rouge, La.: Louisiana State Univ. Press, 1987.

Curtis, Edward P. *The Organization of the British Army Revolution*. New Haven, Conn.: Yale Univ. Press, 1936.

Custis, George Washington Parke. *Recollections and Private Memories of Washington*. New York: World, 1866.

Dalzell, Robert F., Jr. "Constructing Independence: Monticello, Mount Vernon and the Men Who Built Them." *Eighteenth-Century Studies* 26, no. 4 (1993): 543–80.

Dann, John C., ed. *The Revolution Remembered: Eyewitness Accounts of the War of Independence*. Chicago: Univ. of Chicago Press, 1980.

Davies, K. G., ed. *Documents of the American Revolution, 1770–1783*. Colonial Office Series. 21 vols. Shannon: Irish Univ. Press, 1972–81.

Davis, David Brion. *The Problem of Slavery in Western Culture*. Ithaca: Cornell Univ. Press, 1966.

Decatur, Stephen. *Private Affairs of George Washington*. Boston: Houghton Mifflin, 1933.

De Conde, Alexander. *Entangling Alliances: Politics and Diplomacy under George Washington*. Durham, N.C.: Duke Univ. Press.

de Forest, Elizabeth Kellam. *The Gardens and Grounds at Mount Vernon: How George Washington Planned and Planted Them*. Mount Vernon, Va.: Mount Vernon Ladies' Association, 1982.

Dempsey, Janet. "Washington's Last Cantonment." *Journal of the Council on America's Military Past* 17, no. 3 (1990): 52–56.

Detweiler, Susan Gray. *George Washington's Chinaware*. New York: Abrams, 1982.

DeVorsey, Louis. *The Indian Boundary in the Southern Colonies, 1763–1775*. Chapel Hill, N.C.: Univ. of North Carolina Press, 1966.

Dinwiddie, Robert. *Official Records of Robert Dinwiddie, Lieutenant-Governor of the Colony of Virginia, 1751–1758*. 2 vols. Richmond: Virginia Historical Society, 1883–84.

Doerflinger, Thomas M. *A Vigorous Spirit of Enterprise: Merchants and Economic Development in Revolutionary Philadelphia*. Chapel Hill, N.C.: Univ. of North Carolina Press, 1986.

Draper, Theodore. *A Struggle for Power: The American Revolution*. New York: Times Books, 1996.

Drinker, Elizabeth. *Journal*, ed. Henry Drinker Biddle. Philadelphia: Lippincott, 1889.

Dull, Jonathan. *Diplomatic History of the American Revolution*. New Haven: Yale Univ. Press, 1984.

Dwyer, William D. *The Day Is Ours*. New York: Viking, 1983.

East, Robert A. *Business Enterprise in the American Revolutionary Era*. New York: Columbia Univ. Press, 1938.

East, Robert A., and Jacob Judd, eds. *The Loyalist Americans: A Focus on Greater New York*. Tarrytown, N.Y.: Sleepy Hollow Press, 1975.

Edmondson, James H. "Desertion in the American Army during the Revolutionary War." Ph.D. diss., Louisiana State Univ., 1971.

Einstein, Lewis. *Divided Loyalties: Americans in England during the War of Independence*. Boston: Houghton, 1933.

Elkins, Stanley, and Eric McKittrick. *The Age of Federation*. New York: Oxford Univ. Press, 1993.

Engle, Paul. *Women in the American Revolution*. Chicago: Follett, 1976.

Estes, J. Worth. "George Washington and the Doctors: Treating America's First Superhero." *Medical Heritage* 12, no. 1 (1985): 44–57.

Evans, Elizabeth. *Weathering the Storm: Women of the American Revolution*. New York: Scribner's, 1975.

Ferguson, E. James. *The Power of the Purse: A History of American Public Finance, 1776–1790*. Chapel Hill, N.C.: Univ. of North Carolina Press, 1961.

Ferling, J. E. *First of Men*. Knoxville: Univ. of Tennessee Press, 1988.

———. *John Adams: A Life*. Knoxville: Univ. of Tennessee Press, 1993.

Fields, Joseph E., comp. *Worthy Partner: The Papers of Martha Washington*. Westport: Greenwood, 1994.

Fithian, Philip Vickers. *Journals and Letters, 1767–1774*. Ed. J. R. Williams. Princeton: Princeton Univ. Press, 1900.

———. *Journals and Letters, 1773–1774*. Williamsburg: Colonial Williamsburg, 1957.

———. *Journals and Letters, 1775–1776*. Princeton: Princeton Univ. Press, 1934.

Fitzpatrick, John C. *George Washington Himself*. Indianapolis: Bobbs-Merrill, 1933.

Fleming, Thomas. *1776: Year of Illusions*. New York: Morrow, 1975.

———. *Beat the Last Drum: The Siege of Yorktown*. New York: St. Martin's Press, 1963.

———. *The Forgotten Victory: The Battle for New Jersey, 1780*. New York: Readers' Digest Press, 1973.

Flexner, James Thomas. *George Washington*. Boston: Little, Brown, 1965.

Flick, Alexander C. *Loyalism in New York during the American Revolution*. New York, 1901.

———. "New Sources on the Sullivan Campaign of 1779." *New York State Historical Association Quarterly Journal* 10, no. 3 (1929): 185–224.

———. "The Sullivan-Clinton Campaign of 1779." In New York Historical Association, *History of the State of New York*, vol. 4, pp. 185–216. Albany: State of New York, 1934.

Fogg, Jeremiah. *Journal*. Exeter, N.H.: News-Letter Press, 1879.

Fohlen, Claude. "The Impact of the American Revolution Abroad." In *U.S. Library of Congress Symposia on the American Revolution Papers*. Washington, D.C.: Library of Congress, 1976.

Foner, Eric. *Tom Paine and Revolutionary America*. New York: Oxford Univ. Press, 1976.

Foner, Philip S. *Blacks in the American Revolution*. Westport, Conn.: Greenwood, 1975.

———. ed. *Democratic-Republican Societies, 1790–1800*. Westport, Conn.: Greenwood, 1976.

Force, Peter, ed. *American Archives: Consisting of a Collection of Authentic Records, State Papers, Debates, and Letters . . .* 4th ser., Mar. 7, 1774–July 4, 1776, 6 vols.; 5th ser., July 4, 1776–Sept. 3, 1783, 3 vols. Washington, D.C., 1837–1846 and 1848–1853. Referred to as *Am. Arch.*

Ford, Corey. *A Peculiar Service*. Boston: Little, Brown, 1965.

Ford, Paul L. *Washington and the Theater*. New York: Dunlap Society, 1899. Repr. New York: B. Blom, 1967.

Ford, Worthington Chauncey. *Defences of Philadelphia in 1777.* New York: Da Capo, 1971.

———. *Washington as an Employer and Importer of Labor.* Brooklyn, N.Y.: World, 1889.

Fortescue, Sir John William, Sr. *A History of the British Army.* London: Macmillan, 1910–1935.

Fowler, William M., Jr. *Rebels under Sail: The American Navy during the Revolution.* New York, 1976.

Fox, Frederic. "Pater Patria as Paterfamilias." *AH* 14, no. 4 (1963): 32–37, 100–102.

Franklin, Benjamin. *The Papers of Benjamin Franklin.* Ed. Leonard W. Labaree et al. 32 vols. to date. New Haven, 1959–.

Freeman, Douglas Southall. *George Washington: A Biography.* 7 vols. New York: Scribner's, 1948–1957.

French, Allen. *The First Year of the Revolution.* Boston: Houghton, 1934.

Frisch, Morton J. "Hamilton's Report on Manufacturers and Political Philosophy." *Publius* 8 (1978): 129–39.

Garrett, Wendell, ed. "Mount Vernon." *Magazine Antiques* 135, no. 2 (1989): 452–531.

Gates, Horatio. Papers, NYHS.

Gaustad, Edwin S. *Faith of Our Fathers: Religion and the New Nation.* San Francisco: Harper & Row, 1988.

Gilbert, Felix. *To the Farewell Address: Ideas of Early American Foreign Policy.* Princeton: Princeton Univ. Press, 1961.

Gillespie, Michael Allen and Michael Lienesch, eds., *Ratifying the Constitution.* Lawrence, Kansas: Univ. Press of Kansas, 1989.

Gipson, L. H. *The British Empire before the American Revolution.* 15 vols. New York: Knopf, 1966–1970.

Glenn, Patricia. "Wakefield," *Early American Life* 10, no. 2 (1979): 30–33.

Goode, Cecil E. "Gilbert Simpson: Washington's Partner in Settling His Western Pennsylvania Lands." *Western Pennsylvania History Magazine* 62, no. 2 (1979): 149–66.

Goolrick, John T. *The Life of General Hugh Mercer.* New York: Neale Publishing, 1906.

Gottschalk, Louis Reichenthal. *Lafayette: A Guide to the Letters, Documents and Manuscripts in the U.S.* Ithaca: Cornell Univ. Press, 1975.

Gottschalk, Louis and Margaret Maddox. *Lafayette in the French Revolution: From the October Days through the Federation.* Chicago: Univ. of Chicago Press, 1973.

Graham, Gerald S. *The Royal Navy in the War of American Independence.* London: Longman, Green, 1976.

Gray, Lewis Cecil. *History of Agriculture in the Southern U.S. to 1860.* 2 vols. Washington, D.C.: Carnegie Institution, 1933.

Graymont, Barbara. *The Iroquois in the American Revolution.* Syracuse, N.Y.: Syracuse Univ. Press, 1972.

Green, Constance McLaughlin. *Washington: Village and Capital, 1800–1878.* Princeton: Princeton Univ. Press, 1962.

Greene, Nathanael. *Papers.* Ed. Richard K. Showman et al. Chapel Hill, N.C.: Univ. of North Carolina Press, 1976.

Greenman, Jeremiah. *Diary of a Common Soldier in the American Revolution.* Ed. Robert C. Brag and Paul E. Bushnell. De Kalb: Northern Illinois Univ. Press, 1978.

Griffin, Appleton P. C. *Catalogue of the Washington Collection in the Boston Atheneum.* Cambridge, Mass.: Harvard Univ. Press, 1897.

Griffith, Lucille Blanche. *The Virginia House of Burgesses, 1750–1774.* Northport, Ala.: Colonial Press, 1963.

Gross, Robert A., ed. *In Debt to Shays: The Bicentennial of an Agrarian Rebellion.* Charlottesville, Va.: Univ. Press of Virginia, 1993.

Gruber, Ira D. *The Howe Brothers and the American Revolution.* New York: Atheneum, 1972.

Hall, Wilbur C. "Sergeant Champe's Adventure." *WMQ,* 2d ser., 18 (1938): 322–42.

Halleck, Henry W. "Military Espionage," *American Journal of International Law* 5 (1911): 590–603.

Hamilton, Alexander. *The Papers of Alexander Hamilton.* Vols. 1–4. Ed. Harold C. Syrett. New York: Columbia Univ. Press, 1961–1962.

Hamilton, Edward P. *The French and Indian Wars.* New York: Doubleday, 1962.

Hammond, Bray. *Banks and Politics in America from the Revolution to the Civil War.* Princeton: Princeton Univ. Press, 1957.

Hapward, Donald. "The Continental Army at Morristown, 1779–1780." M.A. thesis, Emporia State Univ., 1979.

Harrell, Isaac S. *Loyalism in Virginia*. Durham, N.C.: Duke Univ. Press, 1926.

Harrington, J. C. "The Metamorphosis of Fort Necessity." *Western Pennsylvania Historical Magazine* 37 (1954–1955): 181–88.

Hart, James. *The American Presidency in Action, 1789: A Study in Constitutional History*. New York: Macmillan, 1948.

Hatch, Robert McConnell. *Major John André: A Gallant in Spy's Clothing*. Boston: Houghton, 1986.

Haworth, Paul Leland. *George Washington, Country Gentleman*. Indianapolis: Bobbs-Merrill, 1915.

Heathcote, Charles W. "The Conway Intrigue." *Picket Post* 37, no. 7 (1952): 13–19.

Henderson, H. James. *Party Politics in the Continental Congress*. New York: McGraw-Hill, 1974.

Henriques, Peter R. "An Uneven Friendship: The Relationship between George Washington and George Mason." *VMHB* 97, no. 2 (1989): 185–204.

Herndon, George M. *Tobacco in Colonial Virginia*. Williamsburg, Va.: 350th Anniversary Celebration Committee, 1957.

Higginbotham, Don. *George Washington and the American Military Tradition*. Athens, Ga.: Univ. of Georgia Press, 1985.

———. *The War for American Independence: Military Attitudes, Policies, and Practice, 1763–1789*. Boston: Northeastern Univ. Press, 1983.

———, ed. *Reconsiderations on the Revolutionary War: Selected Essays*. Contributions in Military History No. 12. Westport, Conn.: Greenwood, 1978.

Hilliard d'Auberteuil, Michel. *Essais historiques et politiques sur les Anglo-Americains*. 2 vols. Bruxelles: n.p., 1782.

Historical Manuscripts Commission. *The Manuscripts of the Earls of Dartmouth*. Eleventh Report, Part 5; Fourteenth Report, Part 10; Fifteenth Report, Part 1. 3 vols. London, 1887–96.

Holcombe, Arthur N. "The Role of Washington in the Framing of the Constitution." *Huntington Library Quarterly* 19, no. 8 (1956): 317–34.

Hoppin, Charles Arthur. *The Washington Amnesty and Records of the McClain, Johnson and Forty Other Colonial American Families*. Greenfield, Ohio: n.p., 1932.

Horrell, Joseph, and Richard W. Oram. "George Washington's 'Marble colour'd folio Book': A Newly Identified Ledger." *WMQ*, 3rd ser., 43, no. 2 (1986): 252–66.

Horsman, Reginald. *Diplomacy of the New Republic, 1776–1815*. Arlington, Illinois: Harlan Davidson, 1985.

———. "Thomas Jefferson and the Ordinance of 1784." *Illinois Historical Journal* 79 (1986): 99–112.

Howard, John T. "The Doctors Gustavus Brown." *Annals of Medical History*. New ser., 9, no. 9 (1927): 437–48.

Howe, Herbert B. "Colonel George Washington and King's College." *Columbia Univ. Quarterly* 24, no. 6 (1932): 137–57.

Hume, Edgar E. *Lafayette and the Society of the Cincinnati*. Baltimore: Johns Hopkins Univ. Press, 1934.

Humphreys, David. *Life of General Washington*. Athens, Ga.: Univ. of Georgia Press, 1991.

Hunce, Anthony M. "Washington at Whitemarsh." *Bucks County Historical Society Collection of Papers* 4 (1917): 703–24.

Hunter, William A. *Forts on the Pennsylvania Frontier, 1753–1758*. Harrisburg, Penn.: Pennsylvania Historical Commission, 1960.

Idzerda, S.J., and Robert R. Crout, eds. *Lafayette in the Age of the American Revolution*. 5 vols. Ithaca, N.Y.: Cornell Univ. Press, 1977.

Ifkovic, John. *Connecticut's Nationalist Revolutionary: Jonathan Trumbull, Jr.* Conn. Bicentennial Series, vol. 25. Hartford: American Revolution Bicentennial Committee of Connecticut, 1977.

Innes, Stephen, ed. *Work and Labor in Early America*. Williamsburg: Institute for Early American Study, 1988.

Irving, Washington. *Life of George Washington*. New York: Putnam's, 1857–1858.

Isaacs, Rhys. *Transformation of Virginia, 1740–1790*. Chapel Hill, N.C.: Univ. of North Carolina Press, 1982.

Jackson, John W. *The Pennsylvania Navy, 1775–1781: The Defense of the Delaware*. New Brunswick, N.J.: Rutgers Univ. Press, 1974.

———. *With the British Army in Philadelphia*. San Rafael, Calif.: Presidio Press, 1979.

Jefferson, Thomas. *Papers*. Ed. Julian Boyd et al. 27 vols. to date. Princeton: Princeton Univ. Press, 1950–.

———. *Autobiography*. Ed. Adrienne Koch and William H. Peden. New York: Modern Library, 1944.

———. *Writings*. Ed. A. A. Lipscomb and A. E. Bergh. 20 vols. Washington, D.C.: Thomas Jefferson Memorial Association of the United States, 1903.

Jensen, Arthur L. *Maritime Commerce of Colonial Philadelphia*. Madison, Wis.: Univ. of Wisconsin Press, 1963.

Jensen, Merrill. *Tracts of the American Revolution, 1763–1776*. Indianapolis: Bobbs-Merrill, 1967.

Johnson, Charles F. "Chip Off the Old Jock," *AH* 27, no. 12 (1976): 62.

Johnson, William. *Papers of Sir William Johnson*. Albany, N.Y.: State Univ. of New York, 1921–1965.

Johnston, Henry P. *The Campaign of 1776 around New York and Brooklyn*. New York: Da Capo, 1971.

Jones, Alice Hanson. *Wealth of a Nation to Be: The American Colonies on the Eve of the Revolution*. New York: Columbia Univ. Press, 1980.

Jones, Robert F. *George Washington*. Twayne's World Leader Series, vol. 80. Boston: Twayne, 1979.

Kaminski, John P. *George Clinton: Yeoman Politician of the New Republic*. Madison, Wisc.: Madison House, 1993.

Keane, John. *Tom Paine: A Political Life*. Boston: Little, Brown, 1995.

Ketcham, Ralph. *Presidents above Party: The First American Presidency, 1789–1829*. Chapel Hill: Univ. of North Carolina Press, 1984.

Ketchum, Richard M. *The Winter Soldiers*. Garden City: Doubleday, 1973.

Kimball, Marie G. *The Martha Washington Cook Book*. New York: Coward-McCann, 1940.

Kite, Elizabeth Sarah. *L'Enfant and Washington, 1791–1792*. New York: Arno Press, 1970.

Klein, Milton, and R. W. Howard. *Twilight of British Rule in Revolutionary America: The New York Letter Book of General James Robertson, 1780–1783*. Cooperstown, N.Y.: New York State Historical Association, 1983.

Knollenberg, Bernhard. *Growth of the American Revolution*. New Haven: Yale Univ. Press, 1975.

———. *George Washington: The Virginia Period*. Durham, N.C.: Duke Univ. Press, 1964.

———. *Origin of the American Revolution*. New York: Macmillan, 1960.

Knox, Dudley W. *The Naval Genius of George Washington*. Boston: Houghton, 1932.

Knox, James H. Mason. "Medical History of George Washington." *Bulletin of the Institute of the History of Medicine* 1, no. 6 (1933): 174–191.

Kohn, Richard H. "The Federalists and the Army: Politics and the Birth of the Military Establishment, 1783–1795." Ph.D. diss., Univ. of Wisconsin, 1968.

Konkle, Burton. *Benjamin Chew, 1722–1810*. Philadelphia: Univ. of Pennsylvania Press, 1932.

Kopperman, P. E. *Braddock at the Monongahela*. Pittsburgh: Univ. of Pittsburgh Press, 1977.

Kulikoff, Allan. *Tobacco and Slaves*. Chapel Hill, N.C.: Univ. of North Carolina Press, 1986.

Labaree, B. W. *Patriots and Partisans: The Merchants of Newburyport, 1760–1815*. Cambridge, Mass.: Harvard Univ. Press, 1962.

Labaree, Leonard. "Nature of American Loyalism." American Antiquarian Society, *Proceedings* 54 (1944): 15–58.

Landers, H. L. *The Virginia Campaign and the Blockade and Siege of Yorktown*. Washington, D.C.: U.S. Army War College, 1931.

Larter, Harry C., Jr. "German Troops with Burgoyne, 1776–1777," *Fort Ticonderoga Museum Bulletin* 9 (1952): 13–24.

Lassiter, Francis R. "Arnold's Invasion of Virginia." *Sewanee Review* 9 (1901): 78–93, 185–203.

Leach, Donald Edward. *Arms for Empire*. New York: Oxford Univ. Press, 1973.

Leake, Isaac Q. *Memoirs of the Life and Times of John Lamb*. Albany: J. Munsell, 1857.

Lear, Tobias. *Letters and Recollections of Washington*. New York: Macmillan, 1906.

Leduc, Gilbert. *Washington and the 'Murder' of Jumonville*. Boston: Little, Brown, 1943.

Lee, Henry (Lighthorse Harry). *Memoirs of the War in the Southern Department of the U.S.* Philadelphia: Bradford, 1812.

Leiby, Adrian Coulter. *Revolutionary War in the Hackensack Valley.* New Brunswick, N.J.: Rutgers Univ. Press, 1962.

Levy, Leonard W. "Liberty and the First Amendment, 1790–1800," *AHR* 68 (1962): 22–37.

Lewis, Fielding O. "Washington's Last Illness." *Annals of Medical History,* new ser., 4 (1932): 245–48.

Lewis, Monte Ross. "Betrayal of the Beloved Indians, 1794–1844." Ph.D. diss., North Texas Univ., 1981.

Lewis, Robert. Diary. Mss. Mount Vernon Library.

Lewis, Thomas A. *For King and Country: George Washington, the Early Years.* New York: John Wiley, 1993.

Littlefield, Douglas R. "Eighteenth-Century Plans to Clear the Potomac River: Technology, Expertise and Labor in a Developing Nation." *VMHB* 93, no. 3 (1985): 291–322.

Livingston, William. *The Independent Reflector.* Ed. Milton Klein. Cambridge, Mass.: Harvard Univ. Press, 1963.

Lomask, Milton. *Aaron Burr.* 2 vols. New York: Harper & Row, 1979.

Longden, H. Isham. "The History of the Washington Family," *The Genealogists' Magazine* 1 (1925): 47–54, 109–16; 2 (1926): 12–18.

Loss, Richard. "The Political Thought of President George Washington." *Presidential Studies Quarterly* 19, no. 3 (1989): 471–490.

Lossing, Benjamin Franklin. *Pictorial Field Book of the Revolution.* 2 vols. New York, 1851–52.

Lundin, Leonard C. *New Jersey: Cockpit of the Revolution.* Princeton: Princeton Univ. Press, 1940.

Luzager, John F. "The Arnold-Gates Controversy." *West Virginia History* 27 (1966): 75–84.

McAdams, D. R. "The Sullivan Expedition," *NYHS Quarterly* 54, no. 1 (1970): 53–81.

McBarron, H. Charles. "The American Regiment, 1740–1746." *Military Collector & Historian* 14, no. 3 (1962): 84–86.

McClellan, William S. *Smuggling in the American Colonies at the Outbreak of the Revolution.* New York: Williams Collége Press, 1912.

McColley, Robert. *Slavery and Jeffersonian Virginia.* Urbana: Univ. of Illinois Press, 1964.

McDonald, Forrest. *The Presidency of George Washington.* Lawrence: Univ. Press of Kansas, 1974.

McGuire, Thomas J. *The Surprise of Germantown.* Philadelphia: Cliveden National Trust for Historic Preservation, 1994.

Mackesy, Piers. *The War for America, 1775–1783.* Cambridge, Mass.: Harvard Univ. Press, 1964.

Maclay, William. *Diary.* Baltimore: Johns Hopkins University Press, 1988.

———. *Journal.* New York: A. & C. Boni, 1927.

Madison, James. *Papers.* 17 vols. Chicago: Univ. of Chicago Press, 1962–1991.

Maier, Pauline. *From Resistance to Revolution: Colonial Radicals and the Development of American Opposition to Britain, 1765–1776.* New York: Knopf, 1972.

Marshall, Christopher. *Extracts from the Diary of Christopher Marshall.* Ed. William Duane. Albany, N.Y.: J. Munsell, 1877.

Marshall, Peter. "Lord Hillsborough, Samuel Wharton and the Ohio Grant," *English Hist. Review* 80 (1965): 721–22.

Marx, Rudolph. "A Medical Profile of GW." *AH* 6, no. 8 (1955): 43–47, 106–7.

Mason, George. *Papers.* Ed. Robert A. Rutland. Chapel Hill, N.C.: Univ. of North Carolina Press, 1970.

Mayo, Katherine. *General Washington's Dilemma.* New York: Harcourt, Brace, 1938.

Metzger, Charles H. *The Prisoner in the American Revolution.* Chicago: Loyola Univ. Press, 1971.

Middlekauff, Robert. *The Glorious Cause: The American Revolution, 1763–1789.* New York: Oxford Univ. Press, 1982.

Miller, John Chester. *Origins of the American Revolution.* Boston: Little, Brown, 1943.

Minnesota Historical Society. "Washington and the Potomac: Manuscripts of the Minnesota Historical Society, 1769–1796." *AHR* 28 (1923): 497–519, 705–22.

Monaghan, Frank, and Marvin Lowenthal. *This Was New York*. Garden City, N.Y.: Doubleday, 1943.

Moomaw, William H. "Denouement of General Howe's Campaign of 1777." *English Historical Review* 79, no. 7 (1964): 498–512.

Morgan, Edmund S., and Helen M. Morgan. *The Stamp Act Crisis: Prologue to Revolution*. Chapel Hill, N.C.: Univ. of North Carolina Press, 1958.

Morison, Samuel Eliot. *The Young Man Washington*. Cambridge, Mass.: Harvard Univ. Press, 1932.

Morton, Richard L. *Colonial Virginia*. 2 vols. Chapel Hill, N.C.: Univ. of North Carolina Press, 1960.

Murdock, David H., ed. *Rebellion in America: A Contemporary British Viewpoint*. Oxford: Oxford Univ. Press, 1979.

Naval Documents of the American Revolution. 10 vols. Superintendent of Documents, Washington, D.C., 1964–1973.

Nelson, Paul David. *Anthony Wayne, Soldier of the Early Republic*. Bloomington, Ind.: Univ. of Indiana Press, 1985.

———. *General Horatio Gates*. Baton Rouge, La.: Louisiana State Univ. Press, 1976.

Nelson, William H. *The American Tory*. Boston: Little, Brown, 1961.

———. "New York in the Strategy of the Revolution." In *History of the State of New York*, ed. Alexander C. Flick, vol. 4, 78–83. New York: New York Historical Association, 1933.

Nettles, Curtis P. *The Emergence of a National Economy, 1775–1815*. New York: Holt, Rinehart and Winston, 1962.

Nickerson, Hoffman. *Turning Point of the Revolution*. Boston: Little, Brown, 1928.

Nordham, George W. *The Age of Washington: George Washington's Presidency, 1781–1787*. Chicago: Adams, 1989.

———. *George Washington and Money*. Washington, D.C.: Univ. Press of America, 1982.

Nute, Grace L. "Washington and the Potomac." *AHR* 28, no. 3 (1923): 497–519, 705–722.

Oaks, Robert F. "Philadelphia in Exile: The Problem of Loyalty during the American Revolution." *PMHB* 19 (1972): 298–325.

O'Callaghan, E. B., ed. *Documents Relative to the Colonial History of the State of New York*. 14 vols. Albany, N.Y., 1856–83.

O'Callaghan, Jerry A. "The War Veteran and the Public Lands." *Agricultural History* 28, no. 10 (1954): 163–68.

Ousterhout, Anne M. "Controlling the Opposition in Pennsylvania during the American Revolution." *PMHB* 105 (1981): 3–35.

Packard, Francis R. "Washington and the Medical Affairs of the Revolution," *Annals of Medical History*, new ser., 4, no. 5 (1932): 306–12.

Paine, Thomas. *Collected Writings*. Ed. Eric Foner. New York: Library of America, 1995.

Palmer, Dave Richard. *The Way of the Fox: American Strategy in the War of Independence*. Westport, Conn.: Greenwood, 1975.

Palmer, Gregory. *Biographical Sketches of Loyalists of the American Revolution*. Westport, Conn.: Meckler, 1984.

Paltsits, Victor Hugo. "The Use of Invisible Ink for Secret Writing during the American Revolution." *New York Public Library Bulletin* 39 (1985): 361–64.

Pancake, John S. *1777: Year of the Hangman*. University, Ala.: Univ. of Alabama Press, 1977.

Pape, Thomas, "The Washington Emigrants and Their Parents." *Tyler's Quarterly Historical and Genealogical Magazine* 4 (1922–1923): 359–80.

Pargellis, Stanley M. *Lord Loudoun in North America*. Hampden, Conn.: Archon, 1968.

———. "Braddock's Defeat." *AHR* 40, no. 1 (1936): 259–62.

Parker, Robert. "Journal." *PMHB* 27, no. 10 (1903): 404–420; 28, no. 1 (1904): 12–24.

Parkman, Francis. *Montcalm and Wolfe*. Boston: Little, Brown, 1884.

Patterson, Robert U. "James Craik, Physician General." *Military Surgeon* 70, no. 2 (1932): 152–56.

Peckham, H. H. *The Toll of Independence*. Chicago: Univ. of Chicago Press, 1974.

———, ed. *Sources of American Independence*. 2 vols. Chicago: Univ. of Chicago Press, 1978.

———. *The War for Independence: A Military History*. Chicago: Univ. of Chicago Press, 1958.

———. "British Secret Writing in the Revolution." *Michigan Alumnus Quarterly Review* 44 (1938): 126–31.

Pennsylvania Archives. Ed. Samuel Hazard et al. 9 series. Philadelphia and Harrisburg, 1852–1935.

Pennsylvania, State of. *Colonial Records.* 16 vols. Harrisburg, 1938–53. Includes *Minutes of the Provincial Council of Pennsylvania; Minutes of the Council of Safety; Minutes of the Supreme Executive Council.*

Pennypacker, Morton. *General Washington's Spies.* Brooklyn: Long Island Historical Society, 1939.

Perkins, Bradford. *The First Rapprochement: England and the United States, 1795–1805.* Philadelphia: Univ. of Pennsylvania Press, 1955.

Perry, James R. "Supreme Court Appointments, 1789–1801." *Journal of the Early Republic* 6, no. 4 (1986): 371–410.

Peterson, Merrill. *Thomas Jefferson and the New Nation.* New York: Oxford Univ. Press, 1970.

Pettengill, Ray W., ed. *Letters from America, 1776–1779: Being Letters of Brunswick, Hessian and Waldeck Officers with the British Armies.* Boston: Little, Brown, 1924.

Phelps, Glenn A. "George Washington and the Building of the Constitution: Presidential Interpretation and Constitutional Development." *Congress and the Presidency* 12, no. 2 (1985): 95–109.

Philbrick, Francis Samuel. *The Rise of the West, 1754–1830.* New York: Harper, 1965.

Phillips, Philip Lee. "Washington as Surveyor and Mapmaker." *DAR Magazine* 55, no. 3 (1921): 115–32.

Plumb, J. H. "The French Connection" 35, no. 12 (1974): 27–57, 86–88.

Pogue, Dennis J. "Archaeology of Plantation Life: Another Perspective on George Washington's Mount Vernon." *VC* 41, no. 3 (1991): 74–83.

Pound, Arthur. *Johnson of the Mohawks.* New York: Macmillan, 1930.

Price, Jacob M. *Capital and Credit in British Overseas Trade.* Cambridge, Mass.: Harvard Univ. Press, 1980.

———. "The Rise of Glasgow in the Tobacco Trade, 1707–1775." *WMQ,* 3rd ser., 11, no. 1 (1954): 179–99.

Quarles, Benjamin. *The Negro in the American Revolution.* Chapel Hill, N.C.: Univ. of North Carolina Press, 1961.

Quitt, Morton H. "The English Cleric and the Virginia Adventurer: The Washingtons, Father and Son," *VMHB* 97, no. 4 (1989): 163–88.

Ragsdale, Bruce A. *A Planter's Republic: The Search for Economic Independence in Revolutionary Virginia.* Madison, Wisc.: Madison House, 1976.

———. "George Washington, the British Tobacco Trade and Economic Opportunity in Pre-Revolutionary Virginia." *VMHB* 97, no. 2 (1989): 133–162.

Rakove, Jack N. *Beginnings of National Politics.* New York: Knopf, 1975.

———. *Interpreting the Constitution.* Boston: Northeastern Univ. Press, 1990.

Randall, Christopher Fairbanks. "Sacrificing Theories to Realities: The Problem of Prisoners in the American Revolutionary and Civil Wars." Thesis, Princeton Univ., 1988.

Randall, Willard Sterne. *Benedict Arnold, Patriot and Traitor.* New York: William Morrow, 1990.

———. *A Little Revenge: Benjamin Franklin and His Son.* Boston, Little, Brown, 1984.

———. *The Proprietary House at Amboy.* Trenton: Whitechapel, 1975.

———. *Thomas Jefferson: A Life.* New York: Henry Holt, 1993.

———. "Thomas Jefferson Takes a Vacation," *AH* 47, no. 4 (1967): 74–85.

Randall, W. S., and Nancy Nahra. *American Lives.* 2 vols. New York: Longmans, 1997.

Rice, Howard C., Jr., and Anne S. K. Brown, trans. and eds. *The American Campaigns of Rochambeau's Army, 1780–83.* 2 vols. Princeton: Princeton Univ. Press, 1972.

Rich, Bennett M. *The Presidents and Civil Disorder.* Westport, Conn.: Greenwood, 1990.

Richter, Victor W. "General Washington's Body Guards." *Concord Society Historical Bulletin,* no. 3. [Hoboken, N.J.], 1924.

Riley, John P. "To Quit a Peaceful Abode for an Ocean of Difficulties." *Northern Neck of Virginia Hist. Magazine* 38, no. 1 (1988): 4293–97.

Risch, Erna. *Supplying Washington's Army.* Washington, D.C.: Center of Military History, U.S. Army, Government Printing Office, 1981.

Roberts, Kenneth. *March to Quebec: Journal of the Members of Arnold's Expedition.* New York: Doubleday, 1938.

Roberts, Robert B. *New York's Forts in the Revolution.* Rutherford, N.J.: Fairleigh-Dickinson Univ. Press, 1980.

Roche, John F. *Joseph Reed.* New York: Columbia Univ. Press, 1957.

Rosenblatt, Samuel M. "The Significance of Credit in the Tobacco Consignment Trade." *WMQ,* 3rd ser., 19, no. 3 (1962): 383–99.

Rossie, Jonathan Gregory. *The Politics of Command in the American Revolution.* Syracuse, N.Y.: Syracuse Univ. Press, 1975.

Rossiter, Clinton. *Alexander Hamilton and the Constitution.* Boston: Houghton, 1970.

Royster, Charles. *A Revolutionary People at War: The Continental Army and American Character, 1775–1783.* Chapel Hill, N.C.: Univ. of North Carolina Press, 1979.

Rush, Benjamin. *Autobiography.* Ed. George W. Corner. Princeton: Princeton Univ. Press, 1948.

Russell, E. L. "Lost Story of the Brodhead Expedition." *New York State Hist. Association Quarterly Journal* 11, no. 7 (1930): 252–63.

Ryan, Mary P. "Party Formation in the United States Congress, 1789 to 1796: A Quantitative Analysis," *WMQ,* 3d ser., 28 (1971): 523–42.

Ryerson, Richard A. *The Revolution Is Now Begun.* Philadelphia: Univ. of Pennsylvania Press, 1978.

Sabine, Lorenzo. *Biographical Sketches of the Loyalists of the American Revolution.* 2 vols. Boston: Little, Brown, 1864.

Scharf, John T., and Thompson Westcott. *History of Philadelphia.* 3 vols. Philadelphia: L. H. Everts, 1884.

Scheer, George F., and Hugh F. Rankin. *Rebels and Redcoats.* Cleveland: World Publishing, 1957.

Schmidt, Louis H. "George Washington's Bodyguards Were Wisely Selected and Loyal." *Picket Post* 12, no. 1 (1946): 18–25.

Scott, John A. "Joseph Brant at Fort Stanwyx and Oriskany." *New York History* 19 (1938): 399–406.

Sears, Louis Martin. *George Washington and the French Revolution.* Detroit: Wayne State Univ., 1960.

Selby, John E. *The Revolution in Virginia, 1775–1783.* Williamsburg: Colonial Williamsburg Foundation, 1988.

Seneca. *Morals by Way of Abstracts.* London: Strahan, 1719.

Serle, Ambrose. *The American Journal of Ambrose Serle, 1776–1778.* Ed. E. H. Tatum, Jr. San Marino, Calif.: Huntington Library Press, 1940.

Sharp, James Roger. *American Politics in the Early Republic: The New Nation in Crisis.* New Haven: Yale Univ. Press, 1993.

Shy, John. *A People Numerous and Armed.* New York: Oxford Univ. Press, 1976.

———. "A New Look at Colonial Militia," *WMQ,* 3rd ser., 20 (1963): 175–85.

———. "Quartering His Majesty's Forces in New Jersey." *PNJHS* 78 (1960): 82–94.

Simcoe, John Graves. *Military Journal.* Toronto: Baxter, 1962.

Sims, J. P., ed. *The Philadelphia Assemblies, 1748–1948.* Philadelphia: n.p., 1948.

Slaughter, Thomas. *The Whiskey Rebellion.* New York: Oxford Univ. Press, 1986.

Smith, James Morton. *Freedom's Fetters: The Alien and Sedition Laws and American Civil Liberties.* Ithaca: Cornell Univ. Press, 1956.

Smith, Jean Edward. *John Marshall: Definer of a Nation.* New York: Henry Holt, 1996.

Smith, Joshua Hett. *An Authentic Narrative of the Causes Which Led to the Death of Major André.* New York: Evert Duyckinck, 1809.

Smith, Paul H. *Loyalists and Redcoats: A Study in British Revolutionary Policy.* Chapel Hill, N.C.: Univ. of North Carolina Press, 1964.

———. "The American Loyalists: Notes on Their Organization and Numerical Strength." *WMQ,* 3rd ser., 25 (1968): 259–77.

———. "New Jersey Loyalists and the British 'Provincial' Corps in the War for Independence," *New Jersey History* 87 (1969): 69–78.

Smith, Richard Norton. *Patriarch: George Washington and the New American Nation.* Boston: Houghton/Richard Todd, 1993.

Soltow, J. H. "Scottish Traders in Virginia, 1750–1775." *Economic History Review,* 2d ser., 12 (1959): 83–98.

Sosin, Jack M. *The Revolutionary Frontier, 1763–1783.* New York: Holt, Rinehart & Winston, 1967.

Stanard, Mary N. *Colonial Virginia: Its People and Its Customs.* Detroit: Singing Free, 1970.

Stanley, G. F. "The Six Nations and the American Revolution," *Ontario History* 56 (1964): 217–32.

Stevens, Benjamin Franklin. comp. *Facsimiles of Manuscripts in European Archives Relating to America, 1773–1783.* 35 vols. London: Malby & Sons, 1889–95.

Stewart, Donald H. *The Opposition Press of the Federalist Period.* Albany, N.Y.: State Univ. of New York Press, 1969.

Stillé, Charles J. *Major General Anthony Wayne.* Philadelphia: Lippincott, 1893.

Stinchcombe, William C. *The American Revolution and the French Alliance.* Syracuse, N.Y.: Syracuse Univ. Press, 1969.

Stone, Rufus B. "Brodhead's Raid on the Senecas," *Western Pennsylvania Hist. Magazine* 7, no. 4 (1924): 88–101.

Stryker, William S. *Battle of Monmouth.* Princeton: Princeton Univ. Press, 1927.

———. *Battles of Trenton and Princeton.* Boston: Houghton Mifflin, 1898.

Sturdevant, Rick W. "Quest for Eden: George Washington's Frontier Land Interests." Ph.D. diss., Univ. of California at Santa Barbara, 1982.

Sullivan, John. *Letters and Papers of Major-General John Sullivan, Continental Army.* Ed. Otis G. Hammond. 2 vols. Concord, N.H.: New Hampshire Historical Society Press, 1930–39.

Sweig, Donald M., and Elizabeth S. David. "A Fairfax Friendship: The Complete Correspondence between George Washington and Bryan Fairfax, 1754–1799." *VMHB* 91 (1983): 109–10.

Swiggert, Howard. *War Out of Niagara.* Port Washington, N.Y.: Friedman, 1963.

Sydnor, Charles S. *Gentleman Freeholders: Political Parties in Washington's Virginia.* Chapel Hill: Univ. of North Carolina Press, 1952.

Tebbenhoff, Edward H. "The Associated Loyalists: An Aspect of Militant Loyalism." *NYHSQ* 63 (1979): 115–44.

Tesser, Charles H., ed. *The Sinews of Independence: Monthly Strength Reports of the Continental Army.* Chicago: Univ. of Chicago Press, 1976.

Thacher, James. *Military Journal.* Boston, 1823.

Thane, Elswyth. *Washington's Lady.* New York: Dodd, Mead, 1960.

Thayer, Theodore. *The Making of a Scapegoat: Washington and Lee at Monmouth.* Port Washington: Kennikat, 1976.

Thomas, Augusta Dillman. "Mary Ball: The Mother of Washington," *Picket Post* 12, no. 2 (1980): 4–11.

Thompson, Ray. *Washington at Whitemarsh: Prelude to Valley Forge.* Fort Washington, Pennsylvania: Bicentennial Press, 1968.

Thomson, Harry C. "The First Presidential Vetoes." *Presidential Studies Quarterly* 8, no. 1 (1978): 27–32.

Titus, James R. W. "Soldiers When They Choose to Be So: Virginians at War, 1754–1763," Ph.D. diss., Rutgers Univ., 1983.

Trevelyan, George O. M. *The American Revolution.* 6 vols. London, 1895.

Truman, Harry S. *Where the Buck Stops.* New York: Warner Books, 1989.

Uhlendorf, Bernhard A., ed. *Revolution in America: Confidential Letters and Journals 1776–1784 of Adjutant Major General Bauermeister of the Hessian Forces.* New Brunswick, N.J.: Rutgers Univ. Press, 1957.

U.S. Army. Continental Army. "A Whitemarsh Orderly Book, 1777." *PMHB* 45, no. 7 (1921): 205–219.

U.S. Continental Congress. *Journals, 1774–1789.* Ed. Worthington C. Ford et al. 34 vols. Washington, D.C.: Government Printing Office, 1904–1937.

———. *Letters of Delegates to Congress.* Ed. Paul H. Smith et al. 15 vols. to date. Washington, D.C.: Government Printing Office, 1976–.

———. *Letters of the Members of the Continental Congress.* Ed. Edmund C. Burnett. 8 vols. Washington, D.C.: Government Printing Office, 1921–1936.

Van Closen, Ludwig. *The Revolutionary Journal of Ludwig Van Closen.* Trans. Evelyn M. Acomb. Chapel Hill, N.C.: Univ. of North Carolina Press, 1958.

Van Doren, Carl. *Benjamin Franklin.* New York: Viking, 1938.

———. *Mutiny in January.* New York: Viking, 1943.

————. *Secret History of the American Revolution.* New York: Viking, 1941.

Van Schreeven, William J., et al. *Revolutionary Virginia: The Road to Independence.* 7 vols. Charlottesville: Univ. Press of Virginia, 1973–1983.

Van Tyne, Claude H. *The Loyalists in the American Revolution.* New York: Macmillan, 1902.

Varick, Richard. *Varick's Court of Inquiry.* Ed. Albert Bushnell Hart. Boston: Bibliophile Society, 1907.

Wainwright, Nicholas D. *George Croghan, Wilderness Diplomat.* Chapel Hill: Univ. of North Carolina Press, 1959.

Walker, James W. St.G. "Blacks as American Loyalists: The Slaves' Wars for Independence." *Historical Reflections* 2 (1975): 51–67.

Walker, Lewis Burd. "Life of Margaret Shippen." *PMHB* 24 (1900): 257–67, 401–29; 25 (1901): 20–46, 145–90, 289–302, 452–97.

Wall, C. C. "Housing and Family Life of the Mount Vernon Negro." Unpublished mss., Mount Vernon Library.

————. "Notes on the Early History of Mount Vernon," *WMQ* 3d ser., 2 (1945): 173–90.

Wall, C. C. et al. *Mount Vernon: A Handbook.* Mount Vernon, Va.: Mount Vernon Ladies Association, 1974.

Wallace, Willard M. *Appeal to Arms: A Military History of the American Revolution.* New York: Harper, 1951.

————. *Traitorous Hero: The Career and Fortunes of Benedict Arnold.* New York: Harper & Row, 1954.

Walne, Peter. "The English Ancestry of GW: Some New Evidence," *New England Historical and Genealogical Register* 129, no. 1 (1975): 106–33.

Walpole, Horace. *Letters.* ed. Peter Cunningham. 9 vols. London: Lane, 1857–1859.

Ward, Christopher. *The War of the Revolution.* 2 vols. New York: Macmillan, 1952.

Washington, George. *The Diaries of George Washington.* 6 vols. Ed. Donald D. Jackson and Dorothy Twohig. Charlottesville: Univ. Press of Virginia, 1976–1979.

————. *Journal of the Proceedings of the President, 1793–1797.* Ed. Dorothy Twohig. Charlottesville: Univ. Press of Virginia, 1981–.

————. *George Washington on the Defense of Boston, Cambridge, 4 April 1776.* Boston: Associates of the Boston Public Library, 1972.

————. *Papers of George Washington.* Ed. W. W. Abbot et al. Colonial series, 10 vols., Revolutionary War series, 8 vols to date; Confederation series, 6 vols. to date; Presidential series, 4 vols. to date. Charlottesville: Univ. Press of Virginia, 1983–.

————. *Writings of George Washington from the Original Manuscript Sources, 1745–1799.* Ed. John C. Fitzpatrick. 39 vols. Washington, D.C.: Government Printing Office, 1931–1944.

————. *Writings of George Washington.* Ed. John Rhodehamel. New York: Library of America, 1997.

————. *Writings of George Washington.* Ed. Jared Sparks. 10 vols. Boston: Russell, 1834–37.

Washington, George S. H. Lee. "The Washingtons of Sulgrave." *WMQ,* 2d ser., 17 (1937): 514–22; 19 (1939): 214–25.

————. "Amphyllis Washington, 1602–1655: Her Ancestry and Family Connections," *New England Historical and Genealogical Register* 94 (1940): 251–77, 322–46.

Waters, Henry W. *An Examination of the English Ancestry of George Washington.* Boston: New England Historical and Genealogical Society, 1889.

Webb, Samuel Blachley. *Correspondence and Journals of Samuel Blachley Webb.* Ed. Worthington C. Ford. New York: Wickersham, 1893.

Weems, Mason L. *The Life of Washington.* Ed. Marcus Cunliff. Cambridge, Mass.: Belknap Press of Harvard Univ. Press, 1962.

Weigley, Russell F. *History of the U.S. Army.* New York: Macmillan, 1967.

————. ed. *Philadelphia: A 300-Year History.* New York: W. W. Norton, 1982.

Weiner, Frederick Bernays. "Military Occupation of Philadelphia in 1777–1778." *PAPS* 111 (1967): 310–13.

————. "Washington and His Mother." *AHR* 26, no. 3 (1991): 44–47, 68–70.

Wells, Walter A. "The Last Illness and Death of George Washington." *Virginia Medical Monthly* 53 (1926–27): 629–42.

Wertenbaker, Thomas J. *Father Knickerbocker Rebels: New York City during the Revolution.* New York: Scribner's, 1948.

Whitely, Emily S. *Washington and His Aides-de-Camp*. New York: Macmillan, 1936.

Wickwire, Franklin and Mary. *Cornwallis: The American Adventure*. Boston: Houghton Mifflin, 1970.

Wilkinson, James. *Memoirs of My Own Times*. 3 vols. Philadelphia: Small, 1816.

Willcox, William B. *Portrait of a General: Sir Henry Clinton in the War of Independence*. New York: Knopf, 1964.

———. "The British Road to Yorktown: A Study in Divided Command." *AHR* 52 (1945): 1–35.

———. "British Strategy in America, 1778." *Journal of Modern History* 19 (1947): 97–121.

———, ed. *The American Rebellion: Sir Henry Clinton's Narrative of His Campaign, 1775–1782*. New Haven: Yale Univ. Press, 1954.

———. "Why Did the British Lose the American Revolution?" *Michigan Alumnus Quarterly Review* 62 (1956): 317–24.

Wilstach, Paul. *Mount Vernon*. New York: Blue Ribbon Books, 1930.

Winsor, Justin. "Virginia and the Quebec Bill." *AHR* 1, no. 3 (1895–1896): 436–43.

Wirt, William Henry. *Sketches of the Life and Character of Patrick Henry*. New York: Derby and Jackson, 1859.

Wister, Sally. *Journal*. Philadelphia: Lippincott, 1902.

Wolf, Edwin, II. *The Library at Mount Vernon*. Princeton: Princeton Univ. Press, 1977.

Wood, Gordon. *Radicalism of the American Revolution*. New York: Knopf, 1992.

Wood, W. J. *Battles of the Revolutionary War*. Intro. by John S. D. Eisenhower. New York: da Capo, 1990.

Wright, Albert Hazen. *The Sullivan Expedition of 1779*. Ithaca: Cornell Univ. Press, 1965.

Wright, Esmond. *Washington and the American Revolution*. New York: Macmillan, 1975.

Wright, Robert K., Jr. "Organization and Doctrine in the Continental Army, 1774–1784." Ph.D. diss., William and Mary, 1980.

Zimmer, Anne Y. *Jonathan Boucher: Loyalist in Exile*. Detroit: Wayne State Univ. Press, 1978.

INDEX